Czech (& Central European)
Yearbook of Arbitration

Czech (& Central European)
Yearbook of Arbitration

Volume I

2011

The Relationship between Constitutional Values, Human Rights and Arbitration

Editors

Alexander J. Bělohlávek

Professor
at the VŠB–TU
in Ostrava
Czech Republic

Naděžda Rozehnalová

Professor
at the Masaryk University
in Brno
Czech Republic

JURIS

Questions About This Publication

For assistance with shipments, billing or other customer service matters, please call our Customer Services Department at:

1-631-350-2100

To obtain a copy of this book, call our Sales Department:

1-631-351-5430
Fax: 1-631-351-5712

Toll Free Order Line:

1-800-887-4064 (United States & Canada)

See our web page about this book:

www.arbitrationlaw.com

Printed in the United States of America.
ISBN: 978-1-933833-71-2
ISSN: 2157-9490

JurisNet, LLC
71 New Street
Huntington, New York 11743 U. S. A.
www.arbitrationlaw.com

The title *Czech (& Central European) Yearbook of Arbitration* as well as the logo appearing on the cover are protected by EU trademark law.

Typeset in the Czech Republic by www.jeansolpartre.com

Address for correspondence & delivery of manuscripts
*Czech (& Central European) Yearbook of Arbitration
Jana Zajíce 32, Praha 7, 170 00, Czech Republic*

www.czechyearbook.org

Impressum

Institutions participating in the CYArb Project

Academic institutions

University of West Bohemia in Pilsen, Czech Republic
Faculty of Law, Department of International Law &
Department of Constitutional Law
*[Západočeská univerzita v Plzni, Právnická fakulta.
Katedra mezinárodního práva & Katedra ústavního práva]*

Masaryk University (Brno, Czech Republic),
Faculty of Law, Department of International and European Law
*[Masarykova univerzita v Brně, Právnická fakulta. Katedra
mezinárodního a evropského práva]*

Pavol Jozef Šafárik University in Košice, Slovak Republic
Faculty of Law, Department of Commercial Law and Business Law
*[Právnická fakulta UPJŠ, Košice, Slovensko. Katedra obchodného
a hospodárskeho práva]*

VŠB – TU Ostrava, Czech Republic
Faculty of Economics, Department of Law
[VŠB – TU Ostrava, Ekonomická Fakulta. Katedra práva]

Institute of State and Law of the Academy of Sciences of the Czech Republic
[Ústav státu a práva AV ČR, v.v.i.]

Non-academic institutions participating in the CYArb Project

**International Arbitral Centre
of the Austrian Federal Economic Chamber**
> *[Wiener Internationaler Schiedsgericht (VIAC), Vienna]*

**Court of International Commercial Arbitration attached
to the Chamber of Commerce and Industry of Romania**
> *[Curtea de Arbitraj Comercial Internaţional de pe lângă Camera
> de Comerţ şi Industrie a României, Bucharest]*

**Arbitration Court attached to the Hungarian Chamber
of Commerce and Industry**
> *[A Magyar Kereskedelmi és Iparkamara mellett szervezett
> Választottbíróság, Budapest]*

**Arbitration Court attached to the Economic Chamber
of the Czech Republic and Agricultural Chamber of the Czech Republic**
> *[Rozhodčí soud při Hospodářské komoře České republiky
> a Agrární komoře České republiky, Prague]*

**Arbitration Court attached to the Czech-Moravian Commodity
Exchange Kladno**
> *[Rozhodčí soud při Českomoravské komoditní burze Kladno
> (Czech Republic)]*

ICC National Committee Czech Republic
> *[ICC Národní výbor Česká republika]*

The Court of Arbitration at the Polish Chamber of Commerce in Warsaw
> *[Sąd Arbitrażowy przy Krajowej Izbie Gospodarczej w Warszawie]*

| | |

*Proofreading and translation support provided by: Agentura SPA, s. r. o., Prague,
Czech Republic & TransPerfect Translations, London, UK.*

Contents

CASE LAW

Section A

Current Case Law of the National Courts regarding Arbitration

Contents

Czech (& Central European) Yearbook of Arbitration

BOOKS REVIEWS

NEWS & REPORTS

All contributions in this book are subject to academic review.

List of Abbreviations

AAA	American Arbitration Association
ABGB	Austrian General Civil Code
ADL	Anti-dummy laws
ADR	Alternative Dispute Resolution
APC	Arbitrazh Procedural Code [RUS]
ArbAct	Act No. 216/1994 Coll. of 1 November 1994 on Arbitration and on Enforcement of Arbitration Rulings, as amended [CZE]
ASA	Swiss Arbitration Association
AUT	Austria
BCC	Bulgarian Chamber of Commerce and Industry
BCCIC	Arbitration Court at the Bulgarian Chamber of Commerce and Industry
BGB	German Civil Code
BGH	Federal Supreme Court [DEU]
BGR	Bulgaria
BL	German Constitution [DEU]
BUL	The Republic of Bulgaria
CAN	Canada
CCI	Chamber of Commerce and Industry of the Russian Federation [RUS]
CCP	Code of Civil Procedure
CEE	Central and Eastern Europe
CFI	Court of First Instance [EU]
CIS	Commonwealth of Independent States
CivCo	Act No. 40/1964 Coll., the Civil Code, as amended [CZE]
CJEU	Court of Justice of the European Union
Coll.	Collection of Laws [CZE]
ComC	The Commercial Code [CZE]
ConstCoAct	Act No. 182/1993 Coll., On the Czech Constitutional Court, as amended
CZE	Czech Republic
DEU	Germany
DIS	German Arbitration Institution
ECJ	European Court of Justice
ECR	European Court Reports
ECtHR	European Court of Human Rights
EGBGB	Introductory Act to the German Civil Code [DEU]
ECHR	Convention for the Protection of Human Rights and Fundamental Freedoms (European Convention on the Human Rights)

Czech (& Central European) Yearbook of Arbitration

EU	European Union
FIN	Finland
HRV	Croatia
HUN	Hungary
IACL	Council of the International Association of Constitutional Law
IBA	International Bar Association
ICAA	International Commercial Arbitration Act [BUL]
ICAC	International Commercial Arbitration Court at the Chamber of Commerce and Industry Ukraine
ICAC RF	The International Commercial Arbitration Court at the RF Chamber of Commerce and Industry [RUS], also as MKAS
ICC	International Chamber of Commerce
ICSID	The International Centre for the Settlement of Investment Disputes
IPRG [SUI]	Swiss Federal Code on Private International Private Law (Switzerland)
k.c.	Civil Code [POL]
k.p.c.	Code of Civil Procedure [POL]
LCIA	London Court of International Arbitration
LTU	Lithuania
LVA	Latvia
MDA	Moldova
MINE	Maritime International Nominees Establishment
MKAS	The International Commercial Arbitration Court at the RF Chamber of Commerce and Industry [RUS], also as ICAC RF
MKD	Macedonia
NAFTA	North American Free Trade Agreement
NED	The Netherlands
NEP	New economic Policy
OGH	Austrian Supreme Court [AUT]
OLG	High Regional Court [DEU]
OSŘ [CZE]	Code of Civil Procedure [Czech Republic]
POL	Poland
RF CC	Civil Code of the Russian Federation [RUS]
RUM	Romania
RUS	Russian Federation
SCC	Arbitration Institute of the Stockholm Chamber of Commerce
SVK	Slovak republic
SVN	Slovenia
SWE	Sweden
TFEU	Treaty on the Functioning of the European Union (Lisbon Treaty)
UKR	Ukraine
u.z.n.k.	Act on Suppression of Unfair Competition [POL]
UN	United Nations
UNCITRAL	United Nations Commission on International Trade Law
USA	United States of America
WTO	World Trade Organization
Yale L.J.	Yale Law Journal
Z.z.	Collection of Acts [of the Slovak Republic] [SVK]
ZPO	Code of Civil Procedure [DEU]

Articles

Matej Accetto
The Past and Possible Futures of European Union Judicature

Key words:
EU law | judicial review | European Court of Justice | national courts | preliminary rulings

Abstract | *In many ways, the success of the European Union as a polity is dependent on the effectiveness of its legal order, and that in turn on the effectiveness of its judicature in ensuring observance of EU law. The role played by the European Court of Justice in this respect is a success story; and yet, for more than three decades now, its constant companion have also been the threat of an overflowing caseload and calls for a much needed reform to the system. This paper traces the development of the Luxembourg court system and its various reforms, but also points to their shortcomings – the most general of these being that the changes introduced provide little more than temporary relief. The reason may well be in a (real or perceived) impasse where too drastic a change in any direction would seemingly jeopardise the lauded virtues of the existing system; but it is submitted that the worst outcome would be to stay put, and that changes to the system should be explored where they are most easily implemented and most likely to already have begun – the national courts.*

| | |

Matej Accetto studied law at the University of Ljubljana, taking his LL.B. in 2000; he then received an LL.M. from Harvard Law School in 2001 and a Doctorate in Law from the University of Ljubljana in 2006, where he is Assistant Professor (Docent) of European Law. His other relevant positions and affiliations include an internship at the Court of Justice of the European Union (2003), the Lord Slynn of Hadley European Law Foundation Fellowship (2003–04) and the post-doctoral Monica Partridge Visiting Fellowship at the University of Cambridge, Fitzwilliam College (2006).
e-mail: matej.accetto@pf.uni-lj.si

I. Anamnesis: European Court of Justice: A Supreme Court of the Land

1.01. It is relatively easy to outline the crucial significance of the Court of Justice of the European Union and its jurisprudence for the development of EU law. Firstly, the project of European integration has always been grounded in law: Walter Hallstein, the first president of the European Commission, called the European Economic Community a "community of law" (*Rechtsgemeinschaft*), outlining the various ways in which it should be understood as a "phenomenon of law"[1]. Secondly, while the process of integration was largely driven by the development of its legal order[2], the Court of Justice was at the very core of this legal order[3]. One may quibble whether it was because the Court has single-handedly managed to co-opt the role and convince most of the principle actors into accepting its jurisprudence[4] or because a homogenous legal community overshadowed the other interpretative communities[5], but that makes little difference as even the debate within the wider legal community has largely been influenced (if not guided) by the members of the Court[6].

1.02. In performing its role as both the guardian and the vanguard of EU law, the Court has been directed as well as empowered by a provision which started as Art. 164 EEC and is now Art. 19(1) EU – calling upon it to "ensure that in the interpretation and application of the Treaties the law is observed". This was to be a relatively constrained – even if difficult – mandate to check the abuse of powers and to provide judicial protection to those wronged by the legislative or administrative excesses in the EU legal arena. It was understood as such by Massimo Pilotti in his speech upon

---

[1] WALTER HALLSTEIN, DIE EUROPÄISCHE GEMEINSCHAFT, Düsseldorf & Vienna: Econ Verlag 33–39 (2nd ed. 1974).

[2] On how it has engaged in "community building using the tools of legal integration", see Giorgio Gaja, Peter Hay and Ronald D. Rotunda, *Instruments for Legal Integration in the European Community – A Review, in* 1 INTEGRATION THROUGH LAW: EUROPE AND THE AMERICAN FEDERAL EXPERIENCE, Berlin & New York: Walter de Gruyter 113, 115 et seq. (M. Cappelletti, M. Seccombe, J. H. H. Weiler eds., 2nd ed. 1985).

[3] Even if, remembering the oft-hailed reference to the Court fashioning the fundamental features of this legal order under the cover of benign neglect, its jurisprudence was not always front and centre in the daily news – see Eric Stein, *Lawyers, Judges, and the Making of a Transnational Constitution*, 75 A.J.I.L. 1, 1 (1981).

[4] As stated by Weiler – see Joseph H. H. Weiler, *Journey to an Unknown Destination: A Retrospective and Prospective of the European Court of Justice in the Arena of Political Integration*, 31 (4) J.COM.MAR.ST. 417, 420 (1993).

[5] Harm Schepel and Rein Wesseling, *The Legal Community: Judges, Lawyers, Officials and Clerks in the Writing of Europe*, 3 (2) EUR.L.J. 165, 169 (1997).

[6] See e.g. the list of prominent figures in Armin Von Bogdandy, *A Bird's Eye View on the Science of European Law: Structures, Debates and Development Prospects of Basic Research on the Law of the European Union in a German Perspective*, 6 (3) EUR.L.J. 208, 212 (2000).

being elected the first president of the Court in 1953[7], and expounded by the Court in its very first ruling:[8]

> It is not for the Court to express a view as to the desirability of the methods laid down by the Treaty, or to suggest a revision of the Treaty, but it is bound, in accordance with Article 31, to ensure that [in] the interpretation and application of the Treaty as it stands the law is observed.

But how wide a mandate such a provision may grant in the long run is a story well known to systems of constitutional judicature, and indeed the Court has used it with great aplomb. While it has not – at least not explicitly[9] – called for a revision of the Treaties, it has often effected such "amendments" on its own, either by expanding the purview of their provisions (e.g. the rulings in Meroni[10], ERTA[11] or Marshall[12]) or even by going against the text (e.g. the rulings in Van Duyn[13], Hauer[14] or Les Verts[15]). In brief, the Court was extraordinarily successful in addressing the "constitutional" issues of EU law, establishing EU law as a special supranational legal order and itself as the final arbiter of this order. It did so not by (or even, perhaps, precisely by not) being radical in the legal doctrines it expounded[16] but by acquiring an unprecedented fidelity to and obeisance of its rulings by the Member States[17].

---

[7]   See the excerpt cited in Bo Vesterdorf, *The Community Court System Ten Years From Now and Beyond: Challenges and Possibilities*, 28 (3) Eur.L.Rev. 303, 303 (2003).

[8]   ECJ Judgment of 21 December 1954, Case 1/54, *French Republic v High Authority of the European Coal and Steel Community* [1954] ECR 1, p. 13.

[9]   Opinion 2/94 on Accession by the Community to the ECHR [1996] ECR I-1759, could also be understood as an implicit instruction directed at the Member States to amend the Treaties in order to allow for the accession – see Koen Lenaerts, *Respect for Fundamental Rights as a Constitutional Principle of the European Union*, 6 Colum.J.Eur.L. 1, 1–2 (2000).

[10]   ECJ Judgment of 13 June 1958, Case 9/56, *Meroni & Co., Industrie Metallurgiche, SpA v High Authority of the European Coal and Steel Community* [1958] ECR 133.

[11]   ECJ Judgment of 31 March 1971, Case 22/70, *Commission of the European Communities v Council of the European Communities* [1971] ECR 263.

[12]   ECJ Judgment of 26 February 1986, Case 152/84, *M. H. Marshall v Southampton and South-West Hampshire Area Health Authority (Teaching)* [1986] ECR 723.

[13]   ECJ Judgment of 4 December 1974, Case 41/74, *Yvonne van Duyn v Home Office* [1974] ECR 1337.

[14]   ECJ Judgment of 13 December 1979, Case 44/79, *Liselotte Hauer v Land Rheinland-Pfalz* [1979] ECR 3727.

[15]   ECJ Judgment of 23 April 1986, Case 294/83, *Parti écologiste "Les Verts" v European Parliament* [1986] ECR 1339.

[16]   Ole Spiermann, *The Other Side of the Story: An Unpopular Essay on the Making of the European Community Legal Order*, 10 (4) Eur.J.Int'l L. 763 (1999), attempts to unmask the false "novelty" of the ECJ's approach to the doctrines of supremacy and direct effect by showing how they have already been developed in international law, coming to the conclusion (on p. 781) that, "when compared to the international law of co-operation, as opposed to the international law of coexistence, there was nothing impressive about the general approach adopted by the European Court".

[17]   *Cf.* see Bogdandy, *supra* note 6, at 221.

1.03. However, all this gave rise to that familiar paradox of being a victim of one's own success. While establishing itself as the ultimate arbiter of EU law and that law in turn as the primary "law of the land", the Court found it increasingly difficult to perform its task under Art. 19(1) EU as initially understood: to safeguard the principle of the rule of law and to provide effective judicial protection whenever needed. The biggest (even if not the only) cause of these difficulties is the ever-increasing workload, a common ailment of the European judiciaries, familiar to several national constitutional courts as well as the European Court of Human Rights that are swamped under an increasing number of applications[18] and forced into disposing of them in ways – either via excessively lengthy proceedings or by striking out a large number of applications on procedural grounds – that at least verge on denial of substantive justice.

1.04. Even though the European Court of Justice does not yet face the workload of quite the same magnitude as some national constitutional courts or its Strasbourg counterpart – which, as I will submit later, is in itself a symptom of the problem – it has also found it increasingly hard to cope with the size of its docket. Admittedly, the shortcomings of the extant system of Union judicature have been known for a long while now, and the past few decades have already seen a number of proposals on how to overcome them, some more incremental, others more radical. So far, it was the former which were often adopted and the latter which were largely rejected; but it is the contention of this article that we are at least nearing the time when one of the more radical reforms will be needed if the underlying and self-evident premise of having a functioning system of Union judicature – the respect for the rule of law – is to be maintained. That said, hopefully the development of EU law is also nearing a stage at which more substantial changes to its system of judicial review will become feasible or easier to achieve.

1.05. I will proceed in two steps. First, I will outline the development of the EU court system and its malaise. Then, I will move to the discussion of the proposed remedies, ending with some concluding remarks on the possible outcome of the treatment.

---

[18] One need only see the rising number of pending cases at the ECHR over the last few years: 97,300 pending cases at the end of 2008, 119,300 at the end of 2009 and 139,700 after the first three quarters of 2010. In comparison, 30,163 cases were struck out or declared inadmissible in 2008, 33,065 in 2009, and the number is expected to grow further in 2010. All data taken from annual statistics available at: http://www.echr.coe.int/ECHR/EN/Header/Reports+and+Statistics/Statistics/Statistical+information+by+year (accessed on October 23, 2010).

Czech (& Central European) Yearbook of Arbitration

II. Diagnosis: The Growth and Limitations of the Union Judicature

1.06. It is hard, nowadays, to imagine the apocryphal early days of the European Court of Justice when it received no more than ten new applications per year and when every new application lodged with the Court was at least mentally accompanied by the popping of champagne corks[19]. By 1981, however, the Court already issued 128 judgments in a single year (65 of which were preliminary rulings) and received 339 new applications, with 400 cases (discounting a great number of nearly identical staff cases) pending; in 1999, with a part of the caseload already handled by the (then) Court of First Instance[20], the Court of Justice alone issued 235 judgments (of which 136 were preliminary rulings) and received 545 new applications, with 900 cases pending on the docket[21]. In 2009, with an even greater portion of the burden carried by the (now) General Court and the Civil Service Tribunal, the Court of Justice issued 377 judgments (of which 188 were preliminary rulings) and a number of orders, jointly disposing of 588 cases, while receiving 561 new cases with 741 cases pending resolution[22].

1.07. To put these numbers in context, one can try to match the "demand" for ECJ judgments with their "supply". In the years 1954–59, seven judges (with the assistance of two advocates general) issued 42 judgments; in the years 1985–89 (noting the date of accession of Spain and Portugal), thirteen judges (with six advocates general) issued 1019 judgments;[23] in the years 2000–04, fifteen judges (with eight advocates general) 2392 judgments, opinions and orders;[24] and in the years 2005–09, first twenty-

---

[19] Anthony Arnull, *Refurbishing the Judicial Architecture of the European Community*, 43 (2) I.C.I..Q 296, 297 (1994).

[20] With the Treaty of Lisbon, this court has been renamed as the General Court. When deemed appropriate in the historical context, I will still use the original name, trusting that the reader will not be confused.

[21] *Cf.* Peter Dyrberg, *What Should the Court of Justice Be Doing*, 26 (3) Eur.L.Rev. 291, 294 (2001).

[22] Taken from statistics of judicial activity contained in the 2009 annual report of the Court of Justice, available at: http://curia.europa.eu/jcms/jcms/Jo2_7000 (accessed on October 23, 2010).

[23] *Cf.* a similar point with somewhat different numbers in Paul J. G. Kapteyn, *The Court of Justice of the European Communities after the Year 2000, in* Institutional Dynamics of European Integration, Dordrecht: Martinus Nijhoff Publishers 135, 135 (D. Curtin and T. Heukels eds., 1994).

[24] Due to slightly different ways in which the statistics of the Court has been prepared from 2002 onwards, the data may not be entirely comparable – from 2000 onwards, I use the number of all the judgments, opinions and orders, which may be slightly higher than the number reported earlier as the net figure of completed cases (discounting the joint cases resulting in one judgment). Nevertheless, I think the numbers are not significantly different and merit the comparison between different periods. The data are taken from annual reports available at: http://curia.europa.eu/jcms/jcms/Jo2_11035/rapports-annuels (accessed on October 23, 2010).

five and then twenty-seven judges (with eight advocates general) 2603 judgments, opinions and orders[25]. Put differently, in the first six years, the Court issued one judgment per judge per year; in 1985–89, that number was already fifteen times higher – the Court issued 15 judgments per judge per year; in the 2000–04 period, it was almost 35 decisions (albeit including all judgments, orders and opinions) per judge per year; and in the 2005–09 period, approximately 20 decisions (again including all judgments, orders and opinions) per judge per year.

1.08. The growing docket has been accompanied by the growing duration of the proceedings. This has notably been the case with preliminary rulings which have traditionally received preferential treatment by the Court and have been substantially shorter than direct actions with a comprehensive written stage:[26] on average, the preliminary ruling procedure thus took 6 months in 1975, 9 months in 1980, 13 months in 1983, 18 months in 1988 and 25,5 months in 2003, "catching up" to the lengthier direct actions. Again, the statistics from the last few years is noticeably better: the average duration of proceedings has been dropping between 2003 and 2008 and has temporarily settled at approximately 17 months.

1.09. In general, the last few years seem like a positive trend. The fact that the relevant docket numbers – of cases lodged and resolved – have remained relatively constant over the past decade, with the backlog even somewhat decreasing, that there was a noted decrease in the number of judgments in relation to the number of judges that the Court is churning out annually, and that the duration of proceedings is back where it was in the mid-1980s, this may all give us hope that the major problems of the growing docket are going to be solved. But there are three reasons why this is not necessarily the case.

1.10. Firstly, we are talking about a somewhat anomalous period right after a numerically big enlargement of mostly small states in 2004. This, of course, is not to say that enlargement would by itself imply a smaller docket – on the contrary! Enlargement will normally imply a bigger workload – Craig, for instance, listed it as one of four major reasons for an increasing caseload, alongside an expanding number of EU competences, successful harmonisation of the legal order and an ever greater familiarity with EU law among the members of the bar[27]. Indeed, for one prestigious

---

25   Again, as with the data from the 1980s, some account has to be had of the two enlargements, both the two new judges joining the Court in 2007 and the fact that the effect of ten new judges on the number of cases completed was somewhat delayed as they became involved in new cases.

26   Thijmen Koopmans, *The Future of the Court of Justice of the European Communities*, 11 Y.Eur.L. 15, 17–18 (1991).

27   Paul Craig, *The Jurisdiction of the Community Courts Reconsidered*, *in* THE EUROPEAN COURT OF JUSTICE, Oxford: Oxford University Press 177, 183–184 (G. de Búrca and J. H. H. Weiler eds., 2001). To these, one could add others; Rasmussen, for instance, cites "bad habits" of Member States and EU institutions to resort to the Court of Justice even for the resolution of those disputes that could be resolved politically –

group of commentators, enlargement was identified as the single greatest challenge in terms of docket control[28].

1.11. However, there will inevitably also be a certain delay between the accession of a new Member State and a greater number of applications arriving from that state: the experience with previous accessions has shown that such a delay would normally last between four and five years[29]. Clearly, this effect has also been present in the last two enlargements, both in terms of direct actions (in 2009, out of 142 new actions for failure of a Member State to fulfil its obligations, only 30 were lodged against the most recent twelve Member States) and with regard to the preliminary references coming from the national courts: from 2005 to 2009 (not counting 2004 when only Hungarian courts made two preliminary references), out of 1327 preliminary references only 101 came from these twelve Member States. If we compare this number to the growth of the Court from 15 judges to 27, noting that 90 % of all cases are now being dealt with by chambers of five or three judges, the math becomes even clearer: while these twelve Member States accounted for 8 % of the "demand" for preliminary rulings, their judges constituted an 80 % increase (or 44 % of the new total) in the "supply" capacities of the Court.

1.12. The prediction about an increase in EU law activity after the first five years, however, also seems to be proving true: 48 preliminary references, nearly half of the 101 from the most recent twelve Member States in the five-year period, came in 2009 alone. In that year, these states accounted for 16% of all preliminary references. If we assume that the number of references should normally correlate to the population of a Member State, that percentage is already quite close to their relative size (20% of the entire EU population). The conclusion to draw from all this is that some benefit of relatively small states providing a relatively large number of new judges will remain, but that the long period of cautious familiarisation with EU law in the newest Member States may be coming to the end.

1.13. Secondly, it is inevitable that other factors will continue to expand the docket: the integration of the Member States will continue to deepen, new competences will be acquired b y the Union and new types of controversies will engage the Court (some of which are cited below).

1.14. And, thirdly, if the reason for optimism is the return, in many respects, to the statistics of the mid-1980s, that optimism is slightly misplaced: after all, the 1980s was the period in which the calls for a reform first intensified and led to the establishment of the (then) Court of First Instance. If all

see Hjalte Rasmussen, *Remedying the Crumbling EC Judicial System*, 37 C.M.L.Rev. 1071, 1081 (2000).

[28] A special working group set up by the Commission, which for the most part involved former ECJ judges – see Ole Due et al., Report by the Working Party on the Future of the European Communities' Court System 9–10 (2000), available at: http://ec.europa.eu/dgs/legal_service/pdf/due_en.pdf (accessed on October 23, 2010).

[29] Walter van Gerven, *The Role and Structure of the European Judiciary Now and in the Future*, 21 (3) Eur.L.Rev. 211, 211 (1996); Thijmen Koopmans, *supra* note 26, at 18.

Czech (& Central European) Yearbook of Arbitration

we achieve after all the reforms is to return to the circumstances which required these reforms in the first place, that should be a cause for added concern rather than celebration. One is reminded of how, in the first few years of its operation, when it was dealing with a relatively small number of cases, CFI even called for additional areas of competence to be transferred to it[30], only to regret it a few years later when its wishes were granted and when, upon receiving additional responsibilities, its docket was as full as that of the Court[31].

1.15. Indeed, most of the changes so far have been playing catch-up to the problem of the growing docket, and most provided little more than temporary relief: changes such as the deliberation in smaller chambers, first introduced in 1974 and initiated in practice with the second amendment of the Statute in 1979[32], and then further expanded by the Treaty of Maastricht;[33] the possibility of abolishing the oral stage of the proceedings or resolving preliminary reference by means of a reasoned order in 1990;[34] a number of amendments introduced by the Treaty of Nice to further empower the CFI and the Union legislator in adopting further amendments;[35] or a number of Council decisions aiming to reapportion the burden or bolster the Luxembourg judicature[36].

1.16. It is hard to expect that matters will be helped much by the Treaty of Lisbon, although it includes a few modifications designed to speed up the proceedings (such as when imposing a lump sum or penalty payment upon a Member State in the event of infringement). This is all the less likely because the Treaty also greatly expands the Court's jurisdiction: by giving binding force to the Charter of Fundamental Rights:[37] by abolishing the pillar structure (mostly in relation to the area of freedom, security and justice, but after a transitional period also in criminal matters, even if much less so with relation to the foreign and security policy);[38] and by

---

30   Bo Vesterdorf, *The Court of First Instance of the European Communities After Two Full Years in Operation*, 29 C.M.L.Rev. 897, 905 (1992).
31   See Anthony Arnull, *The Community Judicature and the 1996 IGC*, 20 (6) Eur.L.Rev. 599, 600 (1995).
32   On this see Francis Jacobs, *The Member States, the Judges and the Procedure*, in La Cour de Justice des Communautés Européennes et les États Membres, Brussels: Editions de l'Université de Bruxelles 11, 12 (Institut d'études européennes Université libre de Bruxelles ed., 1981).
33   On this see Anthony Arnull, *supra* note 31, at 600–601.
34   Anthony Arnull, *supra* note 19, at 311.
35   See Paul Craig, *supra* note 27, at 212–213.
36   Such as, e.g., Council Decision 2004/407/EC, Euratom, OJ [2004] L 132, p. 5 (transferring new areas to CFI); Council Decision 2004/752/EC, Euratom, OJ [2004] L 333, p. 7 (establishing the Civil Service Tribunal).
37   The Charter was already anticipated as an important source of the Court's caseload by Peter Dyrberg, *supra* note 21, at 293.
38   Which does not mean that there are no calls for greater involvement of the Court in this area – see Maria-Gisella Garbagnati Ketvel, *The Jurisdiction of the European Court of Justice in Respect of the Common Foreign and Security Policy*, 55 I.C.L.Q. 77, 117–118 (2006).

relaxation of the *locus standi* requirements for private applicants, which also were already envisioned by the Constitutional Treaty and there declared to be "a small step in the right direction and a long way to go"[39].

1.17. The conclusions to draw from the above are simple: it must be – and presumably largely is – accepted that the problem of the growing caseload will not disappear and that the system of EU judicial review needs to be reformed. We can discuss how badly such a reform is needed[40], but most of all what it should entail. It should be accepted that we cannot be satisfied with cosmetic changes which would shorten the proceedings at the expense of the quality of the judicial pronouncements[41]. A more difficult choice may lie between opting for a shock therapy with a comprehensive reform in one sweep or for a series of incremental changes to the existing system – while the latter may be more feasible and politically acceptable, they may not provide any long-term relief[42]. With this in mind, I turn to the discussion of proposed changes to the established judicial architecture.

III. Therapy: Proposed Reforms of the EU Judicial System

1.18. There are a number of possible ways to approach the need for reform of the current system, and I will attempt to structure them into four distinct sets of proposals. The *first*, and one that has also most often been subjected to changes, consists of those proposals aiming to alleviate the judicial burden by refining the organisation and the procedure of the Luxembourg judiciary. As mentioned above, some such proposals have to an extent already been adopted and calls for a new reform may merely wish to have them expanded further[43]. Others include additional proposed changes to the appointment of judges (whether the judges should have

---

[39] Cornelia Koch, *Locus Standi of Private Applicants Under the EU Constitution: Preserving Gaps in the Protection of Individuals' Right to an Effective Remedy*, 30 (4) EUR.L.REV. 511, 527 (2005).

[40] See e.g. David W. J. Scorey, *A New Model for the Communities' Judicial Architecture in the New Union*, 21 (3) EUR.L.REV. 224, 224 (1996), stating that such a reform is "desperately needed".

[41] On this see Catherine Turner and Rodolphe Muñoz, *Revising the Judicial Architecture of the European Union*, 19 Y.EUR.L. 1, 91–93 (1999-2000).

[42] Thus also Takis Tridimas, *Knocking on Heaven's Door: Fragmentation, Efficiency and Defiance in the Preliminary Reference Procedure*, 40 C.M.L.REV. 9, 47 (2003).

[43] Like, for instance, the possibility of doing away with the oral hearing unless asked for with a reasoned request – see Paul Craig, *supra* note 27, at 189; David Edward, *Reform of Article 234 Procedure: The Limits of the Possible*, in JUDICIAL REVIEW IN EUROPEAN UNION LAW, The Hague: Kluwer Law International 119, 139 (D. O'Keefe and A. Bavasso eds., 2000); or by limiting the involvement of advocates general to only the most important cases – see Ole Due et al., *supra* note 28, at 48–49; Walter van Gerven, *supra* note 29, at 222.

longer but non-renewable terms of office[44] and whether the Court of Justice of an ever larger Union should necessarily have judges from all Member States[45]) or to the operation of the Court (such as possibly doing away with the issuing of judgments in all the official languages[46]), even if not all of them would help shorten the proceedings[47]. In any event, such changes have perhaps quite aptly been characterised as "short-termist in the extreme"[48].

1.19. The *second* concerns the relationship between the Court of Justice and the General Court. I already mentioned above that the establishment of a second judicial body was not a long-term solution but rather further compounded the situation, as we now have two courts barely keeping up with a significant caseload and fearing what comes next[49]. Nevertheless, a number of proposed changes have still suggested lessening the burden of the Court of Justice further by increasing that of the General Court in its stead. One strand of these proposals calls for the possibility enabled by the Treaty of Nice but not yet put into practice – that the General Court could also give preliminary rulings. While several former judges and distinguished commentators first opposed such a possibility[50], others advocated it[51] and it ultimately also received a limited endorsement by the Court itself[52].

---

[44]   Walter van Gerven, *supra* note 29, at 221 (calling for a term of 9 years); Ole Due et al., *supra* note 28, at 51 (advocating a term of 12 years); Joseph H. H. Weiler, *Epilogue: The Judicial Après Nice, in* THE EUROPEAN COURT OF JUSTICE, Oxford: Oxford University Press 215, 225 (G. de Búrca and J. H. H. Weiler eds., 2001) (against a renewable term of office).

[45]   David Edward, *supra* note 43, at 135; Thijmen Koopmans, *supra* note 26, at 24–25; Paul J. G. Kapteyn, *supra* note 23, at 139–140; Paul Craig, *supra* note 27, at 192 (calling for a system of rotation).

[46]   David Edward, *supra* note 43, at 131 and 149; Walter van Gerven, *supra* note 29, at 221; Ole Due et al., *supra* note 28, at 44, stated that this accounted for a third of the entire duration of proceedings.

[47]   Limiting the number of judges is of such a type, for instance, as is the possibility of introducing dissenting opinions, already proposed in the 1950s by the Netherlands but rejected by the other States on the premise that the advocates general provide an appropriate second opinion – as per Lagrange in the debate transcript *in* LA COUR DE JUSTICE DES COMMUNAUTÉS EUROPÉENNES ET LES ÉTATS MEMBRES, Brussels: Editions de l'Université de Bruxelles 24 (Institut d'études européennes Université libre de Bruxelles ed., 1981). One of those speaking in favour of introducing them was Joseph H. H. Weiler, *supra* note 4, at 225.

[48]   David W. J. Scorey, *supra* note 40, at 226.

[49]   Of course, while I mostly focus on the analysis of the Court of Justice, most of the points made apply to the General Court as well.

[50]   See Ole Due et al., *supra* note 28, at 22; Walter van Gerven, *supra* note 29, at 214–215; Anthony Arnull, *supra* note 31, at 603–604.

[51]   Takis Tridimas, *supra* note 42, at 20–21; Paul Craig, *supra* note 27, at 205–206; David W. J. Scorey, *supra* note 40, at 228–229.

[52]   For instance in the reflections of the Court of Justice, *The Future of the Judicial System of the European Union*, reproduced *in* THE FUTURE OF THE JUDICIAL SYSTEM

1.20.   The other option in this regard would be to transfer further areas from the jurisdiction of the Court of Justice to the General Court. While some commentators opposed this until the caseload burden was generally alleviated[53], the debate seems to have been won by those advocating further transfers, with the only open issue how broad the transfer should be: according to some, the General Court should deal with all cases involving complex factual considerations[54], according to others with all direct actions[55], while the most radical suggestions would leave only the most important cases to the Court of Justice, with all the others to be resolved by the General Court[56]. Of course, most if not all such proposals were made under the assumption that the Member States would substantially increase the number of judges at the General Court, a possibility also introduced by the Treaty of Nice.

1.21.   The *third* set of proposals is a variation on this theme and contains those calling for the creation of further judicial bodies. The more incremental approach of instituting specialized courts or boards of appeal has long been a viable option: Regulation 40/94/EC on the Community trade mark[57] thus for instance already anticipated the creation of specialized Boards of Appeal, while Regulation 2100/94/EC on Community plant variety rights[58] provided for similar bodies within the Community Plant Variety Office. Already in 1989, the Agreement relating to Community patents (89/695/EEC) concluded at Luxembourg envisioned a Common Appeal Court for Community patents, but it fell far short of obtaining all the necessary ratifications[59]. The establishment of a special European and European Union Patents Court envisioned in the Draft Agreement on the European and Community Patents Court[60] and its positioning *vis-à-vis* the Court of Justice remains one of the hot items on the EU legislative agenda.

1.22.   The more radical proposals, however, suggested that a comprehensive reconsideration of the Union judicature was in order. Should the EU establish new lower, regional courts that would lead to some decentralisation of EU judiciary? Jacqué and Weiler proposed the

---

OF THE EUROPEAN UNION, Portland: Hart Publishing 111, 138 (A. Dashwood and A. Johnston eds., 2001).

53   Walter van Gerven, *supra* note 29, at 215; Anthony Arnull, *supra* note 19, at 305.

54   Paul J. G. Kapteyn, *supra* note 23, at 150–152.

55   Ole Due et al., *supra* note 28, at 23–25; Paul Craig, *supra* note 27, at 193–195.

56   Peter Dyrberg, *supra* note 21, at 297–299. That proposal is similar to the transformation of the ECJ into a proper "constitutional court" of the EU – see text accompanying note 64 below.

57   Council Regulation (EC) No 40/94 of 20 December 1993 on the Community trade mark, [1994] OJ L 11/1.

58   Council Regulation (EC) No 2100/94 of 27 July 1994 on Community plant variety rights, [1994] OJ L 227/1.

59   For more on this, see Walter van Gerven, *supra* note 29, at 216.

60   See the revised text of the Draft Agreement on the European and Community Patents Court and Draft Statute of 23 March 2009, Doc. No. 7928/09 (with the terminology not yet brought in line with the Treaty of Lisbon amendments).

establishment of four (or three) such regional courts which would be competent to issue rulings at first instance in cases arising in their own regions;[61] with others supporting such a possibility[62]. However, it seems that until now those opposing such new courts, including several distinguished former members of the Court[63], have prevailed.

1.23. Another issue has been whether the Union requires a proper "constitutional" court, and several proposals called for a transformation of the Court of Justice into such a constitutional court for the EU, which would also imply a transformation of the General Court into the main judicial engine of the EU[64]. A similar idea with an EU Constitutional Court, the Court of Justice and one or more courts of first instance was allegedly even proposed by the (then) President of the CFI Vesterdorf in 1998[65]. The critics of such proposals claim that EU law does not give rise to purely constitutional cases and that the Court of Justice in any event may not serve as a constitutional court, since that would only further blur the relationship between the European and national court systems[66].

1.24. Which leads us to the *fourth* but perhaps the most important set of proposals – those relating to the role of the national courts. The national courts are naturally far from immune to – or separated from – the judicial control of EU law. They have a general duty to abide by EU law when enforcing the rule of law[67]. Such a duty arises out of the duty of loyal cooperation that was derived from the former Art. 10 EC as well as other general principles of EU law expounded by the Court of Justice. Craig listed them as one of three types of EU courts, alongside the Court of Justice and (now) General Court[68]. In fact, EU lawyers normally understand the national courts to be the *ordinary* Union courts of *general jurisdiction*;[69]

---

61   Jean-Paul Jacqué and Joseph H. H. Weiler, *Sur la voie de l'Union européenne, une nouvelle architecture judiciaire*, 26 (3) R.T.D.E. 441, 446–447 (1990).

62   Paul Craig, *supra* note 27, at 206–208; David W. J. Scorey, *supra* note 40, at 227–228.

63   Ole Due et al., *supra* note 28, at 20–21; Walter van Gerven, *supra* note 29, at 215–217; Thijmen Koopmans, *supra* note 26, at 28–29; Paul J. G. Kapteyn, *supra* note 23, at 148–149. Although Walter van Gerven (and to a lesser extent Thijmen Koopmans) supported the idea of *specialized* regional courts, dealing with technical issues in strictly delimited areas.

64   Notably Jean-Paul Jacqué and Joseph H. H. Weiler, *supra* note 61, at 446; Joseph H. H. Weiler, *supra* note 4, at 221–224; also David W. J. Scorey, *supra* note 40, at 228–230.

65   Hjalte Rasmussen, *supra* note 27, at 1110.

66   Paul J. G. Kapteyn, *supra* note 23, at 147; Walter van Gerven, *supra* note 29, at 215.

67   See more in Christiaan W. A. Timmermans, *Application of Community Law by National Courts: (Limits to) Direct Effect and Supremacy*, in EUROPEAN AMBITIONS OF THE NATIONAL JUDICIARY, The Hague: Kluwer Law International 29, 29 *et seq.* (R. H. M. Jansen, D. A. C. Koster and R. F. B. van Zutphen eds., 1997).

68   Paul Craig, *supra* note 27, at 178–179. Perhaps treating the Court of Justice and the General Court as two distinct types on the one hand and conflating all the national courts into one "type" on the other seems a little strange, but in terms of their duties under EU law, there truly is not much difference among the various national courts.

69   René Barents, *The Preliminary Procedure and the Rule of Law in the European Union, in* EUROPEAN AMBITIONS OF THE NATIONAL JUDICIARY, The Hague: Kluwer

some understand this to be a direct implication of the decision by the drafters of the initial Communities' system against establishing a special "federal" judiciary[70].

1.25. There is no need to rehash here in detail all the duties of the national courts to observe EU law as arising out of the Treaties and in particular the rich jurisprudence of the Court of Justice in this regard. Let us, however, just briefly remind ourselves of two important tenets (and limits) of their duties: they may not by themselves invalidate Union legislation[71], and they must – with the exception of those obvious issues leaving no doubt as to the correct application of EU law[72] – leave the interpretation of EU law to the Court of Justice as well. They both imply the normal means of judicial dialogue between the national courts and the Luxembourg court: the preliminary ruling procedure, which has often been found at the very centre of the proposals for reform.

1.26. A great part of the reason was that preliminary rulings have traditionally been seen as the biggest threat in terms of the growing workload. First making their appearance in 1961, in the 1990s preliminary references accounted for around 60% of the docket and many warned that their share would increase further[73]. Partly, the fear was the result of their growth in absolute terms: comparing the periods from 1980 to 1986 and from 1995 to 1999, i.e. immediately before and after two enlargements and Treaty revisions, the number of preliminary references lodged with the Court in a year on average grew from 113 to 253, an increase of 124%[74]. While their number has somewhat diminished in subsequent years, it has again started to grow in the last few years and passed a new landmark in 2009 with 302 preliminary references lodged with the Court[75].

1.27. On the other hand, preliminary rulings command a lot of attention because they are a cornerstone of developing EU law through the jurisprudence of the Court[76]. If even this cornerstone must be subjected to an uneasy balancing between the length of proceedings and substantive adequacy, there should indeed be cause for concern[77].

Law International 61, 64–67 (R. H. M. Jansen, D. A. C. Koster and R. F. B. van Zutphen eds., 1997); *Cf.* Paul Craig, *supra* note 27, at 178.

[70] Thus René Barents, *supra* note 69, at 64–65, perhaps reading too much into the system set up for what was initially perceived as a very limited economic association of states, federal dreams notwithstanding.

[71] ECJ Judgment of 22 October 1987, Case 314/85, *Foto-Frost v Hauptzollamt Lübeck-Ost* [1987] ECR 4199, paras 14–17.

[72] ECJ Judgment of 6 October 1982, Case 283/81, *Srl CILFIT and Lanificio di Gavardo SpA v Ministry of Health* [1982] ECR 3415, para. 16.

[73] E.g. Peter Dyrberg, *supra* note 21, at 293; Joseph H. H. Weiler, *supra* note 4, at 219.

[74] Calculated from the data in the 2009 annual report, *supra* note 22.

[75] *Ibid.*

[76] Thijmen Koopmans, *supra* note 26, at 29.

[77] *Cf.* Editorial Comments, *The British Suggestions Concerning the Court of Justice*, 16 C.M.L.Rev. 3, 3–7 (1979).

1.28. There have been a number of changes proposed and introduced within the ambit of the existing arrangements, including the *CILFIT* ruling opening a small gap for national courts, at least in principle, to resolve the clear-cut issues of EU law, as well as establishing functional ties of the Court of Justice with the national courts wishing to make a preliminary reference and simplification of the procedure in those cases where preliminary references can be resolved by means of an order[78].

1.29. But there have also been several calls for a more substantial reform, which can be divided into two types. The first concerns proposals to limit access of national courts (either by limiting it to the courts of last instance or by excluding the courts of first instance), something which Rasmussen has called an "eminently suitable remedy"[79] but which seems to have been rejected by the majority in the interest of providing for a unified interpretation of EU law[80].

1.30. A variation of this approach, which would not be based on the formal status of the national court but rather on the individual cases before it, would be to introduce a filtering system whereby the Court of Justice would have the power to choose which references it would admit for consideration. Even though a minority have been in favour of such a system[81], the majority of commentators traditionally felt that it would be too close to US federalism for comfort and would introduce too great a judicial hierarchy into the EU legal order[82], and also that it might provide the Court with a way to avoid addressing difficult issues[83]. However, one of the common reasons stated for the objection was that the current stage of development of EU law did not permit it. Koopmans thus argued that EU law was not yet sufficiently established for such a change[84]. Similarly, while calling for an immediate introduction of docket control, Rasmussen noted that the constraint in the Due report might be interpreted as laying the groundwork for a future reform at a more appropriate moment[85].

1.31. Of course, another option of introducing a filtering system would be for the national courts themselves to apply such a filter[86], which is in fact

---

[78] On this see David Edward, *supra* note 43, at 121–123; *Cf.* Jean-Paul Jacqué, *L'avenir de l'architecture juridictionnelle de l'Union*, 35 (3) R.T.D.E. 443, 445 (1999); Walter van Gerven, *supra* note 29, at 220–221.

[79] Hjalte Rasmussen, *supra* note 27, at 1104.

[80] Ole Due et al., *supra* note 28, at 12–13; Court of Justice, *supra* note 52, at 134–135; Paul Craig, *supra* note 27, at 196; David Edward, *supra* note 43, at 123–125 and 127; Peter Dyrberg, *supra* note 21, at 295; Jean-Paul Jacqué, *supra* note 78, at 447–448.

[81] At least as a possibility to "weed out" the most inappropriate references – Thomas de la Mare, *Article 177 in Social and Political Context*, in THE EVOLUTION OF EU LAW, Oxford: Oxford University Press 245, 248–249 (P. Craig and G. de Búrca eds., 1999); more decisively David W. J. Scorey, *supra* note 40, at 230–231.

[82] Ole Due et al., *supra* note 28, at 21.

[83] Thijmen Koopmans, *supra* note 26, at 29–30.

[84] *Ibid.*, 30.

[85] Hjalte Rasmussen, *supra* note 27, at 1093.

[86] This is advocated by Thomas de la Mare, *supra* note 81, at 247–248.

already an example of the second type of proposals, the one focusing on the "demand" side of the preliminary reference cooperation. Further examples may include those aiming to improve the quality of preliminary references by citing the usefulness of directions given to national courts, identifying best practices, stimulating greater awareness by perhaps temporarily seconding national judges to the Luxembourg courts;[87] and those which call for greater autonomy of national courts when applying EU law, stating that this should be warranted by the greater familiarisation with the field[88].

1.32. Indeed, it seems to be generally accepted that the national courts should assume a more active role in applying EU law[89]. The only unresolved issue seems to be the desired extent of their self-confidence. A minority of commentators goes as far as advocating for national courts to be vested with the right to rule on open issues of EU law themselves, with their rulings open to an appeal via appellate review[90]. A somewhat weaker variation envisions national courts equipping their preliminary references with their own proposed answers, which the Court of Justice could then note and use in the drafting of its ruling[91].

1.33. Following the review above, I wish to conclude with my own observations, and they start where the analysis ended: a significantly stronger role of the national courts is called for, it should be a central issue in the reform debate and it may somewhat paradoxically be required precisely in order to help the Court of Justice perform its duty under Art. 19(1) EU – to safeguard the rule of law in applying EU law. The final part of the paper explains why.

IV. Prognosis: Towards Nationalisation of EU Judicial Review?

1.34. For the last three decades, the Union judicature has been in more or less constant need of reform, and a number of incremental changes have been introduced to try and stem or manage the increasing workload of the Court. But they failed to provide long-term solutions – tinkering will not

---

87 David Edward, *supra* note 43, at 127–129; Paul Craig, *supra* note 27, at 190.

88 Anthony Clarke, *The Application of Community Law by the English Courts*, in EUROPEAN AMBITIONS OF THE NATIONAL JUDICIARY, The Hague: Kluwer Law International 41, 43–44 (R. H. M. Jansen, D. A. C. Koster and R. F. B. van Zutphen eds., 1997).

89 Including a group of distinguished former members of the Court – see Ole Due et al., *supra* note 28, at 14.

90 For a strong support of such a stance, see Arjen W. H. Meij, *National Courts, European Law and Preliminary Co-operation*, in EUROPEAN AMBITIONS OF THE NATIONAL JUDICIARY, The Hague: Kluwer Law International 83, 83–89 (R. H. M. Jansen, D. A. C. Koster and R. F. B. van Zutphen eds., 1997); for a slightly more cautious approach but still amenable to the idea, see Paul Craig, *supra* note 27, at 201–204.

91 Craig opposed such an idea as merely prolonging the time and labour spent on drafting the texts without alleviating the judicial burden of the Court – Paul Craig, *supra* note 27, at 200–201.

do and a more profound reform is needed. That much should surely be recognised by now, so the real question should be: what prevents it?

1.35. Elsewhere[92], I have tried to identify the reasons that made any serious change difficult or nearly impossible, and I identified them as a number of "stalemate positions" on the proper role and functioning of the EU judicial system, where change in either of the two possible directions is perceived as disastrous, even if sometimes thinly veiled as a gift. The first is a seemingly impossible choice between debilitating workload and debilitating decisions, between a selective denial of judicial protection and the slipping quality of judicial pronouncements in trying to keep up with the overflowing workload. The second is a similarly twisted knot of choosing between manageable pragmatism and unmanageable virtuousness, of either opting for pragmatic reform proposals which abandon the substantive virtues of the existing system or remaining faithful to these virtues at all cost, even if that precludes finding any long-term solution to the existing problems. The third, finally, arises out of the fact that any serious reform can only take one of two directions: either the existing Union judicature must be significantly bolstered or the national courts must be greatly empowered to rule on issues of EU law. However, the first option is perceived as a threat of excessive judicial federalisation, while the second seemingly jeopardises the coherence and ultimately effectiveness of EU legal order. Surely, one or the other is inevitable; but they are both undesirable.

1.36. It is this impotent *status quo* – of a severely undernourished Union judicature finding it hard to keep up the increasing workload and the severely restrained national courts muzzled by the *CILFIT* reference requirement and the *Foto Frost* limits on review of legality – which needs to be overcome. And we can start to unravel it by admitting a fact that is always hinted at beneath the surface but seldom openly acknowledged: even as things stand, many of the extolled virtues of the existing system do not work anyway. For instance, when some proposals are criticised as detrimental to the established judicial dialogue between the Court of Justice and the national courts, one could wonder, tongue-in-cheek: what judicial dialogue?

1.37. Let us remind ourselves of the data: in 2009, the Court of Justice received 302 preliminary references, the biggest number so far; and yet, that adds up to one reference per 1.65 million citizens of EU Member States. French courts, for instance, made 28 preliminary references. Are we to assume that, throughout the year and before all French courts, only 28 cases emerged which involved open issues of EU law that would require an authoritative answer by the Court? Or should we admit that the number of national references is so low due to a variety of other reasons: one, that national attorneys often do not raise arguments of EU law and/or national judges do not consider them, or find ways of avoiding addressing

---

92   Matej Accetto, *Double-Headed Trojan Horse*, EUR.ADV. 4, 4–6 (Autumn 2006).

them as not relevant to the decision at issue; another, that national courts in fact already apply some filtering system to decide which questions to refer to the Court, whether we choose to formally acknowledge it or not; and finally, perhaps as a corollary to the previous reason, that sometimes they resolve EU issues by themselves, already assuming a more relaxed interpretation of the *CILFIT* requirements to be able to do so. Otherwise, surely, we should expect thousands rather than a few hundreds of references flooding the Court of Justice every year.

1.38. If we acknowledge this fact, several of the existing arguments are put in a slightly different light. When, for instance, critics of the proposal to limit access to the highest courts alone argue that this would force litigants through the hoops of domestic appeals before they could receive the preliminary ruling and favour the wealthier litigants[93], we can remind them that since 2003, states like Denmark and Finland have produced approximately four preliminary references in a given year – a number which paints somewhat academic both the notion of the negative impact that the proposal would have on the national judicial system and the suggestion that it would significantly help the workload problem. Similarly, when commentators say that the *CILFIT* requirements should not be relaxed[94], we can point out that a strict adherence to its requirements does not take place and would be highly impractical in any event as it would completely swamp the Court of Justice, a fact admitted by the members of the Court[95].

1.39. The upshot of acknowledging this fact is that the reform is not only inevitable, it is also already taking place where it can: at the national court level. We may continue to debate whether or not the requirements limiting the autonomy of national courts should formally be reconsidered, and a few voices at the Court have done precisely that, like AG Jacobs with regard to the *CILFIT* standards in his opinion in the *Wiener* case[96], AG Mengozzi in his opinion in the *Gestoras* and *Segi* cases with regard to the power of national courts to review the acts of the (then) third pillar[97] or very recently AG Villalón with regard to

---

93   E.g. Ole Due et al., *supra* note 28, at 13.

94   E.g. Catherine Turner and Rudolphe Muñoz, *supra* note 41, at 66.

95   In the early 1980s, prior to assuming the role of an advocate general, Jacobs stressed the point with regard to lower-level courts – see the transcript of the debate *in* La Cour de Justice des Communautés Européennes et les États Membres, Brussels: Editions de l'Université de Bruxelles 50 (Institut d'études européennes Université libre de Bruxelles ed., 1981). It was also acknowledged by the Due Working Group – see Ole Due et al., *supra* note 28, at 15; Hjalte Rasmussen said this admission could be welcomed as a "refreshing expression of intellectual plain speaking" – Hjalte Rasmussen, *supra* note 27, at 1088.

96   Opinion of AG Jacobs of 10 July 1997, Case C-338/95, *Wiener S.I. GmbH v Hauptzollamt Emmerich* [1997] ECR I-6495, paras 56–65.

97   Opinion of AG Mengozzi of 26 October 2006, Case C-354/04 P, *Gestoras Pro Amnistía, Juan Mari Olano Olano and Julen Zelarain Errasti v Council of the European Union* [2007]

the *Rheinmühlen I*[98] standards limiting national procedural autonomy in his opinion in the *Elchinov* case[99]. But we should also acknowledge that some such reconsideration is already spontaneously taking place[100], and that calls for greater involvement of national courts in resolving issues of EU law will not only become more frequent and inevitable[101], they will also make ever greater sense if the aspiration for legality and the respect for the rule of law in the operation of the EU legal order is to be taken seriously. The only other alternative, barring the radical approach of introducing a full-fledged "federal" judiciary with a number of inferior Union courts, is to continue living in the pretence (or illusion) that the existing judicial system provides for a suitable level of judicial scrutiny controlling the respect of manifold obligations arising under EU law, and that it will continue to do so through further expansion and deepening of the EU legal order.

1.40. The real challenges of the reform may thus not lie in determining what further tinkering with the structure and organisation of the Luxembourg Court may be attempted to keep its head (just barely) above water, but rather in whether the national courts, already long touted as the ordinary EU courts, are ready to assume the strengthened role that the factual situation demands of them. That understanding should also shift the focus of the debates on EU judicial reform: more efforts should be geared at determining how the national courts are currently coping with EU law and how best to equip – and, perhaps, encourage – them to properly assume such responsibilities. The community of (the rule of) law would deserve as much.

| | |

ECR I-1579, and Case C-355/04 P, *Segi, Araitz Zubimendi Izaga and Aritza Galarraga v Council of the European Union* [2007] ECR I-1657, paras 98–132.

[98] ECJ Judgment of 16 January 1974, Case 166/73, *Rheinmühlen-Düsseldorf v Einfuhr-und Vorratsstelle für Getreide und Futtermittel* [1974] ECR 33.

[99] Opinion of AG Cruz Villalón of 10 June 2010, Case C-173/09, *Elchinov* (not yet reported), paras 23–38. Perhaps unsurprisingly, the Court in its judgment of 5 October 2010 declined Advocate General's invitation to consider the *Rheinmühlen I* standards allowing lower courts to disregard those rulings and directions from higher courts they consider inconsistent with EU law, but many of his arguments echo the appraisal of the state of affairs included here.

[100] *Cf.* Takis Tridimas, *supra* note 42, at 42–44, listing several cases before national courts in evidence of their discretion when applying the *CILFIT* standards.

[101] For a recent example see e.g. Dorota Leczykiewicz, *"Effective Judicial Protection" of Human Rights After Lisbon: Should National Courts Be Empowered to Review EU Secondary Law?*, 35 (3) E.L.REV. 326, 341–348 (2010), arguing that, similarly to the reasoning of AG Mengozzi with regard to the former third pillar mentioned above, the national courts should also be empowered to review EU secondary legislation for compliance with the EU human rights law.

Summaries

FRA [*Le passé et les possibilités d'avenir de l'organisation judiciaire de l'Union européenne*]

À bien des égards, la réussite de l'Union européenne en tant que régime dépend de l'efficacité de son ordre juridique, lequel à son tour dépend de la capacité de son organisation judiciaire à assurer le respect du droit communautaire. Dans ce domaine, le rôle de la Cour de Justice Européenne est une réussite. Pourtant, depuis plus de trente ans maintenant, celle-ci fait sans cesse face à la menace d'innombrables dossiers et demandes de réforme, du reste nécessaire, du système. Cet article retrace le développement du système judiciaire luxembourgeois et ses nombreuses réformes, mais souligne également ses insuffisances, la plus générale étant que les changements introduits n'apportent une amélioration que temporaire. La raison réside peut-être dans le fait que cette question se trouve dans une impasse (réelle ou perçue) où un changement trop brutal dans un sens ou dans un autre compromettrait, semble-t-il, les vertus tellement louées du système existant, mais où l'on suppose que la pire des hypothèses serait de ne rien changer, et qu'il convient d'explorer les modifications du système là où elles sont le plus facilement mises en œuvre et là où elles sont parfois déjà appliquées, en l'occurrence les tribunaux nationaux.

CZE [*Minulý a možný budoucí vývoj soudnictví v Evropské unii*]

Úspěch Evropské unie jako politického zřízení v mnoha směrech závisí na efektivnosti jejího právního řádu, a ta zase závisí na efektivnosti jejího soudnictví při zajišťování dodržování práva EU. Evropský soudní dvůr hraje v tomto ohledu roli úspěšnou; a přesto ho již více než tři desetiletí provází hrozba zahlcení případy a výzvy k tolik potřebné reformě systému. Tato stať sleduje vývoj lucemburského soudního systému a jeho různých reforem, ale také poukazuje na jejich nedostatky – z nichž neobecnějším je ten, že zaváděné změny poskytují pouze krátkodobé řešení vedoucí k úlevě. Důvod může spočívat v (skutečném nebo vnímaném) mrtvém bodě, kde by příliš drastická změna v jakémkoli směru zdánlivě ohrozila pozitiva stávajícího systému; má se však za to, že nejhorší možností je uváznout na místě a že změny v systému by se měly hledat tam, kde je jejich zavádění nejsnazší a kde nejpravděpodobněji již začaly – u národních soudů.

| | |

POL [*Przeszłość i możliwe kierunki rozwoju orzecznictwa Unii Europejskiej w przyszłości*]

Przestrzeganie prawa UE i konsekwencja w jego stosowaniu stanowi klucz do skuteczności Unii jako całości, zaś jego autorytarna ocena tradycyjnie należy do zadań Europejskiego Trybunału Sprawiedliwości. Jednak już od dłuższego czasu sukcesom tej instytucji towarzyszą apele o mniej lub bardziej pilne reformy pozwalające sprostać gromadzącym się sprawom i obowiązkom. Niniejszy artykuł opisuje rozwój istniejącego systemu unijnej kontroli sądowej i próbuje znaleźć przyczyny niepowodzenia dotychczasowych reform w dostarczeniu oczekiwanych długofalowych rozwiązań. Wnioski końcowe zawierają krótką ocenę możliwości zmiany tam, gdzie jest to najłatwiejsze – na poziomie sądów krajowych.

DEU [*Vergangenheit und mögliche Zukunftsalternativen der EU Rechtsprechungssystems*]

Die Einhaltung und konsequente Anwendung von EU-Recht mag für das wirksame Bestehen der EU als solche recht wohl von entscheidender Bedeutung sein, und die Aufgabe, eine verbindliche Beurteilung des EU-Rechts zu unternehmen, ist seit jeher dem Europäischen Gerichtshof anvertraut worden. Seine Erfolge sind jedoch seit langem von Rufen nach mehr oder weniger dringlichen Reformen begleitet, da der Gerichtshof ansonsten nicht mehr mit dem immer voller werdenden Verfahrenskalender und den wachsenden Aufgaben Schritt halten könne. Die vorliegende Arbeit zeichnet die Entwicklung des vorhandenen Normenkontrollsystems der EU nach und versucht die Gründe aufzuzeigen, warum es allen bisher verabschiedeten Reformen nicht gelungen ist, die geforderten nachhaltigen Lösungen zu liefern. Abschließend wird eine knappe Würdigung des Bereichs vorgenommen, in dem ein Wandel am ehesten zu erreichen sein dürfte – dem der nationalen Gerichte.

RUS [*Прошлое и вероятное будущее судебной системы Европейского Союза*]

Соблюдение и последовательное применение законодательства ЕС может быть решающим в плане эффективности Союза в целом, а задача обеспечения авторитетной оценки законодательства ЕС традиционно доверяется Европейскому суду. И все же, длительное время успех его деятельности сопровождается призывами к более или менее срочным реформам, так как ему необходимо поспевать за растущим списком рассматривающихся дел и видов ответственности. В документе прослеживается развитие существующей системы судебного контроля ЕС с попыткой выявить причины, по которым в результате всех проведенных на сегодняшний день реформ не удалось найти востребованные долгосрочные решения. В заключение приведена краткая оценка изменения там, где его можно добиться легче всего, — в национальных судах.

ES [*El pasado y los posibles futuros de la Judicatura de la Unión Europea*]

La observación y la aplicación consistente de la legislación de la UE pueden ser vitales para la eficacia de la Unión en su totalidad, y la tarea de proporcionar una evaluación autoritaria de la legislación de la UE le ha sido encomendada tradicionalmente al Tribunal de Justicia Europeo. Sin embargo, sus éxitos han estado acompañados durante mucho tiempo de solicitudes de reformas más o menos urgentes si se trata de mantener el ritmo de los cada vez mayores legajos y responsabilidades. El artículo sigue el desarrollo del sistema existente de la revisión judicial de la UE e intenta discernir los motivos por los que todas las reformas adoptadas han fracasado en su misión de proporcionar las soluciones a largo plazo solicitadas. Concluye con una breve apreciación del cambio efectivo en aquellos aspectos en que sería más fácil de conseguir: los tribunales nacionales.

Czech (& Central European) Yearbook of Arbitration

Bogusław Banaszak | Łukasz Żukowski

Regulatory Framework and Characteristics of Arbitration Judicature in Poland

Key words:
Constitution
of the Republic
of Poland |
constitutional right
to court proceedings
| arbitration |
arbitrator | arbitration
judicature | request
for arbitration

Abstract | *In Poland, arbitration is considered the best known and most widely used method of out-of-court dispute settlement. The Constitution of Poland of 1997 sets out a comprehensive list of courts, as well as the principle of the exclusivity of the courts in the administration of justice, although it fails to mention arbitration courts. According to the judicature of the Polish Constitutional Tribunal, the justice system should be treated as objective, i.e. as a pursuit devised as a legal means of conflict resolution, and not as subjective, i.e. as the sole jurisdiction of the courts. This means that, from the start, not all cases and disputes concerning the legal situation of an individual necessarily need to be resolved in courts. The primary source of law regulating arbitration courts in Poland is the Civil Code of 17 November 1964, while the date of 28 July 2005 when an amendment to the Code became effective is considered a breakthrough which significantly changed arbitration in Poland. Sources of law other than the Code include a number of acts defining the activities of permanent arbitration courts for resolving disputes of certain kind, including numerous regulations concerning professional corporations. Sources of law regulating arbitration judicature, which are not generally binding, include the rules and regulations of the permanent arbitration courts. The Court of Arbitration at the Polish Chamber of Commerce in Warsaw is the most active permanent arbitration court in Poland.*

| | |

Prof. dr hab. dr h.c. Bogusław Banaszak Professor of Legal Sciences, Professor honoris causa of three Universities, expert in constitutional law; is Head of the Constitutional Law Chair at the University of Wrocław. Prof. B. Banaszak used to be the President of the Polish Legislative Council by the Prime Minister (2006-2010). He is also a member of European Academy of Science, Art and Literature (Paris). Prof. Banaszak has written over 300 publications, including 20 in English and 50 in German, including two highly regarded books on Polish Constitutional Law and International Encyclopedias of Law (Kluwers 2005). He is on the editorial board of several scholarly journals and has given over 60 lectures throughout Europe, Latin- and North America.
e-mail: kaprakon@ prawo.uni.wroc.pl

I. Nature of Arbitration (Arbitration Judicature) in Light of Polish Legal Theory

Dr. Łukasz Żukowski was born in Wrocław in 1975. He completed his MA studies at the Faculty of Law, Administration and Economics of the University of Wrocław in 1999. He is currently employed as Assistant Professor at the Chair of Constitutional Law at the University of Wrocław. Dr. Żukowski is the author of articles concerning Polish constitutional law and human rights. His main area of interest is the constitutional regulation of public funds. His dissertation was devoted to the issue of the Polish central bank's position under constitutional law in the context of Poland's accession to the eurozone.
e-mail:
lzukowski1@wp.pl

2.01. For some time now, out-of-court methods for the resolution of disputes among entities have been increasingly recognised by legal theory and, as a consequence, legal practice; the advantages of such methods in comparison with traditional court proceedings are stressed by advocates of sociological conflict theory. In particular, they argue that an attempt should be made to resolve conflicts (disputes) by other means than by having them examined by a public court. Such methods are generally referred to as ADR – Alternative Dispute Resolution methods, according to U.S. doctrine. In the Polish literature, they are widely defined as the complete set of such proceedings, "the initiation of which depends on the will of the parties, the performance of which takes place outside of common courts, and the desired result of which is a decision made in the course of arbitration, or a settlement achieved by using negotiation or mediation and conciliation procedures"[1].

2.02. The basic range of alternative means of dispute resolution includes negotiation, conciliation, mediation and arbitration. At times, the methods are mixed, combining certain elements of those means listed. In Poland, the most widely known and the most frequently used form of ADR in practice is arbitration, all the more so due to the very long history of arbitration judicature in Poland, especially gaining in importance as a result of the degradation (collapse) of the functioning of the judicial authority.

2.03. It should be noted that the notion of arbitration is generally understood to be the "amicable resolution of disputes between natural and legal entities in civil (business) matters by individuals (arbitrators) and in accordance with (procedural and material) rules, the choice of which is directly or

---

[1] Ryszard Balicki, *Pozasądowe procedury rozwiązywania sporów między jednostkami (Extrajudicial procedures of resolving disputes of the individuals)*, in 2 PRAWA I WOLNOŚCI JEDNOSTKI W KONSTYTUCJI RP (*Rights and Freedoms of the Individuals in the Polish Constitution*), Warszawa: C. H. Beck (M. Jabłoński ed., 2010), see also ANDRZEJ WACH, ALTERNATYWNE FORMY ROZWIĄZYWANIA SPORÓW SPORTOWYCH (*An Alternative Forms Of Resolving Sporting Disputes*), Warszawa: Liber Sp. z o.o. 124 (2005).

indirectly influenced by the parties"[2]. The Code of Civil Procedure[3], on the other hand, uses the term of arbitration judicature, whereas Polish doctrine defines the arbitration court as a non-public court, appointed by the unanimous consent of the parties for the purpose of resolving an existing dispute (or one occurring in the future) due to legal relations, the decision of which will have legal effect equal to a decision of a public court[4].

2.04. Arbitration judicature, both public and non-public, is a common method for out-of-court dispute resolution, known both in the practice and doctrine of various countries. In the definition of arbitration, the doctrine focuses on various elements that could be considered the basic components of this institution. French doctrine assumes it to be a method by which a third party is commissioned by two or more parties with the jurisdictional task of resolving a dispute between them. It also specifies arbitration as a mechanism for solving a problem of at least two entities, adding that an arbitrator is authorised to resolve a dispute due to a private understanding of the parties, and not as a result of the delegation of the state authority. Advocates of *common law* doctrine also stress that the parties involved are not able to resolve the dispute on their own, which is why they agree to have it resolved by a private person, and that the effect would take the form of a decision, and not a compromise reached between the parties to the dispute. German doctrine emphasises that the parties, with their declarations of will, exclude the competence of the public court in that respect, and arbitration judicature constitutes the sum of legal regulations and institutions used for the resolution of disputes, in terms of private law, by private bodies and institutions. German authors only perceive such institutions as arbitration judicature that have been established under an agreement of the parties, and not under a provision of law[5].

2.05. In the Polish literature, various reasons governing the parties' decision to have their dispute resolved by arbitration judicature are stated as well. In general, it may be found that the use of arbitration institutions is accompanied by a critical attitude towards the common courts, considered – especially in business matters – to be inefficient and unable to provide the parties with an expeditious examination and resolution of the matter

---

[2] Karolina Goszka, *Instytucja arbitrażu handlowego (Institute of the Commecial Arbitration)*, 80 (5) EDUKACJA PRAWNICZA 12 (2006).

[3] (43) JOURNAL OF LAWS Item 296 (1964).

[4] See e.g. Tadeusz Szurski, *Arbitraż – skuteczny sposób likwidowania sporów (Arbitration – an effective method of resolving disputes)*, (12) MoP 468 (1998), or ANDRZEJ TYNEL, ROZSTRZYGANIE SPORÓW GOSPODARCZYCH (*Resolving of the Commercial Disputes*), Warszawa: Międzynarodowa Szkoła Menedżerów 9 (1999) and Andrzej W. Wiśniewski, *Charakter prawny instytucji arbitrażu w świetle nowelizacji polskiego prawa arbitrażowego (Legal Nature of an Arbitration Pursuant to the New Polish Arbitration Regulation)*, (2) ADR. ARBITRAŻ I MEDIACJA (2008).

[5] 1-2 ŁUKASZ BŁASZCZAK, MAŁGORZATA LUDWIK, SĄDOWNICTWO POLUBOWNE (ARBITRAŻ), Warszawa: C. H. Beck (2007).

(dispute), as well as being encumbered with excessive formalisation of the procedure. At the same time, the common feature of ADR methods, i.e., arbitration judicature as well, is its efficiency, considerable deformalisation of the proceedings, its non-public nature, and the guarantee of direct participation of the parties authorised to audit the course of the proceedings.

2.06. Therefore, arbitration proceedings are by definition more convenient for the parties due to the fact that they are less formal, quicker and less expensive than the traditional court procedure. Furthermore, the flexibility of arbitration is affected by the possibility for the parties to shape the course of the proceedings. It is also by no means irrelevant that the decision is more compatible with the specific nature of the respective matter due to the expertise of the arbitrators, who do not need to be lawyers, but may be experts in the respective field. Another advantage of arbitration is its confidentiality, pertaining both to the course of the proceedings, as such, and to the decision reached, which is not published, unless approved by the parties[6].

2.07. One other beneficial aspect of arbitration judicature should also be noted. On the one hand, the participants of arbitration proceedings may withdraw and return to the traditional court procedure if they find that the arbitration court does not meet their expectations. On the other hand, the arbitration court's decisions are fully binding for the parties, with legal effect equal to decisions of public courts, although as a rule, decisions of arbitration courts require approval or confirmation of their enforceability in order to gain legal effect equal to the effect of decisions made by public courts[7].

2.08. The autonomous nature of an arbitration court in comparison to a common court is demonstrated, first and foremost, by the need to specify a certain area of activity excluded from the control of the state administration of justice. Therefore, the Polish legislature, following the provisions of the UNCITRAL Model Law, has separated the competence of the arbitration courts from the common courts. According to the provisions of Article 5 of the UNCITRAL Law and Article 1159, Section 1 of the Code of Civil Procedure, a court wishing to intervene in proceedings before an arbitration court must establish statutory authorisation to do so. It is also unacceptable for court proceedings to be initiated before common courts if the matter is governed by an arbitration agreement. Moreover, the independence of an arbitration court in relation to a public court is strengthened – as it is emphasised – by solutions providing the arbitration court with the right to decide on its competence and establishing the principle of independence of an arbitration agreement from the basic agreement, due to which the ineffectiveness of the basic agreement does not affect the effectiveness of the arbitration clause[8].

---

[6] Karolina Goszka, *supra* note 2, at 16.
[7] Łukasz Błaszczak, Małgorzata Ludwik, *supra* note 5, at 19.
[8] *Ibid.*, 21.

2.09. The main prerequisite of arbitration judicature is the freedom of the will of the parties. It is shown both in the decision concerning the resolution of disputes by way of arbitration and in the freedom to decide on the composition of the arbitration team, as well as to choose the law applicable for the purposes of resolving the given matter. The aforementioned features, which appear to be arbitrary, cause difficulties in classifying the institutions of arbitration judicature, not only for the users themselves, i.e., potential and actual parties to disputes resolved by arbitration, but also for legal doctrine. The main question in this respect concerns the legal nature of arbitration. In the Polish literature, it is mainly the ambiguity of the basis of the authority of arbitration courts to act that is noted. Is it more the autonomous will of the parties, or are we dealing with the delegation of state authority here? The nature of arbitration judicature can also be perceived ambiguously: as proceedings under material law or under procedural law. J. Kohler was the first to note that it is necessary to differentiate between the aforementioned aspects, claiming that when qualifying arbitration judicature as an institution of procedural law, we cannot forget that arbitrators only act under an agreement of the parties. However, his suggested differentiation has not been observed by all authors, and the terms "jurisdictional" and "procedural" have been used interchangeably; the issue of the basis of the authority of arbitration courts to act and the issue of the nature of arbitration judicature itself have often been considered together. Therefore, arbitration judicature is still today sometimes declared to be of a "jurisdictional and procedural nature"[9]. However, it seems at present that we should depart from unambiguous delimitations and consider both the contractual and jurisdictional features of arbitration judicature[10]. It is thereby stressed that it would not be possible to have an arbitration function in absolute independence of the national legal system, which is why it is suggested that arbitration be subjected to the law of jurisdiction for the seat of the arbitration court[11].

2.10. Therefore, it seems that the two concepts are not mutually exclusive, but instead complement one another. It appears to be reasonable to analyse arbitration's references to sources of state authority and the organisations thereof. When evaluating arbitration in this context, special attention should be paid to sources of law establishing judicial authority in the Polish legal system, i.e., first and foremost, constitutional regulation.

---

[9]   *Ibid.*, 43.
[10]   See also *supra* note 4.
[11]   Łukasz Błaszczak, Malgorzata Ludwik, *supra* note 5, at 45.

II. Arbitration Judicature and Right to Court Proceedings in Light of Article 45 of the Constitution of the Republic of Poland of 2 April 1997 – Constitutional Foundation of Arbitration in Poland

2.11. Like other methods, arbitration is also considered to be an alternative form in relation to the court (adjudicative) procedure for the resolution of disputes between entities. It is an important relevant feature of ADR, as already mentioned that the parties are free to use these methods in order to resolve the dispute between them. Therefore, one of the issues widely discussed in Polish doctrine is the relation between arbitration judicature (the other ADRs as well) and the constitutional principle of the right to court proceedings, and in a wider perspective, the issue of constitutional grounds for arbitration.

2.12. According to Article 10 of the Constitution of the Republic of Poland of 2 April 1997, judicial power is vested in courts and tribunals (the Constitutional Tribunal and the Tribunal of State). This principle is confirmed by the provisions of Chapter VIII of the basic law of "Courts and tribunals". According to Article 173, "courts and tribunals shall constitute a separate power and shall be independent of other branches of power", which, in accordance with Article 174, "shall pronounce judgement in the name of the Republic of Poland". At the same time, the Constitution only provides courts with exclusivity with respect to the administration of justice, specifying in Article 175 the institutions appointed to implement the administration of justice, i.e., the Supreme Court, the common courts, administrative courts and military courts. It is a closed group, which does not include arbitration courts and other quasi-judicial adjudicating bodies. The basic law provides common courts, by way of asserting competence, with the competence to implement the administration of justice in all matters, except for matters that are statutorily reserved for the competence of other courts, whereas the legal system lacks regulations providing arbitration courts with the competence to examine a given category of matters, e.g. trade or business cases[12]. Furthermore, Article 176 of the Constitution provides a guarantee of at least two stages of court proceedings, i.e., a principle that does not apply for arbitration proceedings (unless otherwise agreed by the parties). Finally, among measures for the protection of rights and freedoms, Article 45 of the Constitution treats the right to court proceedings as a basic measure, stating that "everyone shall have the right to a fair and public hearing of their case, without undue delay, before a competent, impartial and independent court".

---

[12] This issue has been raised by Andrzej Szumański, *Pojęcie, rodzaje, i charakter prawny arbitrażu handlowego (The Concept, Methods and Legal Nature of Commercial Arbitration), in* 8 SYSTEM PRAWA HANDLOWEGO: ARBITRAŻ HANDLOWY (*Commercial Arbitration*), Warszawa: C. H. Beck 48-49 (A. Szumański ed., 2010).

2.13. However, the quoted provisions of the applicable Constitution of the Republic of Poland of 1997 do not show the existence of any contradiction between the indicated constitutional principles (the right to court proceedings) and arbitration judicature. The non-existence of such a conflict has been noted both by doctrine and judicial decisions, including those of the Constitutional Tribunal, referring to the nature and manner of the understanding of the constitutional notion of the "right to court proceedings" and the "administration of justice"[13]. There is no doubt as to the fact that the "right to court proceedings" is integrally connected (by the system) with the judicial administration of justice; at the same time, however, the constitutional right to court proceedings must not be considered equal to the obligation to have every dispute, without exception, examined by a common court[14] In the doctrine, the constitutional notion of the administration of justice is understood in two ways: from subjective and objective perspectives. From the former perspective, it is perceived as being equal to the notion of a state authority (court) implementing the administration of justice[15], provided with the attributes of independence and impartiality. The latter perspective focuses on the nature of the activity in terms of the implementation of the administration of justice, i.e., the resolution of conflicts resulting from legal relations[16], and has been reflected in the judicial decisions of the Constitutional Tribunal. In a decision dated 8 December 1998 (K 41/97), the Constitutional Tribunal found that the administration of justice "should be understood rather objectively as an activity constituting the resolution of legal conflicts, and not subjectively as the exclusive competence of court authorities". Therefore, this means – in the opinion of the Constitutional Tribunal – that not all matters and disputes concerning the legal situations of the entity must be resolved by courts from the very beginning

---

[13] The views of the doctrine have also been indicated by Anna Deryng, *Miejsce sądownictwa polubownego a wymiar sprawiedliwości w świetle zasad konstytucyjnych* (*The place of arbitration in the light of constitutional principles*), (3) ADR. ARBITRAŻ I MEDIACJA (2008); Anna Deryng, *Sąd polubowny a realizacja konstytucyjnej zasady prawa do sądu* (*The arbitration tribunal and the implementation of the constitutional principle of the right to court*), (4) ADR. ARBITRAŻ I MEDIACJA (2009).

[14] LECH MORAWSKI, GŁÓWNE PROBLEMY WSPÓŁCZESNEJ FILOZOFII PRAWA. PRAWO W TOKU PRZEMIAN (*The Fundamental Problems of Contemporary Legal Philosophy. Law in the Course of Transformation*), Warszawa: LexisNexis 236 (1999).

[15] See also BOGUSŁAW BANASZAK, PRAWO KONSTYTUCYJNE (*Constitutional Law*), Warszawa: C. H. Beck 660-661 (2010), and LESZEK GARLICKI, POLSKIE PRAWO KONSTYTUCYJNE. ZARYS WYKŁADU (*Polish Constitutional Law. Outline of Lecture*), Warszawa: K. E. Liber 332 (2007).

[16] See also the comments of Hanna Duszka-Jakimko, Monika Haczkowska, *ADR a zasada prawo do sądu w perspektywie teoretycznej i konstytucyjnej* (*ADR and Principle of the Right to a Court in the Perspective of the Theory and Constitution*), in ALTERNATYWNE FORMY ROZWIĄZYWANIE SPORÓW W TEORII I PRAKTYCE (*Alternative Dispute Resolution in Theory and Practice*), Opole: Wydawnictwo Uniwersytetu Opolskiego 30-31 (H. Duszka-Jakimko, S. L. Stadniczenko eds., 2008).

(Decision K 41/97)[17]. It should be noted that the Polish legal system contains other examples of extra-judicial bodies provided with the authority to resolve conflicts between entities, including, in particular, bodies deciding on the disciplinary liability of members of professional corporations, labour inspectorates or quasi-judicial bodies (e.g. marine chambers)[18].

2.14. Therefore, both the decisions of the Polish Constitutional Tribunal and the European Court of Human Rights allow for the resolution of disputes resulting from legal relations by extra-judicial bodies (not included in the constitutional list of bodies implementing the administration of justice), provided, however, that such a body (court in the material meaning) would guarantee independence and impartiality, and any proceedings held before such a body would be secured by the respective procedural guarantees[19], under which it can be assumed that the proceedings meet the constitutional requirements of a reliable and fair procedure (Article 45 of the Constitution). In proceedings held before arbitration courts, these fundamental rules are implemented by means of the statutory specification of the requirements to be met by arbitrators, and guarantees for respecting the rights of the parties in the course of the arbitration procedure, which shall be referred to below.

2.15. However, the Constitutional Tribunal has indicated that "courts must always have a prevailing position, making it possible to verify the extra-judicial body's decision" (decision dated 8 December 1998)[20]. In the case of arbitration judicature (arbitration), the guarantee is implemented by means of a petition for the reversal of a decision after the occurrence of reasons specified in the law (as discussed in more detail below), as stipulated in Article 1205 of the Code of Civil Procedure (hereinafter referred to as the CCP), and the possibility of the enforcement of arbitration court decisions only after a clause of enforcement has been granted. Therefore, this means that decisions of arbitration courts remain controlled by public courts.

2.16. Interestingly enough, during work on the currently applicable Constitution, it was suggested that it should contain a provision on the possibility of the implementation of the administration of justice to a specific extent by extra-judicial bodies[21]. Although, as already mentioned, the authors of the Constitution have not decided to express such a possibility *expressis verbis*, it seems to be reasonable to search in the provisions of the basic law

---

[17] See also Ryszard Balicki, *supra* note 1.

[18] The existence of such bodies was indicated by the Constitutional Tribunal in its decision of 13 March 1996, K 11/95, finding that "the Polish legal system includes other bodies, the decisions and statements of which can hardly be encompassed by the framework of common courts".

[19] See also Hanna Duszka-Jakimko, Monika Haczkowska, *supra* note 16, at 30-31, and the decisions of the European Court of Human Rights as quoted therein.

[20] See also Ryszard Balicki, *supra* note 1.

[21] See the proposals of Aleksander Ratajczak, *Trzecia władza w Konstytucji* (*Third Power in the Constitution*), (224) "Rzeczpospolita" 17 (1995).

for grounds for the waiver of the parties of the examination of their matter by a public court and for the submission of the matter to an arbitration court. Due to the fact that the choice of an out-of-court resolution of a dispute in the form of arbitration (other ADR forms) remains at the discretion of the parties, such constitutional grounds may be attributed to the principle of freedom (autonomy of a person) as expressed in Article 31, Section 1. It is emphasised that "this freedom includes the right to commission a chosen third party with the resolution of a dispute concerning a subjective right"[22], and entails the waiver of the right to the examination of the matter by a public court, as can be deemed acceptable in light of Article 45 of the basic law. However, it must not be assumed that the submission of a matter for examination by an arbitration court constitutes a waiver of the constitutional right to court proceedings, which – as is reasonably stressed in the doctrine – is a public subjective right, which is neither subject to a statute of limitations, nor allows for the waiver thereof. One should entirely agree with the view that the right to court proceedings in case of the resolution of the matter by an arbitration court is expressed by the possibility of having the decision thereof audited by a common court, based on the generally applicable provisions of the CCP, and not the agreement of the parties[23].

2.17. The difference of opinion in the doctrine with respect to the nature and consequences of a public court's audit of the decision of an arbitration court should be noted. According to the first view, as a result of the audit, access to the public court remains open to a certain extent, while according to the second view, the public court only examines the reliability of the rules of the arbitration proceedings and the compliance of the contents of the decision with the basic rules of the legal system of the Republic of Poland, but does not decide on the subjective rights of the parties[24].

2.18. It seems that the two opinions are similar to some extent, because a public court, revoking the decision of an arbitration court, referring to one of the statutory reasons, indeed does not decide about the subjective rights of the parties, yet such a decision of the court may induce the parties to have the matter examined through the court administration of justice. Secondly, any considerations regarding the relation of arbitration judicature and the traditional court proceedings merely as alternative and complementary solutions are not of great value from the cognitive point of view, and the answer to the question thus asked is rather obvious. There

---

[22] See also Andrzej Szumański, *supra* note 12, at 49. See also Andrzej W. Wiśniewski, *supra* note 4, at 72.

[23] See also ŁUKASZ BŁASZCZAK, MAŁGORZATA LUDWIK, *supra* note 5, at 52-54, and the literature widely cited therein, and also ŁUKASZ BŁASZCZAK, WYROK SĄDU POLUBOWNEGO W POSTĘPOWANIU CYWILNYM (*Arbitration Award in Civil Procedure*), Warszawa: Wolter Kluwers Polska 70-79 (2010).

[24] This firm view has been expressed by Andrzej W. Wiśniewski, *ibid.* The doctrine's view concerning this matter has been discussed by Andrzej Szumański, *supra* note 12, at 49.

is no doubt as to the fact that arbitration judicature (and other ADR) is not able to replace classic court proceedings before common courts, and is only a complementary method. On the other hand, its present and future popularity has two sources: the decrease of the effectiveness of the traditional courts, and – which is no less important – the more general trend toward increasing action on the part of society that accompanies the development of a civil society[25].

2.19. The institution of arbitration judicature – as is reasonably emphasised – "extends (...) the constitutional standard of the right to court proceedings, and is mainly understood as the substantiated right to the implementation of justice, and not only as a formal indication of the right to "court proceedings"[26]. Therefore, in the following considerations, it will be necessary to refer to the procedural guarantees relevant for proceedings held before arbitration courts, the source of which is derived from the requirements of the quoted Article 45 of the Constitution.

III. Sources of Arbitration Law in the Polish Legal System

2.20. The system of sources of law in terms of arbitration judicature in the Polish legal order consists both of international agreements and national legal acts, particularly including code regulations. The acts are included among sources of universally binding law in light of Article 87 of the Constitution of the Republic of Poland. In consideration of the closed system of universally binding acts, the regulations of regular arbitration courts and agreements of the parties as to the course of the proceedings are of a different nature, although they are relevant for the course of the proceedings before arbitration courts[27].

2.21. Due to the limited framework of this document, we will only discuss in detail the sources of national law, in particular, code regulations. The main source of law governing the institution of arbitration judicature (arbitration) in Poland is the Code of Civil Procedure of 17 November 1964, whereas, after the amendment of the Code dated 28 July 2005[28], the subsequent stages of arbitration procedures have been regulated in Part V of the Code under eight titles. It should be noted that the regulation of trade arbitration was planned to be included in a separate act on international trade arbitration, the draft of which was presented to the Sejm in 1998. However, due to the fact that it was not adopted, the institution of arbitration, including trade arbitration, is governed by the CCP. The aim of thoroughly amending the part of the Code

---

25 Lech Morawski, *Proces sądowy a instytucje alternatywne (na przykładzie sporów cywilnych)* (*The Lawsuit and Alternative Institutions (the Examples of Civil Disputes)*), (1) PAŃSTWO I PRAWO 15-18 (1993).
26 See also Hanna Duszka-Jakimko, Monika Haczkowska, *supra* note 16, at 35.
27 See further ŁUKASZ BŁASZCZAK, MAŁGORZATA LUDWIK, *supra* note 5, at 56.
28 (178) JOURNAL OF LAWS Item 1478.

concerning arbitration courts was to achieve the improved adaptation of the legal regulation to the performance of the function thereof with respect to the changes brought about by the transformation of the system, the development of international trade, and foreign investments into Poland. The model solutions of the UNCITRAL law were also taken into consideration at that time. Therefore, the amendment of 2005 revoked, for example, the regulation prohibiting the submission of a matter by the parties for examination by an arbitration court acting in a foreign country (replacing the jurisdiction of Polish courts), if at least one of the parties was not seated or did not conduct its business in a foreign country[29].

2.22. The provisions of the CCP, according to Article 1154, are applied if the place of the proceedings held before an arbitration court is located in the territory of the Republic of Poland, and furthermore, in cases referred to in this part of the code, also if the place of the proceedings held before an arbitration court is located outside of the territory of the Republic of Poland or is not specified. Therefore, the regulation of the CCP after the amendment of 2005 applies both to national arbitration proceedings and international arbitration. The aim of the amended provisions of the CCP, as opposed to the previously applicable provisions, was to establish a solid foundation for international arbitration.

2.23. The non-Code sources governing the institution of arbitration (arbitration judicature) in Poland include a range of acts stipulating the functioning of regular arbitration courts, appointed for the resolution of disputes of a specific type. In particular, the following acts should be named here:

– The Trade Inspection Act of 15 December 2000[30], according to which regular consumer arbitration courts are established at the regional inspectors of the Inspectorate for the purposes of examining disputes that concern property rights, and those that result from contracts for the sale of products and the provision of services concluded between consumers and enterprises;

– The Qualified Sports Act of 29 July 2005[31], under which sports associations may establish regular arbitration courts, for which the provisions of the CCP are applicable. Their jurisdiction includes disputes concerning property related to sports activities. Furthermore, there is a Sports Arbitration Tribunal functioning at the Polish Olympic Committee as a regular arbitration court; no petition may be lodged with a common court for the reversal of the arbitration court's decisions in accordance with the provisions of the CCP, but a cassation appeal may be lodged with the Supreme Court;

---

[29] Andrzej Kąkolecki, Piotr Nowaczyk, *Źródła prawa o arbitrażu handlowym – polskiego i międzynarodowego* (*Sources of the law on commercial arbitration – polish and international*), in Andrzej Szumański, *supra* note 12, at 56.

[30] (4) JOURNAL OF LAWS Item 25, as amended.

[31] (155) JOURNAL OF LAWS Item 1298, as amended.

– The Telecommunications Act of 16 July 2004[32], according to which regular consumer arbitration courts are established at the President of the Office of Electronic Communications for the purposes of examining disputes that concern property rights, and those that result from contracts for the provision of telecommunications services and contracts for the provision of postal services[33].

2.24. Moreover, the functioning of regular arbitration courts is stipulated by numerous statutory regulations concerning professional corporations. This group includes, in particular, the Act on Chambers of Physicians and Dentists of 17 May 1989[34], according to which district medical courts may examine matters as arbitration courts with the written consent of the parties, if the disputes concern the performance of a physician's profession. Similar regulations are also included in: the Act on Self-Governance of Nurses and Midwives of 19 April 1991[35], the Act on the Profession of Veterinary Surgeons and the Chambers of Physicians, Dentists and Veterinary Surgeons of 21 December 1990[36], the Act on Professional Self-Governance of Construction Engineers and Town Planners of 15 December 2000[37], and the Pharmaceutical Chambers Act of 19 April 1991[38/39].

2.25. As already mentioned, the sources of law concerning arbitration judicature, although not of a universally binding nature in light of the Constitution of the Republic Poland, also include regulations on regular arbitration courts. These are acts of internally binding law, and as such, they cannot contain provisions that would contradict the provisions of Part V of the CCP that are of a mandatory nature (*ius cogens* norms). In relation to *ius dispositivum* norms of the CCP, the regulations may contain differing provisions[40].

2.26. The oldest regular arbitration court in Poland is the Arbitration Court at the Cotton Chamber in Gdynia, appointed in 1938 and resolving quality- and trade-related disputes concerning the cotton business. After 1989, i.e., at the beginning of the transformation of the Polish system, other regular arbitration courts began to emerge, particularly including the Arbitration Court at the Polish Bank Association, regular arbitration courts at chambers of lawyers, regional chambers of commerce, regular consumer arbitration courts at the regional inspectors of Trade Inspectorate, and the Arbitration Court at the Polish Chamber of Information Technology and Telecommunications. Apart from the listed courts, there are also

---

[32] (171) JOURNAL OF LAWS Item 1800, as amended.
[33] See further ŁUKASZ BŁASZCZAK, MAŁGORZATA LUDWIK, *supra* note 5, at 67-68.
[34] (30) JOURNAL OF LAWS Item 158, as amended.
[35] (41) JOURNAL OF LAWS Item 178, as amended.
[36] (93) JOURNAL OF LAWS Item 767 (2009).
[37] (5) JOURNAL OF LAWS Item 42, as amended (2001).
[38] (136) JOURNAL OF LAWS Item 856 (2008).
[39] See further Andrzej Kąkolecki, Piotr Nowaczyk, *supra* note 29, at 61-62.
[40] See further ŁUKASZ BŁASZCZAK, MAŁGORZATA LUDWIK, *supra* note 5, at 70.

numerous other regular arbitration courts (approx. several dozens), which, however, do not often perform any activity at all. The most widely known and the most active regular arbitration court in Poland is the Arbitration Court at the Chamber of Commerce in Warsaw[41], examining both national and international disputes[42]. The Arbitration Court at the Polish Confederation of Private Employers LEWIATAN[43] was established not very long ago, in 2005. The Regular Arbitration Court at the Polish and German Chamber of Industry and Commerce should be mentioned as well[44]. Apart from the listed courts, there are also numerous other regular, specialised courts[45].

2.27. In considering the nature of arbitration judicature, and especially its considerably informal nature, the "established customary practice applicable for the given legal relation" is also relevant, which, according to Article 1194, Section 2 of the CCP, is taken into consideration by the arbitration court when resolving a dispute, provided that it does not contradict mandatory provisions of law[46].

IV. Stages of Arbitration Procedure in Light of the Code of Civil Procedure

IV.1. Request for Arbitration

2.28. As already stated, the prerequisite of arbitration judicature is the freedom of the will of the parties, which is manifested in the fact that the parties to a civil law relation may decide that both the dispute existing between them at present and any future disputes shall be resolved without public (common) courts, by means of a request for arbitration, or in other words, by means of entering into an arbitration agreement. The specification of entities that may enter into such agreements (submit their disputes for resolution by arbitration courts) is determined by arbitration capacity, and the types of disputes that may be resolved by arbitration are specified by what is known as arbitration suitability[47].

2.29. As for the first criterion, in light of the applicable provisions of the CCP, a request for arbitration may be lodged both by natural and legal entities, as

---

[41] Established in 1950 as a Board of Arbitrators at the Polish Chamber of Foreign Trade, competent for the resolution of disputes resulting from international business relations. It has been functioning in its present form at the Chamber of Commerce in Warsaw since 1990, see also Karolina Goszka, *supra* note 2, at 15.

[42] Regulations of the Arbitration Court at the Chamber of Commerce, dated January 1, 2007, adjusted to the amended regulation of Part V of the CCP.

[43] Regulations dated February 25, 2005.

[44] Regulations dated January 1, 2009.

[45] For other regular arbitration courts see also Andrzej Kąkolecki, Piotr Nowaczyk, *supra* note 29, at 105-106.

[46] See further TADEUSZ ERECIŃSKI, KAROL WEITZ, SĄD ARBITRAŻOWY (*Court of Arbitration*), Warszawa: LexisNexis 327-328 (2008).

[47] See also Agnieszka Gębala, *Granice dopuszczalności arbitrażu* (*Limits of Arbitrability*), 2 (6) BIULETYN ARBITRAŻOWY 59 (2008).

well as organisational units without legal personality, as well as the National Treasury and government organisational units. These types of proceedings may also apply to the resolution of disputes involving consumers.

2.30. The types of disputes that may be resolved by arbitration are specified by Article 1157 of the CCP, stating that "unless a special provision stipulates otherwise, the parties may submit disputes concerning property rights or disputes concerning non-property rights, which may constitute the subject of a court settlement, except for suits for alimony, for examination by an arbitration court". Therefore, this means that arbitration suitability is broadly defined, but with a limitation stating that the request for arbitration may only apply to disputes concerning the law and not facts, whereas it is irrelevant whether such a dispute would be resolved in procedural or non-procedural proceedings[48].

2.31. Disputes of a non-property nature that may be submitted for examination by an arbitration court include, in particular, disputes concerning rights of a personal nature (Article 23 of the Civil Code) and disputes concerning family relations (e.g. divorce or adoption)[49]. This procedure may also be applied to disputes concerning employment relations, but with a restriction stating that the request for arbitration may only be lodged after the occurrence of the dispute (it cannot apply to future disputes under an employment contract – ineffective arbitration clause).

2.32. The objective limits for the submission of the respective dispute for examination by an arbitration court, as specified in the quoted Article 1157 of the CCP, are binding on the international level as well, because, under the New York Convention, a Polish court may refuse to consider an arbitration agreement or to confirm or execute a foreign arbitration court's decision if the respective dispute is not covered by arbitration suitability under Polish law[50].

2.33. It should be noted that the freedom of the parties not only applies to the choice of this method for the resolution of the dispute (disputes), but also the possibility of freely shaping the elements which are relevant for the arbitration procedure, particularly concerning the number of arbitrators or the method of their appointment[51]. In the absence of a differing opinion of the parties, according to Article 1169, Section 2 of the CCP, three arbitrators are appointed, and the presiding arbitrator is appointed by the arbitrators. If the arbitrators have not been appointed, they are appointed by a common court at the request of a party.

2.34. The prerequisites for the performance of the function of an arbitrator are specified by Article 1170, Section 1 of the CCP, stating that any natural person with full legal capacity can be appointed to act as an arbitrator,

---

[48] *Ibid.*, 64, see also ŁUKASZ BŁASZCZAK, MAŁGORZATA LUDWIK, *supra* note 5, at 90ff.

[49] *Ibid.*

[50] See also Agnieszka Gębala, *supra* note 47, at 64.

[51] See also Ryszard Balicki, *supra* note 1.

irrespective of the person's citizenship, whereas no active public judge may perform the function of an arbitrator. As already stated, the method of appointment of arbitrators may be specified by the parties, unless they fail to do so; then, the method specified in the code is applied (Article 1171, Section 1 of the CCP)[52].

2.35. The autonomy of the parties submitting their dispute for examination by an arbitration court does not allow for the exclusion of the application of fundamental procedural rules, including the requirement of the independence and impartiality of the arbitrator. An arbitrator appointed by the parties is obliged to inform the parties of any circumstances that could cause doubts as to the arbitrator's impartiality or independence. An arbitrator may be excluded at the request of a party if there are reasonable doubts as to the arbitrator's impartiality or independence, or if the qualifications specified in the agreement of the parties are not met[53].

2.36. Furthermore, the parties specify in their decision (arbitration agreement) whether the dispute is to be resolved by a regular arbitration court or an *ad hoc* court, appointed for the purposes of examining a specific dispute.

IV.2. Rules of Proceeding before an Arbitration Court and the Decision of an Arbitration Court

2.37. The code regulation of arbitration is based on two important rules, i.e., the rule of "competence-competence", according to which the arbitration court may decide on its competence, including the existence, validity or effectiveness of the request for arbitration, and the rule stating that the legal importance of the arbitration clause is evaluated irrespectively of the main agreement. This means that the ineffectiveness or expiry of the primary agreement, including the request for arbitration, does not entail the ineffectiveness or expiry of the request itself (Article 1180 of the CCP).

2.38. The parties may agree upon rules of procedure at their discretion, including the adoption of regulations of a regular arbitration court or model regulations for *ad hoc* arbitration at their choice[54]. Unless the parties decide otherwise, the arbitration court may conduct proceedings in the manner considered by the court to be appropriate, and it is not bound by the provisions on proceedings before courts, unless they are of a mandatory nature. However, the court is obliged to observe one of the fundamental rules of reliable proceedings, i.e., the rules of equal treatment of the parties by law (Article 1184 of the CCP). In particular, each party has the right to a hearing and to present its claims, as well as the supporting evidence.

---

[52] The method of appointment of arbitrators in the absence of a differing agreement of the parties is specified by Article 1171 of the CCP.

[53] The exclusion of an arbitrator appointed by the party itself or an arbitrator in the appointment of whom the party was involved may only be requested by the party due to reasons of which the party became aware after the arbitrator's appointment (Article 1174, Section 2 of the CCP).

[54] See also Andrzej Kąkolecki, Piotr Nowaczyk, *supra* note 29, at 59.

2.39. The dispute is resolved in accordance with the law governing the respective legal relation, unless the parties expressly reserved the possibility to decide in accordance with the general rules of law or rules of equity. The agreement concluded between the parties and the usual practice applied for the respective legal relation are always taken into consideration (Article 1194, Sections 1 and 2 of the CCP).

2.40. The requirement that fundamental procedural rules be adhered to, however, while observing the far-reaching autonomy of the parties and the liberalisation of arbitration proceedings, is also demonstrated by the formal requirements concerning the arbitration court's decision (Article 1197). It should, in particular, contain the "motives for the decision", indicating the facts and circumstances relevant to the decision in this matter, although it is not a "statement of reasons" as in the case of a court decision. With this solution, the legislature stresses the separate and specific nature of proceedings held before an arbitration court[55].

2.41. There are no extraordinary measures of appeal against the decision of an arbitration court to a public court; it can only be appealed by a petition for the reversal of the decision issued by the arbitration court in the event of the occurrence of preconditions enumerated in Article 1206 of the CCP. If the parties have agreed that proceedings before an arbitration court are to include more than one stage, the possibility of the reversal of a decision on the basis of a petition applies to the final decision of the arbitration court examining the requests of the parties (Article 1205, Section 2).

2.42. The nature of a petition for the reversal of a decision is complex: it combines the characteristics of an extraordinary measure, which is the petition for the resumption of the proceedings, and a claim aimed at changing the regulatory environment resulting from the decision of the arbitration court[56]. It is relevant that the decision of a common court, made after the examination of the petition, has the nature of a cassation decision, which means that in the model case, the court examines the decision in consideration of the reasons for the reversal of the decision, and not of the substance. Furthermore, the court examining the petition may reverse the decision of the arbitration court, and not only reverse it for the purpose of re-examination, which means that such a decision is eliminated from the legal relations, but the arbitration court is not obliged to re-examine the matter[57].

---

[55] *Ibid.*

[56] See further Tadeusz Ereciński, *Podstawy skargi o uchylenie wyroku sądu polubownego (uwagi de lege ferenda)* (*Principles of the Petition for Annulment of the Arbitral Award (View de Lege Ferenda)*), *in* POLSKIE PRAWO PRYWATNE W DOBIE PRZEMIAN. KSIĘGA JUBILEUSZOWA DEDYKOWANA PROFESOROWI JERZEMU MŁYNARCZYKOWI (*Polish Private Law in an Era of Change. Anniversary Book Dedicated to Professor Jerzy Młynarczyk*), Gdańsk: Wydawnictwo Uniwersytetu Gdańskiego 44 (A. Smoczyńska ed., 2005).

[57] See also Andrzej Kąkolecki, Piotr Nowaczyk, *supra* note 29, at 60.

2.43. However, the doctrine shows some reservations as to the procedure for examining petitions for the reversal of an arbitration court's decision. In particular, as it happens, the duration of examination before common courts is excessively long (from several months to even several years) due to the broad scope of audit of the arbitration court's decision, which in practice is not limited only to the correctness of the procedure (its reliability), but also concerns issues of substance. It is especially true in situations in which the petition allegedly violates the rules of social co-existence[58]. Cases are also prolonged to a significant extent by the fact that decisions of common courts are then appealed to courts of higher instance. Nevertheless, according to Article 1210 of the CCP, the decision of an arbitration court is enforceable, irrespective of the examination of the petition by a common court[59], unless the common court suspends the execution of the arbitration court's decision in a closed session.

2.44. The prerequisites of the petition for the reversal of a decision are specified by Article 1206, according to which a party may request, in the form of a petition, the reversal of the arbitration court's decision, if there was no request for arbitration, the request for arbitration is invalid or ineffective or it lost its effect under applicable law, the party has not been duly informed of the appointment of the arbitrator or of proceedings held before the arbitration court or was otherwise deprived of the possibility to defend its rights, the arbitration court's decision applies to a dispute not covered by the request for arbitration or exceeds the scope of such request for arbitration, the requirements concerning the arbitration court's composition or the fundamental rules of procedure before such court have not been observed as specified by the Act or by the parties, the decision was obtained by means of an offence or if the decision was based on a forged or counterfeit document, or a legally binding decision of a court has been issued in the same matter between the same parties. Moreover, the arbitration court's decision is also reversed if the court finds that, according to the Act, the dispute must not be resolved by an arbitration court (absence of arbitration suitability), and also if the arbitration court's decision contradicts the fundamental rules of the legal order of the Republic of Poland (public order clause).

2.45. A petition for the reversal of the arbitration court's decision may be lodged within three months from the date of delivery of the decision, or if a party requested that the decision be supplemented, rectified or interpreted – within three months from the date of delivery of the arbitration court's ruling concerning this request (Article 1208, Section 1). If the petition is based on the fact that the decision was obtained by means of an offence or if the decision was based on a forged or counterfeit document, or a legally binding decision has been issued in the same matter between

---

[58] See also Rafał Morek, ADR w sprawach gospodarczych (*ADR in Commercial Matters*), Warszawa: C. H. Beck 110-111 (2004).

[59] See also Karolina Goszka, *supra* note 2, at 17.

the same parties, the deadline for lodging the petition is set starting on the date on which the party became aware of this reason. However, the party may not request the reversal of the arbitration court's decision after the expiry of five years from the date of delivery (Article 1208, Section 2).

2.46. The court competent for the examination of the petition for the reversal of the arbitration court's decision is the common court that would be competent for the resolution of the dispute between the parties, if the parties had not requested arbitration (Article 1158). It should be noted that the reversal of the arbitration court's decision does not result in the expiry of the request for arbitration, unless the parties decide otherwise (Article 1211).

2.47. It should be emphasised that the petition for the reversal of the arbitration court's decision, due to the specific characteristics of the institution of arbitration, is of a special (extraordinary) nature, to be used for the protection of a party affected by a gross violation of the arbitration procedure, and it does not constitute another stage of the proceedings. In practice, however, this measure is often treated as such[60].

2.48. The legal effect of the arbitration court's decision or a settlement reached before the arbitration court is equal to a decision of a court or a settlement reached before a court. However, the enforcement of such a decision is only possible after confirmation of the decision (or settlement) by the court or after the court has declared the enforceability thereof (Article 1212 of the CCP). The confirmation or declaration of the enforceability of the arbitration court's decision or a settlement reached before the arbitration court is decided by the court at the request of a party (Article 1213)[61]. The court declares the enforceability of the arbitration court's decision or a settlement reached before the arbitration court, which is enforceable by means of execution, providing them with an enforceability clause (Article 1214, Section 2). The court refuses to confirm or declare the enforceability of the arbitration court's decision or a settlement reached before the arbitration court, if, according to the provisions of the Act, the dispute must not be submitted for resolution by an arbitration court, or the confirmation or execution of the arbitration court's decision

---

[60] See also Ryszard Balicki *supra* note 1; Tomasz Zbiegień, *Skarga o uchylenie wyroku sądu polubownego* (*Petition for Annulment of Arbitral Award*), *in* Międzynarodowy i krajowy arbitraż handlowy u progu XXI wieku. Księga pamiątkowa dedykowana doktorowi habilitowanemu Tadeuszowi Szurskiemu (*International and Domestic Commercial Arbitration at the Beginning of the XXI Century. Commemorative Book Dedicated to Dr. Hab. Tadeusz Szurski*), Warszawa: C. H. Beck 301 and ff. (S. Pieckowski, A. Szumański, J. Poczobut, A. Tynel, P. Nowaczyk eds., 2008).

[61] The application for declaring the enforceability of the arbitration court's decision or a settlement reached before the arbitration court carries a fixed fee of PLN 300, according to Article 24 of the Act on Court Fees in Civil Law Matters of 28 July 2005 ((167) Journal of Laws Item 1398, as amended).

or a settlement reached before the arbitration court contradicts the fundamental rules of the legal order of the Republic of Poland (public order clause of Article 1214, Section 2).

2.49. The court decides whether an arbitration court's decision issued in a foreign country or a settlement reached before an arbitration court in a foreign country is confirmed or declared enforceable after conducting a trial, whereas, irrespective of the aforementioned reasons, the court – at the request of a party – refuses to confirm or declare the enforceability of the arbitration court's decision issued in a foreign country or a settlement reached before the arbitration court in a foreign country, if the circumstances indicated in Article 1215 of the CCP occur[62].

V. Perspectives for the Development of Arbitration Judicature in Poland

2.50. Without any doubt, the transformation of the Polish system and economy created good conditions for the development of arbitration judicature. Further changes in this respect resulted from Poland's accession to the European Union, due to which business increased and new business entities emerged, and as a consequence, business relations became complicated.

2.51. Until 1989, arbitration judicature played a certain role in disputes between natural persons and in international sales. A certain boom in this respect was brought on by the Act on Examination of Matters by Commercial Courts of 24 May 1989[63], which – by means of revoking the anachronistic provisions of the CCP – allowed for the submission of disputes by all business entities for examination by arbitration courts. The changes favoured the establishment of regular arbitration courts for the resolution of business disputes and those occurring at various merchant organisations or professional corporations.

---

[62] It is namely the case if: 1) a party proves that there was no request for arbitration, the request for arbitration is invalid, ineffective or has lost its effect under applicable law, 2) the party has not been duly informed of the appointment of the arbitrator of proceedings held before the arbitration court or was otherwise deprived of the possibility to defend its rights, 3) the arbitration court's decision applies to a dispute not covered by the request for arbitration or exceeds the scope of such request for arbitration; however, if the decision in matters covered by the request for arbitration can be separated from the decision in matters not covered by the request for arbitration or exceeding its scope, the refusal to confirm or declare the enforceability of the arbitration court's decision may only apply to matters not covered by the request for arbitration or exceeding the scope thereof, 4) the arbitration court's composition or the proceedings before this court were not in compliance with the agreement of the parties or, in the absence of an agreement in this respect, were not in compliance with the law of the country in which the proceedings before the arbitration court were conducted, the arbitration court's decision has not become binding for the parties yet or has been reversed, or the execution thereof has been suspended by a court of the country under whose law of or in which this decision was issued.

[63] (33) JOURNAL OF LAWS Item 175.

2.52. The breakthrough date for the development of extra-judicial methods for dispute resolution in Poland is considered to be 28 July 2005, when two acts amending the CCP came into force, i.e., the act implementing the institution of mediation in Polish civil procedure and – as already mentioned – an amendment to the CCP substantially modifying the institution of arbitration in Poland[64].

2.53. However, it should be noted that although international business arbitration does not require any special promotion, arbitration judicature in national business is not a sufficiently known institution, both among business entities and among lawyers. The general criticism of the inefficiency of common courts is not accompanied by any special interest in the application of arbitration clauses in agreements[65]. At present, there are more than 50 regular arbitration courts functioning in Poland, 20 of which are more or less active[66]. According to the statistical data, regular courts examine up to twenty matters a year, whereas – as already mentioned – there is greater activity by the Arbitration Court at the Chamber of Commerce (examining up to several hundred matters a year)[67], and the Arbitration Court at the Polish Chamber of Information Technology and Telecommunications. Thus, the number of matters examined by arbitration courts in relation to the number of matters submitted to common courts is small, which confirms that it is difficult to perceive them today or in the near future as being competitive in relation to the administration of justice by courts. However, we can say that the journey has started, heading towards a point in time when arbitration judicature would serve a complementary function in relation to adjudicative methods. This can even be seen in the fact that, according to the data of the ICC, among 160 countries using its services, Poland is 14th according to the number of parties seeking to make use of the institution of arbitration, and furthermore, Polish arbitration regulations stand 8th among the most frequently selected arbitration laws of the ICC. Polish is more and more frequently used as the language of arbitration[68].

2.54. Therefore, it is predicted that arbitration courts of a specialised nature which could examine complicated business matters will emerge and develop, and thus could constitute a real alternative to the court administration of justice, because without specialised expertise, courts must refer to the opinions of experts in the respective area in each case

---

64 See also RAFAŁ MOREK, MEDIACJA I ARBITRAŻ (*Mediation and Arbitration*), Warszawa: C. H. Beck IX – preface (2006).

65 See also Karolina Goszka, *supra* note 2, at 17.

66 See also Piotr Nowaczyk, *Perspektywy rozwoju sądownictwa polubownego w Polsce* (*Prospects for the Development of Arbitration in Poland*), 4 (1) KWARTALNIK ADR. ARBITRAŻ I MEDIACJA 145 (2009). The author is former President of the Arbitration Court at the Chamber of Commerce.

67 *Ibid.*, 146.

68 See also other detailed information in the work of Piotr Nowaczyk, *ibid.*, 146.

(court experts), which prolongs the proceedings and no doubt increases the costs thereof.

2.55. Undoubtedly, the development of arbitration judicature may also be favoured by the fact that the applicable code regulation (after the amendment of 2005) substantially extended the objective limits of arbitration, i.e., the types of disputes that may be covered by arbitration agreements. The subjective scope of arbitration judicature (arbitration capacity) has also been broadly specified. Obviously, this is not to say that present regulation does not cause any doubts in the practice of its application[69], but it seems that under the influence of the postulates of the practice, some deficiencies or unclear issues can be eliminated in the near future. In practice – as already mentioned – a particularly troublesome issue is the audit of arbitration courts' decisions by common courts, especially the application of the constitutional principle of two stages of court proceedings in this case.

| | |

Summaries

DEU [*Der rechtliche Rahmen und die Natur der Schiedsgerichtsbarkeit in Polen*]

Die bekannteste und in der Praxis am häufigsten zur Anwendung kommende Form der außergerichtlichen Streitbeilegung ist das Schiedsverfahren (Arbitration). Die Verfassung der Republik Polen aus dem Jahre 1997 steckt die Struktur des Gerichtswesens ab und schreibt das Prinzip der Monopolzuständigkeit der Gerichte im Bereich der Rechtspflege fest; die Schiedsgerichte sind allerdings in der Verfassung keinerlei erwähnt. Nach der Rechtsprechung des Verfassungsgerichts geht man freilich davon aus, dass die Ausübung der Justiz objektiv als mit der Beilegung von Rechtsstreitigkeiten befasste Tätigkeit zu betrachten ist, und eben nicht subjektiv als ausschließliche Zuständigkeit der Gerichte. Mit anderen Worten, es ist keinesfalls so, dass sämtliche Streitfälle betreffend die rechtliche Situation einer Gesellschaft von Anfang an von den Gerichten verhandelt werden müssten. Die fundamentale Rechtsquelle, in der das Rechtsinstitut der Schiedsgerichtsbarkeit geregelt ist, ist in Polen die Zivilprozessordnung vom 17. November 1964; als entscheidender Wendepunkt gilt diesbezüglich der 28. Juli 2005: Das Datum, zu dem eine Novelle der ZPO in Kraft trat, die das Rechtsinstitut der Schiedsgerichtsbarkeit in Polen in tiefgreifender Weise neugestaltete. Neben der Zivilprozessordnung ist unter den weiteren Quellen eine Reihe von Gesetzen zu nennen, die sich mit der Tätigkeit der sog. ständigen Schiedsgerichte befasst, welche zur Lösung von

---

[69] Among other issues, because the legislature has not taken a decisive stance, there are doubts as to whether arbitration courts are qualified to examine matters concerning appeals of resolutions by assemblies of capital companies, and subjectively, whether requests for arbitration can be lodged by company officers; see further Agnieszka Gębala, *supra* note 47, at 68.

Streitigkeiten von jeweils spezifischem Charakter eingerichtet wurden; dazu gehören auch gesetzliche Bestimmunten, die für Standes- und Berufsverbände gelten. Zu den Rechtsquellen der Schiedsgerichtsbarkeit ohne allgemein verbindlichen Charakter zählt man außerdem die Schiedsordnungen der ständigen Schiedsgerichte. Das aktivste unter den ständigen Schiedsgerichten ist das Schiedsgericht (Sąd Arbitrażowy) an der Polnischen Wirtschaftskammer (Krajowa Izba Gospodarcza) in Warschau.

CZE [*Právní rámec a povaha rozhodčího soudnictví v Polsku*]
Nejznámější a v praxi nejčastěji používanou formou mimosoudního řešení sporů v Polsku je rozhodčí řízení (arbitráž). Ústava Polska z roku 1997 vymezuje komplexní strukturu soudů a princip monopolu soudů při výkonu spravedlnosti, nezmiňuje se však o rozhodčích soudech. Podle judikatury polského Ústavního soudu je však nutno na výkon spravedlnosti nahlížet objektivně, jako na činnost spočívající v řešení právních sporů, a nikoli subjektivně, jako na výlučnou příslušnost soudů. To znamená, že ne všechny záležitosti a spory týkající se právní situace jednotlivce musí být od začátku řešeny soudy. Základním pramenem práva upravujícím institut rozhodčího soudnictví (arbitráže) je v Polsku občanský zákoník ze dne 17. listopadu 1964, přičemž za průlomové datum je považováno nabytí platnosti novelizace zákoníku dne 28. července 2005, která výrazným způsobem modifikovala institut rozhodčího soudnictví v Polsku. Mimo tohoto zákoníku patří k dalším pramenům práva řada zákonů hovořících o činnosti stálých rozhodčích soudů zřízených k řešení sporů určitého druhu, včetně řady zákonných úprav týkajících se profesních sdružení. K pramenům práva rozhodčího soudnictví, které nemají všeobecně závazný charakter, řadíme také jednací řády stálých rozhodčích soudů. Nejaktivnějším stálým rozhodčím soudem je Rozhodčí soud (Sąd Arbitrażowy) při Polské hospodářské komoře (Krajowa Izba Gospodarcza) ve Varšavě.

| | |

POL [*Ramy prawne i charakter sądownictwa polubownego w Polsce*]
W Polsce najbardziej znaną i w praktyce najczęściej wykorzystywaną formą pozasądowego rozstrzygania sporów jest arbitraż. Podstawowym źródłem prawa regulującym instytucję sądownictwa polubownego (arbitrażu) w Polsce jest kodeks postępowania cywilnego z 17 listopada 1964 r., zmieniony istotnie 28 lipca 2005 r. Do źródeł pozakodeksowych należą także ustawy, przewidujące funkcjonowanie stałych sądów polubownych powołanych do rozstrzygania sporów określonego rodzaju, w tym liczne regulacje ustawowe dotyczące korporacji zawodowych. Do źródeł prawa w zakresie sądownictwa polubownego, nie mających charakteru powszechnie obowiązującego, zalicza się także regulaminy stałych sądów arbitrażowych.

FRA [**Cadres juridiques et caractère de la justice arbitrale en Pologne**]
L'arbitrage est la forme de solution extrajudiciaire des litiges la plus connue et la plus utilisée dans la pratique en Pologne. La source fondamentale du droit régissant l'institution de la justice d'arbitrage en Pologne est le code de procédure civile du 17 novembre 1964, fortement modifié le 28 juillet 2005.

En dehors du code civil, les lois relatives à l'activité des tribunaux permanents d'arbitrage, mis en place pour résoudre les litiges d'un certain caractère, ainsi qu'un grand nombre d'amendements concernant les groupements professionnels représentent d'autres sources complémentaires. Parmi les autres sources de justice arbitrale sans caractère obligatoire, on peut citer les règles de procédure des tribunaux permanents d'arbitrage.

RUS [*Основа права и характер арбитражного правосудия (третейсково разбирательства) в Польше*]

Наиболее значимой и чаще всего применяемой на практике формой внесудебного разрешения споров в Польше является арбитраж. В качестве основного источника права, регулирующего институции арбитражного правосудия в Польше выступает Гражданский кодекс от 17 ноября 1964 года, существенно измененный 28 июля 2005 года. Наряду с кодексом к источникам права также относятся законы, определяющие деятельность постоянных арбитражных судов, сформированных для разрешения определенных видов споров, в том числе целый ряд правовых норм, касающихся профессиональных объединений. К источникам права, регулирующим арбитражное правосудие, которые не носят общеобязательный характер, также относятся регламенты институционных третейских судов.

ES [*Marco legal y características de la jurisdicción arbitral en Polonia*]

En Polonia, el arbitraje es considerado el método más conocido y el más utilizado a la hora de solventar los pleitos de manera extrajudicial. La fuente básica del derecho que regula la institución del arbitraje en Polonia, es el Código Civil del 17 de noviembre de 1964, enmendado considerablemente el 28 de julio de 2005. Además del Código, otras fuente de derecho incluyen leyes que definen las actividades de los tribunales arbitrales permanentes, creados con el propósito de solventar ciertos tipos de pleitos, incluyendo toda una serie de reglamentaciones relativas a las asociaciones profesionales. Las fuentes del derecho de jurisdicción arbitral que carecen de carácter generalmente vinculante, incluyen reglas y reglamentos para tribunales arbitrales permanentes.

Czech (& Central European) Yearbook of Arbitration

Alexander J. Bělohlávek

Arbitration from Perspective of Right to Legal Protection and Right to Court Proceedings (the Right to Have One's Case Dealt with by a Court): Significance of Autonomy and Scope of Right to Fair Trial

Key words:
*party autonomy |
common law | ECHR
| waiver of the right
to court proceedings
| horizontal effect of
law | substantive law |
overriding mandatory
rules | mandatory
rules | continental law
| seat of arbitration |
legal finding | ADR |
independent court |
state court | restriction
of rights | powers of
arbitrators | legal
protection*

Abstract | In the past, states hesitated to recognize decisions of foreign courts on political grounds, as such recognition de facto implied the acceptance of the authority of a foreign state. These obstacles were eliminated by private arbitration, and arbitration, as a means of dispute resolution that replaces state authority, has increasingly been employed where the latter has, for a variety of reasons, proven inefficient and defective. We must strictly distinguish between the right to court proceedings (the right to have one's case dealt with by a court) and the right to legal protection. The right to court proceedings can be waived on the basis of the principle of the autonomy of will (for instance, by means of an arbitration agreement entered into in compliance with the lex arbitri). The right to legal protection cannot be waived. Arbitration is therefore a process of finding and applying the law. However, such legal protection must be approved by the law (laws and regulations) applicable at the seat of arbitration. An arbitration agreement as a manifestation of autonomy only initiates this dispute resolution mechanism within the framework laid down by the lex arbitri. This condition is a necessary prerequisite for attributing legal force to arbitration awards, which are therefore enforceable by public authority. The state assumes no responsibility for the provision of legal protection via private mechanisms (arbitration). Arbitration tribunals do not represent public authority, but are nonetheless instruments of legal protection. While it is permissible for principles of fair trial to be restricted in arbitration, they may not be entirely excluded, and the minimum necessary standard thereof must be preserved.

Alexander J. Bělohlávek
Univ. Professor, Dr.iur., Mgr., Dipl. Ing. oec/MB, Dr.h.c. Lawyer admitted and practising in Prague/CZE (Branch N.J./US), Senior Partner of the Law Offices Bělohlávek, Dept. of Law, Faculty of Economics, Ostrava, CZE, Dept. of Int. and European Law, Faculty of Law, Masaryk University, Brno, CZE (visiting), Chairman of the Commission on Arbitration ICC National Committee CZE, Arbitrator in Prague, Vienna, Kiev etc. Member of ASA, DIS, Austrian Arb. Association. The First Vice-President of the WJA – the World Jurist Association, Washington D.C./USA. e-mail: office@ablegal.cz

I. Nature of Arbitration and Legal Basis for Powers of Arbitrators

3.01. A number of countries have seen significant progress with respect to the general perception of the nature of arbitration[1]. Three to four[2] basic theories have evolved over time, being the contract theory, the jurisdiction theory, the mixed theory and a theory characterizing the substance of arbitration regarding the method of dispute resolution as *sui generis*)[3]. Although the understanding of arbitration from the perspective of public authority is interesting, and it is probably the only point of view that provides answers to a number of questions regarding jurisdiction and the powers of arbitrators, as well as numerous other questions, the author intentionally refrains from elaborating on this issue in any way, because even a brief digression would substantially exceed the limits of the main topic of this article[4]. This article focuses on the nature of arbitration from the perspective of the European Charter on Human Rights, the case law of the European Court of Human Rights (ECtHR), and the influence of such case law on the decision-making practice in certain selected countries as a means of settling the fundamental issues connected with arbitration.

3.02. Like the entire international community, the individual countries have come to realize that litigation (court proceedings) is often unable to provide effective legal protection. Let's look at Germany, for instance. The ECtHR has in a number of cases concluded that the right to a fair trial had been violated due to unreasonably long court proceedings in many countries. This often applied to Germany as well. Indeed, it was a series of complaints lodged against Germany that resulted in a decision adopted by the Grand Chamber of the ECtHR in *Sümerli* v. *Germany* [5], in which the ECtHR actually concluded that German procedural law at that

---

[1] For a detailed historical analysis of arbitration, see, for instance, ILONA SCHELLEOVÁ & KAREL SCHELLE, ROZHODČÍ ŘÍZENÍ (*Arbitration*), Praha: EUROLEX Bohemia (2002). A substantial part of that book is dedicated to the history of arbitration, etc.

[2] Includes the jurisdiction theory, as well as the mixed theory.

[3] For details, see, for instance, Naděžda Rozehnalová, *Rozhodčí řízení – alternativa k řízení soudnímu* (*Arbitration – An Alternative to Litigation*), 5 (4) PRÁVNÍ FÓRUM 121, 121-122 (2008); ALEXANDER J. BĚLOHLÁVEK, ZÁKON O ROZHODČÍM ŘÍZENÍ A O VÝKONU ROZHODČÍCH NÁLEZŮ. KOMENTÁŘ (*Act on Arbitration and on Enforcement of Arbitral Awards. A Commentary*), Praha: C. H. Beck (2004); et al.

[4] Concerning this question, however, see, for instance, the annotations and the analyses of case law presented in this edition of the CYArb (Vol. I), dealing with the relationship between arbitration and constitutional law issues.

[5] *Sümerli* v. *Germany* (dec.), No. 75.529/01, June 8, 2006. After all, German constitutional law fully supports the principle of expeditious proceedings before an independent and unbiased court, and it even expressly incorporates this right in the Constitutions of certain federal states (for instance, Article 51(4) of the Brandenburg Constitution). See, for instance, Council of Europe, Venice Commission, *Can Excessive Length of Proceedings be Remedied?*, (44) SCIENCE AND TECHNIQUE OF DEMOCRACY 164 (2007). This publication issued by the Council of Europe contains a detailed analysis, with national reports filed by ECHR Member States. It is difficult to overlook

time provided no effective remedies[6] for the protection of rights within the meaning of the ECHR. Supporting alternative dispute resolution (ADR)[7] is therefore more than a logical solution. ADR today represents something completely different compared to, for instance, the late 1980s. Whereas, especially at the time of the bipolar global system and many political problems, the main purpose of arbitration and ADR was to solve problems associated with the recognition and enforcement of foreign decisions. Indeed, political reasons justified the approach adopted by the states, i.e. their hesitation to recognize decisions of foreign courts, as such recognition de facto implied the acceptance of the exercise of the foreign state's authority. However, this phenomenon has been gradually eliminated, and arbitration (ADR) has been increasingly employed for completely different purposes. Arbitration has been increasingly used as a substitute for state authority wherever the latter has, for a variety of reasons, proven inefficient and defective.

II. Purpose of Arbitration regarding Court Protection and Constitutional System: The Nature of Arbitration According to Doctrines Applied by Certain Selected Countries

3.03. The case law of many countries offers important guidelines for the definition of the nature of arbitration. It is interesting to note that arbitration is not merely characterized by means of the legal findings reached by the arbitrators (arbitration awards are considered equal to judgments of courts of-law). In the overwhelming majority of countries,

---

the fact that such a situation as regards the length of proceedings, procedural obstacles and other problems with the administration of justice in courts exists in most countries.

[6] Regarding this issue, see an interesting essay by Otakar Hájek, *Winning your case is good, effective remedy is better! Recognition of Foreign Judgments and Arbitral Awards in the Czech Republic*, 4 (8) COMMON LAW REVIEW (2008).

[7] We must emphasize that the conceptual approach to so-called alternative dispute resolution in the individual legal cultures differs. Whereas most countries based on *common law* principles classify arbitration among the means of alternative dispute resolution (ADR), most *civil law* countries conversely separate arbitration from ADR. The purpose is to underline that arbitration is an alternative to litigation, both as concerns the nature and (especially) as concerns the result of the proceedings. Arbitral awards are therefore usually considered to be fully equal to court judgments. This is not to suggest that *common law* does not often arrive at the same conclusion; the underlying concept is different, though. The *common law* regime is (depending on the individual countries) based on the fact that the exercise of judicial authority (power of the courts-of-law as public authorities) has a contractual basis as well, like the exercise of any public authority. Conversely, the doctrine in most *civil law* countries is instead based on the assumption that public authority is derived from state sovereignty as an immanent component of the "state", both from the perspective of international law, and from the purely national and domestic perspective.

the very nature of arbitration (i.e. also from the perspective of procedure) is today compared to litigation (court proceedings) without hesitation. For instance, in comparison with private international law, the nature and purpose of the arbitration agreement is compared to forum selection (choice of court / *prorogation*). Such developments come as no surprise, and they can be traced back to the very beginning of the 19th century. What is probably one of the oldest decisions of this kind comes from Austria: according to the decision of the Austrian Supreme Court (OGH [AUT] of as early as November 4, 1903, *an arbitration award constitutes an enforceable instrument (enforceable title) for and against the parties to arbitration*[8].

3.04. Modern trends in the adjudicative nature of arbitration are evidenced by the progress made in many developed countries. For instance, in **Belgium**: on August 8, 2005, a report was published noting that a Belgian arbitration tribunal is entitled to examine the compliance of the law with the Belgian Constitution[9].

3.05. Indeed, the nature of arbitration in relation to litigation in courts-of-law has been extensively analysed in many court judgments in **Germany** as well. For instance, **OLG** (*High Regional Court*) **Rostock** [DEU] in Case No. 1 Sch. 04/06 of September 18, 2007[10], referring to, *inter alia*, Section 1055 of the German Code of Civil Procedure as the national *lex arbitri* (ZPO [DEU]), delivered the following decision: (approximate translation) [...] *an arbitration award has the same effects as a final and enforceable judgment, and from that perspective* **arbitration performs the same function as legal findings by courts-of-law**[...] *Defective decisions of arbitration tribunals must therefore be perceived in the same manner as defective but final and enforceable decisions of state courts.* Nonetheless, the same court confirmed the prohibition of review of arbitration awards on the merits, stipulating that the purpose of the proceedings on setting aside (annulling) an arbitration award is only the review of compliance with fundamental legal principles, especially procedural principles. As concerns German case law, we ought to mention the decision of **BGH** (*Bundesgerichtshof / German Federal Supreme Court*) **No. III ZB 95/06**[11], according to which the [decision-making of arbitrators] *is an individual process in which the arbitrators form their own opinion on the law as applied to the particular case on the basis of circumstances established by the examination of evidence, the outcome of which is a decision establishing*

---

8   GIUNF, 2477.

9   See Mark Quaghebeur, *Court Seeks ECJ Ruling on Scope of Money-Laundering Directive*, Tax Notes Int'l 304 (July 25, 2005), available at: http://www.vandendijk-taxlaw.be/pdf/Court%20Seeks%20ECJ%20Ruling%20on%20Scope%20of%20Money-Laundering%20Directive.pdf (accessed on September 16, 2010).

10   Stefan Kroell, *Die schiedsgerichtliche Rechtsprechung 2007 (Teil 2)*, 6 (3) SchiedsVZ 119 (2008).

11   (1) SchiedsVZ 40 (2008).

subjective rights. The resolution delivered by **Kammergericht Berlin, Case No. 20 Sch 2/06** of June 15, 2006[12], describes decisions issued in arbitration proceedings as circumstances that are not subject to further proof. In other words, the resolution attributes not only the same effect to arbitration awards, but also considers the nature thereof to be fully comparable to court decisions as concerns the determination of the factual and legal circumstances.

3.06. A landmark decision was adopted by the **Italian Constitutional Court**, Case No. 376 of November 28, 2001, according to which: (approximate translation) *[t]he role of the Constitutional Court is to oversee the legitimacy of the law, i.e. including its compliance with the Constitution and with the fundamental principles of law and state. In that connection, the Constitutional Court also serves as an instrument for the courts-of-law which cannot, in the continental law system, influence the contents of the legal system by their decisions generally applicable in future, ensuring that the legal system is fully compatible with the constitutional laws and the fundamental principles that the law should observe. This is the reason why courts-of-law are entitled to approach the Constitutional Court when applying the law and request that the Constitutional Court intervene, whereby the latter repeals or (depending on the powers with which the Constitutional Court is endowed) amends the respective statute or implementing legislation. **The same right, i.e. the right to approach the Constitutional Court with proposals for repealing any statutes or implementing legislation that the arbitrator considers unconstitutional, and the right to suspend the arbitration proceedings until the Constitutional Court adopts a decision on the respective proposal, must also be provided to arbitrators if the application of the law, the constitutionality[13] of which the arbitrators challenge, should influence the terms of the arbitration award to be issued in the arbitration proceedings.** Arbitrators must possess such a right, because arbitration is subject to principles analogous to those to which litigation is subject, i.e. the principle of independent decision-making and the principle of a fair trial. Furthermore, the scope of such right entrusted to arbitrators is the same, because arbitrators must interpret the law in compliance with the Constitution, and **with respect to the fundamental principle of the application of substantive law, there is no difference between judges on the one hand, and arbitrators on the other.***

3.07. Analogous opinions on the substance and purpose of arbitration are now common in most developed countries. However, we must emphasize

---

12   Adopted from:
http://www.ibr-online.de/IBRUrteile/index.php?zg=9&HTTP_INDEX=Monatsindex
&HTTP_Monat=2006-06&Suchergebnisse=1 (accessed on June 15, 2010).
13   See Jan Ryba, *Posuzování ústavnosti zákonů z hlediska občanského soudního řízení* (*Assessing the Constitutionality of Acts of Parliament from the Perspective of Civil Court Proceedings*), 2 (1) Právní rádce 8 (1994).

that the above-quoted Italian decision is indeed a landmark decision. Nonetheless, the author is of the opinion that the objective is not to endow arbitrators with the status of an authority enforcing public authority (such as judges), but to underline the function of arbitration as an instrument for finding and applying the law, and also to emphasize the nature of constitutional law (constitutional principles) as something that penetrates the entire legal system. Italian arbitrators have, however, voiced certain critical comments, fearing that a potential *explosion* of objections challenging the constitutionality of the interpretation and application of substantive law could result in arbitration becoming too formalistic, and could open the floodgates for (often) unsubstantiated objections raised by the parties, intended solely to slow down the administration of justice. The author, however, has no information suggesting any excessive abuse of this procedure in practice.

III. Right to Legal Protection versus Right to Court Proceedings and Significance of Autonomy

3.08. The European Court of Human Rights (ECtHR) has been regularly dealing with the issue of arbitration, discussing this dispute resolution method in its case law. Logically, the issue of arbitration is being dealt with in connection with the adjudication of complaints of the violation of Article 6(1) of the ECHR[14]. The author believes, though, that the application of the ECHR and of the constitutional principles in general in relation to arbitration cannot be limited to the issue of *fair trial*. These issues are also important from the perspective of the protection (inviolability) of property and other fundamental rights, although according to the author, the case law of the ECtHR, for instance, has been somewhat neglectful of that perspective[15].

3.09. Proceedings at the ECtHR have relatively commonly dealt with the issue of whether and to what extent Article 6(1) of the Convention of the Council of Europe on the Protection of Human Rights and Fundamental Freedoms (ECHR) is applicable to arbitration, and whether and to what extent these standards can be *waived* or contractually modified, meaning the possibility to enter into an arbitration agreement, and possibly also to agree on rules of procedure before the arbitrators. In that regard, the ECtHR also distinguishes, wherever necessary, between *ad hoc* arbitration

---

[14] In general, see, for instance, Vladimír Mikule, *Ještě ke správnímu soudnictví a jeho organizaci* (*More Remarks on Administrative Court Proceedings and the Organization of Administrative Court Proceedings*), 42 (4) PRÁVNÍ PRAXE 185 (1994).
[15] This is not an *omission* on the part of the ECtHR, though. The ECtHR is bound by the text of the complaint addressed to the Court. It is usually the fault of the parties, who often overlook a number of possible constitutional connections and references to other fundamental rights. However, by no means does this only apply to arbitration issues.

proceedings and so-called institutionalized proceedings[16], and devotes its attention to many other questions.

3.10. The right to enter into an arbitration agreement, i.e. waive the right to court proceedings, meaning the protection provided by public authority (judicial authority), is to be found in a different freedom, i.e. the freedom to express one's will[17]. Freedom of will is guaranteed both by constitutional codes of fundamental rights of national origin, and by rules of international origin, in particular, the ECHR[18]. The author is of the opinion that the freedom to express one's will must be understood to be incorporated in the principles of the rule of law;[19] from the perspective of the case law of the Constitutional Court of the Czech Republic, this doctrine must also be perceived as principally delimiting the exercise of state authority *vis-à-vis* the autonomous will of the individual. The autonomy of will and the free independent acts of individuals must be understood both as a restriction on the authority of the state to limit the

---

[16]   See, for instance, Alexander J. Bělohlávek, *Rozhodčí řízení ad hoc vs. řízení před stálými rozhodčími soudy a postavení tzv. rozhodčích center* (*Ad hoc Arbitration v. Arbitration before Permanent Arbitration Courts and the Status of the So-Called Arbitration Centres*), 12 (10) BULLETIN ADVOKACIE 54 (2005); Luděk Lisse, *K právnímu postavení arbitrážních center* (*Regarding the Legal Status of Arbitration Centres*), 13 (1) BULLETIN ADVOKACIE 40 (2006); M. Pavelka, *Rozhodčí řízení před tzv. rozhodčími centry* (*Arbitration before So-Called Arbitration Centres*), 12 (7-8) BULLETIN ADVOKACIE 58 (2005); ROLF A. SCHÜTZE ET AL., INSTITUTIONELLE SCHIEDSGERICHTSBARKEIT, Köln/R.: Carl Heymanns (2006); Vojtěch Trapl, *K otázce zřizování stálých rozhodčích soudů* (*Regarding the Establishment of Permanent Arbitration Courts*), 8 (7) PRÁVNÍ PRAXE V PODNIKÁNÍ 19 (1999); Petr Lachut, *Statut rozhodčího soudu při HK ČR a AK ČR* (*Statute of the Arbitration Court Attached to the Economic Chamber of the Czech Republic and the Agricultural Chamber of the Czech Republic*), (24) DANĚ A FINANCE 5 (1998) et al.

[17]   For details, see Alexander J. Bělohlávek & Tomáš Pezl, *Mezinárodní a tuzemské rozhodčí řízení z pohledu čl. 36 Listiny základních práv a svobod a pravomocí soudů a ústavou garantovaných práv* (*Institut zrušení rozhodčího nálezu v souvislosti se zákazem revision au fond*) (*International and Domestic Arbitration from the Perspective of Article 36 of the Charter of Fundamental Rights and Freedoms and the Jurisdiction of Courts and Rights Guaranteed under the Constitution* (*Annulment of Arbitration Awards in Connection with the Prohibition of Revision au Fond*), 146 (7) PRÁVNÍK 768 (2007). Regarding certain partial issues, see David Slováček, *Ochrana spotřebitele a rozhodčí doložky* (*Consumer Protection and Arbitration Clauses*), 16 (7-8) BULLETIN ADVOKACIE 46 (2009); David Slováček, *Rozhodčí řízení a směrnice o nepřiměřených podmínkách ve spotřebitelských smlouvách* (*Arbitration and the Directive on Unfair Terms in Consumer Contracts*), 18 (9) PRÁVNÍ ROZHLEDY 331, 332 (2010) et al.

[18]   For instance, from the perspective of Article 2(4) of the Constitution [CZE], the contents of which are identical to Article 3 of the Charter of Fundamental Rights [CZE]. For example, Article 2(3) of the Charter of Fundamental Rights [CZE] stipulates that (cit.) *Everyone may do what is not prohibited by Acts of Parliament; and nobody may be compelled to do what is not prescribed by Acts of Parliament*, like in the national constitutional regimes.

[19]   See DUŠAN HENDRYCH & CYRIL SVOBODA, ET AL. ÚSTAVA ČESKÉ REPUBLIKY. KOMENTÁŘ (*Constitution of the Czech Republic. Commentary*), Praha: C. H. Beck 613 (1997).

acts of individual entities other than by an express statutory prohibition or an express statutory order, and as the full respect of the state for the exercise of free will, or respect for the acts of an individual that are not expressly ordered or prohibited (under mandatory or even overriding mandatory rules)[20].

3.11. If both of the abovementioned doctrines, now established in most modern legal systems, collide, the conclusion to be deduced from the conflict (albeit merely putative) must make certain that neither doctrine is suppressed. If we apply that mentioned above to the conflict of free will and the inalienability of rights, we must always presume that the individual's expression of will was performed freely and with full knowledge of the consequences of such expression for the individual. Only in case of doubts about the freedom of the expression of will or its very purpose is it necessary to establish whether this free expression of will has not resulted in renouncing a right to an already constitutionally impermissible extent. The legislative stipulation of the freedom of will also entails the right to make free decisions on whether and in what manner the particular individual will exercise his or her right or abstain from exercising this right[21]. No such step adopted by the individual can generally be described as violating the principle of the inalienability of rights. By defining these fundamental rights and freedoms and the doctrine of the application thereof, the state

---

[20]   See, for instance, the award of the Constitutional Court [CZE], I ÚS 546/03, published *in* 32 (12) SBÍRKA NÁLEZŮ A USNESENÍ ÚSTAVNÍHO SOUDU. For confirmation of the possibility to exclude the jurisdiction of courts as public authorities within the framework of the respective legal system, in terms of the conditions of the objective and subjective arbitrability, in connection with the rules incorporated in Article 36(1) of the Charter of Fundamental Rights [CZE], see, for instance, the decision of the Constitutional Court [CZE], I. ÚS 16/02, according to which (cit.) [...] *The procedural guarantee incorporated in Article 36(1) of the Charter materializes if combined with the constitutional principle enshrined in Article 2(2) of the Charter, because the exercise of the state authority's powers beyond the limit laid down by an Act of Parliament would consequently constitute a failure to protect the law[...]*, i.e. conversely, disrespect for the expression of will of the parties incorporated in the arbitration agreement and permitting *revision au fond* in relation to an arbitral award issued within the limits of the objective and subjective arbitrability would constitute a violation of Article 36(1) of the Charter of Fundamental Rights [CZE] in connection with Article 2(2) of the Charter of Fundamental Rights [CZE] and Article 2(3) of the Charter of Fundamental Rights [CZE], as well as other constitutional imperatives and principles. Also, for instance, František Šamalík, *Lidská práva – základ demokratické legitimity (Human Rights – the Basis for Democratic Legitimacy)*, 133 (1) PRÁVNÍK (1994). Regarding the meaning of overriding mandatory rules, see, for instance, ALEXANDER J. BĚLOHLÁVEK, ROME CONVENTION / ROME I REGULATION. COMMENTARY. NEW EU CONFLICT-OF-LAWS RULES FOR CONTRACTUAL OBLIGATIONS, New York: JurisPublishing (2010), Commentary on Article 9 of the Rome I Regulation; Monika Pauknerová, *Overriding Mandatory Rules and Czech Law*, *in* 1 CZECH YEARBOOK OF INTERNATIONAL LAW: SECOND DECADE A HEAD: TRACING THE GLOBAL CRISIS, New York: Juris Publishing 81 (A. J. Bělohlávek & N. Rozehnalová eds., 2010).

[21]   See, for instance, Ivo Telec, *Přirozené právo osobnosti a jeho státní ochrana (Natural Law of Persons and Its Protection by the State)*, 15 (1) PRÁVNÍ ROZHLEDY 1 (2007).

undertakes to respect such rights. This is primarily a definition of the vertical effect of fundamental rights, i.e. in the relationship of *state* versus *citizen*[22]. The definition of the relationship between citizens (the so-called horizontal effect of law) is generally perceived as secondary. It is therefore not possible to apply a general constitutional doctrine to a relationship between private persons, unless a subjective right of any of the parties is breached by the other party, and unless this breach is at the same time the subject of proceedings before the competent state authority safeguarding the protection to rights[23].

3.12. Now that it is quite clear what the inalienability of rights means, we must proceed to the analysis of the meaning of the generally recognized right to access an independent and unbiased court with a dispute[24]. It is a guarantee provided to individuals (both natural and legal persons), guaranteeing their right to access an unbiased and independent court, in the manner stipulated by the law and for the purpose of defence and/or the exercise of one's right. However, it is a right, not an obligation to protect one's rights by exercising them in court. At the same time, the *forum* making a decision on these rights is subject to the requirement of being independent and unbiased. Last, but not least, both the exercise of such right by the individual, and particularly its award by the court/tribunal are subject to the observance of the prescribed procedure.

3.13. Article 6(1) of the ECHR guarantees the right to a fair and public hearing of the case by an independent and impartial tribunal established by law. The wording of Article 6(1) of the ECHR clearly indicates that it only applies to those institutions that are established by law and for the decisions of which responsibility can therefore be assumed. It is clear that the evaluation of the relationship between the rights incorporated in Article 6(1) of the ECHR depends on whether arbitration awards can be classified (under *lex arbitri* and other national laws and regulations) as decisions issued by public authorities, i.e. authorities established by law and considered tribunals (courts) for the purposes of the

---

22   For instance, Article 1(3) of the Fundamental Act (Grundgesetz) [DEU].

23   See, for instance, Michal Bartoň, *Horizontální působení základních práv jako způsob pronikání ústavního práva do práva obyčejného (podústavního)* (*Horizontal Effect of Fundamental Rights as a Method whereby Constitutional Law Penetrates Sub-Constitutional Law*), *in* INTERPRETACE PRÁVA ÚSTAVNÍMI SOUDY (TEORETICKÉ REFLEXE) (*Interpretation of the Law by Constitutional Courts (Theoretical Essays)*), Plzeň: Nakladatelství a vydavatelství Aleš Čeněk, s.r.o. (K. Klíma ed., 2006).

24   In the Czech Republic [CZE], see Article 36 of the Charter of Fundamental Rights (like other constitutional systems). The respective Article stipulates (cit.) *Everyone may assert, through the prescribed procedure, their rights before an independent and impartial court, and in specified cases, before another body,* and subsequently (cit.) *Unless provided otherwise by an Act of Parliament, a person who claims that his or her rights were curtailed by a decision of a public administrative authority may turn to a court for review of the legality of that decision. However, judicial review of decisions affecting the fundamental rights and freedoms listed in this Charter may not be removed from the jurisdiction of courts.*

ECHR. According to the author, though, such interpretation can only be accepted in relation to the scope of application of the mechanisms designated by the ECHR as international instruments for the protection of fundamental rights (especially the opportunity to address the ECtHR after all remedies at the national level have been exhausted). However, the right to legal protection, as such, is much broader and more extensive. This right cannot be limited to mechanisms (here within the meaning of the ECHR) anticipated by the ECHR or by other acts, whether at the international or national level. The right to legal protection is derived from the very substance of public authority exercised in this or that manner over any and all individuals, depending on their personal status (usually nationality), and/or depending on the place where he she resides, permanently or temporarily. However, public authority is also bound by certain obligations owed to individuals. One of these obligations is the provision of the possibility of legal protection. Public authority is not only the bearer of authority, but also the bearer of obligations *vis-à-vis* those subordinated to it. It does not matter whether we perceive public authority as a contract between the citizen and the state, or as something emanating from the very substance of the state and representing its basic characteristic feature at the same time.

3.14. The author is of the opinion that **we must strictly distinguish between the right to court proceedings and the right to legal protection**. The right to court proceedings represents the right of access to a court or other public authority, **the right to court proceedings can be *waived* on the basis of and to the extent of the autonomy enjoyed by the particular entity (for instance, by entering into an arbitration agreement). Conversely, the right to legal protection cannot be waived.** Such possibility would imply the waiver of one's own personality, prohibited in a modern society. Any substantive right is deprived of its meaning if there are no procedural remedies for the protection thereof, i.e. protection *by legal means*. The author fully approves of the opinion that maintains that, by entering into an arbitration agreement, the person (party to the agreement) waives his or her right to court proceedings, i.e. his or her right to the protection provided by public [procedural] mechanisms. He or she does not, however, waive his/her right to legal protection. Due to and as a result of his or her autonomy of will, the individual or entity, by entering into an arbitration agreement, merely opts for an alternative offered by law just as well, i.e. by the same fundamental right that provides the possibility to access a court-of-law. The state (public authority), therefore, does not restrict the right to legal protection, but only offers alternatives. If the entity exercises his or her autonomy and opts for arbitration, he or she waives the right to court proceedings. However, court proceedings, as a public-law mechanism, will apply whenever the individual or entity fails to exercise their autonomy and freedom of contract or exercise them in a manner not approved by law (usually exceeding the permitted extent or proceeding in such manner that is penalized by invalidity for other reasons). **Based on the above, the author concludes that arbitration is and must be regarded as the process of finding and applying the law, not a mere process of trying to prove the agreement or the terms of the agreement between the parties.** However, it is always such *"legal protection"* that is permitted under the law and applicable at the seat of the proceedings. In other words, arbitration is only permitted to the extent allowed by valid and applicable law. An arbitration agreement as an expression of autonomy only initiates this mechanism, within the limits stipulated by the *lex arbitri*. Only those conditions secure that arbitration awards are endowed with legal force, i.e. that they are enforceable by public authority. It is only natural, though, that the state assumes no responsibility for the provision of legal protection by private mechanisms (in this case through the medium of arbitration). Although arbitral tribunals are not public authorities, they represent an instrument of legal protection. It is therefore a dispute resolution mechanism whereby legal findings are made, the applicable rules are identified, and the law is applied to the established facts of the case, all in a manner approved by the law. In relation to arbitration, public authority usually comes into play only after an arbitration award has been adopted in a manner presumed by the law and in compliance with the law. Mechanisms of public authority are, very exceptionally, also employed in case the basic functions of arbitration proceedings could be put in jeopardy while the proceedings are still pending (especially in the form of support and assistance rendered by courts), or after the arbitration proceedings are terminated, where it is necessary to review whether fundamental principles were observed in the course of the arbitration proceedings (the role of courts as supervisory authorities).

3.15. Finally, we need to point out that certain national rules of *lex arbitri* expressly allow the possibility to agree on a waiver of the right to have the arbitration award set aside by the court. Also, this alternative is by no means rare in national laws. It is, however, only a manifestation of the respect for the individual's autonomy of will. It does not constitute a waiver of the right to legal protection. It is only an accentuation of contractual autonomy as a component of the autonomy of will, with a greater emphasis on the responsibility of individuals for their legal acts (for their conduct)[25]. This alternative is usually subject to the requirement that

---

[25] For example, an interesting decision was adopted by the Latvian Constitutional Court (dec.) 2004-10-01, January 17, 2005. The case concerned the possibility of and the conditions for entering into an arbitration agreement in consumer matters. Like the ECtHR case law and the decisions of the ECJ at that time, the Latvian Constitutional Court stated that anyone can, on the basis of common market conditions, choose to either accept or refuse to enter into an agreement, and either accept or refuse any specific contractual terms and conditions. In other words, nobody is forced to enter into an agreement. *The invisible hand of the market* (which descriptive term was expressly used by the Constitutional Court in their reasoning) thus influences the terms and conditions of concluded agreements, and the market itself provides the parties

the respective proceedings are international proceedings, i.e. the parties to the proceedings are a particular entity and the state in the territory of which the proceedings are held. This is logical, because the state (public authority) is subject to much less responsibility for the performance of its obligations *vis-à-vis* individuals in cases where such an international element is present.

IV. Scope of Right to Fair Trial and Arbitration

3.16. However, even the principles incorporated in the so-called fair trial doctrine both under Article 6(1) of the ECHR and under the individual national laws need not necessarily apply to arbitration at all[26], or they may only apply to arbitration to a limited extent. It is also an expression of autonomy, as well as an expression of responsibility for the individual's own acts. In that regard, the author emphasizes his negative view of the extent of protection accorded, especially by EU law, to individuals in certain specific areas, such as consumer protection, labour law, etc. The extent of protection has become so excessive that, according to the author, it slows down not only economic development, but consequently also social development, which is rather absurd. Indeed, the financial crisis in most EU Member States clearly demonstrates the unreasonable requirements

---

(here the customers/consumers) with the opportunity to decide whether or not to enter into the agreement; the parties must therefore accept both the positive and negative consequences of their decision. If any of the market participants abuses its position with the intention of imposing its conditions on other market participants against their will, then protection against such abuse is to be found exclusively in the mechanisms provided under antitrust laws. At the same time, fully in compliance with the ECtHR case law (especially in terms of the decision in *Suovaniemi v. Finland* and others), the Constitutional Court adjudicated on the issue of successfully challenging the arbitrator for being biased. The decision was issued before the first ECJ decision dealing with arbitration clauses in consumer contracts (*Mostaza Claro* case, 2006), and the court was not lured by the tempting populist tinsel of consumer protection to such extent to which, according to the author's opinion, EU law fell for it, trying to protect the so-called weaker party in a somewhat dogmatic manner. That particular case concerned a motion for repealing Section 132, Para. 3, Part One, Section 233, Para. 6 of the Code of Civil Procedure; in terms of Article 9 of the Constitution, the Constitutional Court declared these provisions in conformity with constitutional law. The electronic version of the decision is available at: www.satv.tiesa.gov.lv/upload/2004-10-01E.rtf (accessed on July 11, 2008). As concerns the case law available at the time the Latvian Constitutional Court was making their decision, see especially the ECJ Judgment of 27 June 2000 in Joined Cases C-240/98 - 244/98, *Océano Grupo Editorial SA* v. *Roció Murciano Quintero* [2000] ECR I-4491, OJ, C 320, 21.10.2000 at p. 4.

26   ECtHR, *Suovaniemi et al.* v. *Finland* (decision on the admissibility), application no. 31737/96, 23 February 1999, (cit.) [...] *A distinction may have to be made even between different rights guaranteed by Article 6. Thus, in the light of the case-law, it is clear that the right to a public hearing can be validly waived even in court proceedings* [...] *The same applies a fortiori, to arbitration proceedings, one of the very purposes of which is often to avoid publicity.* [...].

that are demanded of the public sector and of public finance. The extent is so excessive that the private sector could never meet the requirements. At the same time, it is an approach clearly demotivating, because it merely sets minimum requirements with respect to the responsibility of individuals for their own conduct. From the global and somewhat abstract perspective, it is an approach merely setting minimum requirements with respect to the self-education of individuals in terms of their empirical development. The author generally regards these trends as very negative and decelerating, from the long-term perspective, both economic and social development. The author therefore welcomes, *inter alia*, that the Czech Republic [CZE] rejected the application of the Charter of Fundamental Rights of the EU in connection with the *Lisbon Treaty* (*Treaty on the Functioning of the European Union*), and continues to rely on its own constitutional standards, as well as the standards safeguarded by international agreements.

3.17.   Regarding the scope of the right to a fair trial, it is appropriate to start with the basic framework of the decision-making practice of the ECtHR. The case law of the ECtHR, and before that the European Commission of Human Rights, indicates that where arbitration is conducted on the basis of a voluntary decision of the parties, it is not subject to Article 6(1) of the ECHR, and the acts of the arbitration tribunal are not attributable to the state. According to the ECtHR, the state (public authority) therefore holds no responsibility for the acts of such arbitration tribunal. The author is of the opinion, though, that this does not *ipso facto* mean that such arbitration proceedings can also disregard fundamental principles of a fair trial. But the author disagrees with the opinion that Article 6(1) of the ECHR does not apply to arbitration. Only from the formal point of view does Article 6(1) of the ECHR not apply to arbitration, that is, as concerns the mechanisms incorporated in the ECHR and designed for the enforcement of the right to a fair trial *vis-à-vis* states that are bound by the ECHR. However, the right to a fair trial is not limited to the subject matter of the ECHR. It is a general concept inherent to a developed legal society. Consequently, if Article 6(1) of the ECHR defines the basic scope of the right to a fair trial, then the fact that the ECHR mechanisms are not directly applicable to arbitration does not mean that the fundamental principles of a fair trial should not apply to arbitration either. It only means that the mechanisms provided for in the ECHR as acts of international law do not apply to *voluntary arbitration*. Entering into an arbitration agreement thus does not constitute a waiver of the right to a fair trial. Despite the fact that the procedural mechanisms provided for in the ECHR do not apply to arbitration directly, the case law of the ECtHR still represents an essential benchmark for the assessment of the fundamental principles of a fair trial, including those that must be observed in arbitration proceedings.

3.18.   However, the case law of the ECtHR regarding *fair trial* is being adopted by courts in many *distant countries* as well. For instance, the ECtHR case law regarding arbitration was invoked by the Supreme Court of

Appeal of South Africa in *Telcordia Technologies Inc.* (Delaware [USA]) v. *Telkom SA* [South Africa][27]. This case concerned proceedings at the ICC International Court of Arbitration (with the seat of arbitration in South Africa), in which an English *barrister* acted as the sole arbitrator. The South African court set aside the arbitrator's award for *gross irregularities*. At the same time, however, the same court revoked the authorization of the sole arbitrator and replaced him with a panel of three arbitrators consisting of retired South African judges. The main reason for these measures was, however, disagreement with the decision on the merits. The Supreme Court, as the Court of Appeal, subsequently set aside the decision and declared it to be in breach of the principles of party autonomy in arbitration[28]. The Supreme Court maintained that this approach was in compliance with global practice and international customs and the erudition of foreign and international tribunals. At the same time, the Supreme Court emphasized the interest in supporting the international business system, which ought to be foreseeable in matters of dispute resolution. The internationally recognized standards include the autonomy of the forum and the minimization of court intervention.

3.19. As concerns the requirements of a fair trial in arbitration, the author believes that it is appropriate to make a few notes about the rich and established case law of certain selected countries. Special attention should be paid to Austria. In the author's opinion, Austria boasts one of the most stable systems regulating arbitration, which at the same time is very favourable toward arbitration (the only disadvantage perhaps being the multi-tier court proceedings, especially in connection with the annulment of arbitration awards). In the author's opinion, the Austrian rules are more favourable to arbitration than Swiss law, which is being highlighted in literature as the best place for arbitration (seat of arbitration). It is indeed a very stable system, without the rather surprising decisions that occur, for instance, from time to time, in Swiss practice; at the same time, it is a balanced system. It provides truly equal opportunities, and it is able to reliably protect both parties from very serious flaws in procedure. The author firmly believes that the Austrian case law could well serve as the long-term benchmark for fair trial in arbitration[29]. We must point out, though, that Swiss practice, for instance,

---

[27] Judgment of the Supreme Court of Appeal of South Africa, 26/05, November 22, 2006 [2006] 139 SCA (RSA). The electronic version is available at: http://www.saflii.org/za/cases/ZASCA/2006/112.html (accessed on July 17, 2010).

[28] See Richard H. Christie, *Arbitration: Party Autonomy or Curial Intervention – The Historical Background*, 111 SOUTH AFRICAN LAW JOURNAL 143 (1994).

[29] See, for instance, the following decisions of the OGH [AUT] (Supreme Court of Austria – *Oberstes Gerichtshof*):

➤ Decision of May 3, 1899: The arbitrator must hear the parties personally; authorizing a third party to do so is not allowed. Source: STEFAN RIEGLER, ALEXANDER PETSCHE, ALICE FREMUTH-WOLF, MARTIN PLATTE & CHRISTOPH LIEBSCHER, ARBITRATION LAW OF AUSTRIA: PRACTICE AND PROCEDURE, New York: JurisPublishing 248 (2007), (hereinafter "RIEGLER ET AL., ARBITRATION AUSTRIA").

can also offer very rich case law[30]. According to the author, however, the Swiss case law is not as balanced as the Austrian decision-making

Czech (& Central European) Yearbook of Arbitration

> ➢ Decision of February 26, 1901: An (oral) hearing is not necessary if the parties are allowed to state their case [in a different manner]. Source: GIUNF, 1304.
> ➢ Decision of November 20, 1934: The right to be heard (the right to state one's case) is not violated if the facts of the case are not examined by the arbitral tribunal to the full extent. Source: (10) RSP (1935).
> ➢ 3 Ob 402/37, June 9, 1937: The parties to an arbitration agreement may agree whether a hearing will be held or not. In the absence of such agreement, the decision whether to hold a hearing or not will be made by the tribunal. Source: EVBL 722 (1937).
> ➢ 2 Ob 344/51, November 21, 1951: (i) A simple announcement specifying the time and place of the hearing is a sufficient guarantee of the right to a fair trial; it is not necessary to invite the parties to attend. (ii) The fact that a party was not informed about one or more dates of hearings only constitutes a breach of the right to a fair trial if the other party attended the hearing and the absent party did not have the opportunity to respond to the pleadings of the attending party. (iii) It is not necessary for the presentations of the parties to be witnessed by all members of the arbitral tribunal; the attendance of one of the members of the arbitral tribunal shall suffice. Source: RIEGLER ET AL., ARBITRATION AUSTRIA, 336.
> ➢ 2 Ob 422/54, January 13, 1955: Interrogation of witnesses does not have to be attended by all members of the tribunal; one member shall suffice. Source: JBL 503 (1955).
> ➢ 7 Ob 623/81, September 24, 1981: The arbitrator must inform the parties about any and all changes in the circumstances of the case. If necessary, the parties must have the opportunity to attend the examination of evidence and to make statements regarding such examination. Source: EVBL 77 (1982).
> ➢ 2 Ob 516/84, February 29, 1988: Arbitrators may elect the chairman of the tribunal by drawing lots. Source: RIEGLER ET AL., ARBITRATION AUSTRIA, 248.
> ➢ 3 Ob 1091/9, November 27, 1991: The right to state one's case and consequently the right to a fair trial are not violated if the tribunal ignores a proposal for evidence or if the tribunal fails to examine the facts of the case entirely. However, these rights are violated if the award rests on circumstances or evidence that the parties did not have the opportunity to comment on. Source: RZ 65 (1993).
> ➢ 3 Ob 2374/96f, November 20, 1996: (i) The fact that arbitration proceedings instituted by a limited partnership (Kommanditgesellschaft) as the plaintiff against a partner of this partnership with unlimited liability (general partner/ Komplementär) as the defendant were not attended by the partner of this partnership with limited liability as the second defendant does not constitute a violation of the partnership's right (as a party) to be heard (right to a fair trial); only the party to the proceedings itself possesses this right, not its partners or its representatives. (ii) Compliance with due process must be examined from the perspective of the order articulated in the decision, not the reasons for the decision. Published in: RZ 72 (1997).
> ➢ 6 Ob 186/97i, July 24, 1997: (i) If a party failed to raise the objection in the course of the proceedings that the permanent court of arbitration ceased to exist, the party is barred from making that objection the grounds for the annulment of the arbitral award. (ii) Insufficient assessment of the factual and legal circumstances of the case and the pleadings of the parties does not constitute a violation of fair trial. Source: (19) RdW (1998).
> ➢ 7 Ob 221/98w, December 10, 1998: The right to be heard (the right to state one's case) may also be provided retrospectively in the proceedings on the annulment of the arbitral award. Source: RdW 206 (1999).
> ➢ 3 Ob 35/05a of March 31, 2005: The principles of fair trial are not violated if the arbitrators fail to grant the proposal for examination of evidence or if the facts of the case were not sufficiently established. Source: RIEGLER ET AL., ARBITRATION AUSTRIA, 380.
> ➢ 2 Ob 41/04z, March 17, 2005: Any agreement on the appointment of arbitrators according to which only one of the parties has the exclusive right to appoint the chairman of the arbitral tribunal in case the parties fail to agree on the chairman, and if the chairman is not elected by the other members of the tribunal, breaches Article 6(1) of the ECHR and is therefore null and void. Source: JBL 801 (2005).

30 See, for instance, the decision of the Swiss federal court, according to which the guarantees enshrined in Article 58 of the Federal Constitution and Article 6(1) of the ECHR apply both to state courts and private arbitration tribunals, the decisions of which correspond to the decisions of state courts as concerns the administration of justice and are equal to the decisions of state courts with respect to their finality and enforceability. Arbitral awards must therefore guarantee independent legal findings. Published in: ATF/BGE 117 Ia 166, JdT 1992 I 212, ASA BULLETIN 259 (1992), RDSIE

practice. The measure of support provided to arbitration in any particular country cannot only be measured in quantitative terms, depending on how few arbitration awards are set aside by courts. Conclusions can only be drawn after a thorough analysis of these decisions, and always taking into account how efficient the law is in protecting the parties from very serious flaws. In this particular respect the Austrian practice exhibits, in the author's opinion, a greater degree of stability and transparency, and above all, balance.

V. Approach of the ECtHR (European Commission of Human Rights) to Arbitration

3.20. The ECtHR regards the state not only as the authority enforcing sovereign public authority, but also as the authority guaranteeing the observance of obligations assumed *vis-à-vis* foreign countries. The ECtHR therefore confirms the premise that the state alone is held responsible at that moment. At the same time, the ECtHR sets a high standard of contractual freedom with respect to the individuals' voluntary waiver of court proceedings. Such an approach is important, and it has an impact not only at the level of state responsibility in relation to arbitration conducted in its territory, but also in relation to arbitration conducted abroad[31].

3.21. Judgment in *De Wilde, Ooms et Versyp v. Belgium*:[32] In this case, the ECtHR accepted a very high standard for the restriction of rights, taking into account the significance thereof in a democratic society. It was a decision that, in the author's opinion, suggested that we must strictly distinguish between legal protection and court proceedings. The ECtHR allowed a major restriction of rights in relation to the right to court proceedings, i.e. protection through public authority[33].

---

187 (1993). This opinion was reiterated in another decision published in: ATF 119 II 271, 3b, as well as in another decision in: ATF 112 Ia 166.

[31] The latter aspect is manifested, in particular, in the recognition and enforcement of foreign arbitral awards.

[32] Judgments Nos. 2832/66, 2835/66 and 2899/66, March 10, 1972. See also Thomas A. O'Donnell, *The Margin of Appreciation Doctrine: Standards in the Jurisprudence of the European Court of Human Rights*, 4 (4) HUMAN RIGHTS QUARTERLY 474 (1982), Onder Bakircioglu, *The Application of the Margin of Appreciation Doctrine in Freedom of Expression and Public Morality Cases*, 8 (7) GERMAN LAW JOURNAL (2007) et al. For an annotation of the decision in *De Wilde, Ooms and Versyp v. B*, see, for instance, the Netherlands Institute of Human Rights / Utrecht School of Law at: http://sim.law.uu.nl/SIM/CaseLaw/hof.nsf/e4ca7ef017f8c045c1256849004787f5/ca9ce 8eb36e8cee2c1256640004c2552?OpenDocument (accessed on June 7, 2010).

[33] The ratio decidendi in original (cit.) [...] *Taking into consideration the importance of these rights in a democratic society, the standard of permissibility of the restrictions shall be very high.* [...].

3.22. Judgment in **_Waite and Kennedy v. D_**:[34] In this case, the ECtHR expressed its opinion that no restriction of rights (meaning the right to court proceedings) can follow from the very act of entering into an arbitration agreement. We must always presume that the person is generally not restricting his or her rights (except for the very moment at which the arbitration agreement is concluded). The simultaneous restriction of fundamental rights requires a *lack of action (omission)*. The very possibility of excluding the protection of subjective rights by court proceedings before (state) courts-of-law does not constitute a restriction of fundamental rights. This judgment scrupulously protects the freedom of the expression of will. This freedom includes the possibility of an express renunciation of certain rights. Besides, a restriction of any fundamental right may be in effect insofar as the particular rights are not deprived on their merit[35].

3.23. Judgment in **_Deweer v. Belgium_**:[36] The ECtHR concluded that it is not merely in civil matters (especially in the form of arbitration) that the waiver of the right to court proceedings (waiver of the right to have one's case dealt with by a court)[37] can be found. The ECtHR declared that the waiver of the right to court proceedings is also possible in criminal matters. The waiver is not, in principle, a breach of the ECHR.

3.24. Judgment in **_Lithgow et al. v. United Kingdom_**:[38] According to the ECtHR, the word "tribunal" does not necessarily have to represent a component of the judicial system of a particular country. It can refer to an

---

34 Decision on Complaint No. 26083/94 of February 18, 1999. See, for instance, Markus Rau, *After Pinochet: Foreign Sovereign Immunity in Respect of Serious Human Rights Violations – The Decision of the European Court of Human Rights in the al-Adsani Case*, 6 (6) GERMAN LAW JOURNAL (2002); August Reinisch, *The Immunity of International Organizations and the Jurisdiction of their Administrative Tribunals*, 7 (2) CHINESE JOURNAL OF INTERNATIONAL LAW 285 (2008) et al. Annotation included in the press release of the ECHR Registrar at:
http://www.echr.coe.int/eng/Press/1999/Feb/waite.kennedy%20epresse.html (accessed on July 1, 2008). A more detailed annotation, for instance, is also included in the information database of the Netherlands Institute of Human Rights. The electronic version can be found at:
http://sim.law.uu.nl/SIM/CaseLaw/hof.nsf/2422ec00f1ace923c1256681002b47f1/609 3b338dfb67368c1256727004ba9e5?OpenDocument (accessed on September 1, 2010).
35 The ratio decidendi in original (cit.) [...] *First of all, the restriction of rights cannot follow just from concluding an arbitration court agreement. Secondly, it shall always be presumed that the person has not restricted the rights, with an exception of the time when the activity of him/her does not unequivocally confirm it. Thirdly, such restriction may be in effect insofar as the particular rights are not deprived on their merit.* [...].
36 Decision of February 27, 1980. See (35) ECHR REP., Series A, 25, para. 49.
37 Concerning the concept of *court/tribunal*, see, for instance, the ECtHR decision in *Lithgow et al. v. UK* of June 24, 1986. In that regard, it is necessary to bear in mind that the definitions of *"court/tribunal"* vary to a substantial extent. A differentiated approach to that concept is employed, in particular, by laws and regulations of other than national origin.
38 Decision of June 24, 1986.

entity/individual upon which the exercise of public authority is delegated by the state. However, this does not include cases in which the parties (again as a result of their autonomy) agree to such review[39].

3.25. Judgment in *Bramelid and Malström et al. v. Sweden*:[40] The ECtHR accepted the possibility of renouncing the righ t to court proceedings[41], and highlighted the necessity to distinguish between voluntary and mandatory arbitration. However, if the law requires the parties to submit to arbitration, i.e. the submission to arbitration is not the result of exercising their own autonomy, the mechanisms of the ECHR apply[42]. This particular case concerned mandatory arbitration.

---

[39] It does not matter whether the *lex arbitri* stipulates direct enforceability of an arbitral award, like, for instance, in the Czech Republic (Section 27 of the Czech Arbitration Act, which allows the parties to agree in their arbitration agreement on a review of the arbitral award by other arbitrators), in Austria (Section 607 of the ZPO[AUT]) et al., or whether an exequatur is required, like, for instance, in Germany (Section 1062 et seq. of the ZPO[DEU], or especially Section 1064 of the ZPO[DEU]), or in the U.S. or the UK, provided the applicable statutory conditions under UK law are met. See, for instance, Alexander J. Bělohlávek, *Druhá instance v rozhodčím řízení* (*Appeal in Arbitration*), 4 (6) PRÁVNÍ ZPRAVODAJ 5 (2003); Květoslav Růžička, *Odvolání v rozhodčím řízení?* (*Appeal in Arbitration?*), 9 (4) PRÁVNÍ PRAXE V PODNIKÁNÍ 11 (2000); and Vladimír Balaš, *Možnosti přezkoumání rozhodnutí při řešení sporů v mezinárodním ekonomickém právu* (*WTO, NAFTA, ICSID*) (*The Possibility of Review of Decisions in Dispute Resolution under International Economic Law* (*WTO, NAFTA, ICSID*)), 12 (2) ČASOPIS PRO PRÁVNÍ VĚDU A PRAXI 97 (2004) (the last mentioned author, however, in relation to disputes under international law). See also Klaus P. Berger, *Die Regelung der gerichtlichen Anfechtbarkeit internationaler Schiedssprüche in europäischen Schieds-gerichtsgesetzen*, RIW 850 (1989); W. Laurence Craig, *Uses and abuses of appeal from awards*, ARBITRATION INTERNATIONAL 174 (1998); Květoslav Růžička, *Mezitímní a částečný rozhodčí nález* (*Interim and Partial Arbitral Award*), 5 (4) PRÁVNÍ FÓRUM 153 (2008); Hans-Jürgen Schroth, *Die „kleine Berufung" gegen Schiedsurteile im deutschen Recht*, 5 (6) SCHIEDSVZ 291 (2007); Gökçe N. Uzar, *Rechtsmittel gegen Schiedssprüche nach dem neuen deutschen und türkischen Schiedsverfahrensrecht, in* 19 SCHRIFTEN ZUM VERFAHRENSRECHT, Frankfurt: Peter Lang Verlag (2007) et al. The author maintains that we cannot accept that the issue of the breach of the confidentiality clause incorporated in the arbitration agreement should be discussed before the same arbitrators as the continuation of the former dispute, i.e. we cannot allow any possibility of reopening the previously terminated arbitration or ......(?) the proceedings of any arbitration. See Llewellyn Joseph Gibbons, *Private Law, Public "Justice": Another Look at Privacy Arbitration, and Global E-Commerce*, 15 OHIO STATE JOURNAL ON DISPUTE RESOLUTION 769, 777 (2000).

[40] Decision on Complaints Nos. 8588/79 and 8589/79, December 12, 1983. See (38) ECHR REP., Series DR, 18.

[41] See also JOHN TACKABERRY, RONALD BERNSTEIN & ARTHUR MARRIOTT, BERNSTEIN'S HANDBOOK OF ARBITRATION AND DISPUTE RESOLUTION, London: Sweet & Maxwell 230, marg. 2-623 (2003).

[42] The original version (cit.) [...] *A distinction must be drawn between voluntary arbitration and compulsory arbitration. Normally, Article 6 poses no problem where arbitration is entered into voluntarily.* (...) *If, on the other hand, arbitration is compulsory in the sense of being required by law, as in this case, the parties have no option but to refer their dispute to an arbitration Board, and the Board must offer the guarantees set forth in Article* 6 (1). [...].

3.26. Judgment in *Rychetsky v. Switzerland*:[43] Apart from the nature of arbitration (*mandatory* versus *voluntary*), the applicability of the ECHR also depends on the contents of the *lex arbitri*[44]. *The case concerned the Swiss Intercantonal Agreement on Arbitration*[45] of March 27, 1969. The *Commission* concluded that the state could not be held responsible for arbitration, unless any of the parties requested intervention in the form of public authority[46]. However, the *Commission* emphasized that national courts did not have the opportunity to deal with such case until the complainant himself asked for intervention by public authority (because of the unreasonable length of the arbitration proceedings)[47] and the state is therefore only responsible for delays in proceedings before state authorities. Such a decision was also invoked by the English Supreme Court of Judicature / Court of Appeal (Civil Division)[48] in *Stretford v. The Football Association Ltd.*)[49].

---

[43]   Decision on Complaint No. 10881/84 of March 4, 1987, (51) ECHR REP., Series A DR, 83-93. See also, for instance, Olivier Jacot-Guillardmond, *L' arbitrage privé face à l'article 6 § 1 de la Convention européene des Droits de l'Homme*, in PROTECTING HUMAN RIGHTS: THE EUROPEAN DIMENSION. STUDIES IN HONOUR OF GÉRARD J. WIARDA, Köln: Carl Heymans Verlag KG 202 (Franz Matscher & Herbert Petzold eds., 1988); Charles Jarrosson, *L'arbitrage et la Convention européene des droits de l'Homme*, 4 REV. ARB. 573, 589 (1989); and Fredrik Ringquist, *Do Procedural Human Rights Requirements Apply to Arbitration – a Study of Article 6 (1) of the European Convention on Human Rights and its Bearing upon Arbitration*, Thesis, 2005, the electronic version of which is available at: www.jur.lu.se/.../Examensarbeten.nsf/0/05891BE871840D2EC12571070048DF0C/$File/xsmall.pdf?OpenElement (accessed on July 10, 2008) et al.

[44]   In the published English version (the French version was not considered) (cit) [ ] *in order to answer the question of whether the guarantees secured by Article 6 apply, account must be taken not only of the arbitration agreement between the parties and the nature of the private arbitration proceedings, but also of the legislative framework providing for such proceedings.* [...].

[45]   *Konkordat über die Schiedsgerichtsbarkeit*. This *Konkordat* was replaced with the new Swiss federal regulation of civil court proceedings, with effect since January 1, 2011.

[46]   This case concerned a complaint about delays in arbitration conducted in Switzerland, lodged by a French citizen. It has to be conceded that the arbitration was indeed taking an unreasonably long time.

[47]   The original version in which this decision was published in the abovementioned source (cit.) [...] *The Commission points out that the national courts were not required to deal with the case until the applicant applied to them, i.e. prior to August 30, 1983, on the grounds of undue delay in the arbitration proceedings. It follows that they cannot be held responsible for the period prior to this application* [...].

[48]   The Court was to decide on an appeal against the judgment of the High Court of Justice Chancery Division, [2007] EWHC 479 (Ch). Considering the focus of this contribution, it is appropriate to mention that the subject matter of the English court's decision was also partially an issue of public policy, in connection with certain procedural acts (see, for instance, para. 68 of the appellate court's decision, etc.). The public policy issue was, however, of no special importance in this regard, and therefore the respective decision is not considered in this contribution in that respect.

[49]   Case No. A3/2006/0713/CHANF of March 21, 2007, [2007] EWCA Civ 238, [2007] APP.L.R. 03/21. The judgment can be found at:

3.27. Judgment in *Axelsson et al.* v. *Sweden*:[50] The *Commission* concluded that the restriction of the right to court proceedings as a result of the exercise of contractual autonomy is not contrary to Article 6 of the ECHR. The *Commission* maintains that Article 6 of the ECHR is focused on a legitimate aim and proportionate means of achieving such aim. The *Commission* also did not find any significant interest that ought to be subject to protection by public authority. According to the Commission, autonomy could be restricted in certain specific cases for the purpose of protecting the interests of minority groups. The important thing is, though, that the *Commission* also highlighted the responsibility of those who enter into an arbitration agreement for the consequences of their conduct. The waiver of the right to court proceedings must, nonetheless, meet the following two requirements: (i) the waiver must be made in an unequivocal manner, and (ii) the waiver must not jeopardize an important public interest of any sort.

3.28. Judgment in *Jakob Boss Soehne KG and Others* v. *Germany*:[51] The complainant (a company) in this case voluntarily entered into an arbitration agreement and thereby renounced its right to have its civil rights determined in court proceedings, for the conduct of which the state was responsible under the ECHR. This did not mean, however, that the respondent state's responsibility was completely excluded [...], as the arbitration award had to be recognized by the German courts and given executory effect by them. The courts thereby exercised certain control and guaranteed the fairness and correctness of the arbitration proceedings, which they considered to have been carried out in conformity with fundamental rights, and in the particular case, in conformity with the right of the complainant to be heard.

3.29. Judgment in *Nordstrom* v. *the Netherlands*:[52] The *Commission* accepted the possibility of renouncing the protection guaranteed by Article 6 of the ECHR, emphasizing that it is necessary take into account the contents of the law that allows such procedure. The important thing is that a reasonable degree of control over the arbitration proceedings must be maintained. At the same time, it is necessary to examine whether the control was properly exercised in the particular case [...]. In connection with that particular case, the *Commission* noted that Dutch law contains rules that permit the courts to set aside (quash) arbitral awards on specific grounds. [...] According to the *Commission*, though, the courts do not guarantee that arbitration proceedings comply with Article 6 of

---

www.nadr.co.uk/articles/published/ArbitLRe/Stretford%20v%20FA%202007.pdf (accessed on January 5, 2009), and the electronic version of the decision is also available at: www.portal.nasstar.com/75/files/Stretford%20v-FA%20CA%2021%20Mar%202007.pdf (accessed on January 5, 2009). The court was assessing the length of arbitration proceedings according to the rules of a football association.

50 Decision No. 11960/86, July 13, 1990, (51) ECHR REP., Series DR, 51, 83.
51 Decision No. 18479/91, December 2, 1991, (51) ECHR REP., Series DR, 83.
52 Decision No. 28101/95, November 27, 1996, (87-B) ECHR REP., Series DR, 112.

the ECHR. The author believes, however, that the *Commission* neither excluded nor actually implicitly confirmed that arbitration must also comply with the principles of fair trial. The Commission also confirmed that it is exclusively up to the Contracting State (party to the ECHR) to decide itself on which grounds an arbitral award can be set aside[...].

3.30. Judgment in ***Osmo Suovaniemi et al. v. Finland*** :[53] Apart from accepting the possibility of the waiver of the right to court proceedings, the ECtHR also declared that entering into an arbitration agreement does not constitute a waiver of all the rights enshrined in Article 6(1) of the ECHR; also, the conclusion of the arbitration agreement must be executed in compliance with the *lex arbitri*[54]. *National laws may exclude the possibility of entering into an arbitration agreement in respect of certain disputes (objective arbitrability). The ECtHR stated that the grounds for renouncing the court proceedings can only be inherent in certain features of court proceedings. The ECtHR demonstrated this conclusion on the principle of proceedings held in curia* (with the exclusion of the public)[55].

3.31. Judgment in *Albert and Le Compte, van Leuven, De Meyere v. Belgium*:[56] The ECtHR declared that there would be no sense in the arbitral agreement

---

53 Decision No. 31737/96, February 23, 1999.

54 That is, within the national rules of *lex arbitri* (the applicable national rules regulating arbitrability, as well as other conditions for entering into arbitration agreements).

55 In that part of the judgment, the ECtHR further invoked, for instance, the decision in *Håkansson v. Sweden*. In *B v. United Kingdom*, the ECtHR emphasized that the issue of the publicity of the proceedings before public authorities must be assessed in light of the purpose of these proceedings and always according to Article 6(1) of the ECHR. See [2002] 34 EHRR 19. See, for instance, Alec Samuels, *Current Developments*, 23 (1) STATUTE LAW REVIEW 82 (2002). The decision in *B. v. United Kingdom* has been invoked in many decisions of national courts, for instance, (i) judgment of the Supreme Court of the Judicature Court of Appeal (Civil Division), Case No. A/3/2003/1477 of March 25, 2004 (in (1) *Department of Economic Policy and Development of the City of Moscow*, and (2) *The Government of Moscow v. (1) Bankers Trust company*, and (2) *International Industrial Bank*), [2004] EWCA Civ 314 (also available in an electronic version, for instance, at: http://www.hrothgar.co.uk/YAWS/reps/04a314.htm (accessed on September 17, 2010); (ii) Judgment of the Court of Appeal (UK) of October 16, 2006 in *ASM Shipping Ltd of India* v. *TTMI Ltd of England*, [2006] EWCA Civ 1341; (iii) *Cetelem SA v. Roust Holdings Ltd.*, [2005] EWCA Civ. 618, (iv) *North Range Shipping Ltd* v. *Seatrans Shipping Corporation*, [2002] EWCA Civ 405, and (v) *English v. Emery Reimbold & Strick Ltd*, [2002] EWCA Civ 605 et al.

56 Decision, Nos. 7299/75 and 7496/76, February 10, 1983, (58) ECHR REP., Series A. The merits of the case concerned decisions of the Belgian authorities (self-regulating professional medical body) on the temporary suspension of the right to practice medicine. See ROBERT ESSER, AUF DEM WEG ZU EINEM EUROPÄISCHEN STRAFVERFAHRENSRECHT, Berlin: De Gruyter 567 (2002); GEORGIOS PETROCHILOS, PROCEDURAL LAW IN INTERNATIONAL ARBITRATION, Oxford: Oxford University Press 164 (2004); Jeanine Bucherer, *Die Vereinbarkeit von Militärgerichten mit dem Recht auf ein faires Verfahren gemäß Art. 6 Abs. 1 EMRK, Art. 8 Abs. 1 AMRK und Art. 14 Abs. 1 des UN-Paktes über bürgerliche und politische Rechte, in* 180 BEITRÄGE ZUM AUSLÄNDISCHEN ÖFFENTLICHEN RECHT UND VÖLKERRECHT, Berlin: Springer Verlag 42, Footnote 126 (2005); JOCHEN ABR FROWEIN, DER EUROPÄISCHE GRUNDRECHTSSCHUT UND DIE NATIONALE GERICHTSBARKEIT, Berlin/New York: Walter de Gruyter 22 (1983) et al. The decision is also available in an electronic version

if any of the parties could subsequently, at any later moment, decide to use a particular procedural circumstance as an objection to the arbitral award. It is therefore permitted to limit to a particular stage of the proceedings, for instance, a bias challenge resulting from the arbitrator's relationship to the case or a jurisdictional challenge. According to the ECtHR, the state does not have the obligation to avert every violation of procedural rights, but to secure the possibility of such defence [...].

| | |

Summaries

FRA [*Procédure d'arbitrage du point de vue du droit à la protection juridique et à la procédure judiciaire (droit de chacun pour que son affaire soit examinée par un tribunal): Importance de l'autonomie et l'amplitude du droit à un procès équitable*]

Dans le passé, les États hésitaient, pour des raisons politiques, à reconnaître les décisions des tribunaux d'autres pays, dans la mesure où cette reconnaissance impliquait, de fait, l'acceptation du pouvoir d'un État étranger. L'arbitrage privé a surmonté ces réticences et la procédure d'arbitrage remplace de plus en plus le pouvoir de l'État là où il s'avère, pour un grand nombre de raisons, peu fonctionnel et inefficace. Il est nécessaire de faire une stricte distinction entre le droit à la protection judiciaire et le droit à la protection juridique. Il est possible de renoncer au droit à la protection judiciaire conséquemment à l'autonomie de la volonté (par exemple par un contrat d'arbitrage conclu dans les limites de la lex arbitri). Mais il est impossible de renoncer à la protection juridique. C'est pourquoi la procédure d'arbitrage est une recherche et une application du droit. Il doit cependant s'agir d'une protection juridique approuvée par la loi du lieu de la procédure d'arbitrage. Le contrat d'arbitrage, en tant qu'expression de l'autonomie, ne fait qu'initier ce mécanisme de résolution des litiges, et ce dans les limites définies par la lex arbitri. Ce n'est qu'à cette condition que l'on reconnaît une force juridique aux sentences arbitrales sous forme de force exécutoire à l'aide du pouvoir public. L'État ne porte pas la responsabilité de l'octroi de la protection juridique à l'aide des mécanismes de droit privé (procédure d'arbitrage). Les tribunaux d'arbitrage ne représentent pas le pouvoir public, mais ils sont toutefois un outil de la protection juridique. Les principes d'un procès équitable peuvent être limités dans la procédure d'arbitrage, mais il est impossible de les exclure totalement et il faut en sauvegarder le standard minimal indispensable.

at: http://www.legislationline.org/legislation.php?tid=2&lid=7207&less=false (accessed on July 11, 2008).

CZE [*Rozhodčí řízení z pohledu práva na právní ochranu a práva na soudní řízení (právo každého, aby jeho případ řešil soud): Význam autonomie a rozsah práva na spravedlivý proces*]
V minulosti se státy z politických důvodů zdráhaly uznat rozhodnutí soudů jiných zemí, neboť tím fakticky implikovaly akceptaci cizí státní moci. To překonávalo soukromoprávní rozhodčí řízení a rozhodčí řízení stále více nahrazuje státní moc tam, kde je tato z řady důvodů nefunkční a neefektivní. Je nutno striktně rozlišovat mezi právem na soudní ochranu a právem na právní ochranu. Práva na soudní ochranu se lze vzdát v důsledku autonomie vůle (například rozhodčí smlouvou uzavřenou v mezích lex arbitri). Práva na právní ochranu se vzdát nelze. Rozhodčí řízení je proto nalézáním a aplikací práva. Musí však jít o právní ochranu aprobovanou právem v místě rozhodčího řízení. Rozhodčí smlouva jako výraz autonomie jen tento mechanismus řešení sporů iniciuje, a to v mezích stanovených lex arbitri. Pouze za této podmínky je rozhodčím nálezům přiznána právní síla v podobě vykonatelnosti pomocí moci veřejné. Stát nenese odpovědnost za poskytování právní ochrany pomocí soukromoprávních mechanismů (rozhodčího řízení). Rozhodčí soudy nereprezentují veřejnou moc, jsou však nástrojem právní ochrany. Zásady spravedlivého procesu lze v rozhodčím řízení omezit, nelze je však zcela vyloučit a musí být zachován jejich minimální nezbytný standard.

| | |

POL [*Postępowanie arbitrażowe w perspektywie prawa do ochrony prawnej oraz prawa do postępowania sądowego (prawa osoby do oddania swej sprawy pod rozstrzygnięcie sądu): znaczenie autonomii i zakres prawa do sprawiedliwego procesu*]
Postępowanie arbitrażowe to rozpoznawanie i stosowanie prawa. Jest to instrument zapewniający w sposób alternatywny ochronę prawną w zakresie dopuszczanej przez prawo autonomii umownej. Można zrzec się prawa do ochrony sądowej za pośrednictwem władzy publicznej i w ramach dopuszczalnych przez prawo, jednak nie można zrzec się prawa do ochrony prawnej. Zasady sprawiedliwego procesu można w postępowaniu arbitrażowym ograniczyć, jednak nie można wykluczyć ich minimalnego (obowiązkowego) standardu.

DEU [*Das Schiedsverfahren aus der Sicht des Rechts auf Rechtsschutz und des Rechts auf ein Gerichtsverfahren (das Recht jeder Person, dass ihr Fall durch ein Gericht gelöst wird): Die Bedeutung der Autonomie und der Einfluss des Rechts auf einen fairen Prozess*]
Das Schiedsverfahren ist Findung und Anwendung des Rechts. Es handelt sich um ein alternatives Instrument des Rechtsschutzes im Ausmaß der rechtlich genehmigten Vertragsautonomie. Während man auf den gerichtlichen Schutz durch öffentliche Gewalt in den rechtlich

zugelassenen Grenzen verzichten kann, ist ein Verzicht auf den rechtlichen Schutz unmöglich. Die Prinzipien eines fairen Prozesses können im Schiedsverfahren eingeengt werden; ihr (obligatorischer) Mindeststandard lässt sich jedoch nicht ausschließen.

RUS [*Арбитражное разбирательство с точки зрения права на правовую защиту и права на судебное разбирательство (право каждого человека на рассмотрение его дела в суде): Значение автономии и область действия права на справедливый процесс*]
Арбитражное разбирательство представляет собой поиск и применение закона. Это инструмент предоставления правовой защиты альтернативным путем в пределах договорной автономии, предусмотренной законом. Хотя от права на судебную защиту в органах государственной власти в рамках закона можно отказаться, от права на правовую защиту отказаться нельзя. Принцип отправления правосудия может быть ограничен нормой, предусматривающей арбитражное рассмотрение, но его минимальный (обязательный) стандарт не может быть исключён полностью.

ES [*El procedimiento de arbitraje desde la perspectiva de la protección legal y el derecho a proceso judicial (el derecho de cada uno a que un tribunal enjuicie su caso). Significado de la autonomía y alcance del derecho a un juicio justo o debido proceso*]
El procedimiento de arbitraje es el proceso de verificación y aplicación del derecho. Se trata de un instrumento que proporciona protección legal utilizando una vía alternativa en la extensión de la autonomía contractual legalmente aprobada. Aunque es posible renunciar al derecho de protección judicial por mediación del poder público dentro de los límites estipulados por la ley, no es posible renunciar al derecho de protección legal. En el procedimiento de arbitraje es posible limitar los principios del debido proceso, pero no se puede excluir su norma mínima (obligatoria).

Matija Damjan

Arbitral Interim Measures and the Right to Be Heard

Key words:
interim relief |
interim measures |
right to be heard |
ex parte measures |
preliminary orders |
adversarial procedure
| enforcement |
UNCITRAL Model
Law

Abstract | *If arbitration is to be equally efficient as judicial mechanisms of dispute resolution, it must provide an equivalent system of immediate interim protection of parties' rights and property until the decision on the merits of the case. Therefore, modern arbitration legislations recognise the right of arbitral tribunals to issue interim measures and provide the possibility of enforcement of such measures. A delicate balance needs to be reached between the need for swift action on one hand and the protection of constitutionally guaranteed procedural rights (such as the right to be heard) on the other hand. The article discusses the problems that arise in this sphere, taking into account the latest changes to the UNCITRAL Model Law on Arbitration and their implementation in Slovenian law.*

Matija Damjan, Ph.D.
is a research fellow
at the Institute for
Comparative Law at
the Faculty of Law,
University of Ljubljana.
In his research he
primarily focuses on
the areas of private
and commercial law.
He was a member
of the expert group
that prepared the
draft of the Slovenian
Arbitration Act,
enacted in 2008.
e-mail:
matija.damjan@
pf.uni-lj.si

| | |

I. Introduction

4.01. A party unwilling to participate constructively in arbitration proceedings can obstruct, in various ways, the swift conduct of arbitration and may try to undermine the possibility that the final award, when issued, is brought to full effect[1]. If arbitration is to be equally efficient as judicial mechanisms of dispute resolution, it must therefore provide an effective system of immediate interim protection of parties' rights and property during arbitral proceedings[2]. Modern legislations recognise arbitral tribunals' power to issue interim measures, and allow such measures to be enforced by state courts when necessary. The need for swift action both in granting and in the enforcement of arbitral interim relief, however, may come into conflict with the basic principle of equal treatment of parties, especially in relation to the full opportunity of presenting their case. I will discuss some issues that arise in this sphere, taking into account the United Nations Commission on International Trade Law (UNCITRAL) Model Law on International Commercial Arbitration, especially amendments to it adopted in 2006, which aim to strike a balance between these two requirements and thus facilitate the judicial enforcement of arbitral interim measures internationally. The implementation of arbitral interim relief in the Slovenian Arbitration Act of 2008[3] will also be examined.

II. Power of the Arbitral Tribunal to Order Interim Measures

4.02. Most modern legislations today follow the principle that in the absence of public policy reasons requiring judicial intervention, arbitral tribunals have the power to order interim measures, unless the parties have expressly agreed to exclude such competence. An important factor that contributed to the adoption of this position was Article 17 of the UNCITRAL Model Law, which in the original 1985 version stipulated that, unless otherwise agreed by the parties, the arbitral tribunal may, at the request of a party, order any party to take such interim measure of protection as the arbitral tribunal may consider necessary in respect to the subject matter of the dispute. This provision brought the power to grant interim relief within

---

[1] Material evidence may be hidden or destroyed, assets out of which a subsequent award could be satisfied may be squandered or transferred outside the reach of a jurisdiction that allows effective enforcement of arbitral awards; a party may sustain considerable irreparable damage or irreplaceable loss by the opposite party's actions or omissions before the final award is made.

[2] Julian D. M. Lew, Loukas A. Mistelis, Stefan M. Kröll, Comparative International Commercial Arbitration, The Hague: Kluwer Law International 586 (2003); Rayond J. Werbicki, *Arbitral interim measures: Fact or fiction?*, 57 Jan Disp. Resol. J. 62, 63 (2002).

[3] Zakon o arbitraži (ZArbit), Uradni list RS, št. 45/08.

the tribunal's original jurisdiction that stems directly from the law and does not require a specific mandate in the arbitration agreement[4]. In addition, most of internationally established arbitration rules expressly confer on the arbitral tribunal the power to grant interim relief (e.g. Article 26 of UNCITRAL Arbitration Rules, Article 23 of ICC Rules of Arbitration, and Article 34 of AAA Commercial Arbitration Rules)[5].

4.03. Arbitration laws and private arbitration rules usually do not enumerate the possible types of interim measures or define their content. Legislative acts based on UNCITRAL Model Law have followed its 1985 wording under which arbitral tribunal may issue any measure it deems necessary[6]. The content of the interim protection is thus in principle left to the discretion of the arbitrators, who are not limited by the types of interim measures existing in national legislation[7]. Obviously, from a practical point of view only such measures make sense that either the parties concerned will follow voluntarily, or that may be legally enforced in the courts (i.e. admissible under *lex fori*)[8]. In legal theory, arbitral interim measures are commonly divided by their purpose into several categories, analogous to the types of judicial interim measures that may be issued by the courts[9]. Interim measures may be designed for the following purposes:

   a) to maintain or restore the *status quo* pending determination of the dispute;

   b) to protect against current or imminent harm or prejudice to the arbitral process itself;

   c) to preserve assets out of which a subsequent award may be satisfied; or

   d) to preserve evidence that may be relevant and material to the resolution of the dispute[10].

---

[4] KARL H. SCHWAB, GERHARD WALTER, ADOLF BAUMBACH, SCHIEDSGERICHTBARKEIT, München: C. H. Beck 191 (2000); 12 ROLF A. SCHÜTZE, AUSGEWÄHLTE PROBLEME DES DEUTSCHEN UND INTERNATIONALEN SCHIEDSVERFAHRENSRECHTE, Köln: Carl Heymanns Verlag 237 (2006).

[5] See more extensively at JULIAN D. M. LEW, LOUKAS A. MISTELIS, STEFAN M. KRÖLL, *supra* note 2, at 591-593; William Wang, *International Arbitration: The Need for Uniform Interim Measures of Relief*, 28 BROOK. J. INT'L L. 1059, 1067-1069 (2003).

[6] E.g. Article 20(1) of Slovenian Arbitration Act of 2008.

[7] The English Arbitration Act of 1996 gives two examples of provisional awards that may be ordered by the tribunal: (a) a provisional order for the payment of money or the disposition of property as between the parties, or (b) an order to make an interim payment on account of the costs of the arbitration (Article 39(2)).

[8] KARL H. SCHWAB, GERHARD WALTER, ADOLF BAUMBACH, *supra* note 4, at 192-193; see also STEFAN BANDEL, EINSTWEILIGER RECHTSSCHUTZ IM SCHIEDSVERFAHREN, München: Verlag C. H. Beck 131-195 (2000).

[9] See JULIAN D. M. LEW, LOUKAS A. MISTELIS, STEFAN KROLL, *supra* note 2, at 595; KARL H. SCHWAB, GERHARD WALTER, ADOLF BAUMBACH, *supra* note 4, at 194; ALAN REDFERN, MARTIN HUNTER, LAW AND PRACTICE OF INTERNATIONAL COMMERCIAL ARBITRATION, London: Sweet & Maxwell 350-358 (1999).

[10] *Cf.* revised Article 17 of UNCITRAL Model Law.

4.04. Although the legislations following the 1985 version of UNCITRAL Model Law normally do not set any other conditions for issuing interim measures[11] arbitrators in practice often refer to the relevant rules of national law which apply to the regular courts, simply because such rules are well established and sufficiently elaborated to provide clear guidance in decision making. Nevertheless, at least two general substantive criteria for ordering interim relief may be discerned in international arbitration practice: the measure should not prejudge the final decision on the merits of the case and an imminent risk of substantial or irreparable damage must be present. The proposed requirement that the party requesting interim protection should demonstrate a likelihood of its success on the merits of the claim has been met with mixed reactions. Unlike in litigation, where the judge ordering interim relief is often different from the judge deciding on the merits of the claim, in arbitration, the same tribunal has to address both issues. In order to avoid complaints of bias or prejudging, the arbitrators therefore like to avoid expressing any views on the substance of the dispute before the final decision on the merits[12]. Nevertheless, the new Article 17 A (1)(b) of the Model Law and Article 26 (3)(b) of UNCITRAL Arbitration Rules as revised in 2010 include the controversial criterion of a reasonable possibility of success on the merits. They both expressly provide, however, that the determination on this possibility should not affect the discretion of the arbitral tribunal in making any subsequent determination.

III. Procedure for Issuing Interim Measures

III.1. General

4.05. The determination of the procedure for issuing interim measures is normally left to the agreement of the parties or, in the absence of such an agreement, to the discretion of the arbitrators. In principle, the tribunal may issue an interim measure only upon request by any of the parties[13]. An exception to this general rule are arbitration rules of the World Bank's International Centre for Settlement of Investment Disputes[14], which allow the tribunal to recommend provisional measures on its own initiative or to recommend measures other than those specified in a

---

[11] This has led to divergent explanations in theory. Some authors believe that arbitrators are bound by the same criteria as the state courts; others believe that arbitrators may issue interim measures whenever and whichever they find necessary. See STEFAN BANDEL, *supra* note 8, at 99-104; JULIAN D. M. LEW, LOUKAS A. MISTELIS, STEFAN KROLL, *supra* note 2, at 602-603; ROLF A. SCHUTZE, *supra* note 4, at 239-242.

[12] JULIAN D. M. LEW, LOUKAS A. MISTELIS, STEFAN KROLL, *supra* note 2, at 603-604.

[13] See Article 17(1) of the Model Law, Article 26(1) of UNCITRAL Arbitration Rules, Article 23(1) of ICC Arbitration Rules.

[14] Available at: http://icsid.worldbank.org/ICSID/ICSID/RulesMain.jsp (accessed on October 12, 2010).

request. Such provisional measures, however, only have the legal nature of recommendations and are not binding on either party to the proceedings.

4.06. Another procedural question is whether interim measures may be issued by the president of the arbitration tribunal alone, for instance, when instant action is necessary to prevent imminent harm, but the tribunal cannot meet in time. There is no doubt that the parties may agree to confer such power on the president. Moreover, some authors believe that even in the absence of such an agreement by the parties, the arbitrators may themselves authorise the president to grant interim relief, on the basis of their general competence to determine the rules of procedure (*cf.* Article 19 of the Model Law)[15].

III.2. Ex Parte Measures

4.07. The most contentious issue of the procedure, however, is whether arbitral tribunals should have the competence to issue interim measures *ex parte*, that is, at the request of one party and without giving the party against whom the measure is directed the opportunity to present its case beforehand. National courts often issue injunctions without hearing the opposing party if such measures are necessary to prevent violence or imminent damage, etc. In such a case, giving advance notice of the measure to the opposing party would be counterproductive, since it would give it an opportunity to avoid the effects of the injunction. Adversarial process before the court is therefore only ensured subsequently, when the party has been served the injunction and may object to it.

4.08. A state court may issue an (*ex parte*) injunction even if the dispute at hand is subject to an arbitration agreement. No other body beside the court exists, anyhow, that could grant interim relief before the arbitral tribunal has been drawn up[16]. After the formation of the arbitral tribunal, however, a party may choose to request interim measures either from the court or from the arbitral tribunal. Therefore, it is essential for the party to know which of these two bodies may be reasonably expected to act more expeditiously. Comparatively, most national legislations remain silent on the issue of permissibility of *ex parte* arbitral interim measures. An exception is Austrian civil procedure, which clearly specifies that interim measures may only be issued against a party after its hearing[17] – thereby precluding *ex parte* action by arbitral tribunal. On the basis of a more general formulation of the German law[18], Bandel argues that a subsequent possibility for the opposing party to present its case may be

---

[15] KARL H. SCHWAB, GERHARD WALTER, ADOLF BAUMBACH, *supra* note 4, at 197; for opposing view see STEFAN BANDEL, *supra* note 8, at 79.

[16] Unless, of course, the arbitration agreement provides otherwise, e.g. by authorising the president of a permanent arbitral institution to provide interim protection of parties' rights before the commencement of arbitral proceedings.

[17] »*nach deren Anhörung*«. See Austrian *Zivilprozessordnung* (ZPO) Art. 593 (1).

[18] See German ZPO Art. 1041 (1).

sufficient to ensure adversarial procedure, but acknowledges that this is sometimes difficult to provide[19]. Given that the principle of adversarial process holds even greater importance in arbitration than in judicial procedures, however, many arbitral theorists and practitioners take the view that arbitral tribunals should never issue *ex parte* measures and that immediate interim relief, when required, should only be granted by state courts[20].

4.09. Castello summarizes the following main reasons why the parties might prefer to obtain interim relief from arbitrators rather than from state courts (especially in international arbitration):

1. In some jurisdictions, the courts lack the jurisdiction to order *ex parte* relief, or tend to refuse to grant interim relief in disputes subject to an arbitration agreement (the former *McCreary* doctrine in the US);

2. A court might refuse to grant interim relief in support of an arbitration located abroad;

3. A party may be faced with practical obstacles to access to justice in a foreign country, e.g. the lack of knowledge of the official language of the court or difficulties in finding a local attorney, etc.;

4. A party may wish to preserve the confidentiality of the case by avoiding the public proceedings before a court;

5. A party may question the expertise of national courts required to decide on certain issues, or it might have doubts over the impartiality of national judges, especially if interim relief is sought against a national of the country of the court's venue;

6. Finally, an arbitral tribunal that is already familiar with the facts of the dispute may be able to decide on the request for interim relief much more quickly than a national court that needs to study the case first, and which is often also burdened with a large caseload[21].

4.10. As we may notice, the rationale given in favour of arbitral *ex parte* interim relief is mostly of practical nature, taking into account the typical needs of the parties. The reasons most often stated against arbitral *ex parte* measures, on the other hand, are both practical and doctrinal. Among the practical misgivings is the fact that arbitral interim measures are not directly enforceable. Since the purpose of *ex parte* measures is swift action preventing the other party to avoid the effects of the measure, it seems more efficient to request interim protection directly from a court, which may also enforce its injunction if necessary. A counterargument in favour of arbitral *ex parte* interim measures stresses the fact that parties to arbitration in practice usually comply with interim measures voluntarily, so as not to offend the arbitrators. Subsequent judicial enforcement of arbitral

---

[19] STEFAN BANDEL, *supra* note 8, at 94-95.

[20] JULIAN D. M. LEW, LOUKAS A. MISTELIS, STEFAN M. KRÖLL, *supra* note 2, at 606-607.

[21] James E. Castello, *Arbitral Ex Parte Interim Relief: The View in Favor,* 58-OCT DISP. RESOL. J. 60, 60-61 (2003).

interim measures is therefore not required, and *ex parte* measures achieve the effect sought[22].

4.11. A more doctrinal objection to *ex parte* measures points out that such unilateral action is contrary to the consensual nature of arbitration. As a general rule, arbitrators' contacts with only one of the parties to the proceedings are deemed inappropriate and may constitute grounds for annulment of the arbitral award, especially if the substance of the dispute was discussed. When issuing *ex parte* measures, however, the tribunal always comes into contact with one side of the dispute only. By conducting the evidence and listening to the arguments of the party requesting interim *ex parte* measures, the arbitrators thus find themselves in a situation that would normally constitute grounds for challenging an arbitrator due to doubts as to his impartiality.

4.12. A further procedural argument against *ex parte* action of the arbitral tribunal is that, unlike in judicial proceedings, arbitral interim measures are not subject to appeal, while the final arbitration award can only be challenged on limited grounds. The party against which arbitral interim measure is directed therefore does not enjoy the same level of protection as before a court. Due to the absence of specific remedies, adversarial procedure may only be ensured before arbitral interim measures are issued. Therefore, arbitral interim measures should only be issued after the hearing of the opposing party or, alternatively, after having given that party an opportunity to state its position on the proposed measure in writing[23]. It should be noted, nonetheless, that like national judges, the arbitrators may at any time withdraw an interim measure, either upon objection by a party or at their own motion. On this basis, it is argued by the proponents of *ex parte* arbitral interim relief that such measures do not conflict with the principle of adversarial procedure, as long as the party against whom the measure is directed is given a subsequent opportunity to object to the measure, upon which the tribunal re-examines whether the measure was justified and may immediately revoke or amend it, if necessary[24].

4.13. Finally, the opponents of *ex parte* interim relief emphasise that efficient arbitration must build on the consensus and cooperation of the parties. Arbitral interim measures can only be really effective when arbitrators rely on their ability of persuasion – for which they must deal with both parties. Experienced practitioners are therefore concerned that, by issuing an interim measure at the request of one party, arbitration would lose the

---

[22]   James E. Castello, *supra* note 21, at 66. *Cf.* Yves Derains, *Arbitral Ex Parte Interim Relief: The View Against*, 58-OCT Disp. Resol. J. 61, 62-63 (2003).

[23]   ROLF A. SCHUTZE, *supra* note 4, at 242-243.

[24]   James E. Castello, *supra* note 21, at 66; JULIAN D. M. LEW, LOUKAS A. MISTELIS, STEFAN M. KRÖLL, *supra* note 2, at 607-608; KARL H. SCHWAB, GERHARD WALTER, ADOLF BAUMBACH, *supra* note 4, at 198.

trust of the other party[25]. In the long term, this might subject arbitral awards to more stringent judicial control. For this reason, the critics believe that giving the arbitral tribunal the power of *ex parte* interim relief may turn out to be a poisoned gift causing more harm than good. Instead of giving additional powers to the arbitrators, it would be more efficient to ensure more effective cooperation between national judges and arbitrators in providing interim protection to the parties[26].

III.3. Amendments to the Model Law

4.14. After several years of intense discussion in UNCITRAL's Working Group on Arbitration and Conciliation, the view prevailed that in certain cases, arbitral tribunal's power to grant *ex parte* interim relief is necessary, after all, to ensure a fair outcome of arbitration proceedings. Consequently, a new Chapter IV.A was inserted in the Model Law, which specifies the procedure both for granting and for the enforcement of arbitral interim measures. The new provisions are relatively detailed, especially in comparison with other provisions of the Model Law, which generally leave the procedural arrangements to the agreement of the parties or of the arbitrators[27]. This is the result of UNCITRAL's attempt to formulate a compromise solution that would provide the possibility of arbitral *ex parte* interim relief, but also address the concerns of the opponents.

4.15. The new rules distinguish terminologically between interim measures, which are issued in a regular adversarial procedure (*inter partes*), and preliminary orders, which may be issued by the arbitral tribunal without prior notice to the other party (*ex parte*). Preliminary orders cannot exist independently from interim measures, as a party may make an application for a preliminary order only together with a request for an interim measure (Article 17 B (1)). The term "preliminary order" is used to emphasize its limited nature. An arbitral tribunal may grant a preliminary order provided it considers that prior disclosure of the request for the interim measure to the party against whom it is directed risks frustrating the purpose of the measure. The purpose of such preliminary order is to provide a means for preserving the *status quo* until the arbitral tribunal decides, by issues an interim measure, whether to adopt or modify the preliminary order. Preliminary order can thus ensure immediate *ex parte* effect of the requested interim measure [28].

---

[25] This concern was expressed by the Milan Club of Arbitrators both at its XIII colloquium on interim measures and international arbitration held in October 2002 and at the London Court of International Arbitration in May 2003.

[26] Yves Derains, *supra* note 22, at 63.

[27] The new chapter on arbitral interim measures now consists of 11 articles, which, for instance, makes it longer than the whole chapter on the conduct of arbitral proceedings.

[28] Explanatory Note by the UNCITRAL secretariat on the 1985 Model Law on International Commercial Arbitration as amended in 2006, Vienna: United Nations Publications 31 (2008).

4.16. The substantive conditions for granting preliminary orders are in principle the same as those applying to interim measures, i.e. imminent harm and possibility of the party's success on merits (Article 17 A); the threshold of urgency, however, is increased, as the requesting party must satisfy the tribunal that irreparable harm is likely to result if the preliminary order is not granted immediately. If the necessity of immediate action without notice to the other party is not demonstrated, the arbitrators may decline to issue a preliminary order, and proceed to decide on the requested interim measure in accordance with the regular *inter partes* procedure. Furthermore, the party applying for a preliminary order should, as a rule, provide security in connection with the order unless the arbitral tribunal considers it inappropriate or unnecessary to do so.

4.17. Article 17 C contains safeguards for the party against whom the preliminary order is directed. Immediately after the determination on the application for a preliminary order, the arbitral tribunal must notify the party of the application and of the preliminary order itself. The party must be given an opportunity to present its case at the earliest practicable time and the arbitral tribunal must decide promptly on any objection to the preliminary order. Only after adversarial procedure has been established[29], arbitral tribunal may issue an interim measure adopting or modifying the preliminary order. In any event, a preliminary order has a maximum duration of twenty days, unlike interim measures, whose duration is not limited. After twenty days from the date on which the preliminary order was issued by the arbitral tribunal, the order expires, unless it has been adopted by an interim measure. Finally, while preliminary orders are in principle binding on the parties, they are not subject to enforcement by a court. The Model Law explicitly states that such a preliminary order does not constitute an award (which might be subject to enforcement).

4.18. The party applying for a preliminary order must disclose to the arbitral tribunal all circumstances that might be relevant to the arbitral tribunal's determination whether to grant or maintain the order, and such obligation continues until the party against whom the order has been requested has had an opportunity to present its case. Thereafter, the arbitral tribunal may require any party promptly to disclose any material change in the circumstances on the basis of which the measure was requested or granted. The arbitral tribunal may modify, suspend or terminate an interim measure or a preliminary order it has granted, upon application of any party or, in exceptional circumstances and upon prior notice to the parties, on the arbitral tribunal's own initiative.

4.19. Overall, the Model Law gives arbitrators the power to grant *ex parte* interim relief in the form of preliminary orders if the requesting party demonstrates the necessity of immediate action without prior notice to any other party. However, such orders are limited in time, must be

---

[29] That is, after the party against whom the preliminary order is directed has been given notice and an opportunity to present its case.

Czech (& Central European) Yearbook of Arbitration

reviewed by the arbitral tribunal in adversarial procedure as soon as possible, and are not directly enforceable. These safeguards should ensure that the party against whom the preliminary order is directed does not suffer any damages due to the order, at least until it has had the chance to present its case to the tribunal. In this way, the parties' right to be heard remains guaranteed in arbitral procedure. Of course, the parties may still agree to exclude the arbitral tribunal's power to grant *ex parte* interim relief altogether, should they find such competence unnecessary or inappropriate[30].

4.20. Despite the compromise described, the issue of *ex parte* measures remains controversial. It is interesting to note that the latest revision of UNCITRAL Arbitration Rules, which has aligned the rules on interim measures with those contained in amendments to the Model Law, does not include a provision dealing with preliminary orders. Nonetheless, this does not signal a shift in UNCITRAL's position on the appropriateness of *ex parte* interim relief in arbitration. The omission of a specific provision is due to the finding that, regardless of a specific provision in Arbitration Rules, it would still not be possible for an arbitral tribunal to grant preliminary orders in legal systems that did not allow them. For this reason, the Commission's report emphasises that the power to grant preliminary orders has to be found outside these Rules, e.g. in the relevant arbitration law of the place of arbitration[31].

III.4. Ex Parte Measures in the Slovenian Arbitration Act

4.21. Slovenia was the first country to reform its arbitration legislation on the basis of the amended UNCITRAL Model Law, so one of the issues that had to be decided in preparing draft law was whether to adopt the Model Law's new rules on preliminary orders. The solution eventually enacted in the Arbitration Act of 2008 authorises the arbitrators to grant *ex parte* interim relief; the provisions regulating this competence, however, have not been modelled after the Model Law, but are condensed into a single article that regulates both *inter partes* and *ex parte* arbitral interim measures. The expert group preparing the draft law felt that, since *ex parte* interim relief had not been opposed to by Slovenian arbitration theorists or practitioners, there was no need to regulate this type of arbitral action more extensively than arbitral procedure in general.

4.22. According to Article 20 of the Arbitration Act, unless the parties have agreed otherwise, the arbitral tribunal has the power to issue, at the request of a party, any interim measure it deems necessary taking into account the subject matter of the case[32]. The tribunal may require any

---

[30] *Cf.* James E. Castello, *supra* note 21, at 65-66.
[31] UN DOCUMENT A/65/17 – REPORT OF THE UNITED NATIONS COMMISSION ON INTERNATIONAL TRADE LAW, FORTY-THIRD SESSION (New York, 21 June – 9 July 2010), 21 paras 121-125.
[32] The law does not define the types of possible interim measures, but leaves the definition of their content to the arbitrators' discretion.

party to provide appropriate security in connection with the requested measure[33]. In principle, interim measures may only be issued after the party against whom the measure is directed has been given the opportunity to present its case. Exceptionally, however, if the tribunal finds that immediate intervention is necessary or if the nature of the measure requires so, the arbitral tribunal may issue an interim measure without prior notice to the other party. The law does not distinguish in terminology between interim measures and preliminary orders, but uses the term "interim measure" (*začasni ukrep*) for both types of measures. Nevertheless, the interim measures that have been issued without prior notice to the other party, although binding on the parties, may not be subject to enforcement by a court. The enforcement is only possible after such an *ex parte* measure has been confirmed by the tribunal in adversarial procedure. The arbitral tribunal may modify, suspend or terminate any interim measure it has granted (either *ex parte* or *inter partes*), upon application of any party or, in exceptional circumstances and upon prior notice to the parties, on the arbitral tribunal's own initiative. Unlike the Model Law, the Arbitration Act does not limit the maximum duration of *ex parte* interim measures. This should not imply, however, that such measures might stay valid indefinitely, as the arbitrators are under obligation to conduct the proceedings in accordance with the basic principles of arbitration, which include the equality of parties and their right to be heard (Article 21). Due to the exceptional nature of *ex parte* interim measures, the opposing party must be given the opportunity to present its case as soon as possible.

III.5. Limitations of Arbitral Interim Measures

4.23. In any case, the scope and content of interim protection that may be granted by arbitrators is rather limited in comparison with the jurisdiction of a court. The power of the arbitral tribunal to issue interim measures is always based on the parties' agreement, even if the law presumes such mandate should the parties not exclude it specifically[34]. Due to the consensual nature of arbitral tribunal's powers, all arbitral measures must remain within the limits of the arbitration agreement and may only relate to the dispute to which the agreement applies. The arbitrators cannot order any acts or omissions of third persons who are not parties to the arbitration agreement. An interim measure issued in arbitration proceedings therefore only has the nature of a contractual obligation between the parties to the arbitration, while third parties are not bound by it[35].

---

[33] Taking into account the circumstances of the case, security may be required either from the party requesting an interim measure (to compensate any harm that may arise from the measure) or from the opposing party (to avoid the issuing of the measure).

[34] JULIAN D. M. LEW, LOUKAS A. MISTELIS, STEFAN M. KRÖLL, *supra* note 2, at 588-589; for opposing view see STEFAN BANDEL, *supra* note 8, at 15-16.

[35] See the decision of the Constitutional Court of the Republic of Slovenia, Up 20/99, 25 May 1999, para. 6.

4.24. Of course, arbitration tribunal cannot directly enforce its interim measures[36]. Under the Model Law, measures issued in adversarial procedure may be enforced with the assistance of a court, while interim measures issued *ex parte* are not enforceable at all. Nevertheless, this does not signal that *ex parte* measures are meaningless. The lack of coercive power may be at least partially replaced by persuasive power of the tribunal. If a party fails to comply, this may be considered by the tribunal as evidence of the party's acting in bad faith, and taken into account in deciding on the allocation of costs and expenses of arbitration. Arbitral tribunal may legitimately use all means at its disposal to convince the party to follow the interim measures voluntarily[37].

IV. Enforcement of Arbitral Interim Measures

IV.1. General

4.25. Where parties fail to adhere to arbitral decisions voluntarily, the assistance of courts is necessary for the enforcement. The manner of such judicial support is particularly important in the enforcement of arbitral interim measures, where a swift response is usually required[38]. The UNCITRAL Model Law of 1985 deliberately avoided the issue of enforcement of arbitral interim measures, due to its controversy. Such an approach left the countries adopting the Model Law with three possibilities: that they reserve judicial enforcement only for final arbitration awards; that they allow the enforcement of arbitral interim measures when issued in the form of an arbitral award; or that they lay down specific rules enabling the enforcement of arbitral interim measures even when they are issued in the form of procedural orders[39]. Various regulatory approaches have been used. German[40], Austrian[41], Swiss[42] and English legislation[43], for example, expressly provide that courts may allow the enforcement of arbitral interim measures at the request of either the parties or of the

---

[36] The parties may, however, authorise the arbitral tribunal to impose penalties on the party who fails to comply with an interim measure issued by the tribunal. See Lojze Ude, Arbitražno pravo, Ljubljana: GV Založba 206 (2004); for the US aspect see David E. Wagoner, *Interim Relief in International Arbitration: Enforcement is a substantial problem,* 51-OCT Disp. Resol. J. 68, 69 (1996).

[37] Julian D. M. Lew, Loukas A. Mistelis, Stefan M. Kröll, *supra* note 2, at 594; Karl H. Schwab, Gerhard Walter, Adolf Baumbach, *supra* note 4, at 191, 196.

[38] UN Document A/CN.9/605 – Report of the United Nations Commission on International Trade Law on the work of its thirty-ninth session (New York, 19 June-7 July 2006), para. 88; Rolf A. Schutze, *supra* note 4, at 244.

[39] Julian D. M. Lew, Loukas A. Mistelis, Stefan M. Kröll, *supra* note 2, at 612.

[40] German ZPO, Art. 1041 (2).

[41] Austrian ZPO, Art. 593 (2).

[42] *Bundesgesetz über das Internationale Privatrecht,* Art. 183 (2).

[43] English Arbitration Act, Article 42.

arbitral tribunal[44]. In many other countries, however, the enforcement of arbitral interim measures is not specifically regulated, or is even considered inadmissible.

4.26. In the judicial enforcement procedure, the question arises once again whether the court should always guarantee the parties' right to be heard, or whether it should (in some cases) give priority to a speedy procedure. The German ZPO in principle requires a prior hearing of the opposing party in the recognition and enforcement procedure, but authorizes the president of the competent panel of judges to allow preliminarily the enforcement of arbitral interim measures before having heard the opposing party. Nevertheless, the court may only take the final decision on the enforcement after the other party has been given an opportunity to present its case before the court[45]. The Austrian ZPO provides that the court *may* hear the opposing party before the enforcement of an arbitral interim measure. If the opposing party has not been heard before the decision, it may file an objection against the enforcement order in accordance with the rules of civil execution procedure.

IV.2. Amendments to the Model Law

4.27. The 2006 revision of the Model Law established a new model legislative regime for the recognition and enforcement of interim measures, which was modelled on the regime for the recognition and enforcement of arbitral awards under articles 35 and 36 of the Model Law. The new Article 17 H provides that an arbitral interim measure may be recognized as binding and enforced upon application to the competent court, irrespective of the country in which it was issued[46]. Only interim measures issued after hearing the opposing party may be enforced, while *ex parte* preliminary orders are not subject to enforcement by a court. The grounds listed for refusing recognition or enforcement are the same as those that apply to the recognition or enforcement of arbitral awards, among which is the violation of the right of a party to present its case (which additionally prevents the enforcement of *ex parte* interim measures). Additionally, the recognition or enforcement of an interim measure may be refused if the arbitral tribunal's decision on the provision of security in connection with the interim measure has not been complied with; or if the interim measure has been terminated or suspended by the arbitral tribunal or by a court; or if the interim measure is incompatible with the powers of the court unless the court decides to reformulate the interim measure to the extent necessary to adapt it to its own powers and procedures

---

[44] STEFAN BANDEL, *supra* note 8, at 215-221.

[45] Art.1063(3) ZPO; KARL H. SCHWAB, GERHARD WALTER, ADOLF BAUMBACH, *supra* note 4, at 298-299; STEFAN BANDEL, *supra* note 8, at 208.

[46] This was an important innovation, since the New York Convention on the Recognition and Enforcement of Foreign Arbitral Awards does not apply to the enforcement of arbitral interim measures.

(Article 17 I). The Model Law does not state whether the court may decide without hearing the party against whom the interim measure is invoked, but it follows from Article 17 I (1)(a) that the opposing party should be given the opportunity to request refusal of the enforcement on certain grounds.

IV.3. Enforcement under the Slovenian Arbitration Act

4.28. The new Slovenian law has followed the solution of the Model Law in establishing a unified legislative regime for the enforcement of both domestic and foreign arbitral interim measures. Since the enforcement of interim measures can only serve its purpose if it is relatively fast, the Arbitration Act omits a separate phase of recognition or of declaration of enforceability, which apply to the enforcement of arbitral awards, and allows the entire procedure to take place in a single phase before a local court competent for execution in general. The general rules of civil execution procedure apply, which means that the court issues the enforcement order at the request of one party and without hearing the party against whom the interim measure is invoked. However, the opposing party may object to the order issued, and the enforcement will generally not commence until the court has decided on the objection, unless the courts finds that immediate enforcement is necessary due to the circumstances of the case.

4.29. Article 43 provides that a court may refuse the enforcement of an interim measure on any of the grounds due to which it could refuse the declaration of enforceability of a domestic arbitral award or the recognition of a foreign arbitral award. Since Arbitration Act directly refers to the New York Convention as to the grounds for the refusal of recognition and enforcement of foreign arbitral awards[47], Article 43 in effect expands the use of the Convention so that, under Slovenian law, its rules now also apply to the enforcement of foreign arbitral interim measures. As provided in Article 20, the interim measures issued *ex parte* cannot be subject to enforcement by a court. Additional grounds for the refusal of enforcement due to the provision of security, the termination or suspension of the measure, or its incompatibility with the court's jurisdiction, are closely modelled on the provisions of the Model Law[48]. The party who is seeking or has obtained enforcement of an interim measure must promptly inform the court of any termination, suspension or modification of that interim measure. At the request of a party, the court may at any time terminate or modify the enforcement order. The court may order the requesting party to provide appropriate security in connection with the interim measure.

---

[47] In this respect, the rules of the New York Convention and of the Model Law are basically identical.

[48] Articles 17 I (1)(a)(ii) and (iii), and 17 I (1)(b)(i) of the Model Law.

V. Conclusion

4.30. The new legislative regime for arbitral interim measures established under UNCITRAL Model Law clearly defines the power of arbitral tribunal to grant interim relief and the competence of the courts to assist in enforcement of the measures granted by the tribunal. The recognition of the power to grant *ex parte* interim measures enables the arbitrators to act expeditiously, which is especially important under circumstances where interim protection by a court could not be secured immediately. The power of *ex parte* action, however, does not infringe excessively upon the parties' right to be heard, since the party against whom the measure is directed must be heard by the arbitrators subsequently, and since *ex parte* measures are not enforceable by the courts. It follows that the roles of arbitral tribunals and of state courts in providing interim relief during arbitral proceedings will continue to be complementary, rather than mutually exclusive. To what extent arbitral *ex parte* interim relief will be used in practice will depend on the parties' agreement to grant (or to deny) such powers to the tribunal and on the arbitrators' decision whether to use such powers. No cases have been reported yet concerning arbitral interim relief under the Arbitration Act, so it remains to be seen in what way the new rules will be accepted in practice.

| | |

Summaries

DEU [*Schiedsrichterliche einstweilige Maßnahmen und der Anspruch auf rechtliches Gehör*]
Wenn das Schiedsverfahren ebenso effizient wie gerichtliche Mechanismen der Streitbeilegung sein will, muss man ein gleichwertiges System des sofortigen einstweiligen Schutzes der Rechte und des Eigentums der Parteien bis zur Entscheidung über die Zulässigkeit der Klage ermöglichen. Moderne Vorschriften über das Schiedsverfahren räumen den Schiedsgerichten die Kompetenz ein, einstweilige Massnahmen zu ergehen. Diese unterliegen der Zwangsvollstreckung. Ein feines Gleichgewicht zwischen der Notwendigkeit für schnelles Handeln einerseits und dem Schutz der auf dem Verfassungswege garantierten Prozessrechte (wie etwa das Recht auf rechtliches Gehör) andererseits muss erreicht werden. Der Artikel behandelt einige Probleme solcher Art unter Berücksichtigung der neuesten Änderungen im UNCITRAL Modelgesetz und deren Umsetzung im slowenischen Recht.

CZE [*Předběžná opatření vydávaná v rámci rozhodčího řízení a právo být slyšen*]
Pokud má být rozhodčí řízení stejně účinné jako soudní mechanismy řešení sporů, musí poskytovat ekvivalentní systém okamžité prozatímní ochrany práv a majetku účastníků až do doby vynesení rozhodnutí o skutkové podstatě případu. Proto moderní předpisy o rozhodčím řízení uznávají právo rozhodčích tribunálů nařídit předběžná opatření a poskytují možnost jejich výkonu. Mezi potřebou rychlého zásahu na jedné straně a potřebou ochrany ústavou

zaručených procesních práv (například práva být slyšen) na straně druhé je nutné dosáhnout velice křehké rovnováhy. Článek pojednává o problémech, které se v této oblasti vyskytují, a to s ohledem na poslední změny ve vzorovém zákonu UNCITRAL o rozhodčím řízení a jeho implementaci do slovinského právního řádu.

| | |

POL [**Arbitrażowe środki tymczasowe i prawo do bycia wysłuchanym**]
Współczesne systemy prawne uznają uprawnienia trybunałów arbitrażowych w zakresie orzekania środków tymczasowych i dopuszczają egzekwowanie takich środków przez sądy krajowe. Jednak konieczność sprawnego orzekania oraz wymagania arbitrażowych środków tymczasowych mogą okazać się sprzeczne z niektórymi podstawowymi zasadami arbitrażu, zwłaszcza z równym traktowaniem stron i ich prawem do bycia wysłuchanym. Artykuł omawia powyższe relacje, uwzględniając modelowe prawo UNCITRAL w zakresie arbitrażu oraz jego zastosowanie w słoweńskim prawie.

FRA [**Mesures provisoires dans l'arbitrage et le droit d'être entendu**]
Les législations modernes reconnaissent le pouvoir des tribunaux arbitraux d'ordonner des mesures provisoires et permettent l'exécution de telles mesures par des juridictions étatiques. Cependant, la nécessité d'une action rapide à la fois dans l'octroi et dans l'exécution des mesures provisoires peut entrer en conflit avec certains principes de base du droit de l'arbitrage, notamment l'égalité de traitement des parties et leur droit d'être entendu. Ces relations sont examinées, en tenant compte de la loi-type de la CNUDCI sur l'arbitrage et son application dans la législation slovène.

RUS [**Временные меры арбитражных (третейских) судов и право быть выслушанным**]
Современные законодательства признают право арбитражных (третейских) судов применять временные меры и допускать их принудительное применение судами государства. Необходимость в оперативных действиях при назначении арбитражным судом временных мер и их принудительном применении может противоречить некоторым основным принципам арбитража, особенно в части равенства подхода к сторонам и их права быть выслушанным. Такие взаимосвязи рассматриваются с учетом типового закона ЮНСИТРАЛ, касающегося арбитража, и его применения в словенском законодательстве.

ES [**Medidas provisionales sobre arbitraje y el derecho de ser escuchado**]
Las legislaciones modernas reconocen el poder de los tribunales de arbitraje para proferir medias provisionales y permitir que los tribunales estatales las apliquen. Sin embargo, la necesidad de una acción rápida en la concesión y aplicación de estas medidas provisionales de arbitraje puede entrar en conflicto con ciertos principios básicos del arbitraje, particularmente en el tratamiento igualitario de las partes y su derecho a ser escuchadas. Estas relaciones se debaten teniendo en cuenta la Ley Modelo de la CNUDMI sobre el arbitraje y su implementación en la ley eslovena.

Rainer Arnold | Elisabeth Meindl

The EU Charter
of Fundamental Rights
and Public Policy
in International
Arbitration Law *

Key words:
Public Policy | ordre
public | International
Arbitration |
EU Charter of
Fundamental Rights

Abstract | *There are no doubts about the relevance of public policy as to the recognition of foreign arbitral awards in Germany. As far as the impact of the EU Charter of Fundamental Rights is concerned, it remains unclear to what an extent these rights will coin the national notion of public policy. The bottom line is that the Charter enfolds binding force and modifies the application of substantive legal provisions according to primacy of EU law yet special attention should be drawn to the scope of the Charter, Art. 51. However, as the Charter reflects every EU member states' thinking so it can be argued that it be applicable regardless of any EU law significance of the case when defining the national concept of public policy. The EU Charter might have a decisive influence when it comes to defining a genuine European approach or concept of public policy as well. This concept might be applied as an ordre public international which substitutes national public policy concepts in relation to the recognition of international arbitral awards.*

| | |

Prof. Dr.
Rainer Arnold
Full Professor at
the University of
Regensburg, Chair
of Public Law,
Comparative Law, EU
Law and Economic
Administrative Law,
Jean Monnet Chair
ad personam (Legal
Relations of the EU
with Central, Eastern
and Southeastern
Europe), former Jean
Monnet Chair of EU
Law; for many years
Visiting Professor at the
Universities of Paris I
and Paris II; at various
times Visiting Professor
at the Universities of
Strasbourg, Roma
(La Sapienza),
Bologna; Director
of the German Law
Studies at the Moscow
State Lomonossov
University; Director of
the EU Law Centre at
Bahcesehir University
Istanbul; Corresponding
Member of the Bologna
Academy of Science;
Honorary Member
of the Russian and
Slovenian Association of
Constitutional Law.
e-mail: Rainer.Arnold@
jura.uni-regensburg.de

---

* Prof. Dr. Reiner Arnold contributed the passages
referring to the EU Charter (Chapter 5); Elisabeth Meindl
contributed the passages referring to International Private
Law and Arbitration Law.

Czech (& Central European) Yearbook of Arbitration

I. Introduction

5.01. International private law and international procedural law have always provided public policy rules which allow judges to restrain from rules of a (foreign) legal order which must be applied to the relevant case in favour of (national) fundamental principles if the application of these foreign provisions would lead to a result which is considered to be a manifest violation of those principles[1]. Public policy rules are also relevant in arbitration law. As a result, public policy rules modify arbitration law which is dominated by party authority in favour of fundamental principles of public law, in particular inalienable rights meant to protect the individual[2]. This applies both to procedural aspects of arbitration law and to aspects of the substantive provisions of the legal order to be applied by the arbitral tribunals.

Elisabeth Meindl
Fellow at the Chair
of Public Law/ Jean
Monnet Chair
(Researcher and
Lecturer); 1st and 2nd
State Exam in Law;
work experience
(internship) at Bavarian
EU representation in
Brussels; preparing
a doctoral thesis on
foreign relations of the
German Federation
member states;
research fields: EU
law, Public and Private
International Law,
Arbitration.
e-mail: Elisabeth.
Meindl@jura.
uni-regensburg.de

5.02. The entry into force of the Lisbon Treaty not only created a new structure of the EU albeit the structure of the texts was left unchanged. Art.6 (1)(1) of the EU-Treaty now refers to the Charter of Fundamental Rights of the EU which entered into force the very same moment. This development gives rise to the question whether and to what an extent the fundamental rights contained in the EU Charter are to be considered by the courts or arbitral tribunals when deciding cases which have connections to more than one national legal order. This article is meant to deal with that question and to describe the role of fundamental rights in general and in international arbitration law in particular from the perspective of arbitral proceedings taking place within German territory.

II. International Arbitration Law in Germany

II.1. Regulations to Be Applied in Domestic Arbitration Proceedings

5.03. In Germany, the 10th book of the *Zivilprozessordnung* (Code of Civil Procedure, CCP) refers to arbitral tribunals. The 10th book is applicable if the parties involved have agreed that their conflict be settled by arbitral tribunals which are situated within the German territory, see also Art. 1025

---

[1] Hans-Jürgen Sonnenberger, *in* 10 MÜNCHNER KOMMENTAR, BGB, München: Verlag C. H. Beck, Art. 6 EGBGB, marg. note 2 (5th ed. 2010).

[2] ADOLF BAUMBAUCH, WOLFGANG LAUTERBACH, JAN ALBERS, PETER HARTMANN, ZPO KOMMENTAR, München: Verlag C. H. Beck § 1059 ZPO, marg. note 16 (69th ed. 2011); Norbert Horn, *Zwingendes Recht in der internationalen Schiedsgerichtsbarkeit,* 6 (5) SCHIEDSVZ 209, 209-210 (2008).

I CCP[3]. The German Law differentiates between two types of such party agreements. They are described in Art. 1029 CCP. According to Art. 1029 (2) CCP such an agreement can be included in the contract (*Schiedsklausel*) or can be agreed upon separately i.e. after the conflict has arisen between the parties (*Schiedsabrede*). The 10th book of the CCP provides regulations on the requirements for a binding arbitration agreement, on the formation and on the competence of the arbitration court, Arts. 1034 ff and Art. 1040 CCP Arts. 1042 to 1050 CCP refer to certain procedural aspects. The latter ones in particular intend to stress the principle of party autonomy as a major principle of arbitration law[4] while at the same time some essential principles of procedural law cannot be derogated such as the right to be heard or the principle of party equality, § 1042 I CCP.

Art. 1052 to Art. 1958 CCP provide regulations on how arbitration proceedings are to be resolved and on the effects a final decision of the arbitration court has. According to Art. 1055 CCP, this decision called *Schiedsspruch*, is equivalent to a judgement of state courts which has become legally binding *(rechtskräftig)*. Still, Art. 1060 CCP describes the requirements which have to be met in order to allow one party to enforce the *Schiedsspruch*. In addition, Art. 1060 II CCP also opens up the possibility for the party which has lost in terms of the *Schiedsspruch*, to bring forward objections against it. So does Art. 1059 CCP: On initiative of the party succumbed state courts can be called upon to overhaul the *Schiedsspruch*, which can eventually lead to its annulment. As a result, Art. 1060 II CCP and 1059 CCP warrant state control of arbitration proceedings to a certain extent[5].

II. 2. Regulations concerning an International Background of the Conflict

5.04. International private procedural law, this means rules which help to determine the country whose courts shall be held competent to resolve the conflict which has arisen between the parties, do not necessarily apply to arbitration proceedings. As a result, one has to apply special rules concerning arbitration in that respect. The 10th book of the CCP provides a conflict rule: If the parties decide that their dispute be settled within German territory, Art. 1043 and 1025 CCP (*Territorialitätsprinzip*)[6] the relevant provisions of the CCP, the 10th book, apply to conflicts with an international background.

---

3   ADOLF BAUMBAUCH, WOLFGANG LAUTERBACH, JAN ALBERS, PETER HARTMANN, *supra* note 2, at §1025 ZPO, marg. note 2.
4   *Ibid.*, § 1042 ZPO, marg. note 2.
5   *Ibid.*, § 1059 ZPO, marg. note 1.
6   *Ibid.*, § 1025 ZPO, marg. note 2; ECKART BRÖDERMANN, JOACHIM ROSENGARTEN, INTERNATIONALES PRIVAT-UND ZIVIL-VERFAHRENSRECH (IPR/IZVR), Berlin: Carl Heymanns Verlag 214 (5th ed. 2010); Klaus Reichold, *in* HEINZ THOMAS, HANS PUTZO, ZPO, München: Verlag C. H. Beck § 1025 ZPO, marg. note 1 (30th ed. 2009); Norbert Horn, *supra* note 2, at 213.

5.05. However, international agreements dealing with the question which country's arbitration rules to apply exist. They are prior to the German conflict rule of Art. 1025 CCP within their functional scope[7]. It is noteworthy that the Brussels I regulation which provides rules on how to determine the country whose courts are competent to solve disputes in various civil matters in case they share connections to one EU member state, i.e. if the defendant lives within EU territory (see (8) of the preamble), is not applicable to arbitration proceedings. According to Art.1 par. 2 lit. d) of the regulation, arbitration is excluded from the scope of the regulation[8]. Still, various international agreements have been ratified by Germany so that these must be referred to before applying autonomous rules of the CCP. The most relevant ones are the Convention on the Recognition and Enforcement of Foreign Arbitral Awards (New York Convention)[9] the Geneva European Convention on International Commercial Arbitration (European Convention)[10] and the Agreement relating to Application of the European Convention on International Commercial Arbitration (Application Agreement)[11].

5.06. As far as the question whose country's procedural rules shall be applied, is concerned, the *lex fori* – a principle which is dominant in international civil procedural law, is not necessarily valid in international arbitration law. By contrast, Art. 1042 III CCP and various international agreements leave it to the parties' discretion which procedural rules are to be applied (*freie Rechtswahl*)[12] – regardless of the fact that some central aspects of German arbitration law are regarded to be indispensable, Art. 1042 III CCP. Concerning approaches in that concern in international agreements, Art. IV (1) European Convention and Art. V (1)(d) New York Convention are the most important ones amongst them.

5.07. Another aspect to be considered by the parties is the contract between them and the arbitration court. This contract has to deal with issues such as the composition of the court to decide upon the conflict (*Schiedsrichtervertrag*). Due to a lack of special (arbitration law) conflict rules on how to determine the relevant legal order, international agreements on contract law and German autonomous international private law can be applied. This contract is deemed to be a contract *sui*

---

[7] ECKART BRÖDERMANN, JOACHIM ROSENGARTEN, *supra* note 6, at 213.

[8] See also Peter Schlosser, *„Brüssel I" und Schiedsgerichtsbarkeit*, 7 (3) SCHIEDSVZ 129, 129 (2009); EWALD GEIMER, ROLF A SCHÜTZE, EUROPÄISCHES ZIVILVERFAHRENSRECHT, München: Verlag C. H. Beck Art.1 EuGVVO (3rd ed. 2010).

[9] Convention on the Recognition and Enforcement of Foreign Arbitral Awards of 10 June 1958.

[10] Geneva European Convention on International Commercial Arbitration of 21 April 1961.

[11] Agreement relating to Application of the European Convention on International Commercial Arbitration of 17 December 1962.

[12] ECKART BRÖDERMANN, JOACHIM ROSENGARTEN, *supra* note 6, at 225.

generis[13]. As a result, Arts. 3 and 4 of the Rome I Regulation apply if there is a European connection and Art. 27ff of the Introductory Act to the German Civil Code (*Einführungsgesetz zum Bürgerlichen Gesetzbuch, EGBGB*), which comprehend German autonomous law on contractual obligations *(Vertragsstatut)*.

5.08. Whilst the UNÜ does not contain any regulations on how to determine whose country's substantive provisions shall be applied on the issue to be resolved (*Hauptvertragsstatut,* lex contractus), Art. VII of the European Convention leaves it largely to the discretion of the arbitral tribunal to decide upon that question. By contrast, German autonomous law, Art. 1051 CCP insofar focuses on party autonomy[14]. It is noteworthy that party agreements in that respect are to be seen rather as references to the substantive legal rules of the respective country than as references to its very own conflict rules, see by contrast Art. 4 I 1 EGBGB referring to foreign international private law and its conflict rules.

III. Public Policy Rules in the German Legal Order

5.09. Private international law and private international procedural law do not contain rules in a substantive sense. This denomination is used to describe rules which help to determine which legal order shall be applied in cases which reveal connections to legal orders of several countries[15]. German private international law is – as are others – largely based on the assumption that the legal order which is deemed to have to most relevant connection to the case shall be applied[16]. This approach implies that the very own substantive national rules of the country whose conflict rules are applied, are not deemed to be superior to other countries' legal orders. However, the so-called public policy rules restrain this unbiased approach[17].

5.10. As it is commonly agreed upon, the extent and meaning of what is considered to be part of the essential normative order of a state is not determined by national rules only. Gradually, international and European Union law take an influence as well insofar as they form an integral part of the national legal order in case these international or supranational rules are directly applicable[18]. The following passages are meant to provide an overview over public policy clauses in EU secondary law and in German autonomous private international law.

---

[13] *Ibid.*, 222.

[14] Klaus Reichold, *supra* note 6, at § 1051 ZPO, marg. note 1.

[15] Hans-Jürgen Sonnenberger, *supra* note 1, at Art. 3 EGBGB, marg. note 7.

[16] *Ibid.*, Art. 6 EGBGB, marg. note 2; FLORIAN KIENLE, INTERNATIONALES PRIVATRECHT, München: Vahlen 1, marg. note 2 (2nd ed. 2010).

[17] See FRITZ STURM, GUDRUN STURM, *in* STAUDINGER- EINL ZUM IPR, München: Sellier marg. note 56 (D. Heinrich ed., 2003).

[18] Hans-Jürgen Sonnenberger, *supra* note 1, at Art. 6 EGBGB, marg. note 19, 65; DIETER BLUMENWITZ, *in* STAUDINGER, KOMMENTAR ZUM BGB, München: Sellier Art. 6 EGBGB, marg. note 63 (2003).

III.1. Substantive Law and Public Policy Rules Relevant in Germany

5.11. If that the application of provisions stemming from the one legal order which is deemed to have the closest connection to the conflict leads to a result which manifestly violates the essential principles of the country whose conflict rules are applied, so-called public policy rules allow the judge to abstain from applying these (foreign) provisions[19]. Hence, these clauses take an influence on the resolution of a conflict. The legal order which is applied in general to the case or the substantive regulations agreed upon by the parties themselves are neglected in favour of the essential principles of the country whose judges are to decide about their conflict[20].

5.12. Still, as international integration grows steadily, one has to consider the question as to whether national autonomous private international law is applicable at all or rather derogated by international agreements or EU law, see Art. 3 EGBGB. As a result, Art. 6 EGBGB is only relevant in cases where no other regulations of international private law apply.

5.13. As it is a Member State of the EU, two EU regulations are of great importance for Germany in this respect, commonly referred to as the Rome I[21] and the Rome II[22] regulations. These are based on the Judicial Cooperation in Civil Matters, then regulated in Art. 65 (b) of the EC-Treaty, which corresponds today to Art. 81 (2) (c) of the Functioning Treaty.

III.1.1. Art. 6 EGBGB

5.14. In German private international law, Art. 6 EGBGB contains such a public policy clause. Art. 6 EGBGB states:

> *A provision of the law of another country shall not be applied where its application would lead to a result which is manifestly incompatible with the fundamental principles of German law. In particular, inapplicability ensues, if its application would be incompatible with civil rights.*

As already explicitly mentioned in Art. 6 EGBGB, civil or fundamental rights granted by the German Constitution (BL, *Grundgesetz*) are considered to be an essential part of the fundamental principles of German law[23]. However, it is worth mentioning that these fundamental rights are violated in the sense of Art. 6 EGBGB only if there is a significant

---

19 Hans-Jürgen Sonnenberger, *supra* note 1, at Art. 6 EGBGB, marg. note 2.
20 *Ibid.*
21 Council Regulation (EC) No. 593/2008 of 17 June 2008 on the law applicable to contractual obligations.
22 Council Regulation (EC) No. 864/2007 of 11 July 2007 on the law applicable to non-contractual obligations.
23 Karsten Thorn, *in* OTTO PALANDT, BÜRGERLICHES GESETZBUCH, München: Verlag C. H. Beck Art. 6 EGBGB, marg. note 7 (68th ed. 2009); Karsten Thorn, *in* OTTO PALANDT, BÜRGERLICHES GESETZBUCH, München: C. H. Beck Einl v Art. 3 EGBGB, marg. note 11 (68th ed. 2009).

domestic relevance (*hinreichender Inlandsbezug*) of the conflict[24]. Merely in these cases, national virtues and principles shall be held prior to foreign legal orders.

5.15. Moreover, the European Convention of Human Rights (ECHR) must be considered as well when interpreting the term *fundamental principles*, Art. 6 EGBGB[25]. Consequently, these rights must be taken into account, in fact regardless of a regional or domestic relevance of the conflict in order to avoid any breach of the convention by Germany as a Member State[26]. It is sufficient that a court of a Member State of the Convention is to decide about the case no matter if the country whose legal order is to be applied is bound by the Convention[27].

5.16. Furthermore, the essential principles of European Union law do play an important role as well when it comes to defining what is meant by the term *fundamental principles*: For EU Member States this implies that Fundamental Freedoms as well as fundamental rights referred to by Art. 6 (3) EU-Treaty, which are influenced by the ECHR, are rules to be taken into account when applying their respective public policy clause[28] According the case-law of the Court of Justice of the EU (CJEU), these form an integral part of the national legal order[29]. After the entry into force of the EU Charter, see Art. 6 (1) EU-Treaty, it should be explicitly included when talking about EU law impact on Art. 6 EGBGB.

5.17. Yet a different question is to what an extent the conflict is required to have an *EU law* relevance – with other words, it might be doubted if the Charter is to be applied to every conflict being resolved by an EU Member State court or only to special cases.

5.18. Art. 51 (1)(1) of the EU Charter of Fundamental Rights holds that the EU institutions be bound by the Charter and the member states when implementing EU law[30]. This restrictive approach might imply that – in

---

[24] Karsten Thorn, *in* Otto Palandt, Bürgerliches Gesetzbuch, München: Verlag C. H. Beck Art. 6 EGBGB, marg. note 6 (68th ed. 2009); Dieter Blumenwitz, *supra* note 18, at Art. 6 EGBGB, marg. note 137.

[25] Karsten Thorn, *supra* note 24, at Art. 6 EGBGB, marg. note 7; Florian Kienle, *supra* note 16, at 23, marg. note 55.

[26] Karsten Thorn, *supra* note 24, at Art. 6 EGBGB, marg. note 7; Dieter Blumenwitz, *supra* note 18, at Art. 6 EGBGB, marg. note 74 and 77.

[27] *Ibid.*, marg. note 7; Dieter Blumenwitz, *supra* note 18 at Art. 6 EGBGB, marg. note 75.

[28] Hans-Jürgen Sonnenberger, *supra* note 1, at Art. 6 EGBGB, marg. note 65 and 67; Hans-Jürgen Sonnenberger, *in* 10 Münchner Kommentar, BGB, Einl. IPR, München: Verlag C. H. Beck marg. note 209 (5th ed. 2010); Dieter Blumenwitz, *supra* note 18, at Art. 6 EGBGB, marg. note 79.

[29] Hans-Jürgen Sonnenberger, *supra* note 1, at Art. 6, marg. note 65; ECJ Judgement of 15 July 1964, 6/64, *Flaminio Costa v ENEL* [1964] ECR 1251.

[30] Markus Kotzur, *in* Rudolf Geiger, Daniel-Erasmus Khan, Markus Kotzur, EUV, AEUV: Vertrag über die Europäische Union und Vertrag über die Arbeitsweise der Europäischen Union; Kommentar, München: Verlag C. H. Beck marg. note 10, 11 (5th ed. 2010) and *ibid.*, Art. 51 GR-Charta.

contrast to the ECHR – the EU Charter is only relevant in cases which call for the application of (substantive) provisions implementing EU law. The member states are by no means bound by the Charter in an all-encompassing way. Not any exercise of sovereign power by them is subjected to the EU Charter.

5.19. As a result, in cases without any relevance to EU law – be it cases which involve non-EU Member States' legal orders only, be it where no EU secondary law exists, or cases where Fundamental Freedoms are not threatened at all it may be doubted whether the Charter is applicable at all. It remains to be seen how the discussion will develop in that respect[31].

5.20. It is noteworthy that the fundamental principles of EU law might also be called upon following the basic principles of EU law, such as primacy of EU law. This applies for cases where the substantive rules specified by national autonomous international law are those of an EU Member State: Provisions which are directly applicable, such as these fundamental rights and principles, must be granted primacy as they supersede the national provision in conflict with them[32]. As a result, these principles, which are certainly part of public policy as well, see above, might also be considered without any reference to public policy rules[33]. However, this is not a question of international private law rather than a question of EU law, namely the position of EU law when in conflict with national provisions[34], in our case with those national provisions which are to be applied according to conflict-of-laws rules.

III. 1. 2. Rome I and Rome II Regulations

5.21. The Rome I and Rome II Regulations offer rules on how to specify the legal order whose substantive provisions shall be applied to conflicts between two parties if the conflict is to be dealt with by an EU Member State – or, better put, a court of a Member State except for Denmark[35]. Regulations are binding in their entirety and are directly applicable according to Art. 288 (2) of the Functioning Treaty so that they may be regarded to be part of the German legal order. Whilst the functional scope of the Rome I Regulation can be described as covering contractual commitments, Art.1 (1) Rome I Regulation, the Rome II Regulation is applicable to non-contractual obligations, Art.1 par. Rome II Regulation.

---

31 *Ibid.*, Einf GR-Charta, marg. note 10, 11.

32 Judgement of the the ECJ of February 5, 1963, No. 26/62, *NV Algemene Transporten Expeditie Onderneming van Gend & Loos v Netherlands Inland Revenue Administration* [1693] ECR 1 (26); Dieter Blumenwitz, *supra* note 18, at Art.6 EGBGB, marg. note 84, discussing that approach in the scope of the ECHR.

33 Dieter Martiny, *in* 10 MÜNCHNER KOMMENTAR, BGB, München: Verlag C. H. Beck Art.21 Rom I-VO, marg. note 3 (5th ed. 2010); Hans Jürgen Sonnenberger, *supra* note 28, at Einl. IPR, marg. note 204 and 209.

34 Dieter Martiny, *supra* note 3, at Art. 21 Rom I-VO, marg. note 3.

35 FLORIAN KIENLE, *supra* note 16, at p. 66, marg. note 145a, p. 93, marg. note 195a.

5.22. Art. 21 of the Rome I Regulations holds:

> *The application of a provision of the law of any country specified by this Regulation may be refused only if such application is manifestly incompatible with the public policy (ordre public) of the forum.*

5.23. Art. 26 of the Rome II Regulations holds:

> *The application of a provision of the law of any country specified by this Regulation may be refused only if such application is manifestly incompatible with the public policy (ordre public) of the forum.*

5.24. The Rome I Regulation provides uniform rules to specify the *substantive* legal order to be applied in a certain case, see Art. 20 Rome I Regulation and the identical Art. 24 Rome II Regulation:

> *Exclusion of renvoi*
>
> *The application of the law of any country specified by this Regulation means the application of the rules of law in force in that country other than its rules of private international law, unless provided otherwise in this.*

5.25. However, the judges (necessarily of an EU Member State bound by the Regulation) to decide about the case and who must apply these rules of law specified by the Regulations may refuse to if their application leads to results manifestly incompatible with the public policy of their own country. It is worth mentioning that none of the Regulations refers to a set of rules considered essential by the EU (in the sense of genuine European public policy concept) but to those by the forum state[36]. As a result, the judges must turn to Fundamental Rights and national principles. Nonetheless, essential principles of European Union law do play a vital role in that respect given that these form an integral part of the national legal order, see above[37]. As a result, the above mentioned (twofold) impact of EU law on a case with international relevance applies as well albeit the public policy rules of the regulations are to be applied rather than Art. 6 EGBGB.

5.26. Still, a further aspect is worth mentioning here. The substantive legal rules specified by the regulations must not necessarily stem from an EU Member State, see Art. 2 Rome I and Art. 3 Rome II Regulation. As a result, each of the two legal constructions – one deriving from public policy rules, the other referring to the EU law principle of primacy over national member state law – can become relevant. Yet, in cases where the legal order of a non-Member State must be applied, EU fundamental principles become relevant only via public policy rules.

---

[36] Hans-Jürgen Sonnenberger, *supra* note 1, at Art. 6 EGBGB marg. note 1; Karsten Thorn, *supra* note 24, at Art. 6 EGBGB, marg.note 8; Dieter Blumenwitz, *supra* note 18, at Art. 6 EGBGB, marg. note 79-81, discussing such a genuine European approach.
[37] Dieter Martiny, *supra* note 34, at Art. 21 Rom I-VO, marg. note 3.

III. 2. Procedural Guarantees as Part of Public Policy

5.27. Beyond the functional scope of Art. 6 EGBGB, yet of similar meaning, are rules in international civil procedure law protecting procedural rights which are considered to be part of public policy[38]. The right to be heard, Art. 103 (1) BL (Constitution, *German Grundgesetz*) is an example for this set of provisions[39]. In addition, impartial, independent judges are deemed to be essential as well[40]. They become relevant when it comes to the questions of recognition and enforcement of a foreign judgement[41]. In German autonomous international law, Art. 328 (1)(4) CCP is a key provision in that respect. Still, international provisions, namely EU secondary law, are prior to Art 328 (1)(4) CCP. The Regulations known as Brussels I and Brussels II are worth mentioning, which both refer to violations of public policy as a means to refuse to recognize the decision in question (Art. 34 (1) Brussels I Regulation and Art. 22 (a) Brussels II Regulation).

IV. The Relevance of Public Policy Rules in International Arbitration Proceedings in Germany

5.28. The public policy rules mentioned above are not only relevant in case a state court must decide upon a conflict with international background. The following passages intend to provide an overview to what an extent public policy rules must be taken into consideration by arbitral tribunals. Regardless of the type of arbitral award (domestic or foreign), German literature uses the term *anerkennungsrechtlicher ordre public*[42] in that respect.

IV. 1. Lex Contractus, Arbitral Procedure and Public Policy Rules in Autonomous German Law

5.29. Art. 1051 CCP provides a conflict rule overriding to a large extent those of the EGBGB to specify the country whose legal substantive provisions shall be applied to the conflict if arbitral proceedings take place in Germany[43].

5.30. Still, public policy rules must be complied with by the arbitral tribunals[44]. This requirement is largely implied by the necessity to have

---

[38]   Hans-Jürgen Sonnenberger, *supra* note 1, at Art. 6 EGBGB, marg. note 21; Karsten Thorn, *supra* note 24, at Art. 6 EGBGB, marg. note 1.

[39]   Hans-Jürgen Sonnenberger, *supra* note 1, at Art. 6 EGBGB, marg. note 21; Jens-Peter Lachmann, *Zehn Jahre Rechtsprechung zum 10. Buch der ZPO*, 7 (1) SCHIEDSVZ 9, 17 (2009).

[40]   Dieter Blumenwitz, *supra* note 18, at Art. 6 EGBGB, marg. note 97.

[41]   FLORIAN KIENLE, *supra* note 16, at 190, marg. note 413; Norbert Horn, *supra* note 2, at 209, 212; Dieter Blumenwitz, *supra* note 18, at Art. 6 EGBGB, marg. note 94-95.

[42]   Dieter Blumenwitz, *supra* note 18, at Art. 6 EGBGB, marg. note 100; Norbert Horn, *supra* note 2, at 209, 211.

[43]   Klaus Reichold, *supra* note 6, at § 1051 ZPO, marg. note 1.

[44]   Joachim Münch, *in* 3 MÜNCHNER KOMMENTAR, ZPO, München: Verlag C. H. Beck § 1051 ZPO, marg. note 20 (3rd ed. 2003); ECKHART BRÖDERMANN, JOACHIM ROSENGARTEN, *supra* note 6, at 229, marg. note 786.

the arbitral award recognized in the country where it should be used an enforcement order[45]. In addition, provisions of arbitration law mostly provide regulations laying down reasons for which the arbitral award can be appealed before state courts. This refers to public policy both in a substantive and procedural aspect[46].

IV. 1. 1. Appeal to State Courts against an Arbitral Award

5.31. Although state courts restrain themselves from subjecting arbitral awards issued in Germany, so-called domestic awards, Art. 1025 CCP, to a *revision au fond*[47], Art. 1059 CCP provides for a proceeding to appeal against the award for certain reasons. Art. 1059 (2)(b) CCP refers to public policy in that respect. Once called upon, Courts of Appeal must examine *ex officio* whether public policy rules were obeyed by the domestic[48] award in question.

IV. 1. 2. Recognition and Enforcement of Arbitral Awards

5.32. As to (international) arbitration proceedings taking place in Germany, Art. 1060 (2) CCP, applies, while foreign awards are referred to by Art. 1061 CCP in case one of the parties intends to use it as an enforcement order in Germany[49].

Arbitral awards of German arbitral tribunals
(Domestic awards, *inländische Schiedssprüche*)

5.33. The reasons for which an arbitral awards issued by German arbitral tribunals (domestic awards) might be denied enforceability are equal to those which apply in appeal cases. Art. 1060 (2) CCP refers to Art. 1050 CCP.

Foreign arbitral awards to be recognized and enforced in Germany

5.34. Due to the necessity to have arbitral tribunals' rulings recognized and declared enforceable by the state courts of a different country if it is to gain the function of an enforcement order (*Vollstreckungstitel*), the latter must expressly recognize the awards. Although international agreements and autonomous German law restrain from subjecting them to a so-called *revision au fond* in recognition matters as well[50], some essential requirements must be met. Art. 1061 CCP refers to the conformity of the arbitral tribunal's ruling to public policy of the German legal order, being the very state whose decision of recognition is sought[51].

---

[45] Joachim Münch, *supra* note 44, at § 1051 ZPO, marg. note 20; ECKHART BRÖDERMANN, JOACHIM ROSENGARTEN, *supra* note 6, at 229, marg. note 786.

[46] Klaus Reichold, *supra* note 6, at § 1059 ZPO, marg. note 16; Joachim Münch, *supra* note 44, at § 1059 ZPO, marg. note 42.

[47] Norbert Horn, *supra* note 2, at 209, 215-216; Joachim Münch, *supra* note 44, at § 1059 ZPO, marg. note 2-4.

[48] Klaus Reichold, *supra* note 6, at Art. 1059 ZPO, marg. note 5.

[49] Norbert Horn, *supra* note 2, at 209, 212.

[50] ADOLF BAUMBACH, WOLFGANG LAUTERBACH, JAN ALBERS, PETER HARTMANN, *supra* note 2, at Art. 1061 ZPO marg. note 4.

[51] Dieter Blumenwitz, *supra* note 18 at Art.6 EGBGB, marg. note 99.

5.35. In order to come up to the parties' needs and interests when solving international conflicts, which is foremost that the ruling be accepted in other countries, arbitral tribunals will keep in mind this recognition requirement of conformity to public policy. It is worth mentioning that the persons held responsible to decide upon the case must in a certain way foresee which country's provisions will determine the requirements of recognition and enforceability[52].

IV. 2. International Agreements

5.36. Art. VII of the European Convention leaves it largely to the discretion of the arbitral tribunal to decide upon the question of lex contractus. Art. V (2)(b) of the New York Convention specifies the reasons for which a state court of a Member State of the Convention might deny recognition to an arbitral award issued by an arbitral tribunal of a foreign state no matter if this state is a member to the Convention[53].

IV. 3. The Notion of an "Ordre Public" International or Transnational Public Policy[54]

5.37. The following passage shall discuss whether and to what an extent the application of public policy must be modified if applied by arbitral tribunals. There are several aspects which must be kept in mind.

5.38. Firstly, an aspect which distinguishes conflicts to be resolved by state courts from those to be resolved by (international) arbitral tribunals is the mere fact that public policy rules are applied by arbitral tribunals rather than state courts – that is tribunals or courts not integrated within state jurisdiction[55]. With regard to that difference, it can be argued that arbitral tribunals apply a common international understanding of what public policy means rather than the (national) public policy clauses referred to above[56].

5.39. Secondly, one must also differentiate according to the origin of the arbitral award. Being tribunals beyond state jurisdiction, even domestic awards without any connection to foreign countries must comply with Art. 1060 CCP in order to be declared enforceable by state courts in Germany – so must domestic awards with international connection. Yet, these domestic arbitral awards to be declared enforceable by German courts may differ from each other as well as far as their connection to the

---

52 ECKHART BRÖDERMANN, JOACHIM ROSENGARTEN, *supra* note 6, 229, marg. note 786.
53 ADOLF BAUMBACH, WOLFGANG LAUTERBACH, JAN ALBERS, PETER HARTMANN, *supra* note 2, at Art. 1061 ZPO, marg. note 2.
54 Hans-Jürgen Sonnenberger, *supra* note 1, at Art. 6 EGBGB, marg. note 19 (for further examples how this term is used).
55 Norbert Horn, *supra* note 2, at 211.
56 *Ibid.*, 210-211.

German or European legal order is concerned. The German legal order is not necessarily the one to be applied to the conflict. Foreign awards must comply with Art. 1061 CCP to be recognized and declared enforceable by German courts if they are to be used as enforcement orders according to German law. Still, they might have even closer connection to the German legal order – the *lex contractus* might have even been German law[57].

5.40. As far as foreign awards are concerned, state courts sought for recognition apply the *ordre public international*[58]. This modification means that awards are not considered to infringe public policy even if a German state court would have affirmed a violation of public policy applying Art. 6 EGBGB or Art. 21 Rome I Regulation[59]. Only manifest contradictions to the German legal order which do allow under no circumstances an approval as enforcement order shall be relevant when it comes to the question of recognition[60]. As a result, examination criteria as to whether public policy is infringed in recognition matters can be described to be far less strict[61].

5.41. It is argued that a set of provisions should be defined which unite international, commonly shared values rather than national rules[62]. This leads to the question which rules can be described to make up this *ordre public international* as it is of greatest interest to the parties of arbitration proceedings to be able to have an award recognized by as many states as possible if the award shall be used as an enforcement in a country different to the one where proceedings have taken place.

---

[57] ADOLF BAUMBACH, WOLFGANG LAUTERBACH, JAN ALBER, PETER HARTMANN, *supra* note 2, at Art. 1061 ZPO, marg. note 1.

[58] Dieter Blumenwitz, *supra* note 18, at Art. 6 EGBGB, marg. note 100 101 (with further referrals to jurisdiction in that respect).

[59] BGH NJW 1998, 2358 (2358); BGH NJW 1986, 3027 (3028).

[60] Dieter Blumenwitz, *supra* note 18, at Art. 6 EGBGB, marg. note 101; BGH NJW 1998, 2358 (2358); BGH NJW 1986, 3027 (3028).

[61] Dieter Blumenwitz, *supra* note 18, at Art. 6 EGBGB, marg. note 100; It remains unclear and contested if the same modification applies to domestic arbitral awards. An affirmative answer to this question might indeed base on the first aspect mentioned above and concerning the fact that domestic awards do not necessarily have a closer connection to German law than foreign awards might even have, see above. However, according to recent German jurisdiction, the examination criteria relevant for Art. 1059 CCP, thus when examining domestic awards, only slightly differ from those of Art. 1061 CCP/ Art. 5 (2)(b) of the New York Convention, see ADOLF BAUMBACH, WOLFGANG LAUTERBACH, JAN ALBERS, PETER HARTMANN, *supra* note 2, at Art. 1060 ZPO, marg. note 16; Joachim Münch, *supra* note 44, at Art. 1059 ZPO, marg. note 41-43; Norbert Horn, *supra* note 2, at 216; BGH, NJW 2009, 1215, 1216 (2009).

[62] Norbert Horn, *supra* note 2, at 211; Hans-Jürgen Sonnenberger, *supra* note 1, at Art.6 EGBGB, marg. note 19.

V. The EU Fundamental Rights Charter as a Source of EU Law Based on the European Constitutional Tradition

V. 1. The EU Fundamental Rights Charter

5.42. The EU Fundamental Rights Charter which entered into force 1st December 2009 is the most modern fundamental rights document in Europe. Its modernity lies in the fact that new needs for protection have been integrated into the Charter, such as data protection, possible impacts of biology and medicine on a person, as well as the guarantee of an intact environment. A second fact in this context is the completeness of the fundamental rights system insofar as it is recognized as necessary to extend the protection even beyond the written provisions which do not cover dangers to the individual unknown until now. The effectiveness of the fundamental rights protection is a characteristic of modern European Constitutionalism which also applies to the EU Fundamental Rights Charter.

5.43. A third, functional aspect has to be regarded as being of importance in this context. An advanced understanding of protecting fundamental rights from the intervention of the legislator is manifest: so restrictions of these rights can only be made if a law, an Act of Parliament, gives its permission for that. Furthermore, the very nature of the fundamental rights, the nucleus (*Wesensgehalt*) must not be affected as well as the principle of proportionality. Thus, the three elements of a fundamental rights protection against legislature as developed in modern European Constitutional law are also applicable to the Charter (legal basis, guarantee of the essence of a right, proportionality).

5.44. The EU Charter is also an expression of a common European tradition. It can be seen as a fruit which has been grown on an *European tree.* Thus, the Charter unites several sources of European fundamental rights protections systems such as the ECHR, the European Social Charter, the EU law itself and the national Constitutional law. As a result, the Charter might be a major source of reference when defining a genuine European concept of public policy applied in recognition matters.

5.45. Regarding the various chapters of the Charter, its *European* character will be manifest.
Chapter 1 on dignity seems to be strongly influenced by Art. 1 of the German BL. Both documents place dignity of human beings as a supreme value at the top of all fundamental rights, expressing clearly the anthropocentric approach of the European Union legal order in the same way as the German order does. In the same chapter, the prohibition of torture and degrading treatment, specific aspects of dignity of man, is manifestly drawn from Art. 3 of the ECHR. The rights embodied in Chapter 2 are of classic nature and are very similar to the corresponding national constitutional rights. There is also a correspondence with

the unwritten, judge-made fundamental rights of the supranational Community which have been developed by the CJEU, then called ECJ (European Court of Justice). As they were based on a common European constitutional tradition, they have assumed the essential contents of the national constitutions' rights. Chapter 3 on equality embodies the classic aspects of non-discrimination and prohibition of arbitrariness (*Willkürverbot*). On the other hand, equality is conceived in a modern sense including the protection of weaker groups in the society such as children, aged people, disabled persons and so on. Here, national *and* supranational legal developments are reflected in these provisions. Chapter 4 on solidarity that is on social rights, is mainly influenced by the European Social Charter, a complimentary treaty to the ECHR. Thus, the Charter is the first multi-national document which combines social rights and classic rights meant to protect the individual from state intervention. Chapter 5 on European Union citizenship has been transferred from the EC-Treaty to the Charter. Chapter 6 on justice is clearly drawn from Art. 6 and Art. 7 ECHR and has to be interpreted, as the interpretation rule of the Charter says, in the light of the Strasbourg Court.

5.46. To summarize, it should be stated that the Charter, though it is a source of EU law, has its origin in the most important European documents on the individual's protection. There is a certain predominance of the ECHR and the case-law of the Strasbourg Court of Human Rights which influence the interpretation of national constitutional law as well as of supranational law. It should be said that the Charter is addressed to the EU authorities as well as to Member States insofar as they implement EU law. In purely national matters, the Charter is not applicable, see above.

V. 2. The Charter as a Common European Public Order and as Part of the National Concept

5.47. The question arises whether the Charter could be used as a basis of a European public policy when arbitration of transnational character is executed. Insofar as the arbitration proceedings concern matters of the EU fundamental freedoms such as the transnational movement of goods or services, indeed the EU Charter constitutes the public policy as a limit for arbitration.

5.48. But also if EU related matters are not concerned, the EU Charter is the most adequate document for determining European public policy. It is largely accepted that the ECHR takes part, alongside with the national Constitution, in defining the national concept of public policy. This results mainly from the fact that the Strasbourg Convention is part of the Council of Europe's member states'legal order. The impact on the national concept does not depend on its rank in the internal national order. In Germany, the Convention is equivalent to ordinary federal laws in accordance with the transformation mechanism foreseen by Article 59 (2) BL, but, nevertheless, its impact on the national public order is recognized. It is true that the Convention serves, despite its internal rank, as an instrument of interpretation also for constitutional law, as the presumption of innocence decisions of the Federal Constitutional Court clearly show[63]. This shows the interpretation effect of international instruments, despite its internal rank, on national ordinary as well as on constitutional law.

5.49. A similar interpretation effect can also be stated in the context of the EU Fundamental Rights Charter, independently from its formal applicability, see above. The national public order is a source of national law but defined also from external law. The national concept embraces those values the State adheres to. An EU Member State's legal thinking, in particular its constitutional orientation as to values, is essentially determined by the Charter. Thus, the Convention as well as the Charter are essential factors of influence on the concept of public policy. Thus Germany's value orientation which is expressed by the concept of public order includes national constitutional law as well as the international and supranational documents, mainly the ECHR and the EU Fundamental Rights Charter. As far as possible, the values determined by these documents shall be conceived in a convergent way. European Constitutionalism of today is characterized by strong convergence tendencies in particular in the fields of fundamental rights and Rule of Law. The EU Charter itself intends to harmonize value interpretation with the Strasbourg jurisprudence as to the rights corresponding to the ECHR. Also national constitutional law shows this tendency, both in legal orders where an express harmonization clause exists as in Article 10 (2) of the Spanish Constitution and in orders without such an express clause. The latter, implicitly, seek to make their national fundamental rights compatible with those embodied in international instruments. This furthers indirectly the harmonization of the EU Charter's rights drawn from the national constitutional tradition with the ECHR. As a result, we can state the consolidation of a European Constitutional order which is related to a *three level constitutionalism* with converging value concepts[64] which determine the national public policy as a limit for arbitration.

| | |

---

[63] See 74 Federal Constitutional Court 358, 370; 82 Federal constitutional Court 106, 115.

[64] See Rainer Arnold, *European Constitutional Law: Its notion, scope and finalities,* in New Directions in Comparative Law, Northampton: Edward Elgar Publishing, Inc. 99 – 107 (J. Nergelius, A. Bakardjieva Engelbrekt eds., 2010).

Summaries

FRA [*La Charte communautaire des droits fondamentaux et l'ordre public dans le droit de l'arbitrage international*]

L'importance de l'ordre public ne fait aucun doute en termes de reconnaissance des sentences arbitrales étrangères en Allemagne. En ce qui concerne l'impact de la Charte communautaire des droits fondamentaux, il reste difficile de déterminer dans quelle mesure ces droits déborderont sur la notion nationale d'ordre public. Au minimum, la Charte affecte la force obligatoire et modifie l'application de dispositions légales majeures en vertu de la primauté du droit européen, même si l'Art. 51 de la Charte mérite qu'on l'étudie avec attention. Toutefois, étant donné que la Charte reflète la pensée de chacun des États-membres de la Communauté, il est possible d'avancer que celle-ci est applicable quelle que soit la portée de l'affaire dans le cadre du droit européen quand on défend le concept national d'ordre public. La Charte de l'Union européenne peut avoir une influence décisive lorsque l'on tente de définir une approche européenne authentique, ou même un concept d'ordre public. Ceci permettra alors d'appliquer ce concept en tant qu'ordre public international, en remplacement des concepts d'ordre public nationaux.

CZE [*Listina základních práv Evropské unie a veřejný pořádek v mezinárodním rozhodčím právu*]

V otázce uznávání cizích rozhodčích nálezů nejsou v Německu žádné pochybnosti o relevantnosti veřejného pořádku. Pokud jde o dopady Listiny základních práv Evropské unie, stále není jasné, v jakém rozsahu budou tato práva utvářet národní pojetí veřejného pořádku. Rozhodujícím faktorem je, že Listina zahrnuje závaznost a upravuje uplatnění ustanovení hmotného práva podle prvořadosti práva Evropské unie, nicméně je třeba věnovat zvláštní pozornost rozsahu článku 51 Listiny. Ovšem vzhledem k tomu, že v Listině se odráží uvažování každého ze členských států Evropské unie, je možné tvrdit, že by měla být použitelná při definování národní koncepce veřejného pořádku bez ohledu na důležitost případu podle evropského práva. Listina Evropské unie by mohla mít rozhodný vliv, také pokud jde o definování ryzího evropského pojetí nebo koncepce veřejného pořádku. Tato koncepce používaná již při uznávání mezinárodních rozhodčích nálezů by mohla nahradit vnitrostátní koncepce veřejného pořádku.

| | |

POL [*Karta Praw Podstawowych UE i porządek publiczny w międzynarodowym prawie arbitrażowym*]

Niniejszy artykuł opisuje postanowienia regulujące zasady porządku publicznego obowiązujące w Niemczech. Szczególna uwaga została poświęcona wpływowi prawa międzynarodowego, zwłaszcza zaś prawa UE, na wykładnię oraz zakres wspomnianych zasad. Wpływ obowiązującej od 01.12.2009 roku Karty Praw Podstawowych UE na orzecznictwo w tym zakresie będzie można ocenić dopiero w przyszłości. Zarówno trybunały arbitrażowe, jak i sądy państwowe, muszą przestrzegać zasad porządku publicznego. W artykule opisano szczegółowo owe przepisy obowiązujące w Niemczech, kładąc szczególny nacisk na koncepcję ordre public international i jej zastosowanie w prawie arbitrażowym.

DEU [***Die Charta der Grundrechte der Europäischen Union und der ordre public-Vorbehalt im internationalen Schiedsrecht***]
Nationale ordre public Klauseln erhalten durch völkerrechtliche Bindungen der Staaten neuen Gehalt: Internationale wie auch supranationale Grundsätze prägen den Inhalt der Klauseln. Die Bedeutung der Grundrechte Charta der EU ist noch nicht abschließend geklärt. Da die Charta Ausdruck der Rechtsüberzeugung eines jeden EU Mitgliedstaates ist[65], liegt es jedoch nahe, sie unabhängig von einem EU-rechtlichen Bezug des Falles bei der Bestimmung des nationalen ordre public-Gehaltes heranzuziehen. Ein anerkennungsrechtlicher, modifizierter ordre public wird bereits gegenüber internationalen Schiedssprüchen angewandt. In diesem Zusammenhang könnte die Grundrechte Charta auch bei der Entwicklung eines grenzüberschreitend gültigen, europäischen ordre public – Konzepts Orientierung bieten.

RUS [*Хартия ЕС по правам человека и государственная политика в международном арбитражном праве*]
В статье рассматривается ряд положений, действующих в Германии, которые содержат правила осуществления государственной политики. Особое внимание уделяется влиянию, оказываемому международным правом, а именно, правом ЕС, на толкование и область действия таких правил. Всё еще открытым остаётся вопрос о том, в какой мере Хартия Европейского Союза по правам человека, действующая с 01.12.2009г., будет в этом плане влиять на юрисдикцию. Третейские, а также государственные суды обязаны соблюдать правила государственной политики. Такие положения, действующие в Германии, подробно описаны с акцентом на понятие ordre public international, которое должно быть применено в арбитражном праве.

ES [*La Carta de derechos fundamentales y la Política pública de la UE en la Ley de arbitraje internacional*]
El artículo describe el conjunto de provisiones relevantes en Alemania que contienen normas de política pública. Se dedica una especial atención al impacto que tiene la ley internacional, especialmente la de la UE, en la interpretación y el ámbito de estas normas. Aún queda por ver hasta

---

[65]   Dies gilt jedenfalls vorbehaltlich derjenigen Staaten, die sich die Anerkennung der Charta vorbehalten haben.

qué punto la Carta de derechos fundamentales de la UE vigente desde el 1/12/2009 ejercerá influencia en la jurisdicción a este respecto. Los tribunales de arbitraje, así como las cortes estatales están obligados a obedecer las normas sobre política pública. Estas provisiones relevantes en Alemania se describen detalladamente y se hace un especial hincapié en la noción de un ordre public international que se ha de aplicar en la legislación de arbitraje.

Czech (& Central European) Yearbook of Arbitration

Leonila Guglya
Conflicts of Interest in Arbitration: The News from the Russian Federation

Key words:
*Arbitration |
Arbitrator | IBA
| IBA Guidelines
| Independence |
Impartiality | Conflicts
of interest | Russian
Federation | Chamber
of Commerce and
Industry of the
Russian Federation |
MKAS | Appointing
authority | Disclosure
| Challenge*

Abstract | *Impartiality and independence of arbitrators, standing right at the forefront of the arbitration and, essentially, ensuring its legitimacy, have always attracted attentions of scholars and practitioners. A major breakthrough in terms of development of internationally recognized standards in the area took place in 2004, when the Guidelines on Conflicts of Interest in International Arbitration were published by the IBA. Nevertheless, despite the optimistic expectations of the drafters, the IBA Guidelines had not facilitated the conflicts of interest resolution practice of the courts and tribunals in the Russian Federation. In order to fill the lacuna, in late August 2010 the "Russian version" of the Guidelines – Rules on Impartiality and Independence of the Arbitrators – were adopted by the Chamber of Commerce and Industry of the Russian Federation. The present article is aimed at analysing the reasons underlining the adoption of the Rules, their structural peculiarities, and, most importantly, at scrutinizing the content of the instrument in making an attempt to find explanations for the inclusion of certain provisions thereto, be that by virtue of reference of pre-existing precedents, regional cultural heritage or legal realities. The study proceeds on the comparative edge, contrasting the approach adopted by the Rules with that finding its reflection in the text of the IBA Guidelines.*

Leonila Guglya is a Research Associate in the International Investment Arbitration Project led by Gabrielle Kaufmann-Kohler and Thomas Schultz at the University of Geneva Law School, funded by the Swiss National Science Foundation. She holds an SJD degree from Central European University; LL.M (Geneva Master in International Dispute Settlement – MIDS); LL.M in International Business Law (Central European University); Specialist in Law and LL.B (National University of 'Kyiv-Mohyla Academy') degrees. e-mail: leonila.guglya. alumni@mids.ch

| | |

I. The *Russian Guidelines:* A Tale of the *Rules on Impartiality and Independence of the Arbitrators*

6.01. Some five years after the IBA promulgated its Guidelines on Conflicts of Interest in International Arbitration (hereinafter – the *"IBA Guidelines"*), the Chamber of Commerce and Industry of the Russian Federation (hereinafter – the *"CCI"*) came up with the similar initiative. On 27 August 2010, the President of the CCI, by his Order, promulgated the *"Rules on Impartiality and Independence of the Arbitrators"* (hereinafter – the *"Rules"*)[1]. The Rules were adopted in accordance with the Art. 12 of the Law of the Russian Federation *"On International Commercial Arbitration"*[2] and Art. 8(1) of the Federal Law of the Russian Federation *"On [Domestic] Arbitration Courts in Russian Federation"*[3] (both confirming, that the arbitrator shall be impartial and independent) taking into account current international, foreign and national experiences in dealing with the impartiality and independence of the arbitrators (including the IBA Guidelines).

6.02. The Rules are primarily aimed at prevention and facilitation of the resolution of conflicts of interest, which may arise in practice of the arbitral tribunals seated on the territory of the Russian Federation, both – domestic and international, proceeding in either institutional or *ad hoc* setting[4]. The language of the Rules suggests their application (as a default solution) in the *ad hoc* arbitration (once the assistance of the appointing authority – the President of the CCI – is sought)[5]. Otherwise, the Rules are expected to serve as a *"manual"* for arbitrators and a guidance for the arbitral institutions (*inter alia* when serving as appointing authorities)[6], as well as, where appropriate, for the national courts of the Russian Federation in annulment and recognition and enforcement proceedings.

---

[1] Order of the President of Chamber of Commerce and Industry of the Russian Federation No. 39, of August 27, 2010. The text of the Rules is available in Russian at: http://arbitrage.ru/pravila-o-bespristrastnosti-i-nezavisimosti-treteiskih-sudei (accessed on December 1, 2010). To the best of the author's knowledge, no translation of the Rules into English is yet available.

[2] No. 5338-1, of July 7, 1993.

[3] No. 102-ФЗ, of July 24, 2002.

[4] See the Preamble to and well as Art. 2 of the Rules.

[5] According to Art. 2(2) of the Rules, they are to be used by the President of the CCI in exercising his functions in appointments, challenge and removal of arbitrators, as provided for in Arts. 6(1), 11(3), 11(4), 13(3) and 14 of the Law of the Russian Federation *"On International Commercial Arbitration"*. Such functions are to be exercised, in particular, failing the agreement of the parties over the appointment, challenge or removal of arbitrators respectively.

[6] For the context of the arbitration *proper*, the Rules expressly provide that their application should be limited by the agreement of the parties, relevant arbitration rules and *lex arbitri* (Preamble to the Rules, para. 5; Rules, Art 1(3)).

6.03. As compared to the IBA Guidelines, the Rules have a somewhat broader coverage, addressing not only the circumstances that might indicate potential conflicts of interest, but also a number of the procedural momenta concerning disclosure, pre-appointment contacts between a party and a prospective arbitrator, challenge and removal procedures[7]. It might be suggested that a somewhat extended scope of the Rules, as compared, for instance, to the IBA Guidelines, is permitted (or even supported) by their "*local*" rather the global coverage, encompassing a single jurisdiction (though a sizeable one). Time-wise, the Rules cover the period starting when an offer of appointment has been made to the prospective arbitrator and ending with the completion of the arbitration proceedings[8], this being coherent with the IBA Guidelines[9].

6.04. Whilst being overall more concise in elaborating over the general standards, the Rules, similarly to the IBA Guidelines, contain three lists. The lists, rather conservatively, are referred to via the nature of the circumstances, addressed therein (rather than by the colour as is in case of the IBA Guidelines). Respectively, they deal with the "*Circumstances, which unconditionally bar the arbitrator from participating in the proceedings*"[10]; "*Circumstances necessitating disclosure*"[11] and "*Circumstances that do not need to be disclosed*"[12]. Structurally, the most stringent ("*red*") Russian list differs from its IBA counterpart in that the waiver is not possible should any of the circumstances mentioned therein occur, while on the IBA "*red*" list only four situations are non-waivable, whilst the other fourteen could be subject to the explicit waiver, exercised by the parties[13].

II. The "Jurisdiction-Specific" Instrument: Raison d' Être

6.05. In justification of the adoption of the Rules a reference has been made to the substantial difficulties, arising in practice of the resolution of conflicts of interest issues in Russian Federation, as well as to certain malpractices that were ascertained in the area. Indeed, the problem of absence of a clear guidance as to the scope of permitted relationships between an arbitrator and a party was clearly present in both – Russian arbitration practice and case-law, being also acknowledged by the legal

---

[7] See Rules, Art. 7; Arts. 9-11 (Section III); Arts. 12-13 (Section IV) respectively.

[8] Rules, Art. 1(1).

[9] IBA Guidelines, General Standard I ("*General Principles*").

[10] Rules, Art. 5.

[11] Rules, Art. 6.

[12] Rules, Art. 8. Even despite the absence of the colors in the Rules, the color attributes of the lists, as introduced by the IBA Guidelines, will be used further in the discussion, with "*unconditionally barring*" circumstances being seen in "*red*", "*circumstances necessitating disclosure*" – in "*orange*" and "*circumstances that do not need to be disclosed*"- in "*green*".

[13] IBA Guidelines, General Standard 4 ("*Waiver by the Parties*"), part "*c*".

scholars and practitioners exploring this field[14]. Attempts of search for the impartiality and independence "*standards*" were made, for instance, in the Letter of the Presidium of Higher Arbitrazh Court of the Russian Federation No. 96, entitled "*An Overview of the Practice of Consideration by Russian Arbitrazh Courts of the Disputes, Related to the Recognition and Enforcement of Foreign Court Decisions*", nevertheless, the above instrument (due to its all-encompassing nature) is far from having a comprehensive coverage of the relevant issues.

6.06. In the meantime, no case-law originating from Russian Federation bearing reference to the IBA Guidelines – seemingly a palpable solution for the existing lacuna – is available, even though a group of the Russian experts, consisting of Ilya Nikiforov, Ivan Marisin and Vladimir Khvalei have translated the text of the Guidelines into Russian[15]. A possible reason for the reluctance of the courts and tribunals to resort to the Guidelines could be found in the fact that the regional peculiarities had not found their reflection in the text of the latter, among the other things, because not a single representative of the ex-USSR area (neither, though, of the CEE region) was a member of the respective IBA Working Group[16]. It is undeniably true, that the drafters of the Guidelines, anticipating "*a global*" application thereof, have never excluded the CEE jurisdictions from the coverage of the instrument[17], nonetheless the presentation of the view from the region concerned in the discussions could have helped in both – enriching the document and giving it [more] "*legitimacy*", intensifying its practical use in the respective region.

III. The Specificities of the [Russian] Rules

6.07. Whilst the discussion below is not aimed at analysing each and every peculiarity of the Rules, the most interesting developments will receive their brief reflection. Among those –definitions, which the categories of independence and impartiality received in the text of the Rules, as well as a series of reflections on certain circumstances, having (or to the contrary – not having) the conflicts of interest – raising potential, at least judging from the Russian perspective.

---

[14] See, *inter alia*, Illya Nikiforov, *Interpretation of Article V of the New York Convention by Russian Courts – Due Process, Arbitrability, and Public Policy Grounds for Non-Enforcement*, 25 (6) J.Int'l Arb. 795 (2008).

[15] The Russian text is available on the IBA web page at: http://www.ibanet.org/Publications/publications_IBA_guides_and_free_materials.aspx (accessed on December 1, 2010).

[16] The list of members of the working group could, *inter alia*, be found in the Notes to the text of the Guidelines.

[17] Otto L. O. de Witt Wijnen, Nathalie Voser, Neomi Rao, *Background Information on the IBA Guidelines on Conflicts of Interest in International Arbitration*, 5 (3) B.L.I. 343, 434 (2004), referring, *inter alia*, to the creation of "*standards that could be accepted by different legal cultures*".

IV. An "Innovative" Division: Impartiality versus Independence

6.08. An important achievement of the Rules is their demonstrated ability to draw a dividing line between impartiality and independence, defining each of the categories. The delineation of the type is indeed rare in current legal scholarship, even more so in practice. For example, the IBA Guidelines avoided the issue, sticking to the general notion of "*conflicts of interest*" instead[18].

6.09. Several trends pertaining to the characterization of the independence – impartiality phenomenon are currently dominant in the relevant scholarly writings. A consolidation trend rests on the submission in regard to the absence of an absolute independence and suggests the removal of an [artificial] border between the identity – and relation – based analyses, *inter alia* advocating that certain human interactions (and not just identities, or specificity of the issue concerned) could cause bias in arbitrators. Along these lines, it has even been suggested that

[...] the two crucial words are legally synonymous. In truth, there is only one meaning, deriving its principal force from the word "impartiality"[19].

Alternatively, the ICC Arbitration Rules, at times quite actively criticized for this particular approach, refer only to the concept of independence[20].

6.10. Nevertheless, seemingly siding with the authors agreeing with the idea of proximity and interrelation between the impartiality and independence, though not their interchangeability[21], the Rules have defined the terms. Accordingly, the arbitrator is deemed to be impartial if

He is not directly or indirectly interested in the outcome of the case and does not have predisposed preferences or prejudices towards a certain party to arbitration, its counsel, expert, consultant or witness[22].

---

18 IBA Guidelines, General Standard 2 ("*Conflicts of Interest*").

19 Lord Steyn, *England: the Independence and/or Impartiality of Arbitrators in International Commercial Arbitration, in* ICC BULLETIN SPECIAL SUPPLEMENT: INDEPENDENCE OF ARBITRATORS 94 (2007).

20 Art. 7(1) of the ICC Arbitration Rules (1998). According to the still different view, nonetheless leading to the same conclusion, whilst both independence and impartiality are distinct, it is independence, that has to serve as a basic criterion for assessment, as

Only an independent [Judiciary] is able to render justice impartially on the basis of law, thereby also protecting the human rights and fundamental freedoms of the individual.

Office of the High Commissioner for Human Rights, *Chapter 4, Independence and Impartiality of Judges, Prosecutors and Lawyers, in* HUMAN RIGHTS IN THE ADMINISTRATION OF JUSTICE: A MANUAL ON HUMAN RIGHTS FOR JUDGES, PROSECUTORS AND LAWYERS, Geneva: United Nations Publication 115 (2003), available at: http://www.ohchr.org/Documents/Publications/training9chapter4en.pdf (accessed on December 1, 2010).

21 Naser Alam, *Independence and Impartiality in International Arbitration – an Assessment*, 1 (2) TRANSNATIONAL DISPUTE MANAGEMENT (May 2004).

22 Rules, Art. 4(2).

The arbitrator is considered independent

> *in the absence of such relationship between the arbitrator and the parties to arbitration, their counsels, experts, consultants, witnesses, that could influence the position of the arbitrator concerning the case*[23].

6.11. The above definitions seem to be reasonable. Nonetheless, for the time being, it is uneasy to assess their practical usefulness and significance. Notably, further in the Rules, where the particular circumstances potentially hindering impartiality and independence are discussed, no distinction is made between the two categories. However, possibly, a clearer vision of impartiality and independence might assist those concerned with the scrutiny of the real life situations on their basis in the correct application of the earlier.

V. Certain "Substantive" Standards

6.12. Predictably, the most peculiar traits of the Rules lie in their content[24]. First of all, it is noticeable that whilst the Rules address some of the conflicts of interest areas focused on in the IBA Guidelines – such as relationships between an arbitrator and a dispute, as well as between an arbitrator and a party, arbitrator's interest in the dispute – in a quite similar manner, there are certain areas of the IBA Guidelines which the Rules practically do not address (for instance, a relationship of an arbitrator's law firm with a dispute and parties or a relationship between an arbitrator and an arbitral institution), finally, the Rules concentrate on certain areas to a much more substantive extent than the IBA Guidelines (the relationship between arbitrators, between arbitrators and other professional participants in the case (counsel, experts, consultants), between arbitrators and witnesses).

6.13. Proceeding to a more detailed assessment, it is interesting to see that the two sets of rules reflect different visions of certain phenomena they both touch upon. For example, varied weight is attributed to the statements made by the arbitrator concerning the case he is involved in (the legal assessment of the latter). Whilst under the Rules such statements evidence predisposition of the arbitrator towards the case, necessitating his unconditional withdrawal from the proceedings, under the IBA guidelines they would only fall under the Orange list, mandating disclosure, yet leaving the parties concerned free to decide on the further prospective of the arbitrator's participation in the arbitration. It is indeed difficult to find the reason for this discrepancy of approaches. Possibly, one has to resort to certain cultural perceptions that would give such communications diverse value in each of the contexts. Indeed, an old Russian proverb confirms that it is not possible to remedy something that has already been put down on paper[25].

---

[23] Rules, Art. 4(3).

[24] The list of circumstances, addressed by the Rules in their comparison with those addressed in the IBA Guidelines could be found in the Table I, appended to this Article.

[25] *"Что написано пером – не вырубишь топором"*, Russian proverb.

6.14. Furthermore, as far as the Rules are concerned, no specific significance is attached to the affiliation of the arbitrator with a certain law firm in the cases of involvement of the law firm (via different lawyers thereof or otherwise) in advising or representing one of the arbitrating parties. This approach is contrastingly different once compared to the one adopted by the IBA Guidelines, where a significant attention is devoted to the law firm – related matters. The explanation of the Russian *status quo* should be searched for in the relevant legal framework and practice, in particular – in the essential absence of regulation of rendering of the commercial legal services, which is considered to be just the other type of the entrepreneurial activity, not subject to the professional control mechanism[26]. Consequently, the law firm is seen no differently from enterprises involved in the various other economic sectors, failing to justify any claim for the special (or at least specific) treatment. Demonstrating this exact trend, a single circumstance, that could be read as a "*red*" (or, rather "*orange*") flag for the purposes of the conflicts of interest, addressed in the Art. 6(3)(3) of the Rules, refers to the "*organization*" in which the arbitrator is (or has been) employed, or the association of attorneys to which he is a member – both categories not being tantamount in their structure and context to the "*concept*" of a law firm, yet, arguably, referring, *inter alia*, thereto.

6.15. Proceeding further to the circumstances not addressed (or at least not explicitly addressed) in the Rules, while reflected in the IBA guidelines, special consideration should be paid to the IBA's core "*identity between the arbitrator and the party*" criterion. The Rules touch upon the identity issue only partially, for instance via barring the arbitrator, who has a history of prior involvement in the same proceedings in a "*party*" capacity, from participation in the consideration of the case. Nonetheless, even though the Rules are not detailed enough in this particular respect, it might be presumed, that the only reason thereof is that this strong conflict of interest situation is taken "*for granted*" for the purposes of the impartiality and independence test. An interesting case, *LL.C. "Legal Bureau "Vashe Pravo" v. LL.C. "Ivsilikat"(both – Russian Federation)*, dealing with the challenge of the domestic arbitration award in Russia, where, in the well-reasoned opinion the Russian court has condemned the identity between the arbitrator and the party, demonstrates the above.

---

[26] The only spheres of legal professional activity, regulated in Russian Federation, are notary, public prosecution and advocacy. The latter at times is referred to as the "*Bar Association*", yet in fact does not amount to such, as, according to the Federal Law of the Russian Federation "*On the Activity of Advocates and Advocacy*", No. 63-ФЗ, of May 31, 2002, membership in advocacy is neither mandatory for Russian lawyers, nor serves as a prerequisite for the admission to general legal practice and the right to represent clients in courts (except for in criminal cases). While special qualification exams and fulfillment of a stage requirement are necessary for the admission to advocacy, most lawyers practice without the latter, *inter alia*, via joining the law firms.

6.16. In the case mentioned above, one of the parties, *Ivsilikat*, challenged the award rendered by the Kostroma Economic Arbitration Court at the LL.C. *"Legal Bureau "Vashe Pravo"* (hereinafter – *"Vashe Pravo")*[27], ordering *Ivsilikat* to pay *Vashe Pravo* a monetary sum[28]. Annulment of the award has been sought in reliance on the infringement of the principles of impartiality of the tribunal due to the fact that the arbitration institution had been established by the Claimant (*Vashe Pravo*) and, thus, could not consider the case brought by the latter. The Arbitrazh Court of Kostroma Region set the award aside[29]. The decision of the lower court has been confirmed by the Federal Arbitrazh court of Volgo-Vyatskij circuit[30]. Subsequently, *Vashe Pravo* challenged the above decisions to the Higher Arbitrazh Court of the Russian Federation, alleging that no infringement of impartiality had occurred. *Vashe Pravo* based its submissions on the principle of the overall independence of the arbitration institution, which is bound only by the relevant law and its arbitration rules as well as the principle of competence-competence[31].

6.17. Nevertheless, in the opinion of the Higher Arbitrazh Court, while

> *[...] the legislation of the Russian Federation contains a general requirement that the arbitrator shall be able to provide impartial resolution of the dispute, should not be directly or indirectly interested in the outcome of the case and should be independent from the parties*[32],

the Kostroma Arbitration Court, according to its founding documents, had been established by the sole shareholder of the LL.C *"Vashe Pravo"* – Ms. Halapsina N.V. Ms. Halapsina on her own promulgated the Arbitration Rules and compiled the list of arbitrators, also appointing herself a chair of the said institution. Moreover, according to Art. 34 of the Arbitration Rules of the Court, the arbitrators in each particular case had to be appointed by the chair of the Court. Consequently, the arbitrator for the case at stake, Mr. Kogan B.L., had been appointed by Ms. Halapsina. On the other hand, the same person, Ms. Halapsina, the only shareholder of *LL. C. "Vashe Pravo"* was also the one who signed the claim submitted for consideration to the arbitration institution.

---

[27] Award rendered by the Kostroma Economic Arbitration Court at the LL.C. *"Juridical Bureau Vashe Pravo"*, dated February 15, 2008, in Case No. 1107/13.

[28] The arbitration has been commenced on the basis of the contract for the advisory services, concluded between the parties on September 20, 2004 (No. 83), the arbitration clause (Section 7) of which referred disputes to the Kostroma Economic Arbitration Court.

[29] Decision of the Arbitrazh Court of Kostroma Region of April 11, 2008.

[30] Decision of Federal Arbitrazh court of Volgo-Vyatskij Circuit of June 16, 2008, in Case No. A31-626/2008-20.

[31] Decision of the Higher Arbitration Court of the Russian Federation of November 10, 2008, in Case No.10509/08.

[32] In particular, the court relied on Arts. 8 and 12 of the Federal Law *"On [Domestic] Arbitration Courts in Russian Federation"* and Arts. 7, 9, 17, 19 II of the Arbitration Rules of the Kostroma Economic Arbitration Court attached to the LL.C. *"Juridical Bureau Vashe Pravo".*

6.18. On the basis of the above factual complex, the court found, that an undue connection existed between the arbitrator and the *LL.C.* "*Vashe Pravo*", the arbitrator being subordinated to the claimant, and, in addition, that the resolution of the dispute involving *LL.C.* "*Vashe Pravo*" by the arbitration court it created itself infringes the subjective impartiality principle, necessitating the annulment of the award rendered. This way the Russian courts have clearly demonstrated that the identity between the arbitration institution, an arbitrator and a party will not be tolerated.

6.19. Another interesting aspect of the Rules is their particular attention to the cases of participation of arbitrators in public [professional] events organized and, as the case may be, sponsored by one of the parties – an instance not addressed by the IBA guidelines. The reason for such an emphasis is in two recent cases dwelling on the same issue, considered by the Russian courts – *Yukos Capital S.A.R.L. (Luxembourg) v. OJSC "Oil Company "Rosneft"" (OJSC "Jugueskneftegaz") (Russian Federation)* and – *"Metaltrade Deutschland GMbH Engineering und Handel" (Germany) v. OJSC "Corporation VSMPO – AVISMA" (Russian Federation)* – concerned with the annulment of the awards of MKAS[33] on the basis of lack of independence and impartiality of the arbitrators. In both cases the challenges were based on the [undisclosed in course of the proceedings] fact of participation of the arbitrators in the conferences, organized by one of the parties to arbitration – *Yukos* and *VSMPO – AVISMA*, respectively.

6.20. In scrutinizing the circumstances in each of the cases, the courts have ultimately reached contrasting results. While in *Yukos* the awards have been set aside due to the finding of the indirect interest of the arbitrators concerned (who, allegedly, received certain compensation for their conference presentations) in the outcome of the case[34], in *VSMPO – AVISMA* the courts decided to confirm the award, explaining, *inter alia*, that in order to prove partiality of the arbitrator, the German party had to provide documentary evidence of the fact that the representative of the party involved (or the party itself) was sponsoring the event, rather than just participating in its organization. Without denying at least persuasive effect of the judgment in the *Yukos* case, rendered earlier, and without

---

[33] Awards of MKAS in Cases Nos. 143/2005 and 145/2005, of September 19, 2006 in Case No. 27/2007 of December 17, 2007, respectively.

[34] Decisions of the Arbitrazh Court of the city of Moscow of May 23, 2007, in Cases No. A40-4577/07-8-46 and No. A40-4582/07-8-47, affirmed by the decisions of the Federal Arbitrazh Court of Moscow Circuit of August 13, 2007 and of Higher Arbitrazh Court of the Russian Federation of December 10, 2007 (No. 14956/07). The same awards, however, have been recognized and enforced in the Netherlands, where their annulment at the seat of arbitration was disregarded on the basis of "*partiality*" of the judicial system of the Russian Federation. See Decisions of the District Court of Amsterdam of February 28, 2008, in Case No. LJN BC8150, Decision of the Court of Appeals of Amsterdam of April 28, 2009, in Case No. LJN BI2451, Decision of the Supreme Court of Netherlands of June 25, 2010, ruling the appeal logged by *Rosneft'* inadmissible, as well as Albert Jan van den Berg, *Enforcement of Arbitral Awards Annulled In Russia: Case Comment on Court of Appeal of Amsterdam, April 28, 2009*, 27 (2) J.INT'L ARB. 179 (2010).

touching upon a value of precedent in the Russian legal system, the courts distinguished between the cases on the basis of the sponsorship of the event as opposed to its *"mere"* organization, founding the *"precedent"* inapplicable to the case under their consideration[35].

6.21. The provision, incorporated into Art.8(2)(9) of the Rules, referring the participation of the arbitrator in the *"public events"* organized or supported by the party to the list of circumstances that do not need to be disclosed unless the arbitrator received a remuneration from the party to arbitration or its representative, clearly follows the courts' conclusions in *VSMPO – AVISMA*. Nevertheless, this solution, as is, *inter alia*, demonstrated by the above decision itself, might have certain problems in terms of its practical implementation, to the extent that it is indeed uneasy to define the *"remuneration"* in the context of participation in the *"public events"* (for instance, would the waiver of the conference fees, coverage of the travel or lodging expenses serve as such?), and, even once defined, to prove it with the documentary evidence.

6.22. One can note many more interesting novelties and peculiarities of the Rules, some of which are backed-up by the quite exciting experiences of the national (and, at times, international) arbitration and judicial practice. Among them – an express exclusion of the [*"separate"*] co-authorship, editing and reviewing from the list of the *"suspicious"* circumstances, that need to be disclosed[36], possibly in the outcry of the German case, in which the chairman of the DIS tribunal was unsuccessfully challenged, being an editor of the *DIS Series* containing a piece authored by the respondent's counsel;[37] a regulation of the professor – student and the PhD supervisor – PhD candidate situations[38] (which, potentially, might necessitate an explicit extension to the other situations arising in the educational environment, say that of the classmates, in light of the recent unsuccessful challenge in the ICSID case involving a proximate neighbour of the Russian Federation – *Alpha Projektholding GmbH (Austria) v. Ukraine*[39]), etc. Nevertheless, on balance, the approach, adopted by the Rules, even though indeed to the extent specific, is coherent in spirit with that of the IBA Guidelines. The Rules could be seen as a big pro-arbitration step in the legal framework of the Russian Federation.

---

[35] Decision of the Arbitrazh Court of the city of Moscow of June 23, 2006, in Case No. A40-18045/08-50-180, denying the set aside request, affirmed by the Federal Arbitrazh Court of the Moscow circuit on August 28, 2008. Decision of the Higher Arbitrazh Court of the Russian Federation of November 13, 2008, in Case No. 14732/08 (cassation denied).

[36] Rules, Art. 8(2)(5).

[37] Decision of Higher Regional Court of Frankfurt am Main, Case No. 26 Sch 8/07, of October 4, 2007.

[38] Rules, Arts. 6(3)(9) and 8(2)(2).

[39] *Alpha Projektholding GmbH v. Ukraine*, ICSID Case No. ARB/07/16, Decision on Respondent's Proposal to Disqualify Arbitrator Dr. Yoram Turbowicz of March 19, 2010.

Table I: Circumstances Relevant to the Assessment of the Conflicts of Interest under the Rules on Impartiality and Independence of the Arbitrators and IBA Guidelines on Conflicts of Interest in International Arbitration: A Comparison

Rules on Impartiality and Independence of the Arbitrators	IBA Guidelines on Conflicts of Interest in International Arbitration
RELATIONSHIP OF THE ARBITRATOR TO THE ARBITRAL INSTITUTION	
1. The arbitrator holds a position in the institution which is an appointing authority	
Not addressed	Orange list – 3.5.3.

Rules on Impartiality and Independence of the Arbitrators	IBA Guidelines on Conflicts of Interest in International Arbitration
RELATIONSHIP OF THE ARBITRATOR TO THE DISPUTE	
1. Prior involvement of the arbitrator in the case as a party, counsel, expert, consultant, witness	
Red list [non-waivable] – Art. 5(1)(1)	Red list [non-waivable] -1.1.; [waivable] – 2.1.2. (and 2.1.1.)
2. Prior involvement of the spouse or close family member of the arbitrator in the case as a party, counsel, expert, consultant, witness	
Red list [non-waivable] – Art. 5(1)(1)	Red list [waivable] – 2.3.8.
3. Public Statement, made by the arbitrator about the case, in particular – the legal evaluation of the latter	
Red list [non-waivable] – Art. 5(1)(5)	Orange list – 3.5.2.
4. Public Statement of general nature, made by the arbitrator concerning the legal issue that also arises in the case	
Green list – Art. 8(2)(1)	Green list – 4.1.1.

Rules on Impartiality and Independence of the Arbitrators	IBA Guidelines on Conflicts of Interest in International Arbitration
RELATION OF THE ARBITRATOR'S LAW FIRM TO THE DISPUTE	
1. Prior involvement of the arbitrator's law firm in the case (without the involvement of the arbitrator)	
Not addressed	Red list [waivable] – 2.3.5.

Rules on Impartiality and Independence of the Arbitrators	IBA Guidelines on Conflicts of Interest in International Arbitration
ARBITRATOR'S DIRECT OR INDIRECT INTEREST IN THE DISPUTE	
1. Identity between the party and the arbitrator	
Not explicitly addressed	Red list [non-waivable] –1.1.
2. Shareholding and/or control in the party by arbitrator, his spouse, close family member	
Substantial: Red list [non-waivable] – Art. 5(1)(2)	Red list [non-waivable] –1.1., 1.2., 1.3.; [waivable] – 2.2.1., 2.3.4., 2.3.8., 2.3.9.; Orange list – 3.5.1., 3.5.4.
Not Substantial: Orange list – Art. 6(3)(6)	Green list – 4.5.2.
3. Significant financial interest of the arbitrator or his close family member in the outcome of the dispute	
Red (non-waivable) list – Art. 5(1)(2) [Indirectly]	Red list [non-waivable] –1.3.; [waivable] – 2.2.2.

RELATIONSHIP BETWEEN THE ARBITRATORS	
1. Marriage or close family ties between the arbitrators	
Red list [non-waivable] – Art. 5(1)(3)	Not addressed
2. The co-arbitrators are lawyers in the same firm	
Green list – Art.8(2)(4)	Orange list – 3.3.1.
3. Affiliation between the arbitrators, arbitrator and counsel within the past 3 years (partnership, etc)	
Not addressed	Orange list – 3.3.3.
4. The arbitrator is inferior in terms of the workplace hierarchy to the co-arbitrator or a chair	
Orange list – Art. 6(3)(5)	Not addressed
5. Two or more arbitrators sit together on a different tribunal at the same or different institution	
Green list – Art. 8(2)(6)	Not addressed

RELATIONSHIP BETWEEN THE ARBITRATOR'S LAW FIRM AND A PARTY	
1. Participation of the law firm of the arbitrator in the different unrelated legal proceedings as a counsel for the party opposing a party to the arbitration at stake	
Ongoing: Not addressed	Orange list – 3.4.1.
In past and without the participation of the arbitrator: Not addressed	Green list – 4.2.1.
2. A lawyer in the arbitrator's law firm serves as an arbitrator in the other dispute involving the same party, parties or their affiliates	
Not addressed	Orange list – 3.3.4.
3. A close family member of the arbitrator is a partner/ employee in the law firm representing one of the parties, not participating in such a representation	
Not addressed	Orange list – 3.3.5.
4. Ongoing commercial relations between the arbitrator's law firm and one of the parties or its affiliate	
Significant: Not addressed	Red list [non-waivable] – 2.3.6.
Insignificant: Orange list – Art.6(3)(3)	Orange list – 3.2.1.
5. Involvement of the law firm associated with the arbitrator's law firm in representation of one of the parties	
In case of the fee-sharing: Not addressed	Orange list – 3.2.2.
Without sharing of the fees or other revenues: Not addressed	Green list 4.3.1.
6. Regular representation of the party (or its affiliate) by the arbitrator or by the arbitrator's law firm (without involvement in the dispute at stake)	
Not addressed	Orange list – 3.2.3.

RELATIONSHIP BETWEEN THE ARBITRATOR AND THE PARTY	
1. Employment or contractual (remunerated) ties between the arbitrator and the party to arbitration (or its representative)	
Ongoing: Red list [non-waivable] – Art. 5(1)(4)	Red list [non-waivable] -1.4.; [waivable] – 2.3.2., 2.3.7.
Within the past 3 years: Orange list – Art. 6(3)(1)	Orange list – 3.4.2.
2. Participation of the arbitrator in the different unrelated legal proceedings as a counsel, expert or consultant of one of the parties to arbitration	
Ongoing: Red list [non-waivable] – Art. 5(1)(4)	Red list [non-waivable] -1.4.; [waivable] – 2.3.1., 2.3.7; Orange list – 3.2.3.
Within the past 3 years: Orange list – Art. 6(3)(1)	Orange list – 3.1.1.
3. Participation of the arbitrator in the different unrelated legal proceedings as a counsel for the party opposing the party to the present arbitration (within past 3 years)	
Not addressed	Orange list – 3.1.2.
4. Participation of the arbitrator in the arbitration on a related issue involving one of the parties or its affiliate	
Not addressed	Orange list – 3.1.5.
5. Prior appointment as an arbitrator by the party/ in the case involving the party	
Connected case: Orange list – Art. 6(3)(7)	Not addressed
Unconnected case or connected case commenced simultaneously: Green list – Art. 8(2)(8)	Not addressed
More than 3 occasions: Not addressed	Orange list – 3.3.7.
6. Discussion of the issues, pertaining to arbitration, between the arbitrator and one of the parties (or the counsel of the latter)	
Orange list – Art. 6(3)(8)	Not addressed
7. Close friendship ties between the arbitrator and the individual having controlling influence in the party, its affiliate, witness, expert, unconnected to the professional activity and membership in professional associations and social organizations	
Not addressed	Orange list – 3.4.3.
8. The arbitrator is a former judge, who has heard a significant number of cases involving one of the parties within past 3 years	
Not addressed	Orange list – 3.4.4.
9. Initial contact of the arbitrator with the party prior to the appointment	
Not addressed	Green list – 4.5.1.
10. The arbitrator and a individual having control over the party to arbitration have worked together in the professional capacity	
Not addressed	Green list – 4.5.3.
11. The arbitrator is a consumer of products/ services, offered by the party to arbitration, if such products/ services are acquired by the arbitrator on the conditions, on which such goods and services are offered to the other consumers	
Green list Art. 8(2)(11)	Not addressed
12. The arbitrator participated in public events (conferences, seminars, presentations) organized and financed by the party or its representative, given that the arbitrator was not receiving remuneration from the party or its representative	
Green list – Art. 8(2)(9)	Not addressed

RELATIONSHIP BETWEEN ARBITRATOR AND COUNSEL, WITNESS, EXPERT OR CONSULTANT	
1. Membership of the arbitrator and the counsel of the party in the same law firm/ organization	
Orange list – Art. 6(3)(4)	Red list [waivable] – 2.3.3.
2. PhD Dissertation Supervision, exercised in course of the past 3 years, by the arbitrator over the counsel and visa-versa	
Orange list – Art. 6(3)(9)	Not addressed
3. Close friendship ties between the arbitrator and the counsel, unconnected to the professional activity and membership in professional associations and social organizations	
Orange list – Art. 6(3)(10)	Orange list – 3.3.6.
4. Established relationships between the arbitrators, the arbitrator and the counsel via the membership in professional organization or via prior involvement in the different arbitrations as arbitrators or counsels	
Green list – Art. 8(2)(3)	Green list – 4.4.1./4.4.2.
5. *"Separate"* co-authorship of the one collective work, editing or reviewing of the same work by the two or more arbitrators, an arbitrator and a counsel, expert, consultant, witness	
Green list – Art. 8(2)(5)	Not addressed
6. The counsel of the party is or has been a student in the University where the arbitrator is/ has been a professor	
Green list – Art. 8(2)(2)	Not addressed
7. The arbitrator and the counsel, the expert, the consultant or the witness sat or are sitting on the different arbitration panels in the unconnected dispute	
Green list – Art. 8(2)(7)	Not addressed
8. The arbitrator and the counsel, the expert, the consultant or the witness of the party are mentioned in the same institutional list of arbitrators	
Green list – Art. 8(2)(10)	Not addressed

| | |

Summaries

DEU [*Interessenkonflikte im bereich der Schiedsgerichtsbarkeit: Neues aus der Russischen Föderation*]

Die Unbefangenheit und Unabhängigkeit von Schiedsrichtern – Konzepte, die ganz im Vorfeld der Schiedsgerichtsbarkeit stehen und letzten Endes deren Legitimität gewährleisten – haben stets das Interesse der juristischen Lehre und Praxis auf sich gezogen. Im Jahre 2004 kam es zu einem bahnbrechenden Wandel in Sachen der Entwicklung international anerkannter Grundsätze in diesem Bereich, als die IBA (International Bar Association – der Internationale Rechtsanwaltsverband) ihre „Guidelines on Conflicts of Interests in International Arbitration" (Richtlinien zu Interessenkonflikten in der internationalen Schiedsgerichtsbarkeit) veröffentlichte. Dennoch, und ungeachtet der optimistischen Erwartungen der federführenden Autoren, führten die IBA-Richtlinien nicht zu einer vereinfachten Entscheidungspraxis der Gerichte und Schiedsgerichte in der Russischen Föderation, was Interessenkonflikte anbelangt. Um die Lücke abzudecken, verabschiedete die Industrie- und Handelskammer der Russischen Föderation Ende August 2010 eine „russische Fassung" der Guidelines, bezeichnet als „Regeln für die Unbefangenheit und Unabhängigkeit von Schiedsrichtern". Der vorliegende Artikel ist zielt darauf ab, die Gründe zu analysieren, die der Verabschiedung der Regeln zugrunde lagen, sowie deren strukturelle Besonderheiten, und unterzieht insbesondere den Inhalt dieses Instruments einer genauen Prüfung, um Erklärungsversuche für die Einbeziehung bestimmter Regeln anzustellen – dabei mag es sich um einen Verweis auf hergebrachte Präzedenzfälle handeln, oder um regionales kulturelles Erbe, oder um eine Anerkennung der juristischen Realitäten. Die Studie geht dabei entlang der komparativen Linie vor und vergleicht den von den Regeln gewählten Ansatz mit dem Ansatz, der im Text der IBA-Richtlinien Niederschlag gefunden hat.

CZE *[Střety zájmů v rozhodčím řízení: zprávy z Ruské federace]*
Nestrannost a nezávislost rozhodců, kteří stojí přímo v popředí rozhodčího řízení a v podstatě zajišťují jeho zákonnost, byly vždy předmětem pozornosti akademiků i praktiků. Velkým průlomem v oblasti mezinárodně uznávaných standardů v této oblasti byl rok 2004, kdy Mezinárodní asociace advokátů (IBA) zveřejnila Guidelines on Conflicts of Interest in International Arbitration (Pokyny pro řešení střetů zájmů v mezinárodním rozhodčím řízení). I přes optimistická očekávání jejich autorů však v Ruské federaci nedošlo při řešení střetu zájmů k usnadnění praxe tamějších soudů a tribunálů. Obchodní a průmyslová komora Ruské federace vydala na konci srpna 2010 „ruskou verzi" pokynů – Pravidla nestrannosti a nezávislosti rozhodců, kterými vyplnila aktuálně chybějící úpravu. Tento článek se zaměřuje na rozbor důvodů k přijetí pravidel, jejich strukturální zvláštnosti, a zejména zkoumá obsah tohoto nástroje, přičemž se snaží hledat vysvětlení pro zahrnutí určitých ustanovení do pravidel, ať již odkazem na dřívější precedenty, na regionální kulturní dědictví, nebo na právní reálie. Studie je vypracována jako komparativní, kdy je proti sobě kladen přístup použitý v pravidlech a přístup odrážející se v textu pokynů vypracovaných Mezinárodní asociací advokátů.

| | |

POL *[Sprzeczność interesów w arbitrażu: aktualna sytuacja w Federacji Rosyjskiej]*
Niniejszy artykuł poświęcony jest analizie Regulaminu bezstronności i niezależności arbitrów, zatwierdzonego przez przewodniczącego Izby Przemysłowo-Handlowej Federacji Rosyjskiej w 2010 roku. Omawia on przyczyny jego przyjęcia, szczegółową strukturę oraz powody, dla których konkretne sytuacje określane są jako niosące ryzyko naruszenia bezstronności i niezależności arbitrów. Cechy charakterystyczne rosyjskiego podejścia porównano tutaj z charakterystyką opublikowaną w podobnym dokumencie w 2004 roku przez Międzynarodowe Stowarzyszenie Prawników (IBA).

FRA [*Conflits d'intérêts et arbitrage: Tendances récentes en Fédération de Russie*]

La présente contribution a trait à la mise en oeuvre des Lignes Directrices de l'IBA sur les conflits d'intérêts dans l'arbitrage international en Fédération de Russie. Suite à l'absence d'application par les cours et tribunaux russes des Lignes Directrices de l'IBA, une 'version russe' des Lignes Directrices a été adoptée en 2010 par la Chambre de Commerce et d'Industrie de la Fédération de Russie à travers la formulation de 'Règles d'Impartialité et d'Indépendance des arbitres'. La contribution met en relief les raisons qui ont présidé à l'adoption des 'Règles d'Impartialité et d'Indépendance des arbitres', leurs particularités et traits caractéristiques. Elle met également en exergue le contenu singulier de certaines dispositions et leur spécificité. Enfin, l'accent est mis sur une comparaison entre les Règles d'Impartialité et d'Indépendance des arbitres' et les Lignes Directrices de l'IBA.

RUS [*Конфликт интересов в арбитраже: новости из Российской Федерации*]

Статья посвящена анализу Правил о беспристрастности и независимости третейских судей, утвержденных в 2010 году Президентом Торгово-Промышленной Палаты Российской Федерации. Рассматриваются причины принятия Правил, их структурные особенности, мотивы охарактеризирования тех или иных ситуаций как представляющих риск для беспристрастности и независимости третейского судьи. Особенности Российского подхода сопоставляются с подходом, отображенном в документе схожего характера, опубликованом в 2004 Международной Ассоциацией Юристов.

ES [*Conflictos de intereses en el arbitraje: noticias de la Federación Rusa*]

El artículo analiza las Reglas para la imparcialidad e independencia de los árbitros, aprobadas por el Presidente de la Cámara de comercio e industria de la Federación Rusa en 2010. En ellas, se describen los motivos para adoptar las Reglas, las características estructurales particulares de las mismas y los motivos para la caracterización de determinadas situaciones como riesgos que afectan a la imparcialidad e independencia de los árbitros. Las características particulares del enfoque ruso se comparan con las que aparecen detalladas en un documento similar publicado en 2004 por la International Bar Association (IBA).

Czech (& Central European) Yearbook of Arbitration

Vladimir Khvalei

Constitutional Grounds for Arbitration and Arbitrability of Disputes in Russia and Other CIS Countries

Key words:
Objective arbitrability
| subjective
arbitrability | Russia |
arbitration

Abstract | *Limits of arbitability are based on balance between constitutional right to protect civil rights by any means which are not directly prohibited by the law, which includes the right to submit a dispute to arbitration, and intention of a state to retain control over certain areas of civil and economic activities. Thus, a state could exclude certain type of disputes from arbitrable, which is understood as limits of objective arbitrability. A state also could limit an ability of certain entities to be a party to arbitration, thus limiting subjective arbitrability. The scope of arbitrable disputes defers from a country to country, depending on level of control the state wants to keep over arbitration. However, there are some features common to some CIS countries: Belarus, Kazakhstan, Russia and Ukraine exclude from arbitrable disputes related to immovable property. There is also a tendency to exclude corporate disputes as well.*

| | |

Vladimir Khvalei,
MCIArb, is a partner
in the Moscow
office of Baker &
McKenzie and heads
the firm's CIS Dispute
Resolution Practice
Group. Mr. Khvalei
is Vice-President of
the ICC International
Court of Arbitration,
chairs the Arbitration
Commission of ICC
Russia and is also
included on the
list of arbitrators
of the arbitration
institutions in Austria,
Russia, Belarus and
Kazakhstan.
e-mail:
Vladimir.Khvalei@
bakermckenzie.com

I. A Few Words about the Terms "Arbitration", "Arbitrazh" and "Arbitrability"

7.01. In the Soviet Union, disputes between companies fell under the jurisdiction of so-called "state arbitrazh", which in fact was a department in the government with a status similar to a ministry. To apply the term "arbitrazh," which traditionally applied only for arbitration[1], to a quasi-judicial system can hardly be considered a good idea. However it is unlikely that in Soviet times, given the undeveloped state of arbitration proceedings, that anyone would have paid serious attention to such a terminological error[2]. State arbitrazh in the USSR was subordinated to the USSR Government. Alongside it, some state arbitrazh were subordinated to the governments of the Union republics, to the governments of municipalities, and so forth.

7.02. During the period of Gorbachev's reforms, when much attention was given to the question of separation of powers, it became obvious that the disputes should be resolved not by some ministry or department, but by a court, i.e. a body formally dependent neither on legislative authority, nor on the executive.

7.03. Thus, on the basis of state arbitrazh, a system of commercial courts was created. Due to the collapse of the USSR, this process was completed in the newly created independent states, former Soviet republics. In Belarus, and Ukraine such courts were called "commercial courts"; in Kazakhstan "economic" courts, and only Russia inherited the historic terminological error and continued to use the term "arbitrazh" in reference to state courts dealing with commercial disputes, which are officially called "arbitration courts". This terminological confusion, in practice, creates serious problems, as the dispute resolution clause referring to "arbitration court in Moscow" could be equally interpreted as referring to the state commercial court or to arbitration.

7.04. In order to find a way around the problem, the Russian legal community proposed a new English term for state arbitration courts –

---

[1] For example, in English law the term "arbiter" meant, as of 1549, "a person chosen by two disputants to resolve the dispute", DOUGLAS HARPER, ONLINE ETYMOLOGY DICTIONARY (2001), available at:
http://www.etymonline.com/index.php?search=arbiter&searchmode=none
(accessed on November 30, 2010).

[2] The system of state arbitrazh was created in 1922, after the end of the Russian Civil War, when due to the changeover to the NEP [New Economic Policy] from the policy of so called "military communism" the Soviet Union decided to built a regulated market economy, where the state controlled companies played the main role. At the same time a system of "Arbitrazh" was created. "Arbitrazh" courts formally were not parts of the judiciary and had a status either of "Ministerial Arbitrazh", i.e. the status of department in the ministry in charge of resolving disputes between the state companies of the same ministry or "Inter-Ministerial Arbitrazh" in charge of resolving disputes between the companies subordinated to different ministries. Apparently, applying an analogy with arbitration courts it was decided to name these departments "arbitrazh."

"arbitrazh courts" aimed at distinguishing them from *"arbitration courts"*. That said, in order to rule out completely the possibility of confusion, lawyers often refer to state courts considering commercial disputes as "state arbitrazh courts". Correspondingly, the procedural code which regulates the procedure for considering disputes in state arbitrazh courts is referred to as the Arbitrazh Procedural Code (APC for short).

7.05   Likewise, the word "arbitrability" does not exist in dictionaries of the Russian language; however, recently this term became popular among arbitration practitioners. As far as the meaning of this term varies from jurisdiction to jurisdiction, in this article "arbitrability" will be defined as an "external" restriction of the scope of disputes which may be referred to arbitration, where "external" means a restriction established by law or court practice. Arbitrability could be limited by subject matter of disputes (so called "objective" arbitrability) or by personal capacity to submit disputes to arbitration ("subjective" arbitrability").

II. Constitutional Grounds for Arbitration

7.06.   The Constitution of the Russian Federation not only guarantees protection of human and citizens' rights and freedoms[3], but also sets forth that:[4]

> *Each person is entitled to protect his or her rights and freedoms by any and all means not prohibited by law.*

Thus, the general rule established by the Russian Constitution says that any party is entitled to protect its own rights and freedoms by any means, even if such means are not provided specifically by law, but do not contradict it. Applying to arbitration for protection of a violated right constitutes a means of protection of civil right which is not only not prohibited, but explicitly provided by law.

7.07.   Thus, according to the Civil Code of the Russian Federation:[5]

> *A court, arbitrazh court, or arbitration court (hereinafter: court) shall effectuate the protection of violated or contested civil rights in accordance with the jurisdiction of cases established by procedural law.*

Under the Law "On Arbitration Courts in the Russian Federation," which applies to domestic disputes, any dispute deriving from civil law relations can be referred to an arbitration court unless otherwise established by federal law[6]. The Arbitrazh Procedural Code of the Russian Federation likewise contains the same provision[7].

---

3   Article 45.1 of Constitution of the Russian Federation, 12 December 1993 (*"RF Consitution"*)

4   Article 45.2 of RF Constitution.

5   Article 11.1 of Civil Code of the Russian Federation (*"RF CC"*). Part I adopted by the Federal Law No. 51-FZ of 30 November 1994.

6   Article 1.2 of Federal Law No. 102-FZ "On Arbitration Courts in the Russian Federation" of 24 July 2002 (as amended 27 July 2010).

7   Article 4.6 of Arbitrazh Procedural Code of the Russian Federation, Federal Law No. 95-FZ of 24 July 2002.

7.08. The civil procedural legislation of the Russian Federation states that any dispute subject to jurisdiction of courts of general jurisdiction arising out of civil law relations may be referred by agreement of the parties to arbitration at any moment until the trial court takes decision ending the proceedings on its merits, unless otherwise provided by federal law[8].

7.09. Finally, the Russian Law "On International Commercial Arbitration" also speaks about the possibility of referring to arbitration of those disputes, which involve contractual and other civil law relations arising out of foreign trade and other types of international economic transactions, if a commercial enterprise of at least one of the parties has its place of business abroad[9].Therefore the right to refer a dispute to arbitration constitutes a means of protection of civil rights is established by the Constitution of the Russian Federation, as well as by the Russian federal laws.

7.10. Nonetheless, in Soviet times, due to a variety of reasons, arbitration hardly existed in the USSR, except for the activity of the Foreign Trade Arbitration Commission at the RF Chamber of Commerce and Industry. The development of a market economy after Gorbachev's reforms inevitably led to a situation where, alongside with the appearance of private businesses, arbitration began to develop as an alternative form of dispute resolution. Along with that, such advantages of arbitration as the independence from the state and the impossibility of arbitral awards review on the merits by state courts, aroused serious dissatisfaction among certain people who had previously not had experience with arbitration. In their efforts to prevent the enforcement of awards unfavourable to them, they tried to find a way to establish that arbitration itself was contrary to the Constitution, insofar as it limited a party's right to judicial protection, that is, a resort to a state court.

7.11. This question has repeatedly been the subject of consideration by the Russian Constitutional Court, in particular, upon the application of joint-stock company ALROSA ("AK ALROSA"). In its appeal to the Constitutional Court, AK ALROSA challenged the constitutionality of Article 5 of Russian Federation Law "On International Commercial Arbitration," under which no judicial interference should take place in matters regulated by this Law except in cases when the Law so specifies.

---

[8] Article 3.3 of Civil Procedural Code of the Russian Federation, Federal Law No. 138-FZ of 14 November 2002.

[9] Article 1.2 of Law of the Russian Federation No. 5338-I *"On International Commercial Arbitration"* of 7 July 1993.

7.12. The Constitutional Court rejected the application, stating:[10]

> *Restriction of the competence of courts of general jurisdiction[11] when considering applications for setting aside the ICAC[12] award is in fact a necessary guarantee of the parties' right to freedom of contract and their exercise of the right to judicial protection in that procedural form which was freely selected and which does not rule out the possibility of applying to courts of general jurisdiction concerning matters arising in connection with the consideration of a case by arbitration courts, on grounds specified by the Russian Federation Law 'On International Commercial Arbitration'.*

Previously, the Constitutional Court stated[13] that when entering into contracts with arbitration agreements (clauses), subjects of civil law relations, exercising the right to freedom of contract, voluntarily reject the resolution of disputes by a state court by independently selecting arbitration institutions and appointing arbitrators, and assume the obligations to subordinate themselves to rules regulating the procedure for setting aside and enforcement of arbitral awards. Thus, this cannot be viewed as a breach of constitutional rights. It should be noted that similar situations were subject to some controversies in the other CIS states.

7.13. Thus, for example, the state company Slavutich-Stal, after an award was issued against it under the Rules of the International Commercial Arbitration Court at the Chamber of Commerce and Industry of Ukraine, applied to the Constitutional Court of Ukraine with an inquiry as whether activity of this arbitration court shall not be considered as illegal performance of functions of a state court, although according to the Constitution of Ukraine it did not belong to the country's court system. Fortunately, the Constitutional Court of Ukraine disagreed with the applicant. However, in some countries of the former USSR, the opponents of arbitration were more successful.

7.14. In 2002, the Constitutional Court of the Republic of Kazakhstan found that due to the inadmissibility of waiver of the right to judicial protection, an arbitral award may be appealed on the merits if it contradicts legislation.

---

[10] Ruling of RF Constitutional Court of 20 February 2002, No. 54-O *"On refusal to admit for consideration the application of joint-stock company ALROSA on breach of constitutional rights and freedoms by articles 5 and 34 of Russian Federation Law 'On International Commercial Arbitration'".*

[11] At that time disputes related to setting aside an arbitral award felt within competence of Russian courts of general jurisdiction.

[12] ICAC or, according to Russian acronym *"MKAS"* is the International Commercial Court of Arbitration at the Chamber of Commerce and Industry of the Russian Federation.

[13] Ruling of RF Constitutional Court of 15 May 2001, *On the application of AK ALROSA on breach of constitutional rights and freedoms by articles 35.1 of Russian Federation Law "On International Commercial Arbitration".*

Fortunately, this decision did not last long, and in fact was overruled by the laws *"On Courts of Arbitration"* and *"On International Commercial Arbitration"* passed in December 2004.

7.15. The Constitutional Court of Kyrgyzstan went even further, finding that arbitration courts were not named by Constitution as a part of Kyrgyzstan judiciary system, and thus, they were illegal. This problem, however, was resolved after new article was introduced on 21 October 2007 to the Constitution of the Kyrgyz Republic explicitly stating the possibility of resolution of civil law disputes by arbitration[14]. Fortunately, this kind of approach has already passed into history, and at present hardly anyone will cast doubt on the constitutionality of the existence of arbitration. Nonetheless, it would be incorrect to say that disputes regarding the possibility of referring this or that dispute for arbitration have ceased at all.

7.16. Without pretending to make a comprehensive analysis of regulation of arbitrability, the author will provide below some information as to how this issue is regulated in the Russian Federation, as well as some other CIS countries (Belarus, Kazakhstan, Ukraine).

III. Determination of Applicable Law When Resolving Matters Involving Arbitrability

7.17. The matter of arbitrability of a dispute cannot be discussed in the abstract without any relation to what court or arbitral tribunal will decide on this question. In theory, a dispute on arbitrability may be considered by:

(i) a state court to which has been submitted a claim on a dispute covered by the arbitration agreement, while considering the issue of validity of agreement to arbitrate;

(ii) an arbitral tribunal when its competence is challenged;

(iii) a state court at the place of arbitration, when reviewing an application for setting aside the arbitral award; or

(iv) a state court at the place where recognition or enforcement of a foreign arbitral award is sought.

7.18. In an ideal world, in all the four above cases, both state courts and the arbitral tribunal must come to the same conclusion regarding the arbitrability of the subject of the dispute; however, this is not so. And it is not only because of a different liberal or conservative approach to the interpretation of legislation, which could be taken by different *forums*, but also due to the fact that courts or arbitral tribunals may apply a different law when deciding this issue, and thus come to a different result.

---

[14] Article 38 of the Constitution of the Kyrgyz Republic: *For out-of-court settlement of disputes arising from civil law relations, citizens of the Kyrgyz Republic are entitled to establish arbitration courts. The authority, method of creation and activity of arbitration courts are defined by law.*

III.1. The State Court and the Determination of a Claim's Arbitrability

7.19. The matter of arbitrability of a dispute may arise in the state court if a party has submitted a claim covered by the arbitration agreement, and the other party argues that the state court lacks jurisdiction because of the parties' agreement to resolve this matter by arbitration. According to the New York Convention:

> *The court of a Contracting State, when seized of an action in a matter in respect of which the parties have made an agreement within the meaning of this article, shall, at the request of one of the parties, refer the parties to arbitration, unless it finds that the said agreement is null and void, inoperative or incapable of being performed[15].*

7.20. A similar provision can be found in the European Convention on International Commercial Arbitration of 1961 (the "European Convention")[16], and in the UNCITRAL Model Law "On International Commercial Arbitration" dated 21 June 1985 (hereinafter the "UNCITRAL Model Law"):

> *A court before which an action is brought in a matter which is the subject of an arbitration agreement shall, if a party so requests not later than when submitting his first statement on the substance of the dispute, refer the parties to arbitration unless it finds that the agreement is null and void, inoperative or incapable of being performed[17].*

7.21. The RF Arbitrazh Procedural Code provides that a court shall leave a claim without consideration, which is tantamount to a refusal to examine a case on its merits:[18]

> *An arbitrazh court shall leave a statement of claim without consideration if it finds... that:*
>
> ...
>
> *5) there exists an agreement between the parties to refer the dispute to arbitration ...;*
>
> *6) the parties have entered into an agreement to refer the dispute to arbitration during the court proceedings before the decision is passed ending the proceedings on its merits...*

These provisions therefore oblige a state court to refuse to consider a dispute on the merits given the existence of a valid arbitration agreement. However, this obligation arises solely in case that the court *does not find that the said agreement is null and void, inoperative or incapable of being performed.*

---

15 Article II (3) of 1958 Convention on the Recognition and Enforcement of Foreign Arbitral Awards.
16 Article IV.3 of European Convention.
17 Article 8.1 of UNCITRAL Model Law. See also Article 8.1 of RF Law "On International Commercial Arbitration."
18 Article 148 (5) and (6) of RF APC.

7.22. According to general approach the lack of arbitrability of a dispute covered by the arbitration agreement results in invalidity of the arbitration agreement. Moreover, the wording of the New York Convention and UNCITRAL Model Law allows to conclude that the court must analyse the issue of arbitrability *ex officio*. When assessing the validity of an arbitration agreement, the court should apply not the laws of its own country, but the laws chosen by the parties as applicable to the arbitration agreement or *lex arbitri*[19]. In practice, however, on very few occasions did the parties make explicit choice of the law applicable to an arbitration agreement. Therefore, by default an arbitration agreement is governed by *lex arbitri*, which is logical, as the arbitral award could be set aside only by a state court at the place of arbitration, which will apply its own law when assessing the validity of the arbitration agreement.

7.23. However, when considering the validity of arbitration agreement, in some cases a state court cannot determine the law which shall be applied to the arbitration agreement. For example, if the parties have chosen neither the law applicable to the arbitration agreement nor the place of arbitration, then the place of arbitration and consequently, also the *lex arbitri*, may be determined only after the initiation of arbitration proceedings[20]. If the arbitration has not yet been initiated or remains at the stage where the place of arbitration has still not been designated, the state court will not be able to determine the *lex arbitri* based on the place of arbitration, and therefore will have no choice than apply the appropriate conflict of laws rule of its own country[21].

---

[19] Article V (1a) of the New York Convention states that the law applicable to an arbitration agreement is the law *to which the parties subordinate that agreement, and in the absence of such indication...*the law of *the country where the award was granted*. A similar standard is found in clause 2 of Article VI of the European Convention.

[20] Under the UNCITRAL Model Law, in the absence of parties' agreement on the place of arbitration, the place of arbitration is determined by the arbitral tribunal – Article 20.1; a similar provision is found in the RF Law "On International Commercial Arbitration." According to the ICC Arbitration Rules, in the absence of agreement between the parties the place of arbitration is determined by the Court (Article 14.1).

[21] According to Article VI.2 of the European Convention *In taking a decision concerning the existence or the validity of an arbitration agreement, courts of Contracting States shall examine the validity of such agreement with reference to the capacity of the parties, under the law applicable to them, and with reference to other questions: (a) under the law to which the parties have subjected their arbitration agreement; (b) failing any indication thereon, under the law of the country in which the award is to be made; (c) failing any indication as to the law to which the parties have subjected the agreement, and where at the time when the question is raised in court the country in which the award is to be made cannot be determined, under the competent law by virtue of the rules of conflict of the court seized of the dispute.* Federal Law of Switzerland on International Private Law of 18 December 1987 (Article 178.2): A*n arbitration agreement is valid if it conforms either to the law chosen by the parties, or to the law governing the subject-matter of the dispute, in particular the main contract, or to Swiss law.* The legislation of the Russian Federation applicable to this situation does not contain a conflict rule dealing with arbitration agreements, due to which a Russian court

7.24. Furthermore, according to the European Convention irrespective of the law applicable to the arbitration agreement, the court may declare it invalid if under the laws of the court's country the subject of the dispute cannot be the subject to arbitration[22]. Therefore a state court to which has been submitted a claim on a dispute covered by the arbitration agreement, should apply to the validity of the arbitration agreement:

(i) the law named by the parties as the law applicable to the arbitration agreement;

(ii) in the absence of such, the law of the place of arbitration (*lex arbitri*);

(iii) if it is impossible to determine *the place* of arbitration – the law established in compliance with the conflict rule of the court's country;

(iv) and also in any case the law of the court's country relating to the arbitrability of a dispute.

III.2. Determination of Arbitrability by an Arbitral Tribunal

7.25. An arbitral tribunal may consider the arbitrability of the dispute's subject if one of the parties challenges the jurisdiction of the tribunal, referring to the non-arbitrability as a basis for the invalidity of the arbitration agreement. Even in a case where a party does not challenge the jurisdiction of the arbitral tribunal, the arbitrators are under the duty to do the same *ex officio* and, in principle, may come to the conclusion that they do not have jurisdiction. This follows from the fact that it is believed that the duty of arbitrators is to render a valid award, i.e. an award which will not be set aside by a competent court of the country where the award was issued. The non-arbitrability of a dispute will serve as a ground for setting aside the award by a state court, therefore, the arbitrators themselves must decline their jurisdiction if they find that the dispute it is not arbitrable.

7.26. An arbitral tribunal deciding on the issues of arbitrability shall apply the law chosen by the parties. So, for instance, parties to a contract can state explicitly that both the contract and the arbitration agreement therein shall be regulated by the legislation of the Russian Federation. Based on the autonomy of the arbitration agreement, the parties can also choose as the law applicable to the arbitration agreement a law different from the law applicable to the main contract. Thus, for example, the main contract may be regulated by the laws of the Russian Federation, while the arbitration agreement is regulated by Swedish law.

---

lacks another way out except by applying Russian law to the arbitration agreement, if the parties have not chosen the law applicable to the arbitration agreement, and the place of arbitration is undefined.

[22] Article VI.2 of the European Convention states as follows: *The courts may also refuse recognition of the arbitration agreement if under the law of their country the dispute is not capable of settlement by arbitration.*

7.27. However, parties quite rarely indicate the law applicable to the arbitration agreement. Therefore, practically speaking, in most cases the choice of the law applicable to the arbitration agreement is determined by the choice of the place of arbitration[23]. As mentioned above, in a case when the place of arbitration is not defined by the parties, it is determined either by the arbitration institute or the arbitral tribunal considering the dispute. In view of the foregoing, the arbitral tribunal, when deciding whether the dispute is arbitrable or not, applies a) the law named by the parties, and b) the law of the place of arbitration apply.

7.28. One should also take into account the fact that the ICC Arbitration Rules, for example, impose on the arbitral tribunals a duty to make every effort to make sure that the award is enforceable at law[24]. Due to this, arbitrators should also take into account the arbitrability of a dispute under the law of the country where the arbitral award most likely to be enforced.

III.3. Determination of Arbitrability by a State Court at the Place of Arbitration

7.29. A state court at the place of arbitration may consider matters of arbitrability when evaluating the validity of an arbitration agreement if one of the parties has submitted an application for setting aside the arbitral award. That said the court must consider this issue *ex officio*[25].

7.30. The Russian Federation Law "On International Commercial Arbitration" contains a provision under which the arbitral award can be set aside if the subject of the dispute cannot be referred to arbitration under the laws of the Russian Federation[26]. A similar provision could be found in the Federal Law "On Arbitration Courts in the Russian Federation"[27], applicable to domestic arbitration, as well as in the RF APC[28]. If *lex arbitri* allows to challenge an interim decision on jurisdiction[29], then in that case the state court may consider this matter also if such interim award is challenged. In exactly the same manner as an arbitral tribunal considering a question relating to its own jurisdiction, a state court, in assessing an arbitration agreement, must first apply the law chosen by the parties. In the absence of such a choice a state court must apply the law of the place of arbitration[30].

---

[23] This is also confirmed by the provisions of the New York Convention (Article V (1) (a)), which sets forth that *Recognition and enforcement of the award may be refused... only if that party furnishes... proof that...*
    the said agreement is not valid under the law to which the parties have subjected it or, failing any indication thereon, under <u>the law of the country where the award was made.</u> (emphasis added).

[24] Article 35 ICC Arbitration Rules.

[25] This follows from clause 2 (b) (i) of UNCITRAL Model Law.

[26] Article 34.2.2.

[27] Article 42.2.

[28] Article 233.3.1.

[29] Article 16.3, UNCITRAL Model Law.

[30] Article V (1) (a).

III.4. Determination of Arbitrability by a Court at the Place of Recognition and Enforcement of a Foreign Arbitral Award

7.31. Finally, a competent court can refuse to recognize or enforce a foreign arbitral award if the subject of the dispute is not arbitrable under the law of the country of that court[31].

III.5. Conclusion on Applicable Law When Deciding Matters Related to the Arbitrability of a Dispute

7.32. It thus ensues that when deciding on the matter of arbitrability of a dispute, it is necessary to take into account, above all, the law designated by the parties as applicable to the arbitration, and in the absence of such, the law of the place of arbitration. However, in addition to this, one must not ignore the law of the country of possible recognition and enforcement of the arbitral award, as this matter will certainly arise at a later stage.

7.33. Further, there exists a potential possibility that court of any state which, for some reason or other, will decide on the question of the arbitration agreement's validity and will find the arbitration agreement null and void if the subject of the dispute is not arbitrable under the laws of that state. Finally, when deciding on subjective arbitrability, both the court and the arbitral tribunal must apply the personal law of the party to the arbitration agreement, which, as applied to legal entities, is usually the law of the place where such legal entity is registered[32].

IV. Objective Arbitrability under Russian Law

IV.1. General Provisions of Arbitrability

7.34. According to the Civil Code of the Russian Federation[33] a matter relating to the protection of violated or contested civil rights may be referred to arbitration[34]. Therefore any civil law dispute can be subject

---

[31] This follows from Article V (2) (a) of Article V of the New York Convention: *Recognition and enforcement of an arbitral award may also be refused if the competent authority in the country where recognition and enforcement is sought finds that the subject-matter of the difference is not capable of settlement by arbitration under the law of that country.*

[32] In this sense, Section 48 of the Swedish Law "On Arbitration" of 1999 is instructive: *1. Where an arbitration agreement has an international connection, the agreement shall be governed by the law agreed upon by the parties. Where the parties have not reached such an agreement, the arbitration agreement shall be governed by the law of the country in which, by virtue of the agreement, the proceedings have taken place or shall take place.*
2. The first paragraph shall not apply to the issue of whether a party was authorized to enter into an arbitration agreement or was duly represented.

[33] Article 11.1, RF CC.

[34] According to Article 12 of the Commercial Procedural Code of Ukraine, a dispute falling within the jurisdiction of commercial courts may be referred by the parties for settlement to a court of arbitration, except for disputes for recognition of the invalidity of administrative acts, disputes related to supply contracts for state needs, as well a corporate disputes.

of an arbitration agreement. Exceptions to this general rule may be made only by law[35]. Furthermore, there is no single normative act which would define precisely which disputes in Russia are not arbitrable. The provisions on limiting the referral of disputes to arbitration can be found in the Arbitrazh Procedural Code of the Russian Federation, the Civil Procedural Code of the Russian Federation, and other laws. Furthermore, certain conclusions regarding limitation of arbitrability may be drawn on the basis of an analysis of court practice. Despite the fact that there are serious doubts about authority of Russian courts to limit arbitrability of disputes, from a pragmatic point of view this practice cannot be ignored.

IV.2. Disputes Related to Administrative Relations

7.35. The RF Civil Code directly states that under a general rule, civil legislation does not apply to proprietary rights arising out of administrative relations, including to tax and other financial and administrative relations[36]. This provision is important, since, for example, the legal status of legal entities is defined by its foundation documents, which are registered by state authorities. Although the actions of state authorities might influence the status of a legal entity (for example, in case a claim is presented for liquidation of a legal entity in cases established by law), disputes of this type will not be arbitrable, as they concern administrative relations.

IV.3. Tax Disputes

7.36. Likewise, disputes with the tax authorities concerning payment of taxes are not arbitrable under Russian law, as they arise out of administrative relations. The question quite often arises as to whether disputes between

---

[35] Thus, in the case *Imanagement Services Ltd. v. Cukurova Holding AS* the Moscow City Arbitrazh Court, setting aside the ICAC award, concluded that the dispute considered by the tribunal was not enforceable as it is provided by Articles 11 and 1062 of the RF CC. Article 1062 of the RF CC states that claims arising from gambling are not enforceable. After the 1998 default Russian state courts took a very conservative approach with regard to disputes involving undeliverable forward contracts and qualified them as gambling, thus denying enforceability. When similar disputes were submitted to arbitration, some tribunals, ignoring the practice of Russian state courts, none the less considered such disputes on the merits. In this case the Moscow City Arbitrazh Court set aside the ICAC award, referring to Article 233.3.1 of the RF APC, under which an arbitrazh court sets aside an arbitral award if it finds that the dispute submitted to arbitration may not be the subject of arbitration under federal law. The Federal Arbitrazh Court of the Moscow Circuit, dissenting from the opinion of the Moscow City Arbitrazh Court, said: *The essence of this provision [Article 233.3.1 of the RF APC] lays in the fact that the court must establish the non-arbitrable nature of a dispute, i.e. come to a conclusion that this category of disputes does not fall within the category of disputes of a private-law nature, and therefore the dispute cannot be referred to arbitration, that is, the dispute possesses features of a public nature and therefore cannot be the subject to arbitration. In addition to that, this argument must be underpinned by a reference to a federal law provision that excludes this category of disputes from the competence of arbitration courts.* (Resolution of the Federal Arbitrazh Court of the Moscow Circuit of 29 June 2007 in Case No. KG-A40/4610-07)

[36] Article 2.3 RF CC.

two private entities which have arisen with regard to reimbursement of taxes paid by one party to the contract, and which, according to the contract, should be reimbursed by the other party, are arbitrable. Although a party might claim reimbursement of a paid tax, such dispute is not tax related, and is therefore arbitrable. A tax dispute is in place in the event that the dispute arises between a private entity and tax authorities. Such a dispute is not a civil law one and cannot be the subject of arbitration. A dispute between two private companies does not affect the interests of the state, and therefore does not have a character of a public law dispute. In its essence, it is not a tax dispute but a dispute on contract price or compensation of expenses incurred by one of the parties under the contract. As the parties are entitled to establish any means of determining the price or reimbursing the expenses incurred by the party, nobody can restricts the parties' freedom to include the amount of taxes to be paid in calculation of the price or expenses to be reimbursed.

7.37. This was the main issue in the case *Quattrogemini Ltd. (Finland) v. Neva Chupa Chups JSC (Russian Federation)* when the court considered an application for enforcement of the SCC award in Russia.The facts of the case are as follows: On June 30, 1995, Quattrogemini Ltd. and Neva Chupa Chups JSC entered into a contract for construction of a warehouse for Neva Chupa Chups JSC in St. Petersburg. With time, a dispute arose between the parties as to the payment of amounts in reimbursement for VAT and special tax paid by Quattrogemini Ltd. in respect of imported equipment and materials. On June 15, 1999, the arbitral tribunal acting under the SCC Rules made an award in favour of Quattrogemini Ltd. On October 26, 1999 the St. Petersburg City Court (court of general jurisdiction) decided to enforce the SCC award. Neva Chupa Chups CJSC filed an appeal stating that the tribunal had lacked jurisdiction over the dispute. In particular, it was argued that the tribunal resolved a dispute arising out of a tax relationship which was not arbitrable. The Supreme Court of the Russian Federation dismissed the applicant's arguments[37]. The court pointed out that the SCC tribunal had resolved a dispute arising out of a civil-law relationship, and not a tax relationship and that such a dispute is arbitrable under Russian law. Quattrogemini Ltd in fact claimed reimbursement for the tax amounts paid thereby in the Russian Federation, and not for payment of taxes in Quottrogemini's place and stead, and such reimbursement was to be paid by Neva Chupa Chups JSC in accordance with the contract.

IV.4. Antitrust Disputes

7.38. Disputes involving the antitrust authorities regarding the application of provisions of antitrust law are not arbitrable in Russia because of their public character. The question as to whether private disputes related to the observance of antitrust legislation are arbitrable has

---

[37]   Ruling of the Supreme Court of 20 December 1999 in Case No. 78-G99-7.

not been decided in Russian legislation. Such disputes may arise, for example, if one of the parties to arbitration alleges that some provisions of a contract are not in compliance with the antitrust law provisions and are, therefore, invalid. From a formal point of view, nothing here might affect the jurisdiction of the tribunal to decide on this dispute. However, such issues had not been subject to review by the Russian courts so there is still no clear answer on it. However, Kazakh courts have already expressed their view, and are not in favour of arbitration.

7.39. In the case *State Property and Privatization Committee of the Republic of Kazakhstan v. AES Sentry Power Limited (Ireland) and Tau Power B.V. (Netherlands)*, the Supreme Court of the Republic of Kazakhstan found the arbitration clause in concession agreement invalid[38]. By the contract the Government of Kazakhstan provided AES with two power plants, and the concession agreement, among others, contained some provisions regarding price and tariffs for electricity generated by the plants. The Supreme Court of the Republic of Kazakhstan stated that the regulation of the activity of natural monopolies and the setting of rates and prices for their services falls within the exclusive competence of an authorized state agency. Along with that, the concession contract contained certain provisions on the procedure for determining prices and rates for electricity produced; disputes on this were to be resolved by arbitration. Such provisions, in the view of the Supreme Court of Kazakhstan, created a possibility for transferring regulation of rates and prices from the area of public law relations to that of private law relations. In this way, the activities of energy companies, being natural monopolists, could avoid control from the government.

IV.5. Disputes Related to Privatization of State Property

7.40. It should be noted that concession contracts, as the one considered by the Kazakh Supreme Court in the example above, in Russia shall be qualified as a privatization transaction, and, therefore, shall fall within the exclusive jurisdiction of the state arbitrazh courts. Therefore according to Article 248.1 of the RF Arbitrazh Procedural Code, disputes relating to property that is state-owned by the Russian Federation are subject to the exclusive jurisdiction of arbitrazh courts in the Russian Federation for cases involving foreign parties, including disputes related to the privatization of state property and requisition of the private property for state needs.

7.41. This position is also supported by court practice, where in *State Property Fund of the Kaliningrad Region (Russian Federation) v. Finvest Ltd.* the Kaliningrad Regional State Property Fund went to the Arbitrazh Court of the Kaliningrad Region to invalidate a share purchase-and-sale agreement executed in the course of privatization. The first instance court refused to consider the case, noting that the privatization agreement contained

---

38 Resolution of the Panel for Civil Cases, Supreme Court of Republic of Kazakhstan, 8 January 2004, No. 3a-148/2-03.

an arbitration clause. The Presidium of the Russian Federation Supreme Arbitrazh Court overturned the lower court decision for the following reasons:

> The dispute between the Property Fund and the company cannot, by its very nature, be subject to arbitration, considering that assets owned by a public entity, i.e., the Russian Federation, whose powers to dispose of its property are restricted by privatization legislation, were in the case under review to be taken over for a consideration, i.e., through privatization. Under the Privatization Law, disputes arising out of privatization transactions are subject to state courts. Therefore, the dispute in question may not be subject to private arbitration[39].

IV.6. Disputes Related to Establishment, Restructuring and Liquidation of Legal Entities

7.42. In principle, disputes between shareholders of a company and state authorities in connection with the establishment, restructuring and liquidation of legal entities are of a public-law character, and therefore not arbitrable. According to the RF Arbitrazh Procedural Code[40] disputes related to establishment, liquidation or registration within the Russian Federation of legal entities and registration of self-employed entrepreneurs, as well as challenges to the decisions of the governing bodies of these legal entities, fall within the exclusive jurisdiction of state arbitrazh courts.

IV.7. Disputes Involving Shareholders' Agreements

7.43. The question as to whether disputes involving shareholders' agreements can be referred to arbitration has not been regulated by Russian legislation for very long time. On one hand, such disputes have a civil-law character, and therefore there is no obstacle to their referral to arbitration. However, attempts to prevent situations where fabricated arbitral awards were used by corporate raiders for hostile takeovers, and efforts to protect national entities from the negative foreign arbitral awards have led to the exclusion of this type of dispute from arbitrable disputes.

7.44. In December 2007 the Supreme Economic Court of Ukraine assigned disputes between shareholders (participants) related to their participation in Ukrainian companies, as well as disputes between shareholders and the companies themselves to the exclusive competence of Ukrainian courts[41]. A similar decision was passed by the Plenum of the Supreme Court of Ukraine on 24 October 2008. In 2009, the changes were introduced to

---

[39] Judgment by the Presidium of the Russian Federation Supreme Arbitrazh Court of 10 April 2001 No. 3515/00.
[40] Article 248.5 RF APC.
[41] Recommendations of the Presidium of the Supreme Business Court of Ukraine of 28 December 2007 No. 04-5/14 "*On the practice of applying legislation when considering cases which arise from corporate relations.*"

the Commercial Procedure Code of Ukraine, prohibiting arbitration of any disputes, which arise from corporate relations between a company and its participant (founder, shareholder), including a former participant, or between the participants (founders, shareholders) relating to the establishment, activity, management or termination of their company. The same sort of restriction can also be found in the Law of Ukraine "On Private International Law."

7.45. The legislation of the Russian Federation has not given a final answer on this matter. In 2009, amendments were introduced into various laws aimed at regulating agreements between shareholders, however, there is still no clear answer whether the disputes between shareholders could be submitted to arbitration. If one applies to shareholders' disputes the same pattern as to disputes related to immovable property, then a logical conclusion will be that such disputes are not arbitrable.

IV.8. Disputes Related to Bankruptcy

7.46. The RF Law "On Insolvency (Bankruptcy)" states that bankruptcy cases are reviewed by state arbitrazh courts[42] and may not be referred to arbitration[43]. A similar provision is contained in the legislation of Belarus[44], Kazakhstan[45] and Ukraine[46].

IV.9. Disputes Related to Registrable Rights to Immovable Property

7.47. It should be noted that the legislation of the Russian Federation not only does not contain an explicit prohibition on the referral of civil-law disputes related to immovable property to arbitration[47], but explicitly provides for such possibility[48]. From the other side the RF Civil Procedural Code states that claims for the rights to land plots, subsoil plots, individual water objects, forests, multi-year plantations, buildings, structures, edifices and other objects firmly attached to the ground shall be submitted to courts at the place where said objects are situated[49].

---

[42] Article 6.1 Federal Law No. 127-FZ *"On Insolvency (Bankruptcy)"* of 26 October 2002.

[43] Article 33.3.

[44] Article 3 of the Republic of Belarus Law *"On Economic Insolvency (Bankruptcy)."* See also Aleksandr Korobeinikov, *Certain Matters Relating to the Arbitrability of Disputes Arising in the Course of Economic Insolvency (Bankruptcy)*, 7 (2) "Treteisky Sud" Magazine (2005).

[45] Article 7.5 of Republic of Kazakhstan Law *"On Courts of Arbitration."*

[46] Article 6 of Law of Ukraine *"On Courts of Arbitration."*

[47] As was correctly noted supra by the FAS MO, an exclusion of the arbitrability of disputes must be made only by a federal law.

[48] See Article 25 of Federal Law of 16 July 1998 No. 102-FZ *"On Mortgage (Pledge of Real Estate)"*: *If not provided otherwise by federal law or this Article, a registration record of a mortgage is invalidated within 3 working days after receipt by the registration authority of the application from the legal owner of the mortgage [...] or of a decision by a court, arbitrazh court, or court of arbitration to terminate the mortgage.*

[49] Article 30.1 RF CPC. It should be noted that the legislator does not use the term *"immovable property"* in this Article, and therefore air and sea vessels which, under

7.48. Further, it would be incorrect to think that these provisions exclude these categories of disputes from being arbitrable. The provisions quoted above establish rules that provide which particular court of general jurisdiction (or magistrate) should consider a civil-law dispute if the case falls under the system of courts of general jurisdiction (if it does not have a commercial nature, in which case this dispute is subject to state arbitrazh court if does not contain of arbitration clause). However these provisions of the RF Civil Procedural Code do not deal with the issue whether these categories of disputes should be considered exclusively within the system of courts of general jurisdiction and thus excluding it from those that are arbitrable.

7.49. Unfortunately, in the Russian Federation the possibility of registering rights to immovable property based on an arbitral award was often used by parties for attacks by raiders and illegal takeover of other people's property, which forced the system of state courts to exclude disputes related to registered rights to immovable property from arbitration. For example, on 22 August 2006, an arbitral tribunal acting under the Rules of the Permanent Court of Arbitration at the Astrakhan Chamber of Commerce and Industry granted the claim of Manufacturing Firm "Podvodnik" LLC (hereinafter "Podvodnik LLC") for recognition of its ownership right to unauthorized construction consisting of a bank revetment, fence and gates. The parties to the arbitration agreement and, correspondingly, the arbitration proceeding, were Podvodnik LLC and the Local Government of the city of Astrakhan[50]. Further, for some reason the arbitral tribunal did not take into account that the unauthorized construction was located on a land plot which had earlier been provided by the Astrakhan Local Government to the individual O.V. Klim, who was not a party to the arbitration. Mr. Klim filed an application with the Arbitrazh Court of the Astrakhan Region for setting aside the arbitral award, and the court granted the application.

7.50. There are also quite a number of similar cases, in which arbitration was initiated with the purpose of legalizing illegal construction or to appropriating a third party's property on the basis of the arbitral award[51]. It is obvious that if each of these similar cases had not been left without a proper reaction from the law-enforcement authorities, then the Supreme Arbitrazh Court and Supreme Court would not need to take a restrictive approach with regard to arbitrability of disputes related to immovable property. However, due to a variety of reasons the law-enforcement system could not prevent the seizure of immovable property through the use of fabricated arbitral awards, thus both of the higher judicial instances

Czech (& Central European) Yearbook of Arbitration

---

civil legislation, are classified as immovable property, do not fall under the operation of this Article.

[50] See Resolution of the Federal Arbitrazh Court of the Povolzhsky Circuit of 2 August 2007 in Case No. A06-179/07-9.

[51] See Ruling of the RF Supreme Arbitrazh Court of 15 June 2009 in Case No. 5520/09; Resolution of the Federal Arbitrazh Court of the Povolzhsky Circuit of 24 September 2009 in Case No. A65-9867/2009.

excluded disputes related to rights subject to registration to immovable property from arbitrable disputes[52].

7.51. The Supreme Arbitrazh Court of the Russian Federation stated in 2005 that an arbitration court is not entitled to hand down an award compelling the registration authority to register immovable property on the name of a party to arbitration, because issues related to public-law relations (registration of real estate) cannot be the subject to arbitration[53]. In the same document the Supreme Arbitrazh Court stated that arbitration courts likewise were not entitled to levy execution on pledged immovable property, as these disputes also fall under the exclusive competence of state courts[54]. In 2010, however, the Supreme Arbitrazh Court turned to the Constitutional Court for clarification as to whether an arbitration court has right to decide to levy execution on mortgaged property[55], however, at the time of drafting this article, the Constitutional Court had not expressed its view.

---

[52] However, the issue whether they were authorized to do so is still a subject of heated discussions.

[53] *According to Article 1 of the Federal Law "On Arbitration Courts in the Russian Federation," any dispute deriving from civil law relations may be referred to a court of arbitration, if otherwise is not specified by federal law. This provision of the Law does not affect the operation of any other law of the Russian Federation, under which certain disputes may not be referred to arbitration or may be referred to arbitration only in compliance with provisions other than those contained in the named Law. Proceeding from part 6 of Article 4 of the RF APC, a dispute arising out of civil law relations, which falls under the jurisdiction of arbitrazh courts, may be referred by the parties to arbitration, if otherwise is not specified by federal law. Thus, cases arising from administrative and other public relations, by virtue of these provisions may not be referred to arbitration. Article 2 of Federal Law No. 122-FZ of 21 July 1997 "On State Registration of Rights to Immovable Property and Transactions Therewith" states that state registration is the sole proof of the existence of the registered right and constitutes a legal act of recognition and confirmation by the state of the creation, transfer or termination of rights to immovable property. Proceeding from the mentioned provision, a legal relation related to the registration of an ownership right [to immovable property] has a public character, and the arbitral award ordering the registration authority to undertake appropriate actions [has] public-legal consequences. According to Article 17 of this Law, grounds for state registration of the existence, creation, termination, transfer, and encumbrance of rights to immovable property and transactions therewith are provided by judgments entered in force. This provision evidence that the question of ownership right to immovable property falls within the exclusive jurisdiction of state courts. Given the circumstances set forth, the arbitral award ordering the registration authority to register the ownership right to immovable property on a name of a party to arbitration affects issues of a public character which cannot be submitted to arbitration–* Clause 27 of Information Letter of the Presidium of the RF Supreme Arbitrazh Court of 22 December 2005 No. 96 *Survey of the practice of arbitrazh courts' consideration of recognition and enforcement of awards of foreign courts, of challenges to the awards of courts of arbitration, and of issuance of enforcement orders for enforcement of the decisions of courts of arbitration.*

[54] *Ibid.,* 28.

[55] Ruling of Presidium of the RF Supreme Arbitrazh Court of 18 May 2010 in Case No. 634/10.

7.52. Also, according to the practice of Russian courts, matters relating to the termination or amendment of the term of long-term real estate lease agreements are also not arbitrable, as the rights to lease real estate for a term longer than 1 year are subject to registration with the state authorities[56]. The landmark case to demonstrate this approach of the Russian courts was *Kalinka Stockman* case[57]. In 1997, Kalinka-Stockmann entered into a 10-year agreement for a lease of premises in the „Smolensky Passazh" business complex in central Moscow. The lease provided for the tenant's right to extend the lease term for another 10-year period on the terms and conditions applicable within the past five years of the effective term of the original lease. In 2007, the landlord refused to extend the lease on the agreed-upon terms and conditions and was therefore sued by Kalinka-Stockmann which referred the dispute to arbitration under MKAS (ICAC RF) Rules in accordance with the arbitration clause contained in the lease. On 29 April 2008, the tribunal acting under MKAS Rules rendered an award in favour of the claimant. The award supported the claimant's right to extend the lease term for another 10 year period on the earlier agreed terms and conditions. The tribunal also ordered the respondent to enter into an extension by executing and registering an addendum to the original lease of 1997. On 14 August 2008, the Arbitrazh Court of the City of Moscow set aside the MKAS award. One of the reasons was the fact that the dispute could not be the subject matter to arbitration. The Federal Arbitrazh Court of the Moscow Region supported the position of the trial court[58].

7.53. It is interesting to note that the Supreme Court, in principle supporting the position of the Supreme Arbitrazh Court that disputes related to immovable property are not arbitrable, found a different reasoning. The RF Supreme Court stated that an arbitral award cannot be a basis for registration of rights to immovable property, inasmuch as they do not have "the legal force of a court decision"[59].

7.54. It is worth noting that both the legislation of Ukraine[60], and the legislation of Kazakhstan[61] also exclude disputes involving immovable property from arbitrable disputes.

---

[56] See also an interesting overview of the Russian court practice in Sergey Strembelev, *Arbitrability of disputes about investment in the construction of real estate in Russia,* 27 (2) THE INTERNATIONAL CONSTRUCTION LAW REVIEW (April 2010).

[57] Resolution of Federal Arbitrazh Court of Moscow Circuit of 3 September 2007 No. KG-A40/8370-07.

[58] Ruling No. KG-A40/9294-08-1,2 of 13 October 2008 by the Federal Arbitrazh Court of the Moscow Okrug.

[59] Reply to Question 2 on civil cases in the Survey, appr. by Resolution of the Presidium of the Supreme Council of the Russian Federation of 7 November 2007. The text of the survey was not officially published.

[60] Article 6 of Law of Ukraine *"On Courts of Arbitration,"* Article 77 of Law of Ukraine *"On International Private Law."*

[61] Article 417 of RK CPC.

Czech (& Central European) Yearbook of Arbitration

IV.10. Disputes Related to Registrable Rights to the Results of Intellectual Activity

7.55. The RF Arbitrazh Procedural Code[62] states that disputes related to registration or issuance of patents, registration and issuance of certificates to trademarks, industrial samples, utility models or registration of other rights to the results of intellectual activity which require registration or issuance of a patent or certificate in the Russian Federation are subject to the exclusive jurisdiction of Russian courts. According to the law of Ukraine "On Private International Law," disputes related to the intellectual property rights which require registration or the issuance of a certificate in Ukraine fall within the exclusive jurisdiction of Ukrainian courts[63].

IV.11. Disputes Related to the Issuance or Invalidity of Securities

7.56. According to the Law of Ukraine "On Private International Law," cases related to the issue or invalidity of securities issued in Ukraine are also within the exclusive jurisdiction of the Ukrainian courts[64].

IV.12. Labour Disputes

7.57. According to a general rule, it is believed that labour disputes cannot be the subject of arbitration because they are not classified among disputes of a civil law character. The Law of Ukraine "On Arbitration Courts" explicitly excludes labour disputes from those that are arbitrable[65].

IV.13. Other Cases of Limitation of Objective Arbitrability

7.58. Besides the main cases of limitation of objective arbitrability which to some degree are common to the CIS countries, in some countries one could find also some specific limitations. For example, Russian courts take a restrictive approach with regard to the disputes related to use of pension funds. Thus, in the case *Non-State Pension Fund v. Parma-Management LLC*, a Russian court stated that disputes involving a trust agreement concerning pension reserves were not subject to arbitration[66]. The cassation court noted[67] that the court had correctly applied Federal Law No. 75-FZ *"On Non-State Pension Funds"* of 7 May 1998, providing that a fund's disputes with legal entities and individuals are considered in court[68][which means state courts]. This same law also specifies[69] that a non-state pension fund has right to sign a trust agreement only on terms which are approved by state authorities. Such terms[70] do not envisage the possibility of referring disputes to arbitration.

---

62 Article 248.3 of RF APC.
63 Article 77 of Law of Ukraine *"On International Private Law."*
64 *Ibid.*
65 Article 6 of Law of Ukraine "On Arbitration Courts."
66 Decision of Perm Region Arbitrazh Court No. A50-16146/08 of 27 January 2009.
67 Resolution of Federal Arbitrazh Court of Ural Circuit No. F09-3704/09 of 9 June 2009.
68 Article 37 of Federal Law No. 75-FZ *"On Non-State Pension Funds."*
69 *Ibid.*, Article 25.7.
70 Approved by order No. 134 of Inspectorate of Non-State Pension Funds at Ministry of Labor and Social Welfare of RF, 27 December 1999.

7.58. The legislation of Kazakhstan establishes that only contractual disputes of a civil-law character can be referred to arbitration[71]. Thus, from arbitrable disputes, when they are being considered by internal arbitration, torts are excluded.

7.59. According to the Law of Ukraine "On Arbitration Courts" the following cannot be the subject of arbitration:[72]
   - disputes which arise upon conclusion, amendment, termination or performance of contracts for procurement of goods for state needs;
   - disputes related to state secrets;
   - disputes arising from family legal relations, except for disputes deriving from a marriage contract;
   - disputes which result in the arbitral award ordering the performance of some actions by state authorities or their functionaries when carrying out their official duties.

V. Subjective Arbitrability

V.1. Limitation of Subjective Arbitrability

7.60. The legislation of CIS countries rather infrequently limits the possibility of entities to enter into arbitration agreements. The exclusions sometimes met in practice mainly concern public entities, or situations involving bankruptcy.

V.2. Limitation of Subjective Arbitrability of Public Entities

7.62. The European Convention on International Commercial Arbitration explicitly stipulates that legal entities which, under the national law applicable to them, are considered "legal entities of public law," will have the opportunity to enter into arbitration agreements[73]. Russian law does not restrict the capacity of state entities to conclude arbitration agreements for commercial transactions. However, in some CIS countries one could find restrictions on this matter.

7.63. The law of the Republic of Kazakhstan "On Arbitration Courts" excludes disputes concerning the interests of the state and of state companies, as well as disputes where the parties are natural monopolists and companies occupying a dominant position on the market from domestic arbitration.

---

[71]   Thus, according to Article 6.2 of the Republic of Kazakhstan Law "*On International Commercial Arbitration*," *An arbitration agreement may be concluded by parties in respect of disputes which arose or may arise between the parties regarding some specific civil-law agreement.*

[72]   Article 6 of Law of Ukraine "*On Arbitration Courts*".

[73]   Article II of European Convention. It is true that any state, upon signing the Convention, was entitled to state a reservation about the inapplicability of this provision to the subjects of that state, although de facto such a reservation was stated only by Belgium, whose national legislation at the time it acceded to the European Convention limited the right of public subjects to enter into arbitration agreements. See FOUCHARD GAILLARD GOLDMAN ON INTERNATIONAL COMMERCIAL ARBITRATION, The Hague: Kluwer Law International 140 (E. Gaillard, J. Savage eds., 1999).

That said the law of the Republic of Kazakhstan "On International Commercial Arbitration" does not have similar restrictions.

7.64. According to the law of Ukraine "On Arbitration Courts" disputes where one of the parties is a state authority or a functionary engaged in his or her own administrative functions cannot be the subject of arbitration[74].

V.3. Limitation of Subjective Arbitrability in Case of Bankruptcy

7.65. The legislation of some countries states that companies under bankruptcy proceedings are not entitled to enter into arbitration agreements. In particular, this approach also exists in the Russian Federation. According to a general rule established in Russian Bankruptcy Law, after the court declares a debtor a bankrupt and opens bankruptcy proceedings, all claims of creditors relating to monetary obligations may be made only in the framework of bankruptcy proceedings to a court at the debtor's location[75]. That said, the date for initiating the bankruptcy procedure is the time when the supervision procedure is introduced[76]. As the Constitutional Court of the Russian Federation stated, "the possibility for creditors to present their claims against the debtor outside the frames of the bankruptcy case... would contravene the very essence of a bankruptcy proceeding, exclusively in the course of which the task of proportional distribution among creditors of the entire bankruptcy estate is to be decided..."[77]. By virtue of this, if a bankruptcy procedure is initiated for a Russian company, then the court of arbitration is not entitled to make a decision in regard to a claim brought against the debtor, as such claims should be reviewed solely as part of the bankruptcy procedure in a state arbitrazh court where the debtor is located[78]. Furthermore, according to the court practice in the Russian Federation, the bankruptcy receiver is also not entitled to submit disputes under transactions which he or she signs during liquidation of the company to arbitration[79].

V.4. Other Cases of Limitation of Subjective Arbitrability

7.64. In Kazakhstan disputes in which the interests of under-age minors, as well as persons legally declared to be not of legal capacity, are affected, are also excluded from arbitrability[80].

---

[74] Article 6 Law of Ukraine "*On Arbitration Courts*".

[75] Article 126.1 Federal Law No. 127-FZ of 26 October 2002 "*On Insolvency (Bankruptcy)*."

[76] Resolution of the Federal Arbitrazh Court of the Povolzhsky Circuit of 30 August 2010 in Case No. A5-3748/2010.

[77] Ruling of the RF Constitutional Court of 8 August 2004 No. 254–O.

[78] See Resolution of the Federal Arbitrazh Court of the Povolzhsky Circuit of 30 August 2010 in Case No. A5-3748/2010.

[79] Resolution of Federal Arbitrazh Court of the West Siberian Circuit of 16 October 2009 No. F04-6332/2009; Resolution of Federal Arbitrazh Court of the North Caucasian Circuit of 15 October 2009 No. A53-10285/2009.

[80] Article 6.7 of Law of Republic of Kazakhstan "*On International Commercial Arbitration*," Article 7.5 of Republic of Kazakhstan Law "*On Courts of Arbitration*."

VI. Conclusions

7.65. While resort to arbitration is considered by one of the means of protection private rights guaranteed by Russian Constitution, the scope of arbitrable disputes in Russian is seriously limited by Russian laws and the approach of Russian courts.

7.68. Thus, from civil law disputes, which generally can be subjected to arbitration, are excluded disputes related to a title to immovable property (and other rights to immovable property subject to state registration); disputes related to privatization; disputes related to establishment, reorganization and liquidation of legal entities. The question as to whether disputes between shareholders and between shareholders and a company can be subject to arbitration is still a "grey area". Therefore, a signatory to an arbitration agreement which could be potentially enforced in Russia should double check whether the subject matter of the dispute is arbitrable not only under Russian law, but whether Russian courts allow such disputes to be submitted to international arbitration.

| | |

Summaries

FRA [*Motifs constitutionnels en matière d'arbitrage et arbitrabilité des conflits en russie et dans d'autres pays de la cei*]
Les limites de l'arbitrabilité se fondent sur l'équilibre entre le droit constitutionnel de protéger les droits civiques par tous les moyens non explicitement prohibés par la loi, dont celui de soumettre un litige à l'arbitrage ou l'intention d'un État de conserver le contrôle sur certains aspects des activités civiles et économiques. Ainsi, un État pourrait exclure certains types de litiges du champ d'application de l'arbitrage étant entendu comme les limites de l'arbitrabilité objective. Un État pourrait également limiter la capacité de certaines entités à participer à un arbitrage, en limitant alors l'arbitrabilité subjective. La portée des conflits susceptibles d'arbitrage diffère d'un pays à un autre, en fonction du degré de contrôle que l'État souhaite conserver sur l'arbitrage. Néanmoins, quelques États membres de la CEI présentent certaines caractéristiques communes, notamment la Biélorussie, le Kazakhstan, la Russie et l'Ukraine qui excluent du champ d'application de l'arbitrage les litiges portant sur les biens immobiliers. Il existe également une tendance à exclure les conflits d'entreprise.

CZE [*Ústavněprávní základy rozhodčího řízení a arbitrabilita sporů v Rusku a v jiných zemích Společenství nezávislých států*]
Limity arbitrability sporů v rozhodčím řízení vycházejí z rovnováhy mezi ústavně zakotveným právem na ochranu občanských práv jakýmikoli prostředky, které nejsou přímo zakázány zákonem, což taktéž zahrnuje právo předložit spor k vyřešení v rámci rozhodčího řízení, a úmyslem státu zachovat si kontrolu nad určitými oblastmi občanských a hospodářských aktivit. Stát by tak mohl vyloučit arbitrabilitu určitého typu sporů, což je chápáno jako meze objektivní arbitrability. Stát by také mohl omezit schopnost určitých subjektů stát se účastníkem rozhodčího řízení, čímž by omezil subjektivní arbitrabilitu sporů. Rozsah arbitrabilních sporů se v jednotlivých zemích liší, a to v závislosti

na úrovni kontroly, kterou si chce stát nad rozhodčím řízením ponechat. V některých zemích Společenství nezávislých států však existují určité společné rysy: například Bělorusko, Kazachstán, Rusko a Ukrajina vylučují arbitrabilitu sporů týkající se nemovitostí. Existuje zde také snaha vyloučit z rozhodčího řízení spory právnických osob.

| | |

POL [***Przesłanki konstytucyjne arbitrażu oraz zdatność arbitrażowa sporów w rosji i pozostałych krajach wnp***]
Artykuł na temat ograniczeń obiektywnej i subiektywnej arbitralności w Rosji i innych krajach WNP, który przedstawia zarys historyczny arbitrażu w ZSRR, aktualne podstawy prawne arbitrażu oraz niektóre orzeczenia z konkretnych sporów arbitrażowych.

DEU [***Verfassungsrechtliche Grundlagen für das Schiedsverfahren und Schiedsfähigkeit von Streitsachen in Russland und anderen GUS-Staaten***]
Dieser beitrag über die Beschränkungen der objektiven und subjektiven Schiedsfähigkeit in Russland und einigen weiteren GUS-Staaten verschafft einen Überblick über den historischen Hintergrund der Schiedsgerichtsbarkeit in der Sowjetunion, beschreibt die derzeitigen legislativen Grundlagen für die Grenzen der Schiedsfähigkeit in Streitsachen und zeichnet das Fallrecht zu spezifischen Fragen der Schiedsfähigkeit nach.

RUS [***Конституционные основы арбитража и возможности решения споров в арбитраже в россии и других странах снг***]
Очерк, посвященный ограничениям в отношении объективной и субъективной подсудности арбитражу в России и некоторых других странах СНГ, представляет собой обзор исторических предпосылок арбитража в СССР, нынешних законодательных основ и примеров прецедентного права в вопросах подсудности арбитражу.

ES [***Bases constitucionales para el arbitraje y arbitrabilidad de las disputas en rusia y en otros países***]
Este ensayo sobre la limitación de la arbitrabilidad objetiva y subjetiva en Rusia y en algunos otros países de la Comunidad de Estados Independientes revisa los antecedentes históricos del arbitraje en la URSS, las bases legales actuales para los límites de la arbitrabilidad y alguna jurisprudencia sobre temas de arbitrabilidad en particular.

Karel Klíma

Constitutional Environment and the Phenomenon of Arbitration

Key words:
Adversarial nature
of arbitration |
general principles
of due process |
objective arbitrability
| nature of justice
| concept of "due
process" | arbitration,
jurisdictional theory
| constitutional
nature of arbitration
| constitutional
environment |
constitutional values
| constitutional law |
public policy | model
law | fundamental
human rights

Abstract | *The idea of international arbitration tribunals that use several instruments of international law institutes a "non-governmental" approach to settling private-law disputes (in addition to the perceptibleness of settlement, which may be negotiated outside arbitration proceedings). From the constitutional viewpoint, such an approach relinquishes, to some extent, the right to resort to general courts of law, the principle of fair trial and, to some extent, the principle of appeal. All these factors correspond, more or less, to the organizational and procedural aspects of constitutional law. From the viewpoint of constitutional law, it is difficult to perceive the effects of this agreement as "a derogation of the jurisdiction of the Constitutional Court". More precisely, the issue concerns the lawful use of the arbitration authority of public power with regard to a subject of private law with the possibility (albeit limited) to have the matter "returned" for review by a general court of law.*

**Prof. nzw. et Doc.
JUDr. Karel Klíma,
CSc., dr. hab.** is a
university lecturer
currently leading the
Constitutional Law
Department at the
Law Faculty of West
Bohemian University
in Plzeň; long-time
member of the Council
of the International
Association of
Constitutional Law
(IACL), member
of the Academy of
Comparative Law,
member of the World
Jurist Association and
its President for the
Czech Republic.
e-mail:
khklima@mbox.vol.cz

| | |

I. Introduction

8.01. First, it should be noted that the way the approach to the quest for the content of the title of this article is formulated is neither formally random nor symbolic, and certainly not "solemn", much less "mandatory". It is based on the author's long-standing doctrinal concept clarifying why and how constitutional law is "lit up"[1] in other sectors of the Czech legal system in its established form.

8.02. Constitutional law in its current (modern, highly "internationalized") form is itself subject to being "lit up" (*mirrored, reflected, applied*). It is "lit up from above" by international law, particularly through multilateral international treaties (an example is the European Convention on Human Rights and Fundamental Freedoms) and even EU treaties (naturally, the "Lisbon Treaty"). If we consider the question of what, in terms of values, is essentially the shared content of international pacts (especially since the Second World War), particularly the two European ones mentioned in brackets in the preceding sentence, we arrive at the core values of democratic governance, the guarantee of fundamental human rights concepts and the concept of the (democratic) rule of law[2]. Constitutional systems, in view of the values they affirm, are thus interlinked with international human rights standards and therefore *a high degree of unification of constitutional values*[3] can be seen at international level. *In this respect, there is a certain "lighting-up" in the opposite (vertical) direction, comprising the influence of constitutional values on the material content of certain international treaties.*

8.03. Historically, the spreading characteristic of constitutions (again, especially those of European countries) containing provisions "opening up" the system to international law, or defining the relationship of one's own legal system to an international treaty, customs, organizations, etc., is not at all old. This trend away from "textbook" dualism towards a varying scale of unitary model is undoubtedly being speeded up significantly by the level of development of European economic integration[4].

---

1 This term is used in the case-law of the Czech Constitutional Court. Based on our free, non-authentic own interpretation of this concept, we might say that, in particular, it encompasses the unwritten influence of core value principles, the ideas or concepts of the Constitution, constitutional theory, comparative constitutional law, political theory, etc. – see, for example, our interpretation, particularly as regards Article 9(2) of the Czech Constitution, *in* KAREL KLÍMA ET AL., KOMENTÁŘ K ÚSTAVĚ A LISTINĚ (*Constitution and Charter of the Fundamental Rights and Basic Freedoms: A Commentary*), Plzeň: Vydavatelství a nakladatelství Aleš Čeněk, s.r.o. 78 et seq. (2005).
2 Indeed, the first historical (complete) declaration of human rights is the legendary "Declaration of the Rights of Man and Citizen", as a result of the French Revolution, to a large extent "retroactively" (and officially) "promoted" to the constitutional level by a decision of the Constitutional Council of France from 1971.
3 *Cf.* Boguslaw Banaszak, *Znaczenie porównawczego prawa konstytucyjnego w dobie globalizacji i jednoczenia sie Europy, in* PORÓWNAWCZE PRAWO KONSTYTUCYJNE WSPÓŁCZESNYCH PAŃSTW DEMOKRATYCZNYCH, Warszawa: Wolters Kluwer Polska 31 et seq. (2007).
4 The unusual range of extraordinary derogation by the European Court of Justice merits acknowledgement, in particular the judgment in *Van Gend and Loos*, see KAREL

II. Constitutional and International Legal Framework of Arbitration

8.04. Globally, arbitration has a "supranational" or international (that is, international-law) basis. This can be attributed in part to the fact that the "UNCITRAL Model Law" (hereinafter "UNCITRAL"), relating to international arbitration, has been reflected in many national legal systems "as a principle for the regulation of both international and domestic arbitration (i.e. proceedings without the corresponding international element)"[5]. It is a set of rules which are *recommended*[6] for international commercial law, but, in light of their permeation into the law of numerous UN member states, constitute a special model of "vertical" (naturally) legislative monism. Indeed, this is consistent with the "*pacta sunt servanda*" principle mediated by a more or less (politically) respected and historically the most prestigious international organization (the UN). In terms of the Czech Constitution, this entails one of the many areas of the fulfilment of the principles of international law by Article 1(2): "The Czech Republic shall comply with its obligations under international law"[7].

8.05. However, we cannot directly infer that the application of the UNCITRAL model prevails over the laws of the Czech Republic because this is no "Parliament-approved" international treaty; it is, in fact, "secondary" UN law, and recommendatory at that (the "weight" of the recommendation vague; enforcement is evidently impossible)[8]. Nevertheless, with regard to the respect of constitutional law for international law, we can ask whether the law of a member state is capable of resisting (refusing to give in to, opposing, etc.) the recommendatory principles of an international

---

KLÍMA ET AL., ENCYKLOPEDIE ÚSTAVNÍHO PRÁVA (*Encyclopaedia of Constitutional Law*), Praha: ASPI 173 et seq. (2007).

5   *Cf.* Alexander J. Bělohlávek, Tomáš Pezl, *Mezinárodní a tuzemské rozhodčí řízení z pohledu čl. 36 Listiny základních práv a svobod a pravomocí soudů a ústavou garantovaných práv (institut zrušení rozhodčího nálezu v souvislosti se zákazem revision au fond) (International and Domestic Arbitral Proceeding from the Perspective of the Art. 36 of the Charter of the Fundamental Rights and Basic Freedoms and the Jurisdiction of the Courts and Constitutionally Vested Rights (Institute of the Annulment of the Arbitral Award in Relation to the Prohibition of the Au Fond Revision)*, 146 (7) PRÁVNÍK 768 (2007).

6   *Ibid.*, 763.

7   International commitments are of a varying nature and are not limited solely to international contract law, but also cover international customary law and general principles of law; see KAREL KLÍMA ET AL., KOMENTÁŘ K ÚSTAVĚ A LISTINĚ (*Constitution and Charter of the Fundamental Rights and Basic Freedoms: A Commentary*), Plzeň: Vydavatelství a nakladatelství Aleš Čeněk, s.r.o. 48 (2nd ed. 2009).

8   Interesting in this context is the provision of (now only historical) Section 135(1) of the 1948 Constitution, which provided procedural safeguards for international (private) relations: "The judiciary in civil legal matters shall pertain to civil courts, either ordinary or special courts, or to arbitration courts."

standard. Under Act No. 216/1994 Coll. on arbitration and the enforcement of arbitral awards, as amended (hereinafter the Arbitration Act), the legislature of the Czech Republic generally followed the beaten path established by previous legislation in the form of Act No. 99/1963 Coll. This is certainly no breach of the general constitutional principle above. The overall concept of arbitration rules is not inconsistent with *recommended* international legislation. Respect for international law, however, is a common feature of modern constitutionalism, i.e. of democratic states after the Second World War[9], and in particular of the most recent constitutions after 1990 (the so-called "new democracies")

III. Constitutional Aspects of UNCITRAL

8.06. As mentioned above, although the UNCITRAL Model Law is recommendatory, there are numerous reasons why constitutional law should express the need for major respect for this type of "derived norms" under international law[10]. As the framework of rules (guidelines) for arbitration, including the "national" framework (exclusively), is also geared towards the legal systems of member states (of the UN), it is clear that these rules will not be reflected by the legislature only in the promulgation of a special law (the Arbitration Act in the Czech Republic), including changes in rules and regulations issued, in particular, by permanent arbitration courts[11]. The legislature will also respond in other laws "trespassing" on the judiciary context;[12] important unifying and even test-case decisions of the supreme courts also belong here[13]. However, through numerous provisions the Model Law enters into constitutional

---

[9]   Under Austrian law, acts and deeds may be declared enforceable if such acts and deeds are enforceable under the laws of the State in which they are issued, and if reciprocity is guaranteed by international treaties; see Enforcement Procedure, Law 79/1896, as amended by Act No. 519/1995, Section 79(2).

[10]   In several provisions, the Model Law mirrors other important international agreements, such as the Convention on the Recognition and Enforcement of Foreign Arbitral Awards (1958) – see Decree of the Ministry of Foreign Affairs No. 74/1959, and the European Convention on Commercial Arbitration (1961) – see Decree of the Ministry of Foreign Affairs No. 176/1964, directly binding upon the Czech Republic.

[11]   *Cf.*, for example, the Rules of Procedure of the Arbitration Court attached to the Economic Chamber of the Czech Republic and Agricultural Chamber of the Czech Republic, issued pursuant to Section 13 of the Arbitration Act and published in the Business Journal.

[12]   *Cf.*, for example, the Ukrainian Act on the Recognition and Enforcement of Foreign Court Decisions in Ukraine.

[13]   *Cf.*, for example, Resolution of the Plenary Session of the Supreme Court of Ukraine No. 12/1999 on practical experience from the judicial hearing of proposals for sessions and the enforcement of the decisions of foreign courts and arbitration courts and annulling decisions taken in the context of international commercial arbitration in Ukraine; see also the pilot (and hotly debated in the Czech Republic) Order of the Constitutional Court of the Czech Republic No. IV. ÚS 174/02, filed in Volume of the Collection of Findings and Orders of the Constitutional Court of the Czech Republic No. 27 under number 20.

V. The "Constitutional" Nature of Arbitration as a Means of Dispute Resolution

8.10. It is entirely logical for the basis of a constitutional perspective of arbitration (it is entirely irrelevant whether in proceedings with an international element or in "national" proceedings) to raise the question of its relationship with otherwise exclusive equity in the system of the *state judiciary*, and therefore the relationship between public authority and the decision-making powers of arbitrators.

8.11. The doctrine of constitutional law (in both theoretical and comparative terms), based on the theoretical service of political science, does not insist that the functions of public authority (in particular the public authority of the State) should all be concentrated within the competence of national authorities. For various reasons of efficiency, it places them (by law) into the *decision-making competence* of other types of legal entities, such as municipalities (local public authorities), independent public institutions (e.g. the Supreme Judicial Council in Poland, the Slovak Republic, France and elsewhere), private professional associations (legal activity *ex officio*, notarial activities in probate proceedings, as part of enforcement activity, etc.)[22]. Constitutional systems therefore enable and allow *non-state institutions* to perform certain tasks of public authority, either *"instead of the State"* (e.g. a notary instead of a court official), or *"alongside the State"*, but always within the scope of the envisaged function of State power. This can be shown, for example, in the legislative method of *ensuring the enforceability* of an arbitral award[23].

8.12. In light of the above, we need to look at the phenomenon of arbitration[24]. The constitutional power of democratic states, both in respect to international contract law and in respect to civil and entrepreneurial freedom, as well as, ultimately, effectiveness[25], makes unwritten recognition of arbitration as proceedings *"placed on the same footing as judicial proceedings"*[26] within, of course, a *sui generis* meaning, i.e. in its

---

[22] If the constitutional systems place proposals for the registration of candidates *solely* in the hands of political parties (*cf.* the elections to the Czech Chamber of Deputies), their *statesmanship*, and hence *public aspect*, is constitutionally recognized.

[23] Thus, under Section 44 of Slovak Act No. 244/2002 on arbitration, "a domestic arbitration judgment which has become final shall be enforceable according to special regulations upon expiry of the deadline for compliance in the Slovak Republic." Regarding the conditions for the recognition and enforcement of foreign court decisions, see, for example, the Ukrainian Act on the Recognition and Enforcement of Foreign Court Decisions in Ukraine (Article 2).

[24] However, it is difficult to accept the observation that arbitration courts are inherently "really just a substitute for the state judiciary"; *cf.* JITKA MOTHEJZÍKOVÁ, VILÉM STEINER ET AL., ZÁKON O ROZHODČÍM ŘÍZENÍ. KOMENTÁŘ (*Act on Arbitration. A Commentary*), Praha: C. H. Beck 19 (1996).

[25] Why the State should ensure the professionalism and financial costs of decision-making in all private conflicts.

[26] *Cf.* Alexander J. Bělohlávek, Tomáš Pezl, *supra* note 5, at 770.

public function. This observation does not primarily entail a relationship of such proceedings' "parallel independence" of the State (see below on the possibility of reviewing an arbitral award). At the same time, it cannot be inferred that arbitral awards are "incapable of being decisions of a public authority"[27]. Furthermore, a permanent court of arbitration (e.g. in the Czech Republic) can be established *only* by law (see Section 13(1) of the Arbitration Act)[28].

8.13. With regard to the legislative basis (special legal regulation) and a certain (albeit narrow) possibility for the State to review an award, or the guarantee of the enforceability of awards, arbitration has public elements and, ultimately, a character that clearly places it in parallel with the judicial decision-making of the State. In this respect, the opinion of the Constitutional Court of the Czech Republic that "an arbitrator does not ascertain a right, but rather creates (or possibly solidly builds, clarifies, i.e. settles) an obligation on the parties' behalf" is hardly sustainable[29]. The adversarial nature of arbitration requires a qualified evaluation of the counterparties' arguments, which is impossible without the legal application and systemic assessment of legal concepts.

VI. The Issue of Public Policy

8.14. The structure of Article 34 of the UNCITRAL Model Law, governing possible appeals to an ordinary court seeking a derogation from an arbitral award, is a kind of transfer mechanism which (in paragraph 2) sets out the conditions under which the litigant may lodge an appeal with a court of the State[30], for the sake of example an ordinary court.

8.15. If we exclude from constitutional assessment those conditions of judicial arbitrability which are only of an organizational and procedural nature (a review of the powers or jurisdiction of arbitrators, the prevention of a party from submitting arguments, etc.), the determination of an alleged breach of the "public policy of the State" is a legally highly uncertain issue questioning several branches of law[31].

---

[27] *Cf.* the cited Finding of the Constitutional Court of the Czech Republic No. 20, Vol. 27.

[28] Regarding institutional arbitration, see KVĚTOSLAV RŮŽIČKA, *supra* note 14, at 29.

[29] Like Květoslav Růžička, we do not share this conclusion of the Constitutional Court; *cf.* KVĚTOSLAV RŮŽIČKA, *supra* note 14, at 25 (concerning Order of the Constitutional Court of the Czech Republic IV. ÚS 174/02).

[30] Any comparative specification of the issue as to which court has jurisdiction is beyond the purposes of this article because in this respect the systems of constitutionally close countries, such as the Czech Republic, Germany, France, etc., differ completely.

[31] If we take, as our basis, university pragmatics for the divisions of fields of study (subjects) at law faculties, "public policy" encompasses issues of public international law and constitutional, European, and private (especially commercial) law, and is most useful for actual arbitration practice (for the parties to the proceedings).

8.16. The concept of public policy can evidently be approached from multiple perspectives. From the perspective of constitutional law, this concept can be subsumed in the scope of the term "constitutional system"[32], and as such we directly exclude the reference extreme to beyond the limits of any hypotheticality[33], on the one hand, and "in unacceptable conflict with the law of the State"[34] on the other hand, which makes the interpretation of the concept legislatively "endless"[35].

8.17. If, in this regard, we select the method of systemic inductive confrontation (the meaning of arbitral appellation versus unsurpassable constitutional barriers), it is possible to intercede in favour of a specification of the barriers contained in the constitutional system which must be respected by the parties to arbitration:

a) general principles of due process conditioning democratic statehood, e.g. the equality of the parties;

b) fundamental human rights, and hence *entrepreneurial rights*, when excess threatens the position of the parties, such as the prohibition of debtors' prison or extreme violation of the freedom of contract (acting under duress, blackmail, etc.).

We base the above deduction in part on the issue of *objective arbitrability*, or what type of disputes may be subject to arbitration. In this sense, Czech law laconically establishes the term "property dispute" (Section 2(1) and (2) of the Arbitration Act)[36]. However, (property) disputes arising in connection with the enforcement of a decision or incidental disputes (in insolvency proceedings) are excluded[37].

---

[32]   Here we can clearly agree with Alexander J. Bělohlávek's explanation rather than his alternative version of "social order"; even so, we need not address, for example, political freedoms, elections, local government, etc. See Alexander J. Bělohlávek, Tomáš Pezl, *supra* note 5, at 778.

[33]   Alexander J. Bělohlávek draws attention to this in: *Výhrada veřejného pořádku hmotněprávního a procesního ve vztazích s mezinárodním prvkem (Substantial and Procedural Ordre Public Reservation in the Relations with the International Element)*, 11 PRÁVNÍK 1267-1301 (2006).

[34]   *Cf.* the interpretation of the term *"basis of the legal order of the state"* in any law theory textbook.

[35]   A Hungarian ordinary court cannot (must not) review a foreign arbitral award on its merits, *cf.* Section 74(3) of the Legal Regulation on Private International Law (No. 13/1979).

[36]   For constitutional arguments, a useful definition is provided by Květoslav Růžička, in that *property disputes in legal theory is any dispute, the subject of which relates to property or can be expressed in property values, i.e. particularly in monetary terms; cf.* KVĚTOSLAV RŮŽIČKA, *supra* note 14, at 33.

[37]   Alexander J. Bělohlávek thus admits the arbitrability of disputes *under contracts regarding the holding of office of the governing body or a member of another body of a company (a 'management contract'), various types of mandate relations, etc.; cf.* ALEXANDER J. BĚLOHLÁVEK, ZÁKON O ROZHODČÍM ŘÍZENÍ A O VÝKONU ROZHODČÍCH NÁLEZŮ. KOMENTÁŘ (*Act on Arbitration and on Enforcement of the Arbitral Awards. A Commentary*), Praha: C. H. Beck 33 (2004).

VII. Consideration of the Potential Constitutional and Substantive Legal Effect of Arbitrators' Decision-Making Activities

8.18. One of the reasons set by Czech arbitration rules as a reason for the annulment of an arbitral award can be used as an example. This is Section 31(f) of the Arbitration Act ("an arbitral award orders a party to take action not sought by the beneficiary or to take action which is impossible or illegal under domestic law"). **Again, we are faced with how to address the legislative specification of public policy,** and therefore selected points of (potential) confrontation with certain values of the Constitution. It is necessary, of course, to respect certain impracticality in, or, more mildly speaking, the hypotheticality of the application of such considerations[38]. Yet we not talking about a situation where an arbitral award is challenged on the basis of its merits, but about the potential challenging of the "side effect" of an arbitral award, for example, an arbitration award which goes against the principle of the equality of the parties, harms the privacy and freedom of the parties, harms the content of property rights (*utendi, fruendi...*), is physically impossible to implement, etc[39]. The constitutional content of an award, as to its substance, cannot consequently be excluded (see Article 2(3) of the Charter of Fundamental Rights and Freedoms), but, naturally, our basis is whether an excess has actually occurred, e.g. whether there has been constitutionally inadmissible self-restraint or renunciation (*debtors' prison is conventionally inadmissible*). Here, we are guided by the constitutional emphasis, i.e. Article 36(2), final sentence, which provides that: "[...] However, reviews of decisions relating to fundamental rights and freedoms under the Charter shall not be excluded from the court's jurisdiction." This provision applies only to the administrative judiciary. A systemic interpretation of the Charter's value base leads us to the conclusion, however, that this regulation is part of "public policy"[40].

---

[38] Yet we are not deterred in our thinking even by the pragmatic observation of Alexander J. Bělohlávek that ...*reasons for a review of decisions of the national decisions of ordinary courts, subject to 'public policy', nor is there any logical reason for this in* Alexander J. Bělohlávek, Tomáš Pezl, *supra* note 5, at 774.

[39] Under Article 1150 of the Polish Rules of Civil Procedure, a foreign arbitral award may be enforced in Poland if, *inter alia*, "the parties have had the opportunity to defend themselves or to be represented, or if they have been properly represented".

[40] E.g. Swiss law provides that any claim of a property nature may be a subject of arbitration (Article 177 of the Act on Private International Law).

VIII. The Meaning of "Due Process" for the Arbitration Model

8.19. The concept of "due process" and its inherent components is currently a constitutional phenomenon of the system in place at the Council of Europe which, to varying degrees, vertically enters the constitutional and judicial procedural foundations of Member States[41]. As a judicatory method for the application of the European Convention (especially Article 6 thereof), this doctrine (unlike and as opposed to the UNCITRAL Model Law) is **binding**. It is **directly binding** and, under Article 10 of the Constitution of the Czech Republic, takes precedence over the application of the law as a provision of national origin. The author is naturally aware of a certain aloofness by the European Court of Human Rights concerning judicial review and the use thereof in relation to arbitration[42], and of the voluntary contractual basis for arbitration. The voluntary contractual basis for arbitration should be seen as a dominating constitutional factor giving preference to the private nature of free will.

8.20. Due process should also be viewed as an organizational and procedural system and the regulation of relations between the "public authority" and "persons" (including legal persons). The system of relations conceived as "due process" is therefore part of "public policy" and can be associated, in particular, with conditions for the opportunity of recourse to an [ordinary] court (under Article 34 of the UNCITRAL Model Law)[43]. The concept of "due process" also incorporates the main principles of the judicial process which are implemented by the structure of arbitration; these include the equality of the parties when entering into the arbitration agreement, the right to legal assistance, the adversarial principle, the notification to the parties of all evidence[44]. Under German law, the procedural violation of public policy includes cases where "fundamental rules of procedure

---

[41] Regardless of the type of constitutional culture (*cf.*, for example, the UK Human Rights Act 1998), in particular the constitutional practice of the continental systems has been modified so strongly by the activity of constitutional courts that, on the one hand, there is the text, for example, of Title V of the Charter of Fundamental Rights and Freedoms, and, alongside this, the guidelines of the ECHR in case of the need for a second (review) instance in criminal cases; *cf.* the interpretation *in* KAREL KLÍMA et al., *supra* note 7, at 1293, concerning the ECHR ruling in *Golder* (1975, A-18).

[42] In *Nordström v Netherlands* (decision on admissibility), application no. 28101/95, 27 November 2005, no review of the arbitral award by a court is envisaged, and therefore the States are not required to make amendments; in *Suovaniemi and others v Finland* (decision on admissibility), application no. 31737/96, 23 February 1999, the ECHR goes so far as to prevent the courts from serving as another instance where the unsuccessful party does not objections in the actual proceedings.

[43] Belgium does not engage in this at all; contractually it is also possible to exclude France with regard to relations without an international element.

[44] The jurisdiction of the court is addressed differently if arbitration is handled contractually, and there is no need to construe the risk of "withdrawal from a judge"; the speed of the proceedings is addressed differently. Regarding the constitutional principle

pertaining to the minimum standard of judicial proceedings in the rule of law are breached"[45].

IX. Open (and Certainly Incomplete) Conclusion

8.21. The constitutional environment as a certain harmony of democratic constitutional systems in their current openness to international law and supranational Union units is capable, according to the discussion contained in this article, of viewing, in a respectable light, the phenomenon of *arbitration* in the fully complexity of its private and jurisdictional elements, including the international law element.

8.22. The inductive method of comparative constitutional law, based on model principles of democratic constitutionalism (mainly the continental European "model"), makes it possible to identify and guarantee the contractual nature of arbitration in its effectiveness (positive). It also enables certain fundamental values to be set for the benefits of the public-law judiciary, in its *subsidiary* application, to the quality of arbitration. The use of the *deductive* method of constitutional law in this article might suggest that the "control function" of the (state) judiciary does not require a constitutionally mandatory form in view of the compared implementing legislation in selected countries around the world. Also, regarding the possible appeals "bridge" (the possibility of appealing to a state court), it is better to retain more freedom of contract, and have the state court system intervene only where there clear constitutional abuses exist, i.e. where excesses of a human rights and principally equity nature occur.

8.23. Ultimately, not even the comparatively clear Kelsen (pyramid) model of the constitutional order of the Czech Republic, the Constitution (the chapter on the judiciary), or the Charter (the chapter on the principles of judicial proceedings and the rights of parties) place implementing legislation (especially the Arbitration Act) in conflict[46] with constitutional values. Indeed, the opposite might be true, in that, in terms of content, it is beneficial to the values of international law, which the constitutional order constructively respects.

| | |

---

of the "prohibition of withdrawal from the lawful judge" at ordinary courts, see KAREL KLÍMA, *supra* note 7, at 954 et seq.

[45] According to Alexander J. Bělohlávek, at issue here, for example, is the possibility of commenting on all facts and evidence; *cf.* ALEXANDER J. BĚLOHLÁVEK, *supra* note 37, at 485.

[46] It is thus somewhat paradoxical that the finding of the Constitutional Court of the Czech Republic cited several times above, the purpose of which was to provide a barrier for the admissibility of constitutional complaints, and the content of which does not adequately assess all the values of arbitration, and thus its public elements, essentially underscores the principle of the subsidiarity of the state judiciary in relation to arbitration.

Summaries

DEU [*Verfassungsrechtliches Umfeld und das Phänomen der Schiedsgerichtsbarkeit*]

Der Gedanke der internationalen Schiedsgerichte, mehrere Instrumentarien des internationalen Rechts auszunutzen, konstruiert das „nicht staatliche" Verfahren der privatrechtlichen Streitbeilegung (neben einem Vergleich, den die Parteien auch außerhalb des Schiedsverfahrens vereinbaren können). Verfassungsrechtlich gesehen verzichten sie somit teilweise auf die allgemeine Gerichtsbarkeit, teilweise auf einige Grundsätze des fairen Prozesses und teilweise auch auf die Kassationsprinzipien. Das alles mehr oder weniger auf der Ebene des Verfassungsrechts im organisatorischen und prozessualen Sinn. Verfassungsrechtlich lässt sich diese Vereinbarung letztlich nur schwer als „Derogation der Zuständigkeit des Verfassungsgerichts" verstehen. Es geht eher um eine gesetzlich zugelassene Applikation der Richterfunktion der öffentlichen Gewalt auf ein privatrechtliches Subjekt mit der Möglichkeit (auch wenn nur eingeschränkt) der „Rückgabe" zur gerichtliche Überprüfung.

CZE [*Ústavněprávní prostředí a fenomén arbitráže*]

Myšlenka mezinárodních rozhodčích soudů s využitím několika instrumentarií mezinárodního práva konstruuje „nestátní" způsob rozhodování soukromoprávních sporů (vedle smíru, který strany mohou uzavřít i mimo rozhodčí řízení). Z hlediska ústavního se tak částečně vzdávají přístupu k obecnému soudnictví, částečně se vzdávají některých zásad spravedlivého procesu a částečně i apelační zásady. To vše víceméně v rovině ústavního práva organizačního a soudně procesního. Ústavněprávně chápat tuto dohodu v účincích jako „derogaci jurisdikce ústavního soudu" lze obtížně. Jde spíše o zákonem dovolené užití rozhodcovské funkce veřejné moci na soukromoprávní subjekt i s možností (byť omezenou) jejího „vrácení" k přezkumu obecným soudem.

| | |

POL [*Uwarunkowania konstytucyjno-prawne i zjawisko arbitrażu*]

Doktryna prawa konstytucyjnego (fundamenty teoretyczne i płaszczyzna porównawcza), oparta na teoretycznych poczynaniach nauki o państwie nie upiera się, aby funkcje władzy publicznej koncentrowały się wyłącznie w prerogatywach organów państwowych. Dlatego systemy konstytucyjne umożliwiają i akceptują wykonywanie niektórych zadań władzy publicznej przez instytucje niepaństwowe zamiast władzy państwowej lub „równolegle z nią", jednak zawsze w ramach zakładanej funkcji władzy publicznej. Władza konstytucyjna państw demokratycznych, zarówno w stosunku do międzynarodowego prawa umownego, jak i w stosunku do swobód obywateli i przedsiębiorców, wreszcie – w świetle celu, jakiemu służy, w sposób niepisany uznaje możliwość wyboru postępowania arbitrażowego jako postępowania „stojącego na równi z postępowaniem sądowym".

FRA [*Environnement du droit constitutionnel et phénomène de l'arbitrage*]

La doctrine du droit constitutionnel (fondement théorique et comparatif), s'appuyant sur le service théorique de la science politique, n'exige pas obligatoirement que les fonctions des pouvoirs publics et tout particulièrement de l'État soient entièrement concentrées dans les compétences des organes de l'État. Les systèmes constitutionnels permettent et approuvent ainsi que des institutions non étatiques remplissent certaines missions des pouvoirs publics, et ce à leur place ou « parallèlement », mais toujours dans le cadre de la fonction prévue du pouvoir de l'État. Le pouvoir constitutionnel des États démocratiques, aussi bien dans le respect du droit contractuel international que dans le respect des libertés civiles et entrepreneuriales, mais aussi dans le respect de la rationalité, reconnaît ainsi implicitement la variante de la procédure d'arbitrage en tant que procédure « placée à égalité avec une procédure judiciaire ».

RUS [*Конституционно-правовая среда и феномен арбитража*]

Доктрина конституционного права (теоретических и сравнительных оснований), основанная на теоретических положениях науки о государстве, не настаивает на том, чтобы функции публичной власти, и прежде всего, государства, были полностью сосредоточены в правомочиях государственных органов. Конституционные системы допускают возможность и санкционируют выполнение негосударственным учреждением определенных задач публичной власти – вместо нее, или «наряду с ней» – но лишь в контексте предполагаемых функций государственной власти. Конституционная власть демократических государств как в части международного договорного права, так и в части гражданской и предпринимательской свободы, так, наконец, и в части целесообразности, на неписаном уровне признает арбитражное разбирательство как вариант разбирательства, «поставленный на однин уровень с судебным разбирательством».

ES [*EL entorno constitucional legal y el fenómeno de arbitraje*]

La doctrina del derecho constitucional (su fondo teórico y comparativo) sustentada en el servicio teórico de la ciencia relativa al Estado, no insiste en el hecho de que las funciones del poder público, en particular del Estado, queden concentradas mayormente en las competencias de los órganos públicos. De esta manera, los sistemas constitucionales permiten y aprueban que instituciones no públicas cumplan algunas tareas del poder público, sustituyendo a este último, o encontrándose "al lado del mismo", todo ello no obstante, dentro del marco de la supuesta función del poder público. El poder constitucional de los Estados democráticos , tanto a la hora de respetar el derecho internacional contractual, como al respetar la libertad civil y empresarial, y también finalmente de cara a su conveniencia, de hecho reconoce, de forma no escrita, la variante de procedimiento arbitral como procedimiento "en pie de igualdad con el procedimiento judicial".

Czech (& Central European) Yearbook of Arbitration

Jozef Suchoža | Regina Palková

Reflections on Arbitration Proceedings: A Chance for Dispute Resolution Missed Forever?[1]

Key words:
Arbitration
proceedings
| arbitrator |
independence |
impartiality of
arbitrators

Abstract | *Arbitration practice has been evolving over time, in line with the historical and socio-political backdrop (the latter being an important aspect of commerce and trade in many legal systems), up to a point at which it is common practice for contractual parties to "promise" each other that such disputes as may arise from their business relationship will not be resolved in court proceedings, but be brought before a special body – a permanent arbitration court or an ad hoc arbitrator.*
The institution of arbitration proceedings – as a part of a larger dispute resolution system and an alternative to judicial proceedings in general courts – confronts potential participants in arbitration with a dilemma: which of the dispute resolutions methods on offer should they use?
It is not easy to resolve the above-described dilemma of having to choose in favour of one method of dispute resolution or the other, nor is it easy to come to a final conclusion as to what direction should generally be taken by parties for resolving their disputes, as to what form of dispute resolution could be recommended as "more ideal" – that is, whether to take, at those metaphorical crossroads, the classic (and in some ways safer) route of court proceedings or to venture down a new "turning in the road" and take the risk of experimental alternative dispute resolution.

| | |

Prof. JUDr. Jozef Suchoža, DrSc. is a recognised authority in the field of commercial law. He is a member of the Scientific Council at the Institute of State and Law of the Czech Academy of Sciences in Prague, and an international arbitrator on the lists of arbitrators of the Arbitration Court attached to the Slovak Chamber of Commerce and Industry and of the Arbitration Court attached to the Economic Chamber of the Czech Republic and the Agricultural Chamber of the Czech Republic. He is currently acting as the project manager in charge of a project funded by the Slovak Research and Development Agency (APVV), which focuses on the issue of out-of-court dispute resolution in Slovakia (LPP 0076-09 – Out-of-court/alternative dispute resolution in Slovakia).

---

[1] This article originated in the course of work on the project LPP-0076-09 *"Out-of-court (alternative) dispute resolution in the Slovak Republic"*

I. Genesis of the Problem

9.01. Worldwide interest in the arbitration procedure as an alternative method for resolving legal arguments (disputes, conflicts) between people (but also between legal entities) has undoubtedly been on the rise. What are the causes behind this? From the dawn of history, when barter became an inevitability, humankind has sought a way in which it could resolve and settle mutual interpersonal conflicts as arise from its customary cooperation and its civil (private-law) relations (including commerce and trade), and do so in a reasonable and expeditious manner that is efficient for the disputing parties. This is inherent in the constant striving of people to accomplish simplicity, order, balance, transparency and fairness on the level of natural human interaction. Before state structures came into existence, conflicts between people were resolved by the chieftains (elders) of tribes, by priests, but also by elected arbitrators[2].

JUDr. Regina Palková, PhD is research associate at the Chair of Commercial Law and Economic Law of the Faculty of Law of Pavol Jozef Šafárik University in Košice. She completed her post-graduate studies in 2009. Her research work continues to address issues in the realm of arbitration as well as out-of-court dispute resolution in a more general context. She manages the grant project "Out-of-court (alternative) dispute resolution in Slovakia". e-mail address for contacting both authors: regina.palkova@upjs.sk

9.02. The eldest forms of conciliatory proceedings (arbitrage) in the history of humankind, reaching back as far as the despotic systems of antiquity (in particular in ancient Rome), were not a mere historic relic, but became sort of a spontaneous expression (protest?) against the exclusivity of established (public-law) procedural mechanisms. The elected arbitrator no longer acts as a judge (iudex), but rather like a conciliator (mediator), and the final result of his work is rather a settlement of disrupted relations between the parties to the dispute than a solution (decision) of the dispute imposed from above, i.e., from a position of power, in the form of a judgment (ruling).

9.03. From its very historic inception, the procedure before an elected arbitrator went fundamentally beyond the procedural public-law framework of court proceedings. The legal relevance of such procedures, and the consequences to which they gave rise, were in a certain sense comparable to proceedings in a (state) court[3]. Since the days of ancient Rome, and through the

---

[2] *Cf.* ILONA SCHELLEOVÁ ET AL., ÚVOD DO CIVILNÍHO ŘÍZENÍ (*Introduction to Civil Procedure*), Praha: Eurolex Bohemia, s.r.o. 90 et seq. (2005).
See also HANS HATTENHAUER, EVROPSKÉ DĚJINY PRÁVA (*European History of Law*), Praha: C.H. Beck 29 et seq. (1998).

[3] The complexity of the Roman civil procedure has been pointed out by Prof. JÁN VÁŽNY, ŘÍMSKÝ PROCES CIVILNÍ (*The Roman Civil Procedure*), Praha: Melantrich, a.s. 66 et seq., 70 et seq., 81 et seq. (1935).
See also MILAN BARTOŠEK, DĚJINY ŘÍMSKÉHO PRÁVA (VE TŘECH FÁZÍCH JEHO VÝVOJE) (*The History of Roman Law [in three developmental stages]*), Praha: Academia 85 et seq., 91 et seq. (1988).

subsequent various ways in which Roman law was adopted in continental Europe, especially after the fall of the Western Roman Empire (476 CE), and incorporated into the legal systems of medieval European states, elements of classic Roman private law were demonstrably being carried over and, in a certain sense, modified, including the institution of elected arbitrators, whereas the legal systems of the nascent states and proto-states echoed in one form or another traces of yet more ancient home-grown elements and traditions of law from pre-Christian times[4]. In this context, it appears appropriate to note that most recent research work has shown how out-of-court settlements played their role alongside the dispute resolution in court within the circumstances of Middle-Age Hungary[5].

9.04. The institution of arbitration also found its reflection in the legislation of Austro-Hungary, and here primarily in the statutes for civil court proceedings, i.e., specifically, in the Austrian law on court proceedings in civil legal matters of 1895 and in the Hungarian Act No. I/1911 on the civil court system – laws that remained on the books even during the existence of Czechoslovakia as an independent state, basically up until the passage of Czechoslovak Act No. 142/1950 Coll., which promulgated the Code of Civil Procedure[6].

---

[4] *Cf.* FRANTIŠEK WEYR, TEORIE PRÁVA (*Theory of Law*), Brno-Praha: Nakladatelství Orbis 149 et seq. (1936). In this respect, the author writes: *Roman law has been 'received', as is known, by other (that is, national) systems of law. To the legal scholar, reception cannot mean anything else but the adoption of the content of norms from one legal system in another legal system: in other words, manifestations of that which ought to be are being adopted or, if you will, received. Conversely, the idea of a reception of theories from one legal system by another is nonsensical – after all, as we have already seen, the lawmaker-in-practice (i.e., the maker of that which ought to be, i.e., of legal norms) is in no position to set forth legal theories and provide that they should become binding law, much less to receive theories created by another maker of norms and incorporate them in his own work, i.e., 'his' legal system.*
For the details on how Roman law penetrated the European sphere, see HANS HATTENHAUER, EVROPSKÉ DĚJINY PRÁVA (*European History of Law*), Praha: C. H. Beck 97 et seq. (1998).
[5] See also the intriguing work Adriana Švecová, Tomáš Gábriš, *Riešenie konfliktov v Uhorsku na podklade stredovekej listinnej praxe 13. a začiatku 14. Storočia* (*Conflict Resolution in Hungary on the Basis of the Documentary Record of Medieval Practice in the 13th Century and at the Beginning of the 14th Century*), 19 (40) PRÁVNĚHISTORICKÉ STUDIE 359 et seq. (2009). The authors state:
Conflict resolution is as topical today as it was in the past. It appears that, long before today's legal theory came to witness the boom of out-of-court dispute resolution among the legal and professional community, this form of dispute resolution actually dominated in the Middle Ages.
The authors further elaborate, with reference to TREVOR DEAN, CRIME IN MEDIEVAL EUROPE, Harlow: Pearson Education Ltd. 100-101 (2001): *...out-of-court dispute resolution was the preferred solution for parties to a dispute, seeing as it was faster and cheaper than court proceedings, corruption-proof and offered a greater certainty of higher compensation and actual conciliation between the parties.*
[6] *Cf.* VÁCLAV HORA, ČESKOSLOVENSKÉ CIVILNÍ PRÁVO PROCESNÍ, DÍL III.- OPRAVNÉ PROSTŘEDKY A ZVLÁŠTNÍ ZPŮSOBY ŘÍZENÍ (*Czechoslovak Civil Procedural Law, Vol. III – Remedies and Special Forms of Procedure*), Praha: Všehrd 228 et seq. (1929). In this respect, the author states:

9.05. The process of expansion and, above all, internationalisation of arbitration in former Czecho-Slovakia noticeably gathered steam upon the creation of the Arbitration Court at the Czechoslovak Chamber of Commerce in Prague based upon Act No. 119/1948 Coll., on state oversight over foreign trade and international forwarding relations. This court was renamed the Arbitration Court at the Czechoslovak Chamber of Commerce and Industry in 1978[7]. It should be stressed that this court played an exceptionally important role in the further development and increased institutionalisation of arbitration in what was then Czechoslovakia and its two eventual successor states.

9.06. In this respect, we ought to call to mind the previously implemented changes of civil-law statutes in 1963 and 1964, i.e., the adoption of a new Code of Civil Procedure (Act No. 99/1963 Coll.) and a new Civil Code (Act No. 40/1964 Coll.). During that era and along with these changes, the Czechoslovak concept of, and legal framework for, arbitration procedures also gradually changed. This occurred in a separate law, Act No. 98/1963 Coll., on arbitration in international business dealings and the enforcement of arbitral awards, which built upon its predecessor, Act No. 97/1963 Coll., on international private and procedural law[8].

9.07. Compared to the set of rules contained in Act No. 98/1963 Coll., the current legal framework for arbitration in Slovakia (Act No. 244/2002 Coll., as amended by Act No. 521/2005 Coll. and Act No. 71/2009 Coll.) and in

---

We speak of arbitration proceedings wherever private will entrusts certain private entities with hearing and deciding upon their dispute, thus removing the contested matter from the ambit of general courts. The said private will may manifest itself, above all, in the form of an agreement *of the parties to the dispute, made in writing (577), but may also rest upon* a last will and testament, *as well as in other dispositions or in articles of association (599 Code of Civil Procedure).*

Conversely, Prof. Václav Hora differentiates these arbitration courts of a private nature from what he calls obligatory (authorised) arbitration courts *whose organisation and competencies derive from the sovereign will of the state and who enjoy exclusive jurisdiction over certain matters* (p. 229). Among these courts, he lists, *inter alia*, stock exchange arbitration, arbitration commissions for undertakings with trade-union plant committees, mining arbitration courts and others.

[7]   It ought to be noted, however, that the establishment of a modern system of international commercial jurisdiction in commercial matters (international commercial arbitration) is connected with the creation of the International Chamber of Commerce – ICC in Paris in 1919, where the International Court of Arbitration – ICC Court – was constituted in 1923.

[8]   Act No. 98/1963 Coll. was abolished in the Czech Republic by act No. 216/1994 Coll., on arbitration proceedings and the enforcement of arbitral awards, which is in force to this day. In Slovakia, act No. 98/1963 Coll. was abolished by way of act No. 218/1996 Coll., on arbitration proceedings.

Cf. Vilém Steiner, František Štajgr, Československé Mezinárodní civilní právo procesní (*Czechoslovak International Civil Procedural Law*), Praha: Academia – Nakladatelství Čs. Akademie věd 165 et seq. (1967).

In this work, the authors presented the view that *arbitrators are not bodies of state authority or public administration.* (p. 174).

See also Vilém Steiner, Občianske procesné právo v teórii a praxi (*Civil Procedural Law in Theory and Practice*), Bratislava: Obzor 14 et seq. (1980).

the Czech Republic (Act No. 216/1994 Coll., on arbitration proceedings and the enforcement of arbitral awards) is more comprehensive, and thus applies irrespective of whether arbitration takes place to resolve domestic (property) disputes or international (commercial-law or civil-law) relations[9]. However, the tendency towards legislative 'complexity', towards expanding the sphere (scope of application) of arbitrability, has recently encountered certain difficulties. The reason for this is the divergent character of those disputes which, under existing law, fall within the realm of arbitration proceedings.

9.08. The Slovak lawmaker has long been looking for new models of arbitration procedure, in spite of the fact that the current act on arbitration proceedings from 2002 (itself already the second Slovak arbitration law, which abolished the historically first Slovak act on arbitration proceedings – Act No. 218/1996 Coll. in the wording of Act No. 448/2001 Coll.) has been amended twice already[10]. The first amendment took the form of Act No. 521/2005 Coll., which set forth a twin set of public record – namely, the list of permanent arbitration courts – to be kept in the Commercial Gazette and in a Record kept by the Slovak Ministry of Justice. The second amendment (Act No. 71/2009 Coll.) incorporated several provisions concerning consumers in the act on arbitration proceedings[11].

---

[9] *Cf.* Jitka Mothejzíková, Vilém Steiner, et al., Zákon O rozhodčím řízení a výkonu rozhodčích nálezů. Komentář (*Commentary on the Act on Arbitration Proceedings and the Enforcement of Arbitral Awards*), Praha: C. H. Beck 11 et seq. (1996). For a more detailed view, see Alexander J. Bělohlávek, Zákon O rozhodčím řízení a o výkonu rozhodčích nálezů. Komentář (*Commentary on the Act on Arbitration Proceedings and the Enforcement of Arbitral Awards*), Praha, C. H. Beck 26 et seq. (2004).
See Květoslav Růžička, Rozhodčí řízení před Rozhodčím soudem při Hospodářské komoře České republiky a Agrární komoře České republiky (*Arbitration Proceedings before the Arbitration Court attached to the Economic Chamber of the Czech Republic and the Agricultural Chamber of the Czech Republic*), Dobrá Voda u Pelhřimova: Vydavatelství Aleš Čeněk (2003).
See also Přemysl Raban, Alternativní řešení sporů, arbitráž a rozhodci V České a Slovenské republice a zahraničí (*Alternative Dispute Resolution, Arbitration and Arbitrators in the Czech and Slovak Republic and Abroad*), Praha, C. H. Beck 73 et seq. (2004).
[10] The Czech act on arbitration proceedings and the enforcement of arbitral awards (216/1994 Coll., as amended by Act No. 245/2006 Coll. and Act No. 296/2007 Coll.) has proven more sustainable. It has been in force for 15 years already. Even though the historically first Slovak act on arbitration proceedings of 1996 was passed almost two years before the first Czech law, it was abolished only six years later.
[11] Effective as of July 1, 2009, the amendment expanded the original wording of Section 31 (3) of the act on arbitration proceedings by inserting an additional provision according to which the arbitration court shall also take into consideration the generally binding provisions for the protection of consumer rights, i.e., Section 53 of the Civil Code (on consumer contracts), the Consumer Protection Act (Act No. 250/2007 Coll.), Act No. 266/2005 Coll., on the protection of consumers in financial services sold at a distance, Regulation (EC) 2006/2004 of October 27, 2004, of the European Parliament and the Council, on cooperation between national authorities responsible for the enforcement of consumer protection laws (OJ L 364/11, 12/09/2004).

9.09. The pace of legislation which we could observe in our country from mid-2009 and which was headed towards passage of a third amendment of the act on arbitration proceedings was eventually slowed when the president refused to sign the bill adopted by parliament, and returned it to the legislative body for a new discussion. The proposed amendment to the act on arbitration proceedings conceives of, firstly, new legal institutions such as the "administration of a permanent arbitration court", and, secondly, introduces a special review mechanism for remedying acts of arbitration which go beyond the standard procedural means set out in the act on arbitration proceedings, including the Code of Civil Procedure. Lastly, the concept of the founders' liability "for the activities of the permanent arbitration court and of its arbitrators, including damage caused by the activities of the permanent arbitration court and its arbitrators" is ambiguous. Then there remains a body of other unresolved issues and problems, e.g., the question of which arbitration courts have jurisdiction over consumer disputes or labour-law disputes.

9.10. Aside from legislative aspects, the issue of arbitration proceedings doubtlessly touches upon other interests as well. Firstly, there is the issue of identifying the legal character of the procedure itself, as a specific legal process, within the context of classic civil court proceedings – in short, the issue of localising where contractual arbitration stands within the hierarchy of legal process as such. These are systemic, branch-related questions – that is, questions of legal theory – and they include the root problem of defining arbitration with a view to constitutional and international aspects (including the European context). Building on these, we find that there is yet another issue, the core of which is that we have to arrive at some sort of doctrine (tenets, theory) of arbitration proceedings (both generally and in commercial relations specifically) which also involves bringing order to the relevant scientific findings, the normative (legislative) documentation (incl. foreign sources), and, finally, a comparative review, selection, and hierarchisation of compared (and selected) legal institutions from an international cross-section[12].

For the same reasons, the provision of Sec. 33 of the act on arbitration proceedings was expanded by adding the following: *Also, performance under a consumer contract may not be awarded if that contract is at odds with the generally binding provisions on consumer protection, i.e., in particular, if it contains unacceptable contractual terms and conditions.* Finally, the amendment supplemented the grounds on which action may be filed in the competent court for nullification of a domestic arbitration award, worded as follows: *the decision infringed upon generally binding statutory law for the protection of consumer rights.*

Cf. Regina Palková, *Vybrané problémy rozhodcovskej zmluvy (So zvláštnym zreteľom na oblasť sporov zo spotrebiteľských zmlúv)* (*Selected Issues of Arbitration Agreements [with Special Consideration for Consumer Contracts]*), *in* 62 (2) Justičná revue 225 et seq. (2010).

[12] In this respect, the work by Alexander J. Bělohlávek, Arbitration Law And Practice in the Czech Republic (with Regard to the Arbitration Law in Slovakia), Praha: Linde a.s. 52 et seq. (2009) deserves particular attention.

9.11. Secondly, we are faced with theoretical and legislative issues of arbitrability, i.e., the definition of the scope of those legal relations which fall within the ambit of arbitration proceedings – in the form of a comparative cross-section, and taking into consideration the desired state under future law, as well as such other issues as may be pertinent. The legal position of arbitrators or, as the case may be, permanent arbitration courts in terms of their decision-making practice remains unresolved 'by tradition'.

II. Theoretical Issues of Arbitration Proceedings

9.12. In traditional Czechoslovak procedural doctrine, the arbitration procedure was treated within the context of Czechoslovak civil procedural law, and while it was, e.g., omitted from Part Three of Hora's textbook – special forms of procedure – under doctrinal and pedagogical aspects – it did find its way into the following Part Four, where it was reviewed alongside the syndicalist procedure, the stock exchange arbitration procedure and the arbitration procedure in employment-related disputes[13].

9.13. Hora's approach with respect to the categorisation of arbitration in his standard textbook on civil law – i.e., treating it almost as an afterthought (in a marginal section of the textbook) – becomes understandable when we realise that Prof. Hora considered arbitration procedures to be a part of Czechoslovak civil procedural law only in a broader sense of the term, but not under the aspect of inherent integrity, whereas he reasoned that such procedures take place "before private persons by mutual accord of the parties...". Similarly, Prof. F. Štajgr states that "the procedure before arbitrators is a procedure aimed at deciding a property dispute (which has arisen from international commerce). The arbitrators may substitute for the court, but they are themselves not a court. They replace the court at the will of the parties, and are simply persons who enjoy a certain amount of trust of the parties"[14].

9.14. New views of arbitration – which we may call diametrically opposed to the simplified (austere) understanding of arbitration as some sort of "special" procedure (derived from civil court procedures) – were conditional upon (and heavily influenced by) the expansion of the

---

[13] *Cf.* Václav Hora, *supra* note 6, at 179 et seq. & 228 et seq. Prof. Hora himself has this to say:
Special procedures presuppose a procedure before regular courts. Therefore, the following are not special procedures:
  1. Proceedings before arbitratorarbitrators (even though these are addressed in Book VI. Section 4 of the Code of Civil Procedure), because they take place, by mutual accord of the parties, before private persons, and are governed by principles which are also either stipulated by mutual accord of the parties or by way of the arbitrators' discretionary powers. The activities of regular courts in these proceedings concern only isolated random issues ... and where they do, they remain within the framework of the general principles for regular proceedings.

[14] Vilém Steiner, František Štajgr, Československé mezinárodní civilní právo procesní (*Czechoslovak International Civil Procedural Law*), Praha: Academia – Nakladatelství ČSAV 172 et seq. (1967).

sphere of international arbitration. Within the Czechoslovak context, the legislation on international private and procedural law contained in Act No. 97/1963 Coll., helped a great deal in this respect, as did (building upon the erstwhile law) the legal regulation of arbitration proceedings in international commerce and of the enforcement of arbitral awards codified in Act No. 98/1963 Coll. These laws *de facto* removed the issue of arbitration agreements (in terms of their concept, content and formal requirements) from the scope of classic rules and doctrines of civil procedural law (or rather, elevated the issue beyond that framework)[15].

9.15. The first arbitration laws adopted in the 1990s in the Czech Republic (Act No. 216/1994 Coll.) and in Slovakia (Act No. 218/1996 Coll.) in a sense unified the regime of arbitration proceedings held in international commercial relations and in domestic property disputes, so that the issue of arbitration is (to simplify somewhat) reduced to one of understanding (defining) arbitrability.

9.16. Irrespective of the previous legislative dualism in the Czechoslovak laws on arbitration procedures – i.e., on the one hand, arbitration procedures as stipulated in historic laws on civil court proceedings (and therein labelled as "special"), i.e., categorised as a special form of procedure, and, on the other hand, arbitration procedures in commercial disputes with an international element, legal theory always stressed their commonalities, i.e., in particular, the contractual (consensual) basis of arbitration proceedings.

9.17. The phenomenon of the (arbitration) agreement is the defining element of arbitration proceedings, in terms of how to interpret its legal character, its basic characteristics and the relevant sanctions (consequences of liability) for arbitrators (arbitration courts) who cause damage (in the broader sense of pecuniary loss) to the parties to the proceedings. The arbitration procedure, too, is concerned with the protection of subjective rights of people awarded under the given substantive law and otherwise guaranteed by the supreme laws of the given state[16].

9.18. In connection with the legal framework for arbitration procedures, several questions arise from the broader context, consequences and interpretations of that framework. Taking as their point of departure the very fact of how the laws on arbitration procedures are labelled (e.g., in

---

[15] *Cf.* VILÉM STEINER, OBČIANSKE PROCESNÉ PRÁVO V TEÓRII A PRAXI (*Civil Procedural Law in Theory and Practice*), Bratislava: Obzor 217 et seq. (1980).
Similarly VILÉM STEINER, FRANTIŠEK ŠTAJGR, *supra* note 14, at 165 et seq.

[16] *Cf.* the basic rights and liberties – Article 12 et seq. of the Slovak Constitution (constitutional law No. 460/1992 Coll.).
Similarly Article 20 (right to own property), Article 35 (right to conduct business), Article 46 et seq. (right to protection by courts and other protection by the law), etc.
Cf. also the Charter of Fundamental Rights and Basic Freedoms (in particular Art. 2 et seq., Art. 11, Art. 26, etc.) *in* JIŘÍ NOLČ, ET AL., ÚSTAVA ČR S ÚVODNÍM KOMENTÁŘEM (*The Czech Constitution, with an Introductory Commentary*), Brno: Computer Press, a.s. (2005).
Cf. ROBERT ALEXY, POJEM A PLATNOSŤ PRÁVA (*Concept and Rule of Law*), Bratislava: Kalligram 126 et seq. (2009).

Slovakia, the "act on arbitration proceedings", in the Czech Republic, the "act on arbitration proceedings and on the enforcement of arbitral awards", but finally also the Model law on international commercial arbitration), several interpretations put particular stress on this aspect in the sense that these laws are thought to be of an expressly procedural character. These interpretations overlook the fact that, aside from the procedural aspect, arbitration laws often contain two additional elements: an organisational / institutional element (i.e., the mechanism for creating the position of arbitrators and the institution of permanent arbitration courts), and the element of applicable (governing) substantive law which in the specific case is to be applied, including relevant trade customs, the principles of fair business dealings, and *boni mores*.

9.19. Regarding the procedural side of the law, there are views that would consider the arbitration procedure to fall within the sphere of interest of procedural law as public law. This view disregards the contractual basis of arbitration, which "triggers" not only the mechanism for creating the position of the arbitrator (or of the permanent arbitration court), but also the entire process of hearing and deciding specific disputes before the arbitral tribunal, whereas the procedural steps and measures only superficially resemble proceedings in the general courts (e.g., in the matter of certain identical or similar procedural principles). The procedural aspects of arbitration are closely related to the adequate substantive law from which the claims that are made have been derived. In the older literature, we occasionally encounter the view that all legal procedures (processes) more or less exhibit common features. This concerns especially procedures which take place before the general courts, i.e., the civil court process and the criminal process. In this respect, Prof. Macur voiced the opinion at the time that some sort of general doctrine of procedural law, referred to as Allgemeine Prozessrechtslehre, had been taking shape in Europe since the end of the 19th century[17].

9.20. Other proceedings are an organic part of the "legal process" (as a phenomenon conceived this broadly), such as proceedings before the Constitutional Court, administrative proceedings or proceedings before other governmental bodies (public authorities), disciplinary proceedings,

---

[17] JOSEF MACUR, OBČANSKÉ PRÁVO PROCESNÍ V SYSTÉMU PRÁVA (*Civil Procedural Law within the Legal System*), Brno: Jan Evangelista Purkyně University in Brno 199 et seq. (1975).
Cf. also JOSEF MACUR, SOUDNICTVÍ A SOUDNÍ PRÁVO (*The Judiciary and Judicial Law*), Brno: Jan Evangelista Purkyně University in Brno 45 et seq. (1988).
Similarly JOSEF MACUR, PROBLÉMY VZÁJEMNÉHO POMĚRU PRÁVA PROCESNÍHO A HMOTNÉHO (*Issues concerning the Mutual Relation of Procedural and Substantive Law*), Brno: Acta Universitatis Brunensis 49 et seq. (1993). For a review and reflection on the latter-cited publication of Macur, see Viktor Knapp, *Úvahy o civilním procesu* (*Deliberations on Civil Procedure*), 133 (9-10) PRÁVNÍK 807 et seq. (1994).

etc[18]. According to Prof. Weyr, the bedrock of legal proceedings as such is the creation of norms, i.e., primary, secondary, general or specific norms, whereas the normative process takes place either based upon autonomous or heteronomous principles[19]. In this understanding, the act of entering into a (private-law) contract, including arbitration agreements, is undeniably also a "norm". Understanding the essence of the legal process on the most general level, i.e., "the process as such", entails an analysis of all aspects and dimensions of various manners (kinds) and modalities of legal processes, i.e., also such as do not take place before the general courts (such as, e.g., civil court proceedings or criminal proceedings), but also before other bodies (forums) of the private-law realm (sphere). In its generalised form, the legal process presents itself not merely as a public-law collection of procedural rules – which is only one of several potential options (forms) of legal process – but also has a potential private-law level, e.g., in arbitration[20]. The above allows us to frame the hypothesis that

---

[18] *Cf.* Ján Drgonec, Konanie pred Ústavným súdom Slovenskej republiky (*Proceedings before the Constitutional Court of the Slovak Republic*), Šamorín: Heuréka 251 (2008).

Cf. Radovan Suchánek, *Vliv ústavního soudu na legislativní proces* (*The Influence of the Constitutional Court on the Legislative Process*), *in* II. Nové jevy v právu na počátku 21. století. Teoretické a ústavní impulzy rozvoje práva (*II. New Legal Phenomena at the Beginning of the 21st Century. Theoretical and Constitutional Stimuli for the Development of Law*), Praha: Charles University in Prague 124 et seq. (A. Gerloch, M. Tomášek eds., 2010).

Similarly Viktor Knapp et al., Tvorba práva a její současné problémy (*The Development of Law and Its Current Problems*), Praha: Linde Praha 462 (1998).

See also Marián Ševčík, Správne právo procesné (*Administrative Procedural Law*), Bratislava: Eurounion 177 (2007).

Cf. Lubomír Kubů, Pavel Hungr, Petr Osina, Teorie práva (*Theory of Law*), Praha: Linde Praha 25 et seq. (2007).

[19] František Weyr, Teorie práva (*Theory of Law*), Brno-Praha: Nakladatelství ORBIS 133 et seq. (1936). The author states:

Autonomous principle' here is meant to be understood as the principle whereby a given norm can only come into existence by way of a collaboration of subjects which binds the (future obliged party), i.e., in other words: through which the subject that is the creator of the norm becomes the subject bound by the pertinent obligation.

See also Viktor Knapp, Teorie práva (*Theory of Law*), Praha: C. H. Beck 52 et seq. (1995).

[20] Even though Prof. K. Růžička is not a proponent of what is known as the contractual theory, which substantiates the legal character of the arbitration procedure, he does point out the significance and indeed the priority of the understanding of the parties with respect to the procedural approach (the procedural rules) in arbitration, over and above the UNCITRAL Rules or the Rules of Arbitration of the Arbitration Court.

Cf. Květoslav Růžička, *supra* note 9, at 154 et seq.

Similarly Květoslav Růžička, *K některým otázkám rozhodčího řízení* (*On Certain Issues concerning Arbitration*), 44 (1) Acta Universitatis Carolinae Iuridica- Aktuální otázky mezinárodního práva soukromého (*Current Issues of International Private Law*) 67 (1998). In this respect, the author writes: *Also in the case of international commercial arbitration, the parties are entitled to set rules of procedure for the arbitrators (in the absence of which, the arbitrators determine them themselves).*

the "legal process" (under the aspect of its general definition) should be understood as a category above the level of legal branches, as a category of interdisciplinary nature. Keeping this in mind, we find that certain types of legal processes have an explicitly (non-contentious) public-law character (such as e.g., civil court proceedings)[21], whereas others can hardly be subsumed under the sphere of public law (e.g., arbitration proceedings – contractual arbitrage). The fact is, arbitration also gives rise to additional – one might say, derived – problems, as we shall see in the following section of this paper.

III. The Arbitrator: Selected Issues

9.21. Acting in the role or position of arbitrator within the context of dispute resolution qua arbitration is currently fraught with numerous questions and controversies. With a view to the weight and significance of arbitration proceedings and the nature of its results (in the form of an arbitral award), arbitrators find themselves in a position similar to that of a state judge. It is with some justification that we may call the arbitrator a quasi-judge who was appointed by the contractual parties. This postulate, made at the beginning of this analysis, essentially captures all relevant elements of the role and function of arbitrators within the context of arbitration proceedings, and along with other characteristics of arbitration, differentiates it from other forms of alternative dispute resolution (such as, e.g., mediation). This approach towards arbitration proceedings and towards the position of arbitrators was also expressed in the decision of the European Court of Justice in C-145/96 *von Hoffmann v. Finanzamt Trier*, which held that the "*services of an arbitrator are principally and habitually those of settling a dispute between two or more parties*", which is why they cannot be put on the same level as a lawyer representing and defending the interests of parties[22]. The position of arbitrators is generally a controversial issue which has divided the professional community into two opposing camps. One camp understands the arbitrator to be in the position of a body unto whom the competence of courts has been conferred. This approach is characteristic for what is known as jurisdictional theory. The other ideological platform

---

[21] V. Knapp has this to say concerning this issue:
The court proceedings are therefore above all a formal procedure followed by the court as a body of state sovereignty. This ... emphasises the public-law character of proceedings, and it is precisely this public-law concept that is ... the key to resolving the interaction between civil procedural law (and indeed judicial procedure in general) and substantive law – loco cit. in footnote 15, p. 811
See also František Štajgr, *Některé teoretické otázky civilního práva procesního* (*Certain Theoretical Issues of Civil Procedural Law*), 15 (X) ACTA UNIVERSITATIS CAROLINAE. IURIDICA. MONOGRAPHIA 21 (1969). The author writes: *...Civil procedure law belongs within the sphere of public law, and cannot belong anywhere else.*
[22] PHILIPPE FOUCHARD, EMMANUEL GAILLARD, BERTHOLD GOLDMAN, ON INTERNATIONAL COMMERCIAL ARBITRATION, London: Kluwer Law International 560 (1999).

of legal theorists assumes that the arbitrator acts in the position of someone who has undertaken the task to render a service to the parties. This 'service' is the solution of the dispute which has arisen among the parties. Professional circles in these parts of the world rather identify with the latter position[23]. Of course, as is the case with most contested issues, and thus also with the issue of the arbitrator's role, one will find positions that elude the rigorous understanding of the arbitrator along the lines of the above-cited criteria.

9.22. The selection and appointment of the arbitrator is a central, if not the most important, step in the arbitration procedure, which has far-reaching consequences and influences the entire further course of decision of the dispute[24]. The opportunity to determine one of the authors of the eventual decision is a defining factor of the arbitration system[25]. The option of having the arbitrator appointed by the contractual partners is generally accepted in all legislations which integrate the arbitration procedure into the system of dispute resolution.

9.23. The opportunity to actively influence the choice of the individual (or even the entire arbitral body – tribunal) who is to decide the dispute in question is the most frequently discussed advantage of arbitration procedures. The parties are given the power to influence the resolution of disputes which arise between them in a very substantial manner when they are allowed to appoint a single arbitrator by mutual accord, or even "their own" arbitrator each. Conventional court proceedings prevent the parties to the dispute from exercising any influence whatsoever on the choice of who specifically is going to decide (or partake in the decision of) their dispute.

9.24. The appointment of an arbitrator by mutual accord (consensus) of the parties subsumes two acts which must both (cumulatively) be accomplished: firstly, there is the elementary prerequisite of appointment that the parties have an understanding – consensus – regarding the identity of the arbitrator(s), and secondly, the appointee must accept his appointment. A different matter is the mechanism for establishing a whole arbitral tribunal, in that the selection of the individual arbitrators is followed by the election of a chairperson (presiding arbitrator) by the thus chosen arbitrators. In this case, the parties no longer have any influence

---

[23] For a more detailed account, see: Ján Husár, *Rozhodca v rozhodcovskom konaní* (*The Arbitrator in Arbitration Proceedings*), *in* Arbitráž i mediacja jako instrumenty wspierania przedsiębiorczości: Materiały z Międzynarodowej konferencji naukowej zorganizowanej przez Zakład Prawa Handlowego i Gospodarczego Wydziału Prawa Uniwersytetu Rzeszowskiego w Rzeszowie w dniach 22-23 września 2006 roku, Rzeszow: Facultas Iuridica Universitatis Ressoviensis 63-73 (J. Olszewski, B. Sagan, R. eds., 2006).

[24] Douglas Earl Mclaren, *Party-Appointed vs. List-Appointed Arbitrators: A Comparison*, 20 (3) Journal Of International Arbitration 233 (2003).

[25] Doak Bishop, Lucy Reed, *Practical Guidelines for Interviewing, Selecting and Challenging Party-Appointed Arbitrators in International Commercial Arbitration* 14 (4) Arbitration International 395 et seq. (1998).

on the choice of the third arbitrator, who in most cases will assume the position of the chairperson of the arbitral tribunal and who is chosen by the arbitrators, who were in turn appointed by the parties.

9.25. The above-mentioned partial acts of appointment must ultimately be fulfilled cumulatively, if not at the very same moment. A point of contention will be the moment in which the parties should enter into their agreement on the identity of the person entrusted with resolving their disputes, i.e., the moment in which the parties are to agree on the arbitrator. Several alternative situations may arise in practice. The name of the arbitrator may be contained in the agreement made between the parties itself, in the form of a provision which submits all disputes (or specific disputes) under the decision-making authority of the thus specified individual. If a dispute occurs, then this understanding will qualify as an agreement on the arbitrator (though the acceptance and consent of the appointee to act as arbitrator in the given dispute will still be required). At the same time, it is the undisputed right of the parties to agree, within the context of the arbitration clause contained in their main contract, merely on the fact that their disputes should be resolved before an institution of arbitration, whereas the remaining points will be further specified only in the event that a dispute actually arises. In such a case, the agreement will not contain, and need not contain, any direct specification of the concrete individuals who are to act in the "position" of an arbitrator. We believe that the latter alternative is more efficient in practice, given that it is clearly impossible to anticipate all future situations, so that it is more than unrealistic to rely on the continued availability of the individual appointed in the agreement, given the vagaries of human life[26].

9.26. One of the basic prerequisites for acting as an arbitrator is that the person who is to resolve the dispute between the parties (or partake in the resolution of the dispute, in the case of several arbitrators who reach a decision on an arbitral tribunal) preserves his impartiality and independence.

9.27. In some countries, parties may challenge the choice of arbitrator and the arbitrator's acts for the same reasons for which they may challenge the

---

[26] A similar position has been taken by the Czech Supreme Court in its decision 33 Odo 135/2006 of January 31, 2008. In the light of this decision, *...it has now become apparent that it is not expedient to determine the identity of arbitrator/s as specific private individuals (i.e., by specifying their name, place of residence, date of birth, etc.) without at the same time determining a 'substitute' arbitrator, i.e., a mechanism for selecting an arbitrator for the event that the arbitrator initially specified by the parties did not, or could not, act in this position. If the individual who has thus been determined in the arbitration agreement does not act as the arbitrator, then it is, in the view of the Supreme Court, not permissible that a court should instead appoint the arbitrator.* – Zbyšek Kordač, *Pozor při určování rozhodců!* (*Beware of the Pitfalls in Appointing Arbitrators!*) Available in Czech at:
http://www.epravo.cz/top/clanky/pozor-pri-urcovani-rozhodcu-53952.html
(accessed on September 5, 2010).

acts of judges in deciding a dispute[27]. However, as Redfern and Hunter show, this analogy between the role of arbitrators and the role of judges should not be pushed to such extremes; the aforementioned authors emphatically point out the difference between the respective positions of arbitrator and judge in connection with the character and origin of their competencies and powers. Following tradition, they invoke the need to approach the position of the arbitrator and the position of the judge differently, calling the judge a "servant of the state", and requiring that the judge's duties and responsibilities be derived from this specific character of his work and role. However, in consideration of the essence of the arbitrator's activity, which – as in the case of judges – lies in hearing and deciding disputes, we believe that there exists an undeniable analogy between arbitrator and judge in terms of the need to preserve impartiality and independence.

9.28. The independence and impartiality of courts and judges is a topic that draws a lot of attention, also in the international forum – to wit, in the UN Basic Principles on the impartiality of the judiciary, adopted by the UN General Assembly in November 1985, in Recommendation R/94/12 of the Committee of Ministers at the Council of Europe of December 1994, and in the European Charter on the Statute of Judges (Judges' Charter) approved by the Council of Europe in Strasbourg on 8-10 July 1998. The uncontested principles set out in these international documents and further elaborated upon in national laws and regulations cannot be fully applied to the "statute of arbitrators". The judge is a "servant" of the state, which is why his conduct is subject to more stringent requirements. Judges must act such that the principle of an independent judiciary is not affected, and such that the public trust in an independent and impartial jurisprudence is being strengthened[28]. The way in which a judge behaves and presents himself is under closer scrutiny, given that he must control his conduct even in his private life and during off-duty activities, after taking off the judge's gown, so that the trust in him is not being compromised. Various ethical codes of the judiciary impose obligations on their members regarding their civil life (e.g., the obligation to take into consideration their own trustworthiness in managing their own property and that of their families, or the prohibition of private activities which are in conflict with the dignity of the office of a judge and the trustworthiness of the judiciary, the obligation to set an example, through their civil life and their conduct in public, in terms of good social customs and personal dignity, and the obligation to keep away from company, places and individuals who might compromise them), the professional exercise of the judicial office (e.g., the obligation to refrain from prejudging; the obligation to treat participants

---

[27] Alan Redfern, Martin Hunter, Law And Practice Of International Commercial Arbitration, London: Sweet&Maxwell 199 (4th ed. 2004).

[28] Judicial Code of Ethics – accessible at http://www.vlada.gov.sk (accessed on September 7, 2010).

with patience, dignity and respect, the obligation to see to it that each and every decision be not only factually correct and lawful, but also that its explanation be transparent and compelling), and the obligations *vis-à-vis* one's own profession (e.g., the obligation to show respect and maintain good professional relations with other judges, the obligation to contribute to the creation and perfection of, and the adherence to, ethical rules in the interest of integrity and independence of the judiciary. By contrast, no demands of such breadth can be imposed on arbitrators, given that they are private persons outside their decision-making in the arbitration procedure, in no respect different from any private individual.

9.29. The independence of the judiciary is made manifest in the requirement to be guided only by the best of one's own knowledge and belief in exercising that office. The judge's decision-making must not be influenced by anyone or prone to any such outside influence[29]. We believe that the same construction can also be applied to the position of the arbitrator, who, for the intent and purposes of the case at hand, plays a role which is analogous to that of a judge. In this regard, the defining qualities of the terms impartiality and independence, respectively, are mutually dependent upon each other – one must be fulfilled for the positive existence of the other. Independence is a prerequisite for impartiality, and thus for a fair process, says Čipkár. The independence of the arbitrator is fundamental for observance of the obligation to be impartial in the procedure, and only an independent arbitrator will be able to decide a dispute with impartiality[30]. Similarly, Mokrý also points out the interdependence of these two postulates. He understands an impartial judge to be a person who is not dependent on the matter that is to be heard, the parties to the dispute or their legal counsel, in the sense that he is neutral *vis-à-vis* them, that he has no prejudices, sympathies or antipathies, that the parties are, in his eyes, wholly equal, and that neither of them has any *a priori* advantages, disadvantages, merits or faults[31]. This statement doubtlessly also applies to the impartiality of arbitrators. The contents of the term of impartiality of judges are also made manifest in the case-law of the European Court of Human Rights which held, in *Piersack vs. Belgium*[32], that impartiality must be approached from two different angles[33], in that

---

[29]   Ján Čipkár, Profesijná etika právnika (*The Lawyer's Professional Ethics*), Košice: Pavol Jozef Šafárik University in Košice 125 (2003).
[30]   Emilio Cárdenas, David W. Rivkin, *A Growing Challenge For Ethics In International Arbitration*, in Intercontinental Cooperation Though Private International Law, The Hague: T.M.C. Asser Institute 267 (T. Einhorn, P. E. Nygh, K. Siehr eds., 2004).
[31]   Antonín Mokrý, *Nezávislost a nestrannost soudce – vzájemná souvislost a podmíněnost pojmu (Independence and Impartiality of Judges – on the Interaction and Interdependence of Terms)*, 41 (8) Právní praxe 459 (1993),
[32]   *Piersack v. Belgium* (dec.), No. 8692/79, 1 October 1982.
[33]   Ernest Valko, Branislav Jablonka, *Právo na nestranný súd a jeho uplatnenie prostredníctvom námietky zaujatosti (The Right to an Impartial Court and its Enforcement through the Defence of Bias)*, 7 (6-7) Justičná revue 797 (2004)

a subjective aspect of impartiality must be applied as well as an objective aspect of impartiality. The former covers the personal beliefs of the judge who hears the case, his subjective attitude towards the matter. At the same time and cumulatively, the second, objective element of impartiality must also be present, which entails the provision of sufficient guarantees to rule out any doubt in this respect[34]. An arbitrator will not meet the criteria for impartiality if – as in the analogous case of judges – either element, i.e., the objective element or the subjective element, is not fulfilled.

9.30. Trakman defines impartiality as a state of mind of the individual, whereas it is relevant how this state of mind is evidenced through the arbitrator's conduct which will demonstrate in one way or another that the criteria for impartiality are fulfilled or are not fulfilled. The independence of arbitrators (and its limitations) must be reviewed under the aspect of interpersonal relationships: if the arbitrator is professionally or personally related to any of the parties to the proceedings, or has family bonds or commercial connections to either party, then the requirement for independence on the part of the arbitrator is not met[35]. The arbitrator will not be considered independent, if his personal interests are tied to the interests of one of the parties, e.g., because he provides consulting to one of the parties for consideration in the course of the arbitration proceeding in which he is supposed to act as an arbitrator[36]. Goldman provides an interesting real-life example, in which the objectivity of an issued arbitral award was challenged on grounds of partiality and dependence of one of the arbitrators – whereas the arbitrator was found to lack independence after the issuance of the arbitral award because he was hired into employment by the party favoured by the award only one day later. In practice, it will often be complicated to determine whether a given arbitrator is "dependent" and "partial", i.e., whether he fails to meet the basic postulates which are inseparably tied to the position of any person who is to decide on the rights and obligations of other persons.

9.31. The Slovak Constitution and the Charter of Fundamental Rights and Basic Freedoms warrants that anyone has the right to assert his rights in a lawful manner in an independent and impartial court and, in specified cases, before other bodies of the Slovak Republic. The act on arbitration proceedings stipulates an analogous right to assert, in the spirit of the above, one's rights in an independent and impartial arbitration court or, as the case may be, before an independent and impartial arbitrator or arbitral tribunal. But who is this independent and impartial arbitrator? The provisions of said act which deal with the personal qualities of the arbitrator lacked any explicit requirements of an impartial and

---

[34] *Ibid.*

[35] Leon Trakman, *The Impartiality and Independence of Arbitrators Reconsidered*, 10 INT. ALR 999 (2007).

[36] PHILIPPE FOUCHARD, EMMANUEL GAILLARD, BERTHOLD GOLDMAN, *supra* note 22, at 565.

independent exercise of his office until the passage of the most recent amendment to the act on arbitration proceedings, i.e., Act No. 71/2009 Coll. In connection with the exercise of arbitration duties, the law currently in force now makes the further specification: *the person who accepts the position of arbitrator shall undertake to exercise this office impartially and with due professional care, such that the fair protection of rights and legitimate interests of the participants is warranted and that no infringement of their rights or legitimate interests occurs, and that no rights are being abused to their detriment.*

9.32. Another reference in connection with the requirement of impartial and independent decision-making can be found in Section 6 (3), which requires the judge or other relevant person who appoints the arbitrator to oversee, among other circumstances, the guarantee of impartial and independent decision-making by the chosen arbitrator. Section 9 of the act on arbitration proceedings, which deals with the grounds for challenging an arbitrator, is a provision in which these necessary requirements for efficient and proper performance in the office of an arbitrator are implicit.

9.33. Challenge of the choice of arbitrator is a mechanism as described further below which allows the "sanctioning" of the lack or absence of good judgment on the part of the arbitrator (in the sense of his impartiality and independence). The act on arbitration proceedings requires persons who were appointed as arbitrators to "plead" their lack of independence and impartiality, but immediately informing the parties of all circumstances because of which they should be excluded from hearing and deciding the case, in that there may be doubt of bias with a view to their relationship to the matter itself or to either party. This provision allows us to identify certain criteria which signal unwarranted conduct and relations of the arbitrator towards certain directions (i.e., in particular, the subject matter of proceedings, or one of the contractual parties). From the time of their appointment as arbitrators and throughout the arbitration proceedings, the person who acts as arbitrator must notify the parties of any bias on his part, except for cases in which he already informed the parties of the pertinent circumstances at an earlier point. On the other side, said statutory provision provides the contractual parties with the instrument of challenging an arbitrator by giving notice of their reservations against the arbitrator. It is inherent in the nature of the provision, however, that a party will not invoke bias on the part of "its arbitrator", and that it will invoke bias only for reasons which "surfaced" (or of which the party learned) after the respective person was appointed as arbitrator. But even this ostensibly logical rule does not always apply one hundred per cent.

9.34. Regarding the procedure for challenging arbitrators on grounds of partiality, the law allows the parties to agree on a *modus operandi* for submitting such challenges, either in the arbitration agreement itself or at a later point (though no later than before the arbitration proceedings have actually commenced)[37]. Unless the parties agree otherwise, the arbitration court may continue proceedings while the challenge is being heard, though no arbitral award must be issued until the relevant authority ("selected person", see below) or court decided on the challenge. As a rule, and where this is feasible, the decision on the exclusion of an arbitrator is made by his co-arbitrators. If the challenge is aimed against several members of the arbitral tribunal (i.e., at least two members), then the challenge is to be decided by the chairperson of the respective institution of arbitration. The alternative procedure for challenges which are aimed against the entire arbitral tribunal (or against the single arbitrator) follows logically from the above.

9.35. In the event that the contractual parties have no agreement on how to proceed in the case of a challenge of bias, the act avails of a "default" provision under which that party that wishes to challenge an arbitrator shall send written notice, containing the grounds for challenge, to the selected person, within 15 days from the day on which it learned of the facts and circumstances which disqualify the arbitrator from hearing and deciding the case or which show that the respective person does not meet the criteria for acting as an arbitrator. If no selected person was indicated, then this notice shall be submitted to the court.

9.36. Similarly, the Model Law does not address the issue of independence and impartiality of arbitrators, but includes this matter in the procedure for the "defence of bias", the criteria and prerequisite for which is the existence of circumstances which give rise to justifiable doubts as to the impartiality and independence of the arbitrator[38]. Most international and domestic documents contain direct or indirect requirements with respect

---

[37] Initiation of arbitration proceedings:
Sec. 16 of the Act on Arbitration Proceedings
  (1) Unless where the parties agree otherwise in the arbitration agreement (or at a later point prior to the commencement of arbitration proceedings), the arbitration proceedings in a given dispute shall commence,
    a) if the arbitrators have not yet been appointed: as of the day of service of the claim upon the respective other contractual party;
    b) if the arbitral tribunal is composed of several arbitrators: as of the day of service of the claim upon the presiding arbitrator, and if the presiding arbitrator has not yet been appointed, then upon any of the arbitrators already appointed;
    c) if the arbitral tribunal consists of a single arbitrator: as of the day of service of the claim upon that arbitrator;
    d) if the dispute is resolved by a permanent arbitration court: as of the day on which the claim was submitted to that permanent arbitration court.
  (2) Upon the commencement of arbitration proceedings, the contractual parties become parties to the arbitration proceedings. The claimant is that party which filed the motion for commencement of arbitration proceedings (the "claim"). The defendant is that party against which the claim is aimed.
[38] Article 12 of the Model Law: Grounds for Challenge (Defence of Bias)
  (1) When a person is approached in connection with his possible appointment as an arbitrator, he shall disclose any circumstances likely to give rise to justifiable doubts as to his impartiality or independence. An arbitrator, from the time of his appointment and throughout the arbitral proceedings, shall without delay disclose

to the decision-making of arbitrators in the sense of their impartiality and independence. However, the same documents often fail to provide a definition of what is to be understood by impartiality and independence of arbitrators, so that it is often the courts who "bring to life" specific terms in their decision-making practice.

9.37. The French Cour de Cassation, in the explanation for its judgment in *Ury v. Galeries Lafayette*, elaborates on independence in the sense of the arbitrator's independence of thought –whereas the independence of thought is indispensable for exercising judiciary powers (irrespective of the source of this power) and an elemental trait of arbitrators[39]. Fouchard, Gaillard and Goldman, in analysing the judgments of French courts, have found cross-references to this decision; the Parisian Cour d'Appel repeated this opinion in several of its decisions, and it was also adopted by the authors of other decisions. Indeed, the French courts have in their case-law accomplished a definition of the independence of arbitrators: the independence of arbitrators is an indispensable requirement of their office, as of the moment of their appointment, their role is comparable to that of a judge, and any dependent relationship (especially towards any of the parties) is therefore not permissible[40].

9.38. Also in the Slovak context, the decision-making practice of the courts fosters a clearer understanding of the contents of the terms 'impartiality and independence of the judiciary' (which, *per analogiam*, apply also to arbitrators). A ruling of the Slovak Constitutional Court addressed the independence of judges: *The existence of independence must be determined under the subjective aspect, i.e., based on the personal beliefs and the conduct of the specific judge in the given matter, but also under the objective aspect, i.e., by determining whether the judge provided sufficient guarantee to be able to rule out any doubt in this respect*[41]. Similarly, we find analogous approaches in the case law of courts in other countries.

IV. Concluding Observations

9.39. In recent years, the boom in international commercial arbitration has also prompted theoretical research in the field of arbitration proceedings. In this respect, we have noticed attempts among academic lawyers

---

any such circumstances to the parties unless they have already been informed of them by him.

(2) An arbitrator may be challenged only if exist circumstances that give rise to justifiable doubts as to his impartiality or independence, or if he does not possess qualifications agreed to by the parties. A party may challenge an arbitrator appointed by him, or in whose appointment he has participated, only for reasons of which he becomes aware after the appointment has been made.

[39] PHILIPPE FOUCHARD, EMMANUEL GAILLARD, BERTHOLD GOLDMAN, *supra* note 22, at 562.

[40] *Ibid.*, 565.

[41] Ruling of the Slovak Constitutional Court III ÚS 16/2000 of June 15, 2000, Collections of Rulings and Resolutions of the Slovak Constitutional Court, 2000.

and scholars to form, cultivate and develop a doctrine of (not only international) commercial arbitration, going as far as to create a new legal field (branch) of sorts, known under the moniker "arbitration law". This may indeed be a kind of new legal discipline, a hybrid with elements of several more generally recognised (and, in a sense, "canonised") legal fields.

9.40. The vibrant domestic, but especially foreign publishing activity concerning various aspects of commercial arbitration (known as arbitration studies) bear witness to the relevance, topicality, variety and breadth of scope of the pertinent scholarly and legislative matters (especially under the aspect of *de lege ferenda*). Students across university faculties of law, too, have been showing exceptional interest in the issue. Thanks to the initiative of various committed college teachers, special courses and scientific seminars which focus on international commercial arbitration studies have come into existence at such faculties[42], and remarkable scholarly results have been achieved in this field, also as regards the exchange with international contacts.

| | |

Summaries

FRA [*Les procédures d'arbitrage : une opportunité de résolution des litiges à jamais perdue?*]

La pratique de la procédure d'arbitrage se développe, en accord avec la situation sociale et politique, en tant qu'aspect important de la vie commerciale dans un grand nombre de normes juridiques, à tel point qu'il est devenu courant de voir les contractants se « promettre » mutuellement que les litiges, générés par leurs rapports commerciaux, ne seront pas examinés dans le cadre d'une procédure judiciaire mais soumis à un organe spécifique, un tribunal d'arbitrage ou un arbitre ad hoc.

L'institution arbitrale, en tant qu'élément du système d'examen des litiges et alternative à la procédure judiciaire, pose, devant ses participants potentiels, le dilemme du choix de la méthode d'examen des litiges parmi celles qui sont proposées.

Trancher, de manière univoque, le dilemme du choix de la méthode d'examen des litiges n'est pas simple. Il n'est pas aisé d'arriver à une conclusion finale afin de savoir quelle direction prendre dans la recherche de solution d'un litige par les parties qui s'opposent, quelle forme de solution recommander comme étant « idéale ». Emprunter, au sens métaphorique, la voie classique des procédures judiciaires (dans une certaine mesure la plus sûre) ou prendre un nouveau « tournant » et s'exposer ainsi au risque de résolution du litige par une voie alternative.

---

[42] Specifically also at the faculty of law at Pavol Jozef Šafárik University in Košice.

CZE   [*Rozhodčí řízení - permanentně nevyužitá šance v řešení sporů?*]

Praxe rozhodčího řízení se vyvíjí v souladu s historickým a sociálně politickým pozadím jako důležitý aspekt obchodního života v řadě právních systémů do té míry, že je v současnosti již běžnou praxí, že si smluvní strany navzájem „slibují", že jejich spory vzniklé v rámci jejich obchodních vztahů nebudou řešeny v rámci soudního řízení, ale budou předloženy zvláštnímu orgánu, stálému rozhodčímu soudu, případně rozhodci ad hoc.

Institut rozhodčího řízení jako součást systému řešení sporů a alternativa k soudnímu řízení před tribunály staví před jeho potenciální účastníky dilema, který ze způsobů řešení sporů, jež jsou k dispozici, využít.

Jednoznačně rozhodnout toto dilema možnosti volby ve prospěch některého ze způsobů řešení sporů není jednoduché. Jednoduché není ani udělat celkový závěr o tom, kterým směrem je vhodné se vydat při řešení sporu jeho protistranami, která forma řešení sporů je „ideálnější", a proto doporučeníhodná. Je otázkou, zda se na pomyslné křižovatce při řešení sporu vydat klasickou, v určitém směru i jistější cestou soudního projednávání sporu, nebo zda se vydat po nové „odbočce" a podstoupit tak nástrahy experimentálního řešení sporu alternativní cestou.

|||

POL   [*Postępowanie arbitrażowe – niewykorzystana szansa rozstrzygania sporów?*]

Opracowanie poświęcone jest problematycznym kwestiom postępowania arbitrażowego, których wciąż jeszcze nie udało się rozstrzygnąć z mocą ostateczną. Autorzy zwracają również uwagę na niektóre szczególnie negatywne tendencje w procesie ustawodawczym regulacji prawnej postępowania arbitrażowego na Słowacji. Tym samym próbują przybliżyć szerszym międzynarodowym kręgom specjalistów kierunki regulacji prawnej postępowania arbitrażowego na Słowacji i rozpocząć ewentualną dyskusję merytoryczną na temat utrzymujących się problemów w postępowaniu arbitrażowym.

DEU   [*Das Schiedsverfahren - eine permanent ungenutzte Chance zur Streitbeilegung?*]

Der Beitrag befasst sich mit bestimmten Problemfragen des Schiedsverfahrens, die noch immer ihrer endgültigen Beurteilung harren. Die Autoren heben außerdem einige besonders negative Tendenzen in der slowakischen Gesetzgebung für die Regulierung der Schiedsgerichtsbarkeit hervor. Damit wollen sie nicht zuletzt der breiteren internationalen Fachwelt die Ausrichtung des slowakischen Rechts zum Schiedsverfahren näher bringen und womöglich eine fachlich relevante Diskussion zu den fortwährenden Anwendungsproblemen "in punkto" Schiedsverfahren auslösen.

RUS   [*Арбитражное производство - шанс в разрешении споров утрачен навсегда?*]

В стати рассматриваются спорные вопросы арбитражного (третейсково) разбирательства, которые все еще окончательно не разрешены. Среди прочих аспектов авторы подчеркивают некоторые особо сильные отрицательные тенденции в законодательном процессе праворегулирования арбитража в Словакии. Автори также стремится более широко ознакомить международных специалистов с направлением праворегулирования арбитражного разбирательства в Словакии, и, таким образом, возможно, открыть профессиональную дискуссию по сохраняющимся проблемам применения арбитражного (третейсково) разбирательства.

ES   [*El procedimiento de arbitraje: ¿oportunidad permanentemente desaprovechada en la resolución de litigios?*]

El estudio trata de las cuestiones problemáticas relativas al procedimiento de arbitraje, cuestiones que no terminan de ser resueltas con perentoriedad. Entre otras cosas, los autores destacan algunas tendencias marcadamente negativas en el proceso de la reglamentación legislativa del arbitraje en Eslovaquia. De hecho, los autores intentan acercar al amplio público internacional especializado el encaminamiento de la reforma legislativa, relativa al procedimiento de arbitraje en Eslovaquia y, eventualmente, iniciar un debate científico en torno a los problemas subsistentes de la aplicación del procedimiento de arbitraje.

Jana Koláčková | Pavel Simon
At the Edge of Justice: Arbitration in Unequal Relationships
The Constitutional Limits of Arbitration

Key words:
arbitration |
arbitration award |
unequal relationship
| protection of
consumers, patients
| health insurance
company | health care

Abstract | *The Czech Republic is gradually familiarizing itself with alternative dispute resolution (ADR) methods such as mediation or arbitration. Given that the average duration of proceedings in civil matters before Czech general courts amounts to a full 16 months, it is little wonder that these expeditious methods for settling disputes are appealing to us. ADR offers even more indubitable advantages compared to judicial proceedings, but also harbours significant drawbacks, especially if it is used improperly. Not least for this reason has the European Court of Justice found that arbitration clauses contained in consumer contracts are null and void. Czech courts, too, approach the issue with circumspection, in full awareness of the fact that the risk of a violation of basic rights in such relationships is immense. The Constitutional Court should therefore revise its current approach to the judicial review of arbitral awards (which is currently not permissible).*
The state must ensure that nobody is forced to submit to arbitration. In disputes in which the parties do not enjoy the same bargaining position (i.e., if one party is substantially weaker), the risk that one party is pressured into accepting arbitration is relatively high; the state must therefore warrant that the weaker party's right to due process of law before an independent court (as well as other constitutionally guaranteed rights) are preserved. For this reason, the option to enter into an arbitration clause should be principally ruled out in such cases.

Mgr. Jana Koláčková
Ph. D. student at
Masaryk University
Faculty of Law,
Department
of Constitutional Law
and Political Science,
Consultant at the
Supreme
Administrative Court;
Former Deputy
Minister for Human
Rights and National
Minorities and Director
of Section of Human
Rights of the Office of
the Government.
e-mail: Jana.
Kolackova@nssoud.cz

| | |

JUDr. Pavel Simon
Judge of District Court
of Cheb, currently
assigned to the Czech
Supreme Court.
Author of commentary
on European
International Civil
Procedure Law in
Drápal, Bureš a kol.:
Občanský soudní řád
(Code on Civil
Procedure).
e-mail: Pavel.Simon@
nssoud.cz

| | |

10.01. In July 2009 the Ministry of Health of the Czech Republic announced that a new arbitration tribunal would be established to settle disputes between patients and their health insurance companies concerning payments for health care[1]. According to the press release, the arbitration tribunal will decide whether a patient has the right – on the basis of public insurance – to a medical treatment for free[2]. It is not the first State initiative to promote arbitration, in 2008 the Ministry of Industry and Trade launched a pilot project on alternative dispute resolution in consumer affairs[3]. It has encouraged consumers and sellers of goods or supplier of services about the possibility to resolve their mutual disputes by mediation or arbitration. Both examples have one thing in common – parties involved in the disputes are not equal.

10.02. It goes without any doubts that it is in the best interest of a patient or a consumer to have their disputes resolved quickly, by a specialist of their own choice and in a way which ensures their privacy[4]. However, any decision to undergo arbitration also has negative consequences. The proceedings need not include a hearing; there is no possibility to appeal, parties share the costs of the proceedings regardless of result and they lose the opportunity to challenge the arbitration award in the Constitutional court of the Czech Republic[5]. We can imagine that these consequences are obvious to a health insurance company employing a team of lawyers, but they are hardly obvious to any average patient or consumer.

I. Unequal Relationships

10.03. A relationship between a consumer and a seller of goods or supplier of services is a relationship between two subjects of private law, but it is not a relationship between equal subjects. This is why the policy of protection of consumers was introduced. A relationship between a patient and a health insurance company is very similar and we could find other examples

---

[1] The press release is available in Czech at:
http://www.mzcr.cz/dokumenty/tiskova-zprava-novy-rozhodci-soud-umozni-pacientum-domoci-se-svych-prav_1428_868_1.html (accessed on September 20, 2010).

[2] In the sense of Art. 31 of the Charter of Fundamental Rights and Basic Freedoms.

[3] Information available at:
http://www.mpo.cz/cz/ochrana-spotrebitele/mimosoudni-reseni
(accessed on September 20, 2010).

[4] The three most frequently cited benefits of arbitration. Among others: Alexander Bělohlávek, Tomáš Pezl, *Mezinárodní a tuzemské rozhodčí řízení z pohledu čl. 36 Listiny základních práv a svobod a pravomocí soudů a Ústavou garantovaných práv (Institut zrušení rozhodčího nálezu v souvislosti se zákazem revision au fond) (International and Domestic Arbitral Proceeding from the Perspective of the Art. 36 of the Charter of the Fundamental Rights and Basic Freedoms and the Jurisdiction of the Courts and Constitutionally Vested Rights (Institute of the Annulment of the Arbitral Award in Relation to the Prohibition of the Au Fond Revision)*, 146 (7) PRÁVNÍK 768, 780 (2007).

[5] See among many others: decision of the Czech Constitutional Court, Case No. IV. ÚS 174/02, 15 July 2002.

such as employees and their employer. In an unequal relationship, one party is in a weaker position *vis-à-vis* the second party in terms of both its bargaining power and level of knowledge. This leads the weaker subject to accept terms drawn up in advance by the seller or supplier without being able to influence the content of the terms[6]. Therefore, in a case when a dispute in such a relationship is to be resolved by way of arbitration, it is essential to ensure that the decision of the weaker party to undergo it is motivated by its free and real will.

II. "Case-law" of the Constitutional Court Relating to Arbitration

10.04. We can find approximately 170 judgments rendered by the Czech Constitutional Court relating to arbitration proceedings. None of the constitutional complaints were reviewed in merits; they were dismissed as manifestly ill founded or inadmissible. However it is possible to determine some rules on basis of this "case-law". According to the Constitutional Court it is not admissible to review an arbitration award in law and in facts because: "The Arbitral court has the character of a professional organization providing services for persons who want to make clear and final their legal relations, and therefore the arbitral awards cannot constitute the decision of a public authority pursuant to Art. 87 (1) (d) of the Constitution and Art. 72 (1) (a) of the Act on the Constitutional Court. The arbitrators resolve the dispute if their jurisdiction arises out of a valid arbitration clause concluded between the parties. The arbitrators do not find the law, but they make final and clear the contractual relations of the parties. Their power is not delegated by State, rather it results from the private power of the parties to determine their own destiny. By concluding a valid arbitration clause the parties willingly and consciously waive their right to assessment of the matter by an independent and disinterested court pursuant to Article 36 (1) of the Charter of Fundamental Rights and Basic Freedoms. For the above mentioned reason, the constitutional complaint is aimed against the decision the source of which is not the public authority. It follows from this that the Constitutional Court, which cannot exceed its limits as stipulated by Article 87 (1) (d) of the Constitution, cannot decide on the core of the matter in the case of the filed constitutional complaint[7].

10.05. "The citizen is invited to protect his or her rights using any and all available legal means to force an assessment of the matter by a court if convinced the arbitral tribunal lacked jurisdiction. If the applicant does not consider his signature on the delivery note and invoice as providing a valid basis for

---

[6]   Comp. ECJ Judgment of 27 June 2000, C-240 – C-244/98, *Océano Grupo Editorial and Salva Editores SA et al.*[2000], ECR I.-4941, 25, for relationships involving a consumer.

[7]   Judgment of the Czech Constitutional Court, Case No. IV. ÚS 1357/07, 11 July 2007.

the arbitral tribunal's jurisdiction, he should raise the objection of lack of jurisdiction based on non-existence of the arbitration clause as his act in the arbitral proceedings (Art. 15 (2) of the Act on Arbitral Proceedings). If the objection of the applicant had not been granted and the arbitral award was issued, the applicant, had other means of contesting the conclusion of the arbitral tribunal's jurisdiction, namely to file an application for non-recognition of the arbitral award pursuant to Art. 31 (1) (b) of the Act on Arbitral Proceedings based on the invalidity of the arbitration clause. This reason for setting aside the arbitral award includes also the situation when the arbitration clause does not exist"[8].

10.06. Even in the event that the applicant filed the action for non-recognition of the arbitral award and it was dismissed by the court, the constitutional complaint is admissible only to the extent to which it challenges the court proceedings, not the arbitral proceedings or the arbitral award itself[9]. It means that once the jurisdiction of the arbitral court is validly established, the parties lose the chance to challenge the arbitral award in merits before the Constitutional Court. Moreover, accordingly to the decision of January 28, 2008, Case Number Pl. ÚS 37/08, the arbitrator is not entitled to propose the annulment of a statute or individual provisions thereof (Art. 64 (3) of the Act on the Constitutional Court), because such an interpretation would extend the list of subjects entitled to do so in a constitutionally inadmissible way (Art. 95 (2) of the Constitution). Any proposition of annulment of a statute or a statutory provision filed by an arbitrator should be therefore dismissed as a petition submitted by a person who is clearly not authorized to do so (Art. 43 (1) (c) of the Act on the Constitutional Court).

10.07. It follows from the above, that the jurisprudence of the Constitutional Court is based exclusively on the "theory of contract"[10] and is very rigorous. In the authors´ opinion it does not reflect sufficiently the current situation in the Czech society which is experiencing "an arbitration boom" since in many cases an arbitration clause is imposed on the other/weaker party of contract (it happens often in financial services offered by non-bank subjects[11] but also in consumer affairs in general or in housing affairs). In as early as the 1980s the European Court of Human Rights[12] (ECHR) developed case-law much more sensitive to the criterion of voluntariness of the arbitration proceedings, the Czech Constitutional Court unfortunately does not reflect on it.

---

8 *Ibid.*
9 Alexander Bělohlávek & Tomáš Pezl, *supra* note 4, at 786.
10 It means that arbitration is provided by a private person as a result of a contract of the parties in dispute (Alexander Bělohlávek, Tomáš Pezl, *supra* note 4, at 786).
11 Pavel Uhl, Arbitráž jako symbol hranic práva a jeho proměny, (Post at Jiné právo blog), available at:
http://jinepravo.blogspot.com/2010/03/arbitraz-jako-symbol-hranic-prava-jeho.html (accessed on September 24, 2010).
12 Or more precisely its predecessor – the European Commission for Human Rights.

III. ECHR Case-Law Relating to Arbitration Proceedings

10.08. We can understand the motion of voluntariness of arbitration in two different ways. Arbitration may be made involuntary or compulsory by law (*objective involuntariness*) or by another person/stronger party (*subjective involuntariness*). Since the *Bramelid and Maloström v. Sweden case* of 1982 the European Commission for Human Rights has made a difference between voluntary and compulsory arbitration: "Lastly, there is nothing in the Convention to prevent a person from renouncing the exercise of certain rights guaranteed under Article 6 (1), in the case of a dispute involving civil rights and obligations, provided that the person's decision is taken freely and without coercion"[13]. "A distinction must be drawn between voluntary arbitration and compulsory arbitration. Normally Article 6 of the Convention poses no problem where arbitration is entered into voluntarily. If on the other hand, arbitration is compulsory in the sense of being required by law, as in this case, the parties have no option but to refer their dispute to an arbitration Board, and the Board must offer the guarantees set forth in Article 6 (1)"[14]. Therefore, the ECHR would examine if the award was issued by an independent and impartial body established by law in a fair and public hearing and within a reasonable time.

10.09. According to Besson the Strasbourg Court, and previously the Commission, have addressed the issue of the relationship between objectively voluntary arbitration and human rights in a comprehensive manner. There are several decisions relating to arbitration, but their exact meaning is not always easy to identify. In addition, this case law does not appear always coherent[15]. However we can make a preliminary conclusion by stating that (an objectively) voluntary arbitration proceedings must not

---

[13] *Bramelid and Maloström v. Sweden*, (decision on admissibility), applications Nos. 8588/79 and 8589/79, 12 December 1982.

[14] Article 6(1) of the Convention for the Protection of Human Rights and Fundamental Freedoms provides: "In the determination of his civil rights and obligations or of any criminal charge against him, everyone is entitled to a *fair and public hearing* within *a reasonable time by an independent and impartial tribunal established by law*. Judgment shall be pronounced publicly but the press and public may be excluded from all or part of the trial in the interests of morals, public order or national security in a democratic society, where the interests of juveniles or the protection of the private life of the parties so require, or to the extent strictly necessary in the opinion of the court in special circumstances where publicity would prejudice the interests of justice." *Bramelid and Maloström v. Sweden*, (Report of the Commission), applications nos. 8588/79 and 8589/79, 12 December 1983, D.R. 29, p. 76.

[15] Sébastien Besson, Arbitration and human rights, (Speech given in Vienna on 4 April 2009 at a conference jointly organized by the Young Austrian Arbitration Practitioners and the Young Arbitrators Forum of the ICC), avaible at:
http://www.iccwbo.org/uploadedFiles/
Court/YAF/News/2009,July,Besson_arbitration_HumanRights.pdf
(accessed on September 25, 2010).

fulfil all the requirements of article 6 of the Convention and the Member States have a wide margin of appreciation concerning the judicial review of arbitral awards: "The Commission therefore considers that an arbitral award does not necessarily have to be quashed because the parties have not enjoyed all the guarantees of Article 6 (Art. 6), but each Contracting State may in principle decide itself on which grounds an arbitral award should be quashed"[16]. Nevertheless, the margin of appreciation is not absolute. In the authors' opinion the member state should ensure at least that the award will be quashed if it was issued in a *subjectively* involuntary arbitration proceeding or in a proceeding not reflecting the equality of the parties.

IV. Arbitration and Customer Protection

10.10. The "arbitration boom" mentioned above has been already reflected in decision making of the Czech courts. In December 2009 the District Court in Brno decided[17] that an arbitral clause "agreed" between a customer and a supplier of financial services was absolutely void, because it was unfair to the consumer. The court referred to the Council Directive 93/13/EEC of 5 April 1993 on unfair terms in consumer contracts according to which a clause excluding or hindering the consumer's right to take legal action or exercise any other legal remedy, particularly by requiring the consumer to take disputes exclusively to arbitration not covered by legal provisions should be regarded as unfair (Article 3 (3) and annex (1) (q) of the cited Directive). The court also referred to ECJ judgment of 26 October 2006, C-168/05, *Mostaza Claro* according to which: "a national court seised of an action for annulment of an arbitration award must determine whether the arbitration agreement is void and annul that award where that agreement contains an unfair term, even though the consumer has not pleaded that invalidity in the course of the arbitration proceedings, but only in that of the action for annulment." The protection which the above mentioned directive confers on consumers thus extends to cases in which a consumer who has concluded with a seller or supplier a contract containing an unfair term *fails to raise* the unfair nature of the term, whether because he is unaware of his rights or because he is deterred from enforcing them on account of the costs which judicial proceedings would involve[18].

10.11. The Brno District Court also concluded that it is forbidden to agree arbitral clauses in contracts with consumers *in general* because pursuant Art. 55 (2) of the Civil Code it is inadmissible to make the consumer renounce

---

[16] *Nordström-Janzon and Nordström-Lehtinen v. The Netherlands*, (decision on admissibility), application No. 28101/95, 27 November 1996.

[17] Brno District Court decision, file number 33 Cm 13/2009, 8 March 2010.

[18] ECJ judgment of 21 November 2002, C – 473/00, *Cofidis* [2002] ECR I-10875, para. 34.

his/her right(s) – in this case the right to fair trial before an independent court guaranteed by the Constitution[19]. According to the court it is not reasonable to resolve consumers' disputes in arbitration proceedings and all inappropriate and disproportional provisions should be regarded as unfair (Annex (1) (b) of the Directive 93/13/EEC). The consumer should be protected against the abuse of power by the seller or supplier, in particular against one-sided standard terms contracts and the unfair exclusion of essential rights in contracts. Should the arbitration clause delegate the dispute resolution from the system of independent courts to an *ad hoc* arbitrator with whom the seller or supplier usually cooperates on a long-term basis and who can be dependent financially on him, it is obvious that this represents a one-sided disadvantage to the consumer. The same opinion was used for example in the Brno City Court judgment of 14 December 2009, Case Number 33 C 68/2008, in Zvolen District Court judgment of 8 April 2010, Case number 21Er/1390/2009 or in Prešov Regional Court judgment of 5 May 2010, Case number 3CoE 29/2010[20].

V. Arbitration in Consumers' Disputes in the Czech Republic

10.12. According to the evaluation report of the pilot project of alternative dispute resolution in consumer affairs published by the Ministry of Industry and Trade on 14 October 2010, the pilot phase has shown a real need for alternative dispute resolution mechanisms and especially mediation in this kind of conflicts[21]. Among 2370 filed complaints only one case was resolved in arbitration proceedings despite a relatively high number of arbitral tribunals and arbitrators *ad hoc* involved in the project (59). In the authors'

[19] Directive 93/13/EEC was not properly executed in the Czech legal system, so there is a direct conflict between Art. 31 of the Act No. 216/1994 Coll., on arbitral proceedings and on execution of Arbitral awards and Art. 55 (2) of the Civil Code. See Zdeněk Nový, *Arbitration Clauses as Unfair Contract Term: Some Observations on the ECJ's Claro Case, in* COFOLA 2008: THE CONFERENCE PROCEEDINGS, Brno: Masaryk University 76, 84 (J. Valdhans, R. Dávid, M. Orgoník, J. Neckář, D. Sehnálek, J. Tauchen eds., 2008) or Tereza Kyselovská, *Rozhodčí doložky (nejen) ve spotřebitelských smlouvách a ochrana základních práv (Arbitral Clauses (not only) in Consumer Contracts and the Protection of Basic Rights), in* COFOLA 2009: THE CONFERENCE PROCEEDINGS, Brno: Masaryk University 1107 (R. Dávid, J. Neckář, D. Sehnálek eds., 2009).

[20] All the decisions reflect among other things a common doubt about the quality of arbitration proceedings offered by certain arbitrators *ad hoc*. Link to all of them is available in Pavel Uhl, *Arbitráž útočí a soudy vrací úder* (Post at Jiné právo blog), available at:
http://jinepravo.blogspot.com/2010/06/pavel-uhl-arbitraz-utoci-soudy-vraci.html (accessed on September 26, 2010).

[21] Within the pilot phase 2370 motions were received, 40% of it was resolved either by an advice (694 cases) or by mediation (132 cases). 60% of the cases were not resolved due to inactivity of the other party. Only one case was resolved in arbitration proceedings, two other cases are still pending. The report is available at:
http://www.mpo.cz/dokument79754.html (accessed on September 26, 2010).

opinion the statistic has proved what the above mentioned Directive stipulates – that arbitration was not the appropriate dispute resolution method for conflicts between customer and sellers and suppliers.

10.13. Surprisingly, the report does not reflect the legal context mentioned above and it seems, furthermore, that the Ministry does not want to discontinue promoting arbitration in consumers' affairs *(sic!)*.

VI. Arbitration in Health Care Insurance

10.14. In the authors' opinion arbitration should be used to settle disputes between equal parties. In relationships involving a weaker party the use of arbitration should be forbidden in principle. Consumers are without any doubt vulnerable subjects, and the position of a patient in relation to his/her health insurance agency is even worse. The patient has an obligation arising from law to be insured, but no opportunity to negotiate on the conditions of the contract. The opportunity to change the insurance company is limited by law. Moreover the health insurance agency can impose sanctions on the insured person (e. g. in case of delay with payment).

10.15. The Ministry of Health introduces arbitration proceeding as voluntary, but in a way as a privileged mechanism for resolution of conflicts between the insured and the company on payment for medical treatment. If an arbitration clause in consumer affairs is unfair and therefore void, the same clause in health insurance affairs is still more unfair.

10.16. Arbitration clauses can be agreed probably only in two ways, either during the registration process or after the dispute arises. In the first case the client has no bargaining power because the contract is drawn up in advance. The second situation will occur when an insured person will need – to save his or her health or life – a special and usually very expensive medical treatment which the health insurance company refuses to pay for. It is difficult to imagine another situation in which a person would be more vulnerable. Any arbitration clause signed in such a moment is absolutely void, as the insured patient is actually forced to renounce on his constitutionally guaranteed right to fair trial before an independent court and to agree to undergo arbitration, offering smaller protection to his or her rights. The decision also means that the client loses the possibility of constitutional review relating to his constitutionally assured right to free medical care.

10.17. It is true that nowadays there are no specific mechanisms to resolve such a dispute in proceedings which fulfils the requirements of Article 6 of the Convention and are quicker than ordinary court proceedings. However, there are other methods as to how to resolve this situation and do not breach fundamental rights of citizens. An urgent court proceeding can be introduced, for example. Otherwise, under certain circumstances the "encouragement" to undergo arbitration could by compared to obligatory arbitration in the sense of ECHR case-law.

VII. Conclusion

10.18. We are living a new experience with alternative dispute resolution methods such as mediation and arbitration. With an average court proceeding duration of sixteen months it is understandable that those quick methods seem promising. They have many benefits to bring, but some inconvenience too, especially when they are not performed properly. It is up to everybody to think about the decision and it is up to the State to ensure that nobody is forced to undergo this. In disputes involving non-equal parties the risk of pressure and subjective involuntariness is relatively high; the State should guarantee that the right to a fair trial (and/or other constitutional rights at stake) of the weaker party is not violated. Therefore arbitration in unequal relationships should be forbidden in principle.

| | |

Summaries

FRA [*Arbitrage en cas de rapports inégaux, aux confins de la Justice; Les limites constitutionnelles de l'arbitrage*]

Nous vivons une nouvelle expérience avec modes alternatifs de résolution des conflits (MARC) comme la médiation et l'arbitrage. Avec une durée moyenne de la procédure devant les courts de 16 mois, il est compréhensible que ces méthodes rapides semblent prometteurs. Ils ont de nombreux avantages à offrir, mais aussi des certains inconvénients, surtout quand ils ne sont pas effectuées correctement. C'est pourquoi d'après la Cour de Justice de l'Union Européenne les causes d'arbitrage incluos dans les contrats de consommation sont nulles. Sachant que le risque d'abus des droits fondamentaux est assez important dans les cas analogues, les juridictions tchèques sont aussi prudentes. La Cour Constitutionnelle devrait aussi change son attitude résolue qui exclue la révision au fond des sentences arbitrales.

C'est une tache de l'État pour s'assurer que personne n'est contraint de se soumettre a l'arbitrage. En litiges entre des parties inégales le risque de pression et involontaire subjective est relativement élevé, l'État devrait donc garantir que le droit à un procès équitable devant court indépendant (et / ou d'autres droits constitutionnels en jeu) de la partie faible ne soit pas violée. C'est pourquoi l'arbitrage dans les relations inégales devrait être interdit en principe.

CZE [*Arbitráž v nerovnocenných vztazích – Na hraně spravedlnosti; Ústavní limity rozhodčího řízení*]

Česká společnost se postupně seznamuje s alternativními způsoby řešení sporů (ADR) jako je mediace a rozhodčí řízení. Není se čemu divit, že nám tyto rychlé způsoby řešení sporů připadají lákavé, vždyť průměrná délka řízení před českými soudy v občanskoprávních věcech dosahuje 16 měsíců. V porovnání se soudním řízením nabízí rozhodčí řízení i jiné nesporné výhody, skrývá však i stinné stránky, zvláště pokud je používáno nesprávně. I z toho důvodu Soudní dvůr Evropské unie dospěl k závěru, že rozhodčí doložky obsažené ve spotřebitelských smlouvách jsou nicotné. S vědomím, že v obdobných vztazích je riziko zásahu do základních práv velmi vysoké, přistupují obezřetně k této otázce i české soudy.

Také Ústavní soud by měl tedy přehodnotit svůj přístup k přezkumu rozhodčích nálezů, který je v současnosti vyloučen.
Je úkolem státu zajistit, aby nikdo nebyl nucen podrobit se rozhodčímu řízení. V sporech, ve kterých se strany nacházejí v nerovném postavení (jedna strana je výrazně slabší), existuje relativně vysoké riziko, že slabší strana sporu bude vystavena nátlaku podrobit se režimu rozhodčího řízení. Stát proto musí garantovat, že právo na spravedlivý proces před nezávislým soudem (nebo i jiná ústavně garantovaná práva) slabší strany nebudou narušena. Proto by měla být možnost uzavřít rozhodčí doložku v takovýchto případech v zásadě vyloučena.

| | |

POL   *[Arbitraż w stosunkach nierównoprawnych – na krawędzi sprawiedliwości; Ograniczenia konstytucyjne arbitrażu]*
Alternatywne metody rozstrzygania sporów, takie jak mediacja czy arbitraż to dla Republiki Czeskiej nowe doświadczenie. W sytuacji gdy postępowanie przed sądem trwa średnio 16 miesięcy, nie dziwi fakt, że te szybkie metody wydają się obiecujące. Niosą one ze sobą wiele korzyści, ale także – pewne niedogodności, zwłaszcza, jeżeli nie są prowadzone w należyty sposób. Zadaniem państwa jest dołożenie wszelkich starań, aby nikt nie był zmuszony ich doświadczać. W sporach obejmujących nierówne strony istnieje stosunkowo duże ryzyko nacisku i subiektywnej niedobrowolności; państwo powinno zadbać o to, by nie zostało naruszone prawo do sprawiedliwego procesu (lub inne prawa konstytucyjne) słabszej strony. Z tych powodów arbitraż w przypadku nierównego stosunku stron powinien być z zasady niedozwolony.

DEU   *[Schiedsgerichtsbarkeit in ungleichen Rechtsverhältnissen – am Rande der Gerechtigkeit; Zu den verfassungsrechtlichen Grenzen der Schiedsgerichtsbarkeit]*
Die Tschechische Republik macht mit alternativen Streitbeilegungsmethoden wie z.B. dem Schlichtungsverfahren und dem Schiedsverfahren neuartige Erfahrungen. Angesichts einer durchschnittlichen Prozessdauer für Gerichtsverfahren von 16 Monaten ist es nur verständlich, dass diese raschen Methoden vielversprechend erscheinen. Sie bringen eine Menge Vorteile, allerdings – besonders bei unsachgemäßer Anwendung – auch Ungelegenheiten. Es ist Aufgabe des Staates die Garantie zu gewähren, dass niemand zur alternativen Streitbeilegung gezwungen wird. Bei Streitigkeiten zwischen Parteien, zwischen denen keine Gleichgewicht besteht, ist das Risiko einer Ausübung von Druck oder einer subjektiven Unfreiwilligkeit relativ hoch; der Staat sollte garantieren, dass das Recht der schwächeren Partei für einen fairen Prozess (und/oder andere auf dem Spiel stehende Verfassungsrechte) nicht verletzt wird. Daher sollte die Schiedsgerichtsbarkeit in ungleichen Rechtsverhältnissen prinzipiell untersagt werden.

RUS [*Арбитраж (третейское производство) при неравных отношениях — правосудие на пределе; Конституционные ограничения арбитража*]

Чешская Республика усваивает новый опыт таких альтернативных способов разрешения споров, как посредничество и арбитраж. При средней продолжительности слушаний в суде 16 месяцев становится понятной перспективность таких оперативных методов. При многих преимуществах они также могут приводить и к затруднениям, особенно при их ненадлежащем применении. Именно государство должно позаботиться о том, чтобы такие затрудсния никого не затронули. При неравенстве сторон в спорах риск давления и непроизвольного субъективизма сравнительно велик, и государство должно предотвратить нарушение права более слабой стороны на справедливое судебное разбирательство (и/или других конституционных прав, которые могут подвергаться риску). Поэтому арбитраж при неравенстве сторон должен быть запрещен в принципе.

ES [*Arbitraje en las relaciones desiguales: al límite de la Justicia; Límites constitucionales del arbitraje*]

La República Checa está viviendo una nueva experiencia con los métodos alternos de resolución de disputas como, por ejemplo, la mediación y el arbitraje. Con una duración media de los procedimientos judiciales de 16 meses, es comprensible que estos métodos rápidos parezcan prometedores. Poseen muchas ventajas, pero también algunos inconvenientes, especialmente si no se llevan a cabo correctamente. Es competencia del Estado el asegurar que nadie se vea obligado a someterse a ellos. En disputas que impliquen partes no iguales, el riesgo de presión y de involuntariedad subjetiva es relativamente alto y el Estado debe garantizar que no se infrinja el derecho a un juicio justo (y/u otros derechos constitucionales en cuestión) de la parte más débil. Por tanto, el arbitraje en las relaciones entre partes desiguales en principio debería prohibirse.

Czech (& Central European) Yearbook of Arbitration

Miroslav Slašťan

Acceptance of Human Rights and Constitutional Values in Reviews of Arbitral Awards by the Courts of the Slovak Republic

Key words:
Arbitration court
| arbitral award |
right to a fair trial
| Constitutional
Court | protection
of constitutionality
| review of arbitral
award | Arbitration
Act

Abstract | *This paper examines the development and current state of laws defining Slovak arbitration in the context of the review of arbitral awards permitted under the law. This paper summarizes in particular the case law of the Constitutional Court of the Slovak Republic, which has re-assessed the extend of the constitutional control and abidance of the human rights as applied in the civil proceedings and extended such control also to the arbitral proceedings. It is therefore possible to identify the approach applied to arbitration by the Constitutional Court in conforming to the principle of fair trial and due process of law, provided that the notion of subsidiarity is observed. Subsidiarity is also explained in this document in the context of the particular structure of the Slovak judiciary system and procedural regulations relating to the review of arbitral awards. In its concluding section, the paper recalls recent changes in the arbitral proceedings and the conditions for the review of the arbitral awards with respect to the case law of the European Court of Justice.*

Miroslav Slašťan
is a university lecturer,
currently leading
the International
and European Law
Department at the
Law Faculty at the
Paneuropean University
in Bratislava, Areas
of specialization:
European law and
constitutional law. His
recent research focuses
on judicial protection
of European Union
Law before the Court
of Justice and national
courts of EU Member
States.
e-mail:
miroslavslastan@
gmail.com

| | |

I. Brief Outline of Arbitration Developments and Current Arbitration Legislation in Slovakia

11.01. When considering arbitration legislation in Slovakia, it is worth noting that until 1989 a distinction was made in the former Czechoslovakia between arbitration in international trade, governed by Act No. 98/1963 Coll., and domestic arbitration proceedings required to resolve disputes between former state businesses, governed by Act No. 121/1962 Coll. on economic arbitration. In other words, statutory double-track arbitration was applied. In 1992, the Slovak National Council adopted Act No 9/1992 Coll. on commercial and industrial chambers, which established the Slovak Chamber of Commerce and Industry. Section 16 of this Act enabled the Chamber to establish an arbitration court as a permanent, independent body for the resolution of disputes about asset-related claims by independent arbitrators in accordance with rules on arbitration in international trade.

11.02. Almost two years later, by this time in the independent Slovak Republic, Act No. 120/1994 Coll. was adopted; this was the first piece of legislation to amend the original Act No. 98/1963 Coll. on arbitration. By removing its specific application to international trade, the legislature united trade relations regardless of whether they were of a national or international nature. The first law to comprehensively regulate arbitration in the Slovak Republic according to international standards was Act No. 218/1996 Coll. on arbitration. This legislation facilitated the establishment of permanent arbitration courts by means of a law, i.e. a separate law expressly enabling legal persons set up an arbitration court. In practice, this meant several years of de facto "domination" by a single court in the settlement of arbitration disputes[1].

11.03. After the establishment of the Slovak Republic as an independent state, when the independent Arbitration Court of the Slovak Chamber of Commerce and Industry was created, it was necessary to establish a functioning mechanism in one place (an arbitration court), gain experience, set up a team of experienced arbitrators, and make the business community aware that arbitration was possible and efficient even in the Slovak Republic[2].

---

[1]　Act No. 448/2001 Coll., amending Act No. 218/1996 Coll. on arbitration, also enabled the former Chamber of Commercial Lawyers and the Slovak Agricultural and Food Chamber to establish and maintain a permanent arbitration court at their own expense. These established arbitration courts were obliged to draw up their own statutes and rules of procedure. This complied with the formal requirement of the Arbitration Act (Act No. 218/1996 Coll.) for further arbitration courts to be set up on the basis of authorization under a special law.

[2]　Pavol Erben, *Prehľad vývoja a aktuálny stav právnej úpravy rozhodcovského konania v Slovenskej republike (Overview of developments and the current state of arbitration legislation in the Slovak Republic), in* PODPORA APLIKAČNEJ PRAXE ROZHODCOVSKÝCH

11.04. Act No. 218/1996 Coll. also enshrined, under Section 25, a relatively wide range of reasons for the review and annulment of an arbitral award by an ordinary court:

a) *an award is issued in a case which is excluded from arbitration;*

b) *an award is issued in a case in which a final ruling has previously been delivered by a court or in other arbitration;*

c) *a party to a dispute denies the validity of an arbitration agreement;*

d) *a ruling is delivered on a matter not covered by an arbitration agreement and a party to the dispute has raised this objection in the proceedings;*

e) *a ruling is delivered on a matter which was not the subject of arbitration;*

f) *a party to a dispute required to be represented by a legal representative has not been thus represented, or a person who has not been authorized and whose actions have not been appropriately approved acts on behalf of a party to a dispute;*

g) *not all the appointed arbitrators participate in the delivery of the ruling, or an arbitrator who, as a judge, could be excluded in judicial proceedings due to doubts about his impartiality participates in such delivery of the ruling;*

h) *a party to a dispute is not given the opportunity to prove its claims in issues which could affect any part of the verdict delivered in the award;*

ch) *the law or another substantive regulation of general application is breached in the arbitral award;*

i) *the arbitral award is influenced by a criminal offence for which the offender has been convicted in criminal proceedings.*

It is noteworthy that, despite the legislature's efforts to adopt a modern rule of law, some provisions of the 1996 Arbitration Act were not sufficiently developed, caused doubts in their application or failed to regulate legal relationships with any precision. Certain shortcomings were addressed by an amendment (Act No. 448/2001 Coll.) which clarified a number of issues concerning arbitrators, objections of bias, remedies, the right of the enforceability and legality of rulings, including a modification of the opportunities for a review of an arbitral award (the deletion of the possibilities under subparagraphs e) and ch)).

11.05. The last major amendment t o implement all elements of contemporary arbitration truly rigorously is the currently valid Act No. 244/2002 Coll. of 3 April 2002 on arbitration (the "Arbitration Act"). The legislature based this legislation on the UNCITRAL Rules – Arbitration Rules of the United Nations Commission on International Trade Law, adopted by the UN in 1976. The UNCITRAL Rules form the basis of the current Arbitration Act in the Slovak Republic. Furthermore, this legislation transposes

---

SÚDOV V SLOVENSKEJ REPUBLIKE, Bratislava: EUROIURIS – Európske právne centrum, o.z. 9 (M. Siman ed., 2007).

the general procedural principles of the Rules of Civil Procedure (Act No. 99/1963 Coll.), the 1959 New York Convention on the Recognition and Enforcement of Foreign Arbitral Awards and the 1964 European Convention on International Commercial Arbitration. The above list of legal provisions indicates that they genuinely form comprehensive legislation aiming to encapsulate all phases of arbitration in a single law. Naturally, the law also incorporates other experiences of arbitration practice gained in the Slovak Republic in the period since the adoption of Act No. 218/1996 Coll.

11.06. Furthermore, the Arbitration Act as it currently stands also provides for matters relating to the recognition and enforcement of domestic and foreign arbitral awards in the Slovak Republic. It also precisely defines which disputes cannot be resolved in arbitration. Compared to its predecessor, the current law defines the cases in which a dispute may be settled by ordinary courts and how interim measures are addressed. It also removes the original restriction that arbitration courts may be established only by authorization under a separate law. As a result, any legal person is now entitled, without further limitation, to establish an arbitration court (in Slovakia these currently number around thirty).

11.07. Under the settled case-law of the Constitutional Court of the Slovak Republic (the "Constitutional Court"), the essence of arbitration lies in alternative dispute resolution; the arbitration itself is an alternative to proceedings before the ordinary courts, compared to which it offers the major advantages of flexibility and speed of procedure, informality and lower costs. In these proceedings, the law envisages a minimum of interference by the ordinary courts in the results of arbitration courts' decision-making because, under Section 40 of the Arbitration Act, a domestic arbitral award may be challenged by an action brought to an ordinary court with due jurisdiction only for specifically defined reasons based on respect for legality. Nevertheless, the Constitutional Court has held that, although arbitration can be described as a less complex procedure than proceedings before the ordinary courts, it is necessary to comply with the *principles of justice and legality*. According to Section 51(3) of the Arbitration Act, unless otherwise provided by this law, the arbitration courts apply the provisions of a general legal standard governing the civil process – the Rules of Civil Procedure – on the principle of subsidiarity[3].

11.08. In this respect, all of the Constitutional Court's orders relating to the observance of human rights and constitutional values valid for civil proceedings before an ordinary court are applicable to arbitration and the outcome thereof (in the form of an arbitral award). Moreover, the current Arbitration Act expressly mentions the violation of the principle of the equality of parties to arbitration (Section 17 of the Act) as a ground for

---

[3] See Decision of the Constitutional Court of the Slovak Republic III. ÚS 95/2010 or II. ÚS 173/2010.

annulment of an arbitral award by an ordinary court. An arbitral award may be reviewed on all the grounds on which a retrial may be sought under the Rules of Civil Procedure (e.g. the European Court of Human Rights has held, or has concluded in a judgment, that a court ruling or the preceding proceedings constituted an infringement of the fundamental human rights or freedoms of a party to the proceedings and that the serious consequences of this infringement were not remedied by an award of adequate financial satisfaction, or that an arbitral award is contrary to a decision of the Court of Justice of the European Union[4] or another body of the European Communities).

II. Acceptance of Human Rights and Constitutional Values in Reviews of Arbitration Awards by the Courts of the Slovak Republic

II.1. Definition of the Judiciary in the Slovak Republic

11.09. Title Seven (Judiciary) of Act No. 460/1992 Coll., the Constitution of the Slovak Republic (the "Constitution)", makes a distinction between the two functions of the State in the exercise of judicial power (the judiciary), i.e. the judicial protection of constitutionality (Subdivision One, Articles 124 to 140) and the provision of protection to rights or decisions on guilt and punishment for criminal offences (Subdivision Two, Articles 141 to 148)[5]. As such, the judicial power of the Slovak Republic is vested in two relatively separate components: the constitutional judiciary and the ordinary judiciary. Each component has its own specific functions; the Constitutional Court is an independent judicial body for the protection of constitutionality (Article 124) and the ordinary courts are bodies for the protection of legality (Article 142(1))[6]. It can be concluded that the Constitutional Court is a partner to all ordinary courts and does not base its constitutional position on a hierarchical principle. According to the case-law of the Constitutional Court, the independence of both branches of the judiciary (the Constitutional Court and ordinary courts) is reflected in the fact that each has its substantive scope, defined by the Constitution and laws, which is carried out independently and without the participation

---

[4] For a review of Slovak judicial decisions incompatible with EU law, see Michael Siman, *Sankcie za porušenie práva Únie v právnom poriadku Slovenskej republiky (Penalties for a Breach of Union Law in Slovak National Law)*, in COFOLA 2010: CONFERENCE PROCEEDINGS, 374 Acta Universitatis Brunensis, Brno: Masarykova univerzita 1328 (2010).

[5] IGOR PALÚŠ, ĽUDMILA SOMOROVÁ, ŠTÁTNE PRÁVO SLOVENSKEJ REPUBLIKY (*Constitutional Law of the Slovak Republic*), Košice: Univerzita Pavla Jozefa Šafárika 382 – 383 (3rd ed. 2008).

[6] See Order of the Constitutional Court of the Slovak Republic of 20 August 1998 I. ÚS 52/98.

of the other component. The Constitutional Court is not empowered to act and decide on matters that are entrusted to the jurisdiction of the ordinary courts (Article 142(1) of the Constitution)[7]. The ordinary courts are not empowered to act and decide on matters that are entrusted to the jurisdiction of the Constitutional Court (Articles 125 to 129 of the Constitution)[8]. However, not even this definition is absolute and always specific.

11.10. The Constitutional Court is the only public body of its kind in the Slovak Republic and represents the application of a model of a concentrated and specialized constitutional judiciary[9]. Its supervisory competence in relation to other components (bodies) in the division of powers applies not only to the executive and legislative powers, but also to the judicial power, i.e. the ordinary judiciary. According to the settled case-law of the Constitutional Court, the Constitutional Court is not empowered to review and assess the legal opinions of an ordinary court which, in the interpretation and application of laws, guided it to a decision on the merits of the case. The Constitutional Court fundamentally does not have the right to examine whether or not, in proceedings before the ordinary courts, the facts were properly established and what factual and legal findings were made by an ordinary court on the basis of the facts, i.e. to protect citizens from factual errors of the ordinary courts (e.g. Decisions of the Constitutional Court II. ÚS 21/96, ÚS I. 4/00). In other words, the role of the Constitutional Court is not to represent ordinary courts with the competence to interpret and apply laws. The role of the Constitutional Court is limited to checking the compatibility of the effects of such interpretation and application with the Constitution or any international treaty pursuant to Article 7(4) of the Slovak Constitution, i.e. to provide protection from such interference with rights which is constitutionally indefensible and unsustainable (Decisions of the Constitutional Court I. ÚS 17/01, I. ÚS 13/01 or I. ÚS 120/04).

11.11. The Constitutional Court is empowered to consider only the unconstitutionality of the proceedings of ordinary courts, but not the diversity of their legal views reached on the basis of the interpretation and application of relevant provisions of the law. The application of the law in judicial proceedings and court procedure in accordance with

---

[7] BERNARD PEKÁR, KONTROLA VO VEREJNEJ SPRÁVE V KONTEXTE EURÓPSKEHO SPRÁVNEHO SÚDNICTVA (*Control in Public Administration in the Context of the European Administrative Judiciary*), Bratislava: Univerzita Komenského 112 (2011).

[8] See Order of the Constitutional Court of the Slovak Republic of 20 August 1998 I. ÚS 52/98.

[9] For details on individual models of the constitutional judiciary, see, for example, VOJTĚCH ŠIMÍČEK, ÚSTAVNÍ STÍŽNOST (*Constitutional Complaint*), Praha: Linde 26 (2005), or JÚLIA ONDROVÁ, KONANIE O KONTROLE PRÁVNYCH PREDPISOV PRED ÚSTAVNÝM SÚDOM SLOVENSKEJ REPUBLIKY A ČESKEJ REPUBLIKY (*Proceedings for Checks on Legislation before the Constitutional Court of the Slovak Republic and Czech Republic*), Banská Bystrica: Univerzita Mateja Bela 113 (2009).

a law which is in force and effect cannot be viewed as an infringement of fundamental human rights. For example, failure (the decision not to uphold an application) in proceedings before the ordinary court cannot be regarded as an infringement of a citizen's fundamental rights[10]. The Constitutional Court may not, in any circumstances, examine the observance and application of such provisions of procedural rules which are a manifestation of the independent status of the court and the judge: provisions on the evaluation of evidence, the court's exclusive competence as to the scope of evidence taken, etc[11]. It follows from the Constitutional Court's status that it may review only those decisions of the ordinary courts where an infringement of a fundamental right or freedom has occurred in the preceding proceedings or in the decision itself[12].

II.2. Arbitration Courts and Arbitration in the Context of Human Rights and Constitutional Values

11.12. The introduction of the right to judicial and other legal protection among the human rights protected by the Constitution enhanced the viability of the legal protection not only of human rights, but of all rights deriving from the legal system of the Slovak Republic. Without the realistic assurance of judicial and other legal protection, all other rights would be guaranteed only by voluntary observance thereof, which does not exist in full in any State.

11.13. The constitutional arrangement of the right to judicial and other legal protection has de facto split the regime of legal protection and the constitutional principles relating to them into
  a) the right of access to judicial and other legal protection (Article 46 of the Constitution);
  b) the right to a fair trial (Articles 47 and 48 of the Constitution); and
  c) special rights applicable only to criminal proceedings (Articles 49 and 50 of the Constitution)[13].

The right of access to judicial and other legal protection and, in particular, the right to a fair trial are also the determining maxims for arbitration and its outcome in the form of an arbitral award. The extent to which they are applied can be assessed primarily in the context of the Constitutional Court's case-law in its decision-making activities mainly concerning the review of arbitral awards.

---

[10] See, for example, Order of the Constitutional Court of the Slovak Republic of 30 January 1996 I. ÚS 8/96.
[11] See Order of the Constitutional Court of the Slovak Republic of 28 January 1998 I. ÚS 5/98.
[12] Bernard Pekár, *supra* note 7, at 113.
[13] Ján Svák, Ľubor Cibulka, Ústavné právo Slovenskej republiky (*Constitutional Law of the Slovak Republic*), Bratislava: Bratislavská vysoká škola práva 545 (2006).

11.14. In particular, it should be noted that the review of arbitral awards is a role primarily entrusted to the jurisdiction of ordinary courts (see Sections 40 to 43 of the Arbitration Act) and only subsequently (subsidiarily) does the possibility of a review of an arbitral award by the Constitutional Court come into consideration. The principle of subsidiarity enshrined in Article 127(1) of the Constitution (... *except where another court decides on the protection of such rights and freedoms*) indicates that the Constitutional Court's jurisdiction to protect fundamental rights and freedoms exists only where the protection of such rights and freedoms is adjudicated by the ordinary courts. The Constitutional Court, in establishing such jurisdiction, is guided by the principle that the Constitution calls upon the ordinary courts to protect not only legality, but also constitutionality. Therefore, the Constitutional Court's jurisdiction is subsidiary and comes into play only when the ordinary courts do not have jurisdiction (Decision of the Constitutional Court IV. ÚS 236/07).

11.15. According to the Constitutional Court's settled case-law, the principle of the subsidiarity of jurisdiction represents a constitutional order for each person. Accordingly, anyone who alleges that any of their fundamental rights has been infringed must respect the sequence of such protection, i.e. before filing a complaint with the Constitutional Court, they must seek protection from the public authority whose competence precedes the jurisdiction of the Constitutional Court (Decision of the Constitutional Court IV. ÚS 128/04).

11.16. The Constitutional Court has accepted the observance of the principle of subsidiarity, for example, in relation to an arbitration court's order to stay the arbitration proceedings on account of failure to pay the arbitration fee[14]. The Constitutional Court held that, in essence, this is an interlocutory decision by the arbitration court which, in the circumstances of the case concerned, does not constitute *res judicata*. The Constitutional Court takes the view that arbitration thus concluded cannot be regarded as a definitively resolved case, as complainants have the opportunity to pursue their claims by submitting an application to the arbitration court.

11.17. Therefore, the arguments advancing the right to judicial and other legal protection under Article 46(1) of the Constitution do not apply to all decisions rendered in the arbitration proceedings. In this respect, the Constitutional Court focused on the nature and substance of the arbitration. One of the conditions for the establishment of an arbitration court's jurisdiction is its contractual basis (Section 3 of the Arbitration Act). Under a contract or arbitration clause, the parties freely choose to resolve disputes arising between them in a given contractual or other legal relationship. By entering into a contract or arbitration clause, the parties voluntarily and knowingly relinquish their right to judicial protection through the ordinary courts and assign it instead to an arbitration court,

---

[14] See Decision of the Constitutional Court of 21 September 2010 III. ÚS 335/2010-16.

which is a private entity because, in view of its purpose and nature, it cannot be automatically classified as a public authority.

11.18. In the Constitutional Court's opinion, arbitration takes on a public dimension only when the arbitration court delivers its decision on the substance of the case – its judgment, as Slovak law attaches the quality of enforceability to an arbitral award, which also constitutes an enforcement order. Pending that decision, the proceedings remain within the sphere of the arbitration court and, by nature, are a private relationship. Thus, if a complainant challenges an arbitration court's interlocutory decision – an order to stay the proceedings on account of failure to pay the fee, this is not an order reviewable by another arbitrator (Section 37(2) of the Arbitration Act) or court. Given the stage of the proceedings and situation regarding the circumstances of the case under consideration (a decision not constituting *res judicata*), the Constitutional Court concluded that the complainant had not exhausted all legal means made available to him by law for the protection of his rights (Section 53(1) of the Act on the Constitutional Court), and therefore deemed the complaint to be inadmissible.

11.19. The Constitutional Court also applied the principle of subsidiarity to a constitutional complaint against a follow-up decision of Brezno District Court[15] and Banská Bystrica Regional Court[16] discontinuing enforcement on the grounds that the arbitral award was in contravention of the law. Despite the beneficiary's objection that a bailiff's court lacks jurisdiction to review the substance of the enforcement order, i.e. to address the accuracy of the factual and legal conclusions of the issuing authority, the bailiff's courts argued that Section 45 of the Arbitration Act empowered them to examine the legality of the arbitration court's approach to the arbitration proceedings. A bailiff's court examines whether formal and material conditions for enforcement have been met in its decision-making on the bailiff's application for authorization to carry out enforcement (Section 44 of the Rules of Enforcement), any objection by the liable party to the enforcement (Section 50) and any application by the liable party for the suspension of discontinuance of enforcement (Section 58 of the Rules of Enforcement). The bailiff's court may also, to this extent, examine the enforcement order throughout the enforcement proceedings, and if it is found that the conditions of material or formal enforceability of the enforcement order have not been met, it must provide an adequate procedural response to any findings of illegality in enforcement. The courts consequently declared the enforcement to be inadmissible and halted it in accordance with Section 57(1)(g) of the Rules of Enforcement, in conjunction with Section 45(1)(c) and Section 45(2) of the Arbitration Act, and in accordance with Section 2(a) and (b) of Act No. 258/2001 Coll. on consumer credit. The Constitutional Court reclassified the

---

[15] See Brezno District Court Procedure No. 4 Er 157/08-16 of 27 May 2010.
[16] See Banská Bystrica Regional Court Procedure No. 16 CoE 172/2010-41 of 29 July 2010.

infringement of the right to judicial protection and to the equality of parties to judicial proceedings pursuant to Article 46(1) and Article 47(3) of the Constitution, as identified by the complainant, to the effect that the ordinary courts, by their decisions, had rendered it impossible for the complainant, as the beneficiary, to recover a monetary claim from the liable party as set out in the final arbitral award, i.e. the complainant was deprived of judicial protection in enforcement proceedings and of the opportunity to stand in court in the enforcement proceedings. If the approach taken by a court deprives a party of the opportunity to stand in court, under Section 237(f) of the Rules of Civil Procedure, that party is entitled to lodge an appeal against any decision by the court of appeal. As the complainant failed to appeal, the Constitutional Court deemed the complaint to be inadmissible pursuant to Section 53(1) of the Act on the Constitutional Court[17].

11.20. The principle of subsidiarity must also be applied in relation to objections to a final arbitral award seeking to breach the principle of the equality of parties to arbitration in connection with the insufficiently ascertained facts of the case or different view of the evidence and submissions presented by the other party (which the arbitration court considered legitimate and proven), where the evidence (of equal legal status) submitted by the complainant was not taken into account and no reason was given for this. The Constitutional Court held that, in this case, the complainant was entitled to claim the protection of its fundamental right under Article 46(1) of the Constitution, the infringement of which, according to the complainant, occurred as a result of the arbitration court's award, by bringing an action for the annulment of that decision pursuant to Section 40 (1)(g) of the Arbitration Act, upon which an (ordinary) court with due jurisdiction is entitled and obliged to adjudicate[18].

11.21. The Constitutional Court's settled case-law in cases where it has reviewed the decisions of ordinary courts (Decisions of the Constitutional Court II. ÚS 21/96 and III. ÚS 151/05) should also be applied in cases where evidence has been duly taken if the Constitutional Court is reviewing an arbitral award in terms of compliance with the principles of due process; this is because arbitration is an alternative to proceedings before the ordinary courts. Arbitration courts are also obliged to apply the law in such a way that the exercise of their powers results in a decision which meets the parameters of legality and constitutionality. The Constitutional Court expressly noted that the taking of evidence in arbitration proceedings is governed solely by the *principle of adversarial proceedings*, which means that the arbitration court only takes evidence put forward by the parties (Section 27(1) of the Arbitration Act). For example, if the arbitration court fails to cite provisions

---

[17] See Decision of the Constitutional Court of the Slovak Republic of 10 November 2010 II. ÚS 474/2010-15.
[18] See Decision of the Constitutional Court of the Slovak Republic of 10 December 2009 IV. ÚS 406/09-17.

of generally binding legislation, but sets out the course of evidence-taking and the conclusions drawn in detail, it is not possible to assent to the complainant's allegations of the illegality and validity of the challenged arbitral award to such an extent that would establish the Constitutional Court's jurisdiction to decree that the rights indicated by the complainant have been infringed. In this case, in the Constitutional Court's opinion the arbitration court quite clearly, although relatively simply, presented its findings, which, with regard to the taking of evidence, set out its train of thought quite plainly. Such deficiencies in the statement of grounds of an arbitral award, particularly with reference to the fact that, as a result of decision-making activities in relation to the dispute, it is meaningful, relevant and convincing, cannot indicate a breach of the principles of due process or, by extension, an infringement of the complainant's fundamental right under Article 46(1) of the Constitution[19].

11.22. In particular, we should recall recent developments in arbitration with regard to the possibility of reviewing arbitral awards in the context of European Union law and the case-law of the Court of Justice of the European Union. On 1 July 2009, Act No. 71/2009 Coll., amending Act No. 244/2002 Coll. on arbitration entered into effect. In addition to some major changes (such as the enshrinement of the duty for the arbitration request and arbitral award to be served on the parties in person), the amendment of the Act made it possible for an arbitral award on the performance of a consumer contract to be challengeable by an action for annulment at an ordinary court if consumer protection provisions are breached, as an arbitration court is now obliged to take into account the provisions of generally binding legislation on consumer protection (Section 31 of the Arbitration Act); it is no longer possible for an arbitral award to be attributed with performance under a consumer contract which is contrary to the provisions of generally binding legislation on the protection of consumer rights (Section 33(2) of the Arbitration Act). These changes by the legislature, according to the explanatory memorandum to Act No. 71/2009 Coll., were expressly taken from the case-law of the EU Court of Justice, particularly Judgment of the Court of 6 October 2009, C-40/08, *Asturcom Telecomunicaciones SL v Cristina Rodríguez Nogueira* (ECR 2009, pp. I-09579, hereinafter referred to as "*Asturcom Telecomunicaciones SL*").

11.23. The practices of the arbitration courts, combined with a far-reaching campaign waged by the Ministry of Justice of the Slovak Republic between 2008 and 2010, resulted in the ordinary courts drawing on the ramifications of the *Asturcom Telecomunicaciones SL* judgment almost immediately[20]. For example, it follows from the interlinked rulings of the

---

[19] See Decision of the Constitutional Court of the Slovak Republic of 25 May 2010 III. ÚS 213/2010-16.

[20] See also the temporal effects of preliminary rulings *in* MICHAEL SIMAN, MIROSLAV SLAŠTAN, SÚDNY SYSTÉM EURÓPSKEJ ÚNIE (*The Judicial System of the European Union*), Bratislava: EUROIURIS – Európske právne centrum, o.z. 359 (2010).

Humenné District Court[21] and Prešov Regional Court[22] that the bailiff's application for the authorization of enforcement was rejected because the liable party had been granted consumer credit (amounting to EUR 780.12, and which the liable party had undertaken to repay to the beneficiary together with a contract fee of EUR 49.79 and contractual remuneration of EUR 829.91, i.e. a total of EUR 1,659.83 over 36 monthly instalments payable in accordance with a payment schedule) which contained unfair terms, i.e. arrangements for penalties – contractual fines, and arrangements to secure the credit with a blank promissory note, which were not individually negotiated and caused a significant imbalance in the rights and obligations of the parties to the detriment of the consumer. It was by reference to the requested credit agreement in question that the bailiff's courts discovered the unfair conditions.

11.24. In the opinion of both courts, such unreasonable conditions are null and void and therefore in this part the enforcement order – arbitral award – includes a commitment to consideration which is illegal and contrary to good morals. Similarly, the amount of the contractual penalties awarded under the arbitral award, i.e. EUR 860.51, was deemed by the district court to be totally disproportionate to the amount of the principal of the credit actually granted (EUR 780.12) and contrary to good morals and the law. They justified the refusal to grant authorization for enforcement by reference to Section 45 of Act No. 244/2002 Coll. on arbitration, according to which the court with due jurisdiction to enforce a decision or to order enforcement shall discontinue the enforcement of an arbitral award or enforcement order of its own motion if it discovers an irregularity in the arbitration consisting, *inter alia*, of the fact that the arbitral award orders a party to provide consideration which is objectively impossible, illegal or contrary to good morals. Since, in this case, the enforcement order (arbitral award) requires the liable party to provide consideration which is contrary to good morals, the district court rejected the application for authorization to carry out enforcement by invoking Section 45 of the Arbitration Act and Section 44 of Act No. 233/1995 Coll. on bailiffs and enforcement, as amended (the "Rules of Enforcement"), as the Arbitration Act and Rules of Enforcement complement each other.

11.25. This practice by the ordinary courts also recently underwent constitutional scrutiny. In a complaint to the Constitutional Court, the beneficiary argued that there had been a violation of Article 2(2) of the Constitution (according to which the courts may act only on the basis and within the limits of the Constitution and to the extent and in the manner prescribed by law) because the court had reviewed the credit agreement as a result of incorrectly invoking Section 45 of the Arbitration Act and had thus intervened in a case which had been closed with final effect (by the arbitral award). Section 45 of the Arbitration Act does not enable a bailiff's court to

---

21 See Order of Humenné District Court No 21 Er 536/2009-22 of 3 December 2009.
22 See Order of Košice Regional Court No 5 CoE 4/2010-73 of 15 April 2010.

review an enforcement order, but only to assess the consideration awarded by the enforcement order as such. The legal wording of this provision refers to considerations ordered by an arbitral award, not considerations arising on the legal grounds serving as the basis for the rendering of the enforcement order; the bailiff's court has the jurisdiction (Section 45 of the Arbitration Act), when deciding whether to grant authorization to the bailiff, to examine only whether the consideration ordered by the arbitral award is contrary to good morals, but does not have jurisdiction to review the legal basis on which the right was exercised in arbitration. Only an arbitration court is entitled to conduct a substantive assessment of the case; reassessment by a bailiff's court is precluded by the force of *res judicata*. An ordinary court may review the legal grounds for the consideration ordered under an arbitral award only if the law confers such power on it (Section 40(1) of the Arbitration Act, governing the possibility of bringing an action for annulment of an arbitral award). If the consumer does not bring an action for a review of an arbitral award, the ordinary court cannot remedy this omission or substitute the consumer's general passivity in arbitration (see the *Asturcom Telecomunicaciones SL* judgment). The complainant considered the order of the courts to be inadequate and an infringement of the right to judicial protection under Article 46(1) of the Constitution, especially since it is impossible to ascertain from the statement of grounds of the challenged order how and by what interpretation of Section 45 of the Arbitration Act the court came to identify the phrase "consideration granted by an enforcement order" with the phrase "legal reason for consideration granted by an enforcement order".

11.26. The Constitutional Court, without a closer interpretation of the two controversial laws or case-law of the EU Court of Justice, agreed with the procedure followed by the ordinary courts, judging their considerations to be "logical, and therefore quite legitimate and legally acceptable", and also "adequately justified". Similarly, the Constitutional Court dismissed the grounds for the infringement of the right to the equality of parties in proceedings under Article 47(3) of the Constitution[23] since, according to the complainant, despite the absolute passivity of the other party to the arbitration (the liable party), that party was placed in a position as if it had not filed objections in the arbitration proceedings *per se*. The Constitutional Court rejected the argument that the liable party had benefited from such a procedure, thus breaching the principle of the equality of parties[24].

| | |

---

[23] See Decision of the Constitutional Court of the Slovak Republic of 9 September 2010 IV. ÚS 310/2010-19.

[24] See Decision of the Constitutional Court of the Slovak Republic of 10 November 2010 II. ÚS 474/2010-15.

Summaries

DEU [*Anerkennung der Menschenrechte und Verfassungswerte bei der Überprüfung von Schiedssprüchen durch die Gerichte der Slowakischen Republik*]

Der Beitrag befasst sich mit der Entwicklung und dem aktuellen Stand der Rechtsregelung des Schiedsverfahrens in der Slowakei im Zusammenhang mit dem Recht zur Überprüfung von schiedsgerichtlichen Entscheidungen, die unter dem Gesetz gestattet sind. Der Beitrag resümiert vornehmlich die Rechtsprechung des Verfassungsgerichts der Slowakischen Republik, das seine verfassungsrechtliche Kontrolle und Anerkennung der im Zivilprozess anwendbaren Menschenrechte auch in Bezug auf das Schiedsverfahren neu bewertet hat. Somit ist es möglich, den vom Verfassungsgericht bei Schiedsverfahren angewendeten Ansatz zur Einhaltung des Grundsatzes der Gerechtigkeit und des ordentlichen Rechtsverfahrens sowie der Einhaltung des Subsidiaritätsprinzips zu ermitteln. Dies wird in diesem Beitrag auch im Kontext der besonderen Struktur des slowakischen Rechtssystems und der Prozessvorschriften in Verbindung mit der Überprüfung von schiedsgerichtlichen Entscheidungen erklärt. Im abschließenden Abschnitt des Beitrags werden jüngste Änderungen bei Schiedsverfahren und die Bedingungen für die Überprüfung von Schiedssprüchen in Hinsicht auf die Rechtsprechung des Europäischen Gerichtshofs dargelegt.

CZE [*Uznání lidských práv a ústavních hodnot při přezkumu rozhodčích nálezů soudy Slovenské republiky*]

Tento příspěvek se zabývá vývojem a současným stavem právní úpravy rozhodčího řízení na Slovensku v kontextu právem dovoleného přezkoumání rozhodčích nálezů. Příspěvek shrnuje zejména judikaturu Ústavního soudu Slovenské republiky, který svoji kontrolu ústavnosti a dodržování lidských práv uplatněnou v občanském soudním řízení přehodnotil a vztáhl i na rozhodčí řízení. Je proto možné identifikovat přístup Ústavního soudu při dodržování zásady spravedlnosti a zákonnosti na rozhodčí řízení při současném dodržení zásady subsidiarity. Tu příspěvek taktéž vysvětluje, a to v kontextu jedinečné struktury slovenského soudnictví a procesních předpisů směřujících k přezkoumání rozhodčích nálezů. V závěru příspěvek připomíná aktuální změny rozhodčího řízení a podmínek přezkoumání rozhodčích nálezů vzhledem k judikatuře Evropského soudního dvora.

| | |

POL [*Akceptowanie praw człowieka i wartości konstytucyjnych podczas rewizji orzeczeń arbitrażowych przez sądy Republiki Słowackiej*]

Niniejszy artykuł poświecony jest zmianom i aktualnemu stanowi regulacji prawnych postępowania arbitrażowego na Słowacji w świetle dopuszczalnej przez prawo rewizji orzeczeń arbitrażowych. Artykuł podsumowuje przede wszystkim orzecznictwo Sądu Konstytucyjnego Republiki Słowackiej, który rozszerzył swoją kontrolę zgodności z konstytucją i przestrzegania praw człowieka również na postępowanie arbitrażowe.

FRA   *[Acceptation des droits de l'homme et des valeurs constitutionnelles dans l'examen des sentences arbitrales par les tribunaux de justice de la République slovaque]*
Cette contribution se consacre au développement et à l'état actuel de la réglementation juridique de la procédure d'arbitrage en Slovaquie dans le contexte de l'examen des sentences arbitrales autorisé par la loi. L'article récapitule tout particulièrement la jurisprudence de la Cour constitutionnelle de la République slovaque, qui a étendu également aux procédures d'arbitrage son contrôle de la constitutionnalité et du respect des droits de l'homme.

RUS   *[Соблюдение прав человека и конституционных ценностей при пересмотре арбитражных решений в судах Словацкой Республики]*
Настоящая работа посвящена развитию, а также рассматривает существующую ситуацию в области арбитражного законодательства в Словацкой Республике в контексте допустимого законодательством пересмотра арбитражных решений. В статье, прежде всего, рассматривается правосудие Конституционного Суда Словацкой Республики, который контролирует конституционность и соблюдение прав человека, в том числе и в сфере арбитражного (третейсково) разбирательства.

ES   *[La aceptación de los derechos humanos y de los valores constitucionales al revisar las conclusiones arbitrales por los tribunales de justicia de la República Eslovaca]*
Esta contribución reseña la evolución y el estado actual de la reglamentación legal del procesamiento de arbitraje en Eslovaquia, en el contexto de la revisión de las conclusiones arbitrales que la ley permite. El artículo resume sobre todo la jurisprudencia del Tribunal Constitucional de la República Eslovaca, el cual ha aplicado el control de la constitucionalidad y del cumplimiento de los derechos humanos también al procesamiento arbitral.

Matthias Scherer*
ICSID Annulment Proceedings Based on Serious Departure from a Fundamental Rule of Procedure
(Article 52(1)(d) of the ICSID Convention)

Key words:
ICSID Arbitration |
ICSID Convention
| Annulment of the
Award | Ad hoc
Committees | Article
52(1)(d)

Abstract | *This paper analyses case law on Article 52(1) (d) of the ICSID Convention, according to which an award rendered by an ICSID tribunal can be annulled by an ad hoc Committee on the grounds of a serious departure from a fundamental rule of procedure. To be able to successfully invoke this ground before an ad hoc Committee, the applicant has to demonstrate both that the departure from a rule of procedure is serious and the rule fundamental. These requirements are cumulative. The decisions on annulment which were examined in this paper illustrate that ad hoc Committees interpret narrowly and with great care this ground of annulment because it is related to the principle of due process. An important hurdle to any request for annulment is the wide discretion which arbitral tribunals enjoy in the way they conduct the evidentiary proceedings. The ad hoc Committee in the Azurix case held that "it is only where the exercise of that discretion, in all the circumstances of the case, amounts to a serious departure from another rule of a fundamental nature that there will be grounds for annulment under Article 52(1)(d)". This discretion as well as the professionalism and expertise of the arbitrators sitting in ICSID panels will continue to be the major obstacles for annulment requests on the basis of Article 52(1)(d).*

Matthias Scherer,
Partner, LALIVE
(Geneva). Counsel
and arbitrator
in international
arbitration
proceedings. Member
of the Arbitration
Committee of the
Swiss Chambers
of Commerce, an
associate member
of the ICC Institute,
a vice chair of the IBA
Arbitration Committee,
and serves as Editor of
the journal of the Swiss
Arbitration Association
(ASA Bulletin) and
Co-Editor of the
Swiss International
Arbitration Law
Reports. Matthias
features in the
International Who's
Who of Commercial
Arbitration Lawyers
since its inception
in 2005.
email:
mscherer@lalive.ch

| | |

*   The author wishes to thank Mr Guillaume Aréou and Mr George Walker, Legal Interns at LALIVE for their assistance with the preparation of the paper.

12.01. In 1965, the Convention on the Settlement of Investment Disputes between States and Nationals of Other States (the "ICSID Convention" or the "Washington Convention") entered into force and established the International Centre for Settlement of Investment Disputes (the Centre). The ICSID Convention affords investors of one Contracting State a framework for settling investment disputes with public entities of another Contracting State[1]. Because each Contracting State undertakes to enforce within its territory the pecuniary obligations imposed by an ICSID award "as if it were a final judgment of that State"[2], awards rendered by arbitral tribunals under the aegis of the ICSID Convention are generally final and binding. Article 52 of the ICSID Convention provides for the annulment of an ICSID award under very limited circumstances. In legal systems that are respectful of human rights, the judiciary must abide by certain minimum procedural standards. Thus, Article 6 of the European Convention on Human Rights has spawned a wealth of case law on procedural rights of parties involved in court proceedings. It is not the purpose of this article to contribute to the debate whether the ECHR applies in international arbitration or not. Rather, our goal is to analyze how the ICSID Convention, which creates a self-standing legal system for disputes between States and investors, ensures that arbitral tribunals sitting under the aegis of ICSID respect fundamental rules of due process.

12.02. A party that is dissatisfied with an award rendered by an ICSID Tribunal can file a request for annulment with the ICSID Secretary General. Article 52(3) of the ICSID Convention provides:

> "On receipt of the request the Chairman [of the Administrative Council (i.e. the president of the World Bank)] shall forthwith appoint from the Panel of Arbitrators an *ad hoc* Committee of three persons. None of the members of the Committee shall have been a member of the Tribunal which rendered the award, shall be of the same nationality as any such member, shall be a national of the State party to the dispute or of the State whose national is a party to the dispute, shall have been designated to the Panel of Arbitrators by either of those States, or shall have acted as a conciliator in the same dispute. The Committee shall have the authority to annul the award or any part thereof on any of the grounds set forth in paragraph (1)".

In a sense, *Ad hoc* Committees secure the integrity of the arbitration process. Yet they are not an appellate body and must not review the merits of the award[3]. An annulment request may invoke any combination

---

[1] Article 25 of ICSID Convention related to the jurisdiction of the Centre.

[2] Articles 53 to 55 of ICSID Convention.

[3] In the decision on annulment in the case of *Soufraki*, the *Ad hoc* Committee enumerated three goals that ICSID annulment mechanism seeks to secure: the integrity of the tribunal, the integrity of the procedure and the integrity of the award. Then it stated that an *Ad hoc* Committee "is responsible for controlling the overall integrity of the arbitral process". *Hussein Nuaman Soufraki v. The United Arab States*, ICSID Case No. ARB/02/7, decision on annulment of 5 June 2007, para. 24.

present arguments on that point. The *Ad hoc* Committee held that the granting of the "correction" violated a fundamental rule of procedure, even though the asserted correction was allegedly obvious[16].

12.06. Another decision on annulment arose out of a dispute between Klöckner and the Republic of Cameroon. In the underlying arbitration, Klöckner sought payment of the full price of a fertilizer plant it had constructed in Cameroon. On October 1983, a tribunal rendered an award that Klöckner considered to be systematically hostile to its cause. Alleging a violation of its due process rights, Klöckner challenged this award on three of the five Article 52(1) grounds, namely, the manifestly excessive use of power, the serious departure from a fundamental rule of procedure and the failure to state reasons. Klöckner argued that the tribunal had not truly deliberated, that it was obviously partial, and that it had failed to respect due process. In sum, Klöckner alleged it had not enjoyed the right to be heard.

12.07. The *Ad hoc* Committee disagreed. Observing first that Klöckner had a very personal notion of deliberation, it found that Klöckner's criticism lacked precision and substance and that the arbitral proceedings had in fact been conducted properly. It stated, "[Klöckner] had every opportunity to express itself and present its case"[17]. In this regard, the *Ad hoc* Committee mentioned that a tribunal is not obligated to hear the parties on the reasons it is going to rely on in its decision or bound to select among those arguments put forth by the parties[18]. Secondly, the *Ad hoc* Committee compared the final award's substantial issues with those raised in the dissenting opinion and concluded that Klöckner failed to demonstrate the Arbitral Tribunal's failure to deliberate properly. In view of the confidential nature of deliberations, it is of course difficult for an *Ad hoc* committee to assess the seriousness of the deliberations. Finally, the *Ad hoc* Committee noted that Klöckner did not set forth any criteria the Committee should use in order to assess what qualifies as an adequate deliberative process. For all these reasons, the *Ad hoc* Committee dismissed the allegation of serious departure from a fundamental rule of procedure, but nevertheless annulled the award on the grounds of excessive use of power and failure to state reasons.

12.08. The *Maritime International Nominees Establishment (MINE) v. Government of Guinea* decision remains an important authority on the Article 52(1)(d) annulment ground. In 1984, MINE commenced arbitration against the Republic of Guinea. MINE alleged a breach of contract by the Guinea in the context of a bauxite transportation joint venture. MINE secured an award in its favour rendered on 6 January 1988. The Republic of Guinea sought the (partial) annulment of the performance dispute and the determination of damages. The Republic of Guinea considered that the award was tainted by a manifestly excessive use of power, a serious departure from a fundamental rule of procedure and a failure to state

---

16   *Ibid.*
17   *Klöckner v. Republic of Cameroon*, p. 117.
18   *Ibid.*, 128-29.

reasons. Specifically, the Republic of Guinea objected to the Arbitral Tribunal's use of a theory of damages that neither party had advanced, discussed or had the opportunity to discuss.

12.09. Since the *Ad hoc* Committee annulled the award on the ground of failure to state reasons, it did not examine the alternative grounds for annulment advanced by Guinea, which included serious departure from a fundamental rule of procedure[19]. There exists a close link between these two grounds of annulment. In the case at hand, the Republic of Guinea alleged that the Arbitral Tribunal did not address at least two questions it raised in relation to the calculation of damages[20]. Even if this claim were decided on the ground of the failure to state reason, one must admit that it also concerns the right to be heard. The *Ad hoc* Committee stated that "failure to address these questions [raised by the applicant] constituted a failure to state the reasons on which that conclusion was based"[21]. Guinea's submissions on calculation of damages were of such importance that their acceptance by the Arbitral Tribunal might have changed the outcome of the award. The Arbitral Tribunal had a duty to deliberate upon them even if they were to be ultimately dismissed. Finally, the *Ad hoc* Committee observed that "to the extent that the Tribunal purported to state the reasons for its decision, they were inconsistent and in contradiction with its analysis of damages theories"[22].

12.10. In *Vivendi Universal* (formerly *Compañiá de Aguas del Aconquija*) *v. Argentine Republic*, the dispute concerned the provision of water and sewage services in the Argentine province of Tucumán. The province privatized those services. Then, a new a successive provincial administration took steps which the investors regarded as undermining the concession contract. The concession contract ended and the investors requested arbitration. Compañiá de Aguas del Aconquija alleged that measures taken by the provincial government were attributable to the Republic of Argentina under the terms of the Bilateral Investment Treaty concluded between Argentina and France. On 21 November 2000, the Arbitral Tribunal upheld its jurisdiction but dismissed claims on the merits. On March 2001, Compañiá de Aguas del Aconquija filed an application requesting the partial annulment of the award. Compañiá de Aguas del Aconquija argued that the Arbitral Tribunal analysis of Article 16 (4) of the Concession Contract was not "adequately canvassed in argument"[23]. Compañiá de Aguas del Aconquija also contended that the Arbitral Tribunal's decision arrived unannounced and, consequently, that it had no opportunity "to present arguments on the decision to dismiss

---

[19] *MINE v. Guinea*, para. 6.109.
[20] CHRISTOPH H. SCHEREUER, *supra* note 4, at 989.
[21] *MINE v. Guinea*, para. 6.99.
[22] *Ibid.*, para. 6.105.
[23] *Compañía de Aguas del Aconquija S.A. and Vivendi Universal S.A. v. Argentine Republic*, ICSID Case No. ARB/97/3, Decision on Annulment of July 3, 2002, para. 82.

their claim on the merits"[24]. The *Ad hoc* Committee found no arbitral case law supporting Compañiá de Aguas del Aconquija's allegations. While the *Ad hoc* Committee agreed that the initial tribunal's approach may well have surprised the parties, it did not find that there had been any departure from a fundamental rule of procedure, let alone a serious departure. On the contrary, it considered that "the parties had a full and fair opportunity to be heard at every stage of the proceedings"[25]. Thus, according to *Vivendi v. Argentina Ad hoc* Committee, the failure to anticipate and address an argument that persuades a tribunal cannot form the basis of a successful annulment claim.

12.11. A more recent annulment decision invoking the rule against serious departure is *CDC Group* v. *Seychelles* rendered on 29 June 2005. The dispute arose out of two loan agreements and their related sovereign guarantees made by Seychelles. The Respondent, the Republic of Seychelles, agreed to guarantee *loans* that CDC made to Public Utilities Corporation, a public electric power company. When the latter did not perform its obligations in a timely fashion, CDC sought payment from the Republic of Seychelles which in turn failed to respect its obligations. CDC Group submitted its request for ICSID arbitration and garnered an award in its favour. Dissatisfied with the award, the Republic of Seychelles sought annulment on three of the Article 52(1) grounds.

12.12. The Republic of Seychelles alleged that the Arbitral Tribunal lacked impartiality and did not conduct proper deliberations. Under that theory, the tribunal allegedly failed to answer the questions presented by the parties, to follow the rule of evidence, and to issue a timely award. As for the charge of partiality, the tribunal was accused of committing that violation "when it heard argument on whether or not testimonial evidence needed to be heard at the preliminary hearing because whether the witnesses should be called to testify on its behalf before the Arbitrator was entirely for the Republic"[26].

12.13. The *Ad hoc* Committee pointed out first the weakness of this argument in that the Republic of Seychelles did not object to the improper conduct prior to the tribunal rendering its award[27]. The *Ad hoc* Committee concluded that the record demonstrated that Sir Anthony "served as an unbiased and independent sole arbitrator"[28]. Furthermore, it dismissed the alleged lack of deliberation. The Republic of Seychelles had based that allegation on the fact that the Arbitral Tribunal did not consider relevant matters and pieces of evidence. But the Committee analysed this claim under Article 52(1)(e) and came to the opposite conclusion. The Republic of Seychelles's objection amounted to a mere difference in point of view.

---

24 *Ibid.*, para. 84.
25 *Ibid.*, para. 85.
26 *CDC Group v. Seychelles*, para. 49.
27 *Ibid.*, para. 53.
28 *Ibid.*, para. 54.

Regarding the claim that the Arbitral Tribunal considered irrelevant matters and ignored relevant ones, the *Ad hoc* Committee stated, "again, the Republic [of Seychelles] cites no authority for the proposition that such an error necessitates annulment"[29].

12.14. On 20 February 2004, an ICSID Arbitral Tribunal rendered an award in a case brought by Repsol, acting on behalf of a consortium, against Petroecuador seeking amounts owed for services performed according to the terms of an oil exploration and production contract with the Republic of Ecuador. The award ordered Petroecuador to pay substantial damages. Petroecuador alleged before the *Ad hoc* Committee that the Arbitral Tribunal manifestly exceeded its powers and that it breached a fundamental rule of procedure. It argued that the tribunal's acceptance of Repsol's standing to represent the consortium constituted a serious departure from a fundamental rule of procedure. In its award, the tribunal had highlighted "the lack of evidence to support Petroecuador's argument that Repsol did not have the power to represent the other companies comprising the consortium. Furthermore, the Tribunal considered that all those companies ratified the actions of Repsol through letters signed by their legal representatives"[30]. The *Ad hoc* Committee found no clear evidence of a serious departure from a fundamental rule of procedure[31].

12.15. The allegation of serious departure from a fundamental rule also surfaced in *MTD Equity v. the Republic of Chile*. In that case, MTD and its subsidiaries negotiated two foreign investment contracts with the Chilean Foreign Investment Commission for the development of a self-sufficient township in the city of Pirque, Chile based on a Malaysian model. When the government of Chile subsequently asserted the inconsistency of the project with its urban development policy, MTD filed a request for arbitration. With an award on 25 May 2004, a tribunal held not only that Chile had breached its obligations, but also that MTD had failed to adequately protect itself from inherent investment project risks.

12.16. The Republic of Chile challenged the award on three of the five grounds set out in Article 52(1). It argued that, when finding a breach of the fair and equitable treatment obligation, the Arbitral Tribunal did not "consider or otherwise respond to abundant evidence presented by the Parties with respect to material issues in dispute"[32]. Noting that Chile had developed this line of argument neither in its reply nor during oral arguments, the *Ad hoc* Committee nevertheless analysed it as a potential failure to give the reasons, ultimately concluding that the tribunal's reasoning was sufficiently clear[33].

---

[29] *Ibid.*, para. 78.
[30] *Repsol YPF v. Empresa Estatal Petróleos del Ecuador (Petroecuador)*, ICSID Case No. ARB/01/10, Decision on Annulment of January 8, 2007, para. 77.
[31] *Ibid.*, para. 82.
[32] *MTD Equity Sdn. Bhd. and MTD Chile S.A. v. Republic of Chile*, ICSID Case No. ARB/01/7, Decision on Annulment of March 21, 2007, para. 56.
[33] *Ibid.*, para. 57.

12.17. In addition, the Republic of Chile claimed that the Arbitral Tribunal had ignored Chile's fundamental principle of separation of powers. The *Ad hoc* Committee recognized the distinction between actions taken by different Chilean public officials but disagreed that the tribunal had erred in this way[34]. The *Ad hoc* Committee stressed that, in its award, the tribunal placed considerable emphasis on, and referred four times to, the "unity of State" in making its assessment under the most favoured nation provision of the governing bilateral investment treaty. It explained, "what the Arbitral Tribunal emphasized is the inconsistency of action between two arms of the same government *vis-à-vis* the same investor even when the legal framework of the country provides for a mechanism to coordinate"[35]. Thus, as an active party rather than a passive one, Chile, and not the investor, had a duty to ensure the coherence of actions taken by its various public officials[36].

12.18. Similarly, *Industria Nacional de Alimentos, S.A. (previously Empresas Lucchetti S.A.) and Indalsa Perú S.A. (previously Lucchetti Perú S.A.) v. the Republic of Peru* also concerns an urban zoning decree issued by local authorities. Lucchetti was the owner of property in the City of Lima where it constructed a plant near a protected wetland. On 18 August 1997, the local municipality issued a stop work order to Lucchetti followed by Decree 259 on 16 August 2001 revoking Lucchetti's operating licence. In the preamble of the Decree, it is stated that Lucchetti failed to observe zoning and environmental regulations applicable to the construction of the plant. On December 2002, Lucchetti filed a request for arbitration under the ICSID Convention.

12.19. The Arbitral Tribunal rendered its award on 7 February 2005 concluding that it had no jurisdiction *ratione temporis* to hear the merits of the dispute. Lucchetti sought to annul the award on the following grounds: manifest excess of power, serious departure from a rule of procedure and failure to state reasons. According to Lucchetti, the Arbitral Tribunal exceeded its power "by disregarding [its] offer to prove that the stated reasons for Decree 259 [which was the cause of the annulment of the licence granted to *Lucchetti*] were mere pretexts"[37]. Lucchetti concluded that it had not been given a full opportunity to be heard and also alleged that the tribunal, by its reasoning, violated the presumption of innocence and the requirements of due process. Lucchetti claimed "that it was deprived of a fair opportunity to demonstrate the untruthfulness of the Municipality of Lima's assertions, notably by the Tribunal's refusal to allow it to file a full

---

[34] *Ibid.*, para. 89.
[35] *Ibid.*, para. 87.
[36] *Ibid.*, para. 87-88.
[37] *Industria Nacional de Alimentos, S.A. and Indalsa Perú, S.A. v. Republic of Peru*, ICSID Case No. ARB/03/4, Decision on Annulment of September 5, 2007, para. 47.

Memorial on the Merits before the Tribunal proceeded to a decision on the Preliminary Objections"[38].

12.20. The *Ad hoc* Committee opined, "there is no doubt that what Lucchetti referred to as the Municipality of Lima's subjective assertions did become a crucial element in the Tribunal's ultimate decision"[39] and affirmed that if Lucchetti did not have the opportunity to be heard it would have amounted to a serious departure from a fundamental rule of procedure. However the *Ad hoc* Committee found that Lucchetti had full opportunity to present its case including its argument that the reasons given by Decree 259 were false[40]. The argument of a violation of the presumption of innocence also failed because "the Tribunal did not examine the issue of the alleged illegalities but founded its conclusions on other elements in the preamble to Decree 259"[41]. The Committee dismissed Lucchetti's claims of serious departure from a fundamental rule of procedure and found that the Arbitral Tribunal gave sufficient reasons to explain its conclusion.

12.21. *Rumeli Telekom and Telsim Mobil v. the Republic of Kazakhstan* concerned the alleged expropriation of Rumeli and Telsim's shares in a Kazakh company. These two companies had won the bid for licence to the second largest mobile telephone network in Kazakhstan. An Arbitral Tribunal seized by the two investors concluded that the Republic of Kazakhstan breached its obligations under the Bilateral Investment Treaty. The Republic filed a timely annulment request invoking three of the Article 52(1) grounds. The allegations regarding the serious departure from a fundamental rule of procedure were diverse. The Republic of Kazakhstan alleged that the Arbitral Tribunal lacked impartiality and that it breached the right of Respondent to be heard. It also argued that the Arbitral Tribunal did not take pertinent evidence into account and had not deliberated. The *Ad hoc* Committee concluded that the Arbitral Tribunal is "the judge of the probative evidence"[42]. The Committee had no power to weigh the evidence brought before the Arbitral Tribunal. In the end, there were no annullable elements in the award regarding Article 52(1)(d) and Article 52(1)(e).

12.22. One of the most recent *Ad hoc* Committee decisions regarding a serious departure from a fundamental rule of procedure was handed down on 14 June 2010. It concerned the annulment request brought after the *Helnan International v. The Arab Republic of Egypt* award. The initial dispute arose after Egypt's Ministry of Tourism downgraded the Hotel Shepheard's ratings. An arbitration conducted in December 2004 under

---

[38] *Ibid.*, para. 120.
[39] *Ibid.*, para. 121.
[40] *Ibid.*, para. 123.
[41] *Ibid.*, para. 124.
[42] *Rumeli Telekom A.S. and Telsim Mobil Telekomunikasyon Hizmetleri A.S. v. Republic of Kazakhstan*, ICSID Case No. ARB/05/16, Decision on Annulment of March 25, 2010, para. 104.

the aegis of the Cairo Regional Centre for International Commercial Arbitration "terminated the Management Contract on the ground that it was impossible to execute, and that both parties were responsible for failing to execute the contract"[43]. Helnan thereafter initiated arbitration under the ICSID mechanism. The Arbitral Tribunal decided that it had jurisdiction but dismissed all of the claims on their merits. Helnan sought annulment of the award on three grounds relying first on the fact that the tribunal founded its reasoning upon an issue not submitted by either party. Secondly, Helnan challenged the tribunal's conclusion that "the ministerial decision to downgrade the hotel [...] cannot be seen as a breach of the Treaty by Egypt"[44]. According to Helnan, the tribunal did not support this conclusion and failed to observe a fundamental rule of procedure by neglecting to refer to Helnan's submissions on that issue in the final award. The *Ad hoc* Committee responded with a very limited analysis under Article 52(1)(d) simply stating that Helnan's claim for annulment was not persuasive and that its arguments in fact had been plainly considered by the Arbitral Tribunal[45].

12.23. Lastly, we review two cases concerning awards rendered against the Republic of Argentina caused by its severe economic crisis of 2001. In *Azurix* v. Argentina, the dispute arose in the water services sector whereas *Enron Creditors Recovery Corp. and Ponderosa Assets, L.P.* v. Argentina concerned the transportation and distribution of gas. In an effort to minimize the effects of the crisis, the Argentine government enacted an emergency law that eliminated the government's right to denominate transactions in US dollars and to peg pesos to dollars one-to-one. In the aftermath of this crisis, *Enron* and *Azurix* were two of many ICSID claimants alleging that Argentina breached its contractual and treaty obligations. The ICSID tribunals in both disputes concluded that Argentina had indeed breached its treaty obligations including the principle of fair and equitable treatment.

12.24. The Republic of Argentina sought annulment of the awards on multiple grounds. In the *Azurix* case, Argentina argued that the tribunal had dismissed the evidence it presented consequently violating Argentina's rights of defence and equality[46]. The *Ad hoc* Committee stated that the ICSID Convention provides arbitral tribunals with discretion to grant or deny a party's request. Thus, Argentina's allegation did not amount, in and of itself, to a serious departure from a fundamental rule of procedure. The Committee held, "it is only where the exercise of that discretion, in all the circumstances of the case, amounts to a serious departure from another rule of a fundamental nature that there will be grounds for annulment

---

43 *Helnan International Hotels A/S v. Arab Republic of Egypt*, ICSID Case No. ARB/05/19, Decision on Annulment of June 14, 2010, para. 6.

44 *Ibid.*, para. 28.

45 *Ibid.*, paras 35, 38.

46 *Azurix v. Argentina*, para. 211.

under Article 52(1)(d) of the ICSID Convention"[47]. On the question of the tribunal's refusal to admit certain requests presented by Argentina, the Committee said "it is not the case that a party has the right to demand any evidence at any time without justification. Even where a request is timely, precise and justified, the tribunal may in its discretion reject the request"[48]. Ultimately, the Committee dismissed in its entirety Argentina's request to annul the *Azurix* award.

12.25. The *Enron and Ponderosa v. Argentina* annulment decision made similar conclusions regarding the allegation of serious departure from a fundamental rule of procedure. Enron and Ponderosa argued that the tribunal's admission of a witness statement and an expert report over the objections of Argentina constituted a breach of Article 52(1)(d) of the ICSID Convention. Argentina claimed further that the initial tribunal's decision to close the proceedings in a manner that deprived the Respondent of any further opportunity to challenge any member of the tribunal constituted likewise violated the rule against serious departure from a fundamental rule of procedure. The *Ad hoc* Committee rejected Argentina's argument because it was not clear whether or on what basis Argentina would have raised the challenges it was allegedly precluded from making. Nor was it clear why Argentina had not made such challenges before the proceedings closed[49]. The *Ad hoc* Committee considered "that no tenable basis has been advanced by Argentina for suggesting that the way that the Tribunal exercised its discretion in the circumstances was inconsistent with any principle of equality of the parties or right of defence or fair treatment"[50].

Post-scriptum

12.26. After the completion of the present paper, the decision of the *Ad hoc* Committee in *Fraport AG v Republic of the Philippines*[51] became public. The Committee annulled the award in the underlying proceedings on the basis of Article 52(1)(d) of the ICSID Convention. It found that the Arbitral Tribunal had failed to grant the right to be heard to Fraport in relation to certain evidence produced by the Philippines at a very late stage in the proceedings.

12.27. Given space constraints, it is not possible here to provide a sufficiently detailed overview of the facts of the case to undertake a proper analysis of the decision. Nevertheless, in a nutshell, the Arbitral Tribunal had decided that the Fraport's investment was not made in compliance with

---

47 *Azurix v. Argentina*, para. 210.
48 *Ibid.*, para. 218.
49 *Enron and Ponderosa v. Argentina*, para. 206-12.
50 *Ibid.*, para.193.
51 *Fraport AG v Republic of the Philippines*, ICSID Case or ARB/03/25 (annulment proceedings), Decision of 23 December 2010, chapter IV.B, para. 119-247.

Philippine law and hence did not fall within the scope of the tribunal's jurisdiction under the BIT. The arbitrators found that Fraport had violated the Philippines anti-dummy laws (ADL) by secretly controlling a Philippines entity through undisclosed shareholder agreements. The tribunal heavily relied on documents produced by the Philippines after the closure of the proceedings, in particular a decision of the Philippine prosecutor dismissing a criminal complaint based on the ADL. The Philippines asserted that the prosecutor had access to two documents only, and that he had notably not seen the secret shareholder agreements or other records evidencing Fraport's violation of the ADL. Fraport responded that while they obviously did not know what documents the Prosecutor had access to; he did have access to many more than just the two documents. The arbitral tribunal invited the Philippines to submit evidence as to the prosecutor's file, stressing that this request was not a decision to reopen the proceedings and that the tribunal "merely seeks to complete the evidentiary record which the parties have constituted [with their submissions]". The State filed some 1900 pages of new documents, asserting that that they constituted the entirety of the prosecutorial record. Fraport responded that this was still not the full record. The Philippines admitted as much but added that any omission was unintentional and that they would supplement their production if any additional responsive documents are located. At this stage, the tribunal directed the parties to "cease and desist from sending any further letter to the Tribunal" and then closed the proceedings for good.

12.28. In the award, which was issued a few months later, the tribunal relied, *inter alia*, on the evidence from the prosecutor's file to conclude that Fraport had violated the ADL. It also found that there was no evidence that the prosecutor had seen the critical shareholder agreements.

12.29. The Ad hoc Committee ruled that the tribunal's finding that Fraport had infringed the ADL was an essential part of its decision to decline jurisdiction. According to the Committee, the tribunal could have arrived at a different conclusion had it found that the prosecutor had access to the secret shareholder agreements. It also noted that the evidence from the prosecutor's file on which the tribunal relied had been produced after the hearing and had not been considered by the parties' experts on Philippine law.

12.30. The Committee found that a party's right to be heard – consisting of the opportunity to adduce evidence and argument on its claim and in rebuttal of those of its opponents – constituted a fundamental rule of procedure, as recalled in Article 35(c) of the Model Rules on Arbitral Procedure adopted by the International Law Commission in 1952, on which the drafters of the ICSID Convention relied. Accordingly, the tribunal must afford both parties the opportunity to make submissions if new evidence is received and considered by the tribunal to be relevant. A failure by the tribunal to do so cannot be excused by the fact that both parties were equally disadvantaged.

12.31. The Committee therefore concluded that the tribunal ought not to have considered the new evidence in its deliberations without granting both parties the opportunity to make submissions. According to the Committee, the tribunal should have reopened the proceedings under Rule 38(2) of the ICSID Arbitration Rules. Consequently, the Committee annulled the award on the ground that a serious departure from a fundamental rule of procedure had occurred. It added that a party may lose its right to seek annulment of an award on this ground if it did not raise an objection during the proceedings. However, the Committee concluded that in the case before it, Fraport had not waived its right to invoke the ground for annulment since there had been no decision by the tribunal to which Fraport could object. The tribunal had not communicated whether it needed further clarifications as to the prosecutorial record and had explicitly instructed the parties to refrain from further submissions. (It might however be argued that in such circumstances, the parties should have made a pre-emptive objection to preserve their right to rely on Article 52(1)(d)).

| | |

Summaries

FRA [*Procédure d'annulation CIRDI fondée sur un écart grave par rapport à une règle de procédure fondamentale (Article 52(1)(d) de la Convention CIRDI)*]

Cet article analyse la jurisprudence relative à la Clause 52(1)(d) de la Convention CIRDI, selon laquelle une sentence rendue par un tribunal CIRDI peut être annulée par une Commission ad hoc au motif d'une divergence majeure par rapport à une règle de procédure fondamentale. Pour pouvoir invoquer efficacement ce motif devant une Commission ad hoc, le demandeur doit démontrer que ladite divergence par rapport à une règle de procédure est à la fois grave et fondamentale. Il s'agit d'exigences cumulées. Les décisions d'annulation qui ont été étudiées dans cet article illustrent le fait que les Commissions ad hoc interprètent de façon stricte et minutieuse le motif d'annulation dans la mesure où celui-ci est lié au principe de traitement équitable. La grande liberté d'appréciation dont les tribunaux arbitraux bénéficient dans leur conduite des procédures probatoires constitue un obstacle majeur aux requêtes en annulation. Dans l'affaire Azurix, la Commission ad hoc a soutenu que « ce n'est que lorsque l'exercice de cette liberté d'appréciation, à tous les niveaux de l'affaire, se traduit par une divergence majeure par rapport à une autre règle fondamentale, qu'il existe des motifs capables de justifier l'annulation en vertu de la Clause 52(1)(d) ». Cette liberté d'appréciation, tout comme le professionnalisme et l'expertise des arbitres siégeant aux panels CIRDI, continueront à être les principaux obstacles aux demandes d'annulation fondées sur la Clause 52(1) (d).

CZE [*Řízení o zrušení rozhodčího nálezu před střediskem ICSID z důvodu významného odklonu od základního procesního pravidla (Článek 52 odst. 1 písm. (d) Úmluvy ICSID)*]
Toto pojednání analyzuje rozhodovací praxi související s článkem 52 odst. 1 písm. (d) Úmluvy o řešení sporů z investic mezi státy a občany druhých států (Úmluva ICSID), podle níž může být rozhodčí nález vydaný tribunálem ICSID zrušen výborem jmenovaným ad hoc z důvodů významného odklonu od základního procesního pravidla. Pokud se má navrhovatel úspěšně dovolat tohoto důvodu ke zrušení rozhodčího nálezu před výborem jmenovaným ad hoc, musí prokázat, že předmětný odklon od procesního pravidla je závažný a současně že předmětné procesní pravidlo je zásadní. Tyto požadavky musejí být splněny kumulativně. Rozhodnutí o zrušení rozhodčího nálezu, kterými se tento článek zabýval, prokazují, že ad hoc výbory vykládají tento důvod ke zrušení rozhodčího nálezu úzce a velice opatrně, neboť přímo souvisí s právem na spravedlivý proces. Důležitou překážkou jakékoli žádosti o zrušení rozhodčího nálezu je široká diskreční pravomoc, již mají rozhodčí tribunály k dispozici v rámci vedení důkazního řízení. Ad hoc výbor v případu Azurix rozhodl, že „pouze v případě, kdy uplatnění takovéto diskreční pravomoci s ohledem na všechny okolnosti případu dosahuje závažného odklonu od jiného základního procesního pravidla, budou dány důvody ke zrušení rozhodčího nálezu dle ustanovení článku 52 odst. 1 písm. (d).“ Tato diskreční pravomoc jakož i profesionalita a odbornost rozhodců, kteří jsou členy panelů ICSID, budou i nadále hlavními překážkami pro úspěch žádostí o zrušení rozhodčích nálezů dle článku 52 odst. 1 písm. (d).

| | |

POL [*Postępowanie o uchylenie orzeczenia ICSID w przypadku poważnego odstępstwa od podstawowej zasady proceduralnej (artykuł 52(1)(d) Konwencji ICSID)*]
Niniejsza praca zajmuje się analizą orzecznictwa ICSID w zakresie artykułu 52(1)(d) Konwencji ICSID. Na mocy wspomnianego postanowienia, orzeczenie ICSID może zostać uchylone przez komitet ad hoc, jeżeli nastąpi poważne odstępstwo od podstawowej zasady proceduralnej. Komitety ad hoc opowiadają się za stosunkowo wąską wykładnią niniejszego artykułu i, jak dotąd, żaden z nich nie uchylił orzeczenia ICSID na jego podstawie. Wynika z tego, że, aby powód mógł z powodzeniem odwołać się do tej podstawy przed komitetem ad hoc, musiało wcześniej nastąpić poważne uchybienie w stosunku do prawa do bycia wysłuchanym w procesie arbitrażowym.

DEU [*ICSID Annulment Proceedings based on serious departure from a fundamental rule of procedure (Article 52(1)(d) of the ICSID Convention)*]
Der vorliegende Artikel untersucht die Rechtsprechung von ICSID ad hoc Komitees im Rahmen von Artikel 52(1)(d) des ICSID Übereinkommens. Gemäss dieser Vorschrift kann ein ICSID Schiedsspruch wegen Abweichung von grundlegenden Prozessregeln aufgehoben werden. Bis zum heutigen Tag hat noch kein ICSID ad hoc Komitee einen Schiedsspruch aufgrund

einer Verletzung von Artikel 52(1)(d) aufgehoben. Es kann daraus gefolgert werden, dass nur eine schwerwiegende Verletzung des rechtlichen Gehörs eine Aufhebung nach sich ziehen kann.

RUS   [***Дела об аннулировании решений ICSID (Международного центра по урегулированию инвестиционных споров) с принятием во внимание серьезного отклонения от основополагающей процессуальной нормы (статья 52(1)(d) Конвенции ICSID)***]

В настоящей стати анализируется прецедентное право ICSID из статьи 52(1)(d) Конвенции ICSID. Согласно этому положению решение ICSID может быть аннулировано специально созданным Комитетом в случае серьезного отклонения от основополагающей процессуальной нормы. Комитеты, которые создаются специально для таких случаев, истолковывают эту статью достаточно узко, и на сегодняшний день ни один подобный Комитет не аннулировал решение ICSID на таком основании. А это значит, что для возможности сослаться заявителем на такое основание при обращении в специально созданный Комитет должен быть выявлен факт серьезного нарушения права быть выслушанным на арбитражном процессе.

Thomas Schultz
The Three Pursuits of Dispute Settlement*

Key words:
role of dispute
resolution |
arbitration | mediation |
negotiation | settlement
| rule of law | justice
| satisfaction of the
parties | Owen Fiss

Abstract | *What is dispute settlement? What should we expect or ask from a dispute resolution mechanism? To what extent and with what consequences can we buy dispute resolution, privatise it and remove it from society's purview? Should arbitration be seen as a mechanism that merely does away with disputes, or rather as an instrument of governance? These are some of the principal questions on which this essay seeks to provide some basic structuring reflections. To this effect, the essay envisions three functions that dispute settlement may pursue: the individualised and isolated maximisation of the parties' satisfaction; the sustainment of the rule of law and of predictability; and the enforcement of substantive societal values.*

Thomas Schultz
Swiss National
Science Foundation
Ambizione Fellow,
Graduate Institute
of International and
Development Studies;
Senior Lecturer
(*Maître d'enseignement
et de recherche*),
University of Geneva
Law Faculty; Executive
Director, Geneva
Master in International
Dispute Settlement;
Editorial Director,
Journal of International
Dispute Settlement.
Research supported
by the Swiss National
Science Foundation.
e-mail: thomas.schultz
@graduateinstitute.ch

| | |

*   An earlier version of this essay appeared in *The Roles of Dispute Settlement and ODR*, in ADR IN BUSINESS (A. Ingen-Housz ed., 2nd ed. 2010).

13.01. My aim with this short essay is to outline a triptych on the pursuits of dispute settlement. This triptych is out of necessity a sketch, and its objective is primarily to highlight areas where further work may be useful. But in drawing this sketch, I hope to tackle some structuring ideas for dispute settlement which would allow us to understand arbitration and its confines in a distinctive way.

13.02. This essay's discussion of the pursuits of dispute settlement will draw fairly heavily on Owen Fiss's cardinal exposition of the subject matter 25 years ago, although it will depart from his binomial elaboration at a number of significant junctures[1]. The first pursuit of dispute settlement sketched in this essay is to maximise the satisfaction of the parties to the instant case. It is, then, conducive to immediate peace. The second pursuit envisioned here is the furthering of the rule of law. In this incarnation, the function of a dispute settlement mechanism is to promote formal systemic justice, and hence to sustain some of the basic values of the liberal-democratic tradition. It is, hence, conducive to predictability in the longer term and to treating potential future parties at large as proper responsible moral choosers. The pursuit sketched in the third part of the triptych imagined here is the implementation of substantive societal values inscribed in legal rules. A dispute resolution mechanism would thus be expected to promote the values that society has collectively agreed to embody in authoritative legal texts, which is a pursuit that in the final analysis aims at bringing reality closer to democratically chosen ideals.

13.03. Surely, none of these three pursuits of dispute settlement correctly captures the whole truth of the variegated roles and purposes of any actual dispute settlement system. No actual system can presumably be accurately reduced to any one or even several of these paradigmatic representations. Nevertheless, the purpose of my triptych is simply to offer the simplest possible account of the roles of dispute resolution in a manner that is as bold and contentful as possible, while retaining a reasonable degree of truthlikeness.

13.04. The essay moves in two parts. Reviewing and elucidating Fiss's analysis is the aim of the first part. While Fiss's treatment of this matter is a permanently valuable contribution to the general theory of dispute resolution – one that is too often forgotten or mistakenly thought to be relevant only in the judicial-political context of the 1980s in the United States – his explication of the tension between resolving disputes and justice occasionally lacks analytic purchase. The second part of the essay then delineates further distinctions that lead to the threefold representation already adumbrated.

---

1   Owen Fiss, *Against Settlement*, 93 YALE L.J. 1073 (1984).

I. Fiss's Distinction

13.05. My story starts in 1984. That year, Owen Fiss published a remarkable article in the *Yale Law Journal*, entitled 'Against Settlement'[2]. In this article, which has acquired legendary status in contrarian circles, Fiss dared to go against the grain and raised a forceful voice in the midst of the wind of change that was starting to blow over the court system in the United States. With limited respect for political correctness (a likely valuable source of inspiration for every academic), he cracked open the idea, which was starting to turn into a dogma, that settlement heralds a fairy-tale world of peace and efficiency. For Fiss, the cure that settlement, in the context of mediation or negotiation, might bring to society litigious character would come only at the expense of some of our most sacred values. Brutally simplified, an over-development of settlement as a means of dispute settlement would be reminiscent of a family where the parents systematically negotiate for peace with their children, instead of facing the more draining tasks of parenthood, giving force to the values forming their educational ideals. So Fiss contends, 'ADR is the judicial counterpart to the deregulation movement'[3].

13.06. Fiss's paper 'Against Settlement' was initially presented, provocatively, at a meeting of the American Association of Law Schools intended to celebrate the formation of its new Alternative Dispute Resolution section. Fiss was concerned about the fact that a call was being issued to train students 'for the gentler arts of reconciliation and accommodation', a development advocated by Derek Bok, then President of Harvard University[4]. As David Luban later summarised it, Fiss's point was simply that 'settlements are no cause for celebration'[5] They are merely, as Fiss puts it, 'a capitulation to the conditions of mass society [which] should be neither encouraged nor praised'[6]. When the parties express a preference for settlement, that preference may very well be a 'function of the deplorable character of the options available to them'[7]. Put differently still and to toy with Churchill's famous words, settlements may in many situations of modern, complex society be the worst solution, except for the others that have been tried. Marc Galanter and Mia Cahill present the situation like this:

> *Demand for adjudication-backed remedies is increasing faster than the supply of facilities for full-blown adjudication. ... As society gets richer, the stakes in dispute become higher, and more organizations and individuals can make greater investments in litigation. Expenditures on one side produce costs on the other. ... As the law becomes more*

---

[2] *Ibid.*

[3] Owen Fiss, *Second-Hand Justice?*, Conn. L. Trib. 11 (17 March 1986).

[4] Derek Bok, *A Flawed System*, Harv. Mag. 38 (May-June 1983).

[5] David Luban, *Settlements and the Erosion of the Public Realm*, 83 Geo. L.J. 2619 (1995).

[6] Owen Fiss, *supra* note 1, at 1075.

[7] Owen Fiss, *The History of an Idea*, 78 Fordham L. Rev. 1273, 1277 (2009).

voluminous, more complex, and more uncertain, costs increase. Virtually every "improvement" in adjudication increases the need and opportunity for greater expenditures. Refinements of due process require more submissions, hearings, and findings; elaborations of the law require research, investigation, and evidence. ... There is more of a "settlement range" in which both parties are better off than if they had run through the full course of adjudication[8].

These words seem to echo in the field of international arbitration: mediation and settlement are increasingly considered as ways out of the procedural overheating and cost avalanches in arbitration[9].

13.07. Yet the moral quandary remains at the heart of the promotion of settlement as a method to deal with disputes: while often necessary, settlements represent a step away from law, if we accept the idea of legal philosophers as prominent as Lon Fuller and Matthew Kramer that law has a central guiding role, which it fulfils by setting cognitively reliable guideposts[10]. Embracing the development of settlements without reservations means being happy with the sentiment Fiss calls 'moving a case along' regardless of whether justice has been done or not, instead of confronting the vicissitudes associated with the task of applying the law correctly[11]. So we have come, at some stage, to celebrate the betrayal of the values of the rule of law – perhaps the world's least controversial political ideal – by the eschewal of adjudication, one of the most fundamental mechanisms giving force to the ideal of predictability for guidance. The cause of this, Fiss suggests in essence, lies in the conflation of two roles that dispute resolution may pursue and fulfil. And so he argues that 'In [the] story [told by the ADR movement], settlement appears to achieve exactly the same purpose as judgment'[12]. To mark this division will then be our next task.

13.08. (Fiss, it should be pointed out, uses the concept of 'dispute resolution' in a different way than the generic, overarching meaning that it usually receives, at least in the international context. The latter, more common, meaning of dispute resolution covers the whole variety of procedures leading to the solution of a case, be they judicial or extra-judicial. This is the meaning used for the current chapter. For Fiss, 'dispute resolution' is a synonym to 'Alternative Dispute Resolution' in the sense used primarily in the United States, that is, out of court dispute settlement by arbitration,

---

8   Marc Galanter & Mia Cahill, *'Most Cases Settle': Judicial Promotion and Regulation of Settlements*, 46 STAN. L. Rev. 1339, 1387 (1994).

9   Gabrielle Kaufmann-Kohler, *When Arbitrators Facilitate Settlement*, 25 (2) ARBITRATION INTERNATIONAL 187 (2009).

10   LON L. FULLER, THE MORALITY OF LAW, New Haven: Yale University Press 229 (1969); MATTHEW H. KRAMER, OBJECTIVITY AND THE RULE OF LAW, Cambridge: Cambridge University Press 118 (2007). See also Thomas Schultz, *Some Critical Comments on the Juridicity of the Lex Mercatoria*, 10 Y.B. PR. INT'L L. 667 (2008).

11   Owen Fiss, *supra* note 1, at 1073, 1086.

12   Owen Fiss, *supra* note 3, at 10; Owen Fiss, *supra* note 1, at 1073, 1085.

mediation or negotiation. He opposes it to adjudication, that is, court litigation.)

I.1. Resolving Disputes

13.09. For Fiss, the first role of dispute resolution, in its incarnation as settlement, is merely that: resolving disputes *stricto sensu*. 'What matters' from this perspective, Fiss writes in 1986, 'is not so much the terms of the resolution, but only that the dispute is resolved'[13]. Neutrals in a dispute resolution process espousing this view are 'brokers of deals'[14], their job is to 'maximize the ends of private parties' and to 'secure the peace'[15]. Put more crudely, and with somewhat less enthusiasm, the role of dispute resolution in this incarnation is more simply to move cases along[16]. In an article written on the occasion of a symposium at Fordham Law School marking the 25th anniversary of 'Against Settlement', Fiss insists that the peace achieved by settlements, which he had tentatively admitted 25 years earlier, was in reality 'often a very fragile and temporary peace'[17]. In other words, Fiss considers that settlement, as a method of dispute resolution, ideologically based as it is on 'the supposition of a natural harmony'[18], does not promote wide-scale social peace, but a very specific and individualistic peace: the parties should merely stop 'quarrelling'[19]. The reason why this sort of case-related peace is not conducive to a more general state of social tranquillity is linked to some of law's most basic purposes: the enforcement of our collectively chosen ideals and, more fundamentally, justice[20].

13.10. Fiss further challenges what is probably the most important argument in favour of the desirability of settlement: the fact that it is directly a product of party consent. After all, if a settlement is by definition only possible if the parties agree with the terms of the settlement, and not merely with the terms of the procedure as it would be the case in arbitration for instance, what is there to object to? Leaving aside the empirical question of the conditions under which consent is really given (the problems known as freedom of consent and access to information), two of Fiss's arguments are worth mentioning here.

13.11. First, settlement is not justice. There is simply no reason to conclude, Fiss argues, that the parties believe their settlement to be 'an instantiation of justice or will, as a general matter, lead to justice'[21]. If a bargained-for

---

[13] Owen Fiss, *supra* note 3, at 10.
[14] Owen Fiss, *supra* note 7, at 1280.
[15] Owen Fiss, *supra* note 1, at 1085.
[16] *Ibid.*, 1086.
[17] Owen Fiss, *supra* note 7, at 1277.
[18] *Ibid.*, 1275.
[19] *Ibid.*
[20] H. Lee Sarokin, *Justice Rushed is Justice Ruined*, 38 RUTGERS L. REV. 431 (1986).
[21] Owen Fiss, *supra* note 7, at 1277.

Thomas Schultz

settlement happens to correspond to a rationally established instantiation of justice, then this overlap is merely a matter of luck. Hence, Fiss considers that recourse to settlement is often a 'function of the deplorable character of the options available to them':[22] building on the postulate that the parties to a dispute rarely have a reason not to want justice, a settlement is made *faute de mieux*. The parties simply 'make the best of an imperfect world and the unfortunate situation in which they find themselves'[23]. Settlement is often merely a 'capitulation'[24] before the practical problems faced by the adjudicative system that would, ideally, have instantiated justice.

13.12. Taking the argument further, if parties settle *en masse* in certain domains, or if the settlement rate in given contexts rises significantly, we should perhaps be less than euphoric. It may not be a signal for merriment, but merely a sign that the adjudicative system of *justice* is broken. If there is an increase of settlements within arbitrations, if parties increasingly expect arbitrators to display settlement skills, then we should perhaps not rejoice too quickly, and not marvel at the fact that arbitration becomes more sophisticated, multifaceted and closer to the needs of business. Instead, we should realise that the parties move away from a relatively slow and expensive system of *justice* to a quicker and cheaper system that simply does away with disputes. In the words of William Park, witty as usual, 'An agreement to end hostilities may cost less than arbitration, just as a train trip from London to Paris is cheaper and quicker than a flight from London to Hong Kong'[25]. The parties' consent to settlement may well be the sort of consent one finds in a surrender: if the result is to be praised, it is only because it is economically the best alternative to justice[26].

13.13. Fiss's second argument against the panacea effects of consent builds on these considerations about justice: 'when the parties settle, society gets less than what appears, and for a price it does not know it is paying'[27]. He maintains that, even if the avoidance of adjudication were the parties' true ideal and their desire of settlement not a matter of contingency, then the following problem would still remain: 'Justice is a public good, objectively conceived, and not reducible to the maximization of the satisfaction of the preferences of the contestants'[28].

13.14. To a certain extent, it is hard not to concur in this opinion. Indeed, the parties' quest for efficiency through settlement, in other words their efforts towards their own wealth maximisation, is realised not only at the expense of other forms of their own well-being (such as justice or

---

[22] *Ibid.*

[23] *Ibid.*

[24] Owen Fiss, *supra* note 1, at 1075.

[25] William W. Park, *Arbitrators and Accuracy*, 1 J. Int'l Disp. Settl. 25, 34 (2010).

[26] On the different values pursued in dispute resolution, see for instance Russell Korobkin & Chris Guthrie, *Psychology, Economics, and Settlement*, 76 Texas L.R. 77 (1997).

[27] Owen Fiss, *supra* note 1, at 1085.

[28] Owen Fiss, *supra* note 7, at 1277.

Czech (& Central European) Yearbook of Arbitration

232

fairness)[29]. It also creates negative externalities for society if it becomes overwhelmingly important in a given context. Adjudication is not only necessary for justice to be done in a specific case, but also for justice to be seen to be done – it provides an opportunity for general rules to be applied to specific and individual situations, thus reaffirming and reinforcing law's 'dependable guideposts for self-directed action'[30]. If a dispute settles, it escapes from much of the normative framework and machinery to rule society and to make life in community possible – that is, law. Where settlement starts, law survives only as a shadowy figure lurking in the background, as Bob Mnookin and Lewis Kornhauser put it so eloquently[31]. One should, of course, readily acknowledge that a shadow is better than utter absence. Unconditional supporters of the ADR movement often call for rejoicing and merriment because of law's survival as a shadow in settlement. But I know of no reason why we should not remain hungry for law's full promises. Provided it codes power in a benevolent, not wicked regime[32], law is a common good of moral value[33] as it allows to 'predict and plan'[34], which in turn elevates law's addressees to the dignity of 'responsible moral choosers', to use Matthew Kramer's words[35]. If it is applied competently and impartially, law 'promotes the morally worthy end of upholding the citizens' reasonable beliefs concerning the

[29] See LOUIS KAPLOW & STEVEN SHAVELL, FAIRNESS VERSUS WELFARE, Massachusetts: Harvard University Press (2002).

[30] LON L. FULLER, *supra* note 10, at 229.

[31] Robert Mnookin & Lewis Kornhauser, *Bargaining in the Shadow of the Law*, 88 YALE L.J. 950 (1979).

[32] Indeed, as Matthew H. Kramer has shown, '[law] is indispensably serviceable for the pursuit of benevolent ends on a large scale over a sustained period, but it is also indispensably serviceable for the pursuit of wicked ends on such a scale over such a period': MATTHEW H. KRAMER, OBJECTIVITY AND THE RULE OF LAW, Cambridge: Cambridge University Press 143 (2007). See further MATTHEW H. KRAMER, IN DEFENSE OF LEGAL POSITIVISM, Oxford: Oxford University Press (1999); MATTHEW H. KRAMER, WHERE LAW AND MORALITY MEET, Oxford: Oxford University Press 143-222 (2004); Matthew H. Kramer, *The Big Bad Wolf: Legal Positivism and Its Detractors*, 49 (1) AMERICAN JOURNAL OF JURISPRUDENCE (2004). On law coding power, see MICHEL FOUCAULT, THE WILL TO KNOWLEDGE, London: Penguin Books Ltd. 82, 87, 89 (1978).

[33] EDWARD P. THOMPSON, WHIGS AND HUNTERS, New York: Pantheon Books 265-266 (1975): law is an 'unqualified human good'; NEIL MCCORMICK, RHETORIC AND THE RULE OF LAW, Oxford: Oxford University Press 12 (2005): law is 'a signal virtue of civilized societies'.

[34] BRIAN Z. TAMANAHA, ON THE RULE OF LAW, Cambridge: Cambridge University Press 96 (2004): law 'enhances [its addressees'] dignity ... by allowing them to predict and plan, no doubt a moral positive'.

[35] MATTHEW H. KRAMER, OBJECTIVITY AND THE RULE OF LAW, Cambridge: Cambridge University Press 175 (2007). See similarly Jan Paulsson, *The Power of States to Make Meaningful Promises to Foreigners*, 1 J. INT'L DISP. SETTL. (2010) forthcoming, where he argues, in substance, that adjudication in which a state is dealt with as a normal contractor elevates states to the 'adulthood' of 'making meaningful promises'.

legal consequences of their actions'[36]. Settlement allows us to go back to business, but these lofty ideals are lost.

13.15. Simplified with the utmost terseness, law has public value. Adjudicative dispute resolution mechanisms, as one of the cogwheels of law application, thus also have public value. Settlements, by allowing instant cases to be removed from the ambit of law application, undermine the operations of the rule of law; they decrease the public value of law as an instrument of predictability. For Fiss more specifically, settlements prevent the operations of law application as enforcement of the societal values according to which we agreed to live, which are instantiated as legal rules. This leads to Fiss's second view of the role of dispute resolution.

I.2. Justice

13.16. The second role of dispute resolution according to Fiss, in its incarnation as adjudication, is 'Justice rather than peace'[37]. He puts it thus: the job of legal decision-makers in the adjudicative process 'is not to maximize the ends of private parties, nor simply to secure the peace, but to explicate and give force to the values embodied in authoritative texts such as the Constitution and statutes: to interpret those values and to bring reality into accord with them. This duty is not discharged when the parties settle'[38]. Put differently, the decision-maker in this role is an actor of the state's performance of the social contract: we give up sovereignty to a government, we accept legal limitations on our conduct in return for the assurance that we will be governed according to a defined and agreed set of rules. These rules, Fiss would say, instantiate certain defined and agreed societal values by which we have decided to live. Of course, not all rules carry societal values; many legal rules merely have a coordinating purpose (such as the rule defining when precisely the risk passes from the seller to the buyer). But even in these cases, we should remember that if we are not, as a matter of principle, held accountable for our actions according to initially agreed rules, then we become powerless to make 'meaningful promises', as Jan Paulsson puts it[39]. As he reminds us, in his Holmesian habit to point to simple things that we tend to overlook, if we are not as a matter of principle 'held to a bad bargain', we would 'be stuck in the poverty of a primitive economic system where every transaction is instant – cash and carry'[40].

13.17. Now, what should we think of a dispute resolution mechanism whose only possible successful outcome is that a new promise replaces the failed promise? Perhaps that we should not, for the sake of the socially valuable

---

[36] MATTHEW H. KRAMER, OBJECTIVITY AND THE RULE OF LAW, Cambridge: Cambridge University Press 175 (2007).

[37] Owen Fiss, *supra* note 1, at 1075.

[38] *Ibid.*, 1085.

[39] Jan Paulsson, *supra* note 35.

[40] *Ibid.*

system that makes promises meaningful, be too easily permitted to talk ourselves out of a failed promise by dint of a settlement. Perhaps that if the only recourse we have in a given context is negotiation or mediation, then in this context we simply face, as Jeremy Bentham put it, a 'denial of justice'[41]. Or one can go further: it is the social contract that would founder in such a situation. This is what led to Simon Roberts's understated note that 'consensual agreement has seldom been accorded what one might call "ideological parity" with judgement by legal theorists'[42] and to his somewhat more forceful mention of the 'deep distrust of negotiation and compromise on the part of some who now comment upon them'[43].

13.18. And so Fiss argues that one of the two great roles of dispute resolution, the one played by legal decision-makers in an adjudicative dispute resolution mechanism, is to act as a 'coordinate branch of government'[44]. Dispute resolution is to 'give concrete meaning and expression to the public values embodied in the law and to protect those values'[45], to 'apply and protect the norms of the community'[46], to 'perform a distinctive function within the system of government that is endorsed by the people'[47]. In sum, it is called upon to 'enforce a public morality'[48].

II. Further Distinctions: A Triptych

13.19. When Fiss is understood in the way expounded in the preceding pages, we can perceive the relevance of drawing two analytical dividing lines: the first marks the division between dispute resolution as an instrument to deal with each case in isolation, and dispute resolution as an instrument for induction ('the inferring of future regularities from past regularities'[49]). Within the second category, a distinction may be made between the promotion by induction of procedural justice and of substantive justice. On this basis, I wish to sketch the three main pursuits of dispute settlement as follows:

   (a) The promotion of the satisfaction of the parties to the instant case.
   (b) The promotion of the rule of law.
   (c) The promotion of substantive societal values.

---

[41]   Jeremy Bentham, *Scotch Reform*, in 5 THE WORKS OF JEREMY BENTHAM (SCOTCH REFORM, REAL PROPERTY, CODIFICATION PETITIONS), Edinburgh: William Tait 1, 35 (J. Bowring ed., 1843).
[42]   Simon Roberts, *After Government? On Representing Law Without the State*, 68 (1) MODERN L. REV. 23 (2005).
[43]   *Ibid.*
[44]   Owen Fiss, *supra* note 7, at 1275.
[45]   Owen Fiss, *supra* note 3, at 11.
[46]   *Ibid.*
[47]   Owen Fiss, *supra* note 7, at 1275.
[48]   Owen Fiss, *supra* note 3, at 11.
[49]   MATTHEW H. KRAMER, *supra* note 36, at 23.

II.1. Seeking the Satisfaction of the Parties

13.20. In order to think more fruitfully about dispute resolution as an instrument for party satisfaction, a further division may be advisable: the distinction, present in public international dispute settlement but often ignored in other circles, between a conflict and a dispute. (It is of course not the semantics and terminology that matter here but the distinction itself.) A conflict is a 'general state of hostility between the parties', whereas a dispute is 'a specific disagreement relating to a question of rights or interests in which the parties proceed by way of claims, counter-claims, denials and so on'[50]. At the interstate level, one of the primary aims (historically at least) of dispute settlement mechanisms is precisely to identify and isolate the legal disputes that underlie conflicts – especially armed, or potentially armed, conflicts – and then submitting them to pacific resolution. This transpires for instance in Chapter VI of the UN Charter on the 'Pacific Settlement of Disputes'. If this distinction is perhaps most obvious at the interstate level, because of the extent of the tragedy often involved, it is obviously also applicable to relationships between private individuals, between companies, between a company and a state, and all other variants of business and non-business relationships.

13.21. Accordingly, one may discriminate between dispute resolution mechanisms that, within the context of seeking the satisfaction of the parties to the case, aim at achieving, on the one hand, peace as absence-of-conflict and, on the other hand, peace as absence-of-dispute.

13.22. The existence and inexistence of disputes and conflicts entertain intertwined causal relations. First, disputes can be both the cause and the consequence of conflicts. This much should be obvious. Second, the resolution of a dispute can lead – should hopefully lead – to the disappearance or lessening of the conflict, but it can also have the opposite effect: there are unfortunately many examples in public international dispute settlement where the resolution, by means of adjudication but also mediation and negotiation, of a boundary dispute between two states has led to an increase of the hostilities on the ground. On another level, a divorce by settlement may remove a dispute, or several disputes, but the state of hostility may easily remain or even grow. Or a settlement between two companies, where one company for instance infringed the intellectual property rights of the other, may put an end to that specific dispute, but at the same time fuel the conflict between the companies if one of the parties is left with the impression that it had to throw in the towel, for instance. A bad settlement resolves a dispute, but may have the reverse effect on the conflict. Third, a conflict may in certain situations be resolved while the dispute survives but is simply ignored. The dispute may (the parties still disagree over a specific legal question, but no longer care),

---

[50] JOHN COLLIER & VAUGHAN LOWE, THE SETTLEMENT OF DISPUTES IN INTERNATIONAL LAW, Oxford: Oxford University Press 1 (2000).

whereas the conflict is resolved (the parties are no longer hostile). The differentiation of peace as an absence-of-dispute and peace as an absence-of-conflict leads to a distinction between dispute resolution (*stricto sensu*) and conflict resolution. Both ways of promoting these sorts of peace between the parties, however, seek nothing more than the satisfaction of the parties to the instant case, and may well remain oblivious to the reflected consequences of the resolution of the dispute or the conflict on other addressees of the same normative system.

13.23. A further ramification of party satisfaction as the objective of dispute resolution may be explored: satisfaction cannot be a function of the resolution of the dispute, but of the procedure itself. Indeed, while the resolution of a dispute in and of itself is an objective attainable by dint of a role of the dice or the consultation of an oracle, the search for truth and the provision of a fair hearing are a different matter altogether[51]. To a certain extent, the latter in fact stand in the way of the former: when only the resolution of the dispute matters, then the sole values that should rationally govern the resolution process are finality and efficiency.

13.24. 'Justice delayed is justice denied', says the adage, with all the imperfections and distortions that are normally attached to adages[52]. But in a number of situations (which may of course be extreme situations, but are therefore also particularly useful for purposes of analytical clarity), it may be more important for the parties to participate in a process seeking to establish the truth, to be given a real possibility to express their points of view and to be listened to, than to actually resolve their dispute. To echo a preceding paragraph, one may think of family matters where both parents no longer care to resolve a conflict between them and the many disputes it has spawned, but want to be given a formal and unimpeded possibility to say why they believe they were good parents. Or we may think more gravely of Hannah Arendt when she said (in a perhaps uncharacteristically bold statement), while witnessing the Eichmann trial, that 'everyone, everyone should have his day in court': it may have been more important to let the story of the Holocaust be told than to determine Eichmann's precise liabilities[53]. Such situations may be a partial response to Hamlet's question during his famous soliloquy 'who would bear the whips and scorns of time, ... the law's delay, the insolence of office, ... when he himself might his quietus make with a bare bodkin?'

13.25. William Park, a Shakespeare in his own right in the field of arbitration, describes thus the need for a 'day in court' in the context of arbitration,

---

[51] See generally William W. Park, *Arbitrators and Accuracy*, 1 J. INT'L DISP. SETTL. 25 (2010).

[52] This adage is in fact a rhetorical figure that was used most prominently by British Prime Minister William Gladstone in 1868 in a political speech about the Irish question – a quite different context than the one in which it usually is called upon.

[53] HANNAH ARENDT, EICHMANN IN JERUSALEM, New York: Penguin Books USA Inc. 229 (1994, orig. 1963).

where the tension between finality and economy, on the one side, and truth and fairness, on the other, is a recurring theme:

> *An arbitrator who makes the effort to listen before deciding will enhance both the prospect of accuracy and satisfaction of the litigants' taste for fairness. ... If arbitration loses its moorings as a truth-seeking process, nostalgia for a cheerful golden age of quick results will yield to calls for reinvention of an adjudicatory process aimed at actually getting the facts and the law. ... Much of the criticism of arbitration's cost and delay thus tells only half the story, often with subtexts portending a cure worse than the disease[54]. If simple peace-making were to become the norm, arbitration as a truth-seeking process would need to be reinvented[55].*

13.26. Party satisfaction derived from the procedure itself, as opposed to the resolution it seeks to lead to, may be manifold. A sense that 'justice is being done' is perhaps the most lofty form of satisfaction, but other components often come into the mix. Business parties may for instance oppose a quick and easy settlement, which would have fulfilled their putative aspirations to resolve the dispute, and proceed with a lengthy and costly arbitration because it allows them one of the following: not to show weakness; or to shift the responsibility for the case from business executives to their legal counsel; or to designate the arbitrators as scapegoats for a defeat on the basis of their alleged incompetence and the erroneous arbitral award that ensued; or to fulfil the requirements of an insurance policy that in effect excludes damages incurred by way of settlement; or to satisfy stakeholder demands. If we break up the concept of a party into the actual user of a dispute resolution mechanism (such as a company) and its legal counsel, the interests of the legal profession in a long and costly procedure also becomes apparent. In many of these cases, to varying degrees, the dispute resolution procedure may start following an immanent logic of development and become alienated from its origin as well as from its purpose: peace as absence-of-dispute.

II.2. Sustaining the Rule of Law

13.27. The promotion of the rule of law, I contend, is the second possible pursuit of a dispute settlement system. Even more fundamentally and in terms of political philosophy, a dispute resolution system in this guise aims at the implementation or sustainment or furtherance of some of the core moral-political values of the liberal-democratic philosophical tradition. As Matthew Kramer summarises:

> *[T]he liberal-democratic tradition comprehends thinkers such as John Locke, John Stuart Mill, Immanuel Kant, Friedrich Hayek, John Rawls, and Robert Nozick ... Central to the liberal-democratic tradition*

---

54 William W. Park, *supra* note 51, at 27.
55 *Ibid.*, 53.

has been an emphasis on the liberty and autonomy and dignity of the individual, on the fundamental legal and political equality of persons, on equality of opportunity, ... on the importance of reasoned deliberation and justification in the domain of public power[56].

13.28. These values are crucial for any morally estimable form of governance for variegated reasons, but one only is of particular interest to us here: as has already been briefly mentioned, these values make the addressees of the relevant form of governance responsible moral choosers by allowing them to rationally predict the consequences of their actions. Distortedly simplified, the promotion of these values is intimately tied to the promotion of predictability.

13.29. Matthew Kramer further explains that 'These values come to fruition in the Rule of Law. They are the values whose formal dimensions are enshrined in Fuller's principles'[57]. Simply put, a dispute resolution system that conforms to Fuller's principles sustains the rule of law, which in turn furthers predictability, which brings to fruition the moral-political values of the liberal-democratic tradition. Admittedly, this may benefit from some explanatory comment.

13.30. At the most basic level, we should note that one of the principal differences between (a) dispute resolution seeking the promotion of the rule of law and (b) dispute resolution merely seeking the satisfaction of the parties to a specific case is, as we see, that the former's function is tied to the moral estimableness of the resolution of any given case for all potential parties – the effects of the resolution of one case on other, actual and potential, cases. Such moral estimableness is considered here specifically as the provision of predictability, through induction of general rules, or their precise meanings, from a collection of individually resolved cases: to echo the words used above, the regularities of future case resolutions should be inferable from the regularities of past case resolutions.

13.31. Jan Paulsson captures and illustrates the idea in a plainer way. He explains that in the field of international investments, arbitration is not simply the plaything of the parties – a label typically attached to arbitration – and it should not merely aim at maximising the ends of the parties to each dispute taken individually. As he puts it, 'in the field of international investments, arbitral tribunals are instruments of the rule of law. Their purpose is ... to enable states to make reliable promises. ... International tribunals tend to irritate respondent states [and claimant investors] in individual cases; yet their decisions should be respected in order to achieve the long-term benefits of the rule of law'[58]. What matters here is not the satisfaction of the parties in any individual case, but the overall promotion of the rule of law. Indeed, in the long run the rule of law is infinitely more important for international investments as it removes the

---

56 MATTHEW H. KRAMER, *supra* note 36, at 144.
57 *Ibid.*
58 Jan Paulsson, *supra* note 35.

'cash and carry'[59], 'quick buck'[60] nature of economic transactions in an unreliable environment, that is an insufficiently predictably environment: a 'spectacular rate of return – after which both the investment and the profits vanish'[61].

13.32. So what is the rule of law? In two words: dependable guideposts. In more words, looking to Lon Fuller, clarified by Matthew Kramer, the rule of law (in its meaning as 'formal legality' favoured here[62]) has eight constitutive elements. These, using Matthew Kramer's terminology[63], are (1) governance by general norms, that is the generality of expression and application of the rules that are part of the system; (2) public ascertainability, or the public promulgation of the rules of the system; (3) prospectivity, meaning non-retroactivity of the rules of the systems; (4) perspicuity, that is the formulation of the mandates provided by the legal system in lucid language; (5) non-contradictoriness and non-conflictingness, in other words the normative coherence of legal system; (6) compliability, that is the near absence of unsatisfiable behests; (7) steadiness over time, which calls for 'limits in the pace and scale of the transformations of the sundry norms in a legal system';[64] (8) congruence between formulation and implementation, in other words that the publicly promulgated rules are actually applied and are applied impartially. All these requirements seek to jointly fulfil law's essential function, which is to 'subject [...] people's conduct to the guidance of general rules by which they may themselves orient their behaviour'[65].

13.33. This chapter is scarcely the place for an exhaustive analytical discussion of the different requirements that the rule of law, in its acception favoured here, sets for a dispute resolution system[66]. But one requirement of four of these principles may be outlined here: governance by general norms, public ascertainability, prospectivity and steadiness over time all are principles that are not straightforwardly fulfilled by a dispute resolution method interested only in the parties to the dispute in question. If dispute resolution outcomes are to collectively satisfy these principles, one element in the procedural setup of the system becomes crucial: the precedential force of prior outcomes.

13.34. As an example, the question of whether prior awards in the field of investment arbitration should be given precedential weight has been the

---

59   *Ibid.*
60   *Ibid.*
61   *Ibid.*
62   For other meanings of the rule of law, see BRIAN Z. TAMANAHA, *supra* note 34.
63   MATTHEW H. KRAMER, *supra* note 36, at 103-186.
64   *Ibid.,* 132.
65   LON L. FULLER, *A Reply to Professors Cohen and Dworkin*, 10 VILLANOVA L.R. 655, 657 (1965).
66   For such a survey, see Thomas Schultz, *Arbitration and the Rule of Law*, forthcoming.

subject of heated discussion during the last five years[67]. When investment arbitration is understood in the way favoured here, it seems difficult to eschew the conclusion that a rule of precedent should be practised in the field of investment arbitration. Put boldly, those who oppose the precedential value of arbitral awards in this field further the rule of law's opposite: the rule of men[68].

13.35. Beyond the requirement of the precedential force of prior outcomes, it may simply be adumbrated here, with analytical discussion following elsewhere[69], that other requirements of the eight principles of the rule of law are for instance the following, applicable *mutatis mutandis* to different forms of dispute resolution: public ascertainability requires a wide publication of the outcomes; perspicuity demands detailed reasoned outcomes; non-contradictoriness and non-conflictingness call for *res judicata*, *lis pendens*, derived jurisdiction and, to a certain extent, an appeals mechanism; congruence between formulation and implementation require that adjudication remains overwhelming for any given set of legal situations and thus puts limits to the realm of settlement.

II.3. Promoting Substantive Societal Values

13.36. The promotion of substantive societal values as a third possible role for a dispute resolution system barely requires here any further explanatory comment, as we can embrace Fiss's conception of this role, which I have expounded above[70], with little reservation. It may simply be pointed out that his use of the concept of justice, as a simple opposition to ad hoc peace, may have been given greater analytical purchase if divided into procedural justice, which for instance takes the form of predictability as we have seen in the preceding section, and substantive justice, which is in question here.

13.37. It may also be important to note that justice is here neither *Gerechtigkeit als Rechtsmässigkeit* nor *suum cuique tribuere*, which are two of the great classical conceptions of justice, but a combination of the two.

13.38. The former is based on the tenet that justice (*Gerechtigkeit*) can only be found in conformity to law (*Rechtsmässigkeit*); it conceives of justice *qua* justice according to law, where law stands for the utterances of the sovereign – the law of the state[71]. It is the dominant form of justice for lawyers, who are occupied primarily with the achievement of practical

---

[67] See for instance Gabrielle Kaufmann-Kohler, *Arbitral Precedent·Dream, Necessity or Excuse?*, 23 (3) ARBITRATION INTERNATIONAL 357 (2007).

[68] BRIAN Z. TAMANAHA, *supra* note 34, at 126. On arbitral awards' precedential value, Thomas Schultz, *Some Critical Comments on the Juridicity of the Lex Mercatoria*, 10 Y.B. PR. INT'L L. 667 (2008).

[69] Thomas Schultz, *Arbitration and the Rule of Law*, forthcoming.

[70] See section 'Justice' above.

[71] John Bell, *Justice and the Law, in* JUSTICE: AN INTERDISCIPLINARY PERSPECTIVE, Cambridge: Cambridge University Press 114, 117 (K. R. Scherer ed., 1992).

justice, by focusing on the way in which legal decisions are rendered[72]. Lawyers typically may safely remain agnostic to the values according to which legal rules are created: in the somewhat elliptical words of Pound, 'lawyers are not required to conduct a sit-down strike until philosophers agree' in order to achieve practical justice[73].

13.39. The latter, *suum cuique tribuere*, the most widely shared understanding of justice throughout history, is a 'concern for how resources are allocated'[74], 'how the law ought to allocate entitlements in the first place'[75]. It raises the problem that Kelsen put thus: 'The problem of values is in the first place the problem of conflicts of values, and this problem cannot be solved by means of rational cognition. The answer to these questions is a judgment of value, determined by emotional factors, and, therefore, subjective in character – valid only for the judging subject, and therefore relative only'[76].

13.40. Hence, dispute resolution as a promoter of substantive societal values is meant here essentially as a means to implement the fundamental agreed allocation of entitlements underlying in the legal system of a given society at a given time, which may not yet have translated into positive legal rules.

13.41. This role of dispute resolution puts a limitation on the common idea that as the parties pay for an arbitration, or another dispute resolution mechanism, it is their plaything alone. This limitation is instantiated most obviously through the mechanics of the concept of (substantive) public policy, for instance in arbitration. The question then is whether dispute resolvers should look beyond the narrow requirements of this concept and should take into consideration the social effects of, for example, the outcome of a sports arbitration in a doping case, or the reduction of the differences between social classes by an increased protection of imprudent consumers. Indeed, not all legal questions posed by business disputes relate to rules of coordination. In other words, the role of international dispute resolution as a promoter of substantive societal values in business is a question relating to the ethics of transnational business law. This, however, will be the story for another day.

| | |

---

[72] See generally Niklas Luhmann, *Gerechtigkeit in den Rechtssystemen der modernen Gesellschaft*, 4 RECHTSTHEORIE 131 (1973).

[73] ROSCOE POUND, JUSTICE ACCORDING TO THE LAW, New Haven: Yale University Press 129 (1951).

[74] John Bell, *supra* note 71, at 115.

[75] *Ibid.*

[76] Hans Kelsen, *What is Justice?*, *in* WHAT IS JUSTICE?, London: University of California 4 (H. Kelsen ed., 1957).

Summaries

FRA [*Les trois fonctions du reglement des differends*]
Qu'est-ce que le règlement des différends ? Que pouvons-nous attendre ou exiger d'un système de règlement des différends ? Dans quelle mesure et à quels risques peut-on acquérir la résolution d'un litige, la privatiser et la soustraire à l'intérêt de la société ? L'arbitrage doit-il être compris comme un mécanisme qui met simplement fin à un litige ou plutôt comme un instrument de gouvernance ? Cet article propose une réflexion structurante dont on espère qu'elle pourra contribuer à l'examen de ces questions fondamentales. A cette fin, il brosse les grands traits d'un tableau en trois parties représentant les fonctions qui peuvent être attribuées à un mécanisme de règlement des différends · la optimisation de la satisfaction des parties, la promotion de la 'rule of law' (l'état de droit, avec une minuscule) et de la prévisibilité et, enfin, la mise en œuvre de valeurs sociétales substantielles.

CZE [*Tři snahy o urovnávání sporů*]
Co je urovnávání sporů? Co bychom měli očekávat nebo požadovat od mechanismu urovnávání sporů? V jakém rozsahu a s jakými důsledky můžeme urovnání sporu odkoupit, privatizovat a odstranit ho ze zorného pole společnosti? Mělo by být rozhodčí řízení považováno za mechanismus určený pouze pro řešení sporů, nebo spíše jako nástroj pro rozhodování? To jsou některé z hlavních otázek, ke kterým se tento materiál snaží poskytnout některé základní strukturní úvahy. V této souvislosti materiál předkládá tři základní funkce, které může urovnávání sporů mít: individuální a izolovanou maximalizaci spokojenosti stran; podporu platnosti právních norem a predikovatelnosti; a prosazování hlavních společenských hodnot.

| | |

POL [*Potrójna funkcja rozstrzygania sporów*]
Niniejszy esej wskazuje trzy funkcje, które można przypisać każdemu mechanizmowi rozstrzygania sporów: zindywidualizowaną i odizolowaną maksymalizację satysfakcji stron; utrzymanie rządów prawa i przewidywalności; oraz egzekwowanie podstawowych wartości społecznych. Specyficzna, dominująca funkcja, którą posiada każdy dowolny mechanizm, implicite czy explicite, pociąga za sobą szereg ważnych konsekwencji: na przykład określa idealną rolę, ku której powinien skłaniać się podmiot rozstrzygający w sporze, formę sprawiedliwości i porozumienia, które można osiągnąć, oraz wpisuje systemy rozstrzygania sporów i strony sporu w ramy społeczne.

DEU [*Drei Ziele der Streitbeilegung*]
Der Artikel schlägt drei Funktionen vor, die jeder Streitbeilegungsmechanismus erzielen sollte: Individualisierte und isolierte Maximierung der Befriedigung von Parteien, Beitrag zur Rechtssicherheit und Vorhersehbarkeit sowie Durchsetzung grundlegender gesamtgesellschaftlicher Werte. Dabei zeitigt die vom jeweiligen Mechanismus implizit oder explizit verfolgte spezifische bzw. dominante Funktion eine Reihe bedeutsamer Folgen: So wird z. B. die ideale

Rolle vorgegeben, nach der sich das Verhalten der Schlichter richten sollte, die Form von Gerechtigkeit und Rechtsfrieden, die erzielt werden kann, und die Verortung beider Systeme zur Streitbeilegung sowie der Streitparteien innerhalb der Gesellschaft.

RUS [***Три дела по урегулированию споров***]

В данном очерке рассматриваются три действия, которые могут быть предприняты в механизме разрешения любых споров: максимальное удовлетворение каждой из сторон в отдельности и в частном порядке; соблюдение нормы права и предсказуемости; а также требование соблюдения главных общественных ценностей. Конкретный и преобладающий подход в любом отдельном взятом механизме, будь он неявно или явно выраженным, становится причиной важных последствий: к примеру, на его основе определяется идеальная роль, которой должен придерживаться тот, кто разрешает спор, рамки «корректности» и мирного урегулирования, а также место, отведенное в обществе системам разрешения споров и участникам спора.

ES [***Las tres pretensiones del acuerdo de disputa***]

Este ensayo sugiere tres funciones en las que cualquier mecanismo de resolución de disputas debe centrarse: la maximización aislada e individualizada de la satisfacción de las partes, el mantenimiento del Estado de Derecho y la previsibilidad y la aplicación de los valores fundamentales de la sociedad. La función dominante o específica en la que se debe centrar cualquier mecanismo, sea de forma implícita o explícita, conlleva diversas consecuencias significativas: por ejemplo, determina el papel ideal al que debería tender el comportamiento del resolutor de disputas, la forma de justicia y de paz que se pueden alcanzar y el lugar de ambos sistemas de resolución de disputas y de los disputantes en la sociedad.

Case Law

Section A

Current Case Law of the National Courts regarding Arbitration

1. Bulgaria

Abbreviations used in annotations:

BCC [BUL]	Bulgarian Chamber of Commerce and Industry
BCCIC [BUL]	Arbitration Court at the Bulgarian Chamber of Commerce and Industry
CCP [BUL]	Code of Civil Procedure (1952, 2007)
ICAA [BUL]	International Commercial Arbitration Act

Alexander J. Bělohlávek

I. **Only a Final (Foreign) Arbitral Award Can Be Recognized and Enforced; A Partial Arbitral Award Cannot Be Recognized and Enforced; Conditions for the Recognition and Application of Procedural Regulations Valid in the Place of Recognition (Supreme Cassation Court; 23 February 2009)**

Key words:
partial arbitral award | final arbitral award | lex fori | governing law | procedural regulations | seat of arbitration | New York Convention | certificate of enforceability | obstacle for recognition | recognition and enforcement | outcome of the dispute

Resolution of the Supreme Cassation Court No. 356, Commercial Ref. No. 24/1999, of 23 February 2009 (*A. OOD, USA* v. *K.A., Bulgaria*):[1]

Laws Taken into Account in This Ruling:
➤ Convention on the Recognition and Enforcement of Foreign Arbitral Awards (1958) [New York Convention]: Article 3, Article 5(1)(e);
➤ UNCITRAL Rules on Arbitration (1976): Article 25.

---

[1] Source: APIS 7 PRAVO (*АПИС 7 ПРАВО legal information system*) and Case Law, (9-10) Bulletin of Supreme Cassation Court of Republic of Bulgaria 34 (1998).

Rationes Decidendi:

14.01. Each State Party to the New York Convention recognizes arbitral awards and allows their enforcement in accordance with procedural regulations valid in the territory where recognition and enforcement are demanded. The recognition and enforcement of a foreign award in Bulgaria take place in accordance with Bulgarian procedural regulations.

14.02. Only a final arbitral award is binding for the parties to arbitral proceedings. Only a final arbitral award may be recognized and enforced in Bulgaria.

[**Description of Facts and Legal Issues**]

14.03. The claimant (E. OOD, Croatia) was awarded rights under a partial arbitral award delivered by the Bern Court of Arbitration (Switzerland) and filed a demand with the Sofia City Court for its recognition and enforcement. The Sofia City Court accepted the demand. Its decision was appealed, and the court of second instance (Sofia Appeals Court) annulled the first-instance ruling. The claimant appealed to the Supreme Cassation Court, claiming that the verdict of the Sofia Appeals Court (second instance) is unlawful and that several serious procedural errors had been made. The Supreme Cassation Court confirmed this standpoint.

[**Overview of the Legal Standpoint of the Court**]

14.04. The Supreme Cassation Court ruled that the parties had entered into an arbitration agreement that was subject to the law in the place of the proceedings, as the governing law (a special law under the Convention). The Supreme Cassation Court applied the New York Convention, interpreting it in the sense that every State Party to the New York Convention is to recognize arbitral awards and allow their enforcement in accordance with procedural regulations valid in its territory. Thus, recognition and enforcement are subject to local procedural laws (*lex fori*). In this case, a partial arbitral award did not include a certificate of enforceability issued in the seat of arbitration that would state that the verdict could not be contested in the territory where the arbitral proceedings took place due to the fact that it is a final award. This represents an obstacle for its recognition and enforcement in Bulgaria. Furthermore, the Supreme Cassation Court ruled that **only a final arbitral award is binding for the parties. Only a final arbitral award is subject to recognition and enforcement.** The partial arbitral award delivered in this case did not examine the subject of the dispute to its full extent, as there remained unsettled issues in the dispute between the opposing parties. A decision regarding such issues was liable to overturn the progress of the proceedings and, consequently, the final outcome of the dispute. The Supreme Cassation Court upheld the second-instance verdict, rejecting conclusively the recognition of the relevant partial arbitral award delivered in Switzerland.

Czech (& Central European) Yearbook of Arbitration

II. Arbitration Agreement in the Form of a Reference to General Terms and Conditions; FIDIC Rules (Sofia District Court; 7 November 2008)

Key words:
FIDIC Rules | court jurisdiction | construction work | general terms and conditions

Resolution of the Sofia District Court No. 53,
Civilian Ref. No. 593/2008, of 7 November 2008 (I. vs. H.):²

Laws Taken into Account in This Ruling:
➢ Code of Civil Procedure (current version):³ Article 19(1);⁴
➢ International Commercial Arbitration Act, ICAA [BUL]:⁵ Section 8(1)⁶, Section 10;⁷
➢ Act on Obligations and Agreements:⁸ Section 266(1)⁹.

Rationes Decidendi:
14.05 A valid arbitration clause rules out court jurisdiction. An arbitration clause may be contained in general terms and conditions to which an

---

² One of the parties was a company with its registered office outside Bulgaria. The case was therefore an international dispute regarding a commercial matter. Source: APIS 7 PRAVO (*АПИС 7 ПРАВО legal information system*). The ruling has been identified by Plamen Borissov, Sofia, Bulgaria.

³ Published *in* 59 STATE GAZETTE (*DV / ДВ – Държавен вестник*), (20 June 2007), as amended. Available at: http://lex.bg/bg/laws/ldoc/2135558368 (accessed on December 17, 2010).

⁴ Unofficial translation (cit.) Section 19 – (1) *Parties to a dispute regarding property rights may agree that the dispute will be settled by an arbitration court with the exception of cases where the subject of a dispute is right in rem or the title to real estate, alimony, or rights arising under a labor law relationship.* [...]

⁵ Published *in* 60 STATE GAZETTE (*DV / ДВ Държавен вестник*) (5 August 1988), as amended. The Bulgarian version is available at: http://paragraf22.wap-bg.com/pravo/kodeksi/Otm/gpk.html (accessed on December 17, 2010); the Bulgarian version and an unofficial English translation are available at:
http://www.bcci.bg/arbitration/index.html (accessed on January 12, 2011).

⁶ ICCA [BUL] (unofficial translation in significant part taken from the BCCIC [BUL] website – Chapter II –Arbitration Agreement – [...] Section 8 (1) (*amended by* [Act published in] *Coll., No. 59 of 2007, effective starting on 1 March 2008) A court with which a complaint is filed regarding a dispute that is subject to an arbitration agreement must terminate the proceedings if a party invokes such an agreement during the first verbal hearing. However, if the court finds that the arbitration agreement is invalid, ineffective, or unenforceable, the court continues to examine the dispute.* [...]

⁷ ICCA [BUL] (unofficial translation taken from the BCCIC [BUL] website – Chapter VII – Setting Aside, Recognition and Enforcement of Award – Section 10 – *The provisions of Article 8, para. (1) and Article 9 also apply when an arbitration agreement stipulates that arbitration is to take place in a different country.* Article 9 concerns the powers of Bulgarian courts with regard to preliminary injunctions.

⁸ Published *in* 257 STATE GAZETTE (*DV / ДВ – Държавен вестник*) (22 November 1950). Also available at: http://lex.bg/bg/laws/ldoc/2121934337 (accessed on December 2, 2010).

⁹ The customer's obligation to pay the price for the work (general provision of substantive law).

agreement refers, such as the FIDIC Rules. An arbitration agreement does not have to be entered into separately (explicitly).

[Description of Facts and Legal Issues]

14.06. The parties entered into a contract for construction work in 2005 (the contract concerned the construction of a wastewater treatment facility for two Bulgarian cities). In the contract, the parties agreed to the application of the FIDIC Rules (issued in 1999). The customer failed to pay all the financial obligations arising under the contract, and the contractor claimed their payment in a complaint filed with the Sofia District Court. The customer contested the jurisdiction of the court due to an arbitration agreement included in the FIDIC Rules. The court accepted that a valid arbitration agreement had been entered into and halted the proceeding due to the lack of [its] jurisdiction over the matter.

| | |

III. Party Authorized to Enforce an Arbitral Award; Assignment of a Claim and Burden of Proof (Sofia Appeals Court; 22 February 2007)

Key words:
right of action | burden of proof | duty to submit evidence | writ of execution | authorized person | suability | liable party | legal succession | enforcement of arbitral award | enforcement of a judgment

Resolution of the Sofia Appeals Court Civilian Ref. No. 277/2007 of 22 February 2007 (E.I.AD vs. O.tz.kAD):[10]

Laws Taken into Account in This Ruling:
➢ Code of Civil Procedure (former version that has been replaced by a new law in the interim):[11] Section 237(1)(a), Section 242, Section 243(1), Section 244(1);[12]

---

[10] Source: APIS 7 PRAVO (*АПИС 7 ПРАВО legal information system*). The ruling has been identified by Plamen Borissov, Sofia, Bulgaria. In proceedings before the first-instance court whose verdict was annulled, the parties were in the respective opposite position. The enforcement of the first-instance decision was claimed by "O.tz.kAD".

[11] Published *in* 12 STATE GAZETTE [*DV / ДВ*], (08 February 1952), as amended. Available at: http://paragraf22.wap-bg.com/pravo/kodeksi/Otm/gpk.html (accessed on December 17, 2010).

[12] Individual provisions are not quoted because the law has been repealed and replaced by the new CCP [BUL]. The principles, on which the verdict is based, however, remain preserved in the new Code of Civil Procedure.

> ➤ International Commercial Arbitration Act, ICAA [BUL]:[13] Section 51(1)[14].

Rationes Decidendi:

14.07. When a court has ascertained as part of enforcement proceedings that grounds exist for the enforcement of a judgment (arbitral award), the court must examine the party benefiting from the awarded right and the party against which such a right exists (*right of action* and *suability*).

14.08. A writ of execution may only be issued in favour of a party that is found to possess a right against a party that must submit to the enforcement of a judgment.

14.09. The enforcement of a judgment may be demanded by a person other than a party to arbitral proceedings, specifically, by a party that has been awarded a right under an arbitral award. Such a party, however, must demonstrate its legal succession regarding such a right, where the claimant is subject to the duty to submit evidence (burden of proof). A court examines such a legal succession in enforcement proceedings as part of the exercise of its official authority.

[Description of Facts and Legal Issues]

14.10. The case in question involved the enforcement of a claim concerning the cost of arbitral proceedings. The court of first instance (Sofia City Court) issued a writ of execution in favor of the claimant, "O.tz.**k**", despite the fact that according to the arbitral award the right was possessed by "O.tz.**z**" (a different legal entity). The appeals court annulled the writ of execution (first-instance ruling) because legal succession regarding the right in question had not been examined.

[Comment of the Author of the Annotation]

14.11. Bulgarian law (in the same way as the law of most Central and Eastern European countries) is based on the strict differentiation of legal subjectivity. Save for exceptions, no *piercing the corporate veil* is accepted in contractual relationships. The execution of an arbitral award may be demanded by another person (in this case, a person from the same corporate group), but such a person must demonstrate its legal succession. Such legal succession may be, for instance, the assignment of a receivable.

| | |

---

13 *Supra* note 5.

14 ICCA [BUL] (unofficial translation in significant part taken from the BCCIC [BUL] website – Chapter II –Arbitration Agreement – [...] Article 8 (1) (*amended by* [Act published in:] *Coll., No. 59 of 2007, effective as of 1 March 2008) A court with which a complaint is filed regarding a dispute that is subject to an arbitration agreement must terminate the proceedings if a party invokes such an agreement during the first verbal hearing. However, if the court finds that the arbitration agreement is invalid, ineffective, or unenforceable, the court continues to examine the dispute.*

IV. Examination of Reasons
for Refusing the Recognition /Enforcement
of a Foreign Arbitral Award Based on Objection
Raised by the Party against Whom It Has Been
Invoked (Article 5(1)) and Based
on the Competent Authority (Article 5(2)
of the New York Convention);
Rejection of Arguments on the Merits That Could
Be Used in Arbitral Proceedings
(Sofia City Court; 16 February 2008)

Key words:
arguments on the merits | evidence on the merits | based on an objection |
reasons examined based on official duty | reasons for refusing recognition |
International Court of Arbitration (ICC) | New York Convention | document
forgery | examination of merits | criminal offence | public policy | enforcement
of an arbitral award

Ruling of the Sofia City Court Civilian Ref. No. 62/2007 of 16 February 2008 (*CEZ K.E.Z.G.* and *BT A.* and I.G. vs. *M.Z.P.*):[15]

Laws Taken into Account in This Ruling:
➢ International Commercial Arbitration Act, ICAA [BUL]:[16] Section 51;[17]

---

[15] Source: APIS 7 PRAVO (*АПИС 7 ПРАВО legal information system*). The ruling has been identified by Plamen Borissov, Sofia, Bulgaria.

[16] *Supra* note 5.

[17] ICCA [BUL] (unofficial translation in significant part taken from the BCCIC [BUL] website – Chapter II –Arbitration Agreement – [...] Article 51 (Amended – SG/DV No. 93 of 1993). "(1) Based on an enforceable arbitral award, the Sofia City Court (*Софийски градски съд*) issues a writ of execution at the request of the entitled party. A copy of the arbitral award and a proof of its delivery to the liable party (debtor) must be attached to the request. (2) The international treaties entered into by the Republic of Bulgaria apply to the recognition and enforcement of foreign arbitral awards. (3) *(New, published in Coll., No. 38 of 2001, amended under* [Act published in:], *Coll., No. 59 of 2007, effective as of 1 March 2008).* A request for the recognition and enforcement of a foreign arbitral award may be made to the Sofia City Court, unless otherwise stipulated in an international treaty to which the Republic of Bulgaria is a party. Proceedings on such a request are subject to Articles 118-122 of the Private International Law Act (*Кодекс на международното частно право*) with the exception of the debtor's right to raise an objection on the grounds of the expiration of the debt."

> ➤ Act on International Private Law:[18] Article 117[19], Article 120(1);[20]
> ➤ Convention on the Enforcement of Foreign Arbitration Awards (New York Convention; 1958): Article 3, Article 5.

Rationes Decidendi:

14.12. The reasons for refusing recognition and enforcement according to Article 5(1) of the New York Convention are examined by a court only based on an objection raised by a respondent (liable party).

14.13. The reasons for refusing recognition and enforcement according to Article 5(2) of the New York Convention are examined by a court based on its competence (*ex officio*).

14.14. In recognition and enforcement proceedings, arguments or evidence on the merits are inadmissible if such arguments have not been used by the respondent in the relevant arbitral proceedings despite the fact that such arguments or evidence could have been used. This also applies to facts that may indicate that a criminal offence has been committed (for instance document forgery).

[Description of Facts and Legal Issues]

14.15. The claimants demanded the recognition and enforcement of an arbitral award delivered in proceedings before the International Court of Arbitration (ICC). The respondent defended itself by arguing that the arbitral award was contrary to the Bulgarian public policy; the arbitral award was to be based, among others, on forged documents, where arguments that a criminal offence had been committed were used.

| | |

---

[18] Published *in* 42 STATE GAZETTE (*DV / ДВ – Държавен вестник*) (17 May 2005). It is also available at: http://lex.bg/bg/laws/ldoc/213550365 (accessed on December 12, 2010).
[19] Unofficial translation (cit.) Article 117 – *Judgments delivered and other acts completed by foreign courts and other bodies are recognized and can be enforced if: 1. a foreign court or another body had a jurisdiction pursuant to provisions of the Bulgarian law unless the only reason for foreign jurisdiction in property-related disputes was the nationality of the claimant or the claimant's registration in the country where the court has its seat; 2. the respondent has been delivered a copy of the complaint, the parties have been duly summoned, and no violation of the fundamental principles of Bulgarian law has been committed in relation to their protection; 3. there exists no enforceable ruling of a Bulgarian court in the same matter between the same parties; 4. proceedings are underway before a Bulgarian court regarding the same parties, which began before the foreign proceedings that resulted in the judgment that is to be recognized and enforced; 5. the recognition and enforcement of the judgment are not contrary to the public policy of Bulgaria.*
[20] Unofficial translation (cit.) Article 120 – (1) *A court examines the conditions set out in Article 117 based on its official authority.* [...]

V. The Exclusive Jurisdiction of the Supreme Cassation Court of Bulgaria to Annul Arbitral Awards; Non-Application of the Code of Civil Procedure
(Supreme Cassation Court; 24 February 2009)

Key words:
Supreme Cassation Court of Bulgaria | reasons for annulment of arbitral award | lex specialis | enforceable court decision | review of court decision | special law | exclusion of analogy | exclusive jurisdiction | annulment of an arbitral award | annulment of enforceable ruling | annulment of court ruling

Judgment of the Supreme Cassation Court No. 23, Civilian Ref. No. 44/2009, of 24 February 2009 (*TD "Sh" A* vs. *L.L.K.*):[21]

Laws Taken into Account in This Ruling:
➢ Code of Civil Procedure (current version):[22] Article 303(1) to (6), Article 307(1);[23]
➢ International Commercial Arbitration Act, ICAA [BUL]:[24] Section 47[25].

Rationes Decidendi:
14.16. An arbitral award is the final decision on the merits of a case. The only legal means that can be used against an arbitral award is a request for its annulment.
14.17. A decision on a request for the annulment of an arbitral award can be made exclusively by the Supreme Cassation Court in proceedings that are not a part of the arbitral proceedings (exclusive jurisdiction of the Supreme Cassation Court).

---

[21] Source: APIS 7 PRAVO (*АПИС 7 ПРАВО legal information system*). The ruling has been identified by Plamen Borissov, Sofia, Bulgaria.
[22] *Supra* note 3.
[23] Provisions concerning an extraordinary remedial measure. They allow the Supreme Cassation Court, based on reasons expressly stated under Article 303(1) and Article 307(1), to annul an enforceable court judgment. Article 303(1) of CCP [BUL] defines the reasons for the annulment of an enforceable court judgment, and Article 307(1) sets out the procedural guidelines for the Supreme Cassation Court. Considering the decision in this case (negative outcome, i.e. the legislation was not even used in an analogical manner), the provisions of CCP [BUL] in question are not quoted in this annotation.
[24] *Supra* note 5.
[25] The provision is quoted in connection with an annotation pertaining to a different ruling. The article of ICAA [BUL] in question contains a comprehensive list of reasons for the annulment of an arbitral award.

14.18. An arbitral award may only be annulled based on the reasons set out in the International Commercial Arbitration Act (ICAA [BUL]). The Supreme Cassation Court delivers rulings in accordance with the International Commercial Arbitration Act (ICAA [BUL]), a special law (*lex specialis*) in relation to the Code of Civil Procedure. Hence, the provisions of the Code of Civil Procedure do not apply to the annulment of enforceable court decisions. The provisions of the Code of Civil Procedure do not have to be applied in an analogical manner (per analogiam, in this case the exclusion of analogy).

14.19. Thus, legal standpoints expressed in the different case law of the Supreme Cassation Court are not taken into account during arbitral award annulment proceedings with regard to procedural issues concerning the review of court decisions.

| | |

VI. Payment of a Security as a Prerequisite for a Suspension of the Enforcement of an Arbitral Award; Independence of Arbitral Award Enforcement and Annulment Proceedings (Supreme Cassation Court; 19 March 2009)

Key words:
Supreme Cassation Court | security | prerequisite for a suspension of the enforcement | suspension of enforcement | payment of a security | purpose of security | enforcement of arbitral award | security measure | annulment of an arbitral award

Judgment of the Supreme Cassation Court No. 16, Civilian Ref. No. 199/2009, of 19 March 2009:[26]

Laws Taken into Account in This Ruling:
➤ Code of Civil Procedure (current version):[27] Article 389[28], Article 404(1);[29]

---

[26] Source: APIS 7 PRAVO (*АПИС 7 ПРАВО legal information system*). The ruling has been identified by Plamen Borissov, Sofia, Bulgaria.

[27] *Supra* note 3.

[28] CCP [BUL] (unofficial translation, cit.) Article 389. (1) *To secure its claim, a claimant is entitled to request the issue of a preliminary injunction by a court that has a jurisdiction over the matter at any time during the course of proceedings or by an appeals court at any time after the examination of the matter.* (2) *Security is allowable for all types of litigated claims.* This case concerned a security ordered in connection with the enforcement of an arbitral award.

[29] CCP [BUL] (unofficial translation, cit.) Article 404. The following are subject to compulsory enforcement: 1. enforceable court decisions, enforceable decisions of

> International Commercial Arbitration Act, ICAA [BUL]:[30] Section 47[31].

Rationes Decidendi:

14.20. A decision to suspend the enforcement of an arbitral award may only be made by the Supreme Cassation Court by means of a security measure (exclusive jurisdiction of the Supreme Cassation Court).

14.21. A prerequisite for a suspension of the enforcement of an arbitral award is the payment of a security.

14.22. Arbitral award enforcement and annulment proceedings are two independent proceedings, and the payment of a security or using assets as collateral as part of these proceedings fulfils different purposes. Security relating to the assets of a debtor in enforcement proceedings cannot be accepted as a security in proceedings on the annulment of an arbitral award (in connection with a suspension of enforcement) or a reason for releasing the claimant (applicant) from the duty to pay security in the annulment proceedings.

[Description of Facts and Legal Issues]

14.23. In proceedings on the annulment of an arbitral award, a demand was made for a suspension of the enforcement of the award until the conclusion of the annulment proceedings. The Supreme Cassation Court requested the claimant to pay a security in an amount corresponding to the payment awarded in the arbitral award in respect of which the annulment was demanded. The claimant refused, arguing that its assets (real estate), which had a higher value, had already been distrained as security as part of the enforcement of the arbitral award. The court rejected this argument.

| | |

---

appeals courts awarding a right, imposing an obligation, or affecting property, writs of execution, court settlement records, decisions on writs of execution subject to or based on which a preliminary injunction or immediate execution is imposed, as well as awards delivered by arbitration courts and settlement agreements entered into as part of arbitral proceedings in arbitrable disputes; [...].

[30] *Supra* note 5.

[31] The provision is quoted in connection with an annotation pertaining to a different ruling. The article of ICAA [BUL] in question contains a comprehensive list of reasons for the annulment of an arbitral award.

VII. Initiation of Arbitral Award Annulment Proceedings and Requirements for an Annulment Request; Prohibition of a Review on the Merits (Supreme Cassation Court; 1 December 2009)

Key words:
Supreme Cassation Court | reasons for award annulment | requirements for request | request for annulment of arbitral award | review of award on merits | arbitral award | prohibition of review | annulment of an arbitral award

Judgment of the Supreme Cassation Court No. 106, Civilian Ref. No. 884/2009, of 1 December 2009 (*M "O"* vs. *"O" E.*):[32]

Laws Taken into Account in This Ruling:
➢ Code of Civil Procedure (current version):[33] Article 127(1) and Article 127(2)[34];
➢ International Commercial Arbitration Act, ICAA [BUL]:[35] Section 47[36].

Rationes Decidendi:

14.24. A letter addressed to the Chairman of the Supreme Cassation Court of Bulgaria is not an act that would initiate proceedings on the annulment of an arbitral award.

14.25. A request for the annulment of an arbitral award must conform to the requirements set out in the International Commercial Arbitration Act (ICAA [BUL]).

14.26. The Supreme Cassation Court of Bulgaria may annul an arbitral award only due to the reasons set out in the International Commercial Arbitration Act (ICAA [BUL]). A court may not review an arbitral award on the merits.

---

32 Source: APIS 7 PRAVO (*АПИС 7 ПРАВО legal information system*). The ruling has been identified by Plamen Borissov, Sofia, Bulgaria.
33 *Supra* note 3.
34 CCP [BUL] (unofficial translation, cit.) Article 127. (1) *A complaint must be drafted in the Bulgarian language and must specify the following: 1. the designation of the court; 2. the names and addresses of the claimant and of the respondent, their legal representative or agents, if applicable, and the Personal Identification Number of the claimant and the claimant's fax number and telex address, if applicable; 3. the value of the claim provided that it can be determined; 4. a description of the circumstances that are the basis for the complaint; 5. the claim raised by the claimant; 6. a signature of the person submitting the complaint. (2) Furthermore, the claimant must specify in the complaint evidence and specific circumstances that support its allegations and enclose any and all documents that are to serve as evidence.*
35 *Supra* note 5.
36 The provision is quoted in connection with an annotation pertaining to a different ruling. The article of ICAA [BUL] in question contains a comprehensive list of reasons for the annulment of an arbitral award.

[Description of Facts and Legal Issues]

14.27. A letter was delivered to the Chairman of the Supreme Cassation Court in which the sender claimed the erroneous nature of an arbitral award, requesting its annulment and a new decision on the merits. The arbitral award was enclosed with the letter. The letter was not recognized to constitute a request for the annulment of the arbitral award.

| | |

VIII. National Registration Authority of Top-Level Domain Names and Its Arbitration Board as an Authority Possessing Special Powers, Which Does Not Resolve Disputes in Accordance with the Arbitration Act (Supreme Cassation Court; 30 March 2010)

Key words:
top-level domain name | authority possessing powers | assisting body | consultative body | domain name | arbitration board | arbitral award | court of arbitration | settlement of disputes | annulment of arbitral award

Judgment of the Supreme Cassation Court No. 39, Civilian Ref. No. 115/2010, of 30 March 2010 (*V.V.D.* vs. *BG OOD Register*):[37]

Laws Taken into Account in This Ruling:
➢ Code of Civil Procedure (current version):[38] Article 19(1);[39]
  International Commercial Arbitration Act, ICAA [BUL]:[40] Section 1[41],

---

[37] Source: APIS 7 PRAVO (*АПИС 7 ПРАВО legal information system*). The ruling has been identified by Plamen Borissov, Sofia, Bulgaria.

[38] *Supra* note 3.

[39] Article 19(1) CCP [BUL] is quoted in annotations relating to a different decision. It contains general provisions that define the possibilities regarding the entry into of an arbitration agreement and the objective capacity to arbitrate defined under CCP [BUL].

[40] *Supra* note 5.

[41] ICAA [BUL] (unofficial translation taken from the BCCIC [BUL] website, cit.)
  Chapter I – General Provisions – Art. 1. (1) (Amended – SG No. 93 of 1993). *This Act applies to international commercial arbitration based on arbitration agreements when the place of arbitration proceedings is in the territory of the Republic of Bulgaria.* (2) (Amended – SG No. 93 of 1993), *International commercial arbitration resolves civil property disputes resulting from international trade relations as well as disputes relating to filling gaps in contracts or their adaptation to newly established facts when the domicile or seat of at least one of the parties is not in the Republic of Bulgaria.* [...]

Section 4[42], Section 7(1)[43], Section 47(3), Section 47(4), and Section 47(6)[44].

Rationes Decidendi:

14.28. The arbitration board attached to the national register of top-level domain names (BG OOD Register) is not an arbitration court in the sense of the definition in Section 1 and Section 4 of the International Commercial Arbitration Act (ICAA [BUL]), and its decisions cannot be annulled by the Supreme Cassation Court. A request for the annulment of a decision of the arbitration board in reference to the International Commercial Arbitration Act (ICAA [BUL]) is not admissible.

14.29. This arbitration board does not settle disputes but expresses standpoints of an authority possessing decision-making powers in respect of matters that are in its authority.

14.30. The national register of top-level domain names (BG OOD Register) is an authority that has been entrusted special powers, while the arbitration board is only its assisting [*consultative*] body.

[Description of Facts and Legal Issues]

14.31. The company X Dreams contested the registration of a domain name in the national register of top-level Internet domain names in favour of the company V.V.D. The arbitration board attached to the BG OOD Register ruled that the objection was substantiated, cancelled the original registration, and carried out a new registration in favour of the claimant. V.V.D., the former holder of the domain name, filed a request to the Supreme Cassation Court for the annulment of the arbitration board's decision.

[Overview of the Legal Standpoint of the Court]

14.32. The court ruled that the arbitration board in question was not an authority with a jurisdiction to settle disputes, in this case, a dispute between the companies "X Dreams" and "V.V.D.". The rights of these companies are examined by the Register, which possesses powers to the extent entrusted thereto. The arbitration board has the status of a special assisting body of the BG OOD Register, and it is not a court of arbitration regardless of its designation.

| | |

---

[42] ICAA [BUL] (unofficial translation taken from the BCCIC [BUL] website, cit.) Chapter I – General Provisions – [...] Art. 4. *An Arbitral Tribunal may be either a permanent institution or established to resolve a particular dispute.* [...]

[43] ICAA [BUL] (unofficial translation taken from the BCCIC [BUL] website, cit.) Chapter II – Arbitration Agreement – Art. 7. (1) *An arbitration agreement means the consent of the parties to submit to arbitration the resolution of all or certain disputes that may arise or have arisen between them in connection with a specific contractual or non- contractual legal relation. An arbitration agreement may be an arbitration clause in a contract or a separate agreement.* [...]

[44] The provision is quoted in connection with an annotation pertaining to a different ruling. The article of ICAA [BUL] in question contains a comprehensive list of reasons for the annulment of an arbitral award.

IX. Municipality, State (Foreign State), and State Agency (Foreign State Agency) as a Party to Arbitration in Bulgaria (Supreme Cassation Court; 28 October 2008)

Key words:
capacity to arbitrate | foreign state agency | natural person | municipality | objective capacity to arbitrate | legal entity | acceptability of arbitration agreement | subjective extent | state agency | party to arbitration agreement | party to arbitral proceedings | annulment of arbitral award

Judgment of the Supreme Cassation Court No. 706, Civilian Ref. No. 361/2008, of 21 October 2008 (*Municipality T. vs. M.C.T.*):[45]

Laws Taken into Account in This Ruling:
➢ International Commercial Arbitration Act, ICAA [BUL]:[46] Section 3[47], Section 11(1)[48], Section 47(2), Section 47(3), and Section 47(6)[49].

Rationes Decidendi:
14.33. In arbitral proceedings conducted in accordance with ICAA [BUL], the status of the parties to an arbitration agreement (parties to a dispute) is not of a decisive nature. Decisive is exclusively the acceptability of an arbitration agreement with regard to a specific dispute (objective capacity to arbitrate).

14.34. A party to arbitral proceedings may be both natural person and a legal entity regardless of whether such a party conducts business or not. A party to arbitral proceedings may be a state or a state agency; this also applies to a foreign state or a foreign state agency.

14.35. A municipality may be a party to an arbitration agreement (a party to arbitral proceedings).

---

[45]   Source: APIS 7 PRAVO (*АПИС 7 ПРАВО legal information system*). The ruling has been identified by Plamen Borissov, Sofia, Bulgaria.

[46]   *Supra* note 5

[47]   ICAA [BUL] (unofficial translation taken from the BCCIC [BUL] website, cit.) Chapter I – General Provisions – [...] Art. 3. *The parties to international commercial arbitration may include a state or a state agency.*

[48]   ICAA [BUL] (unofficial translation taken from the BCCIC [BUL] website, cit.) Chapter III – General Provisions – [...] Art. 11. (1) *An Arbitral Tribunal may consist of one or more arbitrators whose number is determined by the parties. When their number is not determined by the parties, an Arbitral Tribunal consists of three arbitrators.* [...].

[49]   The provision is quoted in connection with an annotation pertaining to a different ruling. The article of ICAA [BUL] in question contains a comprehensive list of reasons for the annulment of an arbitral award.

[Description of Facts and Legal Issues]

14.36. "Municipality T" applied for the annulment of an arbitral award which required "Municipality T" to make a financial payment to M.C.T. The claimant argued that the invoked arbitration agreement was invalid and contrary to public order and that the appointment of the arbitration tribunal had been unlawful.

[Comment of the Author of This Annotation]

14.37. The Supreme Cassation Court used a broad interpretation of Article 3 of ICAA [BUL], which expressly states only that a party to an arbitration agreement may be a state or a state agency. This interpretation corresponds to the gradual expansion of both the objective and subjective scope of ICAA [BUL], which originally applied to international commercial disputes exclusively. Its applicability, however, has been expanded, and today, it covers all disputes that are arbitrable in accordance with CCP. According to the current Bulgarian *lex arbitri* laws, an arbitration clause can be agreed with regard to all property-related disputes, regardless of the individual status of the parties to the dispute (agreement) and regardless of whether a dispute is domestic or international. The sole decisive issue is the nature of a dispute and the objective possibilities of submitting such a dispute to arbitration. Thus, individual amendments to ICAA [BUL] have gradually increased its scope without changing the designation of this law, which is now somewhat misleading (the law does not apply the international commercial matters only).

| | |

X. Independence of an Arbitration Clause from the Main Contract and the Duty of a Court to Examine the Validity of an Arbitration Clause before Issuing a Ruling on a Challenge of Jurisdiction (Appeals Court of Veliko Tarnovo; 23 June 2008)

Key words:
main contract | nature of arbitration clause | nature of arbitration agreement | sale and purchase agreement | challenge of jurisdiction | independence of arbitration clause | independence of arbitration agreement | validity of the main contract | validity of the arbitration clause | validity of an arbitration agreement | court jurisdiction | procedural agreement | master agreement | separability | discontinuance of proceedings

Resolution of the Appeals Court of Veliko Tarnovo No. 162, Civilian Ref. No. 335/2008, of 23 June 2008 (F.R.EAD vs. A.i.EOOD):[50]

Laws Taken into Account in This Ruling:
➢ Code of Civil Procedure[51], CCP [BUL]: Article 9(1);[52]
➢ Commercial Code:[53] Section 327(1);[54]
➢ Act on Obligations and Agreements:[55] Section 79(1);[56]

Rationes Decidendi:

14.38. An arbitration agreement (arbitration clause) has the nature of a procedural agreement. An arbitration agreement (arbitration clause) is an agreement that differs from an agreement defining property-related obligations between the contracting parties (the main contract).

---

[50] Source: APIS 7 PRAVO (*АПИС 7 ПРАВО legal information system*). The ruling has been identified by Plamen Borissov, Sofia, Bulgaria. The standpoint of the Appeals Court of Veliko Tarnovo is confirmed by certain judgments of the Bulgarian Supreme Cassation Court, for instance, Ruling of the Supreme Cassation Court No. 9, Commercial Ref. No. 704/2008, (16 February 2009); Source: APIS 7 PRAVO (*АПИС 7 ПРАВО legal information system*).

[51] *Supra* note 3.

[52] Unofficial translation of provisions quoted in an annotation concerning another Bulgarian decision.

[53] Published *in* 48 State Gazette (*DV / ДВ – Държавен вестник*), (18 June 1991). Also available at: http://lex.bg/bg/laws/ldoc/-14917630 (accessed on December 2, 2010). In this case, in connection with claims made under substantive law (for this reason, the provisions are not quoted in this annotation).

[54] The provision defines the buyer's obligation to accept goods and to pay the purchase price.

[55] *Supra* note 8.

[56] The creditor's rights that apply in the event the debtor fails to fulfill its obligation (general provisions of substantive law).

14.39. The validity of an arbitration agreement (arbitration clause) as well as the conditions for its validity are examined independently from the validity of the main contract. An arbitration court must examine the validity of an arbitration agreement before deciding to discontinue proceedings due to a lack of jurisdiction.

[Description of Facts and Legal Issues]

14.40. The parties entered into a master sale and purchase agreement in 2004. Individual purchase contracts were entered into as part of the performance of this agreement. The respondent did not pay for goods supplied after the year 2006. The complaint filed with the court consisted of a claim for the payment of the purchase price. The Veliko Tarnovo District Court (VTDC), as the court of first instance, halted the proceedings due to a lack of jurisdiction, and submitted the case to the Arbitration Court at the Bulgarian Chamber of Commerce and Industry (BCCIC). The claimant insisted, however, that the relationship between the parties in 2006 was no longer subject to the master sale and purchase agreement entered into in 2004, claiming that if the main contract was invalid, so was the arbitration clause. The claimant appealed the court decision to halt the proceedings. The appeals court annulled the verdict of the first-instance court and submitted the case to the court for re-examination.

[Overview of the Legal Standpoint of the Appeals Court]

14.41 The appeals court did not express a standpoint regarding whether in this case an arbitration agreement existed or not. The court ruled, however, that the court of first instance should have examined separately whether the arbitration agreement existed or whether it had expired. The court should not have automatically applied to the validity of the arbitration clause the conclusion relating to the validity of the main contract that contained the arbitration clause. For this reason, the appeals court annulled the first-instance decision and ordered the same court to examine the validity of the arbitration agreement (arbitration clause) independently from the validity of the main contract[57], and, only then, to issue a decision regarding jurisdiction.

[Alexander J. Bělohlávek]

| | |

---

[57] The main contract entered in 2004 was deemed valid by the court of first instance.

2. Czech Republic

Abbreviations used in annotations:
OSŘ [CZE] - Code of Civil Procedure [Czech Republic]

Alexander J. Bělohlávek

I. Prohibition of Reviewing Arbitral Awards on the Merits of the Case (Prohibition of *Révision au Fond*); Review of the Merits in Conflict with the Purpose and Spirit of Arbitration; Transfer of Jurisdiction over the Merits of the Case from the Judge (Court) to the Arbitrator (Czech Supreme Court; October 30, 2009)

Key words:
good morals | reasons for setting aside an arbitral award | nature of arbitration | transfer of jurisdiction | correctness of the arbitral award | factual correctness | prohibition of révision au fond | prohibition of a review on the merits | annulment of an arbitral award

Judgment 33 Cdo 2675/2007 of the Czech Supreme Court of October 30, 2009:[1]

15.01. The fact that the obligation to perform as imposed by an arbitral award is in conflict with good morals is not sufficient grounds to set aside the arbitral award, as reviewing this issue would be tantamount to a review "on the merits", i.e., of the factual correctness of the arbitral award, which is inadmissible.

15.02. Concerning the grounds for setting aside arbitral awards, the lawmaker's intention [and thus the rationale behind the Act on arbitration and on the enforcement of arbitral awards] was to rule out any judicial review of the factual correctness of the arbitral award. This means that the facts of the case as ascertained in arbitration proceedings and the legal assessment of the case are removed from such review. If courts were authorized, in proceedings on the annulment of arbitral awards, to review the award's merits, then the entire legal framework which governs arbitration proceedings would cease to make sense. This follows not least from the

---

[1] Published in the 52 COLLECTION OF COURT DECISIONS AND OPINIONS (2010).

nature of arbitration, which inherently involves the transfer of jurisdiction for hearing and deciding a certain class of disputes from the general courts to the arbitrator, and from the grounds for which arbitral awards may indeed be annulled.

| | |

II. Arbitration Clause as an Integral Part of General Terms of Contract; Prerequisites for Proceedings before a General Court Are Not Met due to Arbitration Agreement (Czech Supreme Court; April 28, 2010)

Key words:
arbitration clause | arbitration agreement | lack of jurisdiction | leasing contract | general terms of contract

Resolution 23 Cdo 4895/2009 of the Czech Supreme Court[2] of April 28, 2010:[3]

15.03. The provision on setting aside [court] proceedings due to an obstacle in the form of an extant arbitration agreement contained in Section 106 (1) of the Code of Civil Procedure[4] constitutes a special arrangement *vis-à-vis* the general provision of Section 104 (1) of the Code of Civil

---

[2] In proceedings on the appeal on questions of law against resolution 20 Co 284/2009-32 of the Prague Municipal Court of August 4, 2009.

[3] Available at the portal of the Czech Supreme Court at: http://www.nsoud.cz/ JudikaturaNS_new/judikatura_prevedena2.nsf/WebSearch/EE8E41F66EFC8F6DC125 772000355CF9?openDocument (accessed on October 9, 2010).

[4] Act No. 99/1963 Coll., as amended, the Code of Civil Procedure (OSŘ [CZE]) (cit.) – Review of the prerequisites of proceedings – [...] Sec. 106 – (1) *The court, upon finding with respect to the respondent's objection (which must be raised no later than on occasion of its first act on the merits) that the matter must pursuant to the parties' agreement in arbitration proceedings, must not hear the matter further and shall set aside the proceedings; however, it shall hear the case if the parties declare that they no longer insist on honoring the agreement. The court shall also hear the matter if it finds that the matter is under Czech law unfit for being subject to arbitration, or that the arbitration agreement is invalid or, as the case may be, does not exist in the first place, or that hearing the case in arbitration would exceed the scope of powers awarded to the arbitrators in the agreement, or that the arbitrators refused to deal with the case. (2) If court proceedings were stayed pursuant to para. (1) and a motion for commencing arbitration proceedings in the same matter is filed, then the legal effects of the original motion are preserved if the motion for the commencement of arbitration proceedings is filed within 30 days from the day on which the court decision to stay proceedings was served. (3) If the arbitration proceedings were commenced before the court proceedings, then the court shall suspend its own proceedings in matters of the non-existence, invalidity, or expiry of the agreement until a decision has been made in arbitration on jurisdiction or on the merits.*

Procedure[5] on the termination of proceedings for lack of jurisdiction. An appeal on questions of law[6] against the resolution of the appellate court which confirmed the first-instance court's decision to set aside proceedings under Sec. 104 (1) of the Code of Civil Procedure is admissible, pursuant to Sec. 239 (2) (a) of the Code of Civil Procedure[7].

15.04. Section 3 (2) of [Czech] Act No. 216/2004 Coll.[8], On Arbitration and the Enforcement of Arbitral Awards, as amended, sets forth that an arbitration clause which is incorporated in general terms of contract that govern the main agreement (to which the said arbitration clause refers) applies (i.e., has been validly agreed) also in those cases in which the written offer to contract (i.e., the written offer of the main agreement with the arbitration clause) has been accepted by the other party in a manner which makes its acceptance of the contents of the arbitration agreement manifest.

15.05. If the "main" agreement (in this case, a "*leasing contract*") expressly states that the terms of contract are attached to the agreement and have been signed by the parties, then these terms of contract form an integral part of the agreement. If the terms of contract contained an arbitration clause and both parties expressed their consent by adding their signatures, then – in line with the explicit arrangement in the main agreement – these terms were an integral part of the agreement and the arbitration clause was thus validly contracted, even if the main agreement itself did not

---

[5]   Act No. 99/1963 Coll., as amended, the Code of Civil Procedure (OSŘ [CZE]) (cit.) – Review of the prerequisites of proceedings – [...] Sec. 104 – (1) *In case of a deficiency with respect to the conditions of the proceedings which cannot be removed, the court shall stay proceedings. If the matter does not lie within the jurisdiction of the courts, or must be proceeded by proceedings before another body, then the court shall refer the matter to the competent body as soon as its resolution to stay proceedings has become final; the legal effects in connection with the filing of the claim (of the motion to commence proceedings) remain preserved. (2) In case of a deficiency with respect to the conditions of the proceedings which can be removed, the court shall take suitable measures to this effect. As a rule, the court may continue proceedings, but must not make a decision on the merits. If attempts to remove the deficiency fail, then the court shall stay the proceedings.* [...]

[6]   Within the context of Czech civil proceedings, the appeal on questions of law is an extraordinary legal remedy. The civil procedure before general courts knows principally two instances. The appeal on questions of law, which is an extraordinary remedy and represents a path to a *notional* third instance, is conditional upon stringent requirements as set out by law.

[7]   The Czech Supreme Court referred to previous decisions, i.e., namely, (●) resolution 29 Odo 1051/2004 of April 28, 2005, published *in* 37 COLLECTION OF COURT DECISIONS AND OPINIONS (2006) and (●) resolution 23 Cdo 1164/2009 of the Czech Supreme Court of December 10, 2009, published on the portal of the Czech Supreme Court, available at: http://www.nsoud.cz (accessed on October 9, 2010).

[8]   (Cit.) Sec. 3 – [...] (2) *However, if the validity of the main contract, of which the arbitration clause is a part, depends upon the validity of the arbitration clause, the arbitration clause shall be held valid if the party challenging the validity of the arbitration clause consented to the main contract in such a way that consent to the arbitration clause resulted from consent to the main contract.*

contain an explicit statement of consent with the arbitration agreement.

15.06. An arbitration agreement does not become invalid merely because it uses an obsolete designation for the arbitration court or for the institution which keeps the list of arbitrators[9], even if the title of that institution has in the meantime changed. Of relevance is alone that the identified entity is still the same. A change in designation of a given institution does not allow for the conclusion that the understanding reached in the arbitral award is indeterminate and inscrutable[10].

| | |

III. Arbitration Clause as an Integral Part of General Terms of Contract; Prerequisites for Proceedings before a General Court Are Not Met due to Arbitration Agreement (Czech Supreme Court; July 27, 2010)

Key words:
contra bonos mores | grounds for an appeal on questions of law | extraordinary remedy | nullity of the arbitration agreement | font used in the arbitration agreement | arbitration agreement, validity thereof | incorrect assessment of the matter | inadmissible performance | impossible performance | right to be heard in the matter | arbitration proceedings | arbitration agreement | defence of nullity | timeliness of the action for annulment | prohibition of révision au fond | prohibition of a review of the award on the merits

Judgment 32 Cdo 761/2009 of the Czech Supreme Court[11] of July 27, 2010:[12]

15.07. The Supreme Court is not authorized to assess the arbitration proceedings in terms of their substance [i.e., the content of the course of proceedings and of the arbitral award], but may only address the issue of whether

---

[9] *Cf.* – as *appointing authority.*

[10] In this respect, the Czech Supreme Court fully endorsed the legal opinion of the court of appeals (second-instance court).

[11] In proceedings on the appeal on questions of law against resolution 18 Co 33/2008-130 of the Hradec Králové Regional Court (as the second-instance court) of July 2, 2008. The first-instance court (the Pardubice District Court) decided by way of judgment 8 C 391/2006-90 of October 29, 2007. The motion for annulment of the arbitral award was dismissed. The Czech Supreme Court also dismissed the appeal on questions of law as extraordinary remedy.

[12] Available on the portal of the Czech Supreme Court at: http://www.nsoud.cz/ JudikaturaNS_new/judikatura_prevedena2.nsf/WebSearch/926B0C2FA161D30FC125 778A002CCB (accessed on October 9, 2010).

the court of appeals[13] properly assessed whether or not the grounds for setting aside the arbitral award were given in the particular case[14]. At the same time, the court of appeals is bound by the reasons which were given for the appeal on questions of law [the latter being an extraordinary remedy] and by how these reasons were defined in terms of substance (Sec. 242 (3) First Sentence of act No. 99/1963 Coll., as amended, Code of Civil Procedure).

15.08. If the appellant, in spite of having had this opportunity, did not invoke the defence of nullity of the arbitration agreement in the proceedings before the arbitrator[15], then these reasons are not available for his appeal in the proceedings on the annulment of the arbitral award[16]. For this reason, it is unnecessary that the courts, in proceedings on the annulment of an arbitral award, consider the substance of reasons given for the nullity of the arbitration agreement (unless this defence has been invoked in the arbitration proceedings themselves)[17].

---

[13] In proceedings on the annulment of the arbitral award.

[14] The appeal on questions of law was filed, and admitted by the Czech Supreme Court, on grounds of *an incorrect assessment of the matter* (i.e., here, in the sense of an incorrect assessment of the reasons for annulment of the arbitral award). In this particular case, the Czech Supreme Court classified the incorrect assessment of the matter as (citing from the reasons of the judgment) *error of the court in applying the law to the ascertained facts of the case. An erroneous application of law is present if the court applied a law or legal regulation other than that which should have been properly applied, or if the court applied the proper law or legal regulation but interpreted it wrongly.*

[15] The appellant objected that the arbitration agreement was invalid in that it had been drawn up in print in an excessively tiny font. In terms of their defense in the arbitration proceedings proper, they had merely referred to the payments which they had made to honour their contractual obligation. At the same time, the appellant stated, without being more specific, that (citing from the reasons of the Supreme Court judgment), *the courts in the Czech Republic rule on anything and everything.* The Hradec Králové Regional Court [CZE] as the second-instance court (court of appeals) found that the arbitration agreement cannot be considered null and void merely because it was hard to scrutinize due to its tiny font. It also stated that drawing up an arbitration agreement with this design is not *contra bonos mores.*

[16] It cannot be ruled out that this postulate will in the near future undergo changes with respect to what is known as consumer contracts. This is because the amendment of the arbitration act which is currently being prepared envisions more stringent conditions for arbitration agreements and for arbitration in the case of disputes as arise from consumer contracts, primarily because of the need to reflect the judicature of the European Court of Justice.

[17] Another issue addressed in the ruling on the merits was that of the timeliness of the action for annulment of the arbitral award (it had been filed after the expiry of the three-month statutory period). The matter was of a specific nature, however, in the sense that the arbitration court decided in a supplementary award on a part of the claim for relief sought which had not been reflected in the original award. That being said, the reasons for this judgment by the Czech Supreme Court offer little room for an assessment of this particular issue (and of how it was handled by the first-instance and second-instance court).

15.09. If the appellant (claimant) is served a resolution by the arbitrator in line with the arbitration clause according to which the former is to take position within a time period of five days or else it will be assumed that they recognized the claim raised in arbitration, then this constitutes sufficient opportunity to be heard, i.e., to make representations regarding the matter in arbitration[18].

15.10. The purpose of arbitration is to transfer the authority to hear and decide certain disputes from the general courts (within whose scope of jurisdiction such matters would otherwise fall) to the arbitrator in their capacity as a private individual. In proceedings on the annulment of an arbitral award, it is therefore not possible to review the substantial correctness of the arbitral award. This also applies with respect to the issue of whether the performances imposed in the arbitral award are in conflict with good morals[19]. Claiming that the performance imposed in the arbitral award was *contra bonos mores* is therefore no reason for annulling an arbitral award on grounds of a legally impossible or inadmissible performance[20].

| | |

The judgments of the first-instance and the second-instance court in the matter have not been published, so we can only rely on the (Supreme Court's) judgment on the appeal on questions of law, in which, as has been stated above, the issue of timeliness of the action for annulment of the arbitral award is mentioned *as an aside*.

[18] The Czech Supreme Court endorsed the findings of the first-instance and the second-instance court.

Act on arbitration and on the enforcement of arbitral awards: Sec. 31 (f) (in informal translation, cit.) *Based on the application of any party, the court shall set aside the arbitral award if* [...] e) *the party was not provided the possibility to be heard by the arbitrators.* On an analogical issue involving judicial proceedings see e.g. Hynek Bulín, *Odnětí možnosti jednat před soudem jako důvod dovolání (K výkladu paragrafu 237 písm. f/ OSŘ* [CZ]) [*Denial of Possibility to Act by the Court On Appeal (On the Interpretation of Section 237 (f) OSŘ* [CZ])], (10) Právní Praxe 622 ff. (1995).

[19] Here the Czech Supreme Court invoked an earlier Supreme Court judgment, 33 Cdo 2675/2007 of October 30. 2009, published in the Collection of Court Decisions and Opinions [CZE], ref. No. 52/2010 (2010).

[20] Act on arbitration and on the enforcement of arbitral awards: Sec. 31 (f) (in informal translation, cit.) *Based on the application of any party, the court shall set aside the arbitral award if* [...] f) *the arbitral award requires the party to satisfy an impossible obligation or an obligation not requested by the claimant or inadmissible pursuant to domestic law,* [...].

IV. Formal Requirements for Arbitration Agreements (Arbitration Clauses); Waiver of the Written Form; Consumer Protection under Special Law, as Opposed to under the Act on Arbitration (Czech Supreme Court; June 29, 2010)

Key words:
arbitration clause | written form | offer to contract | consumer protection | conflict with consumer protection laws | adhesive contract | arbitration agreement | consumer contract | brokerage contract | consent with the arbitration clause | average consumer | contractual structure | conclusion of the arbitration agreement

Judgment 23 Cdo 1201/2009 of the Czech Supreme Court[21] **of June 29, 2010:**[22]

Laws Taken into Account in This Ruling:
➢ Act No. 40/1964 Coll., as amended, the Civil Code: Sec. 34[23], Sec. 55 (1)[24], Sec. 56 (1)[25].

---

[21] In proceedings on the appeal on questions of law (as extraordinary remedy) against resolution 21 Co 245/2008-86 of the Prague Municipal Court of November 11, 2008 (as the second-instance court). These were proceedings on the annulment of the arbitral award on which the Prague 4 Municipal District Court had decided by way of judgment 43 C 48/2006.

[22] Available on the portal of the Czech Supreme Court at: http://www.nsoud.cz/JudikaturaNS_new/judikatura_prevedena2.nsf/WebSearch//1A/DDD7C6E4054CC12 57761003CDF9F?openDocument (accessed on October 9, 2010).

[23] Sec. 34 of act No. 40/1964 Coll., as amended, the Civil Code (cit.) Sec. 34 – *A legal act is a declaration of will aimed at, in particular, the inception, amendment, or expiry of those rights or obligations which are vested in such a declaration by law.*

[24] Sec. 55 of act No. 40/1964 Coll., as amended, the Civil Code (cit.) Sec. 55 – (1) *Terms of consumer contracts must not deviate from the act to the detriment of the consumer. In particular, consumers cannot waive their rights awarded to them by the act or otherwise worsen their contractual position. (2) The terms of consumer contracts mentioned in Sec. 56 shall be considered valid unless the consumer challenges their validity (Sec. 40a). However, if such term directly influences also other terms of the contract, then the consumer may invoke the invalidity of the agreement as a whole. (3) In case of doubts about the meaning of consumer contracts, that interpretation which is more advantageous for the consumer shall apply.*

[25] Sec. 56 of act No. 40/1964 Coll., as amended, the Civil Code (cit.) Sec. 56 – (1) *Consumer contracts must not contain terms that are at variance with the requirement of good faith and mean a considerable inequality in rights and duties of the parties to the detriment of the consumer. (2) The provision of paragraph 1 shall not apply to the terms that define the subject of the performance of the agreement or its price. (3) In particular, the following terms shall be inadmissible: a) terms that exclude or restrict the supplier's liability for acts or omissions resulting in the consumer's death or injury; b) terms that exclude or restrict the consumer's rights in asserting the liability for defects*

> ➤ Act No. 216/1994 Coll., as amended, on Arbitration and on the Enforcement of Arbitral Awards: Sec 3[26].

15.11. If, in proceedings on the annulment of an arbitral award, a court finds that the relation between the parties constitutes a consumer contract, then the court must base its findings regarding the purported conflict with consumer protection laws (and the ensuing nullity of the arbitration clause) on an application of these very laws on the protection of consumers (i.e., in the present case, on Sec. 55 (1) and Sec. 56 (1) of the Civil Code), as opposed to the general requirements for arbitration agreements pursuant to Sec. 3 (2) of act No. 216/1994 Coll. [CZE] / [of the Czech Republic], on arbitration and on the enforcement of arbitral awards, as amended.

15.12. The Czech Act on arbitration and on the enforcement of arbitral awards (Sec. 3 (2) of act No. 216/2004 Coll.)[27] does not condition the effective conclusion of an arbitration agreement with the requirement that the agreement which contains, *inter alia*, the arbitration clause must in a qualified manner make manifest that the parties consented to the arbitral

---

or the liability for damages; c) terms that stipulate that the contract shall be binding for the consumer whilst the supplier's performance is linked to fulfillment of a condition whose realization depends exclusively on the supplier's will; d) terms that allow the supplier not to surrender to the consumer performances previously provided by them even if the consumer does not conclude the contract with the supplier or if they withdraw from it; e) terms that entitle the supplier to withdraw from the contract without any contractual or legal reason, without entitling the consumer to do the same; f) terms that entitle the supplier to terminate a contract that was concluded for an infinite period of time without adequate period of notice, without having reasons worthy of special consideration; g) terms that oblige the consumer to fulfill conditions with which they were unable to acquaint themselves before the conclusion of the contract; h) terms that allow the supplier to change the terms of contract unilaterally without contractually agreed reason; i) terms stipulating that the price of goods or services shall be specified at the moment of their performance or that entitle the supplier to increase the price of goods or services, unless the consumer is entitled to withdraw from the contract if the price previously agreed at the moment of conclusion of the contract is being substantially exceeded at the moment of the performance; j) terms that bind the consumer to fulfill all their obligations even if the supplier has not fulfilled the obligations already arisen to it; k) terms that allow the supplier to assign the rights and duties from the contract without the consumer's consent if the assignment results in a worsening of the enforceability or security of the consumer's claim.

[26] Act No. 216/1994 Coll. of Laws, as amended, on Arbitration and on Enforcement of Arbitral Awards (cit.) Section 3 – (1) *The arbitration clause shall be void unless concluded in writing. The writing may be in the form of a telegram, telex, or other electronic means that allow for the determination of the arbitration clause's content and the identity of the parties to the arbitration clause. (2) However, if the validity of the main contract, of which the arbitration clause is a part, depends upon the validity of the arbitration clause, the arbitration clause shall be held valid if the party challenging the validity of the arbitration clause consented to the main contract in such a way that consent to the arbitration clause resulted from consent to the main contract.*

[27] (Cit.) Sec. 3 – [...] *(2) However, if the validity of the main contract, of which the arbitration clause is a part, depends upon the validity of the arbitration clause, the arbitration clause shall be held valid if the party challenging the validity of the arbitration clause consented to the main contract in such a way that consent to the arbitration clause resulted from consent to the main contract.*

clause as well. It is perfectly sufficient that the arbitral clause be [simply] a part of the main agreement's contents.

15.13. The provision of Sec. 3 of act No. 216/1994 Coll., On Arbitration and on the Enforcement of Arbitral Awards as amended, merely stipulates the formal requirements for arbitration agreements.

15.14. In other words, **Sec. 3 of Act No. 216/1994 Coll., On Arbitration and on the Enforcement of Arbitral Awards, does not set forth any general requirements which would allow for the conclusion that the offer to contract (i.e., to enter into the arbitration clause) was accepted**[28]**, but, in the form of an exemption from the rule, sets out the conditions under which a written offer to contract (i.e., to conclude the main agreement which contains the arbitration clause) may be accepted by the other party in another manner than in writing** (i.e., the offer must be accepted in a form which makes their consent with the arbitration agreement manifest). If the arbitration agreement (or, as it were, the main agreement which contains, *inter alia*, an arbitral clause) was made in writing, then the requirement of the written form has been observed in the terms of Sec. 3 (1) of the cited act. There is therefore no reason to determine whether the prerequisites for an exemption from this rule (as set out in Sec. 3 (2) of the Arbitration Act) were met – much less to conclude the nullity of the arbitration clause on the basis of the latter-cited provision.

15.15. Finally, regarding the issue of whether the contract in question is an individually agreed agreement or a standard form (adhesive) contract, this must be answered based upon e.g. the scope, structure, and choice of font of the contract. Hallmark features of adhesive contracts are e.g. long and unwieldy texts in miniature, hard-to-decipher fonts, or even a mere reference to "general terms of business" (in the same kind of design)[29].

15.16. In circumstances where the arbitration clause is contained in the text as a separate (and, in fact, penultimate) provision, the first words of which ("*Any disputes*" [...]) are highlighted, whereas the immediately following item occupies a single line, followed by the space intended for the leasing customer's signature, there can be no doubt that the recipient of such an offer to contract (the accepting party) consented both to the main agreement and to the arbitration clause contained in the same. It is therefore beyond contention that the parties executed the agreement[30]. In this situation, the claimant (*the party interested in the leasing services*) had to know that they were also entering into an arbitration agreement

---

[28] In this respect, the court of appeals (i.e., the Municipal Court as the second-instance court) erred, in the opinion of the Czech Supreme Court.

[29] In this respect, the Czech Supreme Court also did not endorse the finding of the second-instance court that the agreement was a standard form contract, or adhesive contract, of the type made from time to time between *a commercial entity* and a [final] *consumer*.

[30] In this respect, the Czech Supreme Court referred to the findings made by the same court in resolution 23 Cdo 4895/2009 of April 28, 2010.

(clause); this conclusion must be reached also from the vantage point of what is known as the *average consumer*[31]. Consumer protection has its limits and may in no way be understood to be a defence for frivolous and irresponsible conduct[32]. The argument does therefore not hold that the arbitration clause was placed in the contract without any label or highlight among the contractual provisions in general, and that the contracting party's attention was not drawn to the provision, not even orally.

15.17. The conclusion of whether there existed, on the part of one party, the will to engage in a certain legal transaction (i.e., whether it wished to make a declaration leading to the inception, amendment, or expiry of rights and obligations as vested in such a declaration by law)[33] is a finding *of facts*. In the event that the document which records the declaration of will in and by itself were not sufficient to allow the conclusion that the text contained therein indeed expressed the party's will, one would have to determine the circumstances under which the contract was made or, as applicable and appropriate, the subsequent behaviour of the parties, or such other facts as needed to derive this (or another) conclusion regarding the party's will or, as may be necessary (upon hearing the submitted decisive evidence), arrive at a substantiated conclusion that the burden of proof was not borne. Barring qualified proof to the contrary, the signature on a deed which contains an arbitration agreement means that there exists consent with the arbitration agreement. Therefore, one cannot conclude contrariwise that the arbitration clause was null and void in that it was not executed in a special, qualified manner – after all, the law's only and exclusive requirement is that of the written form[34].

15.18. Upon finding that the brokerage contract that was made between the parties was a consumer contract, the second-instance court (i.e., the court of appeals, i.e., here, the Prague Municipal Court) interpreted Sec. 3 (2) of the act on arbitration [CZE] in a general manner, such that the cited provision calls for a manner of acceptance of the arbitration clause which makes manifest that the other party knew it was entering into an arbitration agreement, and expressed its consent with the same. Upon assessing the matter in line with this provision, the second-instance court held that the requirements for the conclusion of an arbitration

---

[31] The Czech Supreme Court held that this conclusion was all the more pertinent in this case, in which the pertinent party (i.e., the party which received the offer to contract / the *prospective customer*) was a college-educated individual.

[32] With respect to this finding, the Czech Supreme Court referred to another authority, namely, the published commentary on the Civil Code – I JIŘÍ ŠVESTKA, J. SPÁČIL, M. ŠKÁROVÁ, M. HULMÁK ET AL., OBČANSKÝ ZÁKONÍK: KOMENTÁŘ *(Civil Code: Commentary, Vol. I)*, Praha: C. H. Beck 408 (2008).

[33] The provision is cited earlier above in the footnotes to this annotation of the court decision.

[34] As we can see, even in this aspect the Supreme Court was unwilling to endorse the finding of the court of appeals (the Prague Supreme Court as the second-instance court).

agreement (as set out in that provision) were not fulfilled, in that the fact of the claimant's signature on the brokerage contract did not in and by itself allow to assume its consent with the contents of the arbitration agreement. In other words, according to the court of appeals (second-instance court), the signature does not without further allow the conclusion that the claimant knew (had to know) that it entered into such an arbitration clause, and that by signing the agreement, it expressed its consent. The subject matter of the review on questions of law before the Czech Supreme Court was thus limited exclusively to a review of whether this assessment was correct (as opposed to other issues to which the court of appeals (second-instance court) took no recourse in substantiating its decision). The Supreme Court found that the said interpretation of Sec. 3 (2) of Act No. 216/1994 **was incorrect** and that the court of appeals thereby misapplied the law, which is why its decision had to be quashed. In reaching this finding, the Supreme Court did not rule out, however, that consumer protection law may have other demands with respect to the conclusion of the arbitration agreement or, as it were, the validity of an arbitration clause that is incorporated in the main agreement. However, the court would have to so adjudicate based on the interpretation and application of consumer protection laws (in particular, the Civil Code), as opposed to a mere interpretation and application of the general legal framework for arbitration in the Czech Republic, in that the latter contain no such requirement of qualified consent with the arbitration clause contained in the main agreement.

15.19. In interpreting Sec. 3 of Act No. 216/1994 Coll., On Arbitration and on the Enforcement of Arbitral Awards, as amended[35], the Supreme Court found that the purpose of this provision is **solely and exclusively the definition of formal requirements for arbitration agreements**. The arbitration agreement must on pain of nullity be in writing. The written form is observed even if the arbitration agreement is made telegraphically, via teletype, or using electronic means, as long as these allow the recording of the contents of the agreement and the determination of the identity of those who entered into the arbitration agreement[36]. If the arbitration clause forms a part of the terms by which the main agreement (to which the arbitration clause refers) is governed, then the arbitration clause is made validly also if the written offer to enter into the main agreement (along with the arbitration clause) was accepted by the other party in a manner which indicates their consent with the arbitration agreement[37].

---

[35] This provision of the act on arbitration and the enforcement of arbitral awards was in unaltered form in force also at the time at which the arbitral clause under scrutiny (or, as it were, the brokerage contract which contained the arbitral clause) was supposedly agreed between the parties.

[36] The Czech Supreme Court here cites Sec. 3 (1) of Act No. 216/1994 Coll., On Arbitration and the Enforcement of Arbitral Awards, as amended.

[37] The Czech Supreme Court here invokes Sec. 3 (2) of act [CZE] No. 216/1994, as amended, on Arbitration and the Enforcement of Arbitral Awards.

In other words, Sec. 3 (1) of the act on arbitration sets forth that the arbitration agreement must under pain of nullity be made in writing, and sets forth the technical means of communication which may be used to fulfil the requirement of the written form. The second sub-section of the cited provision then stipulates the prerequisites for an exemption from the requirement of the written form for the arbitration agreement, for those cases in which the arbitration agreement has been agreed within the context of the main agreement (i.e., those cases in which the arbitration agreement is an arbitration clause)[38]. For this reason, the Supreme Court quashed the decision of the court of appeals and returned the matter for a new hearing and decision.

| | |

V. Scope of the Arbitration Agreement in Terms of Substance and Interpretation of Same Pursuant to Substantive (Civil) Law; Unjust Enrichment as Subject Matter of Disputes in Arbitration (Arbitrability) (Czech Supreme Court; September 15, 2009)

Key words:
grammatical, logical, and systematic interpretation | verbal expression | verbal interpretation | unjust enrichment | contents of the deed | contents of the declaration of will | legal act | arbitration clause | arbitration agreement | loan agreement | systematic interpretation | rules of interpretation | collateral assignment of rights | suspension of court proceedings | prohibition of a review on the merits | annulment of the arbitral award

---

[38] At this point, the Czech Supreme Court refers to the following published works in its reasons for the judgment:
NADĚŽDA ROZEHNALOVÁ, ROZHODČÍ ŘÍZENÍ V MEZINÁRODNÍM A VNITROSTÁTNÍM OBCHODNÍM STYKU (*Arbitration in International and Domestic Commercial Relations*), Praha: ASPI Publishing 85 (2002), and ALEXANDER J. BĚLOHLÁVEK, ZÁKON O ROZHODČÍM ŘÍZENÍ A O VÝKONU ROZHODČÍCH NÁLEZŮ. KOMENTÁŘ (*Commentary on the Act on Arbitration and the Enforcement of Arbitral Awards*), Praha: C. H. Beck 48 (2004).

Judgment 33 Cdo 4731/2008 of the Czech Supreme Court[39] of September 15, 2010:[40]

Laws Taken into Account in This Ruling:
➢ Act [CZE] No. 40/1964 Coll., as amended, Civil Code: § 35 (2)[41].
➢ Act [CZE] No. 99/1963 Coll., as amended, Code of Civil Procedure: Sec. 106 (1)[42].
➢ Act [CZE] No. 216/1994 Coll., as amended, Act on Arbitration and on the Enforcement of Arbitral Awards.

---

[39] In proceedings on the appeal on questions of law (as extraordinary remedy). Prior to these proceedings on the appeal on questions of law before the Czech Supreme Court, the following courts decided in the matter:

➢ as the first-instance court: the Plzeň-město District Court, which decided to set aside proceedings pursuant to Sec. 106 (1) of the Code of Civil Procedure in 36 C 262/2007-22 of February 21, 2008.

➢ as the second-instance court (court of appeals): the Plzeň Regional Court, in its resolution 13 Co 178/2008-40 of June 27, 2008.

[40] Available in electronic form in the database of decisions on the website of the Czech Supreme Court at: http://www.nsoud.cz/JudikaturaNS_new/judikatura_prevedena2. nsf/WebSearch/04F15EC0A16387D4C12577AF002C5399?openDocument (accessed on October 9, 2010).

[41] Civil Code (cit.) Chapter Four – Legal Acts- Sec. 34 – *A legal act is a declaration of will aimed at, in particular, the inception, amendment, or expiry of those rights or obligations which are vested in such a declaration by law. – Sec. 35 – (1) The declaration of will may be done by acting or omitting; it may be done explicitly or in another way that does not cast doubts on what the participant wanted to express. (2) Legal acts expressed in words shall be interpreted not only according to their verbal expression but in particular also according to the will of the person who engaged in the legal act unless this will is at variance with the verbal expression. (3) Legal acts expressed other than in words shall be interpreted according to what the way of their expression usually means. In the course of this interpretation, it shall be necessary to take account of the will of the acting person and to protect the good faith of the person to whom the act was addressed. [...]*

[42] Code of Civil Procedure (cit.) Sec. 106 – (1) *The court, upon finding with respect to the respondent's objection (which must be raised no later than on occasion of its first act on the merits) that the matter must pursuant to the parties' agreement in arbitration proceedings, must not hear the matter further and shall set aside the proceedings; however, it shall hear the case if the parties declare that they no longer insist on honoring the agreement. The court shall also hear the matter if it finds that the matter is under Czech law unfit for being subject to arbitration, or that the arbitration agreement is invalid or, as the case may be, does not exist in the first place, or that hearing the case in arbitration would exceed the scope of powers awarded to the arbitrators in the agreement, or that the arbitrators refused to deal with the case. (2) If court proceedings were stayed pursuant to paragraph (1) and a motion for commencing arbitration proceedings in the same matter is filed, then the legal effects of the original motion are preserved if the motion for the commencement of arbitration proceedings is filed within 30 days from the day on which the court decision to stay proceedings was served. (3) If the arbitration proceedings were commenced before the court proceedings, then the court shall suspend its own proceedings in matters of the non-existence, invalidity, or expiry of the agreement until a decision has been made in arbitration on jurisdiction or on the merits.*

15.20. Pursuant to Sec. 35 (2) of the Civil Code, legal acts that are expressed verbally must be construed not only based on the verbal expression, but in particular pursuant to the will of the party who engaged in the legal act (unless the will were in conflict with the verbal expression). This rule also applies to the interpretation of arbitration agreements[43].

15.21. Sec. 35 (2) of the Civil Code anticipates that doubts may arise as to the contents of legal acts, and formulates rules of interpretation for this event which determine how the court must remove these doubts through interpretation. The verbal expression of legal acts as recorded in a contract must primarily be interpreted by means of grammatical, logical, and systematic interpretation. In addition, the court is to determine, based upon the evidence heard, the true will of the parties at the time at which they entered into the contract, whereas this will of the parties shall be taken into consideration only to the extent to which it is not in conflict with the verbal expression of the legal act. Pursuant to Sec. 35 (2) of the Civil Code, the interpretation of the substance of a legal act by the courts must not replace or change previously made declarations of will; the application of statutory rules of interpretation is solely to ensure that the contents of a verbally expressed legal act in which the parties concordantly engaged are construed in accordance with the state of affairs at the time of contracting. Where the contents of a legal act are recorded in writing, the determinateness of the expression of the parties' will is inherent in the contents of the deed in which it is recorded.

15.22. In the case under scrutiny here, the arbitration clause (of the same wording in both the loan agreement and the agreement on the collateral assignment of rights made on December 13, 2005) contained an understanding of the parties that [...]*any disputes, disagreements, or claims arising from or in connection with the loan agreement/agreement on the collateral assignment of rights as set out and described in this notarial deed, or from its violation, from the termination of its validity or operativeness, or from its invalidity or inoperativeness, shall be finally decided in arbitration in the terms of act No. 216/1994 Coll., on Arbitration and on the Enforcement of Arbitral Awards.* The interpretation of an arbitration clause with this wording allows for only one conclusion: that the parties expressed their **will to submit any disputes to arbitration** as might arise between them **in connection with the agreements made.** In other words, the arbitration clause **extended both to disputes arising directly from the agreements and to disputes which may merely be connected to the obligations established by the said agreements.** There can in this sense be no doubt that **a dispute concerning the surrender of unjust enrichment in the amount of the difference between the purchase price generated by**

---

[43] It is obvious that the Czech Supreme Court favoured the view – long held by the author of this annotation, for that matter – that the arbitration agreement must at the very least be subjected to an application of the general institutions of substantive law with respect to legal acts.

the respondent when it implemented the collateral assignment of rights and the total amount owed to the respondent by the claimant is also connected to the loan agreement and to the agreement on the collateral assignment of rights.

15.23. Action had been filed on the merits of the case in [a general] court, in spite of the fact that the agreement (here: several agreements) contained an arbitration clause. The respondent made timely use of the defence of lack of jurisdiction of the [general] court, and the court acceded to this objection and set the proceedings aside. The second-instance court (and, with reference to its decision and with respect to the appeal on questions of law (as extraordinary remedy), the Czech Supreme Court) assessed (the merits of) the question of whether the first-instance court had not erred when it set aside the proceedings. In this respect, it also engaged in an interpretation of the arbitration agreement as a legal act. In their legal opinion, the second-instance court (court of appeals) and subsequently the Supreme Court upheld a broad interpretation of the scope of the arbitration agreement in terms of substance, insofar as the expression "disputes arising from or in connection with the agreement/contract" is concerned. Both courts subsumed claims for surrender of unjust enrichment in connection with the legal relation established by such agreements under this expression.

15.24. The above findings were originally made by the court of appeals (second-instance court). The Czech Supreme Court in due course fully endorsed them and dismissed the appeal on questions of law (as extraordinary remedy).

| | |

VI. Arbitral Award Issued in Matters of a Consumer Dispute and Its Assessment in Enforcement Proceedings
(Plzeň-město District Court; November 22, 2010)

Key words:
arbitration clause | offer to contract | arbitration agreement, offer of | court jurisdiction, lack thereof | arbitration clause, validity thereof | arbitration agreement, validity thereof | obstacle to proceedings, in a general court | leasing contract | arbitration agreement | consumer contract | enforcement proceeding | arbitral award

Resolution 73 Nc 671/2009 of the Plzeň-město District Court [...][44] of November 22, 2010:[45]

15.25. The court which decides on a motion for suspension of the enforcement (of a decision) may not review whether the performance imposed by the arbitrator conforms to good morals. The role of the court in enforcement proceedings is not to adjudicate in contentious proceedings (i.e., it does not find itself in the trial stage of proceedings), but merely to enforce what has already been adjudicated.

15.26. It is not proper to deduce from (the not directly applicable) Council Directive 93/13/EEC "alone" that the arbitrator should *not have* the authority to decide disputes from consumer contracts (and thus also from contracts between a commercial entity who offers credit and a private individual (other than an entrepreneur)).

15.27. Under Czech law, the defence of nullity of the arbitral award may only be invoked in *specific proceedings* pursuant to Sec. 31 et seq. of act No. 216/1994 Sb., as amended, i.e., the act on arbitration and on the enforcement of arbitral awards, but not within enforcement proceedings (i.e., the compulsory enforcement of a decision).

| | |

---

[44] In proceedings on the appeal on questions of law against resolution 20 Co 284/2009-32 of the Prague Municipal Court of August 4, 2009.

[45] Borrowed from: Karel Svoboda, *Pohled české soudní praxe na rozhodčí nález týkající se práv ze spotřebitelské smlouvy (The view taken by Czech judicial practice of arbitral awards concerning rights from consumer contracts)*, 19 (11) Obchodní Právo 2-7, 2-3 (2010).

VII. Prohibition of Judicial Review of the Substance of Arbitral Awards; Inadmissibility of Annulment of Arbitral Awards on Grounds of a Conflict with Good Morals (Czech Supreme Court; October 30, 2009)

Key words:
good morals | nature of arbitration | legal assessment | review of factual correctness | factual correctness | annulment of arbitral award

Laws Taken into Account in This Ruling:
➢ Act [CZE] No. 40/1964 Coll., as amended, the Civil Code: Sec. 3 (1)[46]
➢ Act [CZE] No. 99/1963 Sb., as amended, the Code of Civil Procedure
➢ Act [CZE] No. 216/1994 Sb., as amended, Act on Arbitration and on the Enforcement of Arbitral Awards: Sec. 31.

Judgment 33 Cdo 2675/2007 of the Czech Supreme Court[47] of October 30, 2009:[48]

15.28. Taking as our point of departure the nature of arbitration, the purpose of which is the transfer of jurisdiction for hearing and deciding a certain category of disputes from the general courts to the arbitration court, and the reasons for which arbitration awards may be set aside, we may deduce that the intention of the lawmaker was to rule out any judicial review of the factual correctness of the arbitral award. This means that the facts of the case as ascertained in arbitration proceedings and the legal assessment of the case are removed from such review. If courts were authorized, in

---

[46] Civil Code (cit.) Sec. 3 – (1) *The exercise of rights and duties as ensue from civil-law relationships must not groundlessly infringe upon rights and legitimate interests of others and must not be at variance with good morals.* (2) *Individuals and legal entities, state authorities and authorities of territorial self-governance shall see to it that rights from civil-law relationships are not jeopardized or violated, and that potential disputes between the participants are settled primarily by way of amicable agreement.*

[47] In proceedings on the appeal on questions of law (as extraordinary remedy). Prior to the proceedings on the appeal on questions of law before the Czech Supreme Court, the following courts decided on the matter:
 ➢ as the first-instance court: the District Court in České Budějovice, which decided by way of judgment of April 12, 2006, to dismiss the action from annulment of the arbitral award.
 ➢ as the second-instance court (court of appeals): the Regional Court in České Budějovice, which changed the decision of the first-instance court, and changed the arbitral award by way of its decision of February 22, 2007.
The Supreme Court then dismissed the legal opinion of the court of appeals, quashed its decision, and confirmed the legal opinion of the first-instance court.

[48] Borrowed, including the legal proposition, from: Martin Soukup, *"Zrušení rozhodčího nálezu. Rozsudek Nejvyššího soudu České republiky ze dne 30. října 2009, sp. zn. 33 Cdo 2675"* (*"Annulment of an Arbitral Award. Judgment of the Supreme Court of the Czech Republic as of 30 October 2009, docket 33 Cdo 2675/2007"*), 18 (3) Právní Rádce 52-54 (2010).

proceedings on the annulment of arbitral awards, to review the merits of the award, then the entire legal framework which governs arbitration proceedings would cease to make sense[49].

15.29. An arbitral award cannot be set aside by invoking Sec. 3 (1) of the Civil Code, arguing that enforcing the right to performances awarded therein was (with a view to the specific circumstances of the matter) in conflict with good morals and as such inadmissible under domestic law.

| | |

VIII. Court Is Bound by Decision on the Arbitrators' Lack of Jurisdiction Served by Arbitration Panel; Decision-Making by Way of a Jurisdictional Decision; Status of the Arbitration Court Attached to the Economic Chamber of the Czech Republic and to the Agricultural Chamber of the Czech Republic.
(Czech Supreme Court; February 25, 2010)

Key words:
state property | seat of arbitration | jurisdictional challenge | denial of jurisdiction | legal entity | jurisdiction of arbitration court | res iudicata | arbitration court | jurisdictional decision | decision on the merits | resolution | order on jurisdiction | binding power of arbitrators' decision on jurisdiction for the courts | public authority | public powers | annulment of the arbitral award

Laws Taken into Account in This Ruling:
➢ Act [CZE] No. 40/1964 Coll., as amended, the Civil Code: Sec. 18 (1) (d)[50].
➢ Act [CZE] No. 99/1963 Coll., as amended, the Code of Civil Procedure: Sec. 19[51].
➢ Act [CZE] No. 216/1994 Coll., as amended, Act on Arbitration and on

---

[49] It is obvious that the Czech Supreme Court favoured the view – long held by the author of this annotation, for that matter – that the arbitration agreement must at the very least be subjected to an application of the general institutions of substantive law with respect to legal acts.

[50] Civil Code (cit.) TITLE TWO – Legal entities – Sec. 18 – (1) *Legal entities are also endowed with the capacity to have rights and duties.* (2) *Legal entities comprise* a) *associations of individuals or legal entities,* b) *purpose-made property associations,* c) *units of territorial self-governance,* d) *other entities which are defined as legal entities in a law.*

[51] Code of Civil Procedure (cit.) Sec. 19 – *The capacity to be a party in proceedings is limited to those who have the capacity to have rights and duties, and to those who are awarded the capacity to be a party in proceedings by the law.*

the Enforcement of Arbitral Awards: Sec. 13[52], Sec. 15 (1)[53], Sec. 31[54].

➢ Act [CZE] No. 219/2000 Coll., On the Property of the State and its Representation in Legal Relations[55].

Judgment 29 Cdo 1899/2008 of the Czech Supreme Court[56] of February 25, 2010:[57]

15.30. The Arbitration Court attached to the Economic Chamber of the Czech Republic and the Agricultural Chamber of the Czech Republic is a legal entity[58].

15.31. The court is bound by resolutions in which an arbitration court (arbitrator) decides that they lack jurisdiction (Sec. 15 (1) of act No.

[52] Act on arbitration and on the enforcement of arbitral awards [CZE] – Sec. 13 – (1) *Permanent Court of Arbitration may be established only in accordance with the law.* (2) *A permanent court of arbitration may issue their own charter and rules, which must be published in the Official Journal; these rules may determine the procedure for nomination of arbitrators, the number of arbitrators, and they can limit the pool of possible arbitrators to the list held by the permanent arbitral tribunal. The charter and rules may also provide the procedures for administering the permanent court of arbitration as well as other issues connected with the activities of the permanent court of arbitration and the arbitrators, including the rules concerning the costs of the arbitral proceedings and remuneration for arbitrators.* (3) *If the parties agreed on the jurisdiction of a specific permanent court of arbitration, and unless otherwise agreed in the arbitration clause, the parties shall submit to the rules in para. 2 valid at the time of commencement of the arbitral proceedings before the permanent court of arbitration.*

[53] Act on Arbitration and on the Enforcement of Arbitral Awards – Sec. 15 – (1) *Arbitrators are entitled to review their jurisdiction. If they reach the conclusion that they lack the jurisdiction pursuant to the arbitration clause submitted to them, they shall so decide in the form of a decision.* (2) *The objection of lack of jurisdiction based on non-existence, invalidity, or termination of the arbitration clause, unless the invalidity arises from the fact that it was impossible to conclude an arbitration clause in the matter, must be raised as a party's first act in the proceedings.*

[54] A provision cited elsewhere (see the footnotes to another annotated decision).

[55] This provision is merely cited here to provide for a comparison of the legal arrangement of status of the state's property to that of private-law subjects.

[56] In proceedings on the appeal on questions of law (as extraordinary remedy). Prior to the proceedings on the appeal on questions of law before the Supreme Court, the following courts decided on the matter:

➢ as the first-instance court: the Prague 1 Municipal District Court, which dismissed, per judgment 13 C 289/2005-84 of March 15, 2007, the action for annulment of the resolution of the arbitration court in which the latter had denied its own jurisdiction.

➢ as the second-instance court (court of appeals): the Prague Municipal Court which in its judgment 69 Co 340/2007-121 of October 19, 2007, confirmed the decision of the first-instance court.

[57] Borrowed, incl. the legal proposition, from Luděk Lisse, *Nejvyšší soud České republiky: Právní postavení Rozhodčího soudu při Hospodářské komoře ČR a Agrární komoře ČR a vázanost soudu jeho usnesením o nedostatku pravomoci (Supreme Court of the Czech Republic: Legal status of the Arbitration Court Attached to the Economic Chamber of the Czech Republic and Agricultural Chamber of the Czech Republic)*, 2 (11) OBCHODNĚPRÁVNÍ REVUE 329-333 (2010).

[58] It is obvious that the Czech Supreme Court favored the view – long held by the author of this annotation, for that matter – that the arbitration agreement must at the

216/1994 Coll., on arbitration and on the enforcement of arbitral awards).

15.32. (General) courts are endowed with the authority to decide motions for the annulment of arbitral awards, but not resolutions by way of which arbitrators (an arbitration court) decide on their jurisdiction.

15.33. This decision expresses two significant legal propositions brought forward by the Czech Supreme Court – the first of which concerns the legal personhood of the Arbitration Court attached to the Economic Chamber of the Czech Republic and the Agricultural Chamber of the Czech Republic, and the second of which concerns the impossibility to set aside the resolution issued by the arbitration tribunal in the same way in which arbitral awards may (for exceptional reasons exhaustively listed in the law) be set aside pursuant to the Arbitration Act.

15.34. The Arbitration Court attached to the Economic Chamber of the Czech Republic and the Agricultural Chamber of the Czech Republic is one of three permanent arbitration courts in the Czech Republic which have been established by law in accordance with Sec. 13 of the act on arbitration proceedings. It is the largest of them, and annually hears around 3'000 cases (the *annual load of new cases*), and this number has throughout the years been substantially on the rise. However, until recently, it was assumed that this permanent arbitration court has no legal personhood of its own. After all, it was established as *attached to* the Economic Chamber of the Czech Republic and the Agricultural Chamber of the Czech Republic (as of January 1, 1995)[59]. While the Economic Chamber and the Agricultural Chamber are separate legal entities who enjoy their own legal personhood, the law does not expressly stipulate that the Arbitration Court under the *patronage* of these chambers qualifies as a legal entity. After all, under Czech law, legal entities come into existence by way of entry into a public register or record, or by force of law[60]. A loophole of sorts exists in connection with *entities* concerned with the

---

very least be subjected to an application of the general institutions of substantive law with respect to legal acts.

[59] Its engagement builds upon the body of work of the erstwhile Arbitration Court attached to the Czechoslovak Chamber of Commerce and Industry. While the former is not the *legal successor* of the latter, a law was promulgated to preserve the validity of arbitration clauses which were previously (i.e., prior to 1995) agreed for the benefit of the Arbitration Court attached to the Czechoslovak Chamber of Commerce and Industry. In the wake of the legislative change in the Czech Republic, these arbitration clauses are now considered arbitration clauses made for the benefit of Arbitration Court attached to the Economic Chamber of the Czech Republic and the Agricultural Chamber of the Czech Republic. Given that more than 15 years have since passed, there are for all practical purposes no longer any cases in which such "inherited" arbitration clauses make a relevant appearance.

[60] At this point, the author of this annotation has intentionally decided to present a highly simplified interpretation. It can certainly not be the purpose of this *information* to engage in an in-depth interpretation of the Czech Republic's law concerning legal personhood.

administration of state property. However, the Economic Chamber and the Agricultural Chamber are both private-law entities and do not administer state property. The fact that the state has conferred the exercise of public authority in certain matters to the Economic Chamber and to the Agricultural Chamber does nothing to change this fact. But there are no public powers vested in the arbitration proceedings organized by the arbitration court – quite to the contrary, it is, and has always been, the strict interpretation by both the Constitutional Court and the Supreme Court that these proceedings are private-law proceedings. Legal practice has therefore been based on the view that the Arbitration Court attached to the Economic Chamber of the Czech Republic and the Agricultural Chamber of the Czech Republic is not an independent legal entity and does not have legal personhood. This view is shared by the author of this material; I fully agree with the critical views voiced in the publication from which the information on this decision was lifted[61]. The rationale for this view is (again highly simplifying the matter) that the said arbitration court is not a body of public authority, exercises no public powers, and administrates no state property. Nor does the law which created the arbitration court state expressly that the arbitration court was a *legal entity*. In the view of this author, this would be the minimum requirement before we are able to say that the arbitration court is a legal entity (with its own legal personhood) established by force of law. However, the Czech Supreme Court is of the opposite opinion. It reached this decision in connection with **awarding the status of a party to the proceedings to this arbitration court.** Such standing cannot be awarded to anyone who does not enjoy *legal personhood* (either as an individual – a natural person – or, as in this case, a legal person / *legal entity*). The conclusion is quite astonishing, and a matter of interest not least within the context of the discussions concerning the *status* of a number of arbitration courts and centres established abroad and likewise attached to institutions of a type similar to *economic chambers* (*chambers of commerce*).

15.35. Yet another opinion expressed in the said decision by the highest court in the land must be considered of fundamental impact: that according to which it is not admissible to apply the rules on the annulment of arbitral awards *per analogiam* also on decisions reached in the form of resolutions. In connection with this decision, we need to stress that in a number of countries which subscribe to continental legal culture, the issue of jurisdiction of arbitration courts is purely a procedural matter and as such does not qualify as an issue touching upon the merits, an issue of substantive law. Within the legal environment of those countries and their legal systems, it is therefore unusual (and in a number of cases utterly impossible) that the arbitrators decide on their jurisdiction in the form of the arbitral award. This is because in those countries, the decision on the jurisdiction represents a **procedural prerequisite for conducting**

---

[61]   Luděk Lisse, *supra* note 57.

proceedings, which is to be reviewed by the arbitrators (and, by analogy, the courts) always and in all stages of proceedings[62]. They must do so also at the moment in which the issue any decision on the merits. As a rule, it is not necessary that this issue is addressed explicitly or in any great detail in the arbitral award (and it usually never is in cases in which no jurisdictional challenge was raised in proceedings). Of course, this does nothing to change the fact that the defence of lack of jurisdiction must, under most legal systems in place in those countries and/or most rules of arbitration of the permanent arbitration courts, be invoked as one of the first procedural steps of the given party in the matter. This is because it is a principal requirement for jurisdiction to be existent throughout proceedings, i.e., also at the moment in which the arbitrators issue a decision on the merits. At the same time, if the arbitrators answer at any one point the issue of jurisdiction in the affirmative and thereupon proceed to hear the matter, such a jurisdictional decision is not *res iudicata* – precisely because the arbitrators are to review jurisdiction (being a procedural prerequisite) at any time during proceedings. In and by itself, the jurisdictional decision (whether affirmative or negative) therefore cannot be subject to judicial review (in the sense of the institution of a [motion for] annulment of the arbitral award. A review of jurisdiction may only become relevant in connection with a review of the decision on the merits in the form of an arbitral award. And yet, according to the doctrines in force in a number of the said countries, the issue of jurisdiction does not fall within the scope of the term *merits* (as in: the subject matter of proceedings). And where – in the case of international arbitration in such country (as the seat of arbitration) – foreign practice which is based on *common law* doctrine is being applied, according to which jurisdiction is usually an issue of substantive law, so that the decision on jurisdiction is made in an arbitral award, such an award does not constitute a *res iudicata* with respect to the issue of jurisdiction, and the issue of such a decision is not an obstacle to invoking the very same defence again in later proceedings on the annulment of the arbitral award which decide on the merits (or a part thereof) – provided that the relevant procedural prerequisites are met. The *merits* as the subject matter of proceedings are defined solely by the relief sought[63] (or, as the case may be, by the counterclaim).

---

[62] In this regard, there are of course differences to be found between individual legal systems. For instance, under Czech general procedural law (which, by extension, also applies to arbitration), it is indispensable that jurisdiction be given in each individual stage of proceedings, i.e., as of the moment in which proceedings are initiated until their completion. According to the general provisions of Polish law regarding (court) proceedings in civil matters (which constitute a general procedural doctrine), it is indispensable that jurisdiction exist as at the moment in which the proceedings are initiated. However, arbitrators (as well as courts) are in both countries obliged to determine the existence of jurisdiction at any point in the course of proceedings.

[63] It appears expedient to point out that the term *statement of claim* is equivalent to what in a number of countries is understood by the term *request for arbitration*. This is

They essentially are embodied by the rights (=claims) on which a decision is sought. Jurisdiction, which is exclusively understood to be a procedural matter and a *means* for enforcing the aforementioned claims, does not qualify as such *right* (=claim). Where the seat of arbitration is located in one of the countries which endorse such a doctrine (of jurisdiction being a merely procedural issue), it is entirely unnecessary that an arbitral award (e.g. in the form of an interim or partial award) be rendered solely on the issue of jurisdiction, because such a decision would not be recognized as an *award on the merits*, and the subject matter of such a decision is not a *res iudicata*. As a rule, issuing an arbitral award solely on the issue of jurisdiction means an entirely superfluous protraction of proceedings (due to the necessity to meet the pertinent formal requirements, depending on the specific country, and on the specific rules applicable on arbitration). On the contrary, it is entirely sufficient to render a decision in the form of a very simple *resolution*. In addition, in cases in which the arbitrators dismiss the jurisdictional challenge in the course of a hearing, they may do so simply by way of an oral resolution, which is recorded in the records (minutes) of the hearing that are to be drawn up during or after the same[64].

15.36. Within the context of the decision of the Supreme Court annotated herein, we need to mention at least one more thing. In the view of the author of this annotation, the Supreme Court [CZE] fails to sufficiently differentiate between **two different** types of resolution. **The first type** is a resolution which brings an end to arbitration proceedings (Sec. 23 (b) of the Arbitration Act)[65]. I.e., exactly the type of resolution which was issued by the arbitrators that has here come under the scrutiny of the Czech Supreme Court – a typical example being that of the arbitrators

---

because, as a rule, the statement of claim (= request) must contain a precise specification of all claims raised in proceedings, of all allegations of the parties, and of all evidence. Of course, this does not rule out that the parties may be required, depending on the specific progress of proceedings, to supplement further statements and evidence. Even so, the statement of claim must precisely specify all claims (= rights) which are raised in the proceedings and on which a decision is sought.

[64] Regarding this issue, see e.g. Alexander J. Bělohlávek, *Arbitration Agreement, MDR Clauses and Relation thereof to Nature of Jurisdictional Decisions on the Break of Legal Cultures, in* KSIĘGA PAMIĄTKOWA 60-LECIA SĄDU ARBITRAŻOWEGO PRZY KRAJOWEJ IZBIE GOSPODARCZEJ W WARSZAWIE (*Commemorative Book on the 60th Anniversary of the Arbitration Court Attached to the Polish Chamber of Commerce in Warszawa)*, WARSZAWA: SĄD ARBITRAŻOWY PRZY KRAJOWEJ IZBIE GOSPODARCZEJ W WARSZAWIE (*Arbitration Court Attached to the Polish Chamber of Commerce in Warsaw)*, Warszawa: Lexis Nexis Polska Sp. o. o. 411-437 (J. Okolski, A. Całus, M. Pazdan, S. Sołtysiński, T. Wardyński, S. Włodyka eds., 2010).

[65] Act on Arbitration and on the Enforcement of Arbitral Awards [CZE] – Sec. 23 – *The arbitral proceedings terminated by issue of* a) *an arbitral award; or* b) *a decision in the cases when an arbitral award is not issued; the decision must be signed, must include the reasoning, and must be delivered as an arbitral award; if the statement of claim filed with the permanent arbitral tribunal is revoked prior to the establishment of the tribunal or appointment of the arbitrator, the decision on termination of the proceedings is issued and signed by the chairman of the permanent arbitral tribunal.*

Czech (& Central European) Yearbook of Arbitration

accommodating the jurisdictional challenge (by stating that they have no jurisdiction to render a decision on the merits) and therefore setting aside the entire proceedings. Another typical example: the claimant withdraws their claim (maybe with the respondent's consent, depending on the stage and development of proceedings) for whatever reason. Yet another example would be the termination of proceedings due to a failure to pay the fee for arbitration. **The second type** of resolution is a decision on any procedural matter (of the kind which the arbitration senate may issue at any moment during proceedings). This type of *resolution* is not expressly addressed by the Arbitration Act (and the rules of procedure applicable before one permanent arbitration court or the other may modify this type of decision and, in particular, its designation and form), but, in analogy to court proceedings, the designation *"resolution"* is not uncommon. However, these are not *resolutions* which bring an end to proceedings (as in the first case). Of course, in this case, too, the resolution may be one on jurisdiction, but only if the arbitrators find that they do have jurisdiction and/or dismiss the defence of lack of jurisdiction (if raised by one of the parties). But if a motion for annulment cannot be used against a resolution in which the arbitrators deny their own jurisdiction and set the proceedings aside (i.e., a resolution *of the first type*) then this kind of motion also cannot be used to challenge a resolution in which the arbitrators affirm their own jurisdiction (i.e., the *second type of resolution*). It is true that in this *second case*, the jurisdictional challenge may (provided that the pertinent conditions are met) be used later in connection with proceedings on the annulment of an arbitral award (if one is later issued *on the merits*).

| | |

IX. Arbitration Clauses as a Part of General Terms and Conditions of Contract; Arbitration Agreements Causing the Absence of the Prerequisites for Proceedings before a General Court (Czech Supreme Court; April 28, 2010)

Key words:
arbitration clause | lack of court jurisdiction | validity of arbitration clause | validity of arbitration agreement | impediment of court proceedings | leasing agreement | arbitration agreement | general terms and conditions of contract | termination of proceedings

Resolution 23 Cdo 4895/2009 of the Czech Supreme Court (NS ČR)[66] **of April 28, 2010:**[67]

15.37. The provision on the termination of [court] proceedings on grounds of an impediment, consisting of the existence of an arbitration agreement, as set out in Section 106 (1) of the Code of Civil Procedure[68] is a special rule with relation to Section 104 (1) of the Code of Civil Procedure[69],

---

[66] In the proceedings on the second-instance appeal against resolution 20 Co 284/2009-32 by the Prague Municipal Court of August 4, 2009.

[67] Available on the portal of the Czech Supreme Court at: http://www.nsoud.cz/ JudikaturaNS_new/judikatura_prevedena2.nsf/WebSearch/EE8E41F66EFC8F6DC125 772000355CF9?openDocument (accessed on October 9, 2010).

[68] Czech Code of Civil Procedure (cit.) – Review of prerequisites for proceedings – [...] Sec. 106 – (1) As soon as the court determines, with respect to the objection made by the defendant and on occasion of its first step in proceedings in the matter itself, that the matter is to be heard in proceedings before arbiters as per the agreement of the parties, the court may not hear the matter further, but shall terminate the proceedings; it shall hear the matter, however, if the parties declare that they no longer insist on the agreement. The Court shall also hear the matter if it finds that the matter is not fit under Czech law to be the subject matter of an arbitration agreement, or if it finds that the arbitration agreement is invalid or does not in fact exist at all, or that the hearing of the matter in proceedings before the arbiters exceeds the competencies awarded to them in the agreement, or that the arbitration court refused to hear the matter. (2) If proceedings before a court were terminated pursuant to para. 1 and if a motion is filed in the same matter for initiating proceedings before arbiters, then the legal effects of the original motion remain preserved, provided that the motion for the initiation of proceedings before arbiters was filed within 30 days from the day on which the court resolution on the termination of proceedings was served. (3) If the proceedings before arbiters are commenced before court proceedings were opened, then the court shall stay the proceedings on the non-existence, invalidity, or expiry of the agreement, for as long until the arbitration proceedings decide on the jurisdiction or on the merits of the case.

[69] Czech Code of Civil Procedure (cit.) – Review of the prerequisites for proceedings – [...] Sec. 104 – (1) If the lack of prerequisites for proceedings cannot be remedied, then the court shall terminate the proceedings. If the matter does not fall within the scope of jurisdiction of the courts, or if another procedure has priority, then the court cedes the matter to the competent body after the resolution on the termination

which generally governs the termination of proceedings due to a lack of jurisdiction. A review of questions of law[70] aimed against the resolution of the court of appeals that confirmed the resolution of the first-instance court on the termination of proceedings in the terms of Section 104 (1) of the Code of Civil Procedure is permissible under Sec. 239 (2) (a) of the Code of Civil Procedure[71].

15.38. Pursuant to Sec. 3 (2) of [Czech] Act No. 216/2004 Coll.[72], On Arbitration Proceedings and the Enforcement of Arbitral Awards, as amended, an arbitration clause that forms a part of the general terms and conditions of contract by which the main agreement is governed (whereas the arbitration clause refers to the latter in turn) is valid (has been validly agreed) also in those cases in which the written draft of the main agreement with the arbitration clause was accepted by the other party in a manner which shows their consent with the contents of the arbitration agreement.

15.39. If the "main" agreement (here: the "*leasing agreement*") explicitly states that the terms and conditions of contract are attached to the agreement and if the parties signed them, then these terms and conditions form an integral part of the agreement. If the said terms and conditions contain an arbitration clause, and if both parties expressed their consent (by way of their signatures affixed to the said T&C), then the T&C were, as per the explicit understanding in the main agreement, an integral part of the agreement and the arbitration clause was as such contracted validly (even if no additional express consent with the arbitration agreement was given in the main agreement).

---

of proceedings has become final; the legal effects in connection with the filing of the lawsuit (of the motion for initiation of proceedings) remain preserved. (2) If the lack of prerequisites for proceedings can be remedied, then the court shall take appropriate steps and measures to achieve this. In this respect, the court may as a rule continue proceedings but must not decide on the merits of the case. If the attempts to remedy the lack of prerequisites for proceedings fail, then the proceedings shall be terminated. [...]

[70] Within the context of Czech civil procedure, the "*dovolání*" (i.e., an appeal limited to a judicial review of legal questions) is an extraordinary remedy. Civil proceedings before the courts principally have two instances. The judicial review of legal questions, which is an extraordinary remedy and opens the way to a notional, *hypothetical* third instance, is subject to strict statutory criteria.

[71] The NS (ČR) referred to its previous decisions, i.e., (●) 29 Odo 1051/2004 of April 28, 2005, published in: 37 COLLECTION OF COURT DECISIONS AND OPINIONS (2006), and (●) 23 Cdo 1164/2009 by the NS (ČR) of December 10, 2009, published on the web portal of the Czech Supreme Court, available at: http://www.nsoud.cz (accessed on October 9, 2010).

[72] (Cit.) Sec. 3 – [...] (2) *However, if the validity of the main contract, of which the arbitration clause is a part, depends upon the validity of the arbitration clause, the arbitration clause shall be held valid if the party challenging the validity of the arbitration clause consented to the main contract in such a way that consent to the arbitration clause resulted from consent to the main contract.*

15.40. Using an older designation for an arbitration court or an institution that keeps a list of arbitrators[73] does not render the arbitration clause null and void, even if the designation has been superseded by a newer name in the meantime. Of relevance is the unchanged identity of the given entity. A change of name of a given entity does not allow one to conclude that the understanding in the arbitration clause is indeterminate or inscrutable[74].

[*Alexander J. Bělohlávek*]

| | |

---

73 *Cf.* – as *appointing authority*.
74 In this respect, the Czech Supreme Court fully identified with, and endorsed, the legal opinion of the court of (second-instance) appeal.

3. Hungary

Alexander J. Bělohlávek

I. Assessment of Objective and Subjective Arbitrability Based on the Factual Nature of a Claim; Rights *In Rem* versus Contractual Obligations

Key words:
jurisdiction | rights in rem | contractual claims | contractual agreement | contractual obligation | contract for work | price of work | real estate | ownership | nature of claim | substance of the claim | arbitrability | arbitration clause | reject the complaint | actual state of affairs | facticity

Ruling of the Regional Court of Budapest Ref. No. 13.Gf.40.483/2007/7 delivered in 2008:[1]

Laws Taken into Account in This Ruling:
➤ Act No. LXXI of 1994 on Arbitration;
➤ Act No. LXVI of 1997 on the Organization of Courts.

Rationes Decidendi:
16.01. Decisive for determining whether an arbitration agreement applies to a dispute is the actual substance of the claim (*facticity*) and not the formulation of the text of the complaint.
16.02. If a claim is raised in respect of a right *in rem* (in this particular dispute in respect of the ownership of a share in real estate), which in this case would not be subject to an arbitration agreement, but in fact concerns a contractual obligation arising under a contract for work, which contains an arbitration clause, a [general/state] court dismisses the complaint and refers the parties to arbitration.

[Description of Facts and Legal Issues]
16.03. The claimant, the supplier of construction work (the construction of a building), did not receive the full payment of the purchase price. In response, he made a claim requesting its registration in the title certificate for the property (building) to the extent of the claimant's ownership corresponding to the unpaid portion of the agreed price for

---

[1] Source: (*Complex* legal information system) No. BDT 2008.1789; The ruling has been identified and summarized by Dr. Katalin Préda, Attorney, Budapest.

Czech (& Central European) Yearbook of Arbitration

the work. The first-instance court that examined the case rejected the complaint. A second-instance court, however, concluded that the court lacked jurisdiction over this matter because the claim originated under a contractual agreement, a contract for work, where an arbitration clause had been agreed for this type of claim.

| | |

II. A Ruling on the Authority of Arbitrators in the Sense of a Ruling of Procedural Nature against Which a Separate Request for the Annulment of an Arbitral Award Cannot Be Made; Public Policy Exclusively as a Qualified Violation of Fundamental Legal Principles

Key words:
award on jurisdiction | civil law | common law | partial arbitral award | nature of award on jurisdiction | investment securities | interim award | jurisdiction requirement | procedural award on jurisdiction | arbitration clause | decision on the merits | management of investment securities | public policy

Ruling of the Supreme Court of Hungary *(Magyar Köztársaság Legfelsőbb Bíróság)* **Ref. No. Gfv. XI.30.073/2006 delivered in 2007:**[2]

Laws Taken into Account in This Ruling:
➢ Act No. LXXI of 1994 on Arbitration.

Rationes Decidendi:

16.04. Not every violation of the law is a violation of public policy. A violation of public policy must be a considerable violation of a qualified degree that disrupts the fundamental principles of the Hungarian law.

16.05. The fact that a respondent does not oppose a ruling delivered in the course of arbitral proceedings, which concludes that the arbitration tribunal does not have a jurisdiction to resolve a dispute, does not deprive this party of the right to object a lack of jurisdiction in proceedings on the annulment of the arbitral award with regard to the merits of the case. In proceedings on a request to annul an arbitral award, the court examines the validity of the relevant arbitration clause from the position of an official authority.

---

[2] Source: (*Complex* legal information system) No. BH 2007.130. The ruling has been identified by Dr. Katalin Préda, Budapest, Hungary.

[Description of Facts and Legal Issues]

16.06. An agreement on the management of investment securities of the respondent included an arbitration clause. During the arbitral proceedings, the respondent challenged the jurisdiction of the arbitration tribunal. This challenge was dismissed, and the arbitration court delivered a ruling that confirmed its jurisdiction.

[Comment of the Author of the Annotation]

16.07. This ruling fully conforms to the concept of most countries that use a *civil law* system, where *jurisdiction is a purely procedural issue.* The jurisdiction requirement must be complied with throughout the entire proceedings[3]. The fact that arbitrators establish their jurisdiction and deliver a ruling to this effect in the course of proceedings does not necessarily *mean that the jurisdiction ruling is res iudicata.* For this reason, jurisdiction-related decisions are not made, save for exceptions, under interim or partial arbitral awards. As regards arbitration in Central and Eastern European countries, jurisdiction-related decisions are usually made under *a simple* procedural resolution, against which a demand for annulment by a court cannot be made in the same way as against an arbitral award[4]. Simply said, it can be concluded that verdicts of the *award on jurisdiction* type are not issued in these countries because their delivery would be contrary to the concept according to which an award only contains a decision on the merits of a case. In addition, a process in which an arbitral award includes a decision on jurisdiction is lengthy and often thwarts the advantage of arbitration consisting of its flexibility. Thus, an award on jurisdiction is usually delivered in a very informal manner after this issue is examined by arbitrators during the arbitral proceedings (usually as the first prejudicial condition). This approach, which differs from the practice applied in countries influenced by *common law*, stems from the fact that jurisdiction in such countries is (in most cases) an exclusively procedural issue.

| | |

---

[3] A certain exception is Poland, where, in accordance with the procedural rules applied in court litigation, jurisdiction must be determined at the time when proceedings are initiated (a complaint is filed). However, this has no effect on the process, which is the same as in the case of the ruling of the Hungarian Supreme Court referred to in this paper.

[4] An analogical decision conclusion is presented, for instance, in Ruling of the Supreme Court of the Czech Republic Ref. No. 29 Cdo 1899/2008 of 25 February 2010 annotated, *in* Luděk Lisse, *Nejvyšší Soud České Republiky: Právní postavení Rozhodčího soudu při Hospodářské Komoře ČR a Agrární Komoře ČR a vázanost soudu jeho usnesením o nedostatku pravomoci (Supreme Court of the Czech Republic: Legal Status of the Arbitration Court Attached to the Economic Chamber of the Czech Republic and the Agricultural Chamber of the Czech Republic)*, 2 (11) COMMERCIAL LAW REVUE 329-333 (2010), and in this Yearbook (CYArb).

III. Foreign Public Policy versus Domestic Public Policy and the Execution of Foreign Arbitral Awards

Key words:
Foreign arbitral award | foreign public policy | New York Convention | domestic arbitral award | domestic public policy | public policy in Hungary | enforcement | reciprocity

Ruling of the Supreme Court of Hungary (*Magyar Köztársaság Legfelsőbb Bíróság*) Ref. No. Ffv. XI.22.270/2006 delivered in 2007:[5]

Laws Taken into Account in This Ruling:
- ➢ Act No. XX of 1949 on the Constitution of Hungary: Article 57(1);
- ➢ Act No. LV of 1962 on Convention on the Enforcement of Foreign Arbitration Awards (New York Convention of 10 June 1958 on the Recognition and Enforcement of Foreign Arbitral Awards);
- ➢ Act No. LIII of 1994 on the Enforcement of Judgments;
- ➢ Act No. LXXI of 1994 on Arbitration.

Rationes Decidendi:
16.08. Foreign arbitral awards may be enforced as domestic arbitral awards based on the New York Convention.
16.09. The enforcement of foreign arbitral awards in accordance with the New York Convention is allowable even in cases where reciprocity does not apply.
16.10. A violation of a foreign public policy in arbitral proceedings conducted abroad has no effect on the enforceability of an arbitral award in Hungary unless the domestic public policy is violated at the same time (the public policy of Hungary).

| | |

---

[5] *Supra* note 2.

IV. Resignation of an Arbitrator

Key words:
agreement of the parties on course of action | resignation of arbitrator | continuation of proceedings | confirmation of resignation by court | confirmation of resignation by parties | delivery of an arbitral award | annulment of arbitral award

Ruling of the Supreme Court of Hungary *(Magyar Köztársaság Legfelsőbb Bíróság)* **Ref. No. Gfv. XI.30.066/2009 delivered in 2010:**[6]

Laws Taken into Account in This Ruling:
➢ Act No. LXXI of 1994 on Arbitration: Section 21, Section 22, Section 55(1)(d).

Rationes Decidendi:

16.11. An arbitrator can resign at any stage of arbitral proceedings. Arbitrators are not entitled to continue proceedings and to issue a decision in the merits if a member of the arbitration tribunal resigns[7] and the parties do not confirm the termination of such an arbitrator's office[8] or if, in the absence of an agreement, the termination of such an arbitrator's office is not confirmed by a court[9].

16.12. The delivery of an arbitral award by the remaining members of the arbitration tribunal without complying with the requirement set out in the previous paragraph constitutes grounds for annulling the arbitral award[10].

[Description of Facts and Legal Issues]

16.13. According to Section 21 of the Hungarian Arbitration Act, the office of an arbitrator may terminate, among others, by the arbitrator's resignation. Such a resignation, however, must be confirmed by an agreement of the parties or by a court if the parties fail to reach an agreement. In the case in question, one of the arbitrators resigned before the delivery of a decision in the merits. The reason, however, was not the arbitrator's incapacity or failure to meet certain conditions for fulfilling his duties. The parties failed to agree on the confirmation of his resignation. For this reason, the claimant asked a court to confirm the resignation.

| | |

---

[6]   Source: *(Complex* legal information system) No. BH 2010.96. The ruling has been identified by Dr. Katalin Préda, Budapest, Hungary.
[7]   See Section 21, para. 3 of the Arbitration Act.
[8]   The subject of this agreement between the parties is the acceptance or rejection of such an action of an arbitrator.
[9]   See Section 22 of the Arbitration Act.
[10]   See Section 55, para. 1, letter d) of the Arbitration Act.

V. The Legal Force of Arbitral Awards as a Basis for Applying the *Res Iudicata* Principle

Key words:
legal force of an arbitral award | res iudicata

Ruling of the Supreme Court of Hungary (*Magyar Köztársaság Legfelsőbb Bíróság*) Ref. No. Gfv. XI.30.075/2009 delivered in 2009:[11]

Laws Taken into Account in This Ruling:
➤ Act No. LXXI of 1994 on Arbitration.

Rationes Decidendi:
16.14. Awards rendered by arbitral tribunals have the same legal force as court judgments from both the material and procedural viewpoints.
16.15. Matters in respect of which an arbitral award has been delivered are subject to the principle of *res iudicata*. Once decided, a matter cannot be the subject of another complaint.

| | |

---

[11] Source: (*Complex* legal information system) No. EBH 2009.1969. The ruling has been identified Dr. Katalin Préda, Budapest, Hungary.

VI. Discontinuance of Court Litigation due to the Existence of a Valid Arbitration Agreement; Dismissal of Court Action in Respect of a Decision on the Merits

Key words:
dismissal of complaint by a court | legal issues | arbitration clause | main agreement | prohibition of court litigation in respect of a case

Ruling of the Supreme Court of Hungary (*Magyar Köztársaság Legfelsőbb Bíróság*) Ref. No. Gfv. XI.30.252/2007 delivered in 2009:[12]

Laws Taken into Account in This Ruling:
➤ Act No. LXXI of 1994 on Arbitration;
➤ Act No. III of 1952 on Civil Proceedings.

Rationes Decidendi:

16.16. A court without delay dismisses a request as soon as it ascertains that an agreement [*main agreement*] contains a valid arbitration clause.

16.17. A court does not have jurisdiction to settle any legal issues relating to such a legal relationship.

| | |

---

[12] Source: (*Complex* legal information system) No. 2009.186. The ruling has been identified by Dr. Katalin Préda, Budapest, Hungary.

VII. Right to Demand the Annulment of an Arbitral Award; Secondary Participation in Proceedings Is Not One of the Fundamental Rights Protected by the Constitution and No Right Exists to Such Participation That Could Be Claimed by Legal Means

Key words:
persons directly concerned | constitutionally guaranteed right | right to demand annulment | secondary participant | fundamental rights | annulment of arbitral award

Ruling of the Supreme Court of Hungary (*Magyar Köztársaság Legfelsőbb Bíróság*) Ref. No. Gfv. XI.30.003/2008 delivered in 2009:[13]

Laws Taken into Account in This Ruling:
➤ Act No. XX of 1949 on the Constitution of Hungary: Article 57(1);
➤ Act No. LIII of 1994 on the Enforcement of Judgments;
➤ Act No. LXXI of 1994 on Arbitration: Section 55(2)(b).

Rationes Decidendi:
16.18. Only parties and persons directly concerned by the arbitral award are eligible to demand the annulment of an arbitral award.
16.19. A demand for the annulment of an arbitral award cannot be made by a person that has requested participation in the relevant arbitral proceedings (for instance, as a secondary participant) if the person's request has been rejected.
16.20. The right to secondary participation in arbitral proceedings is not one of the constitutionally guaranteed fundamental rights that would have to be respected in every given case. Thus, a person who is not allowed to participate in arbitral proceedings as a secondary participant may not request participation by means of legal action (in this case, an action aimed at the annulment of an arbitral award).

| | |

---

[13] Source: (*Complex* legal information system) No. BH 2009.182. The ruling has been identified by Dr. Katalin Préda, Budapest, Hungary.

Czech (& Central European) Yearbook of Arbitration

VIII. Qualified Violation of Fundamental Rights as a Violation of Public Policy (Ordre Public); Parties to Proceedings on the Annulment of an Arbitral Award; Prohibition to Examine New Evidence in Annulment Proceedings

Key words:
evidence in annulment proceedings | new evidence | arbitral award | conflict with law | share sale and purchase agreement | parties to annulment proceedings | public policy | ordre public | interests protected by law | society interests | fundamental rights | annulment of arbitral award

Ruling of the Supreme Court of Hungary (*Magyar Köztársaság Legfelsőbb Bíróság***) Ref. No. (in two aggregated cases) Gfv. XI.30.016/2008 delivered in 2009.**[14]

Laws Taken into Account in This Ruling:
➤ Act No. XX of 1949 on the Constitution of Hungary: Article 57(1);
➤ Act No. LIII of 1994 on the Enforcement of Judgments;
➤ Act No. LXXI of 1994 on Arbitration: Section 3 to Section 5, Section 55(2)(b).

Rationes Decidendi:
16.21. It is not necessary that all the parties to arbitration take part in proceedings on the annulment of an arbitral award.
16.22. Proceedings on the annulment of an arbitral award may not include the examination of new evidence that has become available only after the delivery of the arbitral award.
16.23. An arbitral award that is contrary to the law does not automatically means a violation of public policy (ordre public). *Public policy is violated only by an arbitral award that violates fundamental rights or fundamental society interests protected by law.*
16.24. An arbitration clause agreed for rights set out in an agreement (in this case, a share sale and purchase agreement) also applies to disputes related to the termination of the agreement.

[Description of Facts and Legal Issues]
16.25. The parties entered into a share sale and purchase agreement. The main purpose was the buyer's intention to acquire machinery included in the company's property. The agreement was terminated by the claimant, and the respondent submitted the case to an arbitration tribunal. The

---

[14] Source: (*Complex* legal information system) No. BH 2009.57 and EBH 2008.1796. The ruling has been identified by Dr. Katalin Préda, Budapest, Hungary.

tribunal ruled in favour of the respondent. The claimant made a demand for the annulment of the arbitral award, arguing, among others, that the arbitration clause did not apply to the matter and that the proceedings were contrary to public policy. The court rejected the demand, and its verdict was upheld by the Supreme Court of Hungary.

| | |

IX. Right to Present a Case (Right to a Fair Trial); An Arbitral Award Must Be Based on the Facts and Legal Issues Examined in Arbitral Proceedings

Key words:
purchase price | purchase agreement | right of a party to present its case | facts of a case | purchase price payment terms | legal status | fair trial | deliberation of arbitration tribunal | annulment of arbitral award

Ruling of the Supreme Court of Hungary (*Magyar Köztársaság Legfelsőbb Bíróság*) Ref. No. Gfv. XI.30.520/2007 delivered in 2008:[15]

Laws Taken into Account in This Ruling:
➤ Act No. XX of 1949 on the Constitution of Hungary: Article 57(1);
➤ Act No. LIII of 1994 on the Enforcement of Judgments;
➤ Act No. LXXI of 1994 o Arbitration: Section 55(1)(c).

Rationes Decidendi:
16.26. An arbitral award may be annulled if an arbitration tribunal delivers a ruling on a factual or legal basis that was not included in the complaint in consequence of which a party is unable to present its arguments.

[Description of Facts and Legal Issues]
16.27. The parties entered into a purchase agreement. The structure of the purchase price to be paid was complicated, and the parties differed in their opinion on the amount of the purchase price and on the payment terms. In proceedings regarding the payment of the purchase price, the arbitration tribunal set the price based on its own estimate in favour of the respondents. The Supreme Court espoused the standpoint of the claimant who, at the same time, demanded the annulment of the arbitral award because the arbitration tribunal, in calculating the purchase price, discovered facts that had not been mentioned by either party. This

---

[15] Source: (*Complex* legal information system) No. EBH 2008.1794. The ruling has been identified by Dr. Katalin Préda, Budapest, Hungary.

way, its verdict was based on facts to which the parties were unable to respond. According to the Supreme Court, the arbitration tribunal should have invited the parties to present their claims in view of the new facts ascertained in connection with the calculation completed by the tribunal, and the arbitration tribunal should have rendered its award only after the parties responded to these facts.

[Comment of the Author of the Annotation]

16.28. The Supreme Court based its verdict on the fact that the case involved a violation of the right to a fair trial (it was not, therefore, an *ultra petita* decision) since the conclusion drawn by the arbitrators did not stem from the facts and legal issues ascertained during the proceedings. The reason was that the parties were unable to respond to arguments subsequently used by the arbitration tribunal in delivering a judgment on the merits.

| | |

X. The Extensive Leeway of Arbitrators for the Determination of the Margin of Freedom Given to Parties for Presenting Their Case (Fair Trial in Arbitral Proceedings); Jurisdiction regarding Claims Raised by Means of Setoff Objection

Key words:
setoff objection | right of a party to present its case | freedom to state one's position | fair trial | setoff | annulment of arbitral award

Ruling of the Supreme Court of Hungary (*Magyar Köztársaság Legfelsőbb Bíróság*) Ref. No. Gfv. XI. 30. 176/2007 delivered in 2007:[16]

Laws Taken into Account in This Ruling:
➢ Act No. XX of 1949 on the Constitution of Hungary: Article 57(1);
➢ Act No. LV of 1962 on the Convention on the Enforcement of Foreign Arbitral Awards (New York Convention of 10 June 1958 on the Recognition and Enforcement of Foreign Arbitral Awards);
➢ Act No. LIII of 1994 on the Enforcement of Judgments;
➢ Act No. LXXI of 1994 on Arbitration.

Rationes Decidendi:
16.29. Arbitrators have an extensive leeway in the determination of the margin of freedom given to parties for presenting their case.

---

[16] Source: (*Complex* legal information system) No. EBH 2007.1705. The ruling has been identified by Dr. Katalin Préda, Budapest, Hungary.

16.30. It is not a violation of the right of a party to present its case [and, consequently, the right to a fair trial in arbitral proceedings] if an arbitration tribunal does not provide a party with a time to respond to the last document submitted by the counterparty as part of the proceedings.

16.31. Arbitral tribunals have the jurisdiction to settle a claim raised as part of proceedings as a setoff objection even though the relevant arbitration clause does not expressly apply to it[17].

[Description of Facts and Legal Issues]

16.32. In this case, the Supreme Court dismissed a request demanding the annulment of an arbitral award based, among others, on a claim that the claimant was not given sufficient time for preparing a statement responding to the last document presented by the respondent during the proceedings.

[*Alexander J. Bělohlávek*]

| | |

---

[17] Although the Supreme Court did not make an explicit statement regarding this issue, claims raised this way must be arbitrable based on objective facts.

Czech (& Central European) Yearbook of Arbitration

4. Poland

Abbreviations used in annotations:

[k.c.]	Civil Code [POL]
[k.p.c.]	Code of Civil Procedure [POL]
[u.z.n.k.]	Act on Suppression of Unfair Competition [POL]
[LCIA]	London Court of International Arbitration

Alexander J. Bělohlávek & Tomáš Řezníček

I. The Possibility of Reaching a Settlement as a Condition of Arbitrability: Irrelevance whether the Subject of Dispute (Settlement) Is a Property or Non-Property Right

Key words:
arbitrability | disposal of rights | court-approved settlement | existence of a legal act | existence of a legal relationship | interim arbitral award | legal circumstances] | factual circumstances | validity of a legal act rules on social coexistence | rights which may be disposed of | property right | non-property right | subject to settlement | admissibility of a settlement | conflict with applicable law | particular settlement | mutual concession | action for enforcement | action for a declaration

Decision of the Supreme Court (*Sąd Najwyższy*) No II CSK 670/09 of 21 May 2010 (parties unknown):[1]

States involved:
[POL] - [Poland]. No link to another State identified in the available summary.

---

[1] Taken from the summary of the decision available at: http://arbitraz.laszczuk.pl/ orzecznictwo/337,postanowienie sadu najwyzszego z dnia 21 maja 2010 r ii csk 670 09.html (accessed on November 17, 2010). The text of the decision in Polish is also printed on the same page. The cited source comes from: Biuro Studiów i Analiz Sądu Najwyższego. This site is an Internet portal of a commercially active entity. It is against the policy of this periodical (CYArb) to refer to such websites and their owners. The authors and editors apologize for this to the owners and operators of the sites cited. Nevertheless, it is clear that the case law of Polish courts here is very well-prepared and up-to-date. Therefore, the authors and editors have used it as the basis for summaries of up-to-date Polish case law relating to arbitration, after verifying the original sources and after authorial and editorial processing.

Laws Taken into Account in This Ruling:

➤ Kodeks cywilny (*Civil Code*) [k.c.] [POL] - Ustawa z dnia 23 kwietnia 1964 r. (Law of 23 April 1964), published in: Dzienik Ustaw, 1964 Nr. 16, poz. 93): Art. 58, Art. 917;

➤ Kodeks postępowania cywilnego (*Code of Civil Procedure*) [k.p.c.] [POL] – Ustawa z dnia 17 listopada 1964 r. (Law of 17 November 1964), published in: Dzienik Ustaw, 1964 Nr. 43, poz. 296: Art. 1157.

Rationes Decidendi:

17.01. The wording "may be subject to settlement" applies to disputes on both property and non-property rights. It is common ground under doctrine and case-law that the parties may seek the award of certain enforcement, a declaration of the existence of a relationship or a right (a declaration of whether or not a right exists here) or the establishment of a particular legal relationship before an arbitral tribunal.

17.02. A grammatical interpretation of Article 1157 k.p.c. [POL][2] shows that, from the perspective of this legislation, it is of fundamental significance whether a dispute on a property or non-property right may be subject to settlement. By contrast, it is entirely irrelevant [...] whether or not the conclusion of a particular settlement (in terms of its content) would be admissible. [...] *The valid conclusion of a settlement is subject to a party's abstract capacity to dispose of its rights* (claims arising from them), rather than just to the possibility of concluding a particular settlement. In other words, it is immaterial whether, within the limits of specific [factual and to some extent legal] circumstances, the parties may conclude a settlement on particular enforcement (content) where such arrangements, from an abstract aspect, may include a legal relationship or rights which may be disposed of by the parties. The content of such arrangements may, in a particular case, be in conflict with applicable law or rules on social co-existence (Article 58, § 1 and 2, k.c. [POL])[3]. Any consideration of the arbitrability of a dispute cannot include an assessment of whether a specific settlement and its content would be inconsistent with the law and whether the precondition of "*mutual concessions*" within the meaning of Article 917 k.c. [POL][4] has been met.

---

[2] *Kodeks postępowania cywilnego* (Code of Civil Procedure) [POL] (Unofficial translation, cit.) Article 1157 *Unless otherwise provided by a special law, the parties may agree that property disputes or non-property disputes, in respect of the subject-matter of which they could reach a settlement, shall be resolved by an arbitral tribunal; this shall not apply to proceedings in matters of maintenance.*

[3] *Kodeks cywilny* (*Civil Code*) [POL] (unofficial translation, cit.) Article 58. § 1. An act in law which is inconsistent with statutory law or is designed to circumvent statutory law shall be null and void unless the appropriate provision envisages a different effect, in particular that those provisions of the act in law which are null and void are replaced by the appropriate provisions of statutory law. § 2. An act in law which is inconsistent with the principles of community life shall be null and void.

[4] *Kodeks cywilny* (*Civil Code*) [POL] (unofficial translation, cit.) *Article 917. By the settlement, the parties shall make mutual concessions within the scope of a legal*

17.03. The fact that a dispute concerns the question of the existence (absence), validity (invalidity), or other defect of a legal act has no effect on an assessment of arbitrability.

| | |

II. The Subject-Matter of an Arbitration Agreement and Arbitrability; A Legal Relationship versus a Claim

Key words:
arbitration agreement | arbitrability | objective arbitrability | disposal of rights | type of legal relationship | types of claims | settlement | settlement of dispute

Decision of the Supreme Court (*Sąd Najwyższy*) No. V CSK 439/09 of 18 June 2010:[5]

Rationes Decidendi:

17.04. The subject-matter of an arbitration agreement is legal relationships, not specific claims arising from such relationships. The possibility of subjecting a dispute to the jurisdiction of arbitrators is abstractly defined for legal relationships, not for the types of claims arising from such relationships (enforcement, a declaration of whether or not a legal relationship or right exists here). The [objective] arbitrability of a dispute depends on the type of legal relationship.

17.05. A precondition of [objective] arbitrability is the abstract possibility of the parties to the dispute to dispose of rights arising from the legal relationship between those parties. In this regard, arbitrability is not dependent on whether the parties can reach a particular settlement. It is therefore irrelevant [...] whether a party itself could conclude and declare that a contract is null and void; [...] the material factor is whether the parties can reach an amicable settlement.

| | |

---

relationship between them in order to eliminate uncertainty as to the claims resulting from that relationship or to secure their performance or in order to evade an existing or potential dispute.

[5] Taken from the summary of the decision available at: http://arbitraz.laszczuk.pl/ orzecznictwo (accessed on November 17, 2010). The text of the decision in Polish is also printed on the same page. The cited source comes from: *Biuro Studiów i Analiz Sądu Najwyższego.*

III. Arbitrability of Claims of Unfair Competition (a Claim for Unjust Enrichment)

Key words:
arbitration agreement | arbitrability | objective arbitrability | disposal of rights | settlement subject to a settlement | dispute settlement | unjust enrichment

Decision of the Supreme Court (*Sąd Najwyższy*) [POL] No. I CSK 120/09 of 2 December 2009:[6]

States involved:
[POL] - [Poland]. No link to another State identified in the available summary.

Laws Taken into Account in This Ruling:
➤ Ustawa o zwalczaniu nieuczciwej konkurencji (*Act on Suppression of Unfair Competition*) u.z.n.k. [POL] - Ustawa z dnia 16 kwietnia 1993 r. (Law of 16 April 1993), published in: Dzienik Ustaw, 1993 Nr. 47, poz. 211: Art. 18;
➤ Kodeks postępowania cywilnego (*Code of Civil Procedure*) [k.p.c.] [POL] – Ustawa z dnia 17 listopada 1964 r. (Law of 17 November 1964), published in: Dzienik Ustaw, 1964 Nr. 43, poz. 296: Art. 1157.

Rationes Decidendi:

17.06. (A claim for unjust enrichment under Article 18(1) (4) u.z.n.k. [POL][7] [Act on Suppression of Unfair Competition], as a dispute on a property right which may be disposed of by the parties, may be subject to settlement. As such, it may constitute the subject-matter of an arbitration agreement (cf. Article 1157 k.p.c.)[8].

17.07. Arbitration agreements [...] clearly relate to disputes arising from or connected with agreements on cooperation in the purchase of goods. The respondent's unfair competition, consisting of the receipt of additional consideration, was not connected [...] with performance under such an agreement, nor did it constitute part of any relationship to the performance thereof, but took place only in parallel to the performance of such an agreement [...]. The claim sought by the party claims hence is not contractual in nature and is unrelated to the content of the agreement, but concerns unfair competition. The parties, upon entering into an arbitration agreement, could hardly be expected to have envisaged

---

6   *Ibid.*
7   [POL] Act on Suppression of Unfair Competition [u.z.n.k.] (*ustawa o zwalczaniu nieuczciwej konkurencji*): Unofficial translation: *In case of unfair competition, an entrepreneur whose interest has been threatened or infringed may seek [...] 4) compensation pursuant to general provisions.*
8   See *supra* note 2.

such conduct and entered into an arbitration agreement on that matter. It clearly follows from the content of the arbitration agreement that it concerned disputes related to the implementation of the agreement, rather than all disputes arising during the implementation thereof.

| | |

IV. The Relevance of a Decision of a Foreign Court to the Recognition and Enforcement of an Arbitral Award; The New York Convention on the Recognition and Enforcement of Foreign Arbitral Awards

Key words:
arbitration agreement | will of the parties | nature of proceedings on annulment | main action | proceedings on the annulment of an arbitral award | foreign arbitral award | exequatur of a decision on annulment

Decision of the Supreme Court (*Sąd Najwyższy*) No. I CSK 159/09 of 6 November 2009:[9]

States involved:
[POL] - [Poland];
[DEU] - [Germany];
[AUT] - [Austria].

Laws Taken into Account in This Ruling:
➤ Kodeks postępowania cywilnego (*Code of Civil Procedure*) [POL] – Ustawa z dnia 17 listopada 1964 r. (Law of 17 November 1964), published in: Dzienik Ustaw, 1964 Nr. 43, poz. 296: Art. 1145 § 1, Art. 1146;
➤ New York Convention on the Recognition and Enforcement of Foreign Arbitral Awards (1958) [Konwencja o uznawaniu and wykonywaniu zagranicznych orzeczeń arbitrażowych (1958 r.)] (Decree of 19 July 1961), published in: Dzienik Ustaw, 1962 Nr. 9, poz 41[10].

---

9   *Supra* note 5.
10   Poland signed the New York Convention on the Recognition and Enforcement of Foreign Arbitral Awards on 10 June 1958; it was ratified on 3 October 1961 and came into force in Poland on 1 January 1962. The text of the Convention was published in Polish in conjunction with the government regulation of 19 July 1961 published in: Dz. U 1962 r. Nr. 9, poz. 41.

Rationes Decidendi:

17.08. A decision on the legal relevance of a particular decision of a foreign court cannot be taken during exequatur procedure as it is impossible to predict what effects of such a decision will be claimed by any applicant (party) in the future and under what circumstances. In this respect, Article 1145 § 1 k.p.c. does not form a basis to dismiss [an application for] the recognition of a decision of a foreign court merely because, in the opinion of the court adjudicating on recognition (in exequatur procedure), the decision will not induce any effects in Poland.

17.09. If the applicant in exequatur procedure (i.e. the person seeking recognition of the decision) was the same party in the [main] action before the Austrian court, it has a legal interest not only in being entitled to bring proceedings in exequatur procedure in Poland, but also, if the conditions laid down in Article 1146 k.p.c.[11] are not met, in being able to claim the recognition of such a decision, i.e. the recognition of the legal effects thereof, in Poland.

17.10. The decision dismissing the application for the annulment of an arbitral award by the court, from a formally procedural perspective, is a decision on the merits and not just a procedural decision[12]. The decision on the application for the annulment of the arbitration award by the court was therefore generally eligible for recognition (it may be subject to *exequatur* procedure). It should be noted, however, that, from the substantive aspect, the dispute was resolved by the award of an arbitral tribunal, the basis of which was the will of the parties expressed by the arbitration agreement.

---

11 [POL] *Code of Civil Procedure* [k.p.c.] Unofficial translation: [Article 1146. § 1. Decision shall not be recognized, if: 1) it is not final in the country where it was issued; 2) it was issued in a case that belongs to an exclusive jurisdiction of Polish courts; 3) a petition commencing the proceedings was not delivered to a defendant who has not entered an appearance on the merits properly and in time enabling to defend himself; 4) the party to a pending proceedings was deprived of the rights to defense; 5) the dispute between the same parties on the same merits was commenced before the Polish courts earlier than before the court of a foreign country; 6) is inconsistent with a previous final decision on the same claim between the same parties issued either before a Polish court or a before the courts of a foreign country that satisfies the conditions for its recognition of the Polish Republic; 7) recognition would be contrary to the fundamental principles of the Polish legal order (public policy). § 2 Any impediment referred to in § 1 point 5 and 6 shall apply accordingly to the case pending before other Polish authority than a court or an authority of a foreign state, and also apply to a decision of other Polish authority than a court or the authority of a foreign state. § 3 The provisions of § 1 point 5 and 6 shall not apply if the court of a foreign country ruled in accordance with the provisions of such a country on national jurisdiction, that the acquisition by a person or a resident of the Polish Republic of succession to property situated at time of death of the deceased in the foreign country].

12 Author's note on this summary: This does not mean that a review on the merits can be carried out in proceedings on an application for the annulment of an arbitral award. An application for the annulment of an arbitral award is a separate claim, initiating a completely new procedure, solely from the perspective of civil procedure. Therefore, a decision on such an application is also a decision on the merits. These merits, i.e. the subject of proceedings for the annulment of an arbitral award, are defined by a forward action for annulment.

In this regard, a decision on an application for the annulment of an arbitral award is only a decision by which the State exercises supervision of (control over) arbitral awards and arbitration in general.

17.11. A decision rendered by a Polish court in proceedings brought by an application for the annulment of an arbitral award must be taken into account in procedure on the recognition of a foreign arbitral award only if so provided by the law applicable to such procedure. According to the k.p.c. and the New York Convention on the Recognition and Enforcement of Foreign Arbitral Awards (1958), a court adjudicating on the recognition of a foreign decision shall take into account, on a motion from a party, a decision annulling an arbitral award. It does so when examining the existence of any grounds for refusal of recognition.

17.12. The basis for the rendering of an arbitral award is the will of the parties. It follows from the nature of the arbitral award and from the role played by the foreign court's decision dismissing the application for the annulment of the arbitral award that there is an insufficient legal basis for the recognition of the foreign court's decision, which is essentially only of a supervisory, rather than a substantive, nature. The connection with an arbitral award and, consequently, not the absolutely individual nature of such a decision of a foreign court on an application for the annulment of such an arbitral award, is primarily an obstacle hindering its assessment as a decision which may be recognized in Poland under Article 1145 § 1 k.p.c.[13].

| | |

V. Obligation of a Party in Proceedings on the Nullity of an Arbitral Award; Nullity of an Arbitration Agreement

Key words:
arbitration agreement | annulment of arbitral award | arbitral award | expiry of arbitration agreement | unenforceability of arbitration agreement | enforceability of arbitration agreement | principle that the court is bound by an application | ineffectiveness of arbitration agreement | governing law | motions of the parties | public policy | Polish public policy

---

[13] [POL] *Code of Civil Procedure* [k.p.c.] Unofficial translation: [The effect in Poland of a foreign judgements incligible for enforcement by means of an execution rendered in civil matters, that are subject to a court proceedings, depends o their recognition by the Polish courts]; Article 1145 k.p.c. was deleted by a law of 5 December 2008 (Dz.U. 2008 r. Nr. 234, poz. 1571).

Decision of the Supreme Court (*Sąd Najwyższy*) of 6 November 2009 No I CSK 121/09 of 23 September 2009:[14]

States involved:
[POL] - [Poland]. No link to another State identified in the available summary.

Laws Taken into Account in This Ruling:
➤ Kodeks postępowania cywilnego (*Code of Civil Procedure*) [k.p.c.] [POL] – Ustawa z dnia 17 listopada 1964 r. (Law of 17 November 1964), published in: Dzienik Ustaw, 1964 Nr. 43, poz. 296: Art. 1206 § 1, Art. 1206 § 2.

Rationes Decidendi:
17.13. Proceedings in respect of an application for the annulment of an arbitral award may be held and a decision may be taken in the case even if it is discovered during these proceedings that the arbitration agreement does not exist, is invalid or ineffective, or has expired under governing law (Article 1206 § 1 point 1 k.p.c. [POL])[15]. The parties may seek annulment of an arbitral award for the above-mentioned reasons.

17.14. A decision on an arbitration agreement's expiry, non-existence, invalidity, ineffectiveness or unenforceability may be taken in proceedings brought by an application for the annulment of an arbitration award only in cases where such a plea [(the expiry of the arbitration agreement etc.)] is lodged by the applicant[16]. In proceedings before a [common] court, the principle that the court is bound by pleas[17] within the limits of the motions brought by the parties applies. The court ex officio takes into account only the factors referred to in Article 1206 § 2 k.p.c. [POL][18].

| | |

---

[14] *Supra* note 5.

[15] [POL] *Code of Civil Procedure* [k.p.c.] Unofficial translation: [Article 1206. § 1. A party may by petition demand that an arbitral award be vacated if: 1) there was no arbitration agreement, or the arbitration agreement is invalid, ineffective or no longer in force under the provisions of applicable law; (...)].

[16] I.e. a person who is in the position of the applicant in proceedings on an application for the annulment of an arbitral award.

[17] I.e. the reasons for which annulment of the arbitral award by the court is proposed.

[18] [POL] *Code of Civil Procedure* [k.p.c.] Unofficial translation: [(...) § 2. An arbitral award shall also be vacated if the court finds that: 1) in accordance with statute the dispute cannot be resolved by an arbitral tribunal, or 2) the arbitral award is contrary to fundamental principles of the legal order of the Republic of Poland (public order clause)].

VI. Prohibition of Review in Relation to the Application of Substantive Law (*Revision Au Fond*) and Limited Exception in the Context of Public Policy

Key words:
arbitration agreement | annulment of arbitral award | principle that the court is bound by an application | governing substantive law | applicable law | motions of the parties | Polish public policy | findings of fact | verification of facts | grounds for annulment of arbitral award | compliance with substantive law | effect of arbitral award | basic principle | principle of law | Polish law | public policy clause

Decision of the Supreme Court No. I CSK 53/09 of 3 September 2009, No. I CSK 53/09:[19]

States involved:
[POL] - [Poland]. No link to another State identified in the available summary.

Laws Taken into Account in This Ruling:
➢ Kodeks postępowania cywilnego (*Code of Civil Procedure*) [POL] – Ustawa z dnia 17 listopada 1964 r. [Law of 17 November 1964], published in: Dziennik Ustaw, 1964 Nr. 43, poz. 296: Art. 1194 § 4, Art. 1206.

17.15. In the opinion of the [common] court adjudicating on the application for the annulment of the arbitral award, it is necessary to determine whether statutory grounds exist for annulment of the arbitral award. A court does not check on the compliance of an arbitral award with substantive law, nor whether the facts found justify the award or whether the facts of the case have been adequately verified.

17.16. Grounds for the annulment of an arbitral award are exhaustively listed in Article 1206 k.p.c. [POL][20]. A court adjudicating on an application for the

---

19 *Supra* note 5.
20 [POL] *Code of Civil Procedure* [k.p.c.] Unofficial translation: [Article 1206. § 1. A party may by petition demand that an arbitral award be vacated if: 1) there was no arbitration agreement, or the arbitration agreement is invalid, ineffective or no longer in force under the provisions of applicable law; 2) the party was not given proper notice of the appointment of an arbitrator or the proceeding before the arbitral tribunal or was otherwise deprived of the ability to defend its rights before the arbitral tribunal; 3) the arbitral award deals with a dispute not covered by the arbitration agreement or exceeds the scope of the arbitration agreement; however, if the decision on matters covered by the arbitration agreement is separable from the decision on matters not covered by the arbitration agreement or exceeding the scope thereof, then the award may be vacated only with regard to the matters not covered by the arbitration agreement or

annulment of an arbitral award is fundamentally bound by the claims put forward by the applicant and thus may annul the arbitral award on the grounds specified in Article 1206 k.p.c. [POL] only where a party relies on them in its application. A court shall ex officio (i.e. with no explicit indication in the application) consider only two grounds for annulment of an arbitral award. These are the grounds referred to in Article 1206 k.p.c. [POL], namely in cases where, under the law, it is impossible to bring a dispute before an arbitral tribunal for resolution (Article 1206 § 2 point 1 k.p.c. [POL])[21] and cases where an arbitral award is contrary to the fundamental principles of Polish law (Article 1206 § 2 point 2 k.p.c. [POL]).

17.17. On the basis of the public policy clause (*klauzula porządku publicznego*) pursuant to Article 1206 § 2 point 2 k.p.c. [POL], an arbitral award shall be set aside where the effects arising from the content of the arbitral award are contrary to any standard regulating a rule regarded as a fundamental principle of law.

17.18. The application of governing substantive *law, compliance with which is* fundamentally ordered by Article 1194 k.p.c. [POL][22], is subject to review by the [general] court adjudicating on an application for the annulment of an arbitral award only where required ex officio by a public policy clause.

| | |

exceeding the scope thereof; exceeding the scope of the arbitration agreement cannot constitute grounds for vacating an award if a party who participated in the proceeding failed to assert a plea against hearing the claims exceeding the scope of the arbitration agreement; 4) the requirements with regard to the composition of the arbitral tribunal or fundamental rules of procedure before such tribunal, arising under statute or specified by the parties, were not observed; 5) the award was obtained by means of an offence or the award was issued on the basis of a forged or altered document; or 6) a legally final court judgment was issued in the same matter between the same parties. § 2. An arbitral award shall also be vacated if the court finds that: 1) in accordance with statute the dispute cannot be resolved by an arbitral tribunal, or 2) the arbitral award is contrary to fundamental principles of the legal order of the Republic of Poland (public order clause)].

21 This is therefore a lack of "objective arbitrability".

22 [POL] *Code of Civil Procedure* [k.p.c.] Unofficial translation: [Article 1194. § 1. The arbitral tribunal shall resolve the dispute in accordance with the law applicable to the given relationship, and if expressly authorized to do so by the parties, in accordance with general principles of law or equity. §2. In any event, however, the arbitral tribunal shall take into consideration the provisions of the agreement and established customs applicable to the given legal relationship].

VII. "Hearing of a Case" in Proceedings on the Annulment of an Arbitral Award

Key words:
hearing of a case by a court | court of first instance | court of second instance |
enforceability | appeal | doctrine | case law | closed session of the court | LCIA

Decision of the Supreme Court No I CSK 538/08 of 24 June 2009:[23]

States involved:
[POL] - [Poland];
[ENG] - [United Kingdom].
The subject of the Polish court's adjudication an application for recognition of an interim arbitral award rendered by the LCIA (London Court of International Arbitration).

Laws Taken into Account in This Ruling:
➢ Kodeks postępowania cywilnego (*Code of Civil Procedure*) [POL] – Ustawa z dnia 17 listopada 1964 r. (Law of 17 November 1964), published in: Dziennik Ustaw, 1964 Nr. 43, poz. 296: Art. 13 § 2, Art. 397, Art. 1214 § 1, Art. 1215 § 1, Art. 1151 § 1.

Rationes Decidendi:
17.19. Under Article 1215 § 1 k.p.c. [POL][24], the court "deciding after a hearing [of a case]", as well as in the preceding Article 1214 § 1 k.p.c. [POL][25], is only the court of first instance.

---

[23] *Supra* note 5.
This was a procedure on the recognition of an English arbitral award in *Elektrim S.A.* The procedure in *Elektrim S.A.* (or specifically Vivendi v Elektrim and others, where a party was the Polish company Elektrim S.A.) comprises a series of proceedings and decisions taking place in numerous states. The first decision in this series was evidently issued in proceedings before the Czech Arbitration Court attached to the Chamber of Commerce of the Czech Republic and Agrarian Chamber of the Czech Republic; it is likely that the decision of this arbitration court was the first to invoke Regulation (EC) 1346/2000 on insolvency proceedings in connection with its effects on arbitration (the Czech decision was issued in January 2008). For more details, see, for example, Alexander Bělohlávek, *Impact of insolvency of a party on pending arbitration proceedings in Czech Republic, England and Switzerland and other countries, in* YEARBOOK ON INTERNATIONAL ARBITRATION, BERLIN: EAP 145-166 (M. Roth and M. Geistlinger eds., 2010) or Alexander Bělohlávek and Tomáš Řezníček, *Dopady rozhodnutí o úpadku a insolvenčního řízení na majetek účastníka na probíhající rozhodčí řízení v lucemburské a mezinárodní praxi ve světle aktuální judikatury některých obecných a rozhodčích soudů (Impacts of Insolvency and Insolvency Proceedings of a Party on Pending Arbitration Proceedings in Domestic and International Experience in the Light of Current Case Law of Particular Courts and Arbitral Tribunals), 2 (9)* OBCHODNĚPRÁVNÍ REVUE 1-14 (2010).
[24] [POL] *Code of Civil Procedure* [k.p.c.]. Unofficial translation: [Article 1215. § 1. The court shall rule on recognition or enforcement of an arbitral award issued abroad or a settlement entered into before an arbitral tribunal abroad after conducting a hearing.].
[25] [POL] *Code of Civil Procedure* [k.p.c.] Unofficial translation: [Article 1214. § 1. The court shall rule in public hearing on recognition of an arbitral award or a settlement

17.20. Article 1151 § 2 k.p.c. [POL][26] clearly provides that the enforceability of a foreign court's decision is "decided by a court after a hearing", without clarifying what stage of court proceedings this imperative of the provision concerns. Regardless of the wording of this provision, neither doctrine nor case law indicates that the court of second instance is obliged to order a hearing after the consideration of a case. On the contrary, it is generally accepted that an appeal, in accordance with Article 397 § 1 k.p.c. [POL][27], in conjunction with Article 13 § 2 k.p.c. [POL][28], should be heard in a closed session of the court. [...] There is no reason for the wording of Article 1215 § 1 k.p.c. [POL] to be interpreted otherwise.

| | |

VIII. Withdrawal of a Plea of the [Non-]Existence of an Arbitration Agreement in Proceedings on the Annulment of an Arbitral Award

Key words:
arbitration agreement | existence of arbitration agreement | non-existence of arbitration agreement | appeal proceedings | withdrawal of a plea | respondent | court of first instance | court of second instance | procedural act | judicial review | withdrawal of an action | assessment of procedural act | legal consequence | justification of plea | lateness of plea | lack of foundation of plea | dismissal of an action

Decision of the Supreme Court No III CZP 29/09 of 4 June 2009:[29]

States involved:
[POL] - [Poland].
No link to another State identified in the available summary.

---

entered into before an arbitral tribunal which is not subject to enforcement. The decision of the court is subject to interlocutory appeal.].

[26] [POL] *Code of Civil Procedure* [k.p.c.] Unofficial translation: [Article 1151. [...] § 2. The court renders the judgement after hearing the case. The decision of a district court on the enforceability is subject to an appeal and the order of the Court of Appeal – cassation appeal; also the reopening of the proceedings that resulted in a final judgement is permitted]; Article 1151 k.p.c. was deleted by a law of 22 December 2004 (Dz.U. 2005 r. Nr 13, poz. 98).

[27] [POL] *Code of Civil Procedure* [k.p.c.] Unofficial translation: [The appellate court resolves the complaint on a closed hearing].

[28] [POL] *Code of Civil Procedure* [k.p.c.] Unofficial translation: [The procedural rules apply accordingly to the other proceedings pursuant to this code unless provided otherwise].

[29] Supra note 5.

Laws Taken into Account in This Ruling:
- ➤ Kodeks postępowania cywilnego (*Code of Civil Procedure*) [POL] – Ustawa z dnia 17 listopada 1964 r. (Law of 17 November 1964), published in: Dzienik Ustaw, 1964 Nr. 43, poz. 296: Art. 203 § 4.

Rationes Decidendi:

17.21. It is permissible for the respondent to withdraw a plea of the [non-]existence of an arbitration agreement in the course of appeal proceedings against a decision of the court of first instance which ruled on the plea.

17.22. In relation to the withdrawal of a plea of the [non-]existence of an arbitration agreement, the provisions of the Code of Civil Procedure do not provide for the requirement of a judicial review, as is the case with the withdrawal of an action (Article 203 § 4 k.p.c. [POL])[30]. The respondent's procedural act consisting of the withdrawal of a plea of the [non-]existence of an arbitration agreement is therefore assessed by the court in the same way as it would consider any other procedural act by a party to the proceedings.

17.23. A plea of the existence of an arbitration agreement may be withdrawn by the respondent only to until such time as this act would result in legal consequences associated with such an act by law. Such a consequence is the dismissal of the action by a court if the plea is justified, or the dismissal of the plea if it is found to be unfounded or late by a court. The moment at which the decision to dismiss or reject the dismissal of an action becomes final is the crucial factor, not the moment when such a decision is issued.

| | |

IX. Arbitrability of Disputes Related to [Business] Companies

Key words:
settlement | arbitration agreement | objective arbitrability | limits of arbitrability | memorandum of association | shareholder

Decision of the Supreme Court No III CZP 13/09 of 7 May 2009:[31]

States involved:
[POL] - [Poland].
No link to another State identified in the available summary.

---

[30] [POL] *Code of Civil Procedure* [k.p.c.] Unofficial translation: [Article 203. § 4. The court may consider inadmissible withdrawal of the petition, waiver or reduction of the claim only if the circumstances of the matter indicate that these conducts are contrary to the law or rules of social interaction or intended to circumvent the law].

[31] *Supra* note 5.

Laws Taken into Account in This Ruling:
- ➢ Kodeks postępowania cywilnego (*Code of Civil Procedure*) [POL] – Ustawa z dnia 17 listopada 1964 r. (Law of 17 November 1964), published in: Dzienik Ustaw, 1964 Nr. 43, poz. 296: Art. 1157, Art. 1163.

Rationes Decidendi:

17.24. Article 1163 § 1 k.p.c. [POL][32] contains no specific rule in relation to Article 1157 k.p.c. [POL][33] setting out the requirement that disputes in respect of which an arbitration agreement has been concluded may be subject to settlement[34].

17.25. The two provisions of the *Code of Civil Procedure* [k.p.c.] cited in the preceding paragraph have completely different subject-matter. Article 1157 k.p.c. [POL] lays down the limits of arbitrability for a dispute by determining, as a major criterion of such arbitrability, [...] the fitness of a dispute for settlement. Article 1163 § 1 k.p.c. [POL], [...] on the other hand, only provides that an arbitration agreement may be contained in the memorandum of association of a [business] company and that it is binding on the company and its shareholders.

17.26. The purpose of Article 1163 k.p.c. [POL] is not to lay down preconditions for the arbitrability of disputes in the relations of a company. This is specifically clear from the fact that Article 1163 § 1 k.p.c. [POL] does not set out the conditions which a dispute [concerning a business] company would have to meet to be arbitrable.

17.27. A special provision in relation to Article 1157 k.p.c. [POL] may be only a provision which deals with (different) treatment of the arbitrability of the dispute.

| | |

---

[32] [POL] *Code of Civil Procedure* [k.p.c.] Unofficial translation: [Article 1163. § 1. An arbitration agreement included in the articles of association or statute of a commercial company concerning disputes arising out of the corporate relationship shall be binding upon the company and its shareholders.].

[33] *Supra* note 2.

[34] This is therefore an issue of "objective arbitrability".

X. Procedural Rules Applicable to Proceedings on an Application for the Annulment of an Arbitral Award; Disputes under a Lease Contract

Key words:
procedural rules | court of first instance | applicable rules | proceedings initiated on a motion | rent | subject of lease | annulment of an arbitral award | fixed term contract | contract of indefinite duration

Decision of the Supreme Court No IV CZ 41/09 of 7 May 2009:[35]

States involved:
[POL] - [Poland].
No link to another State identified in the available summary.

Laws Taken into Account in This Ruling:
> Kodeks postępowania cywilnego (*Code of Civil Procedure*) [POL] – Ustawa z dnia 17 listopada 1964 r. (Law of 17 November 1964), published in: Dzienik Ustaw, 1964 Nr. 43, poz. 296: Art. 23, Art. 715 (this provision has been deleted in the meantime), Art. 1207 § 2.

Rationes Decidendi:
17.28. In accordance with Article 715 k.p.c. [POL][36], which is applicable to this case and the analogy of which is Article 1207 § 2 k.p.c. [POL] for proceedings initiated on a motion [...], procedural rules applicable to proceedings before the court of first instance are applied to proceedings on the annulment of an arbitral award. In this respect, Article 23 k.p.c. [POL][37], among others, should be applied; according to this provision, in disputes on the relinquishment or removal of the subject of lease or sub-lease the subject of the dispute is the amount of rent for the disputed period

---

[35] *Supra* note 5.
[36] [POL] *Code of Civil Procedure* [k.p.c.] Unofficial translation: [Article 715. Proceedings initiated upon the petition on annulment of arbitral award is resolved in accordance with provisions applicable to proceedings of first instance];Article 715 k.p.c. was deleted as part of the reform of arbitration implemented by a law of 28 July 2005 (Dz.U. 2005 r. Nr 178, poz. 1478) repealing Part Three of the k.p.c. (Arbitral Tribunal) in its entirety and replacing it with Part Five. This amendment entered into effect on 17 October 2005.
[37] [POL] *Code of Civil Procedure* [k.p.c.] Unofficial translation: [Article 23. In matters of existence, nullity or dissolution of a tenancy or lease agreement, surrender or recovery of the item that is subject of a tenancy or lease, the amount in dispute is considered to be in case of time-limited agreements – the total rent for the period in question, but no more than a year, in case of agreements for indefinite period of time – the sum of the rent for a period of three months].

(if the contract has been concluded for a fixed period), or the amount of rent for three months (if it has been concluded for an indefinite period).

[*Alexander J. Bělohlávek & Tomáš Řezníček*]
Mgr. Tomáš Řezníček (*1978) works as a legal trainee in the Law Offices of Bělohlávek, Prague, Czech Republic. Graduated from the Law Faculty of Charles University in Prague in 2007, also absolved foreign studies at the Law Faculty of Jagiellonian University in Krakow. Coauthor of various articles with prof. A. Bělohlávek published in professional periodicals in the Czech Republic. Field of interest: Commercial Law, Private International Law, Pharmaceutical Law.
e-mail: tomas.reznicek@ablegal.cz

| | |

5. Russian Federation

Alexander J. Bělohlávek

Key words:
interim award | partial award | decision on the merits | recognition | enforcement | advance on costs

Decision of the High Arbitrazh Court of October 5, 2010 (in *Living Consulting Group v. Sokotel*):[38]

States involved:
[FIN] - [Finland];
[RUS] - [Russian Federation];
[SWE] - [Sweden].

Czech (& Central European) Yearbook of Arbitration

18.01. The supreme Russian arbitration court – the High Arbitrazh Court – **refused to recognize and enforce an interim award concerning an advance on costs of proceedings** which had been issued in SCC proceedings, thus negating the decision of the lower-instance court.

[Author's Note]

18.02. Given that the text of the relevant judgment has not been available at press time of this annotation or, as it were, brief information on the relevant decision, we should refrain from commenting on the basis of insufficient background information. Even so, we can on the other hand say this much: this is not necessarily a decision at odds with doctrines in force in certain countries of the CEE region, but may well be conforming to the concepts recognized in those countries. For one, only decisions on the merits may be subjected to (recognition and) enforcement, and in the said countries, decisions of a procedural character - i.e., any disposition regarding the costs of proceedings (other than a decision on costs which forms an operative part of a decision on the merits) - may therefore often not be recognized as an enforceable decision. Decisions of a procedural nature, among them also advances on costs, are usually made in the form of procedural orders (as opposed to judgments or awards), both in proceedings before general courts and in arbitration. Incidentally, the same will in many cases apply to decisions on whether the given court

---

[38] Tom Toulson, *Russian court refuses to recognise interim award*, GAR (October 29, 2010), available in electronic form at: http://www.globalarbitrationreview.com/news/article/28862/russian-court-refuses-recognise-interim-award (accessed on October 29, 2010). This decision has so far not been published.

has jurisdiction, which in most of these countries are of an exclusively procedural (as opposed to substantive) nature. What we see here is one of the most fundamental differences between the doctrines which are in place in common-law countries on the one hand and continental (civil-law) doctrines (as are applied in CEE countries) on the other hand, namely, the issue of what is the subject matter of interim awards and of partial awards. Whereas interim awards rule on subject matters of a temporary nature, merely serve the purpose of advancing in the given proceedings, represent a kind of temporary technical aid, and therefore cannot be considered a decision on the merits, partial awards by contrast do pass a final decision on the merits (or rather, an independent and severable part of the merits). Another argument in support of the conclusion reached by the Russian court in the said matter is the rather broadly accepted principle that the complainant always pays the full advances on costs. This applies not only almost without exception to proceedings before the general courts, but (in most cases in the above-mentioned countries) also to arbitration proceedings, so that we may without going to far presume this principle to be a fundamental principle of civil proceedings in a broadly conceived sense - i.e., a principle which holds also in proceedings other than court proceedings. The author of this note does not contest that this approach may be used to afford the defendant special protection. However, this conclusion must in no case be made categorically, and certainly not in such stringent terms as presented in the source which informs us of the cited decision of the Russian court[39]. After all, the principle according to which each party pays a pro-rated advance on costs, which is embodied in the rules of proceedings at a number of international arbitration courts, may likewise serve to gain a unilateral advantage for complainants who file clearly frivolous claims. The author would like to stress, though, that these observations can only apply in a general sense, as we must not comment on the specific Russian decision unless and until at least an essential part of it has become available through publication or otherwise.

[Alexander J. Bělohlávek]

| | |

---

[39] *Ibid.*

Section B

Special Case Law of the Courts on the Relation of Arbitration and Constitutional Issues

1. Bolivia

Judgment 0146/2010-R of the *Constitutional Court, Bolivia,* **of May 17, 2010 (parties not identified):**[1]

Rationes Decidendi:

19.01. If agreed in the arbitration agreement that an arbitration centre[2] is to render organisational (administrative) services in connection with the arbitration proceedings (in the capacity of what is known as *case administrator*), then this centre is not authorised to decide on issues pertaining to the merits of the dispute, nor on objections filed by the parties, once the arbitral tribunal is constituted. In accordance with the competence-competence principle[3], decisions on these matters are in the sole competency of the arbitral tribunal.

| | |

---

[1] Source: VIII (10) ITA ARBITRATION REPORT (2010).

[2] Here: *Cámara Nacional de Comercio.*

[3] This principle is also enshrined in Article 32 of Bolivian Arbitration Law No. 1770, pursuant to which the arbitral tribunal has the authority to decide on its own jurisdiction and the challenges regarding the existence, validity and effectiveness of the arbitration agreement.

2. Bulgaria

Constitutional Principles in Case Law
on Arbitration and Arbitral Awards in Bulgaria

Alexander J. Bělohlávek

Abbreviations used in annotations:

BCC   Bulgarian Chamber of Commerce and Industry
BCCIC   Arbitration Court at the Bulgarian Chamber of Commerce and Industry
CCP   Code of Civil Procedure [BUL] (1952, 2007)
ICAA   International Commercial Arbitration Act [BUL]

I. Single-Instance Proceedings for Annulment of Arbitral Awards from Perspective of Constitutional Principles and Protection of Rights (Constitutional Court of the Republic of Bulgaria; October 24, 2002)

Key words:
civil and criminal matters | Appellate court | setting aside | natural and legal person | the structure of court instances | overriding mandatory principle | single-instance system | court of cassation | court of appeal | protection of rights | legal protection | legal certainty | legal person | exercise of rights | judicial system | three-instance system | Constitutional principle

Czech (& Central European) Yearbook of Arbitration

Decision of Constitutional Court of Republic of Bulgaria No. 9, Constitutional Case No. 15/2002 of October 24, 2002:[1]

Laws Taken into Account in This Ruling:
> Constitution of the Republic of Bulgaria:[2] Article 8[3], Article 56[4], Article 117(2)[5], Article 119(1)[6], Article 122(1)[7], Article 124;[8]
> International Commercial Arbitration Act, ICAA [BUL]:[9] Section 47[10].

Rationes Decidendi:

20.01. The number of instances (the structure of court instances) depends on the structure of the judicial system, which is subject to special procedural and other laws. The Constitution does not stipulate a three-instance judicial system as an overriding mandatory constitutional principle. There is no constitutional obstacle preventing the resolution of certain selected civil and criminal matters within the framework of a different system of court instances.

20.02. A single-instance judicial system for proceedings on the annulment (setting aside) of arbitral awards (i.e. exclusion of appeal) does not violate constitutional rights to legal protection.

20.03. The Supreme Court of Cassation is merely a supervisory and appellate court. It does not have jurisdiction to review arbitral awards on the merits. The Supreme Court of Cassation only renders decisions on motions for

---

1 Source: APIS 7 PRAVO (*АПИС 7 ПРАВО legal information system*) and 102 STATE GAZETTE (*DV/ДВ - Държавен вестник*) (November 1, 2002).
2 Promulgated *in* 56 STATE GAZETTE (*DV/ДВ – Държавен вестник*) (July 13, 1991). Also available at: http://lex.bg/bg/laws/ldoc/521957377 (accessed on December 2, 2010). The English version of the following provisions was adopted from the translation of the Constitution of the Republic of Bulgaria on the website of the Bulgarian Constitutional Court, available at: http://www.constcourt.bg (accessed on December 2, 2010).
3 Constitution, Article 8 – *The power of the State shall be divided between legislative, executive and judicial branches.*
4 Constitution, Article 56 – *Everyone shall have the right to a legal defense whenever his rights or legitimate interests are violated or endangered. He shall have the right to be accompanied by legal counsel when appearing before an agency of the State.*
5 Constitution, Article 117 – [...] (2) *The judiciary shall be independent. In the performance of their functions, all judges, court assessors, prosecutors and investigating magistrates shall be subservient only to the law.* [...]
6 Constitution, Article 119 – "(1) Justice shall be administered by the Supreme Court of Cassation, the Supreme Administrative Court, courts of appeal, regional courts, courts-martial and district courts. [...]"
7 Constitution, Article 122 – "(1) Citizens and legal entities shall have the right to legal counsel at all stages of a trial. [...]."
8 Constitution, Article 124 – "The Supreme Court of Cassation shall exercise supreme judicial oversight as to the precise and equal application of the law by all courts."
9 Promulgated in: 60 STATE GAZETTE (*DV/ДВ Държавен вестник*) (August 5, 1988) as amended. Available in Bulgarian at: http://paragraf22.wap-bg.com/pravo/kodeksi/Otm/gpk.html (accessed on December 17, 2010) and in Bulgarian together with an unofficial translation to English at: http://www.bcci.bg/arbitration/index.html (accessed on January 12, 2011).
10 The provision is cited elsewhere in connection with the annotation of another decision. The respective provision of the ICAA [BUL] contains an exhaustive list of grounds for the annulment of arbitral awards.

the annulment (setting aside) of arbitral awards on the grounds expressly specified in the International Commercial Arbitration Act (ICAA [BUL]).

[Description of Facts and Legal Issues]

20.04. The Supreme Court of Cassation applied to the Constitutional Court with a motion that the Act on Amending and Supplementing the International Commercial Arbitration Act (ICAA [BUL]) be declared unconstitutional and repealed[11]. The respective amending statute changed the rules regulating the annulment (setting aside) of arbitral awards, and introduced an exclusively single-instance system for these cases. The claimant (Supreme Court of Cassation) argued that the amendment breached the guarantees safeguarding the exercise of rights by natural and legal persons (Article 56 and Article 122(1) of the Constitution of the Republic of Bulgaria). The claimant further maintained that Articles 119(1) and 124 of the Constitution of the Republic of Bulgaria define the Supreme Court of Cassation as a merely supervisory and appellate court. The claimant also suggested that after the amendment of the ICAA [BUL], the Supreme Court of Cassation would be unable to secure consistency with its own case law as a guarantee of the certainty and foreseeability of the law.

[From the Conclusions of the Constitutional Court of the Republic of Bulgaria]

20.05. The Constitutional Court ruled that the amendment to arbitration law (ICAA [BUL]) did not affect the principle of multi-instance proceedings. The Constitution provides that the number of instances depends on the structure of the judicial system, which is subject to special procedural and other laws. It is not a constitutional principle. The Constitution does not prescribe a three-instance structure as an overriding mandatory principle of legal protection. Therefore, there is no legal obstacle preventing the resolution of certain disputes within the framework of a judicial system different from the three-instance system. This applies to both civil and certain selected criminal cases.

20.06. The Supreme Court of Cassation remains the supervisory and appellate authority, because the respective amendment to the Arbitration Act has not bestowed on the Court any jurisdiction to review arbitral awards on the merits. The Supreme Court of Cassation is only authorized to inquire whether any of the grounds for the annulment of arbitral awards are applicable, the exhaustive list of which is laid down in the International Commercial Arbitration Act (ICAA [BUL]). This amendment by no means affects the rights of natural and legal persons to exercise their respective rights. The reason is that the circumstances assessed by the court under the ICAA [BUL] when ruling on the grounds for the annulment of arbitral awards are examined and must be observed during the arbitration proceedings as well. To the extent covered by these issues

---

[11]   Published *in* 46 STATE GAZETTE (*DV/ДВ - Държавен вестник*) (2002).

(grounds for the annulment of an arbitral award), the proceedings do *de facto* comprise several instances.

20.07. Moreover, if the arbitral award is set aside, the arbitration proceedings are reopened or the interested party can lodge their claims with the court.

| | |

II. Nature of Arbitration – Exclusion of Review on Merits and Ordinary and Extraordinary Remedies (Supreme Court; January 14, 1993)

Key words:
voluntary arbitration | extraordinary review | remedy | authority with special jurisdiction | public authorities | jurisdiction of courts | applicable procedural rules | civil procedure rules/rules applicable to court proceedings | final and binding decision | review arbitral award | commercial arbitration | decision of a state authority | revision au fond | judicial system | court proceedings | contractual nature | public-law nature

Judgment of Bulgarian Supreme Court *(Върховен съд)* **No. 327, Civil Case No. 257/92 of January 14, 1993:**[12]

Laws Taken into Account in This Ruling:
➤ Code of Civil Procedure[13] (repealed version) CCP [BUL]: Article 9(1)[14], Article 225[15], Article 231[16].

Rationes Decidendi:

20.08. An arbitral tribunal in voluntary arbitration is not a judicial authority (such as authorities with special jurisdiction), because of the contractual basis of arbitration. Authorities with special jurisdiction are different,

---

[12] Source: APIS 7 PRAVO [*АПИС 7 ПРАВО legal information system*]; *Case law*, 2 (14) BULLETIN OF SUPREME COURT OF REPUBLIC OF BULGARIA 12 (1993). The decision was pointed out by Plamen Borissov, Sofia, Bulgaria.

[13] Promulgated *in* 12 STATE GAZETTE [*ДВ/ДВ*], (February 8, 1952), as amended. Available at: http://paragraf22.wap-bg.com/pravo/kodeksi/Otm/gpk.html (accessed on December 17, 2010).

[14] CCP [BUL], Article 9 – (Paragraph 1, *amended* [by an act promulgated in:] 55 STATE GAZETTE (*Държавен вестник*) (1992) (approximate translation, cit.) *The parties to a dispute over property can agree that the dispute will be submitted to arbitration; this shall not apply to disputes over rights in rem or ownership of real property, maintenance or rights arising from labor relationships.*

[15] The provision authorized the Supreme Prosecutor or the Chairman of the Supreme Court to apply for a review of any decision of a state authority whereby, in their opinion, the law was intentionally violated. In such cases, they could also discontinue any pending enforcement proceedings. This type of extraordinary review of final and binding decisions used to be and has remained common in certain Central and Eastern European countries. It basically means intervention by public power in purely private disputes in cases of a serious violation of the law (as assessed by the authorized individuals). The motion can therefore only be filed by the Prosecutor or by the Chairman of the Supreme Court (in the individual countries, there existed and sometimes still exist various alternatives as regards the category of individuals authorized to file such a motion). The motion is therefore not filed by the parties. Nonetheless, the parties can give impetus to the process at the authority authorized to file the motion.

[16] A provision regulating extraordinary review initiated by a party with a [legal] interest in the annulment of a final and binding decision and with grounds justifying the extraordinary review.

because they were founded by the state (a state authority). This is not the case with commercial arbitration.

20.09. Awards rendered in [voluntary] arbitration need not comply with judicial practice and are not subject to any ordinary or extraordinary judicial review, nor are they subject to the laws regulating extraordinary review and the annulment of final and binding decisions of public authorities.

20.10. Arbitral tribunals resolve disputes in accordance with their own (internal)[17] rules. The court is not allowed to review arbitral awards from the perspective of their [material] validity, because they were rendered under rules different from the CCP [BUL] [rules applicable to court proceedings], and the parties [having agreed on the arbitral clause] intentionally refused intervention by the courts (prohibition of judicial review of arbitral awards/prohibition of *revision au fond*). Another difference between the two types of proceedings consists of the fact that courts have a varying status within the judicial system (system of public authorities).

[Description of Facts and Legal Issues]

20.11. The arbitral award rendered by the Court of Arbitration at the Bulgarian Chamber of Commerce and Industry [BCCIC] in Sofia was challenged by a motion for review under Section 225 of the CCP [BUL]. The three-member panel refused to grant the remedy;[18] the decision was challenged by another remedial measure and consequently transferred to a panel of the same court consisting of five judges.

| | |

---

[17] This case concerned an award rendered in arbitration held at the Court of arbitration attached to the Bulgarian Chamber of Commerce and Industry. *Own rules* therefore stand for the Rules of this arbitral tribunal on arbitration.

[18] Supreme Court Decree No. 230 of May 18, 1992.

III. Nature of Arbitration and Party Autonomy – Inadmissibility of Extraordinary Remedies against Court Decisions on Annulment of Arbitral Awards as Fundamental Procedural Rule (Supreme Court; June 29, 1993)

Key words:
party autonomy | final decision | extraordinary remedy | procedural inadmissibility | state authority | fundamental breach of procedural rules | annulment/setting aside of an arbitral award

Judgment of Bulgarian Supreme Court *(Върховен съд)* **No. 440, Civil Case No. 286/94 of June 29, 1994:**[19]

Laws Taken into Account in This Ruling:
➤ Code of Civil Procedure[20] (repealed version), CCP [BUL]: Article 9(1)[21], Article 225[22], Article 231[23]
➤ International Commercial Arbitration Act, ICAA [BUL]:[24] Article 47[25].

---

[19] Source: APIS 7 PRAVO *(АПИС 7 ПРАВО legal information system)*; *Case law*, 6 BULLETIN OF SUPREME COURT OF REPUBLIC OF BULGARIA 3 (1994). The decision was pointed out by Plamen Borissov, Sofia, Bulgaria.

[20] *Supra* note 13.

[21] See the note above to another annotated decision regarding Article 9 of the CCP [BUL] (approximate translation of the provision).

[22] See the note above to another annotated decision regarding Article 225 of the CCP [BUL].

[23] See the note above to another annotated decision regarding Article 231 of the CCP [BUL].

[24] *Supra* note 9.

[25] ICCA [BUL] (unofficial translation adopted from the web pages of the BCCIC [BUL], Chapter VII - Setting Aside, Recognition and Enforcement of the Award – Article 47 – (Amended in SG No. 46 of 2002) *The arbitration award may be set aside by the Supreme Court of Cassation if the party requesting that it be set aside proves any of the following grounds: 1) The party was incapable of concluding the arbitration agreement; 2) No arbitration agreement was concluded or it was null and void according to the law chosen by the parties, and failing such a choice, according to this Law; 3) The subject of the dispute was unarbitrable or the arbitration award was in conflict with the public order of the Republic of Bulgaria; 4) The party was not duly notified of the appointment of an arbitrator or of the arbitration proceedings or was unable to take part in the proceedings for reasons beyond its control; 5) The award resolved a dispute not provided for in the arbitration agreement or contains a ruling outside the subject of the dispute; 6) The composition of the Arbitral Tribunal or of the arbitration procedure was not in compliance with the agreement between the parties, unless the said agreement was in conflict with the mandatory provisions of this Law, or failing such agreement, when the provisions of this Law were not applied.*

Rationes Decidendi:

20.12. According to the amendment to the ICAA [BUL] of November 2, 1993, extraordinary remedies against court decisions on the annulment of arbitral awards rendered by the BCCIC [BUL] are inadmissible.

20.13. An arbitral tribunal constituted as a result of party autonomy hears and decides disputes pursuant to its own (internal) rules.

20.14. An arbitral tribunal is not a state authority, and its decisions are not subject to extraordinary remedies; the same applies to court decisions on the annulment of arbitral awards[26].

20.15. The only remedy against an arbitral award is a motion for the annulment of the award by court. The court decision rendered in the annulment proceedings is final.

[Description of Facts and Legal Issues]

20.16. The Sofia Municipal Court dismissed the motion for the annulment of the arbitral award. The party appealed (an extraordinary remedy) to the Supreme Court[27]. The Supreme Court set aside the preceding court decision and remitted the case to the Sofia Municipal Court for a new decision. The Supreme Prosecutor of the Republic of Bulgaria objected that such procedure was fundamentally in violation of procedural rules. The five-member panel of the Supreme Court accepted the objections and quashed the preceding decision of the court as procedurally inadmissible.

| | |

---

[26] See Sections 225 and 231 of the CCP [BUL].

[27] See Section 231 of the CCP [BUL].

IV. Jurisdiction as Procedural *Conditio Sine Qua Non*– Conflict of Jurisdiction between Courts, Other Authorities and Arbitral Tribunals (Supreme Court; June 6, 1995)

Judgment of Bulgarian Supreme Court *(Върховен съд)* No. 508, Civil Case No. 817/95 of June 6, 1995:[28]

Laws Taken into Account in This Ruling:

➢ Code of Civil Procedure[29] (repealed version), CCP [BUL]: Article 9(1)[30] and Article 9(3)[31], 9(4)[32], Article 10;[33]

➢ International Commercial Arbitration Act, ICAA [BUL]:[34] Article 47[35].

Rationes Decidendi:

20.17. Jurisdiction is a procedural *conditio sine qua non*; it is considered to be a prejudicial (preliminary) question.

20.18. The jurisdiction of courts in civil cases can be excluded by an arbitration agreement pursuant to Section 9(3) of the CPC. The existence of such an arbitration agreement constitutes a procedural obstacle, which prevents the court from ruling on any substantive issues, including such issues on which the court would otherwise be obliged to rule *(sua sponte)*.

---

[28] Source: APIS 7 PRAVO *(АПИС 7 ПРАВО legal information system)*; *Case law*, 9 Bulletin of Supreme Court of Republic of Bulgaria, 20 (1995). The decision was pointed out by Plamen Borissov, Sofia, Bulgaria.

[29] *Supra* note 13.

[30] See the note above to another annotated decision regarding Article 9(1) of the CCP [BUL] (approximate translation of the provision).

[31] CCP [BUL] (approximate translation, cit.), Article 9 – [...] (3) *(new, promulgated in the Collection, No. 55 of 1992) Subject to the terms of Paragraphs 1 and 2, the parties have the right to apply to a foreign court for a ruling on a dispute that is not within the exclusive jurisdiction of a Bulgarian court, provided the parties' consent to such procedure is given in writing and is effective under the law of the state of the court. Jurisdiction over a dispute within the jurisdiction of a foreign court can be vested in a Bulgarian court under the same conditions.* This Article allows choice-of-court agreements (so-called *forum selection*).

[32] CCP [BUL] (approximate translation, cit.), [...] (4) *(original Paragraph 2 Coll., No. 55 of 1992) Bulgarian court shall not discontinue or terminate any pending proceedings if it transpires that proceedings in the same case or an associated case have been opened in a foreign court.*

[33] CCP [BUL] (approximate translation, cit.), Article 10 – (1) *The issue of whether jurisdiction over any pending proceedings is vested in a court-of-law [...] or another institution can be determined upon a motion or sua sponte at any point during the proceedings.* (2) *The court order regarding this issue can be appealed in civil proceedings.*

[34] *Supra* note 9.

[35] Article 47 of the ICCA [BUL] contains an exhaustive list of grounds for the annulment of arbitral awards. The provision is cited elsewhere in connection with the annotation of another Bulgarian decision.

20.19. A conflict of jurisdiction between a court and *another authority* shall be assessed by the court *sua sponte* at any point during the proceedings.

20.20. An arbitral tribunal is not *another authority*. A lack of jurisdiction of a court due to the existence of an arbitration agreement is therefore considered by the court exclusively upon request, which must be submitted by the end of the first hearing in the case. If the jurisdictional challenge is not raised by the stipulated deadline, the objection is precluded.

[Description of Facts and Legal Issues]

20.21. "T." Ltd. challenged the decision of the Sofia Municipal Court, whereby the Court dismissed the motion for the discontinuation of the proceedings. The complainant argued that the case fell within the terms of an arbitration agreement. The complainant argued that the decision was unlawful, because the words *another authority* under Article 10(1) of the CPP [BUL] included the BCCIC. The objection of a lack of jurisdiction of the court can therefore be raised at any point during the proceedings. The complainant, however, failed to raise the objection of a lack of jurisdiction of the court due to the existence of the arbitration agreement by the end of the first hearing.

[From the Reasons Presented by the Supreme Court]

20.22. The Supreme Court holds that the court is not bound by the rule under Article 10 of the CCP [BUL]. The rule provides that the court shall assess the question of jurisdiction upon a motion or *sua sponte* at any point during the proceedings. If the court concludes that jurisdiction over the case is vested in another authority, the court discontinues the proceedings. Since the complainant failed to raise the objection of a lack of jurisdiction of the court due to the existence of the arbitration agreement by the end of the first hearing in the case (in court proceedings), the objection is precluded. The reason is that the arbitral tribunal is not *another authority*. The Supreme Court consequently dismissed the appeal.

| | |

V. Purpose of Recognition Proceedings and Prohibition of Material Review– Public Policy and Fundamental Procedural Principles as Condition for Recognition of Foreign Award– The Time Limit for Rendering an Award Agreed by the Parties Cannot Be Extended by a Decision of the Court of Arbitration (Supreme Court; July 28, 2004)

Key words:
temporal restriction | party autonomy | adversarial proceedings | time limit for the rendering of an arbitral award | maximum length of arbitration proceedings | seat of arbitration | ICC International Court of Arbitration | general rule | procedural condition | ICC Rules of Arbitration | equality of the parties | arbitral award | ICC arbitration | special rule | purpose of the recognition proceedings | expiration of the time limit | public policy | enforcement of the award | expiration of the arbitration agreement

Judgment of Bulgarian Supreme Court *(Върховен съд)* No. 630, Civil Case No. 1832/2003 of July 28, 2004 (in *H.T.E.K.Co.V.L.L.,* [Kuwait] v. *T. EAD* [BUL]):[36]

Laws Taken into Account in This Ruling:
➢ Code of Civil Procedure[37] (repealed version), CCP [BUL]: Article 9(2)[38] and Article 10;[39]
➢ Constitution of the Republic of Bulgaria:[40] Article 5(4)[41], Article 121;[42]

---

[36] Source: APIS 7 PRAVO *(АПИС 7 ПРАВО legal information system)*; 4 BULGARSKI ZAKONNIK MAGAZINE 93 (2005). The decision was pointed out by Plamen Borissov, Sofia, Bulgaria.

[37] *Supra* note 13.

[38] CCP [BUL] (approximate translation, cit.), Article 9 – [...] "(2) *(new, promulgated in the Collection, No. 55 of 1992) The arbitral tribunal can have its seat abroad, provided one of the parties has its residence or registered office abroad."*

[39] CCP [BUL] (approximate translation, cit.), Article 10 – "(1) *The issue of whether jurisdiction over any pending proceedings is vested in a court-of-law [...] or another institution can be determined upon a motion or sua sponte at any point during the proceedings. (2) The court order regarding this issue can be appealed in civil proceedings."*

[40] *Supra* note 2.

[41] Approximate translation (cit.), Article 5 – [...] "(4) *Constitutionally ratified and promulgated international treaties binding on the Republic of Bulgaria become part of Bulgarian national law. They prevail over any conflicting national legislation."*

[42] Approximate translation (cit.), Constitution of the Republic of Bulgaria – Article 121 – "(1) *The courts make sure that the parties to court proceedings have equal status and that the proceedings are adversarial. (2) The purpose of court proceedings is to establish the objective truth. (3) Hearings in all courts are public; the law provides for*

> ➢ Convention on the Recognition and Enforcement of Foreign Arbitral Awards (New York Convention; 1958): Article 2, Article 5.

Rationes Decidendi:

20.23. The recognition and enforcement of foreign court decisions and foreign arbitral awards represent separate proceedings provided for in the CCP [BUL]. The purpose of these proceedings is not to revisit the merits of the case, but to determine whether the foreign decision complies with the binding provisions of Bulgarian laws and regulations and with public policy.

20.24. The maximum length of arbitration proceedings (the time limit within which the arbitral award must be rendered) agreed by the parties cannot be unilaterally extended. This time limit cannot be unilaterally extended by the court of arbitration, nor by the arbitration tribunal.

20.25. An arbitral award rendered after the expiration of the time limit agreed by the parties is in breach of the procedure agreed by the parties and results in the expiration of the arbitration agreement (as a condition for arbitration) in consequence of the lapse of time.

20.26. The court dismisses the motion for the recognition and enforcement of a foreign arbitral award if the contents of the award and the procedure by which the award was rendered are in conflict with national public policy.

20.27. The breach of the principles governing adversarial proceedings and the failure to provide the space necessary for the defense of rights in the proceedings constitute a violation of public policy.

[Description of Facts and Legal Issues]

20.28. The Sofia Municipal Court recognized an arbitral award rendered by the ICC International Court of Arbitration (in ICC arbitration proceedings). The Court also passed a decision regarding the enforcement of the award. The appellate court set aside the decision of the court of first instance and denied the recognition of the award. That decision was appealed to the Supreme Court of Cassation. The Supreme Court upheld the decision of the appellate court and denied both the recognition and enforcement of the award.

[Author's Note]

20.29. This arbitral award is of fundamental significance for emphasizing the principle of party autonomy and for stipulating the limits of such autonomy. Even the arbitral tribunal (in the present case, the ICC International Court of Arbitration) is prohibited from extending the time limit for rendering the arbitral award. The tribunal is authorized to make decisions on the extension of the time limit for the award, which is explicitly provided for under the ICC Rules of Arbitration and which lasts six months. The

exceptional situations when the public can be denied access. (4) Court judgments and awards must contain reasons."

Bulgarian Supreme Court therefore concluded that an express agreement of the parties (as a special rule) on the maximum length of the arbitration proceedings (the maximum time limit for the award) prevails over the arbitration rules (as a general rule). The arbitration agreement expires together with the expiration of the agreed time limit; according to the Bulgarian Supreme Court, the jurisdiction of the arbitral tribunal expires at the same moment as well.

20.30. This decision introduced another important standard, namely the standard of principles of national (Bulgarian) public policy. This standard must be observed even if the seat of arbitration is abroad (not in Bulgaria) if the arbitral award is to be recognized and enforced in Bulgaria. Apart from the emphasis placed upon the importance of party autonomy, the decision also highlights the principle of equality of the parties and the principles of adversarial proceedings. Equality and adversarial proceedings are incorporated in Article 121(1) of the Bulgarian Constitution as general requirements of court proceedings. However, the Supreme Court applied this principle as a fundamental principle for all adversarial proceedings, including arbitration. These principles form part of Bulgarian public policy. Although the decision does not explicitly address the issue, we can presume that Bulgarian public policy also comprises certain other principles incorporated in Article 121 of the Constitution, despite the fact that these principles are only expressly stipulated for court proceedings; namely, the principle of establishing the objective truth as the purpose of court proceedings (or rather adversarial proceedings), and the obligation to give reasons for a decision. A contrary conclusion can be drawn with respect to the principle of publicity of proceedings under Article 121(3) of the Bulgarian Constitution. The latter provision explicitly allows a statutory exception.

20.31. Although arbitration in Bulgaria (alongside the Czech Republic, as concerns countries of Eastern and Central Europe) is based on a contract, the adversarial nature of these proceedings is not disputed.

| | |

VI. Violation of Public Policy as a Manifest Breach of Overriding Mandatory Public-law Rules Based on Constitution– The Merits of the Case Cannot Be Reviewed, Not Even During the Process of Examining Public Policy Violations (Supreme Court of Cassation; October 31, 2008)

Key words:
overriding mandatory rules | purchase price | Constitution of the Republic of Bulgaria | public law rule | subject matter of the dispute | review of an arbitral award | review on the merits | violation of public policy | damage | public policy | prohibition of review | basis of the legal system | manifest violation/ manifest breach | setting aside of an arbitral award

Judgment of Supreme Court of Cassation No. 689, Commercial Case No. 360/2008 of October 31, 2008:[43]

Laws Taken into Account in This Ruling:
➢ Constitution of the Republic of Bulgaria;[44]
➢ International Commercial Arbitration Act, ICAA [BUL]:[45] Section 47(3)[46].

Rationes Decidendi:
20.32. A violation of public policy constitutes a breach of overriding mandatory public-law rules based on the Constitution of the Republic of Bulgaria. The breach must affect rules that represent the basis of the legal system[47].
20.33. The court is prohibited from reviewing the merits of the arbitral award and examining the subject matter of the dispute, even if the purpose is to establish whether or not the award violated public policy.
20.34. The court is only entitled to set aside an arbitral award on the basis of grounds expressly specified in the International Commercial Arbitration Act (ICAA [BUL]). A violation of public policy constitutes one of these grounds. The violation of public policy must be manifest, without the necessity to examine the decision on the merits.

---

[43] Source: APIS 7 PRAVO (*АПИС 7 ПРАВО legal information system*). The decision was pointed out by Plamen Borissov, Sofia, Bulgaria.
[44] *Supra* note 2.
[45] *Supra* note 9.
[46] The provision is cited elsewhere in connection with the annotation of another decision. The respective provision of the ICAA [BUL] contains an exhaustive list of grounds for the annulment of arbitral awards.
[47] Likewise, Judgment of the Supreme Court of Cassation No. 728, Commercial Case No. 896/2007 of December 31, 2008 (in *Sh. AD* v. *ET "L"*). The decision also upheld the court practice with respect to the legal opinion presented in the following *rationes decidendi*. In the present case, however, the Court set aside the arbitral award, though not for a violation of public policy, but for the nullity of the arbitration agreement.

[Description of Facts and Legal Issues]

20.35. In the proceedings before the Supreme Court of Cassation, the claimant moved for the annulment (setting aside) of the arbitral award, under which the claimant had been ordered to pay compensation for damage caused by the delay in payment of the purchase price. The claimant argued that the decision was in violation of public policy, because he had not been in delay on the performance of his obligations under the contract.

[From the Reasons Presented by the Court]

20.36. The Court dismissed the proposal and held that no grounds for the annulment of the award were established, because a review on the merits is prohibited even in proceedings on the annulment of the arbitral award.

| | |

VII. Public Policy as Expression of Fundamental Substantive and Procedural Principles, Protecting Fundamental Values, Legal Ideas and Values of State and Society (Supreme Court of Cassation; February 9, 2009)

Key words:
values of society | adversarial proceedings | objective truth | legal ideas | subject of the arbitration proceedings | equality of the parties | decision on the merits | public policy | fundamental values | basic principles of law | substantive and procedural law

Judgment of Supreme Court of Cassation No. 6, Commercial Case No. 696/2008 of February 9, 2009 (in *C. EAD* v. *E. OOD I.T.*):[48]

Laws Taken into Account in This Ruling:

➢ Code of Civil Procedure (current version):[49] Article 235;[50]

---

[48]   Source: APIS 7 PRAVO (*АПИС 7 ПРАВО legal information system*), The decision was pointed out by Plamen Borissov, Sofia, Bulgaria.

[49]   Promulgated in: 59 STATE GAZETTE (*DV/ДВ - Държавен вестник*) (June 20, 2007), as amended. Available at: http://lex.bg/bg/laws/ldoc/2135558368 (accessed on December 17, 2010).

[50]   CCP [BUL] (approximate translation, cit.), Article 235 – "(1) *The decision shall be rendered by the court panel that attended the final hearing in the case.* (2) *The court shall base its decision on the facts of the case that the court accepted as established, as well as on the applicable provisions of the law.* (3) *The court shall also take into consideration circumstances that occurred after the claim was lodged, provided they have a bearing*

> International Commercial Arbitration Act, ICAA [BUL]:[51] Section 47(3)[52].

Rationes Decidendi:

20.37. The term "public policy" refers to fundamental principles of the Bulgarian legal system and protects fundamental values that must be observed. These include principles of both substantive and procedural law, and express basic legal ideas and values of state and society. Such principles include, *inter alia*, the principle of the rule of law, the determination of the objective truth, the equality of the parties in the proceedings, the principles of adversarial proceedings, etc. A violation of the principle of equality of the parties in arbitration constitutes grounds for the annulment of the arbitral award.

20.38. The court is not allowed to examine the decision on the merits and revisit the case that was the subject of the arbitration proceedings.

[Description of Facts and Legal Issues]

20.39. The claimant (C. EAD) applied for the annulment (setting aside) of an arbitral award, under which the claimant had been ordered to secure the free access of the respondent's clients to a particular facility and to discharge certain financial obligations. The claimant argued that the arbitral tribunal violated the principles of adversarial proceedings and the equality of the parties, which constitutes a violation of public policy and grounds for the annulment (setting aside) of the arbitral award. The Supreme Court of Cassation dismissed the motion. The Court held that the decision on the merits could not be reviewed. The violation of public policy would therefore have to be manifest and serious. The Court also elaborated on the term *"public policy"* as summarized above.

[*Alexander J. Bělohlávek*]

| | |

---

on the subject matter of the dispute. (4) *The decision, together with the reasons, shall be rendered in writing. (5) The court shall pronounce its decision together with the reasons no later than 1 month following the final hearing in the case. The decision shall be published in a public and freely accessible register of court decisions."*

51 *Supra* note 9.

52 The provision is cited elsewhere in connection with the annotation of another decision. The respective provision of the ICAA [BUL] contains an exhaustive list of grounds for the annulment of arbitral awards.

3. Canada

Key words:
death threat | enforcement of foreign arbitral award | estoppels | arbitration
proceedings | venue of hearing

Judgment C51225 of the Ontario Superior Court of April 29, 2010,
with respect to the decision of the *Ontario Court of Appeal, Canada*
(in matters of *Donaldson International Livestock Ltd. v. Znamensky*
***Selekcionno-Gibridny Center LLC*):[1]**

Rationes Decidendi:

21.01. In proceedings on the recognition and enforcement of foreign arbitral
awards[2], the court must hear and decide on the objection that one
party in arbitration received a death threat which discouraged them from
participating in oral hearings before the arbitral tribunal. Since the death
threat affected the party's willingness to participate in the arbitration
proceedings, the application of issue estoppels would have resulted in a
violation of the principle of due process.

21.02. If the other party to the arbitration proceedings (i.e., the one which
purportedly issued death threats to the other party) proposes that witness
testimony be heard, e.g. with the aid of videoconferencing technology,
this does not in and of itself constitute a change in the venue of hearing
[Moscow], as this is merely a change of the location in which the respective

---

[1] Published *in* 2010 ONCA 303. Other sources: (i) VIII (10) ITA Arbitration
Report (2010), (ii) ILO (*International Law office*), Arbitration (June 24, 2010);
available in electronic form at: http://www.internationallawoffice.com/newsletters/
detail.aspx?g=e11aa880-4755-451b-ae83-e3466adbaa9a (accessed on October 17,
2010).
[2] This particular case concerned the recognition and enforcement of two arbitral
awards issued in proceedings before the International Commercial Arbitration Court
("ICAC") at the Chamber of Commerce and Industry of the Russian Federation.
The venue of arbitration was Moscow, the governing law was the law of the Russian
Federation. The decision on recognition and enforcement was published in: (2009) O.J.
No. 4011, and annulled by the judgment of the Ontario Superior Court of April 29,
2010, annotated above.

witness or party would give their testimony. For this reason, the offer to proceed in such manner [i.e., to hear testimony via videoconferencing] is not enough to eliminate the death threat[3].

| | |

---

[3] On similar issues, see also DENIS MACEOIN, SHARIA LAW OR "ONE LAW FOR ALL?", London: Civitas (2009). This publication calls for a denial of recognition in the United Kingdom of decisions in arbitration proceedings under Sharia law (whereas such recognition is sought for the purpose of enforcement under the Arbitration Act of 1996), arguing that basic human rights may be violated in connection with death threats in these arbitration proceedings (the author correctly notes that Sharia law does not always differentiate clearly between mediation and arbitration). That being said, it must be noted that the author, Denis MacEoin, is primarily concerned with arbitration in family-law matters. With respect to family-law issues, see also Robert Verkaik, *Court rules Islamic law discriminatory*, THE INDEPENDENT ON SUNDAY (October 23, 2008), available in electronic form at: http://www.independent.co.uk/news/uk/home-news/court-rules-islamic-law-discriminatory-969777.html (accessed on October 17, 2010).

4. Czech Republic

Abbreviations used in the annotations:

ArbAct [CZE]   - Act No. 216/1994 Coll. of 1 November 1994 on Arbitration and on Enforcement of Arbitration Rulings, as amended

CivCo [CZE]   - Act No. 40/1964 Coll., the Civil Code, as amended

ConstCoAct [CZE] - Act No. 182/1993 Coll. on the Czech Constitutional Court, as amended.

IPRG [SUI]   - Swiss Federal Code on Private International Private Law (Switzerland)

Arbitration in the Case Law of the Constitutional Court of the Czech Republic with regard to the Nature and Purpose of Arbitration

Alexander J. Bělohlávek & Tereza Profeldová

Key words:
exequatur | ICC Rules on Arbitration | substantive-law | effect of substantive law | insolvency proceedings | jurisdictional theory | bankruptcy | inspection authority | matrimonial dispute | international law | seat of arbitration | determining the content of agreement | general court | responsibility of arbitrators | responsibility of state | information duty | EU law | negative prescription | progress of arbitration | arbitration agreement | contract theory | court protection | permanent court of arbitration | state authority | state court | sovereign power | effect of filing a complaint | Constitutional Court of the Czech Republic | constitutional court | recognition of arbitration ruling | public authority | enforcement of arbitration ruling | enforcement of a decision | principles of justice | annulment of arbitration ruling

I. Legal Foundation – Nature of Arbitration in the Czech Republic – Critical Comments on Constitutional Case Law

22.01. Arbitration is defined in Act No. 216/1994 Coll. of 1 November 1994 on Arbitration and on Enforcement of Arbitration Rulings, as amended ("ArbAct [CZE]"). According to Section 2, paragraph 1 of ArbAct [CZE], parties may agree that matrimonial disputes between them, with the exception of disputes arising in connection with the execution of a judgment in incidental disputes[1], the hearing and settlement of which would otherwise be in the jurisdiction of a court[2], is to be decided by one or several arbitrators or a permanent court of arbitration[3] (arbitration agreement).

22.02. According to the authors, a number of additional arguments can be found in support of the jurisdictional basis of arbitration in the context of the Czech legal system: (●) Filing an [arbitration] complaint[4] has the same effect as a complaint filed with a general court. (●) According to Section 16 of ArbAct [CZE], which stipulates that if a party raises its claim before arbitrators within the prescription or preclusive period and if arbitrators rule not to have jurisdiction over the matter, or if an arbitration ruling is annulled and a party files another complaint or a demand for the continuation of proceedings with a court or another applicable authority within 30 days after receiving a notice of a lack of jurisdiction or of the annulment of an arbitration ruling, the substantive-law effects of a filed complaint remain preserved[5]. (●) Similarly, an arbitration ruling, which cannot be further reviewed or in respect of which the deadline for making a request for review has elapsed[6], comes into effect on the day of delivery

[1] The term incidental dispute need to be understood (in a simplified manner) as a dispute regarding the exclusion of property and/or rights, including receivables, from the assets of a bankrupt and/or situations where such property or rights are to become a part of a bankrupt's assets.

[2] In connection with the preparation of an amendment to ArbAct [CZE], there have been thoughts to expand objective arbitrability, so that it will apply not only to property-related disputes that are (in the absence of an arbitration agreement) in the jurisdiction of courts, but also to property-related disputes that are in the jurisdiction of other bodies of public authority. A typical example is the numerous disputes in the field of telecommunications, which have up to now been in the jurisdiction of the *Czech Telecommunication Authority*.

[3] So-called *"permanent courts of arbitration"* are defined in Section 13 of ArbAct [CZE]. This provision is referred to in connection with [the current general] case law of Czech courts regarding arbitration. Permanent courts of arbitration may be established in the Czech Republic solely based on the law, a fact that underlines the state's qualified interest in guaranteeing certain standards on the part of government-certified arbitration courts, where such institutions cannot be established without a legal framework. The authors opine that if arbitration were based solely on the contractual agreement of parties, such an involvement by the state would be superfluous. Thus, the authors believe that the quoted legislation is an argument supporting the jurisdictional or (at least) mixed basis for arbitration in the Czech Republic.

[4] Compare: *Request for arbitration.*

[5] This mainly concerns the effect of interruptions of prescription periods as a result of the initiation of proceedings (filing a complaint). As regards this issue, it needs to be pointed out that the Czech law, similarly as the *civil law* of most other countries, is based strictly on the notion that *negative prescription* is a substantive act as opposed to a procedural act.

[6] According to Section 27 of ArbAct [CZE], the parties to an arbitration agreement may agree that an arbitration ruling will be reviewed by other arbitrators. Such a review would constitute a sort of second instance. It should be pointed out, however, that this possibility is used to a limited extent. One of the authors has participated in several

of an enforceable court ruling and is legally enforceable[7]. A paper version of an arbitration ruling must be delivered to the parties; after delivery, it is supplemented by a legal effectiveness clause[8]. Thus, an arbitration ruling issued in the Czech Republic is not subject to any exequatur, and when it comes to legal effect (upon its delivery to the parties), it is enforceable, and its execution can be requested through bodies of public authority. The concept of *legal force* is typical for the jurisdictional and adjudicative nature of proceedings. It would be difficult to find an analogy if the outcome of arbitration were understood exclusively as a certain qualified agreement of the parties on the settlement of a dispute defined by an arbitrator in an arbitration ruling[9]. An arbitration ruling delivered by an arbitrator can therefore be regarded as a jurisdictional act[10], to which the legislation confers the nature of an enforceable judgment already at the time it is delivered to the parties, i.e. at the time when it comes into legal force. (●) This issue is related to the fact that the state retains the authority to conduct a retroactive inspection in connection with the annulment of an arbitration ruling by a court in accordance with Sections 31 and following of the Arbitration Act. (●) Arbitrators cannot proceed in their role entirely without restrictions. On the contrary. They are legally required to settle disputes in accordance with valid laws, unless they are expressly empowered by the parties to deliver a ruling based on [the principles] of justice[11]. It can be therefore concluded that the

hundred arbitrations in the last two decades, mostly as an arbitrator or a member of an arbitration tribunal, and only encountered a review of an arbitration ruling according to Section 27 ArbAct [CZE] on two occasions.

[7] See Section 28, paragraph 2 of ArbAct [CZE].

[8] See Section 28, paragraph 1 of ArbAct [CZE].

[9] Similar concepts exist in the law of other countries, even though it differs from country to country what the nature of the applicable concept is and to what extent it does or does not support the jurisdictional basis of arbitration. In the author's opinion, however, it is indecisive.

For instance:

Article 193, paragraph 3 of IPRG [SUI] (unofficial translation, cit.) *At the request of a party, an arbitration tribunal confirms that a ruling has been issued in accordance with the provisions of this Act; such a confirmation has the same effect as the depositing of the ruling* [with a court].

[10] An act of the application of the law.

[11] See Section 25, paragraph 3 of ArbAct [CZE]. (cit.) *In the practice of arbitration, arbitrators observe the substantive law that is decisive for a dispute; they may, however, decide a dispute according to the principles of justice, but only if they are expressly authorized to do so by the parties. In the sense of Section 37 of the Arbitration Act, in arbitral proceedings with an international element, arbitrators decide a dispute in accordance with the law selected by the parties. A selected law or the law applicable based on collision laws means substantive law unless the choice of the parties indicates otherwise; consideration is not given to conflicting regulations of the law chosen by the parties or a law that is applicable on another basis. If the parties do not choose substantive law in the abovementioned manner, the arbitrators use the law of the country that is determined in accordance with domestic collision legal regulations.*

mission/purpose of an arbitrator is to engage in law finding, similarly as a judge (of a general/state court). Permanent arbitration courts must keep on file arbitration rulings with a legal effectiveness clause as well as all documents describing the progress of arbitral proceedings for 20 years after they come into legal force. (●) In addition, arbitrators participating in "*ad hoc*" arbitral proceedings must within 30 days after the legal force of an arbitration ruling submit to the custody of the district court, in the jurisdiction of which the arbitration ruling is delivered, the arbitration ruling bearing a legal effectiveness clause as well as documents describing the progress of the applicable arbitral proceedings[12]. This obligation to submit arbitration rulings to court custody does not apply only if an arbitration ruling is delivered outside the Czech Republic[13]. Moreover, the Arbitration Act contains supplementary provisions that require (an agreement of the parties regarding the method for the conduct of arbitral proceedings is preferred) an analogical application of the Civil Procedure Code in the event that the parties do not agree on the method for the conduct of arbitral proceedings[14]. Even though an arbitrator does not have to apply the procedural regulations set out in the Civil Procedure Code analogically without further consideration, in judicial practice, arbitrators often resort to this legislation or, as a minimum, take it into consideration. (●) [General] courts fulfil other supportive functions in the arbitration process since arbitrators are, for instance in the sense of Section 20, paragraph 2, entitled to make a demand to the applicable [general/state] court to carry out procedural actions that arbitrators are unable to conduct on their own. A court must comply with their demand, unless the relevant procedural act is not allowable under the law, where a court makes all the decisions necessary for conforming to the request.

---

[12] This applies to *ad hoc* proceedings only. In proceedings before one of the three permanent courts of arbitration in the Czech Republic, arbitration rulings are not deposited with a court. In the event that arbitrators do not fulfill the obligation to deposit with a court an arbitration ruling delivered in *ad hoc* proceedings, their failure to do so has no effect on the validity and legal force of the arbitration ruling. Even though the author has not encountered such a case (no such case has been documented), there may exist liability for damage caused by the failure to fulfill the legal obligation to deposit an arbitration ruling with a court. In such a case, the lawful requirements for claiming damages would have to be met. According to the authors, however, such liability would not be contractual liability stemming from an agreement; it would be non-contractual liability because the prevalent legal opinion in the Czech Republic says that arbitrators do not have any contractual relationship with the parties to arbitration. Further, this fact tends to provide an argument in favor of the jurisdictional theory as opposed to the contractual theory with regard to the basis and nature of arbitration.

[13] In Section 29, paragraph 1 and paragraph 2 of ArbAct [CZE].

[14] See Section 44 of ArbAct [CZE] (cit.) *Unless otherwise stipulated in this Act, the provisions of the Civil Procedure Code shall apply mutatis mutandis to court litigation conducted in accordance with this Act.*

22.03. According to the authors, defining and approaching arbitration this way suggests that the law entrusts/delegates to private entities, under the applicable regulations, the exercise of some of its powers relating to the settlement of disputes. Incidentally, this conclusion is accepted by the majority (save for exceptions) of professionals in the Czech Republic[15]. Some authors (commentators) do not deny the effects of the role and function of the state on arbitration in the Czech Republic, but they lean toward a mixed theory of arbitration, mainly pointing out that even though the appointment of an arbitrator or an arbitration tribunal has a private nature and arbitration may only be initiated and conducted based on an existing agreement of the parties, arbitration itself retains its "public-law character". The state on the one hand exercises its oversight powers *vis-à-vis* arbitration courts and helps through state courts wherever arbitrators are unable to complete certain tasks, and, on the other hand, it confers the same effects, subject to certain conditions, to arbitration rulings as to judgments delivered by courts[16].

22.04. Despite the abovementioned relatively intensive discussions about the prospects of instituting greater control over arbitration, it needs to be said that the official case law of Czech courts attributes clearly contractual nature to arbitration. According to the following (referred to below) rulings, activities conducted by arbitrators cannot be classified as law finding; they consist of clarifying/rectifying an existing contractual relationship in representation and based on the free will of the parties. As regards this issue, however, the Constitutional Court of the Czech Republic failed in 2002[17] to determine whether on this basis, a *"simple"* agreement between parties may gain the status of an enforceable ruling (the Czech law does not require any exequatur decision) Another issue is the extent to which the ruling in question, delivered by the Constitutional Court of the Czech Republic in 2002, needs to be understood as an expression of a binding legal (constitutional) opinion, since none of subsequently delivered rulings have made any attempt to assume an independent approach to the issue, and merely echo the fundamentally important ruling of 2002. Verdicts delivered at a later date obviously do not aspire to express a standpoint with regard to the nature of arbitration; they are essentially judgments that deal with the issue under discussion from the viewpoint of the authority (jurisdiction) of Constitutional Court of the Czech Republic to hear and decide particular constitutional complaints. In general, there are numerous opinions (especially abroad) that expressly state that an arbitration tribunal

---

[15] See, for instance, ZDENĚK KUČERA, MEZINÁRODNÍ PRÁVO SOUKROMÉ, *(International Private Law)*, Brno: Nakladatelství Doplněk 401 (5th revised and supplemented ed. 2001); Květoslav Růžička, *K otázce právní povahy rozhodčího řízení (Regarding the Issue of the Legal Nature of Arbitration)*, 5 BULLETIN ADVOKACIE (2003).

[16] NADĚŽDA ROZEHNALOVÁ, PRÁVO MEZINÁRODNÍHO OBCHODU *(Law of International Trade)*, Brno: MU v Brně 456-457 (2004).

[17] Resolution of the Constitutional Court of the Czech Republic, Ref. No. IV.ÚS 174/02, of 15 July 2002.

is not a court in the sense of the applicable law of the country in question, but, taking into account the nature of arbitration per se, insist that some concepts which define civil legal proceedings need to be applied to it in an analogical manner. Courts (i.e. other than constitutional courts, according to the Czech legal terminology so-called *general courts*) often refer to the case law of the Constitutional Court of the Czech Republic. Nonetheless, arbitration is in fact attributed purely adjudicative importance due to the fact that it is deemed to represent an alternative to court litigation. Numerous verdicts (including rulings delivered by the Supreme Court of the Czech Republic) subject arbitrators to essentially the same requirements as judges participating in court litigation. A typical example is the requirement contained in a ruling of the Supreme Court [CZE], which obliges arbitrators to fulfil the so-called *duty to inform*, which (very simply said) consists of the obligation to inform a party that it will not discharge the burden of proof so as to prevent *surprising decisions* and to provide the parties with effective opportunities for procedural defence. This information duty has been the subject of extensive discussions and has been strongly criticized by arbitrators. Nevertheless, it is this legal standpoint of the Supreme Court [CZE] (similarly as a number of other legal opinions expressed in extensive case law) which clearly confirms that courts base their actions on the jurisdictional theory and the notion that arbitrators have a comparable status as courts (so-called *general/state courts*). Arbitrators, naturally, do not possess any public authority. Still, they are required to comport, in many regards, in the same manner as the judges of *general/state courts*.

22.05. At the same time, it needs to be pointed out that according to a relatively common opinion, arbitrators must apply law to its full extent, including, for instance, regulations of *European law* (EU law)[18]. A typical example is the doctrine employed in connection with the effect of bankruptcy and/or another qualified decision made in connection with the bankruptcy of a person that is a party to arbitration. Not many people in the Czech Republic dispute the standpoint that such a case is fully subject to the effects of Article 15 of Council Regulation (EC) No. 1346/2000 on

---

[18] There are, however, other opinions even though they are advocated by a minority. See, for instance, Květoslav Růžička, *Neaplikování 'Římů' v tuzemském rozhodčím řízení (Non-application of Rome I and Rome II in National Arbitration Proceedings)*, 7 (10) Právní fórum 470-478 (2010), which, as regards this issue, expresses doubts with regard to the determination of the governing law in disputes with an international element. The same problem is dealt with, albeit with a somewhat different conclusion, for instance, by Alexander J. Bělohlávek, *Law Applicable to the Merits of International Arbitration and Current Developments in European Private International Law: Conflict-of-Laws Rules and the Applicability of the Rome Convention, Rome I Regulation and Other EU Law Standards in International Arbitration*, in 1 Czech Yearbook of International Law, New York: JurisPublishing Inc. 25-46 (N. Rozehnalová, A. Bělohlávek eds., 2010).

insolvency proceedings[19], in contrast to, for instance, opinions harboured by many specialists in England[20].

22.06. The authors believe that no matter what effort is used to *separate* in any way arbitration from state power, it is always state power (public authority) that defines the legal framework within which it is willing to accept arbitration. Attempts to portray arbitration as a sort of denationalized process are chimerical. Although the authors do not consider this trend positive, it is necessary to acknowledge the actual state of the legal and commercial environment on the global scale, where it may be somewhat upsetting to conclude that the willingness to fulfil one's obligations in today's world is very distant from the model state of affairs. For this reason, it is difficult to imagine that a claimant would initiate formal action (whether court litigation or arbitration) without

---

[19]   It was in the Czech Republic, where arbitrators, most likely for the first time, applied Council Regulation (EC) No. 1346/2000 to specific arbitration that concerned a series of disputes between Vivendi and Elektrim (Poland) (Elektrim S.A. was declared bankrupt in Poland in August 2007). For a highly anonymized summary of the decision rendered by arbitrations in the Czech proceedings, see ALEXANDER J. BĚLOHLÁVEK, ARBITRATION LAW AND PRACTICE IN THE CZECH REPUBLIC (WITH REGARD TO THE ARBITRATION LAW IN SLOVAKIA), Praha: Linde 263-272 (2009). Only a relatively long time after the matter was examined by arbitrators in the Czech Republic, rulings were delivered in ICC proceedings, proceedings before a Swiss federal court, proceedings before a British court, etc., which have in the interim become relatively well known and have been debated quite extensively. Compare, for instance, with Domitille Baizeau, *Arbitration and Insolvency: Issues of Applicable Law*, in NEW DEVELOPMENTS IN INTERNATIONAL COMMERCIAL ARBITRATION, Zürich: Schulthess (C. Müller and A. Rigozzi eds., 2009). In particular, conclusions can be drawn from comparing them with the following rulings: Arbitration Court attached to the Economic Chamber of the Czech Republic and Agricultural Chamber of the Czech Republic, Arbitration Ruling of 15 January 2008 in Case 135/2006; High Court of Justice, Syska v. Vivendi Universal SA et al, Judgment of October 2, 2008, [2008] EWHC 2155 (Comm); Court of Appeal (Civil Division), Syska v. Vivendi Universal SA et al, Judgment of 9 July 2009 [2009] EWCA Civ 677; Swiss Supreme Court, Vivendi et al v. 4A 428/2008 of 31 March 2009, First Civil Law Division of the Swiss Federal Tribunal. English and Swiss decisions both referred to as the Elektrim disputes. As regards the term "court", as employed in Article 15 of Council Regulation (EC) No. 1346/2000, as a term qualitatively different from the general definition of this term in Article 2 of the quoted regulation, see, for instance, ALEXANDER J. BĚLOHLÁVEK, EVROPSKÉ A MEZINÁRODNÍ INSOLVENČNÍ PRÁVO. KOMENTÁŘ. *(European and International Insolvency Law. A Commentary.)*, Praha: C. H. Beck (2007), see comments on Article 15.

[20]   Compare, for instance, with Alexander J. Bělohlávek & Tomáš Řezníček, *Dopady rozhodnutí o úpadku a insolvenčního řízení na majetek účastníka na probíhající rozhodčí řízení v tuzemské a mezinárodní praxi ve světle aktuální judikatury některých obecných a rozhodčích soudů (Impacts of Insolvency and Insolvency Proceedings of a Party on Pending Arbitration Proceedings in Domestic and International Experience in the Light of Current Case Law of Particular Courts and Arbitral Tribunals)*, 2 (9) OBCHODNĚPRÁVNÍ REVUE *(Commercial Law Review)* 1-14 (2010), or Alexander J. Bělohlávek, *Impact of Insolvency of A Party on Pending Arbitration Proceedings in Czech Republic, England and Switzerland And Other Countries*, in YEARBOOK ON INTERNATIONAL ARBITRATION, Berlin: European Academic Press 145-166 (M. Roth and M. Geistlinger eds., 2010).

a guarantee that a decision in the matter in question will be enforced by the public power for the needs of [the possible] future enforcement (execution) of such a decision. It is only public authority that, through a country's legal system, determines whether and under what conditions the powers of arbitrators are recognized and, more importantly, whether and under what conditions the enforcement of rulings delivered by arbitrators is accepted. Such a legal framework, which derives exclusively from national laws (i.e. a country's lawmaking power and the political and legal standpoint of every individual state as regards the enforcement of *justice* and *law finding*, is often of fundamental importance for deciding the country where international arbitration is to take place in the sense of the seat of arbitration.

| | |

II. Important Rulings of the Constitutional Court

II.1. Resolution of the Constitutional Court of the Czech Republic Ref. No. IV ÚS 174/02 of 15 July 2002[21]

22.07. The chairman of the arbitration tribunal, which delivered a ruling in this case, stated with regard to the constitutional complaint in question that his legal opinion had not been consulted with the other members of the "former" tribunal, that the opinion reflected his personal views, and that it cannot be interpreted as the arbitration court's standpoint in the sense of Section 30, paragraph 3 of Act No. 182/1993 Coll. on the Czech Constitutional Court, as amended (*ConstCoAct* [CZE])[22]. The tribunal that heard the dispute had been appointed by the parties in an *ad hoc* manner and cannot be regarded in the same way as a tribunal of a general court. An arbitration court is a private entity that despite being designated as a court does not belong to the system of courts of law, in the sense of the definition of the judiciary system in the Act on Court and Judges, and it is not a body of public authority. It is a specialized organization providing services to persons that want an arbitrator to clarify and stabilize their legal relationship. The nature of arbitration stems from an agreement

---

[21] Published *in* 27 COLLECTION OF VERDICTS AND RESOLUTIONS OF THE CONSTITUTIONAL COURT OF THE CZECH REPUBLIC [CZE], Resolutions Ref. No. 20, pp. 257 and following.
[22] ConstCoAct [CZE] Section 30 – [...] (3) *A state body or a government authority is represented in proceedings before the Constitutional Court by a person authorized to act on behalf of such a state body or of a government authority in accordance with special regulations, unless otherwise stipulated in this Act. This provision does not prejudice the right of a state body or of a government authority to be represented by an attorney to the extent set out in special regulations.* [...]

that delegates the will of the parties, where the outcome is a rectifying activity in the sense of Section 585 of Czech Act No. 40/1964 Coll., the Civil Code, as amended (*CivCo* [CZE])[23]. The outcome is a qualified form of an obligation that it is binding as such. An arbitrator does not engage in law finding but establishes (defines, clarifies, i.e. sets right) a contractual relationship in representation of the parties. Thus, the power of an arbitrator is not the delegated sovereign power of a state; it stems from the private right of the parties to determine their destiny, where the exercise of this right is entrusted to the arbitrator. An arbitration ruling is not delivered by an arbitration court but by arbitrators. It is enforceable as a result of the enforceability of the obligation established by the arbitrators who represent the parties. From this viewpoint, the Arbitration Court attached to the Economic Chamber of the Czech Republic and Agricultural Chamber of the Czech Republic cannot be the subject of a constitutional complaint.

22.08. Furthermore, the Constitutional Court examined whether the arbitration ruling in question is an enforceable decision of a body of public authority in the sense of Article 87, paragraph 1, letter d) of the Czech Constitution (*Constitution* [CZE])[24] or in the sense of Section 72, paragraph 1, letter a) of ConstCoAct [CZE][25], where the court concluded that the Arbitration Court attached to the Economic Chamber of the Czech Republic and Agricultural Chamber of the Czech Republic is not a body of public authority, and, consequently, its arbitration rulings cannot constitute decisions of a body of public authority in the sense of the aforestated provisions of the Constitution [CZE] and ConstCoAct. According to Section 1 (2)(b) of the Rules of the Arbitration Court attached to the Economic Chamber of the Czech Republic and Agricultural Chamber of the Czech Republic, this arbitration court decides disputes if its authority regarding a dispute stems from a valid arbitration agreement entered

---

[23] CivCo [CZE] Settlement, Section 585 – (1) *Under a settlement agreement, the parties may define their mutual rights that are disputed or dubious. An agreement, under which the parties are to define any and all rights, does not concern rights a party could not have taken into consideration. (2) If an existing obligation has been established in writing, a settlement agreement must also be executed in writing; the same applies to an agreement relating to an obligation that has expired. (3) An existing obligation is replaced by the obligation that ensues from the settlement.*
[24] Constitution [CZE] Article 87 – (1) *The Constitutional Court decides* – [...] *d) a constitutional complaint against an enforceable ruling and another action of bodies of public authority into constitutionally guaranteed rights and freedoms,* [...]
[25] ConstCoAct [CZE] Section 72 – (1) *Eligible to file a constitutional complaint is* a) *a natural person or a juridical person pursuant to Article 87, paragraph 1, letter d) of the Constitution, provided that such a person claims that under an enforceable verdict in proceedings to which it was a party, under a measure, or under another action of a body of public authority (hereinafter referred to as an "action of a body of public authority"), the person's fundamental right or freedom guaranteed under the constitutional order have been violated (hereinafter referred to as "constitutionally guaranteed fundamental right or freedom"),* [...].

into between the parties. In this sense, the opinion [of the Constitutional Court expressed in the ruling under discussion] corresponds to the abovementioned statements of the chairman of the arbitration tribunal who maintains that the nature of arbitration stems from an agreement delegating the will of the parties, where the outcome is a form of qualified obligation that is binding as such. An arbitrator does not engage in law finding, but establishes (defines, clarifies, i.e. rectifies) a contractual relationship in representation of the parties. Thus, the power of an arbitrator is not the delegated sovereign power of the state, but is derived from the private right of the parties to determine their destiny.

22.09. The authors consider this ruling highly controversial. It is likely that the Czech Republic is one of the last two European countries where this doctrine is formally endorsed, as most other countries (in numerous cases based on verdicts of constitutional or superior courts) recognize arbitration as an alternative to court litigation and a method for finding and applying law. The other such country is Bulgaria, where this doctrine essentially stems from the provisions of the Bulgarian Arbitration Act. It needs to be mentioned, however, that the verdict of the Czech Constitutional Court is more than eight years old. Since then, arbitration has gone through hardly imaginable development, and moderate estimates indicate that some 100,000 disputes are settled in arbitration in the Czech Republic every year. Exact statistics are not available because arbitration rulings delivered in the Czech Republic (*domestic arbitration rulings*) are directly enforceable and require no exequatur (recognitory) verdict of Czech courts. It is estimated, however, that this number is considerably higher. Furthermore, a significant portion of these disputes is cases heard in *ad hoc* proceedings (outside one of the three permanent courts of arbitration). For illustration, it needs to be said that, for instance, one of the permanent courts of arbitration, the Arbitration Court attached to the Economic Chamber of the Czech Republic and Agricultural Chamber of the Czech Republic, processes several thousand disputes on an annual basis. In 2010 alone, there were approximately 3,000 new disputes (the exact quantity was unknown at the time of writing this chapter)[26]. It is a trend of the last approximately five to eight years, when the number of civil asset disputes

---

[26] This quantity is beyond comparison. It needs to be mentioned that the development has been similar in some other Central and Eastern European countries. A comparable situation exists, for instance, in Bulgaria. However, the absolute number of disputes settled in arbitration is considerably lower (by several orders). On the other hand, a comparison of the development of the number of disputes, as presented, for instance, the Arbitration Court at the Bulgarian Chamber of Commerce and Industry in its presentation documents, shows that the development is similar to that in the Czech Republic as to the progress of the increase in the number of disputes. The authors believe that Bulgaria will develop similarly as the Czech Republic as far as the absolute numbers are concerned within approximately the next four to five years, provided that standard statistical methods are used and the local specifics are taken into account where applicable.

resolved in arbitration has been increasing every year. This situation is essentially the result of a campaign launched to promote arbitration after the new Arbitration Act (ArbAct [CZE]) was passed in 1994. In contrast to the previous law, this piece of legislation has allowed the hearing of so-called *domestic disputes*[27] in arbitration. Moreover, it appears that the nature of arbitration was not analysed in depth prior to the delivery of the abovementioned resolution of the Czech Constitutional Court. It seems, on the contrary, that the decision was made in a somewhat hasty fashion. It needs to be stressed, that the matter in question, which was examined by the Constitutional Court, involved damages claimed from arbitrators in connection with a verdict delivered in a specific dispute. It is obvious that to a certain extent, the Constitutional Court's ruling was delivered under pressure caused by fears that claims may be made against the government in connection with the exercise of *quasi-judicial power* under the state's supervision. For this reason, the state endeavoured, in delivering this verdict, to *free itself* from any responsibility for the progress and outcome of arbitration in the sense of liability relating to property. Furthermore, it is evident that the Constitutional Court's judgment uses a significant portion of the arguments used by the arbitrators who were the respondents in the proceedings. At least two of them favoured the traditional contractual doctrine. Their statements, which rejected entirely the jurisdictional nature (in the sense of rejecting the application of law and, conversely, in the sense of *finding the content of the agreement of the parties*), were nevertheless to a large extent affected by their personal interests, namely defence against the specific complaint in this matter. It is quite understandable that these statements were accepted by the Constitutional Court as a relatively simple line of arguing to protect the state from possible claims that could be raised against it if any accountability for arbitration were acknowledged. Since the delivery of this judgment in July 2002, no tribunal of the Czech Constitutional Court has examined in depth the nature of arbitration (including the nature of arbitration agreements and arbitration rulings) in any way whatsoever. On the contrary, the Constitutional Court continues to refer (with some exceptions) to the verdict of July 2002. As mentioned above, it is paradoxical that this resolution of the Constitutional Court is also invoked by general courts despite the fact that they often inadequately and strictly insist that arbitration conform to the same standards as those that apply to court litigation.

22.10. According to the authors, the verdict in question is flawed and illogical from the doctrinal viewpoint. In essence, it suggests complete *injustice*. The Czech constitutional system guarantees in the Charter of Fundamental

---

[27]   Arbitration has a long tradition in the Czech Republic (formerly in Czechoslovakia). However, the previous law, Act No. 98/1963 Coll., allowed solely disputes relating to international trade to be settled in arbitration. Arbitrability was expanded to a significant extent only starting on 1 January 1995, when ArbAct [CZE] came into force.

Rights and Freedoms the right of every person to approach an independent court or another "authority" in the event of a dispute[28]. The Czech Republic gives extensive support to arbitration. Its stance is fully based, for instance, on the principle of separability, the principle of *Kompetenz-Kompetenz*, the principle of prohibition of *revision au fond* (prohibition of a review of an arbitration ruling in proceedings pertaining to the cancellation of the arbitration ruling or in proceedings related to execution)[29]. **Likewise, it is fully recognized that by entering into an arbitration agreement, the parties waive the right to court litigation, i.e. the right to have a case examined by a body of public authority, as this right is guaranteed in Article 36 of the Charter of Fundamental Rights and Freedoms [CZE][30]. However, if arbitration were not to provide a qualitatively adequate alternative to court litigation, a party to an arbitration agreement would be entirely stripped of legal protection in the event that arbitration did not involve law finding, but only consisted of *determining the content of a contractual relationship between the parties*[31].** Such a situation is intolerable in the modern world governed by the principle of rule of law. From the constitutional viewpoint, it is therefore necessary to regard arbitration only as an alternative to litigation before [general/state] courts. Thus, arbitration involves law finding, and entering into an arbitration agreement does not deprive any person of legal protection. Nonetheless, a person would be stripped of legal protection and his fundamental civil rights if arbitration consisted of no more than *determining the content of the legal relationship between the parties* without the actual and proper application of law.

---

[28]   The Charter of Fundamental Rights and Freedoms is a part of the constitutional system of the Czech Republic based on Resolution of the Presidium of the Czech National Council No. 2/1993 Coll. of 16 December 1992 on the Proclamation of the Charter of Fundamental Rights and Freedoms as a part of the constitutional order of the Czech Republic, as amended by Constitutional Act No. 162/1998 Coll. (cit.) PART FIVE – Right to Court and Other Legal Protection, Article 36 – (1) Every person may claim his rights, using the prescribed procedure, before an independent and impartial court and, in prescribed cases, before another authority. (2) A person who claims that his rights have been violated by a decision of a body of public administration may approach a court and demand a review of the lawfulness of such a decision, unless the law stipulates otherwise. It is prohibited, however, to exclude from the powers of a court the review of decisions pertaining to fundamental rights and freedoms, as defined in the Charter. (3) Every person is entitled to compensation for damage incurred by same as a result of an unlawful decision of a court, another state authority, or a body of public administration or by an erroneous official procedure. (4) Conditions and details are defined by the law.
[29]   See, for instance, Alexander J. Bělohlávek & Tomáš Pezl, *International and Domestic Arbitration from the Perspective of Article 36 of the Basic Rights and Freedoms Law, Court Jurisdiction and the Rights guaranteed by the Constitution (Set-Aside of an Award in respect to the Prohibition Revision au fond)*, 146 (7) Právník 768-802 (2006).
[30]   The provision is quoted above in the footnotes relating to this chapter.
[31]   This issue is presented in Resolution of the Czech Constitutional Court Ref. No. IV ÚS 174/02 of 15 July 2002.

22.11. The fact that arbitration involves law finding (application) (by settling disputes according to the law) is confirmed by ArbAct [CZE], which allows the delivery of judgments based on the principles of justice (*ex aequo et bono*), but only if the parties expressly agree to such an approach. Otherwise, arbitrators must apply the valid law (i.e. they must identify the valid law, determine its content, and apply it fully to the ascertained facts of the case). It needs to be mentioned, however, that agreements empowering arbitrators to settle a dispute according to *the principles of justice* are exceptional in actual practice. The *resolving nature* of the arbitration process is confirmed by the terminology employed by ArbAct [CZE], which consistently uses the term "resolve". In this regard, it should be mentioned that during recent discussions about a major amendment to the *ICC Rules on Arbitration*[32], the fact that in the English version the term "*to settle*" will most likely be replaced by the term "*to resolve*" was not disputed, which clearly confirms the trend that has become prevalent in international practice during approximately the last two decades, namely a trend that maintains that arbitration is a form of law finding as opposed to *the mere determination of the content of the contractual relationship between parties.*

22.12. In view of these facts, the authors opine that a fundamental constitutional standpoint on the nature of arbitration has not been expressed in the Czech Republic thus far. Nevertheless, it needs to be taken into account that a constitutional viewpoint has been articulated in the way indicated by the corresponding resolutions of the Czech Constitutional Court annotated in this chapter.

II.2. Resolution of the Constitutional Court of the Czech Republic Ref. No. II ÚS 3059/08 of 15 January 2009

22.13. The Constitutional Court refers to its earlier verdicts[33], which were based on the premise that the role of an arbitration court or an arbitrator to deliver decisions originates from an agreement that delegates the will of the parties, and the outcome is a qualified form of an obligation. An arbitrator (court of arbitration) does not engage in law finding, but establishes (determines, clarifies, i.e. rectifies) a contractual relationship in representation of the parties. Its authority is not the delegated sovereign power of the state; it stems from the private right of the parties to determine their destiny.

---

32   It is expected that the process will be completed in the course of 2011.
33   See Resolution of the Constitutional Court of the Czech Republic, Ref. No. I. ÚS 339/02, Ref. No. IV. ÚS 511/03, Ref. No. III. ÚS 166/05, and Ref. No. III ÚS 145/03.

II.3. Resolution of the Constitutional Court of the Czech Republic Ref. No. I ÚS 339/02 of 26 January 2004

22.14. The fulfilment of the constitutional requirements in proceedings before an arbitrator or a court of arbitration is guaranteed by the possibility to have a ruling reviewed by a court[34] in accordance with Part Four of Act No. 216/1994 Coll. on Arbitration and on Enforcement of Arbitration Rulings (compare with the reasons set out in Section 31 of Act (Czech Republic) No. 216/1994 Coll. on Arbitration and on Enforcement of Arbitration Rulings, as amended (ArbAct [CZE])[35]. According to Part Four of ArbAct [CZE][36], a verdict delivered by a court may be contested by means of a constitutional complaint (compare with Resolution Ref. No. III. ÚS 460/01)[37]. The claimant did not take advantage of this option and did not exhaust all procedural means provided by the law to protect the claimant's rights in the sense of the abovementioned Section 75 (1) of ConstCoAct [CZE][38] in conjunction with Section 72, paragraph 2 of ConstCoAct [CZE][39]. This fact renders the claimant's constitutional

---

[34] Already the formulation suggests that the purpose and sense of this section of ArbAct [CZE] was clearly misunderstood, as the case does not involve any review in the sense of an analogy with a *higher instance* (in comparison with court litigation). The sole purpose is giving the parties the possibility to seek protection in the event some of the basic principles of arbitration are violated.

[35] ArbAct [CZE]: Annulment of an arbitration ruling by a court and a halt of an order execution of a ruling – Section 31: *A court annuls at the request of any party an arbitration ruling in the event that* a) *the ruling has been delivered in a case in respect of which a valid arbitration agreement cannot be entered into,* b) *an arbitration agreement is invalid due to other reasons, has been cancelled, and/or does not apply to the agreed matter,* c) *an arbitrator has participated in hearing the case who has not been authorized to be act as an arbitrator pursuant to an arbitration agreement or based on other facts or was not qualified to act as an arbitrator,* d) *the arbitration ruling was not delivered by the majority of arbitrators,* e) *the party was not provided with the possibility to discuss the matter before arbitrators,* f) *the arbitration ruling requires a party to perform in a way that was not demanded by the eligible party or to perform in a way that is impossible or disallowed under the domestic law,* g) *it is established that there exist reasons due to which a demand can be made for re-opening the proceedings in civil court proceedings.*

[36] Part Four of ArbAct [CZE] defines the annulment of an arbitration ruling by a court (both the reasons for and the consequences of the annulment of an arbitration ruling).

[37] Published *in* 24 Collection of Verdicts and Resolutions of the Constitutional Court, Resolution No. 41, pp. 563 and following.

[38] ConstCoAct, Section 75 – Inadmissibility of a Constitutional Complaint (1) A constitutional complaint is inadmissible if the claimant has not exhausted all procedural means afforded by the law for the protection of the claimant's rights (Section 72, paragraph 3); this does not apply to an extraordinary remedial measure, which the body that issues a decision in respect of same may refuse as inadmissible due to reasons determined at its discretion (Section 72, paragraph 4).[...]

[39] ConstCoAct [CZE] Constitutional complaint – Section 72[...] (2) Unless otherwise specified in this Act, a constitutional complaint is subject to the general provisions of this Act pertaining to a complaint, and the person filing a constitutional complaint (hereinafter referred to as "claimant") is subject to the general provisions of this Act pertaining to a petitioner. [...]

complaint unacceptable according to Section 43 (1) (e) of ConstCoAct [CZE].[40]. The nature of arbitration, albeit in matters otherwise heard before general courts, stems from the desire of the parties to delegate contractually the settlement and resolution of their disputes, whether factual or legal, to a third party. The outcome of arbitration (arbitration ruling) is a qualified form of an obligation that is binding as such. An arbitrator clarifies an existing contractual relationship in representation of the parties and not as a representative of the state. Hence, the power of an arbitrator is not the delegated sovereign power of the state; it stems from the private right of the parties to determine their destiny[41].

II.4. Resolution of the Constitutional Court of the Czech Republic Ref. No. IV.ÚS 511/03 of 4 December 2003

22.15. The Constitutional Court maintains the standpoint that an arbitration tribunal established as an *ad hoc* tribunal based on being appointed by the Chairman of the Arbitration Court attached to the Economic Chamber of the Czech Republic and Agricultural Chamber of the Czech Republic is a private entity, is not a part of the judiciary system defined under Part Four of the Constitution [CZE] and under the Act on Courts and Judges, and is not a body of public authority. The nature of an arbitration court is that of a specialized organization providing services to persons who want an arbitrator to clarify and stabilize their legal relationship, which means that arbitration rulings delivered by a court of arbitration and arbitration tribunals appointed in an *ad hoc* manner cannot be considered to constitute decisions of a body of public authority in the sense of Article 87 (1)(d) of the Constitution [CZE][42] and in the sense of Section 72 (1) (a) of ConstCoAct [CZE][43]. Arbitrators resolve disputes if their authority regarding a particular dispute stems from a valid arbitration agreement entered into by the parties. In this regard, the nature of arbitration derives from an agreement delegating the will of the parties, where its outcome is a qualified form of an obligation that is binding as such. Arbitrators (in the same way as arbitration courts) do not engage in law finding; they establish (determine, clarify, i.e. rectify) a contractual relationship in representation of the parties. Their authority is not the delegated sovereign power of the state; it stems from the private right of the parties to determine their destiny. An obligation ascertained by arbitrators is enforceable due to the enforceability of the obligation agreed by arbitrators in representation of the parties.

---

[40] ConstCoAct [CZE], Section 43 – (1) *Outside a verbal hearing without the presence of participants, a presenting judge refuses in a resolution a complaint, [...]* e) *if the complaint is inadmissible, unless otherwise stipulated in this Act.*[...]

[41] This section of the verdict contains a reference to Resolution of the Constitutional Court of the Czech Republic [CZE], Ref. No. IV. ÚS 1/4/02 of 15 July 2002.

[42] Quoted above in this chapter.

[43] *Ibid.*

II.5. Resolution of the Constitutional Court of the Czech Republic Ref. No. III.ÚS 166/05 of 29 April 2005

22.16. Resolution of the Constitutional Court Ref. No. IV. ÚS 174/02 states that a court of arbitration, and therefore also an arbitrator, is not a body of public authority, and, consequently, its arbitration rulings cannot be regarded as decisions of a body of public authority according to Article 87 (1)(d) of the Czech Constitution and according to Section 72 (1) (a) of ConstCoAct [CZE]. Arbitration courts and arbitrators resolve disputes if their authority regarding to a given dispute stems from a valid arbitration agreement entered into by the parties. The nature of arbitration is based on an agreement delegating the will of the parties, and its outcome is a qualified form of an obligation that is binding as such. An arbitrator does not engage in law finding, but establishes (determines, clarifies, i.e. rectifies) a contractual relationship in representation of the parties. Hence, its authority is not the delegated sovereign power of the state, but derives from the private right of the parties to determine their destiny. This standpoint is embraced by the Constitutional Court of the Czech Republic [CZE] with regard to the submission concerning this particular matter. For this reason, the complaint was deemed to be outside the jurisdiction of the Constitutional Court of the Czech Republic [CZE], and it was rejected as such [Section 43 (1)(d) of ConstCoAct][44].

II.6. Resolution of the Constitutional Court of the Czech Republic Ref. No. III.ÚS 145/03 of 12 September 2003

22.17. The question whether an arbitration ruling (delivered by a court of arbitration) is an enforceable verdict of a body of public authority according to Article 87 (1)(d) of the Constitution [CZE][45] and according to Section 72 (1)(a) of ConstCoAct [CZE][46] was examined by the Constitutional Court already in its Resolution Ref. No. IV. ÚS 174/02 of 15 July 2002, where the court concluded that it is not because a court of arbitration cannot be considered to constitute a body of public authority. The Constitutional Court [CZE] based its deliberation on the fact that the nature of arbitration stems from an agreement delegating the will of the parties, where the outcome is a qualified form of an obligation that is binding as such. An arbitrator does not engage in law finding, but establishes (determines, clarifies, i.e. rectifies) a contractual relationship in representation of the parties, and his authority is not the delegated sovereign power of the state, but derives from the private right of the parties to determine their destiny. In this resolution, the Constitutional

---

44 *Ibid.*
45 *Ibid.*
46 *Ibid.*

Court made a reference to its Resolution Ref. No. III. ÚS 460/01[47] of 1 November 2001, stating that if a different conclusion regarding the nature of arbitration rulings were reached, i.e. if it were determined that an arbitration ruling is an enforceable decision of a body of public authority, the court would be forced to reject the constitutional complaint in accordance with Section 43 (1)(e) of ConstCoAct [CZE][48] as inadmissible due to the fact that the measures referred to in Section 75, paragraph 1 of ConstCoAct [CZE][49] have not been exhausted because the claimant had freely made the choice to resort to arbitration as opposed to having recourse to court litigation. The Constitutional Court [CZE] has no reason to deviate from the aforestated conclusions in the case under review even though the court is aware that conflicting opinions exist in legal theory regarding the nature of facultative (international) arbitration[50]. However, if this issue were regarded from the viewpoint of international (public) law, where this criterion is decisive with respect to the functioning of arbitration in actual practice, it is necessary to adopt the standpoint of the party [to these proceedings] that arbitrators as well as permanent institutional courts of arbitration do not act as bodies of the state, and arbitration and acts completed as part of arbitral proceedings are not considered the exercise of state power[51]. It follows from this conclusion that, save for exceptions (see below), actions completed by arbitrators or arbitration courts cannot be attributed to a particular state. In other words, parties may resort to either court litigation or arbitration as regards resolving their disputes, provided that the relevant legal requirements are complied with. In the latter case, however, parties are or must be aware that the role of the state is not limited only to creating a legal framework in which arbitration functions, but also, more importantly, that state involvement in specific matters is only possible *ex post* and consists of annulling an arbitration ruling or halting the execution of a court ruling, where such a course of action is possibly only in certain cases[52] in respect of which rights must be (first) claimed before the applicable general court and, only then or only if all means of legal protection have been exhausted, before the Constitutional Court. The Constitutional Court [CZE] considers as inadequate the claimant's line of arguing consisting

---

47 Published *in* 24 COLLECTION OF VERDICTS AND RESOLUTIONS OF THE CONSTITUTIONAL COURT , Resolution Ref. No. 41 (2002).

48 *Supra* note 42.

49 Quoted above.

50 This part of the verdict of the Constitutional Court of the Czech Republic refers to the following publication: NADĚŽDA ROZEHNALOVÁ, PRÁVO MEZINÁRODNÍHO OBCHODU *(Transnational Law of International Trade)*, Brno: Masaryk University 142 (1994).

51 This part of the verdict of the Constitutional Court of the Czech Republic refers to the following publication: ZDENĚK KUČERA, MEZINÁRODNÍ PRÁVO SOUKROMÉ *(Private International Law)* Brno: Addendum 394 (1994) and following.

52 Refers to Sections 31 and following of ArbAct [CZE].

of references to the case law of the European Court of Human Rights. The first case involved arbitration that was not facultative but obligatory in respect of which it is necessary to take into account, as regards the protection of fundamental rights and freedoms, that a forced "transfer" of certain disputes to arbitration cannot release the state from the fulfilment of its obligations set out under Article 6 of the European Convention on Human Rights, where the state is responsible for arbitration as if it were one of "its" bodies. The situation is similar in the second case, where the matter of the claimants was heard by a body (*Arbitration Tribunal*) established under the 1977 Act whose powers included setting the amount of compensation for the claimants' nationalized assets in a potential dispute. For this reason, the relevant "arbitration" actions (the case involved a special judiciary body) in this case can be undoubtedly attributed directly to the state with all the relevant consequences ensuing from this fact.

II.7. Resolution of the Constitutional Court of the Czech Republic Ref. No. II ÚS 2169/07 of 3 September 2007

22.18. As regards this matter, the Constitutional Court of the Czech Republic [CZE] refers to its earlier verdicts[53], where the court based its conclusions on the fact that the authority of an arbitration court or an arbitrator to resolve disputes stems from an agreement that delegates the will of the parties, where the outcome is a qualified form of an obligation. An arbitrator (court of arbitration) does not engage in law finding, but establishes (determines, clarifies, i.e. rectifies) a contractual relationship in representation of the parties. Hence, its authority is not the delegated sovereign power of the state, but it derives from the private right of the parties to determine their destiny. For this reason, the Constitutional Court of the Czech Republic [CZE] could not examine the complaint because it would be reviewing a decision of an entity other than a body of public authority. In proceeding this way, the court would go beyond the bounds set out in Article 87 (1)(d) of the Constitution [CZE][54]. As a result, the Constitutional Court could not but reject the complaint in accordance with Section 43 (1)(d) of ConstCoAct [CZE][55] based on its lack of jurisdiction over the matter.

---

[53] Refers to, in particular (as an example), these resolutions of the Constitutional Court of the Czech Republic: Ref. No. I. ÚS 339/02, Ref. No. IV. ÚS 511/03, Ref. No. III. ÚS 166/05, and Ref. No. III ÚS 145/03.

[54] See *supra* note 42.

[55] *Ibid.*

The accountability of arbitrators for their actions is approached in a similar manner in the judicial practice in the Czech Republic. This issue can be illustrated, for instance, by Ruling of the Supreme Court of the Czech Republic [CZE] Ref. No. 32 Cdo 1044/2005 of 28 November 2007, which is based on the abovementioned Resolution of the Constitutional Court of the Czech Republic [CZE] Ref. No. IV.ÚS 174/02 and concludes that arbitration rulings delivered by arbitration tribunals or single arbitrators representing the Arbitration Court attached to the Economic Chamber of the Czech Republic and Agricultural Chamber of the Czech Republic are arbitration rulings of this court of arbitration. They are not rulings delivered by arbitrators[56]. The fact that rulings of the arbitration tribunal of the Arbitration Court attached to the Economic Chamber of the Czech Republic and Agricultural Chamber of the Czech Republic are attributed to the arbitration court shows that arbitrators are not liable for damage caused by the delivery of verdicts because they make decisions in the name of the arbitration court. Thus, a claim cannot be raised against an arbitrator in a dispute concerning compensation for damage. There exist no doubts as regards this issue as far as the private-law basis of liability for damage is concerned. Liability for damage is a concept of contractual law that corresponds to the contractual nature of arbitration. It can be therefore concluded that similarly as other countries, there exists no consistent opinion and uniform doctrinal approach in the Czech Republic as regards the nature of arbitration.

[*Alexander J. Bělohlávek & Tereza Profeldová*]
Mgr. Tereza Profeldová (*1978) works as a legal trainee in the Law Offices of Bělohlávek, Prague, Czech Republic and is a graduate of the Faculty of Law of Charles University in Prague. Field of Interest: Private international law, arbitration and IP rights.
e-mail: tereza.profeldova@ablegal.cz

| | |

---

[56] Refers to Resolution of the Constitutional Court of the Czech Republic [CZE] Ref. No. IV ÚS 174/02.

5. Hungary

Abbreviations used in the annotations:
[HUN] - Hungary

Fundamental Rights in the Arbitration Case Law of Hungarian Courts

Alexander J. Bělohlávek

I. Arbitration Courts and the Judiciary – "Independence and Equivalence"

Key words:
jurisdiction of arbitrators | jurisdiction of courts | interpretation of the law | public policy | independence of courts | independence of arbitration courts | prohibition of revision au fond | prohibition of review on the merits

Ruling of the Supreme Court of Hungary (*Magyar Köztársaság Legfelsőbb Bíróság*) **Ref. No. Gfv.VI.32.866/2001:**[1]

Laws Taken into Account in This Ruling:
➤ Act No. XX of 1949 on the Constitution of Hungary;
➤ Act No. LXXI of 1994 on Arbitration;
➤ Act No. LXVI of 1997 on the Organization of Courts.

Rationes Decidendi:

23.01. Courts (general/state courts) may not intervene in arbitral proceedings in the event a valid arbitration clause exists.

23.02. Arbitration courts are not a part of the judiciary and are not subject to the oversight authority of the Supreme Court of Hungary.

23.03. Courts may not intervene in arbitration even in respect of a complaint filed in relation to an arbitral award[2] on the grounds that an arbitral award has violated public policy[3] due to the fact that the arbitral award is contrary to a previously delivered verdict of a [general/state] court regarding an issue that is of material importance for settling the dispute.

---

[1] Source (*Complex* legal information system): No. EBH 2002.772. The ruling has been identified by Dr. Katalin Préda, Attorney, Budapest.

[2] In this case, the Court of Arbitration attached to the Budapest Bar Association.

[3] In this case, public order relating to substantive law. The case involved an examination of amendments to an agreement that contained an arbitration clause, where the claimant maintained that the agreement had been *amended without the claimant's knowledge.*

23.04. Courts, including the Supreme Court (of Hungary), do not have the right to overturn a decision made by arbitrators on the merits.

23.05. In the same way as courts that constitute the judiciary system, arbitration courts have the authority to interpret the law and legal regulations (individual laws).

[Description of Facts and Legal Issues]

23.06. The Arbitration court attached to Budapest Bar Association issued an order to make a financial payment. The claimant maintained that the award delivered by the arbitration court violated public policy because it was contrary to a former verdict of a court.

[Overview of the Legal Standpoint of the Court]

23.07. The first-instance court dismissed the demand for the annulment of the arbitral award, arguing that arbitration courts are independent and their authority to deliver verdicts is outside the jurisdiction of [general/state] courts. The claimant filed an appeal to the Supreme Court, maintaining that the general provisions of the relevant agreement contained an arbitration clause and that the arbitration clause had been amended without the claimant's consent. The verdict states that every court, including a court of arbitration, has the right to interpret the law. Under the Act on Arbitration, courts cannot change arbitral awards on the merits, and, as regards the issue under discussion, not even the Supreme Court has the right to intervene in the matter. The ruling of the first-instance court was therefore upheld.

| | |

II. Parties to Arbitral Award Annulment Proceedings; Exercise of Rights in Litigation

Key words:
Jurisdiction | annulment of arbitral award | right of action | nature of claim | actual state of affairs | facticity

Ruling of the Pécs Regional Court Ref. No. Gpkf. IV.30.014/2005 delivered in 2006:[4]

Laws Taken into Account in This Ruling:
➢ Act No. XX of 1949 on the Constitution of Hungary: Article 57;
➢ Act No. LXXI of 1994 on Arbitration: Section 55(1);
➢ Act No. III of 1952 on Civil Proceedings.

---

[4] Source (*Complex* database): No. BDT 2006.1356. The ruling has been identified and summarized by Dr. Katalin Préda, Attorney, Budapest.

Rationes Decidendi:

23.08. A demand for the annulment of an arbitral award may only be made by a party (participant) to the relevant arbitral proceedings or by a person that is subject to an obligation imposed by the arbitral award, provided that the arbitral award has been delivered to such a person.

23.09. A person that is not a party (participant) to proceedings, is not subject to any obligation imposed by an arbitral award, and has not been delivered the arbitral award does not have the right to demand the annulment of the arbitral award even if the arbitral award contains a reference to such a person.

[Description of Facts and Legal Issues]

23.10. An arbitral award contained a reference to a [legal] person that was not a party to the arbitration proceedings. This person was referred to as an entity possessing the right to cancel or terminate an agreement signed between the parties to the dispute (participants in the proceedings). Following the delivery of the arbitral award, this person demanded its annulment by filing a complaint with a court (arbitral award annulment proceedings).

[Conclusions Drawn by the Arbitration Court]

23.11. The first-instance court dismissed the demand for the annulment of the arbitral award because the claimant (legal person) had not participated in the arbitration process and was not a party subject to any obligation imposed by the arbitral award. The same verdict was issued by the second-instance court that examined an appeal regarding this case. This court stated that a third party (a person other than a party to arbitration) does not have the right to demand the annulment of an arbitral award even if it is referred to in the arbitral award but is not required to fulfil an obligation under the arbitral award. In its ruling, the court referred to the provisions of Section 55(1) of Act No. LXXI of 1994 on Arbitration[5].

---

5   Selection of Corresponding Provisions in the Hungarian Arbitration Act:

Section 55   [Right of Action and Reasons for Annulment of Arbitral Award]

(1) A participant in proceedings as well as a person concerned by an arbitral award may within 60 days after the delivery of the arbitral award file a complaint with a court requesting the annulment of the arbitral award provided that:

a)   the party that entered into the arbitration agreement was not eligible to exercise rights or qualified to complete legal acts;

b)   the arbitration agreement is written up according to the law to which it was subject; in the absence of such a reservation, it is invalid under the Hungarian law;

c)   a party has not been informed of the appointment of an arbitrator or of the initiation of arbitration in accordance with the applicable rules or has been otherwise prevented from the possibility to defend itself in the matter;

d)   the arbitral award has been delivered in respect of a dispute for which an arbitration agreement cannot be entered into or to which the provisions of the arbitration agreement do not apply; if the award also concerns issues not defined under the arbitration agreement, provided that the decisions

III. Application of Mutual Legal Assistance Treaties to the Recognition and Enforcement of Court Judgments with Regard to Arbitral Awards that Have a Nature Comparable to a Court Judgment; Priority of Laws on the Recognition and Enforcement of Court Judgments if They Are More Advantageous than the New York Convention

Key words:
nature of arbitral award | exceptions from recognition rules | exceptions from enforcement rules | foreign arbitral award | judgment recognition | enforcement of judgments | recognition of arbitral award | enforcement of arbitral award | recognition conditions | enforcement conditions | mutual legal assistance | general nature of legal aid agreement | more advantageous conditions

Ruling of the Regional Court of Debrecen Ref. No. Pkf.III.20.503/2005 Delivered in 2006:[6]

Laws Taken into Account in This Ruling:
➢ Act No. LV of 1962 on the Convention on the Enforcement of Foreign Arbitration Awards (New York Convention of 10 June 1958 on the Recognition and Enforcement of Foreign Arbitral Awards);

---

pertaining to issues covered by the arbitration agreement are separable from provisions to which the arbitration proceedings did not apply, the annulment of the arbitral award may only be demanded in respect of the last mentioned parts of the award,
e) The composition or deliberation of the arbitration court was not compliant with the agreement of the parties – with the exception of cases where such an agreement is contrary to the applicable provisions of this Act – or, in the absence of such an agreement, was not compliant with the provisions of this Act.
(2) The annulment of an arbitral award may be demanded on the grounds that:
a) the disputed matter cannot be made subject to the jurisdiction of an arbitration court in accordance with the law of Hungary, or
b) The arbitral award is contrary to the Hungarian public policy.
(3) The elapsing of the deadline referred to in paragraph (1) results in the expiration of the right. In the event a supplementary arbitral award is delivered, the deadline derives from the delivery of such an award.
[...]
Section 58   [Effects of Arbitral Award]
An arbitral award has the same effect as an enforceable *court judgment*; its enforcement is subject to regulations governing the enforcement of court judgments.
[6]   *Ibid.*

> ➤ Act No. XVI of 2002 on Legal Aid between Hungary and Ukraine (this Act promulgates the mutual legal assistance treaty between the two countries into Hungarian law): Article 16[7], Article 17[8];
> ➤ Act No. LIII of 1994 on the Enforcement of Judgments: Article 10, Article 15, paragraph a), Article 16, paragraph a), Article 205, Article 208;
> ➤ Act No. LXXI of 1994 on Arbitration.

States involved:
[HUN] - [Hungary];
[UKR] - [Ukraine].

Rationes Decidendi:

23.12. If an enforceable arbitral award has the nature of a court judgment for the purposes of its enforcement, regulations pertaining to the enforcement of court rulings may be applied to such an award, including a mutual legal assistance treaty(in this case, an agreement between Hungary and Ukraine) that guarantees the enforceability of court judgments.

23.13. Due to the nature of an arbitral award, which is qualified as identical to a court judgment for enforcement purposes, regulations pertaining to the enforcement of foreign arbitral awards (in this case, the New York Convention on the Recognition and Enforcement of Foreign Arbitral Awards) are used together with regulations pertaining to the enforcement of court judgments, where those regulations apply that allow recognition and enforcement to a larger extent.

[Description of Facts and Legal Issues]

23.14. The dispute, which involved a claimant from Ukraine and a respondent from Hungary, was resolved by a Ukrainian arbitration court. The respondent was required to pay a financial obligation as well as the cost of the proceedings. The claimant applied in Hungary for the enforcement of the arbitral award delivered in Ukraine, referring to the mutual legal assistance treaty between Hungary and Ukraine, which guarantees the enforceability of court judgments, and to the Act on the Enforcement of Court Judgments. The claimant maintained that **if an enforceable arbitral award has the nature of a court judgment for the purposes of its enforcement[9], the matter is covered by regulations governing the enforcement of court judgments**, including the mutual legal assistance treaty that guarantees the reciprocal enforcement of court judgments. The

---

7   Quoted in full (in translation) below the annotation of the verdict.
8   *Ibid.*
9   Hungarian Act No. LXXI of 1994 on Arbitration: Section 58 [Effects of Arbitral Award]: *The effect of an arbitral award is the same as the effect of an enforceable court judgment; its enforcement is subject to the regulations governing the enforcement of court judgments.*

first-instance court in Hungary accepted this argument. In an appeal, the respondent objected that the mutual legal assistance treaty only applies to court judgments and not to arbitral awards. The appeals court dismissed this argument and upheld the ruling of the first-instance court.

[Overview of the Legal Standpoint of the Court]

23.15. According to the verdict of the court of second instance (appeals court), the mutual legal assistance treaty between Ukraine and Hungary has a general nature and, therefore, can be applied to the enforcement of arbitral awards. Further, the court took into account the New York Convention on the Recognition and Enforcement of Foreign Arbitral Awards, which identifies exceptions from the obligation to recognize and enforce foreign arbitral awards; however, none of these exceptions could be applied in this particular case. Moreover, this case was subject to the mutual legal assistance treaty between Hungary and Ukraine under which enforceability is defined in broader terms than is the case with the New York Convention. Hence, the court accepted the claimant's argument that if an arbitral award is to have an effect analogical to a court judgment, its recognition and enforcement may be subject to the provisions of international agreements on the recognition and enforcement of foreign verdicts, provided that the standard is more advantageous for court judgments. Even though none of the exceptions set out for recognition and enforcement under the New York Convention applied in this case, the standard of the mutual legal assistance treaty between Hungary and Ukraine was more advantageous[10]. Thus, the international agreement in question offered better conditions. However, this verdict goes much further than the clause setting out the provisions on more advantageous conditions pursuant to the New York Convention. The Hungarian court went as far as to give the same importance to judgments delivered by foreign courts and to foreign arbitral awards as long as they have effects analogical to court judgments. Without exaggeration, this verdict can be considered *groundbreaking*, as it testifies to the fact that arbitral awards are given maximum support in Hungary. At the same time, the judgment shows that the nature and purpose of arbitration are considered equivalent to court litigation.

[Selection of Corresponding Provisions in the Hungarian Act]
- ➢ Act No. XVI of 2002 on Legal Assistance between Ukraine and Hungary[11].

---

[10] Hungarian Act No. XVI of 2002 on Legal Assistance between Hungary and Ukraine (this law implements the mutual legal assistance treaty between the two countries), specifically Articles 16 and 17.

[11] This law promulgates the mutual legal assistance treaty between the two countries into the law of Hungary.

Article 16 - Recognizable and Enforceable Decisions

(1) Under the conditions laid down in the Agreement, one Contracting Party recognizes and enforces the following judicial decisions issued by the other Contracting Party:

a) Decisions in civil matters concerning property claims, including orders confirming a settlement between the parties to the dispute;

b) Decisions in criminal matters concerning claims for damages; and

c) Decisions ordering a claimant, who has been granted an exemption from providing security for the costs of legal proceedings or an advance payment of court costs pursuant to Article 2, to pay the costs of the proceedings.

(2) The Contracting Parties mutually recognize judicial decisions concerning non-property claims in civil matters.

(3) Judicial decisions satisfying the conditions laid down in the Agreement must be recognized and enforced if they become final and enforceable after the Agreement comes into effect.

Article 17 – Conditions for Recognition and Enforcement

The decisions stated in Article 16 shall be recognized and enforced on the following conditions:

a) If the decision is final and enforceable in accordance with the laws of the Contracting Party on whose territory the decision was reached;

b) If the court of the Contracting Party on whose territory the decision was reached has jurisdiction in accordance with the laws of the Contracting Party on whose territory recognition and enforcement is requested;

c) If the party against whom the decision was reached and who did not take part in the proceedings was duly summoned, and if the party that does not have capacity to bring proceedings and against whom the decision requested to be enforced was reached was able to duly represent himself;

d) If between the same parties in the same case the court of the Contracting Party on whose territory the decision must be recognized and enforced has not previously reached a final decision or proceedings have not previously been initiated before the court of the said Contracting Party in the same matter; and

e) If the recognition and enforcement of the decision is not contrary to the fundamental principles of the legal system of the Contracting Party on whose territory the decision must be recognized and enforced.

| | |

IV. Importance of Autonomy and the Possibility to Restrict (Exclude) Certain Constitutionally Guaranteed Fundamental Rights; Fair Trial and Public Policy

Key words:
autonomy of parties | impartiality | public policy violation | violation of fundamental rights | legal protection | fair trial | constitutional law | public policy | waiver of right | fundamental rights | fundamental legal principles | annulment of arbitral award | gross violation

Ruling of the Supreme Court of Hungary (*Magyar Köztársaság Legfelsőbb Bíróság*) Ref. No. Gfv. XI.30.226/2005 delivered in 2006:[12]

Laws Taken into Account in This Ruling:
➢ Act No. XX of 1949 on the Constitution of Hungary: Article 57(1);
➢ Act No. LXXI of 1994 on Arbitration.

Rationes Decidendi:
23.16. In arbitral proceedings, it is permissible to restrict some constitutional rights with regard to the process of law finding. Public policy violation only as an especially serious violation of rights.
23.17. Arbitration restricts or excludes, in a constitutionally conforming manner, certain fundamental rights guaranteed by the constitution with regard to legal protection[13].
23.18. An assertion claiming the absence of fair and impartial trial in arbitration does not mean that the public policy of [Hungary] has been violated at the same time.
23.19. A violation of fundamental rights may represent a violation of the public policy of [Hungary]. However, a violation of public policy is committed only if fundamental legal principles are violated.

[Description of Facts and Legal Issues]
23.20. A contract for construction work contained an arbitration clause. The claimant made a claim for a financial payment under this contract before

---

[12] Source: (*Complex* legal information system) No. EBH 2006.1429. The ruling has been identified by Dr. Katalin Préda, Budapest, Hungary.
[13] The party that filed the demand with the court for the cancellation of the arbitral award maintained that the arbitral proceedings had not been impartial and fair, resulting in a violation of Article 57(1) of the Hungarian Constitution, where the provisions of Article 57(1) guarantee, among others, the right to have claims examined by an impartial and fair court or another body. The same section of the Constitution of Hungary guarantees the public hearing of cases. The Hungarian Supreme Court ruled, fully in accordance with the case law of ESLP, that these rights can to some extent be restricted by entering into an arbitration agreement.

an arbitration court. The arbitration tribunal accepted the claim. In proceedings on the annulment of the arbitral award, the first-instance court concluded that an examination of all the arguments used against the arbitral award uncovered a violation of the right to a fair trial guaranteed under Article 57(1) of the Hungarian Constitution. The court annulled the arbitral award, but the Supreme Court overturned this verdict and decided that the arbitral award would remain in effect. The reason was that the Supreme Court concluded that by agreeing to an arbitration clause, the parties to some extent waived, in a constitutionally conforming manner, some of the principles of fair trial. This way, the court emphasized the importance of the autonomy of the parties. A violation of public policy only occurs if a violation is committed of fundamental legal principles without which the rule of law could not exist.

[*Alexander J. Bělohlávek*]

| | |

6. Poland

Alexander J. Bělohlávek & Tomáš Řezníček

I. Judicial Protection of the Rights of the Parties: Effective Arbitration Clause as a Restriction on the Constitutional Right of Judicial Recourse

Supreme Court (*Sąd Najwyższy*) Decision, Case No. II CSK 263/08 as of 30 October 2008:[1]

Key words:
arbitration clause | permanent arbitration court | constitution | judicial protection | restriction

States involved:
[POL] - [Poland]. From the available annotation a relationship with another country not found.

Laws Taken into Account in This Ruling:
➢ Konstytucja RP (*Constitution*) [POL] – Konstytucja Rzeczypospolitej Polskiej z dnia 2 kwietnia 1997 r. (Law as from 2 April 1997), published in: Dziennik Ustaw, 1997 Nr. 78, poz. 483: Art. 45 ust. 1;
➢ Kodeks postępowania cywilnego (*Code of Civil Procedure*) [k.p.c.] [POL] – Ustawa z dnia 17 listopada 1964 r. (Law as from 17 November 1964), published in: Dziennik Ustaw, 1964 Nr. 43, poz. 296: Art. 1161 § 1, Art. 1161 §3, Art. 1162 §1, Art. 1165 §1, Art. 1165 §2, Art. 1167, Art. 1167.

---

[1] Taken from the decision summary available at: http://arbitraz.laszczuk.pl/orzecznictwo/252, postanowienie sadu najwyzszego z dnia 30 pazdziernika 2008 r ii csk 263 08.html (accessed on December 13, 2010). On the same page is also available the text of the original decision in Polish. Cited source came from the Biuro Studiów i Analiz Sądu Najwyższego. The site is domain of commercial active entity. Contradicts the policy of this periodical (CYArb) to refer to such websites and their owners. Authors and editors therefore apologize the owners and operators of sites cited. It is clear the site contains very well prepared and updated case law of the Polish courts. Therefore the author and editors have used it as the basis for the current annotation of the Polish judicial law relating to arbitration, after review of the original sources, as well as the author and editorial processing.

Rationes Decidendi:

24.01. An effective arbitration clause requires **the appointment of an arbitration court given the task of resolving a dispute.**

24.02. Pursuant to Article 1161, Sections 1[2] and 3[3] of the Code of Civil Procedure, the parties may submit a dispute for resolution by a permanent arbitration court or by an appointed court [*ad hoc*]. The clause is required to take the written form (Article 1162[4] of the Code of Civil Procedure). In case a permanent arbitration court is chosen pursuant to Article 1161, Section 3 of the Code of Civil Procedure, the clause should indicate the court, which must be considered a pertinent part of such contract. Indicating a permanent arbitration court should be specific enough so that the permanent arbitration court can be identified, i.e. it should at least include the seat of the permanent arbitration court and the name thereof, should there be more than one arbitration court in the given location.

24.03. Any interpretation of contractual provisions with regard to dispute resolution in specific cases by an arbitration court should be precise, **since such contract, to certain extent, forms a restriction on the right to trial as guaranteed by Article 45, Section 1 of the Polish Constitution[5],** pled in the cassation appeal. Therefore, the scope to which the parties limit their right to judicial protection of their rights calls for precise interpretation.

| | |

---

[2] [POL] *Code of Civil Procedure* [k.p.c.] Author's translation: [*Article 1161, Section 1-* The submission of a dispute for resolution by an arbitration court is subject to an agreement by and between the parties, indicating the subject of the dispute or the legal relationship from which the dispute arose or may arise (an arbitration clause).].

[3] [POL] *Code of Civil Procedure* [k.p.c.] Author's translation: [*Article 1161, Section 3-* The arbitration clause may indicate a permanent arbitration court as the court of proper jurisdiction for dispute resolution. Unless the parties have decided otherwise, they shall be bound by the rules and regulations of the permanent arbitration court effective as of the date of signing the arbitration clause.]

[4] [POL] *Code of Civil Procedure* [k.p.c.] Author's translation: [*Article 1162, Section 1-* The arbitration clause should be in writing. Section 2- The requirement as to the form of the arbitration clause is also satisfied in the case of a clause included in any written communication or representation exchanged between the parties or made through means of remote communication allowing a record to be made of the contents thereof. Any reference in a contract made to a document containing the provision on submitting disputes for resolution by an arbitration court shall satisfy the requirement as to the form of the arbitration clause, provided that the contract is made in writing and the reference is made in such manner that the clause is incorporated into the contract.]

[5] [POL] *Constitution* Author's translation: [*Article 45, Section 1-* Every person has the right to a fair trial and to an open hearing without unreasonable delay by an independent, sovereign and impartial court of proper jurisdiction.]

II. Autonomy in Arbitration Procedure: Scope of Review of Arbitration Awards

Supreme Court (*Sąd Najwyższy*), Docket V CZ 42/08 as of 9 July 2008:

Key words:
review of arbitral award, review | civil-law | autonomy of arbitral proceedings | arbitral proceedings, function | auxiliary function of court

States involved:
[POL] - [Poland]. From the available annotation a relationship with another country not found.

Laws Taken into Account in This Ruling:

➢ Kodeks postępowania cywilnego (*Code of Civil Procedure*) [k.p.c.] [POL] – Ustawa z dnia 17 listopada 1964 r. (Law as from 17 November 1964), published in. Dziennik Ustaw, 1964 Nr. 43, poz. 296: Art. 1205[6], Art. 1206[7].

---

[6] [POL] *Code of Civil Procedure* [k.p.c.] Author's translation: [Article 1205,
Section 1- An award delivered by an arbitration court in the Republic of Poland may only be annulled by a court in proceedings initiated as a result of a filed challenge of the award and under the provisions hereunder. Section 3 If the parties agreed that the proceedings before the arbitration court should include more than one instance, then provisions in Section 1 herein refer to the final award of the arbitration court ruling with regard to the claims of the parties.]
[7] [POL] *Code of Civil Procedure* [k.p.c.] Author's translation: [Article 1206, Section 1- A party can challenge the arbitral award if: 1) an arbitration clause was missing, it was invalid, ineffective or became null and void under governing law, 2) the party was not given proper notice of the appointment of the arbitrator or about the arbitration proceedings, or was otherwise unable to present its case before the arbitration court, 3) the arbitration award refers to a dispute not contemplated in or not falling within the terms of submission to arbitration; however, if the decision in cases included in the arbitration clause can be separated from decisions in cases not included therein or in excess thereof, the award can only be challenged to the extent of cases not included therein or in excess thereof; any instance of exceeding the arbitration clause does not constitute grounds for a challenge thereof if the party involved in the proceedings did not file any complaint with regard to the examination of claims exceeding the extent of the arbitration clause; 4) the requirements as to the composition of the arbitration authority or the basic rules of conduct before the court pursuant to the provisions of law or defined by the parties were not followed, 5) the award was obtained based on a criminal act or it was based on a counterfeited or manipulated document, or 6) a binding ruling was awarded by a court in the same case between the same parties.*
Section 2- An arbitral award may also be unnulled if the court decided that: 1) under provisions of law, the dispute is not able to be resolved by an arbitration court, or 2) an arbitral award is in conflict with the basic principles of the legal order of the Republic of Poland (public order clause).*]

Rationes Decidendi:

24.04. Arbitration is afforded broad **autonomy** in full compliance with the intentions of the legislature to **significantly restrict the control functions of the common court**. **The basic aim** of such legal regulation is to ensure **expeditious proceedings** in civil-law dispute resolution, and not **to introduce an additional stage of pre-court proceedings**. Parties submitting disputes to arbitration thus have to account for these conditions, which also include a minimal level of external control over.

| | |

III. Constitutional Right to Fair Trial: Fundamental Principles of Legal Order; Public Policy Clause

Supreme Court (*Sąd Najwyższy*), Docket No. I CSK 535/09 as of 9 September 2010 Case No. I CSK 535/09:

Key words:
arbitral award | recognitition of arbitral award | arbitration clause | reasoning of arbitrator | Constitution | fair trial | constitutional principles | fundamental principles | public policy

States involved:
[POL] - [Poland]. From the available annotation a relationship with another country not found.

Laws Taken into Account in This Ruling:
➤ Konstytucja RP (*Constitution*) [POL] – Konstytucja Rzeczypospolitej Polskiej z dnia 2 kwietnia 1997 r. (Law as from 2 April 1997), published in: Dziennik Ustaw, 1997 Nr. 78, poz. 483: Art. 45 ust. 1;
➤ Kodeks postępowania cywilnego (*Code of Civil Procedure*) [k.p.c.] [POL] – Ustawa z dnia 17 listopada 1964 r. (Law as from 17 November 1964), published in: Dziennik Ustaw, 1964 Nr. 43, poz. 296: Art. 1206 § 2.

Rationes Decidendi:
24.05. A challenge to an arbitral award is an extraordinary means of appeal used to annul the decision, should it be justified by at least one of the grounds exhaustively set out in Article 1206 of the Code of Civil Procedure.

24.06. A common court examining the challenge is bound by the grounds pled by the claimant. It only *ex officio* considers two grounds defined in Article 1206, Section 2[8] of the Code of Civil Procedure, i.e. the inability of the arbitration court to resolve a dispute and the conflict of arbitral award with fundamental principles of the legal order of the Republic of Poland.

24.07. The review of an arbitral award as to a conflict thereof with the fundamental principles of the legal order only refers to the contents thereof, and not to the regularities of arbitration proceedings or the composition of the arbitral authority [...]. An arbitral award may be annulled on grounds of the legal order clause in the event it is decided that the contents thereof include results that are not in compliance with a regulatory norm considered as one of the **fundamental principles of the legal order applicable in Poland. [...] These principles include not only constitutional principles, but also guiding principles of individual bodies of law.**

24.08. Requirements for persons acting as arbitrators should go hand in hand with the right of the party to the proceedings to be notified of all possible links of such persons to subjects involved in the proceedings. It is at the discretion of the party to the proceedings to judge such circumstances as the grounds for appointing an arbitrator or for asking for the exclusion thereof. The self-assessment of the arbitrator is irrelevant, since the essence of diligent proceedings lies in the external judgment of other subjects. [...] The fundamental principles of legal order also include, as defined in Article 45, Section 1[9] of the Constitution of the Republic of Poland, the right to a trial, which entails the right of a party to have their case examined by an independent court in fair proceedings.

| | |

---

8   [POL] *Code of Civil Procedure* [k.p.c.] Author's translation: [Article 1206, *Section 2- An arbitral award may also be overruled if the court decided that: 1) under provisions of law, the dispute is not able to be resolved by an arbitration court, or 2) an arbitral award is in conflict with the fundamental principles of the legal order of the Republic of Poland (public order clause).*]

9   [POL] *Constitution* Author's translation: [*Every person has the right to a fair trial and to an open hearing without unreasonable delay before an independent, sovereign and impartial court of proper jurisdiction.*]

IV. Fundamental Principles of the Legal Order: Arbitration Award That Infringes the Guiding Legal Principles

Supreme Court (*Sąd Najwyższy*) [POL], Docket V CSK 8/08 as of 11 June 2008:

Key words:
arbitral award | annulment of arbitral award | arbitral proceedings | arbitration court | constitution | legal order | fundamental principles of the legal order | public order | redress | rule of law

States involved:
[POL] - [Poland]. From the available annotation a relationship with another country not found.

Laws Taken into Account in This Ruling:
➢ Kodeks postępowania cywilnego (*Code of Civil Procedure*) [k.p.c.] [POL] – Ustawa z dnia 17 listopada 1964 r. (Law as from 17 November 1964), published in: Dziennik Ustaw, 1964 Nr. 43, poz. 296: Art. 1206 § 2.

Rationes Decidendi:

24.09. The review of the subject matter of the arbitral award by common law is limited to an assessment of whether or not the delivered award infringes any principles of the legal order. The legislature applies the term of "fundamental principles of the legal order" (Article 1206, Section 2, Item 2[10] of the Code of Civil Procedure), which expressly indicates that we are dealing with such an infringement of regulations in material law that leads to the violation of the principles of the rule of law (law and order), and the delivered arbitral award violates the fundamental legal principles applicable in the Republic of Poland, it harms the governing legal order, and thus violates the systemic, political, social and economic principles.

24.10. Fundamental principles of the legal order essentially include the principle of redress for damage. Unarguably, the compensation should match the damage.

24.11. Any legal action performed to evade the regulatory prohibition against deducting any claims from a composition arrangement violates the public order clause.

| | |

---

10   [POL] *Code of Civil Procedure* [k.p.c.] Author's translation: [*Article 1206, Section 2- An arbitral award may also be annulled if the court decided that: 1) under provisions of law, the dispute is not able to be resolved by an arbitration court, or 2) an arbitral award is in conflict with the fundamental principles of the legal order of the Republic of Poland (public order clause).*]

Czech (& Central European) Yearbook of Arbitration

V. The Scope of the Term "Public Policy": Constitutional and Other Guiding Principles

Supreme Court (*Sąd Najwyższy*), Docket I CK 412/03 as of 9 March 2004:

Key words:
recognition of arbitral award | Constitution | freedom of contract | New York Convention | principles, constitutional | fundamental principles | principles governing individual areas | of law | recognition

States involved:
[POL] - [Poland]. From the available annotation a relationship with another country not found.

Laws Taken into Account in This Ruling:
➢ Kodeks postępowania cywilnego (*Code of Civil Procedure*) [k.p.c.] [POL] – Ustawa z dnia 17 listopada 1964 r. (Law as from 17 November 1964), published in: Dziennik Ustaw, 1964 Nr. 43, poz. 296: Art. 1146 §1, Art 1148 §2 and 3[11], Art. 1151 §2[12];
➢ Konwencja o uznawaniu i wykonywaniu zagranicznych orzeczeń arbitrażowych (1958 r.) (*Convention on the Recognition and Enforcement of Foreign Arbitral Awards*) (Decree as from 19 July 1961), published in: Dzienik Ustaw, 1962 Nr. 9, poz. 41:[13] Article V[14].

---

[11] [POL] *Code of Civil Procedure* [k.p.c.] Author's translation: [*Article 1148, Section 2- The court issues its ruling after the hearing in the presence of a prosecutor. Section3-The court decision may be subject to review, while the final ruling may be subject to a petition to resume the proceedings.*]

[12] [POL] *Code of Civil Procedure* [k.p.c.] Author's translation: [*Article 1151, Section 2- The court issues its ruling after the hearing. An appeal against the execution decision may be lodged, while the final ruling on the subject matter may be challenged with a petition to resume the proceedings.*]

[13] Poland signed New York Convention on the Recognition and Enforcement of Foreign Arbitral Awards on 10 June 1958 and ratified it on 3 October 1961 whereas on 1 January 1962 it came into force in Poland. The text of the Convention was published by Decree of 19 July 1961 (Dz. U 1962 r. Nr. 9, poz. 41).

[14] *Convention on the Recognition and Enforcement of Foreign Arbitral Awards*, in original english version: *Art. V:*
1. Recognition and enforcement of the award may be refused, at the request of the party against whom it is invoked, only if that party furnishes to the competent authority where the recognition and enforcement is sought, proof that: (a) The parties to the agreement referred to in article II were, under the law applicable to them, under some incapacity, or the said agreement is not valid under the law to which the parties have subjected it or, failing any indication thereon, under the law of the country where the award was made; or (b) The party against whom the award is invoked was not given proper notice of the appointment of the arbitrator or of the arbitration proceedings or was otherwise unable to present his case; or (c) The award deals with a difference not contemplated by

Rationes Decidendi:

24.12. The term "public order" mainly includes all principles contained in Constitution, as well as principles governing individual areas of law. [...] Under contractual civil-law relationships [...], one should first name the principle of the autonomy of the parties' will and of the equality of subjects, since these are the principles that would be used, should the Polish court itself apply laws under which the foreign arbitral award was made.

24.13. If a foreign court ruling is a manifestation of a legal institution recognized in Polish law, then such ruling may not be perceived in light of its contradiction with fundamental principles of legal policy, and so the provisions of Article 1146, Section 1, Item 5[15] of the Code of Civil Procedure may not stand in the way of the recognition of the foreign court ruling.

24.14. The material foundation of the delivered arbitral award remains beyond the scope of judgment in a case regarding the enforceability of an arbitral award made abroad.

24.15. The legislature allowed for two separate procedures for challenging decisions containing a ruling on a foreign award: decisions on the recognition of a foreign court award are challenged by lodging an appeal and appeal proceedings, while decisions on the enforceability of a foreign arbitral award are challenged by making a complaint and complaint proceedings. Having these different regulations for the procedure for

---

or not falling within the terms of the submission to arbitration, or it contains decisions on matters beyond the scope of the submission to arbitration, provided that, if the decisions on matters submitted to arbitration can be separated from those not so submitted, that part of the award which contains decisions on matters submitted to arbitration may be recognized and enforced; or (d) The composition of the arbitral authority or the arbitral procedure was not in accordance with the agreement of the parties, or, failing such agreement, was not in accordance with the law of the country where the arbitration took place; or (e) The award has not yet become binding on the parties, or has been set aside or suspended by a competent authority of the country in which, or under the law of which, that award was made. 2. Recognition and enforcement of an arbitral award may also be refused if the competent authority in the country where recognition and enforcement is sought finds that: (a) The subject matter of the difference is not capable of settlement by arbitration under the law of that country; or (b) The recognition or enforcement of the award would be contrary to the public policy of that country.

15 [POL] *Code of Civil Procedure* [k.p.c.] Author's translation: [*Article 1- A ruling is recognized subject to the reciprocity rule, if: 1) the ruling is binding in the country where it was delivered; 2) under Polish law or under an international agreement, the case is not subject to the sole jurisdiction of Polish courts or of third country courts; 3) a party was not deprived of the chance to present its case, and in case it was without procedural capacity – of proper representation; 4) the case was not legally decided before a Polish court, or it was not brought before a Polish court appointed to issue a ruling thereon before the ruling of the foreign court became legal; 5) the ruling is not in conflict with the fundamental principles of the legal policy of the People's Republic of Poland; or 6) for the rendering of the ruling, Polish law was applied where applicable, unless the foreign law applied does not significantly differ from Polish law* .]

challenging first-instance court rulings results in the means of challenge with regard to recognition being examined during the appellate procedure, while a challenge with regard to enforceability is reviewed in a complaint procedure.

| | |

VI. Constitutional Order of Priority of Legal Acts: The Requirement of Written Form under the New York Convention

Supreme Court (*Sąd Najwyższy*), Docket IV CSK 200/06 as of 22 February 2007:

Key words:
conclusion of arbitration clause | form of arbitration clause | validity of arbitration clause | ad hoc arbitration court | function of arbitration court | interpretation of arbitration clause | permanent arbitration court | seat of arbitration court | constitution | constitutional order | Directive 93/13 | priority of legal acts | New York Convention

States involved:
[POL] - [Poland];
[USA] - [United States of America].

Laws Taken into Account in This Ruling:
➢ Konstytucja RP (*Constitution*) [POL] – Konstytucja Rzeczypospolitej Polskiej z dnia 2 kwietnia 1997 r. (Law as from 2 April 1997), published in: Dziennik Ustaw, 1997 Nr 78, poz. 483: Art. 91 ust. 1;
➢ Konwencja o uznawaniu i wykonywaniu zagranicznych orzeczeń arbitrażowych (1958 r.) (*Convention on the Recognition and Enforcement of Foreign Arbitral Awards*) (Decree as from 19 July 1961), published in: Dzienik Ustaw, 1962 Nr. 9, poz. 41: Article II (1) and (2);
➢ Kodeks postępowania cywilnego (*Code of Civil Procedure*) [k.p.c.] [POL] – Ustawa z dnia 17 listopada 1964 r. (Law as from 17 November 1964), published in: Dziennik Ustaw, 1964 Nr. 43, poz. 296: Art. 1162;
➢ Council Directive 93/13/EEC of 5 April 1993 on unfair terms in consumer contracts [*Directive 93/13*], published in: Official Journal L 095 , 21/04/1993 p. 0029 - 0034: Art. 6 (2).

Rationes Decidendi:

24.16. If any proceedings in which Article 1162, Section 2[16] of the Code of Civil Procedure should be applied were initiated after the effective date of the amendment act, then pursuant to Article 2[17] [act of July 28, 2005 amending the act – Code of Civil Procedure – own insertion] it is acceptable, and the complex nature of the submission to arbitration clause, which combines the qualities of a material law and procedural contract, does not form any obstacle to apply the inter-temporal provision included in the procedural act.

24.17. The constitutional order of the priority of legal acts (Article 91, Section 1[18] of the Constitution) calls for a review of formal requirements mainly under the New York Convention, which names in Article II, Sections 1 and 2[19] the requirement of the written form in the wider meaning, also including the exchange of letters and telegrams.

24.18. An arbitration clause is subject to the choice left to a professional – the respondent company, void of any indication as to the rules governing decisions of the American Arbitration Association, imposing foreign laws on a client where they significantly differ from the European legal framework, additional difficulties in claim resolution connected with the different legal system, distance and costs, as well as notorious difficulties in receiving an American entry visa – which all creates an environment that must be regarded as an unfair clause within the meaning of Directive

---

[16] [POL] *Code of Civil Procedure* [k.p.c.] Author's translation: [*Article 1162, Section 2- The requirement as to the form of the arbitration clause is also satisfied in the case of a clause included in any written communication or representation exchanged between the parties or made through means of remote communication allowing a record to be made of the contents thereof. Any reference in a contract made to the document containing the provision on submitting disputes for resolution by an arbitration court shall satisfy the requirement as to the form of the arbitration clause, provided that the contract is made in writing and the reference is made in such manner that the clause is incorporated into the contract.*]

[17] [POL] *Act amending Code of Civil Procedure* [Ustawa z dnia 28 lipca 2005 r. o zmianie ustawy - Kodeks postępowania cywilnego (Dz.U. 2005 nr 178 poz. 1478)] Author's translation: [*Article 2- Arbitral proceedings and court proceedings regarding the effectiveness and enforceability of an arbitral award or regarding a challenge to the arbitral award initiated prior to effective date hereof proceed in line with the previous provisions.*]

[18] [POL] *Constitution* Author's translation: [*Art. 91 § 1-A ratified international agreement published in the Journal of Laws of the Republic of Poland forms a part of the national legal order and is indirectly applied, unless the application thereof is subject to issuing an act.*]

[19] *Convention on the Recognition and Enforcement of Foreign Arbitral Awards* in original english version: [*Art. II. 1.-Each Contracting State shall recognize an agreement in writing under which the parties undertake to submit to arbitration all or any differences which have arisen or which may arise between them in respect of a defined legal relationship, whether contractual or not, concerning a subject matter capable of settlement by arbitration. 2. The term „agreement in writing" shall include an arbitral clause in a contract or an arbitration agreement, signed by the parties or contained in an exchange of letters or telegrams.*]

93/13 EEC. The arbitration clause imposed on the respondent party constitutes an unfair contractual provision and creates an environment that is in conflict with Article 6, Section 2[20] of the Directive and justifies withdrawal from the obligatory submission to arbitration.

24.19. The interpretation of Article II, Sections 1 and 2 [Convention on the Recognition and Enforcement of Foreign Arbitral Awards made on June 10, 1958 in New York – own insertion] prevents us from assuming that, without setting aside the meaning of the regulation, the act of making a contract implicitly satisfies the requirement of the regular written form. There is also no reason to recognize the contents displayed on a website as being akin to the written form, especially bearing in mind that the provisions of the Convention ignore detailed issues with regard to the time, place and manner of receipt of a template available online.

24.20. Pursuant to the provisions therein [Article 1162, Section 2 of the Code of Civil Procedure – own insertion], the written form of submission to arbitration is also satisfied if the clause was included in letters and representations exchanged between the parties through means of remote communication allowing a record to be made of the contents thereof, or if the written contract incorporates a separate document containing a provision on submitting disputes to arbitration. Visiting a website with a template contract addressed to an unspecified forum of readers and confirming online one's will to enter into the contract does not form a representation allowing a record to be made of the contents thereof. In particular, computer "confirmation" itself – as opposed to the standard electronic signature with the basic, i.e. minimal degree of credibility – does not form the basis for identifying or reproducing the contents of such representation. The requirement would be satisfied, however, if the representation were sent by electronic mail (an e-mail), which allows for identification of the sender.

| | |

---

[20] *EEC Directive 93/13:* [*Art. 6 (2) - Member States shall take the necessary measures to ensure that the consumer does not lose the protection granted by this Directive by virtue of the choice of the law of a non-Member country as the law applicable to the contract if the latter has a close connection with the territory of the Member States.*]

VII. The Court Cannot Examine the Essence of the Matter of the Arbitration Award; Resignation of Arbitrators as the Withdrawal from the Contract

Supreme Court (*Sąd Najwyższy*), Docket C III 143/33 as of 16 February 1934:

Key words:
arbitral award | recognition of an arbitral award | resignation of arbitrator

States involved:
[POL] - [Poland]. From the available annotation a relationship with another country not found.

Laws Taken into Account in This Ruling:
➤ Ustawa Postępowania Cywilnego dla Cesarstwa Niemieckiego (*Code of Civil Procedure of German Empire*) [niem.p.c.] [POL] – Ustawa z dnia 30 stycznia 1877 roku (Law as from 17 November 1964): Art. 1026[21], Art 1032[22], Art 1033[23], Art 1044[24].

---

[21]   [POL] *Code of Civil Procedure of German empire*] [niem.p.c.] Author's translation: [*Article 1026- No legal consequences may be derived from a contract on the arbitral settlement of future disputes, if such contract does not refer to a specific legal relationship and legal disputes arising therefrom.*]

[22]   [POL] *Code of Civil Procedure of German empire*] [niem.p.c.] Author's translation: [*Article 1032- An arbitrator may be excluded on the same grounds and under the same conditions that apply to the exclusion of judges. Exclusion may also be applied to arbitrators who were not selected in a compromissory contract, and they unreasonably delay fulfilling their obligations. Exclusion may also be applied to women, juveniles, the deaf, the mute and to persons deprived of honorary civic rights.*]

[23]   [POL] *Code of Civil Procedure* [k.p.c.] Author's translation: [*Article 1033- A compromissory contract is deemed null and void, should the parties thereto ignore one of the following cases: 1) when specific persons are selected in the compromissory contract to act as arbitrators, and one arbitrator dies or for any other reason resigns or refuses to assume the post of arbitrator, or withdraws from the contract made therewith, or ultimately unreasonably delays fulfilling obligations thereof; or 2) when arbitrators inform the parties of the equal division of votes.*]

[24]   [POL] *Code of Civil Procedure of German empire*] [niem.p.c.] Author's translation: [*Article1044- In the case indicated in the above article herein, litigation to annul the arbitral award should be initiated within the preclusive term of one month. The term begins on the day on which the party becomes aware of the grounds for annulment, but no later than the executive decision becomes final. After ten years from the day the verdict became final, litigation may not be initiated. In case the arbitral award is annulled, the executive decision is simultaneously annulled.*]

Rationes Decidendi:

24.21. A public court was only able to recognize an arbitral award as enforceable in full, or refuse to recognize the award as enforceable, also in full, because it is not the business of a public court, when examining the case of the recognition of an arbitral award as enforceable, to analyze whether and to what extent the grounds for the award are well or ill founded, and whether and to what extent the position in making the calculation was proven or recognized by the parties, nor to analyze the subject matter of the dispute at all.

24.22. The arbitration court may apply Section 319 of the German Code of Civil Procedure, i.e. correct obvious calculation errors, typos, etc. It may not, however, change the subject matter of the ruling once it has been delivered to the parties, unless the parties agree to such change.

24.23. Resignation from the mandate is considered to be the declaration of the arbitrators who refuse to fulfill their duties that they withdraw from the contract made with the parties that bound them to resolve dispute.

24.24. Pursuant to the declaration of the arbitrators as to their resignation from their mandate and made in the presence of the parties, i.e. as to their withdrawal from the contract on acting as arbitrators, the arbitration agreement is deemed null and void under, Section 1033 of the German Code of Civil Procedure.

24.25. In light of a null and void arbitration agreement, the arbitrators who resigned from their mandates have no legal grounds to re-assume their rights and obligations at the unilateral request of the claimant without the consent of the respondent, as they did.

[*Alexander J. Bělohlávek &Tomáš Řezníček*]

| | |

Section C

Case Law of the Arbitral Tribunals

All quoted rulings and legal sentences have been anonymized to the maximum possible extent. To this end, legal sentences and explanations have been considerably abbreviated and modified. For the needs of anonymization, some data may have been deliberately altered, where such changes have no effect on the legal pertinence of the analysis of the specific issue expressed, in particular, by legal sentences. Quotes and annotations relating to judicial practice are non binding and cannot be construed as a reference to a law source or an obligatory interpretation of the law. Further, legal opinions voiced by arbitrators are, as a rule, of an individual nature, and arbitration courts composed of different arbitrators may come to significantly different conclusions. Moreover, the quoted rulings of [state] courts cannot be considered a binding legal source in the Czech Republic, even though their considerable importance for the standardization of the current legal practice cannot be denied.

Czech (& Central European) Yearbook of Arbitration

Czech Republic

Vít Horáček

File No.: Rsp 405/2009
Date of Arbitration Award (Final Award): 3 August 2010

Claimant:	*[X] Swiss legal entity*
Respondent:	*[Y] A Czech branch of a major German bank*
Jurisdiction:	*Arbitration Court Attached to the Commercial Chamber of the Czech Republic and to the Agrarian Chamber of the Czech Republic*
Place of Arbitration:	*Prague, Czech Republic, Seat of the Arbitration Court*
Applicable law:	*Czech law pursuant to an agreement of the parties (choice-of-law clause in the agreement)*
Language of the proceedings:	*Czech*

Type of Agreement under Which the Parties Raised Their Claims:
➤ Loan Agreement signed in 2002
➤ Debt Assignment Agreement – so-called *Cession Agreement* ("*Abtretungsvertrag*")

I. Demonstration of the Legal Identity of the Parties in the Proceedings; Requirements for the Formality/ Non-Formality of Evidence Demonstrating the Legal Identity of the Parties; Procedure for Demonstrating the Legal Identity of the Parties

Rationes Decidendi:

25.01. In arbitral proceedings, individual parties have the primary responsibility to verify the legal identity of their counterparties, and they must raise objections in a qualified and specific manner.

25.02. It would be contrary to the principle of the lesser formality of arbitral proceedings if the Tribunal demanded that the parties demonstrate their legal identity in a highly formal manner despite the fact that there exist no apparent doubts regarding the legal identity of the parties, and, furthermore, basic information on the parties is available from public and publicly accessible registers. Such a formal and excessive requirement is a demand of a party requiring the counterparty to demonstrate its legal identity by means of a certified abstract from the Company Register bearing an apostille in accordance with the [Hague] Convention Abolishing the Requirement of Legalization for Foreign Public Documents of 6 October 1961[1], where no apparent doubts exist with regard to the legal identity of such a party, and no factual objections are claimed by the party that requires demonstrating the legal identity in this manner.

[Description of Facts and Legal Issues]

25.03. The Respondent objected that the Claimant had not duly demonstrated its legal identity during the proceedings because it did not present an officially certified abstract from the Company Register bearing an apostille in accordance with the [Hague] Convention Abolishing the Requirement of Legalization for Foreign Public Documents of 6 October 1961.

25.04. The Tribunal rejected this objection because the Tribunal itself had verified, online and using the subsequently provided abstract from the Swiss Company Register, that the Claimant duly existed. Moreover, the objection in question needs to be viewed as being entirely formal and clearly intentional. A demand that the legal identity of a party to arbitral proceedings be demonstrated by means of an appropriately legalized document, in this case (as per the demand in question) a document bearing an apostille, does not stem from any legal standard that would be binding for the arbitrators. Naturally, the arbitrators must examine the legal identity of the parties in an adequate manner. However, it is in no way necessary that arbitrators insist on demonstrating legal identity in the same way as, for instance, it is required in court litigation because it is the parties themselves who should not only demonstrate their legal identity, but also *raise objections* regarding doubts about the legal identity of *their counterparties*. This did in fact happen in the processing of the case in question, as the Respondent raised objections with regard to the Claimant's legal identity. It is impossible, however, to accept objections that are very clearly intentional in the sense of lacking any substantiation of *qualified doubt*. It is because **if the Tribunal itself has no doubts regarding the legal identity of a party based on other facts, which the Tribunal did not have in this case, and if there exist no circumstances based on which the Tribunal would have such doubts, the counterparty's objection, consisting of** *only a highly formal approach to demonstrating legal identity*, **cannot be accepted provided that no doubts otherwise exist with regard to the existence of such a legal identity. On the contrary, such an objection (as the objection raised by the Respondent in this case) would have to be supported by entirely specific and substantiated doubts regarding**

---

[1] Convention (Hague Conference on Private International Law) Abolishing the Requirement of Legalization for Foreign Public Documents of 5 October 1961. For the Czech Republic, as a place of proceedings in the matter in question examined in arbitration, the Convention became valid on 16 March 1999. Its Czech translation was promulgated as an annex to the Ministry of Foreign Affairs Bulletin No. 45/1999 Coll.

the legal identity of the Claimant. It needs to be said, however, that the Claimant presented a certified abstract from the Company Register, albeit somewhat late, only after the first hearing but fully in accordance with the procedural requirements presented by the Tribunal at the end of the first hearing. As specified above, the Claimant is a Swiss legal entity, and general incorporation data registered in the Company Registers of individual cantons of the Swiss confederation can be obtained from a public database accessible through the Swiss federal (government) server at www.admin.ch. This database is generally considered a reliable source. The relevant data from this database (to the minimum extent necessary for these proceedings and for determining general information) were verified by the Tribunal automatically already during the preparations for the hearing. At the same time, it is not necessary that such standard and often administrative preparations completed by arbitrators be mentioned in any way whatsoever. On the contrary, arbitrators assume that it is the parties to arbitration who use an active approach (in contrast to standard court litigation) to verifying the legal identity of their counterparties and who raise objections in this regard if there are **qualified and substantiated doubts** about the legal identity of the respective counterparty. Nevertheless, such qualified and substantiated doubts must be established to a sufficient degree of certainty. If doubts are not adequately supported and if there are no other circumstances requiring a significantly more formal approach, it would be highly unusual and beyond the requirement for the informal nature of the practice of international arbitration to demand the demonstration of the legal identity of the parties in a highly formal manner despite the absence of doubts (whether on the part of the Tribunal or based on definite assertions of the individual parties), which means that such a formal approach was clearly superfluous in this case.

| | |

II. Deficiencies in the Designation of the Parties in the Complaint; Substantive Legitimacy of the Parties; Principle of Non-Formality/Lesser Formality of Arbitration; Designation of Parties to Proceedings

Rationes Decidendi:

25.05. A demand concerning so-called the *substantive legitimacy of parties* includes the requirement that a party to arbitral proceedings must be the person who bears the [substantive] rights or obligations.

25.06. If it is clear who is or may be the *bearer* of the rights (without the delivery of a prejudgment in the dispute) and such a party is only erroneously designated in the complaint (instead of a foreign corporation, the complaint only specifies a branch that does not have an actual legal identity) and if, in fact, no doubts exist regarding who such a party is and who may be the *bearer* of rights or obligations (for example, in view of very precise specifications ascertained from records kept in the Company Register regarding the branch and the entity that has established the branch), such a formally erroneous designation of the party cannot be considered a defect of the arbitral proceedings. Rejecting a complaint solely on the grounds that a party is identified as a *branch of a foreign corporation* without a legal identity, even though the *bearer* of rights can only be the *foreign corporation* in question, where it is clear and where it follows from the records in the Company Register, would go against the principle of the non-formality of arbitral proceedings.

[Description of Facts and Legal Issues]

25.07. The Respondent objected that the party designated in the complaint as the Respondent is not a subject of law [in the sense of *being the beneficiary of a right*][2] and, as such, cannot be designated as the Respondent in the complaint[3]. The Tribunal expressed its conviction, taking into consideration the non-formal nature of arbitral proceedings, that this designation [*Bank XXX, Branch YYY, Identification Number: xxx*[4],

---

2   The bearer of rights is the bank itself and not one of its branches.

3   Rules, Sec. 16(1) (cit.) Sec. 16 [Statement of Claim] – (1) *Arbitral proceedings shall be commenced upon a statement of claim being filed with the Arbitration Court.* [...].
Rules, Sec. 17(1) (cit.) Sec. 17 [Contents of the Statement of Claim] – (1) *The statement of claim shall contain:* a) *names of the parties including identification numbers, if assigned, and personal identification numbers of the parties - natural persons, if known,* b) *addresses of the parties, relief claimed, signature of the Claimant.* [...].

4   The so-called *Identification Number* (in Czech commonly abbreviated as "IČ" and formerly "IČO") is one of the main identifiers of any business/economic entity. It is assigned automatically upon the establishment of an entity (legal entities) or upon the issue of a business permit (natural persons, entrepreneurs who do not have the status of a legal entity). Identification Numbers are assigned by the Czech Statistical Office through the Company Register or other public registers (legal entities) or through trade licensing authorities or other authorities that issue or certify business permits

with its registered office at Street 000, 000 00 City, Czech Republic, incorporated in the Company Register maintained by the aaa Court in bbb, Section ccc, File 0000] is entirely sufficient, particularly because it allows identifying the party very clearly with no uncertainty whatsoever. It needs to be emphasized that **(i)** when an Identification Number is entered into the search engine of the Company Register, an abstract from the Company Register in the Czech Republic corresponding to the certificate of incorporation[5] of the applicable legal entity appears; **(ii)** the Respondent was designated correctly and in accordance with the Company Register in the actual Loan Agreement, and the Respondent clearly raised no objections against this fact when entering into the Loan Agreement. It is necessary to concur with the Respondent that proceedings may only be conducted against a **subject of law**, which is not a branch of a foreign bank but the actual *foreign bank*. In this regard, both the Respondent and the arbitrators fully agree that this issue has been relatively unambiguously settled in the domestic [Czech] judicial practice, i.e. the practice of the Czech judiciary[6], which is, as far as these fundamental questions are concerned, certainly a part of and, as a minimum, the basis for the interpretation of the governing (Czech) law. If, however, only a branch of the bank is designated as a party in the complaint (the Respondent), even though all the abovementioned sources

---

(entrepreneurs who are not legal entities). Identification Numbers are also assigned to legal entities that are not entrepreneurs. The Identification Number must be strictly differentiated from the number under which entrepreneurs (legal entities) are registered in the Company Register or other public registers. The Identification Number remains the same throughout the existence of a legal entity (the duration of the business permit of a natural person) and does not change after a relocation of the registered office or other changes that may take place in respect of a business (corporation, any other business entity, or any legal entity) during its existence. In addition, the Identification Number is an important identifier in cases of corporate changes, changes of registered office, or changes of the commercial name (appellation) of a business, as it definitely and in an error-free manner designates the legal identity of a specific entity. The system of so-called *identification numbers* exists in a number of Eastern and Central European countries. The Identification Number is one of the essential identifiers required for a number of legal acts. Most Western European countries and countries outside Europe do not employ an identification symbol of this kind. In addition, entities registered in the Company Register or another public register are assigned a number under which their entry in the register is made. Unlike the Identification Number ("IČ"/"IČO"), however, the registration number may change, especially when the jurisdiction of the applicable authority that maintains the registry changes due to a relocation of the registered office or a jurisdiction change or as a result of a corporate transformation (change from one type of corporation into another type, where the *identity of the entity's substance* remains unchanged).

5   Data from the Company Register can be obtained through the website of the Czech Ministry of Justice at www.justice.cz. Data are provided free of charge, and the database has been fairly reliable and regularly updated in recent years. Abstracts obtained by electronic means are not legally binding unless certified or issued directly by a court or one of the certified authorities in the Czech Republic (*Czech POINTs*).

6   See the below-quoted judicial practice of Czech courts and of the Constitutional Court of the Czech Republic.

clearly indicate and it is verifiable in a problem-free (especially using the Company Register) and unquestionable manner who this *subject of law* is, it would be more than contravening the practice of international arbitration if, for instance, the arbitrators refused to hear the matter or even rejected the complaint solely due to the fact that the Respondent was not designated in an entirely exact manner, but only through its branch[7]. It is difficult to imagine that in this case, there could exist any doubts regarding an entity that has specific rights or obligations, i.e. an entity against which the Claimant intended to raise its claims *by legal means* through contradictory arbitral proceedings. In addition, the Claimant rectified this deficiency in the course of the proceedings. This case needs to be fundamentally regarded from the viewpoint that the form of the complaint, as submitted by the Claimant with regard to the *designation* of the Respondent, took its formal procedural effect starting at the very beginning of the proceedings *ex tunc*. Any other conclusion regarding this issue would, under the given circumstances, constitute unacceptable excess from the viewpoint of both the practice of international arbitration, the essence of this case, and the domestic arbitration practice with regard to *domestic* disputes (i.e. disputes *without an international element*).

[Judicial Practice of Czech Courts and of the Constitutional Court of the Czech Republic in Relation to the Issues under Discussion]

1. **Standpoint of the Civil and Commercial Law Collegium of the Supreme Court of the Czech Republic, File No. Cpjn 30/97 of 3 September 1997:**[8]

25.08. A legal entity with a branch office that constitutes an organizational unit is designated, in a dispute concerning such a branch office, as a party to the proceedings stating the commercial name and registered office (Section 79 (1), second sentence of Act No. 99/1963 Coll., as amended – the Civil Procedure Code) and in matters arising from business dealings also by its Identification Number and, if applicable, other information necessary for its identification (Section 79 (1), third sentence of Act No. 99/1963 Coll., as amended – the Civil Procedure Code). The fact that a dispute concerns a branch office can be expressed by attaching information on the detached division to the designation of the relevant party; this may also stem from other facts stated in the complaint. The court will halt proceedings due to the non-fulfilment of the requirements for inclusion in the proceedings only if it is unquestionable that the branch office only has been designated as a party to the proceedings. The same applies if a legal entity has another organizational unit, which the law requires to be registered in the Company Register.

---

7   The Tribunal therefore had no doubts about who this *subject of law* was.
8   The standpoint is also published in the Collection of Civil Law Rulings and Opinions of the Supreme Court of the Czech Republic under Ref. No. R 41/1997 civ.

2. Ruling of the Supreme Court of the Czech Republic, File No. 32 Odo 945/2002:

25.09. The fact that an organizational unit of a foreign legal entity located in the Czech Republic is registered in the Company Register does not mean that such an organizational unit has a legal identity and is a qualified party to proceedings.

3. Ruling of the Supreme Court of the Czech Republic, File No. 20 Cdo 2380/1998:

25.10. A branch office does not qualify as a party to proceedings. The rights or obligations pertaining to a branch office apply to a person of which the branch office is an organizational unit. As to matters concerning the branch office, the qualification to be a party to proceedings only lies with such an entity and not with its branch office. Note by the author of the annotation: The term *branch office* is used for *independent divisions* of domestic corporations located in a different place in the Czech Republic. *Branches* of foreign companies are referred to using the designation *organizational unit.*

25.11. As in other cases, in proceedings concerning the enforcement of a ruling, a legal entity that has a branch office as its organizational unit is designated, in matters concerning such a branch office, as a party to the proceedings by means of its commercial name and registered office (Section 79 (1), second sentence of Act No. 99/1963 Coll., as amended – the Civil Procedure Code). The court will halt proceedings due to the non-fulfilment of the requirements for inclusion in the proceedings only if it is **unquestionable that the branch office only has been designated as a party to the proceedings**[9].

25.12. The fact that the designation of the liable party in a draft order for the execution of a ruling is deficient from the viewpoint of its accuracy and completeness, where such a deficiency is not corrected by the entitled party in the course of proceedings before courts at both levels, can only result in the conclusion that there is another deficiency in the proceedings liable to result in an incorrect decision.

25.13. If the designation of the liable party in a draft order for distrainment based on data from the Company Register has served from the beginning solely for the purposes of identifying a branch office and does not coincide, even in part, with the designation of a corporation (the commercial name, registered office, and Identification Number were different) and if the entitled party stated in the course of the proceedings that it believed that the legal identity had a branch office, it is unquestionable that only the branch office has been designated as a party to the distrainment proceedings.

---

[9] The arbitration court had no doubts regarding the bearer of rights in the matter in question.

4. Award of the Constitutional Court of the Czech Republic, File No. ÚS 338/97 (Regarding the Right to Court and Other Legal Protection):

25.14. Even though the Constitutional Court endorses the standpoint of general courts that it is not up to a court of law to educate claimants about substantive law, including issues relating to substantive legitimacy, it does not mean that a court should not inform a claimant about the correct designation of parties, including situations that involve a complaint against a person that is not eligible to be a party to the proceedings. The Constitutional Court harbours this opinion because the qualification to be a party to proceedings is a procedural prerequisite for proceedings examined by a court based on its official authority, where its absence leads to a halt of the proceedings. In consequence, a court should provide the claimant with an opportunity to rectify the situation prior to halting the proceedings. The Constitutional Court has voiced this opinion several times in its awards, and there is no reason why it should diverge from its established judicial practice. In this specific case, the failure to fulfil the information obligation by the court can be qualified as the court's incorrect action in the sense of Section 237 (1)(f) of Act No. 99/1963 Coll., as amended – the Civil Procedure Code. Since the court's failure to meet the information obligation in the course of the proceedings deprived the parties of the opportunity to have the matter heard before the court, the conditions for the admissibility of an appeal have been fulfilled from the viewpoint of the rule of substantive law.

| | |

III. Debt Assignment; Preservation of the Arbitration Clause in the Event of Debt Assignment; Absence of Active Legitimacy due to Non-Receipt of Debt from Legal Predecessor; Objection concerning Absence of Active Legitimacy Combined with the Objection concerning the Absence of Authority (Jurisdiction) of the Arbitration Court; Subjective Arbitrability; Principle of Separability – Separation of the Arbitration Clause from the Principal Agreement

Rationes Decidendi:

25.15. A substantive-law objection against the absence of active legitimacy of the Claimant (in this case an objection against the invalidity of the debt assignment agreement) must also be examined from the viewpoint whether the subjective arbitrability of the dispute exists and, consequently, whether the arbitration court has the relevant authority. It is necessary to differentiate between the substantive and procedural consequences of such an objection.

25.16. If arbitral proceedings are subject to the requirement of non-formality, this requirement needs to be applied to submissions and pleas of the parties, and these must be regarded from the viewpoint of their actual content.

25.17. In the concept of the Czech legal doctrine and the doctrines of most Central and Eastern European countries, authority (jurisdiction) is fundamentally a procedural issue, and it is not decided in arbitral proceedings in the form that is required for examining the actual dispute (a decision is not made by means of an arbitral award, but by means of a resolution). However, if assessing the authority (jurisdiction) [also] depends on certain factual and substantive issues, the authority (jurisdiction) may be determined conclusively only in the award pertaining to the dispute, where it is regarded as a prejudicial issue. It would go against the principle of the economic efficiency and uniformity of proceedings to insist, in such cases, on reviewing and deciding authority (jurisdiction) prior to examining the dispute, as a number or perhaps the majority of issues are to be supported by evidence both with regard to authority (jurisdiction) and the claims of the parties in the actual dispute. This has no bearing on the nature of examining authority (jurisdiction) in respect of deciding procedural aspects.

25.18. The arbitration clause is binding for legal successors, provided that legal succession originates as a result of debt assignment and provided that the parties were aware of the existence of the arbitration agreement.

25.19. The principle of *separability* (independence of the arbitration clause from the principal agreement) needs to be applied to both the original agreement (the loan agreement in this case) and the debt assignment agreement.

25.20. If there are no reasons testifying to the invalidity of the arbitration clause itself, the authority (jurisdiction) of the arbitration court is deemed established, including the assessment of the validity of the principal agreement and the debt assignment agreement.

25.21. An agreement on the method for settling disputes is a qualitative attribute of a contractual relationship.

[Description of Facts and Legal Issues]

25.22. The Respondent has objected that the **Claimant does not possess active legitimacy because it has not duly acquired the debt from its legal predecessor**. The Tribunal examined this objection, concluding that the *Assignment Agreement ("Abtretungsvertrag")* without any doubt shows that both parties intended to assign the debt in question (it is irrelevant how they regard it from the legal viewpoint). Both parties have signed the agreement of their own free will, and the agreement is valid and effective.

Even though the Respondent explicitly objected only the absence of passive legitimacy as a result of the *non-receipt of the debt from its legal predecessor*, the Tribunal had to examine whether this objection also casts doubt on the authority (jurisdiction) of the arbitrators. **This is because if arbitral proceedings are subject to the principle of non-formality, this principle needs to be commensurately applied to pleas and submissions of the parties** if a certain circumstance is entirely clear and establishing no doubts from the legal viewpoint. As regards this issue, the Tribunal had to conclude that the objection against the *non-receipt of the debt from the legal predecessor*, as presented by the Respondent, is, at the same time, an objection against the absence of the Respondent's succession to the arbitration agreement contained in the original principal agreement (*Loan Agreement*) in the form of an arbitration clause. As regards this issue, the arbitrators harbour the unanimous opinion, which, incidentally, is not questioned in the practice of arbitral proceedings in the Czech Republic (the place of proceedings in this case), that an **arbitration clause also binds the legal successor, provided that the legal succession is the result of debt assignment and provided that the parties were aware of existence of an arbitration agreement**. An agreement on the method for settling disputes and, consequently, the method for enforcing law selected by the parties [choice-of-forum clause] is one of the qualitative aspects of an obligation (debt), i.e. the qualitative aspects of the contractual relationship. The objection under discussion, however, needed first to be divided into its substantive-law aspect in the sense of the potential absence of the Respondent's substantive legitimacy on the one hand and the absence of subjective arbitrability (i.e. the absence of authority/jurisdiction) on the other hand[10]. In addition, issues relating to subjective arbitrability need to be singled out for an examination of the authority (jurisdiction) of the arbitrators in a form sufficiently specific to allow determining whether the legal successor of

---

[10] In the concept of the Czech law as well as the doctrines of most Central and Eastern European countries, authority (jurisdiction) is considered to be an issue of strictly procedural nature, regardless of whether authority (jurisdiction) is determined based on factual and/or substantive legal questions or not. For this reason, decisions relating to authority (jurisdiction) as a rule have the form of a procedural resolution and never the form that is prescribed for a ruling in the relevant dispute. Thus, decisions in arbitral proceedings are never *awards pertaining to authority*, but resolutions only. A decision pertaining to authority (jurisdiction) never has, as a procedural issue, the character of a *matter judged* (*res iudicata*) because authority (jurisdiction) must exist at any time during proceedings, and arbitrators (similarly as judges) are entitled and obligated to examine and assess authority (jurisdiction) always and at any point during proceedings, often based on their official power. This does not cast doubt on the procedure where the Parties are allowed to object the absence of authority until a certain time only. As regards the time by which the conditions relating to authority (jurisdiction) must be fulfilled, the procedural requirements of individual countries differ to some extent. For instance, while the Czech law requires that authority (jurisdiction) must be established all the way through proceedings, according to the Polish procedural law, authority (jurisdiction) must be established at the beginning of proceedings.

the original creditor under the *Loan Agreement* (the Respondent in these proceedings) has also assumed obligations arising from the arbitration agreement. Such strict differentiation is necessary, among other reasons, in view of the separability principle, which ensures that the arbitration agreement (arbitration clause) is independent of the principal agreement. Not only is this principle internationally recognized, but it is also a notion generally supported by both the form of the Czech *lex arbitri* and the Czech legal doctrine on the whole. In considering the question whether the assignment of the debt to the Respondent also involved legal succession as regards the arbitration agreement, the Tribunal had to, in view of the abovementioned principle of *separability*, focus on the validity of the *assignment* itself, i.e. the *Assignment Agreement*, particularly from the viewpoint of its fulfilment of the substantive conditions of a legal act. In examining this issue, the Tribunal therefore had to conclude that there were no circumstances that would, in this case, suggest that the Respondent, as the assignee, had not assumed the rights or obligations of the original party to the arbitration agreement. Finally, the Tribunal opined that in this regard, there was an absence of a qualified assertion of the party. If the Tribunal reached this conclusion, it had to assume that the Respondent (as a party to these specific proceedings) was bound by the arbitration agreement, which establishes the authority (jurisdiction) for hearing this dispute. This partial conclusion does not necessarily mean that, from the viewpoint of substantive law, the debt assignment itself was valid and effective in respect of the *principal agreement*, i.e. the *Loan Agreement*. This conclusion is also supported by the principle of *separability*, i.e. the independence of the arbitration agreement from the principal agreement, which must be consistently applied to assignment as it is to other cases. Hence, if the Respondent did intend to cast doubt by objecting the *non-assignment of the debt* the subjective arbitrability of this dispute, such an objection must be rejected and refused due to the aforestated reasons. [...]. From the procedural viewpoint, however, it should be mentioned that the issue of authority (jurisdiction), as regards the potential absence of subjective arbitrability, as may follow from the objection against the substantive legitimacy of the Respondent, could have been decided conclusively by the arbitrators only in a ruling deciding the dispute itself, albeit, naturally, as one of prejudicial questions. It is because the problem under discussion cannot essentially be examined in the way it was presented, let alone decided separately from analysing the facts of the case and the legal aspects of the dispute. Such a *separate assessment* is obviously possible; however, it would be more than abstract as far as the procedural aspects of the case are concerned, and it would only result in increasing the formality of the proceedings. Finally, the fact itself that the Respondent did not explicitly object the absence of authority (jurisdiction), but objected the absence of its legitimacy, which included (based on the opinion of the arbitrators explained above) in fact an objection against the absence of authority (jurisdiction), testifies to the fact that the Respondent was well aware of this inseparability as regards the process of assessing the factual and legal (both substantive and procedural) aspects pertaining to substantive legitimacy on the one hand and subjective arbitrability in this case on the other hand.

| | |

IV. Obligatory Nature of Business Terms / General Terms and Conditions; Necessary Requirement for Qualified, Specific, Definite, and Legally Relevant Objection against the Obligatory Nature of Business Terms as a Prerequisite for Effective Procedural Defence; General Terms and Conditions as a Part of the Standard Contractual Practice between Entrepreneurs and Persons Other than Entrepreneurs in Some Sectors, Such as Banking and Insurance

Rationes Decidendi:

25.23. An objection raised by a party with the intention to cast doubt on the validity and obligatory nature of general terms and conditions, albeit in the agreement such a party declared to consider the general terms and conditions a part of the agreement and accepted a hard copy of the general terms and conditions, needs to be rejected as irrelevant unless it is presented together with a specific and qualified assertion and evidence able to cast doubt on the obligatory nature of the general terms and conditions (such as misinformation, lack of freedom to express will at the time of signing the agreement, etc.).

25.24. The general terms and conditions referred to in an agreement are a part of the contractual relationship. Their contents must be demonstrated by the party that invokes the general terms and conditions in the proceedings.

25.25. An advantage of the procedural principle is the possibility to observe the immediate reactions of the parties to inquiries made and other actions taken during a hearing. Already the manner in which a party immediately, without having time for considering the line of its legal argumentation, responds to questions and other actions may be very important for examining the facts of the case. The immediate nature of such reactions may demonstrate relevant facts devoid of legal tactics. The entire legal irrelevance of a certain immediate statement of facts not supported by any evidence or qualified defence may clearly show that the party simply does not have a legal argument that would cast doubt on the applicable fact in a legally significant manner.

25.26. The use of general terms and conditions needs to be considered a part of standard business dealings. In some sectors, such as banking or insurance, the use of general terms and conditions is commonplace in contracting practice where contractual relationships do not necessarily involve entrepreneurs. In these areas, the practice is widely known, essentially as an inherent part of negotiating and entering into agreements with banks, even to *persons with average knowledge of the underlying issues* (non-entrepreneurs, i.e. *consumers*).

[Description of Facts and Legal Issues]

25.27. As to the General Terms and Conditions of the Respondent, a reference needs to be made particularly to Article [xxxxxxx][11] of the Loan Agreement, which expressly states that: "...the *Bank's General Terms and Conditions* apply in a supporting manner so long as they do not contravene the provisions of this Agreement. By signing the Agreement, the Beneficiary of the Loan also confirmed to have received one copy of this Agreement and of the General Terms and Conditions". This clause clearly shows that [DDDDD][12], in entering into the *Loan Agreement*, was aware that the contractual relationship in question was, in addition to the *Loan Agreement* itself, also subject to the *General Terms and Conditions* ("GTC") and that it was aware of the GTC, as it has received them together with an original counterpart of the *Loan Agreement*. During the second hearing in this matter, the Claimant rejected the obligatory nature of the GTC in response to a question asked by the Tribunal regarding the GTC, stating that it had not received any GTC. Further, the Claimant also refused the notion that the GTC would constitute a part of the contractual agreement in the legal relationship in question. In contrast, the Respondent maintained the opposite, stating in respect of the contents of the GTC that it had erroneously assumed that the GTC had already been automatically added to the file by the Claimant, which was primarily responsible for keeping evidence on the contractual relationship between the parties, and if that was not the case, that the corresponding text of the GTC would be added to the file and for the purposes of serving as evidence. The text of the GTC was submitted by the Respondent immediately after the second hearing. The Tribunal had to reject strongly the Respondent's line of argumentation (defence) regarding the claimed absence of the obligatory nature of the GTC. The fact that a party expressly states in an agreement (the *Loan Agreement* in this case), that is not only in the GTC, that the GTC validly complement the agreed wording of the particular agreement and specifically affirms to have received a copy of the GTC cannot lead to any conclusion other that the GTC are valid and binding for the applicable contractual relationship. The arbitrators naturally do not question the theoretical and hypothetical possibility that a party that

---

[11] Omitted in order to anonymize the ruling.
[12] Legal predecessor of the party to the proceedings.

enters into (signs) an agreement containing a declaration (clause) with a text corresponding to the above interpretation of the section of the *Loan Agreement* pertaining to the GTC has not actually been informed of the text of the GTC, where it is hypothetically possible that the text of the GTC has not in fact been handed over to the party. There may exist a number of factual and legally qualifiable situations, ranging from a *simple* mistake to an actual *physical lack of freedom* to express one's will. The same approach could be used to cast doubt on the obligatory nature of the specific and definite text of the GTC, where the party with procedural interest in doing so would subsequently have to submit evidence demonstrating what text of the contractual conditions is valid and binding for the applicable relationship. The Claimant, however, did not present such qualified defence. Regarding this issue, the Respondent did not discharge the burden of proof and, furthermore, failed to fulfil the burden of assertion. In contradictory proceedings, the advantage of the procedural principle is, principally, the fact that the Tribunal that has the authority (jurisdiction) to hear and settle a dispute can, among others, evaluate the immediate response of parties to inquiries, ascertained (asserted, evidenced) facts, etc. An immediate reaction is often very important, as it allows the Tribunal to form a realistic opinion about the facts of the case. The Claimant's defence regarding the GTC, as presented in the form of the reply to the specific question asked by the Tribunal, could not be, in the procedural circumstances, understood in a way other than highly premeditated and entirely irrelevant from the legal viewpoint (in the sense of the *plea* in question). It is because if the Tribunal accepted the line of argumentation used by the Claimant during the second hearing in the form of the reply to the inquiry about the GTC and rejected the GTC as a part of the substantive-law status of the contractual relationship, it would cast doubt on the very basis of contractual legal relationships, i.e. the notion that reflect the expression of the will and the consequences of legally relevant actions taken by parties to private-law relationships. Moreover, the Claimant was probably taken by surprise by the inquiry about the GTC. Regardless of the fact that the Tribunal, which asked this question, had to examine this matter based on its official duty, as it is a part of examining the contractual status of a legal relationship, it should have been, naturally, the Claimant itself who should have been prepared to answer such a question. It is because an explicit reference to the GTC is contained in the *Loan Agreement* the text of which had been made available to the Claimant, where the use of general terms and conditions is an ordinary instrument in today's contract law. Besides, it is a part of the banking as well as, for instance, insurance practice and a standard in a number of other business fields, where the use of business terms and conditions is a standardized *general part* of agreements as their routinely and often automatically used aspect. This practice is, particularly in the banking sector and in financial agreements, commonly known essentially to every entrepreneur, including those who are *starting out*, i.e. this practice is, as an essentially immanent aspect of negotiating and entering into agreements with banks, widely known even to *people possessing only average knowledge of the matter* (non-entrepreneurs, i.e. *consumers*). The Claimant is, however, an internationally active and experienced business, a legal entity. Thus, the Claimant's effort to *defend itself against the application of the GTC to the legal relationship under examination*, as presented by the Claimant in these proceedings, must be rejected as entirely irrelevant and deliberate, where there can be no doubt whatsoever regarding the insignificance of the Claimant's assertions in this context from the legal viewpoint.

[Determination of Governing Substantive Law in Arbitral Proceedings]

25.28. The dispute in question involved a relationship with a so-called *international element* (substantive-law and procedural international element), which mainly stems from the location of the registered office of the parties in relation to where the proceedings were held[13]. A part of the contractual agreement negotiated by the parties in the *Loan Agreement* was a choice-of-law clause under which the parties agreed to the Czech law (*lex electa*). No doubts were raised regarding this fact in the course of the proceedings. In their assertions, the parties expressly called upon the Czech law and presented their arguments in accordance therewith. Hence, the parties not only did not cast doubt on the choice of law, but also approved this choice by the way in which they presented their legal arguments. The legal arguments presented in the dispute were undoubtedly very important, and the approach used by the parties essentially explicitly reiterated what was agreed under the agreement [with regard to the governing law].

25.29. The Tribunal also examined what law should apply in the event the *Loan Agreement* and/or the *Assignment Agreement* were invalid or ineffectual in any way in respect of their legal effect on the parties to the dispute. From this point of view, it was also concluded that the agreement is subject to the Czech law[14]. If the case involved unfair enrichment resulting from the absence of a title, the Tribunal would have had to, in examining the choice of law, take into account where such unfair enrichment took or could have taken place, whether and what relationship existed between the parties, and other similar issues. Essentially all the circumstances that could be considered, albeit only theoretically, to constitute a limit determining the governing substantive law pointed to the Czech Republic and its legal

---

[13] The Loan Agreement was entered into in 2002. As regards the prospective application of the *Rome Convention* [defining the governing law for contractual agreements], the time applicability requirement, as a minimum, has not been fulfilled (*ratione temporis*). The Czech Republic has acceded to the *Rome Convention* only on 1 July 2006.

[14] The Tribunal based its decision on the fact that the consequences, if applicable, of the invalidity of the Loan Agreement or of the Assignment Agreement would be subject to the law agreed for these agreements as long as they were valid.

system. In the dispute under discussion, regardless of what is or could be the legal basis for the Claimant's claim, if such a claim exists, however, the arbitrators had to conclude that the substantive-law status of this case was subject to the Czech law as the law of choice. It is because the Czech law was either expressly chosen in an agreement (*lex electa contractuali*) or under an otherwise expressed arrangement of the parties as a result of the explicit legal argumentation of the parties to the dispute, which relied on the Czech law exclusively. Considering the merit of this dispute, arguments stemming from and references made to the Czech law can be considered neither accidental nor negligible. On the contrary, this case involved such a clearly and explicitly expressed will of the parties, where the parties felt to be bound by the Czech substantive law, that there can be no doubts whatsoever regarding the choice of law. As regards settling the dispute between the parties, it is, consequently, entirely unimportant whether the will of the parties was expressed in the agreement or at any time thereafter (in the course of the proceedings). It was an expression clear, incontestable, and not establishing any doubts. Only as a supporting argument, it needs to be mentioned that if the legal basis stemmed only from the contractual relationship established under the *Loan Agreement* and the *Assignment Agreement*, the Loan Agreement, which establishes a so-called *absolute transaction*, is related, generally speaking with regard to its collision status, to the place where the registered office of the financial institution is located, i.e. the registered office (and the local law) of the creditor, i.e. the bank's branch. Even in this case, however, an examination of the collision law points to Czech substantive law. There is no doubt that the dispute is subject to the substantive law of the Czech Republic.

| | |

V. Importance of the Judicial Practice of General Courts; Content of Governing Law; Negative Prescription in Relation to Unjust Enrichment; Nature of Legal Relationship (Commercial Legal Relationship and the Application of the Commercial Code versus the Provisions of the Civil Code); Legal Certainty of the Parties; Predictability of Judgments Issued in Arbitral Proceedings; Predictability as a Constitutional Category of Fair Trial

Rationes Decidendi:

25.30. Arbitrators are under no obligation to observe the judicial practice of general and arbitration courts in other matters. As regards judicial practice that is established, of long-term nature, and repeatedly expressed by the judiciary (such as the supreme court in the country of the law that governs a contractual relationship), however, such judicial practice constitutes an important interpretative source, and disregarding it may constitute a violation of the principle of predictability of judgments.

25.31. Despite the formally non-obligatory nature of judicial practice, the actual importance of the legal practice of the judiciary is very high.

25.32. The predictability of judgments is one of the hallmarks of the rule of law and, at the same time, one of the principles of contradictory proceedings.

25.33. Diverging from clear and long-standing judicial practice relating to substantive law is possible essentially only when such a course of action is warranted by the special or exceptional factual and/or legal circumstances of a dispute, which may lead to an opinion that differs from the standpoint that stems from the judicial practice of general courts.

[Description of Facts and Legal Issues]

25.34. The arbitrators concurred that it was necessary to endorse the different standpoints in the theory and in the practice with regard to unjust enrichment in commercial relations. The basic differences concern the issue of negative prescription that is the fact whether the expiration of claims relating to unfair enrichment in business dealings should be subject to the provisions of the Civil Code or of the Commercial Code. Unfair enrichment is a *sui generis* concept that defines in a comprehensive manner all issues related to this concept [solely] in the Civil Code [and not in the Commercial Code][15]. Hence, the Tribunal admitted and some of its

---

[15] The subject of the dispute in this case was whether the definition of negative prescription set out in the Civil Code or in the Commercial Code should be applied.

The Czech Civil Code (Act No. 40/1964 Coll., as amended) contains a comprehensive definition of unfair enrichment, including so-called objective periods (negative

members even harboured the opinion that thanks to the special nature of the concept of unfair enrichment and its complexity, a special definition of the expiration of the corresponding claims, as stipulated in the Civil Code [with regard to issues relating to unfair enrichment], would not make sense, and the [entire] concept of unfair enrichment would be, as a *sui generis* concept, essentially ineffective in commercial legal relationships with regard to its special nature [and the legal consequences]. On the other hand, it is obvious that the Commercial Code is the main act defining commercial relationships from the legal viewpoint, and, despite the fact that it does not contain explicit provisions on unfair enrichment, this case involves unfair enrichment between entrepreneurs. This interpretation is reflected in a prevalent way in the currently relatively stable judicial practice of domestic (Czech) courts as regards the application of the Czech law as the law of choice, as evidence by a number of published verdicts of the Supreme Court of the Czech Republic.

25.35. The Tribunal consisted of persons who possess both practical and academic experience; for this reason, it took into account both their theoretical opinions and the development of judicial practice. Following an extensive discussion, the Tribunal concluded that it was necessary to consider negative prescription, as well as other matters, of claims relating to unfair

---

prescription counted from the time when unfair enrichment occurred) and so-called *subjective periods* (negative prescription counted from the time when the entitled party learned that unfair enrichment has taken place and of the party that has gained *unfair enrichment* to its detriment). These periods that concern unfair enrichment are special periods defined in relation to the notion in question (*unfair enrichment*). These periods are shorter than the general prescription periods that apply to contractual relationships pursuant to the Commercial Code.

As a rule, the Czech Commercial Code (Act No. 513/1991 Coll., as amended) is the law that governs contractual relationships between entrepreneurs entered into in connection with their business activity. The case in question involved a so-called *banking transaction*, which is considered under the Czech law a so-called *absolute transaction* that is always subject to the Commercial Code. However, the Commercial Code does not contain any provisions defining *unfair enrichment*. This concept is defined, as a special concept, in the Civil Code only.

Even though the case under discussion is governed by the Commercial Code overall, unfair enrichment also occurs in commercial-law relations. Thus, the subject of the dispute was whether the *entire legal definition of unfair enrichment* contained *only* in the Civil Code should be used, including *shorter* negative prescription periods, or whether the basis of the definition contained in the Civil Code should apply as to the *principles of unfair enrichment*, and whether expiration should be subject to the general, *longer* period set out in the Commercial Code. The judicial practice of the Supreme Court of the Czech Republic favors the latter alternative (longer expiration period as per the Commercial Code) in the case of a relationship between entrepreneurs that is otherwise governed by the Civil Code. In this case, the Tribunal also preferred this alternative, even though it expressed doubts regarding this course of action. The reason was the fact that the Tribunal considered the issue relatively clearly deliberated by the Supreme Court of the Czech Republic, and diverging from this judicial practice, no matter how incorrect or problematic it may have been deemed by the arbitrators, would represent casting doubt on the notion of legal certainty and the predictability of judgments.

enrichment in commercial legal relationships in accordance with the general definition of negative prescription contained in the Commercial Code [even though the Commercial Code does not otherwise contain any provisions on unfair enrichment, which was the subject of this dispute]. However, the Tribunal did not come to this conclusion as a result of espousing one of the abovementioned views on this matter as a *legally correct* opinion, but because the judicial practice, in particular, of the Supreme Court of the Czech Republic needs to be considered essentially constant as regards this specific issue. Even though there are rulings that support the necessity to apply the special provisions of the Civil Code, they have to be considered essentially *suppressed* at the present time in their doctrinal form. In contrast, the judicial practice that maintains that the relevant issue, which concerns relations between entrepreneurs, is subject to the commercial-law definition of negative prescription needs to be clearly considered as the judicial practice that is currently (not only in a short-term perspective) established and fundamentally and strictly prevalent if not exclusive. It is a legal opinion expressed repeatedly by the Supreme Court of the Czech Republic. The way this legal standpoint has crystallized in the framework of the decision-making practice of general courts in the Czech Republic is so clear that it most likely constitutes a case where such interpretation can be considered a part of the valid law even though, naturally, the judicial practice of general courts does not formally constitute a source of law. **From the factual viewpoint, however, the importance of judicial practice is very high at the present time.** In addition, the issue is so disputable that the judicial practice, in examining this and other similar problems, logically must play an important role in essentially every legal system, whether precedent-based or other. Hence, in the judicial practice in question, the issue is a *part of the law*, i.e. a *part of the substantive-law status* of the claims made in these proceedings. Under these circumstances, however, the Tribunal could not but accept this standpoint without expressing *approval* or, in contrast, *disapproval*. It is because in matters concerning *law per se*, the doctrinal approach of the *Tribunal* needs to be considered essentially irrelevant. **Even though the arbitrators are not fundamentally bound by the judicial practice of general courts, by overlooking or disregarding the legal practice in question, the arbitrators would in this case renounce one of the principles of the rule of law and, consequently, one of the principles of the contradictory process – the principle of predictability that is fundamentally important, where predictability, as a category of today's constitutional principles, is a notion that the arbitrators in this case not only could not have disregarded, but simply had to take into account.** In a situation where the Supreme Court of the Czech Republic, as essentially the *highest authority* of the adjudication system in the structure of general courts, interprets the issue in question so as to favour the application of the commercial-law definition of negative prescription, even in cases of unfair enrichment [defined exclusively in the Civil Code], adopting an opposing viewpoint would constitute a violation of the principle of predictability. Hypothetically, there may exist an opportunity for an individual viewpoint of arbitrators that would differ from the stance of the Supreme Court of the Czech Republic, if the factual and other legal circumstances provided evidence of exceptionality or some exceptional facts and, at the same time, such facts would lead to such an opposing conclusion. Nonetheless, there are no such facts. For this reason, the Tribunal, to conform to the requirement for the predictability of judgments delivered in contradictory proceedings, which the arbitrators consider these proceedings to be, espoused the standpoint of the Supreme Court of the Czech Republic, which has been repeatedly confirmed in the Supreme Court's rulings. Thus, the Arbitrators concluded that the "legal definition of negative prescription in the Commercial Code is of a comprehensive nature, and the absence of an explicit definition of the beginning and length of the prescription period needs to be dealt with, in commercial relations between entrepreneurs, in accordance with the general provisions contained in Section 391[16] and Section 397 of the Commercial Code". The prescription period therefore lasts four years[17].

[*Vít Horáček*]

Dr. Vít Horáček is a partner of the law firm Glatzová & Co. in Prague, Czech Republic. He took his doctorate in law in 1993 at Charles University in Prague. He pursued post-graduate studies at the University of Birmingham and other law faculties abroad. Before joining Glatzová & Co., Dr. Vít Horáček worked for law firms in London and Glasgow. His practice focuses on M&A, telecommunications and IT, real-estate, utilities, intellectual property, banking, capital markets and labour law and acts as international arbitrator. He speaks Czech, English, German, French and Russian.

e-mail: Vit.Horacek@glatzova.com

| | |

---

[16] Act (of the Czech Republic) No. 513/1991 Coll., as amended (cit.) Part 3 – [Beginning and Duration of Negative Prescription Period] - Section 391 - (1) As to rights claimable before a court, the negative prescription period starts on the day when the right can be claimed before a court of law, unless this Act specifies otherwise. (2) As to rights to complete a legal act, the negative prescription period starts on the day when the act can be completed, unless this Act specifies otherwise.

[17] Act (of the Czech Republic) No. 513/1991 Coll., as amended (cit.) Section 397 – Unless the Act specifies otherwise in respect of individual rights, the negative prescription period lasts four years.

Dan Podstatzky – Lichtenstein

Autonomy of Parties and of Arbitral Tribunal in Arbitration and Responsibility of Parties for Procedural Strategy – Defence against Abuse of Purpose of Proceedings (Arbitral Award; Arbitration Court Attached to the Economic Chamber of the Czech Republic and Agricultural Chamber of the Czech Republic; Rsp 752/09; August 2010)

Parties: [X] v. [Y] – Czech companies[1]

Jurisdiction: *Arbitration Court Attached to the Commercial Chamber of the Czech Republic and Agricultural Chamber of the Czech Republic*

Place of
Arbitration: *Prague; Czech Republic, Seat of the Arbitration Court*

Applicable Law: *Czech law pursuant to an agreement of the Parties (choice-of-law clause in the agreement)*

Language of
Proceedings: *Czech*

Type of Agreement between Parties from Which Dispute Arose.
➢ Contract for Work signed in 2006

I. Meaning of Multi-tiered Dispute Resolution Clause

Key words:
maturity of a claim | implied waiver | adversarial proceedings | terms of the agreement | adjudication process | non-satisfaction of a condition | improper conduct | willingness to enter into settlement negotiations | enforceability | waiver of a condition | genuine interest | tacit amendment of agreement | purpose of arbitration | effects of an arbitration agreement | conclusion of contract | multi-tiered dispute resolution clause | meaning of agreement | interest of the parties in settlement | frustration of the purpose of proceedings | abuse of rights | enforceability of a claim

---

[1]   The conclusions of the arbitral tribunal on the individual issues are also applicable to international proceedings. Czech arbitration laws do not distinguish between domestic and international proceedings. The Act on Arbitration and Enforcement of Arbitral Awards contains special rules regarding international elements in connection with the recognition and enforcement of arbitral awards, the determination of the applicable law, and precedence accorded to international treaties.

Rationes Decidendi:

26.01. The parties' undertaking in a dispute resolution clause to attempt to reach an amicable settlement before initiating any other procedure is not a condition precedent for the arbitrability of a dispute (so-called subjective arbitrability). This clause does not postpone the effective date of the arbitration agreement or the enforceability thereof. This clause does not limit the arbitrability of the dispute. It is a condition upon which the maturity of the claim depends, meaning the enforceability thereof.

26.02. Unless the parties themselves invoke the failure to satisfy the condition requiring that an attempt be made to reach an amicable settlement of the dispute and exhibit their willingness to negotiate an amicable settlement, the only possible conclusion is that they have thereby implicitly waived this condition and *de facto* modified the terms of the agreement.

26.03. The party seeking to invoke the failure to satisfy the condition for the resolution of the dispute in adversarial proceedings (arbitration) by arguing that no settlement negotiations were held should at the same time prove their bona fide (not only formal) readiness to hold effective negotiations on the amicable settlement of the dispute.

26.04. If any of the parties raises an objection of the violation of the multi-tiered dispute resolution clause prior to filing a statement of claim, the arbitral tribunal should usually also inquire whether the only purpose of the objection is to postpone the decision, i.e. whether it is mere an obstruction and the abuse of the party's rights. The arbitral tribunal ought to employ all instruments at its disposal in order to prevent that.

[Description of Facts and Legal Issues]

26.05. The arbitration clause contained the following agreement of the parties (cit.) *The parties undertake to resolve any potential disputes arising from the Contract always by **mutual negotiations first**. The parties have agreed that any potential dispute shall be finally settled in arbitration before the permanent Arbitration Court attached to the Economic Chamber of the Czech Republic and Agricultural Chamber of the Czech Republic in Prague, according to its Rules.*

[From the Legal Conclusion of the Arbitral Tribunal]

26.06. A clause stipulating that the parties shall **first attempt to resolve the dispute through mutual negotiations** is fairly typical, and unfortunately often unsuitable (*pathological*). Whether the parties' desire to achieve the possible amicable settlement of their disputes expressed at the conclusion of the contract was serious or not (which is usually legally irrelevant), the clause is most often restrictive and disadvantageous for the parties. If the parties have a genuine desire to reach an amicable settlement, they usually endeavour to achieve such settlement without being forced to do so by an explicit clause incorporated in their contract. Conversely, if one of the parties concludes that it is necessary to file a claim with the tribunal, this usually serves as an indication that the party does not consider any other option to be viable.

26.07. The parties never argued, and the arbitral **tribunal did not establish, that the parties attempted to reach** an amicable settlement of the dispute. In compliance with the extensive international practice in arbitration, the arbitral tribunal did not interpret the contractual obligation of the parties to settle the dispute amicably as a condition of the arbitrability of the dispute (so-called subjective arbitrability).

26.08. The arbitral tribunal in said case also did not attribute any meaning under substantive law to the contractual commitment of the parties to attempt to reach an amicable settlement. A contrary conclusion would require the fulfilment of two prerequisites: first, the parties themselves would have to invoke the failure to satisfy the condition and thereby clearly stipulate that they insist on the performance thereof.

26.09. Adherence to the mechanisms agreed in 'multi-tiered dispute resolution clauses' cannot be imposed on the parties. Even if the failure to observe the agreed procedure is invoked by any of the parties, the arbitral tribunal should inquire whether this constitutes an *abuse of rights*. The terms of the agreement have crucial importance for arbitration, but we must strictly distinguish between the exercise of rights and an obvious attempt to postpone the resolution of the dispute, or even to frustrate the purpose of the arbitration proceedings.

26.10. If – in this case, naturally only hypothetically – the respondent raised such an objection, it would only constitute an obstruction to the adjudication process, because adherence to the procedure of *negotiations between the parties* would apparently fail to have a positive effect of any sort. Consequently, by their very approach to the dispute, the parties themselves have implicitly waived the condition of entering into amicable settlement negotiations prior to initiating any adversarial adjudication process (arbitration).

| | |

II. Withdrawal of Counterclaim, Form of Decision on Withdrawal of Claim, *Lis Pendens*, Status of Counterclaim and Objection of Set-off and Danger of Judgment *Ultra Petita*

Rationes Decidendi:

26.11. If the respondent withdraws their counterclaim during the proceedings, before the nature of their claim is determined (an objection of set-off or a counterclaim) and before the respondent settles the fee for their counterclaim, the counterclaim will be entirely disregarded in the proceedings. The tribunal therefore makes no decision on the admissibility of the counterclaim and no decision on the admissibility of the withdrawal.

26.12. The respondent's claim has not yet been submitted to arbitration (has not become the subject matter of the proceedings), nor have the conditions for adjudicating on the claim been fulfilled. The claim must be entirely disregarded (as if it were never lodged). The counterclaim does not even constitute *Lis Pendens*, should that obstacle become applicable (under any circumstances) at any time until the moment the conditions for adjudicating on the counterclaim are met. These conditions include, in particular, a precise specification of the counterclaim and a description of the factual and legal circumstances, the submission of evidence, the payment of the fee for the counterclaim, and the admission of the counterclaim by a decision of the arbitral tribunal.

26.13. It shall suffice if the arbitral tribunal takes note of the withdrawal of the counterclaim during the proceedings in an informal manner that does not leave any doubt that the claim will be disregarded in the proceedings. At every stage of the proceedings, it must be clear beyond any doubt that claims will be dealt with in the proceedings (in connection with the facts of the case and the legal issues involved).

26.14. If during the proceedings (especially in the award) the arbitral tribunal took into account a procedural defence in the form of a procedural objection of set-off, although the objection in fact constitutes a counterclaim, without the procedural conditions for adjudicating on the counterclaim being met and despite the fact that the *cross-claim* was classified as a counterclaim by the tribunal and the respondent was invited to fulfil the applicable procedural conditions, the arbitral award would certainly be considered a decision *ultra petita*.

[From the Factual and Legal Circumstances and from the Procedural Conclusions of the Arbitral Tribunal]

26.15. The respondent lodged their own claims against the claimant in defence of their case without making any distinction between the individual rights asserted in the proceedings. The arbitral tribunal concluded that the claims raised in the defence constituted a counterclaim, not a procedural objection of set-off. The stage of the proceedings, as well as the other circumstances of the case, would probably allow the tribunal to treat this *cross-claim* exclusively as a counterclaim. The respondent was warned thereof at the beginning of the hearing. The arbitral tribunal reserved the right to make a decision on the nature of this defence and on the admissibility of the counterclaim only after all the stipulated procedural conditions had been satisfied. Above all, the respondent should have provided a precise classification of their claim from the factual and legal perspective, specified evidence supporting this *cross-claim*, and paid the requisite fee.

| | |

III. Party Autonomy (Responsibility of Parties for Proper Presentation of Facts and Submission of Evidence in Proceedings) and Procedural Fiction

Rationes Decidendi:

26.16. If a party refers to its previous submissions (especially written pleadings) during the hearing, and if the other parties are undoubtedly acquainted with these submissions and the contents thereof, these previous submissions in their entirety are deemed incorporated in the party's presentation at the hearing. This theory is based on the procedural fiction that these previous submissions were also presented in their entirety at the hearing, and the principle of party autonomy was observed with respect to their contents as well.

[From the Course of the Proceedings and the Conclusions of the Arbitral Tribunal on Procedural Issues]

26.17. During the hearing, the parties did not insist on a full reading of their previous pleadings. Both parties declared that they were acquainted with the contents of the other party's submissions and referred to their own previous submissions. If a party to a dispute refers during the hearing to its previous submissions (whether written pleadings, as in the present case, or any other submissions), and if the other parties are undoubtedly and fully acquainted with the contents of these submissions, it is not necessary to insist on any oral presentations. Even a very informal reference to these submissions will suffice. These previous submissions of the parties are thereby incorporated in the *oral presentation* at the hearing and establish a *procedural fiction* that the contents of these submissions were fully presented at the hearing. These submissions are therefore considered *heard (discussed)* at the hearing, and the principle of party autonomy in proceedings is fully observed, without any prejudice to the requirement of maximum flexibility and efficiency, which ought to be observed in arbitration (as opposed to litigation) to a much higher degree and intensity.

| | |

IV. Discretionary Power of Arbitral Tribunal to Classify, Even in Course of Final Evaluation Preceding Award, Any Particular Document Presented in Evidence as Mere Statement of Fact Made by Party, Lacking Force of Evidence

Key words:
arbitrators | evidentiary force | submission | delay | acquainting oneself with a document | contractual penalty | statements of fact made by the parties | warning to the parties | hearing | defect | final evaluation

Rationes Decidendi:

26.18. The arbitrators also have discretion to determine whether to assess any particular documents, due to the nature and contents thereof, as documentary evidence or as a statement of fact made by the party.

26.19. The arbitral tribunal is free to make such an evaluation as late as during the final evaluation of evidence and of the entire arbitration proceedings. The fact that the respective document was previously (for whatever reasons) formally designated as *documentary evidence* is irrelevant.

26.20. The arbitrators must only make sure that the parties have the opportunity to acquaint themselves with the respective document and to comment on the document in their submissions.

[From the Course of the Proceedings and the Conclusions of the Arbitral Tribunal on Procedural Issues]

26.21. The respective document was a list of defects [in construction works], an overview of delays in remedying the individual defects, and a specification of the contractual penalties demanded by the claimant in respect of the partial breaches of the contractual obligations. This document was submitted as documentary evidence and the contents of the material was read *in evidence* during the hearing, in particular, during the taking of evidence. Only during the final evaluation (after the hearing and the taking of evidence was closed) did the arbitral tribunal conclude that the document was merely a unilateral act of the party, without any qualified support in the contract in terms of any evidentiary force. The tribunal therefore determined that the document was merely part of the party's

Czech (& Central European) Yearbook of Arbitration

submissions, only expressed in a *different documentary form* (separate from the party's formal pleadings in the case). It is not necessary to warn the parties of such a partial conclusion.

| | |

V. Lack of Any Legal Qualification (Knowledge of Law) of the Party's Representative (Counsel) Is Irrelevant – Free Evaluation (Interpretation) of Legal Circumstances and a Higher Degree of Responsibility of Parties in Commercial Relationships with respect to Acts Binding on Parties

Key words:
autonomous evaluation | due diligence | uniform meaning of terminology | mandatory rules | qualification | inappropriate expression | common language | commercial relationships | expert terminology | mistake | validity of an act | entrepreneur | mandatory due care | employment relationships | language of law | fact of law | legal act | legally relevant conduct | legally relevant expression | expression of will | relevant circumstances | applicable law | specific terminology | generally used terminology | lack of ambiguity | free evaluation | binding force of the act over the parties | knowledge

Rationes Decidendi:

26.22. From the perspective of substantive law it is completely irrelevant whether a particular act (legal act) is performed by a person with or without any legal qualification. The only decisive element is whether the act results in the establishment of a legally relevant fact. It must therefore be a valid act binding on the party.

26.23. If we were to accept the argument that legal acts performed [on behalf of a party] by persons with legal qualification (knowledge of the law) must be distinguished from legal acts performed by persons lacking such qualification (knowledge), we would undermine the very basis of liability [of persons/parties] for legally relevant acts.

26.24. The only important concern is whether the persons who perform the act have legal capacity and whether the act is binding on the contracting party (party to the dispute) both from the perspective of applicable law and with regard to the particular facts of the case.

26.25. The contents of any legal act, as well as any other legal fact important for the assessment of any particular dispute, is subject to the autonomous and free evaluation (interpretation) of the arbitral tribunal alone. The arbitral tribunal is, however, bound by the general legal postulates in terms of the lack of ambiguity of the expression of will, the lack of ambiguity of the contents thereof, and a potential mistake made by the recipient of the *offer* (i.e. the addressee of the particular expression of will made by the other party), etc.

26.26. Commercial relationships are a category that, more than any other, usually requires us to abstain from attributing any significance to the legal qualification (or lack thereof) of the [natural] person acting on behalf of the party. The mandatory due care (*due diligence*) of every entrepreneur should generally include the obligation to make sure that the acts binding on the entrepreneur comply with the requirements of validity and enforceability; without prejudice, however, to the right and obligation of the *forum* to identify and evaluate (interpret) the *actual contents of legally relevant expressions of will*.

26.27. A lack of any legal qualification could only be relevant, to a certain extent, if the respective party is not an entrepreneur. However, the law provides other mechanisms for protecting the participants in these cases, for instance, consumer protection, special types of protection in employment relationships, etc. Besides, even relationships between entrepreneurs are often subject to mandatory rules of applicable law, the purpose of which is to make sure that the parties act in a certain manner or that their expressions of will are interpreted in a certain manner. These situations aside, the arbitral tribunal has no or only a negligible possibility to take into account the lack of any legal qualification of the persons whose acts are binding on the entrepreneur (the party) under the law.

26.28. Arbitration is a suitable platform for taking into account the specific terminology used in certain industries (specialized terminology, expert terminology), which would have a different meaning in common language or in the language of law. However, the terminology must generally be used in the respective industry, and the contents and uniform meaning of the terminology must be undoubtedly known to all parties. If that is not the case (as in this dispute), the inappropriate use of certain phrases must burden the party that actually used the phrases.

[From the Factual and Legal Circumstances and from the Procedural Conclusions of the Arbitral Tribunal]

26.29. The party insisted that the lack of any legal qualification of the persons who had drawn up the list of defects of the construction had to be taken into consideration. The arbitral tribunal did admit that construction works and the documentation accompanying such works are often influenced by a lack of any knowledge of the law, and sometimes even a lack of the ability to envisage the legal consequences of certain words and phrases. But this cannot have any bearing on the binding force of such acts. Such acts must primarily be evaluated (interpreted) from the perspective of the applicable law. Every entrepreneur is obliged to make sure that his or her employees or other persons acting on behalf of the entrepreneur express the contents of their acts in a proper and legally relevant manner. This forms part of the mandatory duty of care binding on every entrepreneur. For instance, the entrepreneur should give proper instructions to the persons acting on his or her behalf, prepare draft phrases to be used in standard documents accompanying the construction, and depending on the importance of the planned assignments, secure the attendance of a person with sufficient qualifications, or at least training.

| | |

VI. Response of Arbitral Tribunal to Withdrawal of Proposal of Evidence and Responsibility of Parties for Own Procedural Strategy

Key words:
proposal of evidence | responsibility of the parties | responsibility for procedural strategy | procedural strategy | taking of evidence | witness | interrogation of an expert witness | expert report

Rationes Decidendi:

26.30. A proposal of evidence presented by one of the parties automatically becomes part of the procedural strategy of the other party to the dispute at the moment of presentation.

26.31. It is to be expected that a party to the dispute will reasonably respond to the change in the proposal of evidence made by the other party. If the other party fails to respond to a negative procedural proposal, i.e. the withdrawal of the previously presented proposal of evidence, for instance, by submitting the same evidence itself, we can also presume that the party agrees and did not intend to use the evidence for its own procedural strategy. The arbitral tribunal is therefore not obliged to respond to the negative procedural (evidence) proposal in any special (express) manner, i.e. approve of or take into account the withdrawal. It shall suffice if the arbitral tribunal informally takes note of the withdrawal and dismisses it from further consideration.

26.32. The parties assume a much higher responsibility for their procedural strategy in arbitration. If any of the parties withdraws its previously presented proposal of evidence, the other party cannot expect that the arbitral tribunal will explicitly respond to the proposal of evidence (the withdrawal thereof), unless the party explicitly declares that it insists on the evidence and thereby makes it its own proposal of evidence.

26.33. This applies to all types of evidence (other than documentary evidence) filed in arbitration; in particular, expert reports, examinations of expert witnesses, examinations of witnesses, etc.

26.34. This shall not affect the power of the arbitral tribunal to request that any of the parties present particular facts in a prescribed manner or submit evidence, nor does it affect the power of the arbitral tribunal to take evidence *sua sponte*, especially if the tribunal deems the evidence necessary for sufficient consideration of the case and proper adjudication on the merits.

| | |

VII. Significance of Petition for Insolvency and Incidental Dispute over Claim Submitted to Arbitration – Significance of Prejudicial (Preliminary) Issues and Objective Arbitrability Thereof

Key words:
objective arbitrability | incidental dispute | petition for insolvency | assets in insolvency | insolvency proceedings | irrelevant circumstance | dispute over property | objective arbitrability | legitimacy of the petition for insolvency | prejudicial perspective | declaration of bankruptcy | subject matter of proceedings | subject matter of a dispute | facts of the case | bankruptcy | outcome of the insolvency dispute | withdrawal of the petition for insolvency | special law | enforcement

Rationes Decidendi:

26.35. The arbitral tribunal has no possibility to assess the legitimacy of the petition for insolvency (motion for a declaration of bankruptcy) lodged by one of the parties against the other party to the dispute with the insolvency court.

26.36. The grounds for [a declaration of] bankruptcy and all the other issues are provided for in a special law[2], which also specifies the details of the mechanisms for evaluating and adjudicating such petitions. Only [insolvency] courts-of-law have jurisdiction over all issues related to petitions for insolvency, which is exclusive jurisdiction.

26.37. Act [CZE – *Czech Republic*] No. 216/1994 Coll., on Arbitration and the Enforcement of Arbitral Awards, as subsequently amended (ArbAct), Section 2(1) of the ArbAct, provides as follows (cit.): "*The parties may agree that their disputes over property, except disputes arising from the enforcement of decisions and except incidental disputes, which would otherwise fall within the jurisdiction of the courts, shall be decided by one or more arbitrators or by a permanent arbitral institution* [...]." The only possible interpretation of this provision is that the exclusive forum for

---

[2] Act [CZE] No. 182/1996 Coll., on Insolvency Proceedings, as subsequently amended.

adjudicating on any and all incidental disputes (*disputes over the assets in insolvency*) is a court-of-law, and this exclusive jurisdiction would also apply if the arbitral tribunal were to rule on the legitimacy of the petition for insolvency or the circumstances associated with the filing of the petition, albeit as a prejudicial (preliminary) question. This excludes the objective arbitrability of these matters.

26.38. If the arbitral tribunal were to conclude that the determination of any issue that is the subject matter of an incidental dispute constitutes a prejudicial (preliminary) question crucial for the resolution of the dispute, the tribunal would have to await the outcome of this incidental dispute.

26.39. The fact that a petition for the declaration of bankruptcy (petition for insolvency) lodged with the insolvency court by one of the parties to arbitration against the other party was withdrawn renders this fact irrelevant *vis-à-vis* the factual circumstances of the dispute currently pending before the arbitral tribunal.

26.40. The fact that no insolvency proceedings are ongoing, as well as the fact that no incidental dispute is pending, or that it was terminated without any decision on the merits, *ipso facto* supports the irrelevance of the argument that the contested claim (receivable) was [some time in the past] the subject of a petition for insolvency.

[From the Factual and Legal Circumstances, Procedural Situation and Partial Opinions of the Arbitral Tribunal]

26.41. The party argued that its claim existed, and supported that argument by the fact that part of the claim was already paid. The other party argued that the payment was made under the pressure of a petition for the declaration of bankruptcy (petition for insolvency) lodged against that party (in connection with the particular claim). The party alleged that that procedure was an abuse of rights and unfair practice. The only purpose of the partial payment was, allegedly, to prove in the insolvency proceedings that the party was capable of meeting its obligations and to avert the declaration of bankruptcy. However, the arbitral tribunal found no pending insolvency proceedings and thus no incidental disputes, and therefore regarded the arguments concerning the petition for insolvency as irrelevant. These circumstances would only be relevant for arbitration if any incidental disputes were pending before the insolvency court, and if the incidental disputes were over the same claim being the subject matter of the dispute submitted to such arbitration. The arbitral tribunal does not attribute any significance to the motives for filing the petition for insolvency and asserting the claims that are the subject matter of the dispute submitted to arbitration.

[Regarding the Term "Property Rights" Pursuant to Czech Law][3]

26.42. Substantive rights are the subject matter of the dispute. **The Civil Code [CZE] (CivCo[CZE])** uses the term 'property' law in several paragraphs. The definition of the term 'property' under the CivCo[CZE] has crucial importance in other areas of law that use this term. Section 1(2) CivCo[CZE] provides (cit.) *The CivCo[CZE] regulates **property relationships** of natural persons and legal entities, **property relationships** between these persons and the state, as well as relationships following from the right of persons to protection, unless these relationships are regulated by special law.* The cited provision defines the scope of the CivCo[CZE]. It follows from the language thereof that civil law includes the regulation of both property relations between subjects having equal standing, as well as personal law. All provisions of the CivCo[CZE] should therefore belong to the area of either property or personal law. Moreover, the CivCo[CZE] includes general provisions common to the area of private law as a whole. These include the definition of the following terms: natural person, legal entity, representation, legal act, prescription, and statute of limitations. However, the CivCo[CZE] does not use the term 'property', but only defines the scope of civil legal relations in Section 118 CivCo[CZE] – these include goods, rights, and other property values, if admissible based on the nature thereof, apartments and non-residential premises. Goods are divided into moveables and immoveables. In a similar way, in the author's opinion, it is possible to define the term 'property'. The term 'property' usually means both moveable and immoveable goods, rights, and other property values belonging to a certain subject. The things are either controllable material goods or controllable resources serving people's needs. Liabilities are, in particular, bank deposits, other accounts, the right to the payment of dividends, and the right to have certain obligations fulfilled. The definition of the term 'other property values' is another issue. Values exist that cannot actually be possessed, because they are not material goods. We can only imagine them, but these values are measurable, and are not liabilities. It is possible to determine their value or price, and they have certain economic importance. For example, 'other property values' can include the right of authorship and the author's right for remuneration from the repetitive sale of his or her creative work, contributions to businesses and cooperatives, expertise, and contributions from silent partners in accordance with the Commercial Code. Therefore, the term 'property' defined in this way represents the set of assets that a certain subject owns or disposes of. The CivCo also uses the term 'property rights' in other places, for example, in Section 100(2) on prescription (cit.) *All property rights are subject to prescription*

---

3 Adopted from: ALEXANDER J. BĚLOHLÁVEK, ARBITRATION LAW AND PRACTICE IN THE CZECH REPUBLIC: WITH REGARD TO ARBITRATION LAW IN SLOVAKIA, Praha: Linde (published in seven languages – English, German, French, Spanish, Polish, Russian, Ukrainian, 2009), chapter analyzing Section 2 of the ArbAct [CZE].

with the exception of an ownership right [...]. Another example is Section 150(4) CivCo[CZE]e on the settlement of the joint property of spouses (cit.) *If the settlement of the joint property of spouses was not carried out on the basis of an agreement within three years from the day on which the joint property of spouses was terminated, or if no application for settlement was filed with the court within three years of when the joint property of spouses was terminated, the following presumption shall apply: for movable goods, the spouses shall be presumed to have settled the movable goods according to the law of the state in which each spouse uses the movable goods as an exclusive owner for their own needs or for the needs of his or her family or household. Other movable goods and real estate shall be considered co-owned by the spouses, and their shares shall be presumed to be equal; the same rule shall also apply to other property rights, receivables, and obligations common to both spouses.* Similarly, one can, for example, refer to Section 153(1) CivCo[CZE] on pledge right (cit.) *The subject of pledge may be movable goods or real property, an enterprise or another aggregate thing, a set of goods, a receivable or another property right where it is admitted by the nature thereof, an apartment or non-residential premises owned according to special law, an ownership interest, a security, or an industrial property right.* From the point of view of the CivCo[CZE], property rights can be divided into absolute property rights and relative property rights. An absolute property right is an ownership right, in particular, which represents the exclusive ownership of goods. Furthermore, there is a right *in rem* (right to the things belonging to someone else) belonging to absolute property rights, which is a right corresponding to an encumbrance, lien, or pledge. Relative property rights are rights arising from contract law. These rights, unlike absolute property rights, do not have effect *erga omnes*, but only effect against the other party to a contract, and the obligation corresponding to these rights can either be non-acting or acting. This division of property rights into absolute and relative property rights is also made in foreign law (e.g. the *German Civil* Code (BGB) or the *Austrian General Civil Code* (ABGB), which considers substantive rights, together with contract law, to be the nucleus of property rights).

26.43. **The Code of Civil Procedure CCP[CZE]**, as the rules of procedure applicable to civil proceedings, uses the same term 'property rights,' namely in connection with the enforcement of the decision. As already stated above, property rights are rights on which a monetary value can be placed, and as such may be used to satisfy a creditor if the debtor does not willingly fulfil his or her obligations, even when faced with an enforceable decision against him or her. The enforcement of decisions for the fulfilment of a monetary obligation may always be enforced by acting against other property rights. According to Section 320(1) CCP[CZE] (cit.) *he enforcement of the decision may be ordered by involving rights other than the wage, monetary liability, or claim stipulated in Section 299 CCP[CZE], if it concerns a right on which a monetary value can be placed,* *and such right does not pertain to the debtor, but is transferable to another person.* There are many rights having property value. This method of execution is typical when the obliged person has a right to the release or delivery of moveable goods against his or her debtor.

26.44. **The Commercial Code (ComC[CZE])** uses the terms 'property rights' or 'property' as well, but like other laws, it does not provide any definition, nor are the judicial decisions very extensive in this regard. The ComC [CZE] is a law distinct from the CivCo[CZE], and regulates entrepreneurs and relations between them. The provisions of the Civil Code may apply to these relations, unless special law stipulates otherwise. It is necessary to take the specific position of the entrepreneurs into account. The definition of the terms 'property' and 'property relations' as included in the paragraphs above may also apply to the property and property relations and property rights of entrepreneurs, but with certain minor variations. Section 6 ComC [CZE] includes the definition of the term 'business property.' This basic definition of 'property' is the same as the definition of this term in the **Civil Code**. The difference is that in the case of natural persons who are entrepreneurs, only property belonging to the entrepreneur and used for business, not all property, is included within this term. In the case of legal entities, this does not apply, and the business property includes all property of the legal entities. This definition of property in accordance with the ComC[CZE] has to be taken into account, in particular, if we speak about an entrepreneur's property, or property situation, and his or her property rights. Consequently, in the case of natural persons, this does not involve, for example, the regulation of all his or her property relations, but only those that are connected with business in accordance with this definition. However, we must also take into account the sense of the term 'property,' and property relations in other laws, such as the Act on Bankruptcy and Settlement [CZE].

| | |

VIII. Significance of Tribunal's Request to Parties to Submit Supplementary Evidence

Key words:
supplementary evidence | proposal of evidence | adversarial proceedings | rejection of evidence | responsibility of the parties | responsibility for procedural strategy | procedural fiction | procedural strategy | procedural representative/ counsel | professional procedural representative/professional counsel | close the hearing of the case | rejection of evidence

Rationes Decidendi:

26.45. The parties' statement that they do not propose any further evidence in the proceedings principally implies that the parties (together with the arbitral tribunal) presume that any and all of the evidence submitted so far was either admitted and heard or rejected. We could therefore presume that there remained no piece of evidence submitted by the parties that was not addressed in compliance with the prescribed procedure (admitted and heard or rejected).

26.46. The *forum's* inquiry addressed to the parties, asking "whether they have any proposals for supplementing evidence," usually means, in any adversarial proceedings, *the so-called last chance* to submit evidence. At the same time, this request automatically implies that the *forum* considers any and all submitted evidence to have either been admitted and heard or rejected, and that the *forum* intends to close the hearing of the case. This does not apply if the *forum* reserves the right to decide on any particular piece of evidence at a later stage.

26.47. The parties must be expected to have reasonable experience in adversarial proceedings. The level of such experience in arbitration is significantly higher than in litigation (court proceedings), due to the degree of responsibility assumed by the parties in arbitration for their procedural strategy. The maximum level of experience can be expected of those parties who are represented in the respective proceedings by professional counsel. If any of the parties believes that any particular piece of evidence has been omitted, the party should point this piece of evidence out in its response to the *forum's* request to propose supplementary evidence. Silence on the part of the party in this situation constitutes a *procedural fiction* that indicates that the party acknowledges that any and all evidence submitted so far has been properly dealt with.

| | |

IX. Scope and Contents of Obligation of Arbitral Tribunal to Guide Parties in Course of Arbitration Proceedings towards Amicable Settlement of Dispute – Differences between Status of Arbitrator and Status of Mediator

Key words:
mediation | mediator | conclusions on the merits | equality of the parties | decision on the merits | (amicable) settlement | conciliation | amicable settlement of a dispute | closing the hearing of the case | preferential treatment of a party

Rationes Decidendi:

26.48. Where the arbitral tribunal guides the parties towards an amicable settlement of their dispute, the tribunal is not allowed to presume any decision on the merits. The arbitral tribunal lacks the power to do so.

26.49. The arbitral tribunal must discharge its statutory obligation (i.e. guide the parties, during the proceedings, towards a potential amicable settlement of the dispute) in a manner principally different from conciliation or mediation.

26.50. Although the Act (ArbAct[CZE]) lays down an explicit obligation to guide the parties towards an amicable settlement of their dispute, the status of arbitrators differs from the status of mediators. Unlike mediators, arbitrators are prohibited from expressing their own legal opinion of the merits of the case during the proceedings. At every least the guidance must not be specific enough for the parties to have a precise idea of the final disposition of the case before the hearing is closed.

26.51. The arbitrator must in no case allow that his or her legal opinions, however expressed during the proceedings, enable the parties to anticipate the outcome of the dispute to such an extent that would give an unfair advantage to one of the parties. That would violate one of the fundamental principles of arbitration, namely the equality of the parties.

26.52. The instruments available to the arbitral tribunal with respect to its obligation to guide the parties towards an amicable settlement of their dispute are usually limited to certain procedural options offered to the parties with a view to an eventual amicable settlement of their dispute. The scope of these options and the particular instruments employed by the arbitral tribunal usually depend on the immediate assessment of the readiness (willingness) of the parties to settle.

26.53. If the approach of the parties suggests that an amicable settlement is impossible, and the parties even explicitly refuse any amicable settlement, the arbitral tribunal usually has no effective instruments with which to induce the parties to settle the dispute amicably. Unreasonable pressure on the parties to settle could also indicate the tribunal's unwillingness to deal with and adjudicate on the dispute.

[From the Procedural Circumstances of the Proceedings]

26.54. In response to the arbitral tribunal's inquiry, the parties stated that it was impossible to amicably settle the dispute submitted to arbitration. This was absolutely clear throughout the proceedings. The arbitral tribunal repeatedly attempted to persuade the parties to seek an amicable settlement of the dispute. The tribunal tried to draw their attention to the potential drawbacks of adjudication on the merits, as well as the consequences of the possible (alternative) conclusions on the merits. In that respect, the tribunal repeatedly presented the parties with the suitability of an amicable settlement of their dispute, describing the potential substantive conclusions at an abstract level of alternatives. The tribunal explicitly emphasized the procedural options available to the tribunal with respect to the procedural support to the parties in connection with an amicable settlement. The parties showed absolutely no readiness (willingness) to reach an amicable settlement. Having ascertained the parties' approach, the arbitral tribunal merely provided the parties with detailed information about the procedural options available to them in case they decided to enter into settlement negotiations during the proceedings.

[Dan Podstatsky – Lichtenstein]

JUDr., MUDr. Dan Podstatsky-Lichtenstein, (*1968), graduated from Faculty of Law of the University of West Bohemia (Pilsen, Czech Republic) and from Third Faculty of Medicine, Charles University (Prague, Czech Republic). Currently attorney at law, arbitrator active in Vienna and Prague, also member of the Appellate Board of the Ministry of Health of the Czech Republic and Counsellor of Minister of Health of the Czech Republic for the Issues of the Legislature. Coordinator of the Arbitration Rules of the Arbitration Court attached to the Economic Chamber of the Czech Republic and Agricultural Chamber of the Czech Republic for the so called refund disputes in the health service.

e-mail: dan.lichtenstein@lichtensteinoffice.com

| | |

File No.: Rsp 800/2009
Date of Arbitration Award (Final Award): 5 June 2010

Claimant:	*[X] Polish Entrepreneur*
Respondent:	*[Y] Czech Entrepreneur*
Jurisdiction:	*Arbitration Court Attached to the Commercial Chamber of the Czech Republic and to the Agrarian Chamber of the Czech Republic*
Place of Arbitration:	*Prague, Czech Republic, Seat of the Arbitration Court*
Applicable law:	*Czech law pursuant to an agreement of the Parties (choice-of-law clause in the agreement)*
Language of the proceedings:	*Czech*

Type of agreement under which the parties raised their claims:
➢ Exclusive Sales Agreement signed in 2004

I. Multi-Tiered Clauses; Amicable Dispute Settlement; Condition in Arbitration Clause; Claim Suability/Maturity; Substantive-Law Nature of Condition; Arbitrability; Authority

Rationes Decidendi:

27.01. A condition, if applicable, in an arbitration clause requiring the parties to attempt to settle a dispute in an amicable manner prior to filing a complaint is a prerequisite for the substantive-law maturity (suability) of a claim. It is not a condition concerning authority (arbitrability), which is in the Czech Republic as well as in most other Central and Eastern European countries an exclusively procedural issue as opposed to being an issue of substantive law.

27.02. The claim suability condition must be sufficiently definite and must identify a specific mechanism for such an action of the parties, so that its potential non-fulfilment could result in the rejection of a claim on the grounds of non-maturity (premature claim).

27.03. Accepted as evidence that a party has attempted to settle a dispute in an amicable manner may be any fact, for instance, the Claimant's notice requesting the payment of debt to which the Respondent fails to respond.

[**Description of Facts and Legal Issues**]

27.04. The agreed arbitration clause reads as follows (cit.) *"Any dispute arising under or in connection with this Agreement, if not settled by mutual negotiation, shall be resolved conclusively by the Arbitration Court attached to the Commercial Chamber and to the Agrarian Chamber of the Czech Republic in accordance with its Rules by one or several arbitrators. The Parties undertake to carry out an arbitration award without delay. A complaint requesting the execution of an arbitration award may be filed with any general court with relevant jurisdiction".* The clause therefore contains provisions (i.e. its wording indicates the will of the parties to proceed in the agreed manner) stipulating that any potential dispute arising under the Exclusive Sales Agreement would be **first resolved by negotiation and only if it cannot be settled this way, the dispute would be submitted to arbitration**. The presented documents did not clearly show whether any negotiations had taken place between the parties with regard to the payment of the debt or whether the Claimant had only served the Respondent notices requesting the payment of the debt, submitted as evidence under Exhibits No. 1 and No. 2 (Claimant's notice requesting the payment of balance owed dated [xx xx 2009] and the Claimant's notice requesting the payment of the balance owed dated [xx xx 2009]), where these documents can be considered an effort or the first step leading to the negotiation of an out-of-court settlement of the dispute. As regards the question whether and to what extent *negotiations* between the parties could have affected, if applicable, the premature filing of the complaint, if it is not documented that such negotiations have taken place and have not resulted in the settlement of the dispute, it needs to be concluded that such an obstacle to the potential premature filing of the complaint does not exist in the case since the wording of the arbitration clause does not establish a sufficiently definite substantive condition that would postpone the suable maturity of the claim raised in these proceedings (for instance, stipulation under what conditions negotiations should take place and by what deadline, a *specific result* is to be achieved, etc.). A refusal to hear the case and issue a ruling regarding the complaint would be on the verge of *denegatio iustitiae* (refusing justice).

II. Standard Business Practice; Entry into Agreement; Master Agreement; Specific Contracts

Rationes Decidendi:

27.05. Arbitrators must take into account the standard business practice not only in view of the governing law, but, primarily, also in consideration of the *European Convention on International Commercial Arbitration* of 1961, provided that the registered office/domicile of both contracting parties is located in a country that is a signatory of this Convention.

27.06. A conclusively entered into agreement in the sense of Section 275, paragraph 4 of the *Commercial Code* (Czech Republic)[4] must set out the will of the contracting parties (from the viewpoint of its definiteness and comprehensibility) defining the relevant proposal to enter into an agreement and whether the parties are willing to accept such a proposal.

27.07. Of material nature for determining the origination of an agreement in this way is also the time of the conclusive action with regard to the proposal to enter into the agreement from the viewpoint of the timeliness of its acceptance.

27.08. An agreement can be entered into conclusively if it is not precluded by the context of the proposal or if it conforms to the practice established by the contracting parties or standard business practices, as set out in Section 264 of the *Commercial Code* (Czech Republic)[5]. In such a case, however, such a will to approve a proposal must be expressed properly, i.e. without objections, changes, or additions and in a timely manner, that is by the deadline that is binding for the party submitting the proposal.

27.09. In addition to actual acceptance, an actual offer exists in commerce, where the offering party proposes the entry into an agreement by a specific action, such as supply. The execution of an actual offer (its delivery to the counterparty) does not constitute a complete actual agreement because the proposal for entering into an agreement must first be accepted, and only then, the agreement is executed.

[Description of Facts and Legal Issues]

27.10. Based on the documents submitted by the Claimant and statements made by the parties to the dispute, the Tribunal has concluded that agreements were in this case entered into in a conclusive manner, where the Claimant responded to the Respondent's demand for certain goods by their delivery. This course of action did not contravene the Master Exclusive Sales Agreement.

| | |

---

4 Act (Czech Republic) No. 513/1991 Coll., the Commercial Code, as amended (cit.) Section 275 – [...] – (4) Taking into account the content of a proposal to enter into an agreement or as a result of a practice established between contracting parties or taking into account the applicable standard practice pursuant to this Act, a party to which a proposal is intended may express consent to the proposal by completing a certain act (for instance, the sending of goods or the payment of a purchase price) without notifying the proposing party. In such a case, the acceptance of a proposal comes into effect at the time such an act is completed, provided that it is completed before the deadline for accepting the proposal.

5 Act (Czech Republic) No. 513/1991 Coll., the Commercial Code, as amended (cit.) Section 264 - (1) In determining the rights and obligations arising from a contractual relationship, consideration is also given to the standard business practices existing in general in the applicable business sector unless such practices are contrary to the contents of an agreement or violate the law. (2) The standard business practices that are to be observed pursuant to an agreement take priority over the provisions of this Act that are not of a compulsory nature.

III. Change of Relief Sought; Failure to Pay the Fee for Arbitral Proceedings; Non-Payment of Fee; Halt of Proceedings

Rationes Decidendi:

27.11. A failure to pay the fee for arbitral proceedings or a part of the fee, following a notice sent to the Claimant, needs to be understood as if the Claimant were no longer interested in having the matter (a part of the matter) heard.

27.12. If the Claimant during the proceedings changes the relief sought and thereby increases its claim without paying the fee for such an increase and without responding in any way to the Tribunal's notices, the arbitrators will, without further notice, halt the proceedings pertaining to the relevant part of the complaint (in respect of which the Claimant has increased its claim) without examining the matter even if they have already accepted a change of such a complaint.

27.13. In the course of the proceedings, the Claimant increased its claim with regard to late payment interest. This partial change, i.e. increase, of the complaint was admitted under a procedural resolution issued by the Tribunal on [xx xx 2009]. Considering that one of the fundamental prerequisites for hearing and settling a dispute by the Tribunal is the payment of the fee for arbitral proceedings as well as the flat fee covering the administrative expenses incurred by the Arbitration Court, of which the Claimant was expressly informed by the Tribunal under procedural resolutions dated [xx xx 2009] and [xx xx 2010], where the matter cannot be examined and a ruling issued before the assessed fee for arbitration and the flat fee for the administrative expenses incurred as part of the arbitral proceedings are paid, the Claimant was invited under the Tribunal's above resolutions to pay the sums in question, where it was stated that if the additional amounts were not paid in both cases, the proceedings could be halted in accordance with Section 2, paragraph (1) and Section 9, paragraph (8) of the Rules on the Cost of Arbitral Proceedings. The Claimant did not respond to these notices in any way whatsoever and failed to pay the additional amount of the fee for arbitration and the flat fee for the Tribunal's administrative expenses by the set deadline. Hence, the Tribunal had to conclude that the conditions for hearing and delivering a ruling regarding this part of the relief sought had not been fulfilled.

| | |

IV. Contractual Fine; Adequacy of Contractual Fine; Adequacy Criteria

Rationes Decidendi:

27.14. Arbitrators are entitled to examine the adequacy of the amount of a contractual fine even if no objection is raised with regard to this issue. The possibility to examine the adequacy of a contractual fine particularly (but not only) from the viewpoint of the customary commercial practice and business ethics is a part of the application of substantive law to the subject of the dispute. Arbitrators apply substantive law in their position as an official authority and, for this reason, they are entitled and obligated to examine the amount of a contractual fine within the confines of substantive law.

27.15. As regards examining the adequacy of the amount of a contractual fine, the absolute amount is not decisive as a rule, provided that the relevant agreement defines only a mechanism for calculating a contractual fine.

[Regarding the Contractual Fine Pursuant to Czech Law]

27.16. As regards a contractual fine, it is particularly necessary to examine the adequacy of its amount. If a contractual fine is not defined by a specific sum and its amount depends on the duration of delay, the inadequacy of the contractual fine cannot be claimed solely based on its absolute amount, as supported by the established judicial practice of Czech courts.

[Related Judgments of [General/State] Courts of the Czech Republic]
Ruling of the Supreme Court of the Czech Republic, File No. 32 Odo 1299/2006 of 24 July 2007:

27.17. An agreed flat contractual fine could be (taking into consideration, at the same time, all circumstances of the given case) considered inadequate in relation to the proportion of the value of the secured receivable and the amount of the contractual fine the debtor would have to pay in such a case for, for instance, only several days of delay. The same evaluation criterion, however, cannot be used if a contractual fine securing a receivable reaches a certain amount as a result of a protracted delay on the part of the debtor; in this case, the amount of the contractual fine depends fully on the time during which the debtor fails to fulfil the obligations secured by the contractual fine – the longer the delay, the higher the contractual fine. In other words, it cannot be concluded that a contractual fine is inadequate based on the total amount thereof, if it results from a protracted delay and the consequent accrual of the contractual fine by otherwise adequate "daily increments".

Ruling of the Supreme Court of the Czech Republic, File No. 32 Cdo 2926/2007 of 27 September 2007:

27.18. *The inadequacy of a contractual fine cannot be derived from its total amount if it is the result of a protracted delay and its consequent accrual by otherwise adequate "daily increments".*

Ruling of the Supreme Court of the Czech Republic, File No. File No. 33 Odo 236/2005 of 27 February 2007, and Ruling of the Supreme Court of the Czech Republic, File No. 33 Odo 810/2006 of 27 July 2006:

27.19. A contractual fine agreed at the rate of 0.5% of balance owed per day of delay is not (taking into account the circumstances of the case) inadequately high, and the provisions pertaining to the contractual fine in such an amount therefore are not and cannot be invalid pursuant to Section 39 of the Civil Code due to being contrary to good morals.

| | |

Books Reviews

Andrzej Szumański & Others
Commercial Arbitration

*Andrzej Szumański & Others, Arbitraż handlowy [**Commercial Arbitration**], in 8 System prawa handlowego [**System of Commercial Law**] Warszawa: C. H. Beck, (Stanisław Włodyka ed., 2010),1200 pp., ISBN: 978-83-255-1234-7.*

Authors of the Individual Chapters: Prof. UJ Dr. Hab. Sławomir Dudzik, Dr. Maria Hauser, Mec. Andrzej Kąkolecki, Prof. AM w Gdyni Dr. Hab. Mirosław H. Koziński, Adw. Maciej Łaszczuk, Adw. Piotr Nowaczyk, Adw. Sylwester Pieckowski, Adw. Paweł Pietkiewicz, Prof. Dr. Hab. Jerzy Poczobut, Dr. Paweł Podrecki, Dr. Marek Porzycki, Adw. Justyna Szpara, Prof. Dr. Hab. Andrzej Szumański, Dr. Maciej Tomaszewski, Prof. UW Dr. Hab. Andrzej Wach, Dr. Andrzej W. Wiśniewski, Prof. Akademii L. Koźmińskiego Tadeusz Wiśniewski, Dr. Gabriel Wujek.

*System prawa handlowego [**System of Commercial Law**]*, a series of books published by C. H. Beck, Poland, is an excellent, integrated and very well structured collection of works presenting Polish legal practice and doctrine (with a major part also devoted to the comparative international perspective) in the individual branches of commercial and economic law. It is a representative series, offering a commentary on the individual sources, and thereby demonstrating how theory can be combined with practice[1]. We can definitely confirm that the entire series is of very high quality. This holds especially true for Volume 8, published in 2010, which is devoted to commercial arbitration.

We must also point out that the authors represent the best from Polish science and practice of arbitration, and other works of the same authors are cited in international literature as well.

The first achievement to be mentioned in this review is the book's very well arranged structure. The opening chapters focus on the concept and fundamental principles of arbitration, as well as the application of substantive standards;[2] the subsequent parts of the book concentrate on procedure. The last part of Volume 8 deals with special types of proceedings, maritime arbitration[3], corporate disputes[4], disputes in the construction industry, sport[5], domain name

---

[1] The other series, for instance, the System of Civil Law, the System of Criminal Law, etc., are just as outstanding.

[2] For instance, Chapter 4 by Jerzy Poczobut. The application of various internationalized standards (so-called *soft law*) in arbitration is analyzed in great detail in Chapter 1 by Andrzej Szumański.

[3] Chapter 13 by Mirosław H. Koziński.

[4] Chapter 15 by Andrzej W. Wiśniewski.

[5] Chapter 16 by Paweł Podrecki.

dispute resolution[6], investment protection[7], etc. However, there is one specific commendable issue that deserves special attention. The concept of the work, as such, as well as the individual chapters, illustrate the differences between the territorially conditioned customs (usages) in arbitration very well. Arbitration is a highly internationalized branch of law. Nonetheless, certain international sources, although written by highly renowned and globally recognized authors, are based on a somewhat false presumption that certain principles applied in *common law* countries are also principles accepted in *worldwide (global)* arbitration practice. This is far from the truth. Countries of Central and Eastern Europe represent a region in which arbitration has become extremely popular, and the increase in the number of disputes in this region is enormous. Poland, which has adopted the UNCITRAL Model Law after the amendment of the Code of Civil Procedure in 2005[8], is a typical example. The total volume of disputes submitted to arbitration in this region greatly exceeds the number of arbitration proceedings held in a number of countries of Western Europe. Nonetheless, these arbitration proceedings exhibit a number of specific features typical for continental procedural systems, which, in certain cases, principally refuse *common law* doctrine in arbitration. Arbitration in these countries retains the character of a very informal, and an especially cheap and fast method of dispute resolution; this applies to Poland too. ***Arbitraż handlowy***, edited by **Professor A. Szumański**, does not deny these differences, and endeavours to underline the comparison, especially in those areas that exhibit regional differences. At the same time, however, the publication does not deny the existence of other approaches and other doctrines employed in the international practice, and often analyses, in a very cautious and professional manner, and with knowledge of both theory and practice, their advantages and disadvantages, especially in connection with territorial contingency. Poland definitely does not belong to the category of countries that would strive to refuse, or even deny some of the truly internationalized standards. On the contrary, Poland has always been able to make use of all positive and practical international trends, and incorporate them into its own practice. This publication duly reflects all these factors. For instance, the construction industry in Poland has extensively applied the FIDIC contractual standards, which naturally influences arbitration as well. This book has devoted an entire chapter to this particular industry[9].

Although the main topic of the publication is arbitration, it does not disregard ADR[10], including mediation. Mediation, together with other forms of ADR, has

---

6   Chapter 17 by Andrzej Wach.
7   Chapter 18 by Mirosław H. Koziński.
8   International sources are analyzed in a very well structured Chapter 2 by Andrzej Kąkolecki and Piotr Nowaczyk.
9   Chapter 14 by Gabriel Wujek.
10 Chapter 19 by Sylwester Pieckowski. We ought to point out that, as opposed to most *common law* countries, *civil law* countries, and especially the countries of Central and Eastern Europe, do not classify arbitration as an ADR method. The reasons why these countries always refer to "*arbitration* and *ADR*" are therefore terminological and conceptual. Contrary to arbitration, *mediation* is deemed to be an *ADR* method.

not reached a particularly high stage of development in the countries of Central and Eastern and Europe, although not for a lack of the necessary legal basis. This is in contrast to arbitration, which is a widespread dispute resolution method. The book, however, provides a very nice description of mediation and other ADR methods, and a pertinent classification of these methods within the entire dispute resolution system in Poland (and also the status of mediation in neighbouring countries to some degree).

The book offers a very good overview of the Polish practice, even from the comparative perspective. Both Polish and international resources (literature) are cited in great detail and to a substantial extent. This cannot be said of the Polish case law, though, which is a pity, because Poland boasts rich and stable jurisprudence. Nonetheless, the commentary in the individual chapters *de facto* incorporates the relevant case law (only citation is scarce). This is perfectly clear from the text itself. On top of that, decisions of Polish courts are not a binding source of law. Indeed, this also holds true for the other countries of Central and Eastern Europe, as well as for most *civil law* countries. Nevertheless, court decisions still play an important *de facto* role in these countries too. If nothing else, case law indicates and thereby consolidates the decision-making practice But, as we have mentioned before, the individual chapters make it clear that the authors are well acquainted with the case law and take it into account in their work. It certainly was not left out of consideration. It would only be more helpful if it were cited explicitly. The scope and stability of case law in certain areas are considered (by the international practice) to be the *benchmark* of the status and stability of the particular legal system. This applies all the more to highly internationalized areas, such as arbitration[11], Polish case law meets these requirements, and it is therefore a pity that explicit citations were not included in the book more often. Nonetheless, this *shortcoming* does not degrade the contents of the book.

A minor disadvantage is the rich, yet less well organized index at the end of the book. The reason is that each chapter basically has its own index. The index for the entire publication (an index of *key words*) is too short to some degree, and can hardly be used for the intended purposes. It more resembles a table of contents, only *structured in a different manner*, arranged into a system of key words. The table of contents in the front section of the book is, however, very detailed and makes it clear at first glance what topics are analyzed in the individual chapters and how extensively. Unfortunately, if the reader is looking for a particular concept and is trying to locate the places at which the concept appears throughout the book, he or she can hardly succeed and must always go through the particular topic in the appropriate chapters. The index is therefore closer to indices published in English or American books. Readers in continental Europe expect a much more detailed index in a publication of this kind and scope. Nonetheless, this (probably) *formal shortcoming* is outweighed by a very well structured table

---

[11] For instance, extensive case law is emphasized as a positive factor in connection with the choice of the seat of arbitration in relation to Austria and Switzerland.

of contents. The TOC is divided into parts, chapters and subchapters, and is very detailed and well marked. The layout and the graphics of each page often enable the reader to identify, without the need to study the respective paragraphs in great detail, the concepts on which the authors elaborate, and the extent to which the particular topic is analysed.

[*Alexander J. Bělohlávek*]

| | |

Alexander J. Bělohlávek
Reflecting the Conflict-of-Laws Standards or Rules of the European Union in Arbitration?

- *Rome Convention / Rome I Regulation. Commentary: New EU Conflict-of-Laws Rules for Contractual Obligations. Vol. I and II, New York: JurisPublishing, Inc., 2010, pp. CLXXIII and 2908., ISBN: 978-1-57823-322-9.*

- *Rozporządzenie Rzym I. / Konwencja rzymska. Komentarz. [Rome Convention / Rome I Regulation. Commentary], Vol. I and II, Warszaw: C. H. Beck Sp.z o.o., 2010, pp. CL and 2691. ISBN: [Vol. I.] 978-93-255-2165-3, [Vol. II] 978-93-255-2166-0.*

- *Европейское международное частное право — договорные связи и обязательства [transcript – Evropejskoje meždunarodnoje častnoje pravo – dogovornyje svjazi i objazatelstva; European Private International Law – Contractual Relations and Obligations][1], Vol. I and II, Kiev: Taxon, 2010, 3296 pp., ISBN: 978-966-7128-75-3, ВВК [ББК] 67.312.2.*

The Czech version of Professor Bělohlávek's Commentary is a well known publication among legal experts (at least Czech lawyers)[2]. The Czech version of the publication is probably the very first comprehensive commentary on Rome I Regulation[3] published in an European Union country and it is much appreciated that these two volumes are Czech and were published as early as 17 December 2009, i.e. on the outset of application of the particular Community (EU law) act. The Rome I Regulation is undoubtedly a landmark act in private international law (conflict-of-laws) for all EU countries (except Denmark). Only a year later, in late 2010, the author published the other language versions of the same Commentary, namely the English, Polish and Russian versions. However, there are certain differences between the last three versions and the very first one (the Czech edition); the former are already updated according to legal developments in the EU refering to the Treaty on the Functioning of the European Union. In addition, the Polish version includes references to Polish law.

---

[1] The Russian version does not refer in the title to *Rome Convention / Rome I Regulation* expressly, but it is the same title as the English and Polish issues (as well as the Czech one).

[2] The Czech title: Řімská úмluva / Nařízení Řím I: Komentář v širších souvislostech evropského a mezinárodního práva soukromého – vydání k 17. 12. 2009 (*Rome Convention / Rome I Regulation: Commentary in broader context of the European and International Private Law – Issue as of 17 December 2009*), Praha: C. H. Beck 2684 (2009).

[3] *Regulation (EC) No 593/2008 of the European Parliament and of the Council of 17 June 2008 on the law applicable to contractual obligations (Rome I)*, L 177 Official Journal 6-16 (2008).

Using the opportunity of this review, however, I would like to underline those aspects which are not obvious from the title of the book itself and which are nonetheless extensively covered in the Commentary. The Commentary is not limited to the interpretation of the individual provisions of the Rome Convention[4] and the Rome I Regulation; it offers a much broader analysis of the individual branches of law encompassed by these Community acts: for instance the continuous comparison with the standards of all conventions adopted so far within the HCCH (Hague Conference on Private International Law), the extensive commentary on unilateral obligations, agreements on the constitution of trusts, the detailed analysis of the law on family relationships and status and legal capacity issues with an international element (in connection with the interpretation of the scope of both acts, the Convention and the Regulation), the relationship between EC/EU law, treaties and domestic law etc. From my point of view and from the perspective of this review, which I would like to emphasize, a significant aspect of the book is the presented comparison with the arbitration practice. The very fact that the author focuses on these issues in his Commentary together with court (litigation) practice is most commendable. Arbitration as a dispute resolution mechanism is sometimes described as trendy. Without delving into any argument with such allegations in this review, the international practice basically unanimously confirms that arbitration is the most widespread alternative to litigation both in international (cross-border) trade and in domestic disputes in a number of countries. Most of the highly renowned publications deal either with litigation, or with arbitration; a comparative analysis is rather unique. Without thereby concurring in all of the author's statements in the Commentary regarding the determination of the law applicable in arbitration, this comparative approach must definitely be acknowledged.

Application of the provisions of the Rome I Regulation in litigation is (within the scope of this Regulation) mandatory. No clear answer, though, has been provided with respect to the question of whether these provisions are binding on arbitral tribunals rendering their awards within EU countries. The international practice is apparently inclined towards the conclusion that these provisions are not binding on arbitral tribunals, only on courts. The author of the Commentary, leaning towards the jurisdictional basis of arbitration, does not deny the flexibility of arbitral tribunals in determining the applicable [substantive] law, yet highlights the use of conflict-of-laws rules applicable in the seat of arbitration also in the arbitration proceedings. He thereby disregards the fact that a number of domestic arbitration laws also expressly provide to arbitral tribunals a rather broad discretion in determining the conflict-of-laws rules applied in order to determine the applicable law. The arbitrators' autonomy, in my opinion, also implies the possibility of a sufficiently broad employment of other methods if determining the so-called law applicable in arbitration. The author has not expressed a definite conclusion suggesting that arbitrators are also under the obligation to

---

4   *Convention on the law applicable to contractual obligations* of 19 June 1980 and the First protocol on the interpretation of the 1980 Convention by the Court of Justice as well as Second protocol conferring on the Court of Justice powers to interpret the 1980 Convention; Consolidated version in: Official Journal C 334, 30/12/2005 P. 0001.

apply the EU/EC private international laws, although this conclusion could be implied in the author's statement that these laws are also included in the national rules of the Member States applicable to the solution of the so-called conflicts of laws. The author's standpoint, fairly critical of a number of EU standards, rather indicates that he recommends the application of the domestic conflict-of-laws provisions in the seat of arbitration and supports this conclusion (probably) with the need for legal certainty for the parties. I believe that arbitrators have much broader discretion than the author of the Commentary suggests. The author thereby somewhat avoids a straightforward answer to the question of whether EU conflict-of-laws rules must be applied in arbitration or not, although he simultaneously acknowledges that arbitration is excluded from the scope of EU law and also takes into account the broad discussion about the proposal of the Commission for the enlargement of Article I of the Brussels I Regulation, including a meticulous analysis of the Heidelberg Report, national reports to the particular proposal etc[5]. In my opinion, the author should pay more attention, for instance, to the potential existence of public interest in the application of such EU law instruments as for instance Council Regulation (EC) No 1346/2000 on insolvency proceedings on the one hand and those areas in which the parties' freedom of choice dominates on the other hand, as the latter are dominating principle under the Rome Convention and the Rome I Regulation.

Nonetheless, the books are fairly unique as regards the space devoted to the law applicable to the arbitration agreement. The author correctly underlines the principal difference between the law applicable to the arbitration agreement and the law applicable to the merits of the dispute (to the main contract according to the principle of separability), see especially the commentary on Article I of the Rome Convention as well as the Rome I Regulation. We can agree with the author's approach which would be rather unique even for detailed monographs on arbitration. That is, we must first analyse the nature of the arbitration agreement, i.e. whether it is a procedural agreement, a contract subject to substantive law or a special type of contract, and to what extent the conclusions on this issue could be influenced by lex arbitri and other standards applicable and used in arbitration. Such a detailed commentary on the law applicable to the arbitration agreement is therefore unique and ought to be appraised as a valuable asset to the Commentary.

[*Květoslav Růžička*]
Professor, Dr. of law, Ph.D.; Department of Int. Law, Faculty of Law, University of West Bohemia and the Dean of the same Faculty of Law; Dept. of Commercial Law, Faculty of Law Charles University in Prague, lecturing private international law and international civile proceedings, arbitration, international commercial law, arbitrator.

| | |

---

[5]   All three language versions (English, Polish and Russian) were published in late 2010 and it is logical that the author could not incorporate the decision of the *Commission* which, in September 2010, accepted the negative comments presented by the Member States regarding the enlargement of the scope of the *Brussels I Regulation* to include arbitration (elimination of the negative exception).

News & Reports

Amendment of the Slovak Arbitration Act of 9 March 2010 Has Not Been Signed by the President of the Slovak Republic

Slovak legislature prepared and debated, during the legislative procedure in 2010, a definitely revolutionary amendment to **Act No. 244/2002 Z.z.**[1] (in the original version adopted on 3 April 2002) **on Arbitration.** This last amendment was actually approved on 9 March 2010 by the National Council of the Slovak Republic[2] and was supposed to enter into force (become applicable) on 1 July 2010. However, the amendment **has not entered into force yet because the President** of the Slovak Republic **refused to sign the Bill.** The new regulation has always received only a lukewarm acceptance; the critics have especially pointed out the **excessive regulation imposed on the arbitration proceedings.** Critics have mainly emphasized that the Amendment could consequently deprive this alternative dispute resolution method of its appeal due to the restrictions which were supposed to be newly introduced. This analysis does not aim at evaluating the proposed changes as to their actual contents, i.e. with regard to their contribution to the arbitration practice in Slovakia. The proposed changes are described and evaluated in this short information solely from the perspective of their connection to the doctrinal approaches to arbitration and the nature of this dispute resolution method. The Amendment generally anticipated more rigorous supervision over permanent arbitration courts, especially as concerns arbitration courts or arbitration proceedings dealing with disputes from **consumer contracts and labor disputes.** The control function (including the power to impose sanctions) of the Ministry of Justice of the Slovak Republic as the supervisory authority was to be augmented as well. The newly introduced method of establishment of permanent arbitration courts, i.e. **under (by) a statute,** can indeed be considered a fundamental [*planned*] novelty[3]. The reason is that Slovakia still belongs to the category of countries with a fairly unrestrained regime of establishing arbitration courts as permanent arbitration institutions (identically to, for instance, the Russian Federation as well as other CEE countries). This newly proposed rule was clearly inspired by the laws of the *Czech Republic*

---

[1]   *Z.z.=Zbierka zákonov (Collection of Acts* [of the Slovak Republic]) as the obligatory publication source in which all primary legislation of the Slovak Republic is promulgated. Promulgation of these laws is the *condicio sine qua non* of their applicability.

[2]   *National Council of the Slovak Republic* is the legislative authority of a parliamentary nature (*cf.* Parliament).

[3]   See Section 12(1) of the Slovak Arbitration Act, the new final sentence of which was supposed to be (cit.) „*Stály rozhodcovský súd môže byť zriadený aj zákonom pri právnickej osobe, ktorá sa na účely tohto zákona považuje za zriaďovateľa.*" ("*Permanent arbitration court can also be established with a legal person which will be considered its founder for the purposes of this Act.*").

Czech (& Central European) Yearbook of Arbitration

where permanent arbitration courts can be established only under (by) a statute[4]. Some authors believed that the already mentioned control function of the state, together with the effort to introduce and to enforce certain minimal standards to be observed by all arbitrators, could in the future have the result of transferring the resolution of disputes arising from a particular category of obligations / legal relationships to arbitration; the jurisdiction of permanent arbitration courts over such disputes would be expressly provided for. This situation would probably leave no doubts that arbitrators are endowed with jurisdiction to decide certain particular disputes delegated to them by the state and therefore no doubts about the jurisdiction approach to arbitration as such.

The Amendment stipulates responsibility of the founder of an arbitration court for the observance of any and all obligations stipulated in connection with the activities of the arbitration court. The Amendment has expressly introduced the possibility of filing complaints against the conduct of arbitration courts. Such complaints may be targeted at the violation of the right to have one's dispute resolved without undue delays, at the violation of the principles of dignity of arbitration by persons participating at the performance of the arbitration court's duties, or at other shortcomings in the arbitration court's practice which are connected to pending cases or to the conduct of arbitrators, the Board of Directors of the arbitration court or members of the Board, or other persons participating at the arbitration court's activities. The Amendment expressly stipulated that the resolution of complaints against the conduct of the arbitration court and requests for review of such resolution are reasonably subject to the provisions of special laws, such as for instance Sections 63 through 70 of Act No. 757/2004 Coll., on Courts and Amending and Supplementing Certain Laws, as subsequently amended, and Act No. 9/2010 Coll., on Complaints. The reference to the Courts Act, or rather its analogous application, clearly confirms that the legislature perceives arbitration in the jurisdiction sense. This approach is further supported by the possibility to lodge a request that the complaint be reviewed by the *Ministry of Justice* in case the complaint concerns proceedings in a consumer contract case and the complainant is not satisfied with the resolution of his or her complaint by the arbitration court / or by the founder of the arbitration court. The founder of an arbitration court should further be obliged to submit information about the founder's activities and about the activities of the permanent arbitration court established by the founder and the court's arbitrators; such information was to be submitted to the *Ministry of Justice of the Slovak Republic* on request. At the same time, the Amendment planned to introduce an obligation binding on the arbitration courts and requiring them to submit annual reports to the *Ministry of Justice of the Slovak Republic* regarding the resolution of consumer disputes[5].

---

4   See Section 13 of the Czech Act No. 216/1994 Coll., on Arbitration and Enforcement of Arbitral Awards.
5   See Section 15b(2) of the Slovak Arbitration Act in terms of the respective amendment which stipulates (cit.) *Zriaďovateľ je na základe podkladov ním zriadeného rozhodcovského súdu povinný vyhotoviť a predložiť ministerstvu správu o činnosti stáleho*

Special rules were to be adopted in connection with decisions in *consumer disputes*. The Amendment anticipated the introduction of special powers granted to a *consumer protection association* which was to be entitled to submit claims with the competent court on the basis of which the court could order the founder of the arbitration court to ensure that each of the founder's permanent arbitration courts abstains from making decisions in consumer disputes. Such measures would be adopted if the conduct of these arbitration courts resulted in repeated violation of consumer rights. When adopting its decisions, the court should especially take into account whether the arbitration court has ever been, in the past, reprimanded for any such violation of the rights of the parties to a consumer dispute by any court or control authority and whether the founder of the respective arbitration court could have been informed thereabout. Apart from that, the Amendment anticipated the introduction of special requirements regarding the form and the contents of arbitration clauses in consumer contracts (not as an arbitration clause but exclusively as a contract incorporated in a separate document). With respect to the discussion about the nature of arbitration in *Slovakia*, we need to draw your special attention to the fact that according to the draft Amendment, resolution of consumer disputes was to be reserved exclusively for permanent arbitration courts which would have to obtain and maintain throughout the proceedings, until the resolution of the particular dispute, a license to decide consumer disputes, granted by the *Ministry of Justice of the Slovak Republic*. We must also point out that the granting of the license was supposed to be subject to and conditional upon the satisfaction of fairly rigorous requirements. One of the mandatory requirements was to be, for instance, a permanently available deposit of 200,000 EUR which would secure financial obligations associated with the founder's liability for the functioning of the permanent arbitration court. Apart from specific requirements regarding the qualification of arbitrators deciding consumer disputes (the qualification criteria for arbitrators were to be stipulated directly by the Act, i.e. these were not supposed to be requirements determined by agreement of the parties to the dispute in accordance with their interests), the Amendment aimed at a significant restriction of the freedom of the parties as regards their agreements

---

rozhodcovského súdu pri rozhodovaní spotrebiteľských sporov v rozhodcovskom konaní za kalendárny rok, a to najneskôr do 31. marca nasledujúceho kalendárneho roka; súčasťou tejto správy musia byť aj informácie o podaných sťažnostiach a o vybavovaní sťažností na postup rozhodcovského súdu vrátane výsledkov vybavovania z hľadiska opodstatnenosti podaných sťažností. V tejto lehote je zriaďovateľ povinný správu predložiť iným orgánom verejnej moci, ak to ustanovuje osobitný predpis. (Based on the background materials of the arbitration court established by the founder, the founder is obliged to draw up and submit to the Ministry an annual report on the functioning of the permanent arbitration court related to the resolution of consumer disputes in arbitration; the report must be submitted no later than 31 March of the following calendar year; the report must also include information about lodged complaints against the procedure adopted by the arbitration court and information about the resolution of such complaints, including information about the complaints being justified or unjustified. The founder is obliged to submit the report to other public authorities by the same deadline if required under any special laws or regulations).

on the method of processing the dispute. The Amendment stipulated, without exceptions, that the arbitration rules in consumer disputes must not deviate, to the detriment of the consumer, from the civil (court) procedure rules for first instance proceedings. Similar restrictive interference by the state were to be introduced in the resolution of labor disputes as well.

All the above mentioned circumstances would at first sight undoubtedly indicate that arbitration in *Slovakia* exhibits the characteristics of a jurisdiction. However, it is appropriate to use the conditional mood because on the other hand, the Amendment also incorporated an element typical for the contractual doctrine and supporting – on the contrary – the contractual nature of the relationship between the arbitrators and the parties. The newly included Section 15c of the Slovak Arbitration Act was supposed to introduce an express civil liability of the arbitrator for damage caused by his or her actions[6]. This means beyond all doubt that the performance of the arbitrators' duties is not shielded by any immunity similar to the immunity of judges. Despite this application of civil law to one of the aspects of the relationship between the arbitrator and the parties to the dispute, I am of the opinion that we cannot conclude that there exists any general civil-law relationship between these entities/persons because we must take special account of the fact that a **substantial part of the arbitrator's duties (including his or her relationship and obligations *vis-à-vis* the parties to the dispute) is laid down by the Act itself, without the possibility to deviate from these rules.** It will no doubt be interesting to watch the developments regarding this Bill in the future, i.e. which direction the arbitration law in Slovakia takes.

[*Alexander J. Bělohlávek & Tereza Profeldová*]

| | |

---

6   (Cit.) *Zriaďovateľ zodpovedá za činnosť stáleho rozhodcovského súdu a jeho rozhodcov vrátane škody vzniknutej z činnosti stáleho rozhodcovského súdu a jeho rozhodcov; tým nie je dotknutá zodpovednosť rozhodcu za škodu podľa Občianskeho zákonníka. Ak o rozhodcovskom rozhodnutí rozhodovali viacerí rozhodcovia, za nezákonné rozhodcovské rozhodnutie nezodpovedá rozhodca, ktorého pri hlasovaní o príslušnom rozhodcovskom rozhodnutí prehlasovali ostatní rozhodcovia a ktorý pripojil k zápisnici o hlasovaní svoje odchylné stanovisko. (The founder assumes liability for the functioning of the permanent arbitration court and its arbitrators including any damage caused by the activities of the permanent arbitration court and its arbitrators, without prejudice to the liability of arbitrators for damage under the Civil Code. If the arbitral award was a collective decision of more arbitrators, the arbitrator who was outvoted by the other arbitrators and who attached his or her dissenting opinion to the minutes of the voting is not liable for the unlawful arbitration award.)*

Report on the "Law, Economics and Arbitration" Conference Marking the 60th anniversary of the Court of Arbitration at the Polish Chamber of Commerce in Warsaw

On 18 November 2010, an academic conference on "Law, Economics and Arbitration" was held in the halls of the Royal Castle in Warsaw as part of the celebrations for the sixtieth anniversary of the Court of Arbitration (the "Court") at the Polish Chamber of Commerce in Warsaw (the "PCC"). The main objective of the conference, as expressed in its theme, was to emphasize the relationship between law and economics. As the content of the speeches shows, the organisers also wished to confirm that the Court at the PCC has always tried to be, and continues to be, at the centre of discussion on the law and the economy.

The conference, which was organised under the patronage of the President of Poland, brought together numerous lawyers and businessmen and was attended by both representatives of the highest state authorities, including the President of Poland himself, the Minister of Justice, and representatives of local government authorities, the Constitutional Tribunal and the Supreme Court, as well as academics from numerous centres of learning and practitioners such as attorneys-at-law, common court judges and arbitrators, some from other countries.

The inaugural lecture, delivered by **Professor Józef Okolski[1]**, the honorary President of the Court of Arbitration at the PCC, dealt with the history of the Court. The message of the lecture was that, in all our activities, we should always remember what we owe to our predecessors, and our duty towards posterity. The conference was organised for precisely that reason. Professor Okolski pointed out that, during the period when Poland had a planned, centralised economy, the Court was an enclave of private law, including with regard to

---

[1]   Professor Józef Okolski completed legal studies (1962) and acquired further academic titles (Ph.D. in 1971, doctor hab. in 1977, associate professor in 1988 and full professor in 1995) at the Faculty of Law and Administration of the Warsaw University. In the period 1990-1993 he was a deputy rector of Warsaw University; 1993 – 1999 Dean of the Faculty of Law and Administration of the Warsaw University; 1983-2010 (still) Head of the Department of Trade Law in the Institute of Civil Law at the Warsaw University; 1999-2007 President of the Court of Arbitration at the PCC; the honorary President of the Court of Arbitration at the PCC; 2001-2007 rector of the College of Public Administration in Ostrołęka (he was also a co-founder). Author of more than 100 scholarly publications (83 individual and 20 as a co-author), including 5 books (3 monographs), editor and co-author of 2 Trade Law academic handbooks, numerous publications: articles, glosses and other works in Polish, and other languages. The Professor was a lecturer in USA (St. Louis and Gainsville University of Florida). For several years Professor has also been a lecturer at the faculty of international comparative law in Strasbourg. He is a member of Académie Internationale de Droit Comparé.

commercial relations with other countries. This was due to the efforts of the various presidents of the Court, who developed its foreign contacts. In this way, alongside law faculties of educational institutions, the Court became a mechanism for absorbing contemporary private law solutions developed abroad into the Polish legal system. The Court also helped to uphold the three great values of private law: private property, contracts as sources of an obligation, and civil liability. Professor Okolski noted that because the Court operated in this way during the time of the People's Republic of Poland, the turning point that came with the systemic changes at the end of 1989 was not a great shock for it, but only the beginning of a further stage in its development, which is still continuing to this day. He concluded by expressing his hope that in the future the distinguishing feature of the Court will be maintained, i.e. the legal, economic and commercial dimensions being combined by the best Polish and foreign lawyers and economists.

The next speaker, **Professor Marek Safjan**[2], spoke on "The Europeanisation of Private Law – Evolution or Revolution, from the Standpoint of Adjudication". He pointed out that the activities of the Court of Arbitration at the PCC are aligned with contemporary ideas emphasising the importance of alternative mechanisms in procedures for settling disputes. He highlighted tendencies in European law and the case-law of the European Court of Justice (the "ECJ") which affect arbitration. In particular, he addressed the idea that common law stands against national law, showing how that concept has evolved and its current relevance. He stressed that the increasingly close links in the realm of the economy, culture and systemic institutions require common legal foundations. Like never before, contemporary Europe requires that a new legal culture be built, based on common principles and structures. This need is dictated not only by pragmatic considerations associated with the principles of the functioning of the common market, but also more far-reaching ideas defining the vision of a united continent.

---

[2]   Since 7 October 2009 Prof. Marek Safjan has acted as a Judge at the Court of Justice of the European Communities. Marek Safjan was a Judge of the Constitutional Tribunal from 1997 to 2006 and President of the Constitutional Tribunal from 1998 to 2006. He graduated from the Faculty of Law and Administration of Warsaw University in 1971; judge's certificate – 1973; juris doctor degree – 1980; habilitated doctor's degree – 1990; professor of legal sciences - 1998. Between 1993 and 1996 he served as Director of the Institute of Civil Law of Warsaw University. From 1996 to 1997 he was a deputy rector of Warsaw University and is a professor in the Chair of Civil Law of that University. He represented Poland in the Committee on Bioethics of the Council of Europe. He is a chairperson of the Scientific Council of the Administration of Justice Institute, and is engaged in the work of Committee on Ethics in the Science at the Polish Academy of Sciences. He is also a corresponding member of the Polish Academy of Science and Arts. He is a member of: Association Internationale de Droit, Ethique et Science (since 1990), Académie Internationale de Droit Comparé (since 1995) and Association Henri Capitant des Amis de la Culture Juridique Française, in which he served as Secretary-General of the Polish Section from 1994 to 1998. He is also a member of the Helsinki Committee in Poland. He is an author of around 150 scholarly publications, including 18 books on civil law, medical law and the EU law.

Furthermore, the process underway in contemporary Europe is peculiar in that the creation of a new, common legal space assumes that the separateness of national systems will be maintained. This is partly due to the interaction of private law and the ECJ. Professor M. Safjan also stressed that the boundary separating private and public law is often invisible and it is inevitable that their mechanisms and methods will permeate across that boundary. Originally, private law had its own objectives. Today, the mechanisms of European private law are dominated by the goals and assumptions that the European Union sets itself. Private law is becoming increasingly similar to public law, because it is becoming a means of achieving the higher objective which is the common market. The autonomy, contractual freedom and formal equivalence of entities under European law are ceding priority to tendencies whereby the position of market participants is being equalised.

Professor Safjan pointed out new challenges facing European law:

- the horizontal operation of the basic principles of European law (that possibility is accepted in ECJ case-law);
- the broadening of the scope of protection of basic rights, and
- the broadening of the sphere of private law, which European law affects.

He added that those challenges give rise to a risk of the principle of contractual freedom being restricted. He stressed that there is also a danger of the pluralism of national systems being transformed into a mere façade concealing a different reality which is subordinated to the centralised European legislator. He finished by highlighting two tendencies: the Europeanisation of private law and the privatisation of European law. The first emphasizes the achievement of goals associated with the construction of a common legal sphere, and therefore imposes tasks which deviate from private law; ECJ case-law should moderate that tendency. The second manifests itself in the traditional goals of private law being emphasized. Summing up, he expressed his conviction that there is a need for a wide, open discussion on how the goals of private law in the EU should be created and established.

The next speaker, **Professor Witold Orłowski**[3], spoke on "Law and Economics – Interdependencies and Relationships". He emphasized that although there is no doubt that law and economics are separate fields, they exert a powerful influence on one another, pointing out the distance dividing economists and lawyers, particularly regarding language. Both lawyers and economists communicate

---

[3] (Born 1962) Professor of economics, working mainly on the economics of transition and the European integration of Central and East European countries. Founder of NOBE (Independent Centre for Economic Studies), one of Poland's leading economic think-tanks, and the Dean of the Business School of the Warsaw University of Technology. Chief economic advisor to PwC Polska. Member of the Economic Council of the Prime Minister, special advisor to the EU Commission, deputy chairman of the Board of Trustees of the National Museum in Warsaw. Former economic advisor to the president Aleksander Kwaśniewski. Author of 8 books and 150 scientific publications. Popular economic commentator and columnist of major Polish newspapers.

with different, insular languages. On the other hand, arbitration is an area which justifies, even forces, close cooperation. He remarked that many indicators can be cited which show that countries which do not have a good legal system pay for its inadequacies in economic terms. He ended his talk by calling for the creation of good law which is favourably disposed to the free market, adding that this will not be possible without dialogue between lawyers and economists.

Professor Stanisław Sołtysiński[4] spoke on "Arbitration at the Dawn of a New Era – Convictions and Challenges", presenting the advantages and disadvantages of arbitration. He pointed out that arbitration is an institution based on trust, which requires that lawyers openly inform their clients of the features of arbitration.

He also said that arbitration proceedings before the Court of Arbitration at the PCC are usually shorter than proceedings before a state court; in order to ensure that proceedings are not slowed down, some foreign courts require that candidates for the position of arbitrator provide information on their professional obligations for the next few months, adding that such a rule was worth considering. Professor Sołtysiński also stressed that representatives of international companies stated in a survey that it is more important for them for a ruling to be fast and final than correct and consistent with existing case-law.

He went on to say that the costs of arbitration are usually higher than those of proceedings before a state court, citing surveys carried out among managers of legal departments of international corporations, whose increasing arbitration costs are more a cause for concern than the possibility of proceedings being prolonged. With regard to the issue of the selection of an adjudicating panel, he pointed out the need for more precise rules relating to conflicts of interests

---

[4] Professor Stanisław Sołtysiński completed legal studies (1961) and acquired further academic titles (Ph.D. in 1965, doctor hab. in 1970, associate professor in 1979 and full professor in 1988) at the Law and Administration School of Poznań University. He completed postgraduate studies at the London School of Economics (1966-67) and at Columbia University in New York, where in 1973 he was awarded the title of Master of Laws (LL.M). Professor Sołtysiński is a renowned specialist in civil law, intellectual property rights, commercial law and foreign investment law. For a number of years prior to the 1989 system transition, Professor Sołtysiński successfully reconciled his academic activity with counselling services rendered to Polish and foreign entities with respect to, inter alia, East-West trade, technology transfer and investment. Professor Sołtysiński is an active participant in international arbitration. His name appears on the official list of the Arbitration Court at the Polish Chamber of Commerce, the International Arbitration Court at the Austrian Chamber of Commerce, and the American Arbitration Association. He served as a member of arbitral panels and legal counsel in over a hundred arbitration cases both in Poland and abroad. In the years 1991 and 1992, he represented the Polish Government during negotiations leading to Poland's association with the European Community. He is a former Dean of the Law School of Poznań University and Visiting Professor at the University of Pennsylvania Law School (1975-1991) and the College of Europe in Bruges (1991-1995). As a long-term member of Poland's Legislative Council, Professor Sołtysiński has provided advice to the Polish Government on how to revise Poland's laws to stimulate foreign trade and investment. He is the author of more than a dozen books and over 250 publications on commercial law, intellectual property, antitrust law, and civil law and arbitration.

and for a wider scope of information provided to parties by candidates for the position of arbitrator.

Professor Sołtysiński criticised investment arbitration, saying that its deficiencies include a lack of consistent case-law or an answer to the basic legal issues of whether a breach of a contractual obligation by a state automatically constitutes a breach of an international agreement, and what states can cite the *"state of necessity"* clause. He also touched on the relationship between treaties on protecting investments and EU law. He finished by saying that the current scope of the control exercised by the common court system over the arbitration court system should be maintained, since it eliminates the irregularities which can sometimes occur in arbitration. Summing up, he stressed how important it is for the common court and arbitration court systems to co-exist in a reasonable manner.

Professor Mirosslaw Wyrzykowski[5] spoke on the issue of the constitutionalization of legal thought, which is manifested in the amicable co-existence of the constitutional court and other public entities. This concept should be understood to mean the direct influence of the constitution on the addressees of its provisions, i.e. the "constitution" in the broad sense, including case-law, legal doctrine and the international context. Professor Wyrzykowski also pointed out that a good constitution is built on basic legal principles; it legitimizes and at the same time limits authority, guarantees the liberty and rights of the individual, creates conditions for the furthering of common interests, guarantees the independence of the courts, judges and the court system and ensures a minimum internal morality of the law. The purpose of all this is to create a moral, intellectual and cultural climate in the state and society, so that individuals have a sense of security and that the effectiveness of the mechanisms of the state's operation

---

[5] Judge of the Constitutional Tribunal from 2001 to 2010. In 1971 graduated from the Faculty of Law and Administration of the Warsaw University; *juris* doctor's degree - 1975, habilitated doctor's degree – 1986; professor of the Warsaw University - 1991, chairing the Comparative and Economic Law Division of the Institute of Legal Administrative Studies at the Faculty of Law and Administration of the Warsaw University. From 1996 to 1999 Deputy Dean and from 1999 to 2001 Dean of the Faculty of Law. In 1988-1990 Head of the Department of Constitutional Freedoms and Rights in the Office of the Commissioner for Citizens Rights. In the period 1990-1993, and 1996-2001 member of the Prime Minister's Legislative Council. From 1996 to 2001 Director of the Centre for Constitutionalism and Legal Culture at the Public Affairs Institute. In the period 1999-2001 member of the Legal Advisory Committee of the Minister of Foreign Affairs. In the period 1990-1995 a professor at the Swiss Institute of Comparative Law in Lausanne and since 1997 visiting professor of the Central European University in Budapest. Lecturer among others at universities of Paris (Sorbonne), Bonn, Sydney, Konstanz, Bayreuth. Member of the Legal Science Committee of the Polish Academy of Sciences. President of the Polish Section of the International Legal Sciences Association. Member of several scientific councils such as Legal Sciences Institute of Polish Academy of Sciences, National School of Public Administration, Institute of Sciences on State and Law and the Legal Administrative Studies Institute at the Warsaw University. Author of numerous publications (monographs, articles, and other works in Polish, and other languages) on administrative and constitutional law.

is ensured, and the principle of cooperation and trust is upheld. Constitutional thought determines the content of constitutional culture. In turn, constitutional culture encompasses ideas, values and also abilities and emotions associated with the functioning of the constitution.

Professor Wyrzykowski then pointed out ways in which the constitution exerts an influence, particularly the constitutional thought of courts. He stated that the constitutional thought of judges manifests itself in legal questions, the most frequently used institution in proceedings before the Constitutional Tribunal (the "CT"), and in the consequences of judgements of the CT being taken into consideration in its adjudication practice. He also discussed examples of the constitutionalization of political thought. He finished by mentioning the considerable effect of the constitutionalization of thought on the legislative process.

Professor Fryderyk Zoll[6] spoke on "Drafts of European Contract Law and Arbitration Practice". He identified the framework of the common contractual law system, explaining that, in the context of legal unification in Europe, the laws of EU Member States are inconsistent; in order to eliminate conflicts, a set of rules for a common reference system has been drawn up relating to contractual law, together with a justification and comparative law commentaries, which would act as a source of EU law creation. At the same time as the framework of a common reference system was being drafted, work was commenced on the idea of an "optional instrument", which was intended to be a set of contractual laws which the parties could choose irrespective of national systems.

Prof. Zoll then posed the question of how those sets of rules could affect arbitration practice. In the context of the intensive trade conducted within the EU, the application of foreign law is a problem which arises on a daily basis. Establishing the content of foreign law is not only costly, but often leads to the law being wrongly applied. For that reason, Professor Zoll suggested that an attempt should be made to encourage the use of an optional instrument within the EU, which courts of individual Member States would treat as their own law; he believes that one advantage of the European framework for a common reference system is its completeness. It currently encompasses not only contractual law, but also torts and unjust enrichment.

The President of the Court of Arbitration at the PCC, **Marek Furtek**, spoke on "The Court of Arbitration at the Polish Chamber of Commerce – Experiences

---

6 Professor Fryderyk Zoll completed legal studies (1992) and acquired further academic titles: juris doctor degree – 1997 and habilitated doctor's degree – 2002 at the Faculty of Law and Administration of Jagiellonian University in Krakow. Professor Zoll is an associate professor at the Faculty of Law and Administration of Jagiellonian University in Krakow – Faculty of Civil Law (from 2006). Currently he is a guest professor at the University of Osnabrueck (Mercator Program) and from October 2011 he will be a professor of Private Polish Law, Comparative Law and European Law at the University of Osnabrueck. Member of Deutsch Polonische Juristen Vereinigung. Author of numerous publications: monographs, articles, and other works in Polish, and other languages.

and Prospects", announcing that work is to be commenced on new documents of the Court and the continuation of measures aimed at making Warsaw more prominent as an arbitration venue. He also pointed out that arbitration has long been used for more than merely resolving civil disputes; it is now often used as a technique for settling investment disputes or public contracts in the broad sense. He called for debate on the Polish model of arbitration law, also stressing that building an environment which is favourable for arbitration cannot involve challenging the current model of control, as exercised by common courts. He finished by reminding the conference that the Court is the common property of the arbitration community and then appealed to the participants to join in the discussion on the further functioning of the Court, which may be reflected in new rules.

The President of Arbitral Council, **Andrzej Kalwas**[7], thanked the attendees for coming and stated that the lectures had shown that "Law, Economics and Arbitration" was a good choice as the theme of the conference; only if we acquire in-depth knowledge of the law and economics can we correctly conduct and assess arbitration disputes.

Once the agenda had been completed, the conference participants received a commemorative book containing articles by academics and practitioners (both Polish and foreign) on issues related to national and international commercial arbitration.

*[**Dr Piotr Bielarczyk**]*
Lecturer at the Department of the History of Political and Legal Doctrine at the Faculty of Law and Administration of the University of Warsaw and an attorney-at-law with FKA Furtek Komosa.
email: pbielarczyk@fka.pl

| | |

---

[7] Minister of Justice 2004-2005. President of National Bar of Legal Counsels 1995-2004. Dean of Warsaw Chamber of Legal Advisors 1983-1995. Judge of the State Tribunal 1989-1991 and 2002-2004. Co-founder of National Chamber of Commerce in Warsaw. Chairman of the Arbitration Board at the Court of Arbitration at the Polish Chamber of Commerce. Member of editorial committees of numerous legal journals. Member of Executive Council of European Association of Labour Law Advisors (affiliated with the European Union). Admitted to the Bar of Legal Advisers (District Chamber of Legal Advisors in Warsaw) in 1965. Specializes in administrative law, corporate and commercial law and employment matters. Expertise in anti-trust law.

Participant's Perspective: The Conference on the Commemoration of the 60th Anniversary of the Arbitration Court Attached to the Polish Chamber of Commerce, Warszawa 18 November 2010

The Arbitration Court at the National Chamber of Commerce organized an international conference on the commemoration of its 60 years of existence[1].

The conference, attended by leading representatives of both theory and practice, major arbitrators, representatives of permanent arbitration courts from many countries as well as the representatives of significant Polish institutions (Supreme Court, Supreme Administrative Court, Constitutional Court and others), was held under the auspices of the President of the Republic of Poland in the prestigious building of the king's castle in the centre of Warsaw. Those lecturers who presented the main speeches were also champions of Polish theory and practice.

Professor dr hab. Marek Safjan, currently the Polish judge at the *Court of Justice of the European Union*, addressed very important issues in his lecture on *Europeizacja Prawa Prywatnego* (*Europeanization of Private Law*). He mentioned a number of rather critical issues in his highly doctrinal and thoroughgoing speech. In connection with constitutional principles (and other issues), he emphasized that EU law should strive to fulfill its main and primary objective which ought to be superior to the basic constitutional principles. EU law should be focused on the protection of interests of the European Union, whereas constitutional regimes usually focus on the protection of interests of individuals. The authors of this brief annotation of the conference, together with a number of other participants at the conference, do not identify with such a strictly articulated opinion. The reason is that this could have the result of the European Union eventually turning into something completely detached from EU citizens and striving to achieve abstract objectives artificially created by the Brussels administration. Such a conclusion is hardly acceptable (which a number of other participants confirmed in their discussions with the authors of this annotation at the conference) and it is rather alarming that this opinion was presented by a judge of the *Court of Justice of the European Union*. The difference between the application of standards of the European Charter and the standards of the

---

[1] The electronic version of the press release available for instance (i) at: http://www.kurier365.pl/index.php?option=com_k2&view=item&id=2598:jubileusz-sadu-arbitrazowego-przy-kig&Itemid=129&tmpl=component&print=1 (accessed on November 27, 2010), or (ii) at: http://www.prawnik.pl/wiadomosci/z_ostatniej_chwili/124674,Sad-Arbitrazowy-przy-KIG-obchodzi-60-lecie-.html (accessed on November 27, 2010).

European Convention of Human Rights is therefore quite clear. After *Professor Safjan*'s speech the authors, as citizens of the *Czech Republic*, had to admit that the Czech Republic, together with certain other countries, was quite correct to make reservations to the Lisbon Treaty meaning the refusal to apply the *European Charter*. However, the authors of this annotation would like to point out that the speech was rather long and *Professor Safjan* analysed that issue, as well as other issues, from many perspectives. The evaluation we have presented here therefore represents only one approach to a partial issue which *Professor Safjan* addressed. We can only hope that the paper presented by *Professor Safjan* at the conference will soon be published so that these very important opinions can be subject to a qualified and objective assessment.

Professor Dr.iur. Stanisław Jerzy Sołtysiński, LL.M. in his lecture on *Arbitraż u progu nowego wieku: wyznania i wyzwania* (in translation – *Arbitration at the Threshold of a New Century: Hope and Challenges*) emphasized the main advantages of arbitration, in particular efficiency, cost effectiveness and expertise of arbitrators. However, he critically commented on the fact that these as well as other advantages of arbitration are presently often suppressed, especially at the international level. We can only agree; it has to be admitted that arbitration in many other countries has become very complicated and predominantly highly expensive *machinery*. If there are any efforts striving to preserve arbitration in its original form, they are to be found in the countries of *Eastern and Central Europe*. Arbitration in these countries has been undergoing rapid developments and it has helped to solve thousands of disputes every year in a number of countries; the reason is that it is a very flexible solution which does not allow for any major and complicated stratagems and the costs of arbitration in these countries usually remain below the level of costs associated with litigation in court (on top of the fact that arbitration is also faster, more professional and more flexible). In connection with high costs, Prof. Sołtysiński quoted several interesting statements, for instance the statement by one of the leading experts, *Marriott*, who mentioned that due to high legal fees *proceedings* [=arbitration proceedings] *in big and well-known world centres* [cities] *are becoming unsustainable.*

Prof. Sołtysiński, however, mentioned a number of important issues concerning the so-called *investment disputes* which represent a significant problem especially for the countries of *Eastern and Central Europe*. He criticized especially the inconsistency in finding the law in investment disputes and the fact that despite extensive case law on investment protection disputes, the international decision-making practice has not provided a clear, unambiguous and generally applicable answer to many fundamental questions, for instance whether the breach of an individual contract automatically constitutes breach of a BIT etc. The system of treaties providing for investment protection and support as well as the mechanisms of investment protection was also subject to the speaker's criticism. He emphasized that this system had introduced a system of the so-called *positive discrimination* vis-à-vis foreign investors; in other words, these systems have the result of the domestic investors being often discriminated against, compared to foreign investors. Domestic investors hardly ever have the same means of protection as foreign investors. In this connection, *Professor Sołtysiński* mentioned a number of well-known and *evergreen* decisions in investment disputes. As concerns the system of investment protection at the European level, *Professor Sołtysiński* did not hesitate to call this system harmful and therefore unfair to *domestic investors* and suggested that this system should be replaced by a different one.

Professor Sołtysiński generally addressed another important issue, in particular the finding of law and application of substantive law by arbitrators. He stressed what the authors of this information principally agree with. He denied that apart from procedural laws, the arbitrators are not bound by substantive law. He believes that arbitrators *have no license to violate substantive law*. The authors of this information cannot, however, fully concur in *Professor Sołtysiński*'s opinion that the dominance of autonomy in arbitration on one hand calls at the same time necessary for the court revision possibility on the other one. We do not agree with this opinion if it should have the result of more extensive control exercised by courts-of-law *vis-à-vis* the factual and legal assessment of the case by arbitrators, compared to the level currently set as the general international and especially European standard. To some extent, though, even this requirement could be accepted providing it did not result in any significant delay or formalization of the resolution of disputes which the parties primarily submit to arbitrators.

Another very interesting speech was presented by **Professor dr hab. Mirosław Wyrzykowski** – judge of the Polish Constitutional Court on – **Konstytucjonalizacja myślenia prawniczego (Constitutionalization of Legal Thinking)**. Professor Wyrzykowski's contribution was interesting especially if perceived as a contrast to and a sort of a *continuation* of the ideas mentioned by *Professor Sołtysiński*. Whereas *Professor Sołtysiński* spoke of the creation of an imaginary category of *second-degree citizens* (in connection with the application of certain legal and procedural mechanisms of the protection of rights), *Professor Wyrzykowski* went even further, from the perspective of general protection of rights, and spoke of the de facto creation of *third-, fourth- and fifth-degree citizens*, applicable to the citizens of the *new EU Member States*. According to *Professor Wyrzykowski*, this is the result of a drastic deficit in constitutionalist thinking. The authors of this information therefore perceive the contribution and the opinions of Professor Wyrzykowski as directly opposite to the ideas presented by *Professor Safjan* in his speech on the defence of EU law. *Professor Wyrzykowski*, though, attempted an interesting definition of the *constitutionalization* and *constitutionalistics*. According to *Professor Wyrzykowski*, these concepts well exceed mere constitutional laws and *formulae*. These concepts are associated with *constitutionalist ideas and thoughts, securing the protection of rights, constitutional cultural climate*.

Further speeches were presented for instance by Dr hab. Fryderyk Zoll, Professor at the Jagielloń University, who gave a lecture on **Projekty europejskiego prawa umów a praktyka arbitrażu (European Contract Law and Arbitration Practice Projects)**, and other major experts. Among a number of other participants, the conference was attended by, for instance, Krzysztof Hubert Łaszkiewicz,

Secretary of the Office of President of the Republic of Poland, Senator Jan Wyrowiński, Piotr Kluz on behalf of the Polish Ministry of Justice, Bohdan Zdziennicki, President of the Constitutional Court, prof. dr hab. Lech Gardocki, President of the Supreme Court, prof. dr hab. Tadeusz Ereciński, Chairman of the Civil Division of the Supreme Court, Andrzej Arendarski, Chairman of the Polish Chamber of Commerce and many others. The conference was opened with a letter of greetings from the President of the Republic of Poland, Bronisław Komorowski [2]. The conference was presided by Dr Marek Furtek, chairman of the Arbitration Court at the Polish Chamber of Commerce, Prof. dr hab. Józef Okolski, Honorary President, and Andrzej Kalwas, Chairman of the Arbitration Board at the same Arbitration Court.

[*Alexander J. Bělohlávek & Tomáš Řezníček*]

| | |

International Symposium
Selected Issues of Commercial Law in a Broader Context: A Report

The international symposium was held in the pleasant setting of Hotel Patria in Štrbské Pleso in the High Tatras from 26 to 28 October 2010. The program of the symposium focused on commercial law.

The event was organized by the Commercial and Financial Law Department of the Law Faculty of University of Pavel Jozef Šafárik in Košice (UPJŠ) in cooperation with the State and Law Institute of the Czech Academy of Sciences as part of the projects APVV-0381-07 ("Effectiveness of Damage Liability Models for Persons with Qualified Authorization") and LPP-0076-09 ("Out-of-Court/Alternative Settlement of Disputes in Slovakia").

The objective of the organizers was to continue a tradition that began in 1970s when the first conference for legal theoreticians and scholars was held with the participation of representatives of the judiciary, prosecutors, lawyers, and other legal professionals.

The symposium was opened by the technical supervisor, Jozef Suchoža, who greeted the guests and participants. His address was followed by a presentation by the Dean of the Law Faculty of UPJŠ in Košice, Mária Bujňáková. Following the introduction, the specialist part of the program of the symposium began, which consisted of four thematic blocks.

The first day was dedicated to systemic issues of commercial law in the context of EU law. This first block of lectures was launched by Oľga Ovečková with a presentation focused on the Regulatory Powers of Commercial Law at Present. Afterwards, the participants heard other lecturers from the Czech Republic and Poland, namely Cezar Kosikowski from the University of Bialystok who spoke about State Economic Interventionism under the EU law and Ján Matejka who presented a paper examining the harmonization of laws in the Czech Republic.

The activities of the working group responsible for drafting the European Model Company Act (EMCA) were presented by Mária Patakyová from the Law Faculty of the Comenius University. The linguistic aspects of EU documents and their direct impact on enterprises conducting business in a Member State were analysed by Ján Bárta from the State and Law Institute of the Czech Academy of Science. Ludmila Lochmanová from the Law Faculty in Olomouc presented a paper targeting the key principles of the Public Procurement Act.

The first day of the symposium was concluded by a presentation of Wojciech J. Katner from the Lodz University who spoke about the Polish law regulating lease agreements. His presentation also included a brief overview of an amendment to the Polish Civil Code which is being drafted, where Mr. Katner assumed a critical standpoint regarding the planned changes.

The second day included two thematic blocks. The first one focused on Theoretical, Legislative, and Application Problems of Commercial Arbitration, including International Arbitration. The morning program was opened by a presentation of an international guest, Přemysl Raban, who spoke about current problems in the alternative settlement of disputes. He was followed by Alexander J. Bělohlávek with a paper entitled Basic Principles of International Arbitration – Some Trends in the Dislocation of Liability and Sanctions. The third lecture was given by Jozef Suchoža who analysed traditions and innovations in arbitral proceedings.

Following a discussion about the introductory presentations, the conference continued by a lecture presented by Alexander Škrinár, the Chairman of the Arbitration Court attached to the Slovak Bar Association. His contribution focused on problems relating to the creation of permanent courts of arbitration, where he tackled numerous pressing issues and presented *de lege ferenda* ideas aimed at improving the functioning of arbitration courts in Slovakia and increasing their credibility among both laymen and professionals.

Regina Palková from the UPJŠ Law Faculty pointed out in her presentation problems relating to the out-of-court settlement of disputes in Slovakia, mentioning some aspects of a recent draft amendment to the Arbitration Act.

The second specialized block was concluded by Tomáš Horáček, an arbitrator at the Arbitration Court attached to the Economic Chamber of the Czech Republic and the Agricultural Chamber of the Czech Republic, who presented a paper responding to mediation- and arbitration-related problems His lecture was followed by a discussion that mainly focused on issues concerning arbitration courts and current problems relating to reviews of arbitration rulings delivered by execution courts in consumer disputes.

The third thematic block was dedicated to Selected Issues of Liability in Commercial Law (covering also *de lege ferenda* issues). The afternoon program was opened by Ján Husár with a lecture focused on liability for the management of another person's assets. His presentation was followed by Milan Hulmák who focused on issues relating to pre-contractual liability (*culpa in contrahendo*) in the law of the Czech Republic with an emphasis on the planned amendment to the Czech Civil Code. Milan Ďurica presented a paper dealing with the sanction liability of trustees in bankruptcy proceedings and restructuring processes.

Subsequent presentations were given by specialists from the UPJŠ Law Faculty in Košice. Juraj Špirko spoke about the liability of members of the governing bodies of corporations and cooperatives, Janka Vykročová analysed liability for damage with regard to the provision of investment services, and Kristián Csach examined in depth the liability of auditors with regard to laws relating to corporate governance, focusing on the historical development and ramifications of this liability as well as on current laws and problems. Liability regarding the organization of professional sports events was examined by Jozef Čorba, presenting an overview of the current state of affairs in both domestic and foreign laws.

Czech (& Central European) Yearbook of Arbitration

The third thematic block and the second day of the symposium was concluded by a presentation of Alexander Bröstl, an attorney, who analysed issues relating to liability for damage caused by an invalid legal act.

The second day of the conference included an entertainment program that was opened by the Dean of the UPJŠ Law Faculty, Mária Bujňáková. During the evening, participants continued informal discussions in the pleasant surroundings of Štrbské Pleso.

The final day of the international symposium was dedicated to the Tribune of Young Adepts of Legal Science as part of which the new generation of law researchers from several universities and academic centres presented the results of their work. There were delegates from all the three countries participating in the symposium.

An issue frequently mentioned in discussions about the presented topics as well as in informal debates was the question of current amendments to private-law legislation. The symposium was beneficial thanks to the fact that it allowed the participants to exchange their views and experiences not only with their domestic counterparts, but also *vis-à-vis* specialists from other countries where similar laws exist. Those who were unable to attend the symposium can read the papers contributed by lecturers in the collection of scientific papers, which was, untraditionally, published before the symposium. The guests appreciated this activity of the organizers, as they received the publication at the beginning of the symposium.

The conference was closed by prof. Suchoža who thanked all participants, organizers, and sponsors of the event. In his final speech, he expressed a desire to continue the renewed tradition of this international symposium and, possibly, to expend the conference to the entire V4 region. He bode farewell to the guests with a wish that they would come again next year.

[*Mária Ivanecká*]
Law Faculty, University of Pavel Jozef Šafárik *in Košice, Slovak Republic.*
E-mail: maria.ivanecka@upjs.sk

| | |

Current Events, Past & Ongoing CYIL / CYArb Presentations

I. Current Events

Selected Scientific Conferences, Seminars, Academic Lectures and Other Professional Events and News in the Development of Arbitration and ADR in the Particular Countries[1]

I.1. [CZECH REPUBLIC]

PRAHA [CZE] 23 and 24 April 2010

The Faculty of Law, Charles University in Prague, hosted an **international conference** on "*Mediation in Civil and Commercial Disputes*". The conference was opened by Prof. Giuseppe De Palo (JAMS ADR Center, Italy), Prof. Dr.Iur. Aleš Gerloch, *Dean of the Faculty of Law, Charles University in Prague*, Dr.iur. Martin Vychopeň, Chairman of the *Czech Bar Association*, and Dr. iur. Tomáš Lichovník from the *Union of Judges of the Czech Republic*. The first day of the conference witnessed a demonstration of the mediation procedure[2], interview with Bruce Edwards and a round table concerning Mediation in Central Europe[3].

---

[1] Contributions mentioned herein represent a selection from papers related to arbitration. CYArb editors hereby apologize to the lecturers for omitting some of them and their topics due to the limited space provided for this section. Editors referred especially to published and other accessible information. Readers are specifically warned that the information about papers presented at the individual conferences and other academic and scientific events is only a selection and definitely does not provide a full report on the entire proceedings and the academic scope of each particular event.

[2] Active participation of the following experts: Dr. Adi Gavrila, Romania, Dr. Roman Rewald, Poland, JUDr. Vít Horáček, Czech Republic, JUDr. Antonín Mokrý, Czech Bar Association, Prague, Czech Republic, Dr. Helena De Backer, Belgium.

[3] The round table was attended by: Mgr. iur. Dana Potocková, Czech Republic, Dr.iur. František Kutlík, Slovak Republic, Dr. Roman Rewald, Poland, Dr. Adi Gavrila, Romania,

A plenary session on the *"Perspectives of ADR in the Czech Republic"*[4] and subsequent parallel workshops in two panels were scheduled for the second day of the conference. The first panel concentrated on the following topics: basic mediation styles and skills[5], mediation practice in Slovakia[6], lawyer as the dispute resolution authority[7], psychological barriers preventing settlement (conclusion of agreement)[8] and mediation and judges[9]. The parallel workshops in the second panel focused on the following issues: preparing for mediation[10], mediation techniques for lawyers[11], enforceability of mediation agreements in the EU[12], advanced mediation techniques[13] and ADR in the construction industry[14].

PRAHA [CZE] 17 May 2010

National Committees of ICC in the Czech Republic and in Poland organized a joint academic colloquium focused on the updating of the ICC Rules on Arbitration; the conference was intended solely for members of the arbitration commissions of these two ICC National Committees due to the still confidential nature of the preparatory works on the amendment of said ICC Rules.

BRNO [CZE] 28 May 2010

International Conference on Mediation held under the title *„Mediace – cesta ke spravedlnosti aneb řešení sporů v 21. století"* [*"Mediation – the Road to Justice aka Dispute Resolution in the 21st Century"*] under the auspices of **the Minister of Justice and the Mayor.**

Dr. iur. Martina Doležalová, Czech Bar Association, Prague, Czech Republic, Dr. Bojana Jovin-Hrastnik, Slovenia and Dr.iur. Marie Brejchová, Czech Republic.

4   The following experts addressed the plenary session: JUDr. Tomáš Horáček, Faculty of Law, Charles University in Prague, Czech Republic, Mgr. iur. Šárka Hájková, Union of Judges, Czech Republic, JUDr. Martina Doležalová, Czech Bar Association, Prague, Czech Republic, Mgr. iur. Robert Cholenský, Czech Republic and Mgr. iur. Dana Potocková, Czech Republic.

5   Under the guidance of Mgr. iur. Martina Kykalová, Czech Republic.

6   Under the guidance of JUDr. František Kutlík, Slovak Republic.

7   Under the guidance of: Dr. Helena De Baker.

8   Under the guidance of: Prof. Giuseppe De Palo, JAMS ADR Center.

9   Under the guidance of: Dr. Machteld Pel, Mgr. iur. Šárka Hájková, Union of Judges, Czech Republic, JUDr. Jaromír Jirsa, Municipal Court in Prague, Czech Republic and JUDr. Martina Kasíková, District Court for Prague-East, Czech Republic.

10   Under the guidance of Mgr. Robert Cholenský, Mediation Institute.

11   Under the guidance of Mgr. iur. Dana Potocková, Conflict Management International.

12   Under the guidance of Prof. Maria Pilar Canedo, Deusto University.

13   Under the guidance of Bruce Edwards, JAMS.

14   Under the guidance of Dr. Peter Kamminga, Gould Center, Stanford University Law School and Dr. Paulo Cecchi Dimeglio, Gould Center, Stanford University Law School.

BRNO [CZE] 25 November 2010 and 7 December 2010
Seminar: **Arbitration – an Effective Instrument for the Resolution of Claims**[15]

BRNO [CZE] 25 November 2010
Workshop: **Arbitration – an Effective Instrument of Prevention against Debtors**[16]

BRNO [CZE] 13 December 2010 and PRAHA [CZE] 14 December 2010
Seminar: **All about Arbitration**

[CZE] Preparatory Works on the Amendment of the Czech Arbitration Act

According to the Programme Statement of the Cabinet[17] newly constituted in summer 2010 after the Parliamentary elections held in late May 2010, the Cabinet undertook to implement an amendment to the Arbitration Act. Preparatory works on this amendment were initiated in October 2010 under the auspices of the Minister of Justice of the Czech Republic, with the participation of other ministries and representatives of both theory and practice. The progress and the results of these works have not been published yet.

---

[15] A similar event is planned also for 11 January 2011 and 8 February 2011.
[16] A similar event is planned also for 17 February 2011.
[17] In an interview for the economic weekly EURO printed in the edition of 27 September 2010, the Minister of Justice of the Czech Republic [CZE] stated (approximate translation, cit.) Question by EURO, a weekly magazine: *The Programme Statement of the Cabinet emphasizes the amendment of the Arbitration Act as one of its priorities Why are the current rules no longer considered satisfactory?* Answer by the Minister of Justice (approximate translation, cit.) *We are only at the stage of contemplating the amendment. We are mainly concerned about consumer credits because disputes from such contracts are often submitted to arbitration based on the arbitration clause incorporated in these contracts. And it is, unfortunately, very often the case that the arbitrator in such disputes is either related to or even employed with the credit provider. It is justified to have serious doubts about a just and fair resolution of the dispute by such a person. This is the reason why we are seriously concerned about the current state of affairs and contemplate several alternative solutions. I honestly admit that it will be very difficult to adopt such rules which will not prohibit arbitration in consumer credit disputes altogether and which will at the same time introduce clear rules. If we prohibit arbitration in connection with consumer loans, all these cases will fall on our courts and Czech justice will slow down. However, if we do not find any other solution, I am willing to discuss such prohibition. Although I consider it to be the most extreme solution.* Full text of the interview in Czech available at the website of the Ministry of Justice of the Czech Republic at: http://portal.justice.cz/Justice2/MS/ms.aspx?o=23&j=33&k=53 72&d=313695 (accessed on November 20, 2010). The interview clearly indicates that the main objectives are special rules focused on consumer protection (the so-called *consumer contract* arbitration).

I.2. [SLOVAK REPUBLIC]

ŠTRBSKÉ PLESO [SVK] 26 – 28 October 2010

International symposium **Obchodné právo a jeho širšie kontexty. Zborník vedených prác. [Commercial Law and its Broader Contexts. Collection of Scientific Works]** organised by the Department of Commercial Law, Faculty of Law, PJ Šafárik University, Košice [SVK] jointly with the Institute of State and Law, Academy of Science Czech Republic [CZE][18].

Selected contributions on arbitration (in alphabetical order):

> ➤ Alexander J. Bělohlávek, *Základní zásady mezinárodního rozhodčího řízení: Některé trendy v dislokaci odpovědností a sankcí [Basic Principles Of International Arbitration: On Certain Trends Regarding The Shift Of the Burden Of Liabilities And Sanctions]*.

> ➤ Tomáš Horáček, *Dohoda o narovnání a její uplatnění v rámci alternativních způsobů řešení soukromoprávních sporů [Settlement Agreement And Its Application In Alternative Resolution Of Private Disputes]*.

> ➤ Pavol Kubíček, *Činnosť Rozhodcovského súdu SOPK a jej legislatívny rámec [Activities of the Arbitration Court Attached to the Slovak Chamber of Commerce and Industry and Their Legal Framework]*.

> ➤ Regina Palková, *Rozhodcovské konania a mediácia z pohľadu súčasnej legislatívy a praxe (Quo vadis mimosúdne riešenie sporov?) [Arbitration and mediation from the perspective of current legislation and practice (Quo vadis, alternative dispute resolutions?)]*.

> ➤ Přemysl Raban, *Současné problémy alternativního rozhodování sporů v našich zemích [Current Problems of Alternative Dispute Resolution In Our Countries]*.

> ➤ Jozef Suchoža, *Tradície a inovácie v rozhodcovskom konaní (legislatívně peripetie a aplikačné paradoxy [Traditions and Innovations in Arbitration (Legislative Peripetia and Application Paradoxes]*.

> ➤ Alexander Škrinár, *Vybrané aplikačné problémy kreovania stálych rozhodcovských súdov a niektoré problémy rozhodcovského konania [Selected Application Problems Of Establishing Permanent Arbitration Courts And Certain Problems Related to Arbitration Proceedings]*.

---

[18] Conference Proceedings: JOZEF SUCHOŽA, JÁN HUSÁR, OBCHODNÉ PRÁVO A JEHO ŠIRŠIE KONTEXTY. ZBORNÍK VEDENÝCH PRÁC (*Commercial Law and its Broader Contexts. Collection of scientific works)*, Košice: Univerzita Pavla Jozefa Šafárika v Košiciach (2010). The particular Conference Proceedings published within the public grant APVV-0381-07 and Nr. LPP-0076-09.

I.3. [CROATIA]

ZAGREB [HRV], 2-3 December 2010

18th Croatian Arbitration and Conciliation Days

I.4. [POLAND]

WARSZAWA [POL], 18 November 2010

Conference on the Commemoration of the 60th Anniversary of the Arbitration Court Attached to the Polish Chamber of Commerce

WARSZAWA [POL], 17 March 2010

Conference on **Rozwiązywanie sporów w transakcjach M&A. Taktyki, wyzwania, metody obrony** [Dispute Resolution in M&A. Tactics, Challenges and Defense Methods][19]

WARSZAWA [POL], 15 December 2010

KIG organized an international conference on the recognition and enforcement of arbitral awards from the perspective of the 50th anniversary of the New York Convention.

I.5. [RUSSIAN FEDERATION]

MOSCOW [RUS], 30 November 2010

Session of the Arbitration Commission of the ICC National Committee of the Russian Federation, attended by the representatives of the ICC National Committee Czech Republic, focused on the cooperation of both National Committees.

MOSCOW [RUS], 1 December 2010

The ICC National Committee of the Russian Federation, in cooperation with two major law offices, organized an international conference on "**International Arbitration and State Courts: Balance of Interests**". The speakers at the conference included for instance *Jason Fry*, Secretary General ICC International Court of Arbitration, *Sir Anthony Colman*, *Dominique Hascher* and others.

---

[19] Information about the conference: Katarzyna Michałowska, *Sprawozdanie z konferencji „Rozwiązywanie sporów w transakcjach M&A. Taktyki, wyzwania, metody obrony"* (Warszawa 17.3.2010 r.). (*Report form Conference „Dispute resolution in M&A. Tactics, Challenges and Defense Methods*), 3 ADR ARBITRATION AND MEDIATION 193-205 (2010).

II. Past and Ongoing CYArb and CYIL Presentations

II.1. Past Presentations in 2010

The CYArb [Czech (& Central European) Yearbook of Arbitration] and the Parallel Project (Periodical) the CYIL [Czech Yearbook of International Law] Were Presented Jointly with Their Publisher (Juris Publishing Inc.) at the Following Events in 2010:

➢ *The Washington D.C. XVIIIth International Congress of the International Academy of Comparative Law*, Washington D.C. [USA]

➢ *The 74th The Hague ILA Conference*, The Hague [NED]

➢ *The IBA [International Bar Association] Annual Conference*, Vancouver [CAN], 3 – 8 October 2010

➢ The International Conference of the Faculty of Law, Trnava University in Trnava [SVK] *"Dies Iurisprudentiae Tyrnaviensis" – "Law in the European Perspective"*, 23 and 24 September 2010

➢ The International Conference of the Faculty of Law, Comenius University in Bratislava [SVK] *"Law as a Unifying Factor of Europe – Jurisprudence and Practice"*, 21 – 23 October 2010

➢ *The International Symposium regarding Selected Commercial Law Issues in a Broader Context* organised by the Department of Commercial Law, Faculty of Law, P. J. Šafárik University in Košice [SVK] jointly with the Institute of State and Law, Academy of Science Czech Republic [CZE], Štrbské Pleso (Tatry) [SVK] 26 – 28 October 2010

➢ *The JURIS Conference on Cross-Examination in International Arbitration*, Vienna [AUT], 5 November 2010

II.2. Ongoing Presentations in 2011

The CYArb and the CYIL Plan to Hold for Presentation (Among Others) at the Following 2011 Events:[20]

➢ The *14th Annual IBA International Arbitration Day*, Seoul [Republic of Korea], 3-4 March 2011

➢ The *WJA* (World Jurist Association) *Conference on International Arbitration and ADR – The Impact on the Rule of Law*, Port Louis [Mauritius], 5-7 April 2011

---

20 Further events (international conferences and congresses) scheduled.

- ➤ The *JURIS Fifth Annual Investment Treaty Arbitration Conference*, Washington D.C. [USA], 5 April 2011

- ➤ The *JURIS Seventh Annual Leading Arbitrators' Symposium* on the Conduct of International Arbitration, Vienna [Austria], 18 April 2011

- ➤ The *IBA/AAA/ICDR Arbitration Conference*, New York City [USA], 13 June 2011

- ➤ The *JURIS Conference on Cross-Examination in International Arbitration*, New York City [USA] at the Harvard Club, 14 June 2011

- ➤ The *WJA* (World Jurist Association) *24th Biennial Congress on the Law of the World*, Prague [CZE], 23 – 28 October 2011

Selected Bibliography of Czech and Slovak Authors for 2010

Opening Remarks:
This overview lists only works published in 2010. The individual chapters into which this overview is divided always cover both substantive and procedural issues.

Titles in translations are for reference only.

I. [CZECH REPUBLIC] – Titles Published within the Czech Republic

I.1. Monographs

Alexander J. Bělohlávek, Ochrana přímých zahraničních investic v Evropské unii [*Protection of Foreign Direct Investments in the European Union*], Praha: C. H. Beck, 2010, ISBN: 978-80-7400-345-5[1].

I.2. Periodicals, Collections and Conference Proceedings

Radovan Dávid, David Sehnálek, Jiří Valdhans (eds); Dny práva 2010 / Days of Law 2010 (fourth annual international conference) Conference proceedings, Brno [CZE]: Faculty of Law, Masaryk University, 2010, ISBN: 978-80-210-5305-2[2].

---

[1] Publication issued in Czech. Polish and Russion language versions also published in 2010 (Russian version in: Kiev [Ukraine]: Taxon and Polish version in: Gliwice [POL]: Wydawnictwo Wokol nas [Publishing House]). See below the separate sub-chapter on the titles of Czech authors published outside the Czech Republic.
[2] Available at: http://www.law.muni.cz/content/en/proceedings (accessed on November 17, 2010). Abstracts of the Conference proceedings available also in hard-copy.

Selected Contributions[3]

Section: Arbitration – Parties Autonomy and Mandatory Rules of Procedure

> ➤ Alexander J. Bělohlávek, *The Scope of Autonomy In Appointment of Arbitrators: The Decision in the „Jivraj" case as an Eruption in Stable Axioms of Arbitration.*
> ➤ Christian W. Konrad, *Reform of the EU Investment Policy – BIT by BIT.*
> ➤ Filip Černý, *Demonstration of the Investor's Autonomy in Investment*
> ➤ *Arbitration as a Determining Factor of the Nature of the Investment.*
> ➤ Hany Elmanaily, *Electronic Arbitration Agreement.*
> ➤ Zbyšek Kordač, *Arbitrators' Power From Comparative View.*
> ➤ Naděžda Rozehnalová, *The Interaction Between Forum Arbitri and Procedural Rules of the State.*
> ➤ Miluše Hrnčiříková, *Consolidation of Arbitral Proceedings as a Safeguard of Justice.*
> ➤ Regina Palková, *The Enforcement of Arbitral Awards in the Present Practice of Slovak Courts.*
> ➤ Jan Havlíček, *Parties as a Domis Litis in Arbitration.*
> ➤ Slavomír Halla, *Binding Nature of Parties' Autonomy in Arbitration.*
> ➤ Lucia Kováčová, *Delivery Issue in Arbitration.*
> ➤ Martin Orgoník, *European Doctrine of Arbitrability of Competition Law v. Procedural Limits Legis Forum in International Arbitration Proceedings.*
> ➤ Jaroslav Králíček, *Restriction of Consumer´s Autonomy alias Application of Procedural Rules of Arbitration.*
> ➤ Radka Chlebcová, Karla Hýblová, *Special Features of Arbitration in Common Law.*

Section: Individuals and International Public Law and European Union Law – Recent Situation

> ➤ Ivan Cisár, *Status of Arbitrator in Public International Law.*

Section: Significance of Soft Law in Commercial Law Context

> ➤ Eva Večerková, *Legal and Non-legal Regulation of Misleading and Comparative Advertising.*
> ➤ Dana Ondrejová, *Soft Law on The Last Way.*
> ➤ Josef Šilhán, *Soft Law with Hard Core Effects.*
> ➤ Vítězslav Šemora, *On the General Application of Legally Unenforceable Instruments Adopted by Administrative Authorities.*
> ➤ Ján Husár, *The Use of Clauses in Shaping the Content of Commercial Contracts.*

---

[3] Detailed list of participants and their contributions see separate part of the publication.

> ➤ Bohumil Havel, *Reasonable Expectations as Soft Law?*
> ➤ Lenka Doubravová, *Code of Conduct and Decision Making (Not Only) for Courts.*
> ➤ Ľubomír Klčo, *Normativity of the Legal Document – UNIDROIT Principles 2004.*
> ➤ Petra Novotná, *The FIDIC Suite of Contracts: Selected Issues.*
> ➤ Tomáš Hülle, *Piercing of the Corporate Veil and „the End of Independence of Entities Establishing Group of Companies".*
> ➤ Karel Marek, *Business Practices, General Terms and Conditions and Interpretation Rules.*

Bulletin advokacie [*Bulletin of the Czech Bar*], Praha: Česká advokátní komora [*Czech Bar Association*], 2010, ISSN: 1210-6348[4]

Jana Horská, Jakub Burian, *Rozhodčí doložka ve spotřebitelských smlouvách ve světle aktuální judikatury českých soudů a ESD [Arbitration Clause in Consumer Contracts in Light of the Recent Case-law of Czech Courts and the ECJ].* No. 4, pp. 22-23.

Robert Pelikán, *Ještě k neplatnosti rozhodčích doložek a k „právním názorům" [More comments on the invalidity of arbitration clauses and on „legal notions"].* No. 9, pp. 40-42.

Přemysl Raban, *Autorizovaní rozhodci nebo adjudikátoři? Je efektivně zajištěna spravedlnost ve spotřebitelských vztazích [Authorized Arbitrators or Adjudicators? Is Justice in Consumer Relations Efficiently Safeguarded].* No. 6, pp. 15-22.

Tomáš Sokol, *Opět k (ne)platnosti rozhodčích doložek ve prospěch soukromých „rozhodčích soudů" [Another article regarding the (in)validity of arbitration clauses favouring private „arbitration courts"].* No. 6, pp. 22-24.

Zuzana Valoušková, *O neplatnosti rozhodčích doložek ve prospěch soukromých „rozhodčích soudů" [On the Invalidity of Arbitration Clauses Concluded in Favor of Private "Arbitration Courts"].* No. 5, pp. 35-37.

Obchodněprávní revue [*Commercial Law Review*], Praha: C. H. Beck, 2010, Vol. 2, ISSN: 1803-6554[5]

Alexander J. Bělohlávek, Tomáš Řezníček, *Dopady rozhodnutí o úpadku a insolvenčního řízení na majetek účastníka na probíhající rozhodčí řízení v tuzemské a mezinárodní praxi ve světle aktuální judikatury některých*

---

[4] Papers published in Czech with abstracts in a foreign language. Abstracts in English and in German.
[5] Papers published in Czech. Abstracts in English, sometimes in German.

obecných a rozhodčích soudů [*Impacts of Insolvency and Insolvency Proceedings of a Party on Pending Arbitration Proceedings in Domestic and International Experience in the Light of Current Case Law of Particular Courts and Arbitral Tribunals*]. No. 9, pp. 1-14[6].

Jana Heboczková, *Autonomie vůle rozhodců při určení rozhodného práva pro meritum sporu při absenci volby práva stranami v mezinárodním rozhodčím řízení* [*The Autonomy of the Arbitrators' Will in Determining the Law Applicable to the Merits of the Case in the Absence of Choice by the Parties in International Arbitration*]. No. 7, pp. 202-208.

Milan Hulmák, Blanka Tomančáková, *Rozhodčí řízení jako vhodný prostředek řešení sporů mezi dodavatelem a spotřebitelem* [*Arbitration as a Suitable Method of Resolution of Disputes Between the Supplier and the Consumer*]. Part I: No. 6, pp. 168-174; Part II: No. 7, pp. 189-202[7].

Obchodní právo [*Commercial Law*], Praha: Prospektrum, 2010, Vol. 19, ISSN: 1210-8278[8]

Alexander J. Bělohlávek, *Pojem investice z pohledu mezinárodně právní ochrany (podmínky ratione materiae, ratione tempori a ratione voluntatis pro využití mechanismů mezinárodní ochrany investic). I. část* [*Qualification of investment for its international protection (Requirements ratione materiae, ratione tempori and ratione voluntatis to apply the system of the international investment protection). Part I*]. No. 3, pp 2-26.

Alexander J. Bělohlávek, *Pojem investice z pohledu mezinárodně právní ochrany (podmínky ratione materiae, ratione tempori a ratione voluntatis pro využití mechanismů mezinárodní ochrany investic). II. část* [*Qualification of investment for its international protection (Requirements ratione materiae, ratione tempori and ratione voluntatis to apply the system of the international investment protection). Part II*]. No. 4, pp 2-18.

Jan Hušek, *Zrušení rozhodčího nálezu soudem – včasnost návrhu: Anotace a poznámka k rozhodnutí Nejvyššího soudu z 29. dubna 2010, sp. zn. 23 Cdo 2672/2008* [*Annulment of Arbitral Awards by Court – Timeliness of the Claim: Annotation of and Commentary on the Decision of the Supreme Court of 29 April 2010, file no. 23 Cdo 2672/2008*]. No. 10, pp. 20-24[9].

Luděk Lisse, *Rozhodčí doložky ve spotřebitelských smlouvách* [*Arbitration Clauses In Consumer Contracts*]. No. 9, pp. 2-12.

Tomáš Pohl, *Otazníky v řízení před rozhodci* [*Uncertainties In Proceedings Before Arbitrators*]. No. 6, pp. 10-18.

---

6   Abstract in English.
7   Abstract in German. The article was drafted with the assistance of the grant provided by Grantová agentura České republiky (Czech Science Foundation) No. P408/10/0914.
8   Papers published in Czech. Abstracts in English. Issued monthly.
9   In the case law section – without annotation. Material only in Czech.

Právní fórum [*Legal Forum*], **Praha: Wolters Kluwer ČR, a.s., 2010, Vol. 7, ISSN: 1214-7966**[10]

Alexander J. Bělohlávek, *Rozhodčí řízení v tzv. smluvních vztazích spotřebitelského typu* [*Consumer Contract Arbitration*]. No. 3, pp. 89-99.

Robert Cholenský, *Nové pojetí povinnosti mlčenlivosti a legislativní předpoklady mediace* [*New Concept Of the Duty of Confidentiality And Legislative Prerequisites for Mediation*]. No. 3, pp. 128-132.

Tomáš Horáček, *Mediace v soukromoprávních věcech jako předmět samostatné právní úpravy* [*Mediation in Private Law Matters Regulated under Special Laws and Regulation*]. No. 3, pp. 123-128.

Dušan Hrabánek, *K náležitostem rozhodčích smluv a činnosti soukromých rozhodčích soudů* [*Regarding the Essentials of Arbitration Agreements and the Functioning of Private Arbitration Courts*]. No. 3, pp. 139-143.

Michal Janovec, *Zrušení rozhodčího nálezu soudem* [*Annulment of an Arbitral Award by Court*]. No. 4, pp. 181-184.

Bohuslav Klein, *Proč mnozí dští oheň a síru na rozhodčí řízení, když jde o božskou instituci?* [*Why so Many People Breathe Fire and Brimstone on Arbitration Procedure When It Is a Heavenly Institution?*]. No. 3, pp. 100-105.

Zbyšek Kordač, *Zkušenosti se současnou právní úpravou a praxí alternativních metod řešení sporů v USA* [*Experience with Current Laws and Practice of Alternative Dispute Resolution in the U.S.A.*]. No. 3, pp. 133-138.

Luděk Lisse, *Rozhodčí doložka ve spotřebitelských smlouvách a judikatura ESD* [*Arbitration Clause in Consumer Contracts and the ECJ Case Law*] No. 12, pp. 581-591.

Naděžda Rozehnalová, Jan Havlíček; *Rozhodčí smlouva a rozhodci ve světle některých rozhodnutí ... aneb quo vadis ...?* [*Arbitration Agreement and Arbitrators in the Light of Certain Judgments or else Quo Vadis?*]. No. 3, pp. 114-119.

Květoslav Růžička, *Neaplikování „Římů" v tuzemském rozhodčím řízení* [*Non-application of Rome I and Rome II in National Arbitration Proceedings*]. No. 10, pp. 470-478.

Klára Spirová, *Alternativní způsoby řešení sporů – mediace* [*Alternative Dispute Resolution Methods – Mediation*]. No. 3, pp. 119-122.

Jozef Suchoža, Regina Palková; *Právna úprava rozhodcovského konania v Slovenskej republike (niektoré úvahy jej zdokonalenia)* [*Arbitration Law in the Slovak Republic (Ideas for Improvement)*]. No. 3, pp. 106-114.

Martin Šmerda, *Zamyšlení nad jedním soudním rozhodnutím – nefér útok na rozhodčí řízení* [*Essay on a Judgment – an Unfair Attack against Arbitration Proceedings*]. No. 4, pp. 176-180.

Pavel Varvařovský, *Rozhodčí řízení v judikatuře Ústavního soudu* [*Arbitration in the Case Law of the Constitutional Court*]. No. 3, pp. 143-146.

---

10 Papers published in Czech. Abstracts in English.

Radka Zahradníková, *Právní úprava arbitráže ve Francii a její potenciální vliv na připravovanou novelu zákona č. 216/1994*[11] [*Arbitration Law in France and its Potential Influence on the Pending Amendment of Act No. 216/1994*]. No. 4, pp. 184-189.

Právní rádce [*Legal Advisor*], Praha: Economia, 2010, Vol. 18, ISSN: 1210-4817[12]

Filip Čeladník, *Opomíjená mediace v občanských a obchodních věcech* [*Neglected Mediation in Civil and Commercial Matters*]. No. 2, pp. 11-13.

Luděk Lisse, *Rozhodčí doložky arbitrážních center ve světle recentní judikatury* [*Arbitration Clauses of Arbitration Centers in Light of Recent Case-law*]. No. 10, pp. 4-11.

Tomáš Pohl, *Otazníky v řízení před rozhodci* [*Uncertainties in Proceedings Before Arbitrators*]. No. 5, pp. 29-34.

Přemysl Raban, *Je efektivně zajištěna spravedlnost ve spotřebitelských vztazích?* [*Is Justice in Consumer Relations Efficiently Safeguarded?*]. No. 2, pp. 46-52.

Martin Soukup, *Zrušení rozhodčího nálezu. Rozsudek Nejvyššího soudu České republiky ze dne 30. října 2009, sp. zn. 33 Cdo 2675* [*Annulment of an Arbitral Award. Judgment of the Supreme Court of the Czech Republic as of 30 October 2009, docket 33 Cdo 2675/2007*]. No. 3, p. 52-54.

Pavel Vrcha, *K problematice určení (jmenování) rozhodce a stanovení procesních pravidel rozhodčího řízení* [*Regarding the Designation (Appointment) of Arbitrators and the Determination of Procedural Rules Regulating Arbitration Proceedings*]. No. 3, pp. 14-20.

Právní rozhledy [*Law Review*], Praha: C.H.Beck, 2010, Vol. 18, ISSN: 1210-4817, reg. No. of the Ministry of Cultural Affairs: E 6318[13]

Ladislav Derka, *Je platná rozhodčí smlouva v případě neplatného určení rozhodce (rozhodců)?* [*Is the Arbitration Agreement Valid if the Designation of Arbitrator(s) is Invalid?*]. No. 6, pp. 215 et seq..

Mirek Katzl, *K otázce vymahatelnosti rozhodčích smluv v USA* [*Enforceability of Arbitration Agreements in the USA*]. No. 24, pp. 872-876.

---

[11] Act No. 216/1994 is a [Czech] statute regulating arbitration and enforcement of arbitral awards. Intensive works on a Government Bill amending said law have been ongoing since autumn 2010.

[12] Papers published in Czech.

[13] Papers published in Czech.

Luděk Lisse, *K otázce platnosti rozhodčí smlouvy v případě neplatného určení rozhodce* [*Regarding the Validity of Arbitration Agreements in Case of Invalid Appointment of Arbitrator*]. No. 13, pp. 473-478.

David Slováček, *Rozhodčí řízení a směrnice o nepřiměřených podmínkách ve spotřebitelských smlouvách* [*Arbitration and the Unfair Terms in Consumer Contracts Directive*]. No. 9, pp. 331 334.

I.3. Other Publications (incl. E-Sources)

Petr Bezouška, Jan Kocina, *Právní povahu rozhodčího řízení – aplikační problémy* [*The Nature of Arbitration – Practical Issues*]. No. 16, pp. 585-588.

Jan Havlíček, *Ochrana spotřebitele v rozhodčím řízení* [*Consumer Protection in Arbitration*][14].

Petr Holeček, *Otázka doručování v rozhodčím řízení a možnost ustanovení opatrovníka* [*The issue of service in arbitration and the possibility t appoint a curator*]. eLAW.cz, 21. I. 2010.[15]

Jan Hrabec, *Jeden případ libovůle obecného soudu ve vztahu k rozhodčímu řízení* [*Arbitrariness Regarding Arbitration – One Judgment*]. No. 22, pp. 818-820.

Martin Kohout, *Aplikace důvodů zvláštního zřetele hodných podle ustanovení § 150 O.S.Ř. v řízení o zrušení rozhodčího nálezu* [*Application of Reasons Worthy of Special Consideration According to the Article 150 Civil Procedure Act in Proceedings of Annulment of Arbitral Award*], 3 (4) Právo 41-46, 2010, ISSN: 1802-9116.

Tereza Kyselovská, *Vybrané otázky arbitrability sporů a internet* [*Selected Issues of Arbitrability of Disputes and Internet*], in COFOLA 2010: the Conference Proceedings, Brno: Masarykova univerzita [*Masaryk University*] 868-880, 2010, ISBN: 978-80-210-5151-5[16].

Bořivoj Líbal, *Malé zamyšlení nad použitím rozhodčích doložek* [*Short Essay on the Application of Arbitration Clauses*][17].

---

[14] Published in Czech; the electronic version available at:
http://www.pravnik.cz/a/300/ochrana-spotrebitele-v-rozhodcim-rizeni.html
(accessed on December 28, 2010).
[15] Published in Czech; the electronic version available at:
http://www.elaw.cz/cs/ostatni/
163-otazka-dorucovani-v-rozhodcim-rizeni-optarovnik.html
(accessed on December 28, 2010).
[16] Published in Czech; the electronic version available at:
http://www.pravnik.cz/a/300/ochrana-spotrebitele-v-rozhodcim-rizeni.html
http://www.law.muni.cz/sborniky/cofola2010/files/sbornik/sbornik.pdf
(accessed on December 28, 2010).
[17] Published in Czech; the electronic version of the article available at: http://www.epravo.cz/top/clanky/male-zamysleni-nad-pouzitim-rozhodcich-dolozek-60721.html
(accessed on December 28, 2010).

Tomáš Palla, *Zneužívání rozhodčích doložek – stále nevyřešený problém* [*Abuse of Arbitration Clauses – An Ongoing Problem*][18].

Lukáš Ryšavý, *Pravomoc rozhodců pro rozhodování majetkových sporů. Některé problematické okruhy rozhodčího řízení* [*Jurisdiction of Arbitrators over Property Disputes. Selected Problems Affecting Arbitration*], 5 (1) Acta Iuridica Olomucensis, Olomouc [*Czech Republic*]: Palacký University 141-146, 2010, IdN: 61989592.

Matěj Šuster, *Pozor na rozhodčí doložky ve smlouvách o úvěrech* [*Beware of Arbitration Clauses in Credit Contracts*][19].

I.4. Books (Monographs) and Articles by Czech Authors Published Abroad and Bibliography on Arbitration in the Czech Republic Published Abroad

Monographs

Alexander J. Bělohlávek, Ochrona bezpośrednich inwestycji zagranicznych v Unii Europejskiej [*Protection of Foreign Direct Investments in the European Union*], Gliwice [Poland]: Wydawnictvo Wokol nas [Publishing House], 2010. ISBN: 978-83-88-199-11-0[20].

Alexander J. Bělohlávek, Защита инвестиций, право Европейского Союза и международное право [Transcript - Zaschita investicij, pravo Evropejskogo Sojuza i mezhdunarodnoje pravo; Protection of Foreign Direct Investments in the European Union], Kiev [Ukraine]: Taxon - (Таксон) [Publishing House], 2010, ISBN: 978-966-7128-78-4, BBK [ББК] 67.312.2.

Other Publications

Alexander J. Bělohlávek, *Czech Republic, in* Arbitration 2010 – Global Arbitration Review – Edition *Getting the Deal Through*, London: Publishing house: Law Business Research 95-100, 2010.

Alexander J. Bělohlávek, *Arbitration in the Czech Republic, in* Loukas Mistelis, Laurence Shore, Hans Smit; World Arbitration Reporter, CZE 1 – CZE 128, 2nd ed. 2010.

---

18 Published in Czech; the electronic version of the article available at: http://www.epravo.cz/top/clanky/rozhodci-dolozky-ve-spotrebitelskych-smlouvach-ano-ci-ne-55269.html (accessed on December 28, 2010).

19 Published in Czech; the electronic version of the article available at: http://www.penize.cz/18995-pozor-na-rozhodci-dolozky-ve-smlouvach-o-uverech (accessed on December 28, 2010).

20 Publication issued in Polish. Czech and Russion language versions also published in 2010 (Czech version in: Prague: C. H. Beck and Russian version in: Kiev [Ukraine]: Taxon). See below the separate sub-chapter on the monographs published within the Czech Republic.

Alexander J. Bělohlávek, *Arbitration Agreement, MDR Clauses and Relation thereof to Nature of Jurisdictional Decisions on the Break of Legal Cultures*, in Józef Okolski, Andrzej Całus, Maksymilian Pazdan, Stanisław Sołtysiński, Tomasz Wardyński et Stanisław Włodyka (eds.), Księga pamiątkowa 60-lecia Sądu Arbitrażowego przy Krajowej Izbie Gospodarczej w Warszawie [*Commemorative Book On the 60th Anniversary Of The Arbitration Court Attached To The Polish Chamber Of Commerce in Warszawa*], Warszawa: Sąd Arbitrażowy przy Krajowej Izbie Gospodarczej w Warszawie [*Arbitration Court Attached To The Polish Chamber Of Commerce in Warszawa*] / LexisNexis Polska Sp. o.o. 411-437, 2010, ISBN: 978-83-931891-0-6.

Pavel Dobiáš, Petr Dobiáš; *Die Schiedsfähigkeit von Streitigkeit über Immobilien in der Tschechischen Republik* [*The capacity to arbitrate the disputes over real-estates in the Czech Republic*], 6 eastlex, pp. 226-229, 2010.

Alexandr Mareš, *eu Domain Names Disputes Resolution*, in Józef Okolski, Andrzej Całus, Maksymilian Pazdan, Stanisław Sołtysiński, Tomasz Wardyński et Stanisław Włodyka (eds.), Księga pamiątkowa 60-lecia Sądu Arbitrażowego przy Krajowej Izbie Gospodarczej w Warszawie [*Commemorative Book on the 60th Anniversary of the Arbitration Court Attached to the Polish Chamber of Commerce in Warszawa*], Warszawa: Sąd Arbitrażowy przy Krajowej Izbie Gospodarczej w Warszawie [*Arbitration Court Attached to the Polish Chamber of Commerce in Warszawa*] / LexisNexis Polska Sp. o.o. 542-558, 2010, ISBN: 978-83-931891-0-6.

For further publications of Czech authors also issued in the Slovak Republic – see below.

II. [SLOVAK REPUBLIC]

Monographs, Collections and Conference Proceedings

Slávka Michančová, Renáta Dolanská (eds.), Súčasnost a perspektívy probácie a mediácie [*Current Situation and Perspectives of Probation and Mediation*], Prešov / Slovenská republika: Prešovská univerzita v Prešove [*University in Prešov / Slovak Republic*], 2010, ISBN: 978–80–555–0162–8.

Selected works published in the particular book on arbitration and ADR:

➢ R. Brzobohatý, Lenka Poláková, *Modely mediace – výzvy a perspektívy pro řešení sporů* [*Models of Mediation – Challenges to and Perspectives of Dispute Resolution*].

➢ Tomáš Horáček, *Aktuální otázky vzdělávání mediátorů v ČR* [*Current Topics Regarding the Education of Mediators in the Czech Republic*], pp. 291 et seq.

➢ Ernest Kováč, *Etický kódex mediátora* [*Code of Ethics for Mediators*], pp. 127 et seq.

Jozef Suchoža, Ján Husár (eds.), Obchodné právo a jeho širšie kontexty. Zborník vedených prác [*Commercial Law and its Broader Contexts. Collection of Scientific Works*], Košice / Slovenská republika [*Slovak Republic*]: Univerzita Pavla Jozefa Šafárika v Košiciach [*Pavel Jozef Šafárik Univerzity in Košice / Slovak Republic*], 2010, ISBN: 978-80-7097-838-2.

Selected works published in the particular book on arbitration and ADR:

➢ Alexander J. Bělohlávek, *Základní zásady mezinárodního rozhodčího řízení: Některé trendy v dislokaci odpovědností a sankcí* [*Basic Principles Of International Arbitration: On Certain Trends Regarding the Shift of the Burden of Liabilities and Sanctions*], pp. 96-120.

➢ Tomáš Horáček, *Dohoda o narovnání a její uplatnění v rámci alternativních způsobů řešení soukromoprávních sporů* [*Settlement Agreement and its Application in Alternative Resolution of Private Disputes*], pp. 146-157.

➢ Pavol Kubíček, *Činnosť Rozhodcovského súdu SOPK a jej legislatívny rámec* [*Activities of the Arbitration Court Attached to the Slovak Chamber of Commerce and Industry and Their Legal Framework*], pp. 72-78.

➢ Regina Palková, *Rozhodcovské konania a mediácia z pohľadu súčasnej legislatívy a praxe (Quo vadis mimosúdne riešenie sporov?)* [*Arbitration and mediation from the perspective of current legislation and practice (Quo vadis, alternative dispute resolutions?)*], pp. 131-145.

➢ Přemysl Raban, *Současné problémy alternativního rozhodování sporů v našich zemích* [*Current Problems of Alternative Dispute Resolution in Our Countries*], pp. 72-78.

➢ Jozef Suchoža, *Tradície a inovácie v rozhodcovskom konaní (legislatívne peripetie a aplikačné paradoxy)* [*Traditions and Innovations in Arbitration (Legislative Peripetia and Application Paradoxes)*], pp. 85-95.

➢ Alexander Škrinár, *Vybrané aplikačné problémy kreovania stálych rozhodcovských súdov a niektoré problémy rozhodcovského konania* [*Selected Application Problems of Establishing Permanent Arbitration Courts and Certain Problems Related to Arbitration Proceedings*], pp. 121-130.

Bulletin slovenskej advokacie [*Bulletin of the Slovak Bar*], **Bratislava: Slovenská advokátska komora** [*Slovak Bar Association*], **2010, Vol. 16, ISSN: 1335-1079**

Beáta Swanová, *Mediácia a premlčanie* [*Mediation and Limitation of Actions*]. No. 7-8, pp. 17 et seq.

III. [BULGARIA]

BULGARIA (2010), *Note General Editor, in* Jan Paulsson (ed.), 58 International Handbook on Commercial Arbitration, Kluwer Law International 1984, Last updated: March 2010 Supplement No. 58.

Lazar Tomov, *Bulgaria, in* Arbitration 2010 – Global Arbitration Review – Edition *Getting the Deal Through*. London: Publishing house: Law Business Research 68-73, 2010[1].

IV. [CROATIA]

Elma Beganovic, *Croatian Law On Arbitration And Uncitral Model Law On International Commercial Arbitration, in* Young ICCA Blog, 15 November 2010[2].

Alan Uzelac, *Croatia, in* World Arbitration Reporter (WAR), Huntington, New York: Juris Publishing, Inc., 2nd ed. 2010.

Landmark Victory for the Republic Croatia, 13 (4) International Arbitration Law Review (Int. ALR), 2010.

---

[1] Published in English.
[2] The electronic version available at: http://www.youngicca-blog.com (accessed on November 27, 2010).

V. [HUNGARY][3]

Monographs and Collections

Éva Horváth, Nemzetközi választottbíráskodás [*International Arbitration*], Budapest: HVG-ORAC, 2010, ISBN: 978-963-258-100-2.

Katalin Ligeti, Confidentiality of awards in international commercial arbitration, Budapest: CEU, Budapest College, 2010. CEU Legal Studies Department master theses; 2010/12[4].

Other Publications (Other than Monographs)

Éva Horváth, *A választottbírósági törvény „születéséről"* [*About the „birth" of the Hungarian Arbitration Act*], XVIII (3) Gazdaság és Jog, Budapest: HVG-ORAC 22-26, 2010, ISSN: 1217-2464.

Katalin Murányi; György Wellmann, *Szemelvények a Legfelsőbb Bíróság választottbíráskodást érintő gyakorlatából* [*Extracts from the Supreme Court Case Law Concerning Arbitration*], *in* XVII (2) Gazdaság és Jog, Budapest: HVG-ORAC 21-24, 2010, ISSN: 1217-2464.

Róbert Szakál, *Együttműködési kötelezettség kontra felróhatóság* [*Obligation to cooperate versus attributability*], *in* XVIII (4) Gazdaság és Jog, Budapest: HVG-ORAC 24-26, 2010, ISSN: 1217-2464[5].

Róbert Szakál, *Felmondási jog korlátozása a sportolói szerződésekben.* [*Restriction of the Right to Rescission in Sports Contracts*], *in* XVIII (2) Gazdaság és Jog, Budapest: HVG-ORAC 24-27, 2010, ISSN: 1217-2464[6].

Tímea Váci, *Céges jogviták: per helyett mediáció vagy választott bíróság* [*Business litigation: Mediation or Arbitration Instead of Litigating*], *in* 24 (15) Adó, Budapest: CompLex 74-75, 2010, ISSN: 0238-3950.

---

[3] Research completed with the assistance of Dr. Katalin Préda, Budapest, Hungary.
[4] The electronic version available at: http://www.etd.ceu.hu/2010/ligeti_katalin.pdf (accessed on November 27, 2010).
[5] Article on the case law of the Arbitration Court attached to the Hungarian Chamber of Commerce and Industry.
[6] Article on the case law of the Arbitration Court attached to the Hungarian Chamber of Commerce and Industry.

VI. [LATVIA][1]

Inese Druviete, *Pagaidu tiesību aizsardzības līdzekļu loma šķīrējtiesas veselībā* [*Role of Temporary Remedies in the "Health Status" of Arbitration Court*], 36 Jurista vārds, Riga: Latvijas Vēstnesis 631 et seq., 2010[2].

Torgāns Kalvis, *Valstiskā uzraudzība pār šķīrējtiesas spriedumu tiesiskumu* [*States Supervision over the Legality of Decisions of Arbitration Courts*], 34 Jurista vārds, Riga: Latvijas Vēstnesis 629 et seq., 2010[3].

Jāni Lapsa, *Šķīrējtiesas process: aktualitātes un nepieciešamās izmaiņas* [*Arbitration: Current Status and Changes Needed*] 28 Jurista vārds, Riga: Latvijas Vēstnesis 623 et seq., 2010[4].

VII. [LITHUANIA]

Deividas Soloveičikas, *Viešųjų pirkimų ginčų arbitruotinumo problematika* [*Possible solution of public procurement cases in arbitration*], 75 Teisė, Vilnius [LTU]: Vilniaus Universiteto leidykla, 2010[5].

VIII. [POLAND][6]

Monographs

Łukasz Błaszczak, Wyrok sądu polubownego w postępowaniu cywilnym [*Arbitration Award in Civil Proceedings*], Warszawa: Wolters Kluwer Polska sp. z o.o., 2010.

Andrzej Szumański, 8 Arbitraż handlowy [*Commercial arbitration*] of Stanisław Włodyka (ed.) *System prawa handlowego* [*Commercial Law System*], Warszawa: C. H. Beck 1.200, 2010, ISBN: 978-83-255-1234-7[7].

---

1 Selected by Veronika Leja, Riga, Latvia.
2 The electronic version available at:
http://www.juristavards.lv/index.php?menu= auth&id=216097
(accessed on December 1, 2010).
3 The electronic version available at:
http://www.juristavards.lv/index.php?menu= auth&id=215393
(accessed on December 1, 2010).
4 The electronic version available at:
http://www.juristavards.lv/index.php?menu= auth&id=213128
(accessed on December 1, 2010).
5 The electronic version of the annotation available at:
http://www.leidykla.vu.lt/mokslo-darbai/teise/teise-2010-75-tomas/soloveicikas-d-viesuju-pirkimu-gincu-arbitruotinumo-problematika (accessed on November 17, 2010). The article was pointed out to us by G. Uleviciute (ECOVIS, Vilnius, Lithuania).
6 Polish bibliography concerning arbitration and ADR for 2008 and 2009 also available in: Andrzej PASEK. *Bibliografia arbitrażu i mediacji za lata 2008-2009*), 2 ADR. ARBITRATION AND MEDIATION 35-61 (2010).
7 Published in Polish.

Józef Okolski, Andrzej Całus, Maksymilian Pazdan, Stanisław Sołtysiński, Tomasz Wardyński et Stanisław Włodyka (eds.), Księga pamiątkowa 60-lecia Sądu Arbitrażowego przy Krajowej Izbie Gospodarczej w Warszawie [*Commemorative Book On the 60th Anniversary Of The Arbitration Court Attached To The Polish Chamber Of Commerce in Warszawa*], Warszawa: Sąd Arbitrażowy przy Krajowej Izbie Gospodarczej w Warszawie [*Arbitration Court Attached To The Polish Chamber Of Commerce in Warszawa*] / LexisNexis Polska Sp. o.o., 2010, ISBN: 978-83-931891-0-6.

Authors of the Individual Chapters:

➢ Artur Barczewski; Bogudar Kordasiewicz, *Dopuszczalność wydawania wyroków przez tzw. kadłubowe zespoły orzekające ("truncated tribunals")* [*Admissibility of Issuing Awards by the So-Called Truncated Tribunals*], pp. 201-216.

➢ Alexander J. Bělohlávek, *Arbitration Agreement, MDR Clauses and Relation thereof to Nature of Jurisdictional Decisions on the Break of Legal Cultures*, pp. 411-437.

➢ Piero Bernardini, *Cost and Time of International Arbitration. The Point of View of the Arbitrator*, pp. 438-446.

➢ Piotr Bielarczyk, *Rozstrzyganie sporów arbitrażowych według zasad słuszności w oparciu o polski porządek prawny* [*Arbitration Dispute Resolution in Accordance with Equity Principles on the Basis of the Polish Legal Order*], pp. 151-156.

➢ Michał Bieniak, *Sąd polubowny a postępowanie upadłościowe.* [Arbitration Court and Bankruptcy Proceedings], pp. 671-675.

➢ Jens Bredow, *Arbitrating Shareholder Resolution Disputes in Germany: The New DIS-Supplementary Rules for Corporate Law Disputes ('DIS-SRCoLD')*, pp. 469-502.

➢ Louis B. Buchman; Eric Loquin, *L'arrêt West Tankers vu de France.* [Arbitration Award in the West Tankers vs. France Case], pp. 503-512.

➢ Andrzej Całus, *Sprawa zdatności arbitrażowej w prawie angielskim i w prawie amerykańskim (federalnym i stanowym)* [*The Issue of Arbitrability in English and (Federal and State) American Law*], pp. 513-541.

➢ Giovanni de Berti, *A Profile of the Chamber of Arbitration of Milan in its Thirty-Fifth Year*, pp. 447-468.

➢ Grzegorz Domański, *Arbitrzy w traktatowym arbitrażu inwestycyjnym - kilka refleksji praktycznych* [*Arbitrators in Treaty-Based Investment Arbitration – a Few Practical Reflections*], pp. 349-358.

➢ Marcin Dziurda; Adam Olszewski, *Pozycja prawna i kompetencje Prokuratorii Generalnej w arbitrażu* [*Legal Status and Powers of the Attorney General Office in Arbitration*], pp. 157-169.

➢ Beata Gessel-Kalinowska Vel Kalisz, *Class action arbitration - perspektywy rozwoju w polskiej praktyce arbitrażowej* [*Class Action Arbitration – Development Perspectives in the Polish Arbitration Practice*], pp. 170-178.

➤ Tomasz Gizbert-Studnicki, *Interpretacja orzeczeń arbitrażowych z punktu widzenia teorii prawa* [*Interpretation of Arbitration Awards from the Point of View of the Theory of Law*], pp. 739-750.

➤ Włodzimierz Głodowski, *Orzekanie przez sąd polubowny w przedmiocie swojej właściwości i kontrola tych orzeczeń przez sąd państwowy* [*Arbitration Court Ruling on its Jurisdiction and Control of Such Rulings by the State Court*], pp. 676-690.

➤ Maciej Jamka, *Dowód z zeznań świadka w krajowej i międzynarodowej praktyce arbitrażowej* [*Evidence in the Form of Witness Testimony in Domestic and International Arbitration Practice*], pp. 179-190.

➤ Witold Jurcewicz, *Rozstrzyganie sporów w systemie „ostatniej oferty" (baseball arbitration)* [*Dispute Resolution in the "Final Offer" System (Baseball Arbitration)*], pp. 191-200.

➤ Andrzej Kąkolecki, *Praktyki arbitrażu* [*Arbitration Practices*], pp. 35-50.

➤ Bartosz Krużewski, *Biegły w postępowaniu arbitrażowym* [*An Expert in Arbitration Proceedings*], pp. 217-231.

➤ Anna Krysiak; Marek Wierzbowski, *Bezstronność i niezależność jako kluczowe cechy każdego arbitra* [*Impartiality and Independence as the Key Characteristics of any Arbitrator*], pp. 359-375.

➤ Maciej Łaszczuk; Justyna Szpara, *Czy autonomia stron w ustalaniu reguł postępowania przed sądem polubownym jest ograniczona w czasie?* [*Is the Autonomy of Parties by Determination of the Rules of Procedure before the Arbitration Court Limited in Time?*], pp. 280-292.

➤ Małgorzata Manowska, *Wybrane zagadnienia dotyczące zarzutu potrącenia w postępowaniu arbitrażowym.* [*Selected Problems Concerning Set-Offs in Arbitration Proceedings*], pp. 232-241.

➤ Alexandr Mareš, *eu Domain Names Disputes Resolution*, pp. 542-558.

➤ Rafał Morek, *Wielostopniowe klauzule rozwiązywania sporów w praktyce kontraktowej i orzecznictwie wybranych systemów prawa kontynentalnego* [*Multistage Dispute Resolution Clauses in Contractual Practice and Case Law of Selected Systems of Continental Law*], pp. 51-67.

➤ Józef Okolski; Małgorzata Wach, *Zasada Kompetenz-Kompetenz w prawie arbitrażowym, ze szczególnym uwzględnieniem regulacji Sądu Arbitrażowego przy Krajowej Izbie Gospodarczej* [*The Kompetenz-Kompetenz Principle in the Arbitration Law with Particular Account Taken of The Regulations of the Court of Arbitration at the Polish Chamber of Commerce*], pp. 242-255.

➤ Marcin Olechowski, *Prawo właściwe do oceny skutków uznawanego międzynarodowego wyroku arbitrażowego* [*Law Applicable to the Assessment of the Effects of a Recognized International Arbitration Award*], pp. 573-585.

➤ Piotr Olkowski; Mikołaj Strojnowski; Krzysztof Wiater, *Zakres swobody arbitra przy ustalaniu i stosowaniu właściwego prawa materialnego* [*The Scope of Arbitrator's Freedom by Determination and Application of the Applicable Substantive Law*], pp. 385-407.

➢ Paweł Pietkiewicz, *Postępowanie przed sądem polubownym. Poszukiwanie dokumentów u strony postępowania oraz u osoby trzeciej* [*Proceedings Before an Arbitration Court. Searching for Documents from a Party to the Proceedings and from a Third Party*], pp. 256-279.

➢ Aleksander Proksa, *Z problematyki formy zapisu na sąd polubowny* [*Certain Issues Relating to the Form of the Arbitration Agreement*], pp. 117-133.

➢ Michał Romanowski, *Znaczenie niezależności i bezstronności arbitra w postępowaniu arbitrażowym w świetle konstytucyjnego prawa do sądu* [*Significance of Arbitrator's Independence and Impartiality in Arbitration Proceedings in the Light of the Constitutional Right to Be Heard by a Court*], pp. 376-384.

➢ Wojciech Sadowski, *Sąd polubowny jako sąd prawa Unii Europejskiej* [*Arbitration Court as an EU Law Court*], pp. 68-84.

➢ Józef Jan Skoczylas, *Charakter prawny zapisu na sąd polubowny a autonomia regulacji prawnej arbitrażu (po nowelizacji z 2005 roku)* [*Legal Character of the Arbitration Clause and the Autonomy of the Legal Regulation of Arbitration (after the 2005 Amendment)*], pp. 134-147.

➢ Grzegorz Suliński, *Spór wielostronny przed sądem polubownym na przykładzie sporu z art. 175 k.s.h.* [*A Multiparty Dispute Before an Arbitration Court as Exemplified by a Dispute Under Article 175 of the Commercial Companies Code*], pp. 293-303.

➢ Marek Świątkowski, *Dlaczego Polska nie jest stroną Konwencji waszyngtońskiej o rozstrzyganiu sporów inwestycyjnych?* [*Why is Poland not a Party to the Washington Convention on the Settlement of Investment Disputes?*], pp. 632-649.

➢ Krystyna Szczepanowska-Kozłowska, *Obowiązek zachowania poufności w międzynarodowym arbitrażu handlowym* [*The Confidentiality Obligation in International Commercial Arbitration*], pp. 304-312.

➢ Andrzej Szlęzak, *Zdatność arbitrażowa w sporach o ustalenie nieważności umowy - komentarz do orzeczenia Sądu Okręgowego w Toruniu z 21 grudnia 2009 r. oraz Sądu Najwyższego z 21 maja 2010 r.* [*Arbitrability in Lawsuits for Determining Invalidity of Contracts - Comments to Decisions of Regional Court in Toruń of 21 December 2009 and the Supreme Court of 21 May 2010*], pp. 313-320.

➢ Maciej Szpunar, *Stosowanie prawa konkurencji Unii Europejskiej przez sądy arbitrażowe* [*Application of EU Competition Law by Arbitration Courts*], pp. 614-631.

➢ Andrzej Szumański, *Problem dopuszczalności modyfikacji treści umowy w wyroku sądu arbitrażowego w świetle prawa polskiego* [*The Issue of Admissibility of Modifications to the Contents of a Contract in the Arbitration Awards in the Light of Polish Law*], pp. 321-332.

➢ Anna Giulia Tevini, *Die Anerkennung und Vollstreckung von Schiedssprüchen in der Volksrepublik China* [*Recognition and Enforcement of Arbitration Awards in the People's Republic of China*], pp. 650-668.

➤ Andrzej Wach, *Międzynarodowy i krajowy arbitraż sportowy* [*International and Domestic Sport Arbitration*], pp. 85-101.

➤ Tomasz Wardyński, *Kilka uwag o istocie arbitrażu* [*A Few Remarks on the Essence of Arbitration*], pp. 102-114.

➤ Karol Weitz, *Uchylenie wyroku sądu polubownego z powodu prawomocnego wyroku sądu (art. 1206 § 1 pkt 6 k.p.c.)* [*Setting Aside of an Arbitration Award Due to a Final Court Judgment (Article 1206 § 1 (6) of the Civil Procedure Code)*], pp. 691-705.

➤ Andrzej W. Wiśniewski, *Zasada równości stron w umowie o arbitraż oraz w procesie powoływania zespołu orzekającego: art. 1161 § 2 oraz art. 1169 § 3 k.p.c.* [*Parties Equality Principle in the Arbitration Clause and in the Adjudication Tribunal Appointment Procedure: Article 1161 § 2 and Article 1169 § 3 of the Civil Procedure Code*], pp. 333-346.

➤ Andrzej Zielony, *Kilka uwag o naturze skargi o uchylenie wyroku sądu polubownego (z uwzględnieniem aspektów historycznych i prawnoporównawczych). [A Few Remarks on the Nature of the Petition To Set Aside an Arbitration Award (Taking into Account the Historical and Legal Comparative Aspects)*], pp. 706-732.

ADR Arbitraż i Mediacja [*ADR Arbitration and Mediation*], Warszawa: C. H. Beck, 2010, ISSN: 1898-942X[8]

Arkadiusz Bieliński, *Rola i pozycja profesjonalnego pełnomocnika w ramach procedur alternatywnego rozwiązywania sporów* [*Role and Position of a Professional Attorney in ADR Procedures*]. No. 2, pp. 5-13.

Łukasz Błaszczak; Krystian Mularczyk, *Sprawozdanie z konferencji arbitrażowej pt. „Wybrane problemy arbitrażu - forum praktyków" (Warszawa 17. 3. 2010 r.)* [*Report on the Arbitration Conference "Selected Arbitration Issues - Practitioners' Forum" (Warszawa 17 March 2010)*]. No. 3, pp. 191-192.

Aleksandra Budniak, *Die Einbindung mediative Elemente in das polnische und das deutsche Gerichtsverfahren in Zivilsachen*. No. 1.

Berenika Kaczmarek-Templin, *Kilka uwag o elektronicznej postaci umowy o arbitraż w kontekście przepisów regulujących formę zapisu na sąd polubowny* [*Several Remarks on the Electronic Form of an Arbitration Agreement in the Context of the Provisions Regulating the Form of an Arbitration Clause*]. No. 3, pp. 17-29.

Karolina Mania, *ODR (Online Dispute Resolution) – podstawowe zagadnienia* [*ODR (Online Dispute Resolution) – Key Issues*]. No. 1, pp. 73-83.

Karolina Mania, *ODR (Online Dispute Resolution) w sporach konsumenckich* [*ODR (Online Dispute Resolution) in Consumer Disputes*]. No. 2, pp. 15-21.

---

[8] Quarterly. Papers published in Polish.

M. Miszkin-Wojciechowska, *Prawne gwarancje poufności mediacji gospodarczej i cywilnej – ocena regulacji prawa polskiego na tle wybranych rozwiązań w prawie obecnym.* [*Legal Guarantees of Commercial and Civil Mediation Confidentiality – Comparing Polish Provisions of Law with Selected Foreign Laws and Regulations.*]. No. 2 (10).

Andrzej Pasek, *Bibliografia arbitrażu i mediacja za lata 2008-2009,* [*Arbitration and Mediation Bibliography of 2008-2009*]. No. 2 (10).

Przemysław Pest, *Religijne uwarunkowania arbitrażu w krajach islamskich* [*Religious Determinants of Arbitration in Islamic Countries*]. No. 2, pp. 63-71.

Mateusz Pietraszewski, *Zapis na sąd polubowny jako klauzula abuzywna* [*Arbitration Clause as an Abusive Clause*]. No. 2, pp. 73-89.

Paweł Pietkiewicz, *Egzekwowalność decyzji Komisji rozjemczych w umowach FIDIC.* [*Enforceability of the arbitration Commissions decisions on FIDIC contracts*], No. 1.

Mateusz Pietraszewski, *Glosa do uchwały Sądu Najwyższego z 7 maja 2009 r.* [*Commentary to the Resolution of the Supreme Court of 7 May 2009*]. No. 3, pp. 89-98.

Michał Romanowska, *Miejsce mediacji wśród ADR w Wielkiej Brytanii i Polsce* [*The Role of Mediation in ADR in Great Britain*]. No. 1.

Rafał Schmidt, *Postępowanie pojednawcze* [*Conciliatory proceedings*]. No. 2 (10).

Rafał Schmidt, *Nadanie klauzuli wykonalności ugodzie zawartej przez mediatorem.* [*Confirmation on Enforceability Given to a Settlement Reached in Front of a Mediator*]. No. 1.

Katarzyna Schubert-Panecka, *Mediation bei deutsch-polnischen Kindschaftskonflikten.* No. 1 (9), 2010.

Ewelina Wętrys, *Skuteczność zapisu na sąd polubowny spółki zależnej wobec spółki dominującej* [*Effectiveness of the Arbitration Agreement of a Subsidiary Towards a Dominant Company*]. No. 3, pp. 141-190.

Rafał Wojciechowski, *Przepisy nowozelandzkiej ustawy o arbitrażu. Przekład z wprowadzeniem* [*Provisions of the New Zealand Arbitration Act. Translation with an Introduction.*]. No. 2, pp. 123-140.

Arbitration e-Review, 2010, Warszawa: Sąd Arbitrażowy przy Krajowej Izbie Gospodarczej [*Court of Arbitration attached to the Polish Chamber of Commerce*] in LexisNexis Polska

Yuliya Chernykh, *Poufność czy jawność w arbitrażu inwestycyjnym - perspektywa Ukrainy* [*Confidentiality or Publicity in Investment Arbitration: Ukraine's Perspective*]. No. 3, pp. 38-42, 2010.

Paweł Cioch, *Orzeczenie Sądu Arbitrażowego ds. Sportu w sprawie A/1480/ Pistorius przeciwko IAAF z 16.5.2008 r.* [*Award of the Court of Arbitration for Sport in case A/1480/Pistorius vs IAAF of 16 May 2008*]. No. 1, pp. 57-72.

Maria Hauser-Morel, *Uprzednio wyrażane poglądy jako podstawa wyłączenia arbitra - uwagi w świetle decyzji ICSID w sprawie Urbaser* [*Previously Expressed Views as the Grounds for Exclusion of Arbitrator – comments in the light of the decision on the ICSID Urbaser case*]. No. 3, pp. 32-37.

Mikołaj Jasiak, *Reforma prawa arbitrażowego w Hiszpanii* [*Arbitration Law Reform in Spain*]. No. 3, pp. 51-52.

Marek Neumann, *Orzeczenie Szwajcarskiego Trybunału Federalnego ws. Atlético v. Benfica: Uchylenie orzeczenia arbitrażowego na podstawie klauzuli porządku publicznego.* [*Swiss Federal Tribunal Set Aside an Arbitral Award on Public Policy Grounds*]. No. 3, pp. 49-50.

Piotr Nowaczyk, *Nowy Regulamin UNCITRAL od kuchni* [*New UNCITRAL Arbitration Rules from the Backstage*]. No. 3, pp. 16-20.

Adelina Prokop, *Regionalne Centrum Arbitrażowe w Kuala Lumpur: Nowy Regulamin UNCITRAL już stosowany w praktyce arbitrażowej.* [*Kuala Lampur Regional Centre for Arbitration: New UNCITRAL Arbitration Rules Already in Force*]. No. 3, pp. 24.

Maciej Tomaszewski, *Regulamin Arbitrażowy UNCITRAL 2010* [*2010 UNCITRAL Arbitration Rules*]. No. 3, pp. 5-15.

Biuletyn Arbitrażowy [*Bulletin on Arbitration*], Warszawa: LexisNexis Polska Sp. z.o.o. 2010[9]

Brady J. Collins, *Multi-step Dispute Resolution under the American Arbitration Association.* No. 2 (14), pp. 68-71.

Andrzej Kąkolecki, *Gorący temat konferencji w Wiedniu – taktyki guerilli w arbitrażu* [*Hot Topic at the Vienna Conference – Guerilla Tactics in Arbitration*]. No. 2 (14), pp. 82-86.

A. D. Kubś, *Arbitraż w Islandii — Wywiad z Haraldurem Ingi Birgissonem* [*Arbitration in Iceland — Interview with Haraldur Ingi Birgisson*]. No. 2 (14).

Rafał Morek, *Przegląd orzecznictwa Sądu Najwyższego i sądów apelacyjnych* [*Selected Supreme Court and Appelate Courts Decisions*]. No. 2 (14), pp. 87-90.

Rafał Morek, *Przegląd orzecznictwa Sądu Najwyższego i sądów apelacyjnych* [*Selected Supreme Court and Appelate Courts Decisions*], No. 3 (15), pp. 116-119.

Peter Taero Nielsen, *Arbitration in Denmark – a General Overview and Some Peculiarities.* No. 2 (14), pp. 72-78.

---

[9]   Issued by Sąd Arbitrażowy przy Krajowej Izbie Gospodarczej (*Court of Arbitration attached to the Polish Chamber of Commerce*) in LexisNexis Polska.

Piotr Nowaczyk, *Arbitraż instytucjonalny czy ad hoc - wystąpienie na konferencji „Tsunami sporów przed nami" zorganizowanej przez SIDiR, FIDIC i ICC Poland 21 stycznia 2010 roku* [*Institutional or ad hoc Arbitration – Speech at the Conference „A Tsunami of Disputes Ahead" Organized by SIDIR, FIDIC and ICC Poland on 21 January 2010*]. No. 2 (14), pp. 49-59.

Łucja Nowak, *Kwestia wyłączenia arbitrażu z zakresu obowiązywania rozporządzenia 44/2001 – sprawa West Tankers i sprawozdanie Komisji* [*Exclusion of Arbitration from the Scope of Regulation No. 44/2001 – West Tankers Case and Report of the Commission*]. No. 1, pp. 65-79.

Barbara Skardzińska, *Język w międzynarodowym arbitrażu handlowym,* [*Language in International Commercial Arbitration*]. No. 1, pp. 80-92.

Tomasz Strumiłło, *Skutki prawne wyroku arbitrażowego* [*Legal Effects of an Arbitral Award*]. No. 3, pp. 96-115.

Maria Szymańska, *Zmiana Regulaminu Arbitrażowego UNCITRAL – rezultaty 51 sesji Grupy Roboczej* [*Revision of the UNCITRAL Rules – the Results of the 51st Session of the Working Group*]. No. 1 (13), pp. 43-47.

Maria Szymańska, *Zmiana Regulaminu Arbitrażowego UNCITRAL – rezultaty 52 sesji Grupy Roboczej* [*Revision of the UNCITRAL Arbitration Rules – Results of the 52nd Session of the Working Group*]. No. 2 (14), pp. 60-67.

Maria Szymańska, *Zmieniony Regulamin Arbitrażowy UNCITRAL - rezultaty 43 sesji UNCITRAL* [*Revised UNCITRAL Arbitration Rules - the results of the 43rd session of UNCITRAL*]. No. 3, pp. 69-95.

Andrzej Tynel, *Kompetencja Rady Arbitrażowej w postępowaniu przed Sądem Arbitrażowym przy KIG* [*Jurisdiction of the Arbitral Council in the Proceedings before the Court of Arbitration at the PCC*]. No. 1, pp. 39-42.

Monika Weingärtner, *Ujawnienie elektronicznych informacji w arbitrażu międzynarodowym* [*Electronic Discovery in International Arbitration*]. No. 1, pp. 48-64.

Karol Weitz, *Klauzula porządku publicznego jako podstawa uchylenia wyroku sądu polubownego na tle praktyki sądów (Wykład i dyskusja na Kolegium Arbitrów 21 października 2009 roku)* [*Public Policy as a Ground for Setting Aside of an Arbitral Award in Courts' Practice – Lecture by Karol Weitz and Discussion at the Meeting of Arbitrators, 21 October 2009*]. No. 1, pp. 13-18.

e-Przegląd Arbitrażowy, 2010, Vol. 1

J. E. Beerbower, *Dispute Resolution in M&A Transactions*, Warszawa, 13-14 May 2010, No. 2 (2).

P. Bytnerowicz, *Termin na zgłoszenie roszczenia wzajemnego w postępowaniu arbitrażowym według Regulaminu ICC* [*The Final Date For Notification of the Counterclaim in the Arbitration Proceeding Under the ICC Rules*]. No. 2 (2).

Mateusz Dubek, Łukasz Rozdeiczer, *Sprawa Jukosu: Rosja jest związana Traktatem Karty Energetycznej* [*The Yukos Case: Russia Bound by Energy Charter Treaty*]. No. 1, pp. 51-52.

Klaudia Frątczak, *Nowy regulamin IBA o postępowaniu dowodowym w arbitrażu międzynarodowym* [*New IBA Rules of Taking Evidence in International Arbitration*]. No. 2 (2).

Klaudia Frątczak, *Orzeczenie Szwajcarskiego Trybunału Federalnego w sprawie 4A_428/2009* [*Swiss Federal Tribunal's Decision of 26 October 2009 (4A_428/2009)*]. No. 1, pp. 55-56.

Beata Gessel-Kalinowska vel Kalisz, XX. *Kongres ICCA, Rio de Janeiro, 23-26 maja 2010 r.* [*ICCA Congress in Rio de Janeiro, May 23-26, 2010*]. No. 2 (2).

Maria Hauser-Morel, *Międzynarodowy Sąd Arbitrażowy ICC* [*ICC International Court of Arbitration*]. No. 1, pp. 35-39.

Maria Hauser-Morel, *Nowe „Oświadczenie akceptacji, dyspozycyjności i niezależności" arbitra* [*The New „statement of acceptance, availability and independence" of the arbitrator*], Międzynarodowej Izby Handlowej, e-Przegląd Arbitrażowy. No. 2 (2), 2010.

Mikołaj Jasiak, *Arbitraż w sporze granicznym między Słowenią a Chorwacją* [*Arbitration in the Border Dispute between Slovenia and Croatia*]. No. 2 (2), 2010.

Michał Jochemczak, *Sprawa Dallah Real Estate v Pakistan* [*Dallah Real Estate v Pakistan Case*]. No. 2 (2).

Marcin Kałduński, *Sprawa Austrian Airlines v. Słowacja* [*Austrian Airlines v. Slovakia Case*]. No. 2 (2).

Izabela Kowalczuk, *Zmiana taryfy opłat ICC* [*Changing ICC Tariffs*]. No. 2(2).

Michał Pochodyła, *London Court of International Arbitration*. No. 1, pp. 40-43.

Katarzyna Michałowska, *Nadużycie prawa dostępu do arbitrażu w międzynarodowych sporach inwestycyjnych* [*Abuse of rights of access to international arbitration in investments disputes*].No. 2 (2), 2010.

Łucja Nowak, *Nowe europejskie ustawy arbitrażowe: Szkocja i Irlandia.*[*New European Arbitration Acts: Scotland and Ireland*]. No. 1, pp. 49-50.

Sylwester Pieckowski, *Projekt kodeksu dobrych praktyk stałych sądów polubownych* [*The draft of the Code of Good Practices of the permanent Arbitration Courts*]. No. 2 (2), 2010.

Michał Pochodyła, *London Court of International Arbitration*. No. 1(1).

Wojciech Sadowski, *Wpływ postępowania upadłościowego w Polsce na postępowania arbitrażowe prowadzone za granicą: uwagi na kanwie sprawy Elektrimu* [*The Impact of Insolvency Proceedings in Poland on Arbitration Abroad Demonstrated by the Elektrim Case*]. No. 2 (2).

Stanisław Sołtysik, *Protocol to Promote Efficiency in International Arbitration – recepta na przewlekłość arbitrażu?* [*Protocol to Promote Efficiency in International Arbitration – the Remedy to Sluggish Arbitration?*]. No. 2 (2).

Justyna Szpara, *Nieważność zapisu na sąd polubowny w zakresie sporów dotyczących prawa Unii Europejskiej: orzeczenie angielskiego High Court w sprawie Accentuate v Asigra Mandatory* [*EU regulations invalidate arbitration clause where parties chose non-EU law: decision of High Court in Accentuate v Asigra case*]. No. 1 (1).

Andrzej W. Wiśniewski, *Arbitraż międzynarodowy w prawie polskim: podstawowe problemy* [*International Arbitration under Polish Law: Basic Problems*]. No. 1, pp. 11-27.

Andrzej W. Wiśniewski, *Fast-track, czyli arbitraż przyspieszony – po polsku* [*Fast-track, ergo expedited arbitration - the Polish way*]. No. 2 (2), 2010.

PPC, 2010

Paweł Grzegorczyk, *W ramach której z podstaw kasacyjnych należy zarzucać naruszenie przepisów regulujących warunki uznania orzeczenia sądu państwa obcego lub wyroku sądu polubownego wydanego za granicą?* [*Which Cassation Ground Should Be the Basis for the Plea of Infringement of the Provisions Regulating the Conditions of Recognition of a Foreign Judgment or a Foreign Award?*]. No. 1, pp. 77-82.

Aleksander Proksa, *Orzecznictwo Sądu Arbitrażowego przy KIG - SA 128/08* [*Awards of the Court of Arbitration at the PCC - SA 128/08*]. No. 3, pp. 120-135.

PPH, 2010

Michał Jochemczak, *Attorney-client privilege w międzynarodowym postępowaniu arbitrażowym* [*Attorney-Client Privilege in International Arbitration Proceedings*]. No. 3, pp. 37-44.

Michał Pełczyński, *Umowna zmiana właściwości miejscowej sądu delibacyjnego w sprawie o uznanie wyroku arbitrażowego* [*Contractual Change of Court's Venue in Proceedings on Recognition of Arbitration Award*]. No. 10, pp. 37-42.

Prawo Europejskie w Praktyce [*European Law in Practice*] 2010

Robert Siwik, *Zapis na sąd polubowny w umowach konsumenckich – wnioski z najnowszego orzecznictwa ETS* [*Arbitration Clause in Consumer Agreements – Conclusions Drawn from the Latest ETS Case Law*]. No. 3, pp. 37-43.

Robert Siwik, *Prawo właściwe dla umowy o arbitraż w międzynarodowym i krajowym arbitrażu handlowym* [*Law Governing the Arbitration Agreement in International and Domestic Commercial Arbitration*]. No. 10, pp. 51-55.

Glosa, 2010

Paweł Błaszczyk, *Glosa do uchwały SN z dnia 7 maja 2009 r., III CZP 13/09. Zdatność arbitrażowa sporów ze stosunku spółki handlowej* [*Capacity to Arbitrate over Corporate Disputes – Commentary on the Supreme Court Resolution of 7 May 2009, III CZP 13/09*]. No. 1, pp. 22-29.

Andrzej Szumański, *Glosa do uchwały SN z dnia 7 maja 2009 r., III CZP 13/09. Sąd polubowny a ugoda sądowa* [*Court of Conciliation and Court Settlement – Commentary on the Supreme Court Resolution of 7 May 2009, III CZP 13/09*]. No. 1, pp. 14-21.

Other Publications

Armen Artwich, *Application of the Delocalization Theory in Current International Commercial Arbitration Practice.* Prz. Prawn. UW, No. 1-2, pp. 130-143, 2010.

Andrzej Bartosiewicz, *Arbitraż domenowy WIPO* [*WIPO Domain Arbitration*], AZ News, 11 August 2010[10].

Dariusz P. Kała, *Skarga o uchylenie wyroku sądu polubownego (cz. I, cz. II)* [*Petition to Set Aside an Arbitration Award (part 1 and part 2)*], 106 (1), 107 (2) Radca prawny 58-64.

Robert Siwik, *Zapis na sąd polubowny w umowach konsumenckich - wnioski z najnowszego orzecznictwa ETS* [*Arbitration Clause in Consumer Contracts – Conclusions on Latest ECJ Findings*], 3 Prawo Europejskie w Praktyce [*European Law In Practice*], 2010.

Michael Wietzorek, *New Arbitration Law in the Republic of Georgia.* Kluwer Arbitration Blog[11].

---

[10] The electronic version available at: http://aznews.pl/2010/08/arbitraz-domenowy-wipo (accessed on November 17, 2010).
[11] The electronic version available at: http://kluwerarbitrationblog.com/blog/2010/09/01/new-arbitration-law-in-the-republic-of-georgia (accessed on November 27, 2010).

IX.   [ROMANIA][12]

Monographs[13]

Alina Mioara Cobuz-Bagnaru, Arbitrajul ad-hoc conform regulilor Comisiei Natiunilor Unite pentru Dreptul Comercial International [*Ad hoc arbitration according to the United Nations Commission on International Trade Law rules*], Bucuresti: Universul Juridic, 2010.

Titus Prescure, Arbitrajul comercial - Modalitate alternativă de soluţionare a litigiilor patrimoniale [*Commercial Arbitration – Alternative approach to resolving patrimonial disputes*], Bucuresti: Universul Juridic, 2010.

Gabriel Tiţa-Nicolescu, Tratat de dreptul afacerilor. Vol. 1 – Persoanele juridice. [*Business Law Treatise. Volume I – Legal Persons*], Bucuresti: Wolters Kluwer, 2010.

Curierul Judiciar [*Legal Courier*], Bucharest, Vol. 2010, ISSN: 1582-7526[14]

Cristian Gheorghe, *Limitele arbitrajului în materie societară* [*The limits of arbitration in company matters*]. No. 8.

Gabriel Mihai, *Arbitrajul comercial între libertatea convenţională şi constrângerile ordinii publice* [*Commercial Arbitration - between conventional liberty and the constraint of public order*]. No. 10.

Cristiana Stoica, *Noile reglementări privind arbitrajul* [*New regulations regarding arbitration*]. No. 7.

X.   [SLOVENIA]

Spomenka Hribar, *Vsakdo se bo na referendumu moral odločiti sam: oktroirani arbitražni sporazum* [*Everyone will have to make up their own mind at the referendum: the imposed arbitration agreement*], 52 (122) Delo 16-17, 2010, ISSN: 1580-3007[15].

Metka Penko-Natlačen, Andrej Friedl, Igor Knez, Gregor Golob, Simon Žgavec, Peter Rižnik, Vesna Uršič, Marko Djinović, Amela Žrt, Alternativno

---

[12] For further articles on arbitration in Romania see also *Revista Română de Arbitraj* issued by the International Commercial Arbitration attached to the Chamber of Commerce and Industry of Romania, see the electronic version available at: http://arbitration.ccir.ro/engleza/index.htm (accessed on November 27, 2010).

[13] All titles published in Romanian. The research for CYArb performed by Dr. Ligia Catuna, Timisoara, Romania.

[14] All titles published in Romanian. The research for CYArb performed by Dr. Ligia Catuna, Timisoara, Romania.

[15] The published material is informative and serves popularization purposes. This published information was pointed out to us by Mojca Muha (Senica), Ljubljana, Slovenia based on the research in the NUK database.

Czech (& Central European) Yearbook of Arbitration

reševanje delovnopravnih sporov s podporo socialnega dialoga[16] [*Alternative dispute resolution of labour law disputes with the help of social dialogue*][17], Ljubljana: Gospodarska zbornica Slovenije 162, 2010, ISBN: 978-961-6666-36-7[18].

Jože Pirjevec, *Enajsta božja zapoved: meje, začrtane po 2. svetovni vojni, se ne spreminjajo : zgodovinar Jože Pirjevec o arbitraži* [*The eleventh commandment: borders made after WWII do not change: Jože Prijevec History on arbitration*][19], 52 (116) Delo 14-15, 2010, ISSN: 1580-3007[20].

Zlatko Šabič, *Referendum o zaupnici slovenskim političnim elitam: arbitražni sporazum* [*Referendum on vote of confidence to Slovenian political elites: arbitration agreement*], 52 (122) Delo 14-15, 2010, ISSN: 1580-3007[21].

Zlatko Šabič, *Mednarodna razsežnost arbitražnega sporazuma* [*The international component of the arbitration agreement*], 52 (122) Delo 5, 2010, ISSN: 1580-3007[22].

Peter Toš, *Dobra odločitev zahteva presojo vseh dejstev : arbitražni sporazum* [*A good decision demands taking account of all facts: arbitration agreement*], 52 (116) Delo 12-13, 2010, ISSN: 1580-3007[23].

Aleš Zalar, Bojana Jovin Hrastnik, Zakon o alternativnem reševanju sodnih sporov (ZARSS) s komentarjem. Zakon o mediaciji v civilnih in gospodarskih zadevah (ZMCGZ) s komentarjem. Zakon o arbitraži (ZArbit) s pojasnili. Serie Zbirka Nova slovenska zakonodaja / GV [*Law on alternative resolution of court disputes with commentary. Law on mediation in civil and commercial matters with commentary. Law on arbitration with commentary*], Ljubljana (Slovenia): GV založba 212, 2010, ISBN: 978-961-247-144-6[24].

---

[16] A study elaborated under the 305/ARDS 2009-2011 Project.

[17] Regarding labour ADR.

[18] This publication was pointed out to us by Mojca Muha (Senica), Ljubljana, Slovenia based on the research in the NUK database.

[19] The published material is informative and serves popularization purposes. This published information was pointed out to us by Mojca Muha (Senica), Ljubljana, Slovenia based on the research in the NUK database.

[20] Interview. Interviewee: J. Pirjevec, interviewer: B. Šuligoj.

[21] The published material is informative and serves popularization purposes. This published information was pointed out to us by Mojca Muha (Senica), Ljubljana, Slovenia based on the research in the NUK database.

[22] The published material is informative and serves popularization purposes. This published information was pointed out to us by Mojca Muha (Senica), Ljubljana, Slovenia based on the research in the NUK database.

[23] The published material is informative and serves popularization purposes. This published information was pointed out to us by Mojca Muha (Senica), Ljubljana, Slovenia based on the research in the NUK database.

[24] This publication was pointed out to us by Mojca Muha (Senica), Ljubljana, Slovenia based on the research in the NUK database.

Important Web Sites

http://www.czechyearbook.org/

Czech Yearbook of International Law® and **Czech (& Central European) Yearbook of Arbitration**

The website is currently available in sixteen languages: English, Bulgarian, Czech, Chinese, Japanese, Korean, Hungarian, German, Polish, Romanian, Russian, Portuguese, Slovenian, Spanish, Ukrainian, Vietnamese. This website allows access to the annotations of all core articles and to information about the authors of these articles as well as to the entire remaining contents (except core articles) of both yearbooks (CYIL and CYArb).

I. [CZECH REPUBLIC]

- http://www.cnb.cz
  Česká národná banka
  (Czech National Bank as the Central bank of the Czech Republic)[1].

- http://www.compet.cz
  Office for the protection of competition[2].

- http://www.concourt.cz
  The Constitutional Court of the Czech Republic[3].

- http://www.csesp.cz
  Czech Society for European and Comparative Law[4].

- http://www.csmp-csil.org
  The Czech Society of International Law[5].

- http://www.czech.cz
  Portal „Hello Czech Republic". Basic information about the Czech Republic and news interesting for foreigners. Rather a promotional portal[6].

- http://www.czso.cz
  Czech Statistical Office[7].

- http://dtjvcnsp.org
  Česko-německý spolek právníků. [Czech-German Lawyers Association]. Deutsch-Tschechische Juristenvereinigung e.V[8].

- http://ekf.vsb.cz
  Faculty of Economics, VŠB Technical University of Ostrava[9].

---

1 Website available in English and Czech.
2 Website available in English and Czech. Basic laws and regulations on the protection of competition in the Czech Republic are also available at the website, both in Czech and in English (unofficial translation).
3 Website available in English and Czech. Part of the (significant) case law also available in English.
4 Website available in English and Czech.
5 Website available in Czech. In English only a brief summary of the web pages.
6 Website available in English, Czech, French, German, Russian and Spanish.
7 Website available in English and Czech.
8 Website available in German.
9 Website available in English and Czech. Some information (regarding post-graduate studies) also available in German. Department of Law see http://en.ekf.vsb.cz/information-about/departments/structure/departments/dept-119 (in English).

- http://ftp.pse.cz/Info.bas/Cz/Predpisy/brs_statut2.pdf
  Statute of Burzovní rozhodčí soud při Burze cenných papírů Praha, a.s.
  [Exchange Court of Arbitration at the Prague Stock Exchange][10].

- http://www.hrad.cz
  Website of the Office of the President of the Czech Republic[11].

- http://www.icc-cr.cz
  ICC National Committee Czech Republic.

- http://www.iir.cz
  Institute Of International Relations Prague[12].

- http://www.ilaw.cas.cz
  Ústav státu a práva Akademie věd ČR, v.v.i. [Institute of State and Law of
  the Academy of Sciences of the Czech Republic][13].

- http://www.jednotaceskychpravniku.cz
  Jednota českých právníků [Czech Lawyers Union].

- http://www.icc-cr.cz
  ICC National Committee Czech Republic.

- http://justice.cz
  Czech justice portal including both courts and the Ministry of Justice,
  prosecution departments, Judicial Academy, Institute of Criminology
  and Social Prevention, as well as the Probation and Mediation Service
  and the Prison Service[14].

- http://www.law.muni.cz
  Faculty of Law, Masaryk University, Brno[15].

- http://www.mzv.cz
  Ministry of Foreign Affairs of the Czech Republic[16].

---

[10] The Statute is available in Czech. One of the three permanent arbitration courts established in the Czech Republic by law (statute), in compliance with Section 13 of Act No. 216/1994 Coll., on Arbitration and Enforcement of Arbitral Awards, as subsequently amended.

[11] Website available in English and Czech. This website also allows access to the personal webpage of the President of the Czech Republic.

[12] Website available in English and Czech. This Institute was founded by the Ministry of Foreign Affairs of the Czech Republic.

[13] Website available in English and Czech.

[14] Website available in Czech. The individual websites of the institutions covered by this portal also contain pages or summary information in English.

[15] Website available in English and Czech.

[16] Website available in Czech. Important information from this portal also available in English.

Czech (& Central European) Yearbook of Arbitration

- http://www.nsoud.cz
  The Supreme Court of the Czech Republic[17].

- http://www.nssoud.cz
  The Supreme Administrative Court of the Czech Republic[18].

- http://www.ochrance.cz
  Public Defender of Rights (Ombudsman)[19].

- http://www.ok.cz/iksp/en/aboutus.html
  Institute of Criminology and Social Prevention[20].

- http://portal.gov.cz
  Portal of the Public Administration[21]. This website allows access to the websites of most supreme public administration authorities (including ministries).

- http://www.prf.cuni.cz
  Faculty of Law, Charles University in Prague[22].

- http://www.psp.cz
  Parliament of the Czech Republic. Chamber of Deputies[23].

- http://www.rozhodcisoud.cz
  The Arbitration Court attached to the Czech-Moravian Commodity Exchange Kladno[24].

- http://www.senat.cz
  Parliament of the Czech Republic. Senate[25].

- http://www.society.cz/wordpress/#awp
  Common Law Society[26].

---

[17] Website available in Czech. Some basic information also in English and French.
[18] Website available in English and Czech.
[19] Website available in English and Czech.
[20] Website available in English and Czech.
[21] Website available in English and Czech.
[22] Website available in Czech. Basic information available in English.
[23] Website available in English and Czech.
[24] Website available in English and Czech. Website of one of the three permanent arbitration courts established in the Czech Republic by law (statute), in compliance with Section 13 of Act No. 216/1994 Coll., on Arbitration and Enforcement of Arbitral Awards, as subsequently amended. This arbitration court was established by Act No. 229/1992 Coll., on Commodity Exchanges, as subsequently amended.
[25] Website available in English and Czech.
[26] Website available in Czech.

- http://www.soud.cz
  Arbitration Court attached to the Economic Chamber of the Czech Republic and Agricultural Chamber of the Czech Republic[27].

- http://www.umpod.cz
  Office for International Legal Protection of Children[28].

- http://www.upol.cz/fakulty/pf
  Faculty of Law. Palacký University, Olomouc.

- http://www.vse.cz
  The University of Economics, Prague[29].

- http://www.zcu.cz/fpr
  Faculty of Law, Western Bohemia University in Pilsen[30].

II. [SLOVAK REPUBLIC]

- http://www.concourt.sk
  Constitutional Court of the Slovak Republic[31].

- http://www.flaw.uniba.sk
  Faculty of Law, Comenius University in Bratislava (SVK)[32].

- http://iuridica.truni.sk
  Faculty of Law, Trnava University in Trnava (SVK)[33].

- http://www.justice.gov.sk
  Ministry of Justice of the Slovak Republic[34].

---

27   Website available in English, Czech, German and Russian. Website of one of the three permanent arbitration courts established in the Czech Republic by law (statute), in compliance with Section 13 of Act No. 216/1994 Coll., on Arbitration and Enforcement of Arbitral Awards, as subsequently amended. This arbitration court was established by Section 19 of Act No. 301/1992 Coll., on the Economic Chamber of the Czech Republic and the Agricultural Chamber of the Czech Republic, as subsequently amended.
28   The Office is the Central authority responsible for protection of children in civil matters having cross-border implications. Website available in English and Czech.
29   Website available in English and Czech.
30   Website available in Czech.
31   Website available in English and Slovak.
32   Website available in English and Slovak.
33   Website available in English and Slovak.
34   Website available in English and Slovak. This website also allows access to the following portals: Courts, Slovak Agent before the European Court for Human Rights, Slovak Agent before the Court of Justice of the European Union, The Judicial Academy.

Czech (& Central European) Yearbook of Arbitration

- http://www.nbs.sk
  Národná banka Slovenska (National Bank of Slovakia as the Central bank of Slovak Republic)[35].

- http://www.nrsr.sk
  National Council of the Slovak Republic (*Slovak Parliament*)[36].

- http://www.prf.umb.sk
  Faculty of Law. Matej Bel University, Banská Bystrica (SVK).

- http://www.prezident.sk
  President of the Slovak Republic and Office of the President (SVK)[37].

- http://www.test.sopk.sk
  The Court of Arbitration of the Slovak Chamber of Commerce and Industry in Bratislava[38].

- http://www.uninova.sk/pf_bvsp/src_angl/index.php
  Faculty of Law, Pan European University (SVK)[39].

- http://www.upjs.sk
  Faculty of Law, Pavol Jozef Šafárik University in Košice (SVK)[40].

- http://www.usap.sav.sk
  Institute of State and Law, Slovak Academy of Science[41].

III. [AUSTRIA]

- http://www.arbitration-austria.at
  Österreichische Vereinigung für Schiedsgerichtsbarkeit. Austrian Arbitration Association[42].

- http://www.internationales-schiedsgericht.at
  Wiener Internationalen Schiedsgerichts (VIAC). Vienna International Arbitral Centre (VIAC)[43].

---

35 Website available in English and Slovak.
36 Website available in English, French, German and Slovak.
37 Website available in English and Slovak.
38 Website available in Slovak. Some basic information available in English.
39 Website available in English, German and Slovak.
40 Website available in English and Slovak.
41 Website available in Slovak.
42 Website available in English and German.
43 Website available in English, Czech, German and Russian.

IV. [BLR] – [BELARUS]

- http://www.cci.by/ArbitrCourt/AboutCourt_en.aspx
  International Arbitration Court attached to the Belarusian Chamber of Commerce and Industry[44].

V. [BGR] – [BULGARIA]

- http://www.bcci.bg/arbitration/index.html
  Arbitration Court at the Bulgarian Chamber of Commerce and Industry.

- http://www.lex.bg
  Information server on Bulgarian law.

VI. [ESTONIA]

- http://www.koda.ee
  Arbitration Court attached to the Estonian Chamber of Commerce and Industry[45].

VII. [CROATIA]

- http://www2.hgk.hr/en/about_cce.asp?izbor=pac
  The Permanent Arbitration Court at the Croatian Chamber of Commerce[46].

VIII. [HUNGARY]

- http://www.mkik.hu/index.php?id=1406
  Court of Arbitration attached to the Hungarian Chamber of Commerce and Industry[47].

- http://www.mkik.hu/index.php?id=1409&print=1
  Act LXXI [Hungary] of 1994 On arbitration. Nonofficial English translation published on the portal of the Hungarian Chamber of Commerce. [Law on arbitration].

---

[44] Website available in English and Russian.
[45] Website available in English, Estonian and Russian.
[46] Website available in Croatian. Basic information available in English. See the English presentation of the arbitration court at the website.
[47] Website available in Hungarian. Basic information available in English.

IX. [LATVIA]

- http://www.chamber.lv
  The Arbitration Court of the Latvian Chamber of Commerce and Industry LCCI[48].

X. [LTU] – [LITHUANIA]

- http://www3.lrs.lt/pls/inter3/dokpaieska.showdoc_l?p_id=56461
  Law on Commercial Arbitration of The Republic of Lithuania No I-1274 as of 2 April 1996[49]. Official translation by Lietuvos Respulikos Seimas (on the portal of the Parliament of the Republic of Lithuania).

- http://www.arbitrazas.lt
  Vilniaus komercinio arbitražo teismas. Vilnius Court of Commercial Arbitration[50].

XI. [MACEDONIA]

- http://www.mchamber.org.mk/%28S%28crtmab45gznlucyny5lvrven%29%29/default.aspx?lId=2&mId=50&smId=0
  The Permanent Court of Arbitration attached to the Economic Chamber of Macedonia [Стопанската комора на Македонија][51].

XII. [MOLDOVA]

- http://www.arbitraj.chamber.md/index.php?id=93/
  Curtea de Arbitraj Comercial International pe linga Camera de Comert si Industrie a Republicii Moldova. The International Commercial Arbitration Court of the Chamber of Commerce and Industry of the Republic of Moldova[52].

---

48   Website available in English, Latvian and Russian.
49   Published in: Parliamentary record, 1998-04-01, Nr. 4 (*Teisės aktą priėmė - Lietuvos Respublikos Seimas*).
50   Website available in English, Lithuanian and Polish.
51   Website available in English and Macedonian.
52   Website available in English, Moldovan and Russian.

XIII. [POLAND][53]

- http://www.sakig.pl/
  Sąd Arbitrażowy przy Krajowej Izbie Gospodarczej w Warszawie[54].
  (Court of Arbitration at the Polish Chamber of Commerce in Warsaw.)

- http://www.iccpolska.pl/
  Polski Komitet Narodowy Międzynarodowej Izby Handlowej. Polish ICC National Committee.

- http://oirp.bydgoszcz.pl/index.php?page=statut_2
  Sądu Polubowny przy Okręgowej Izbie Radców Prawnych w Bydgoszczy.
  Court of Arbitration attached to the Regional Chamber of Legal Advisors in Bydgoscz[55].

- http://www.gca.org.pl/x.php/1,392/Arbitraz.html
  Sąd Arbitrażowy przy Izbie Bawełny w Gdyni. Arbitration Court attached to the Gdynia Cotton Association.[56]

- http://oirp.gda.pl/portal-dla-przedsiebiorcow/sad-polubowny
  Stały Sąd Arbitrażowy przy Okręgowej Izbie Radców Prawnych w Gdańsku. Permanent Court of Arbitration attached to the Regional Chamber of Legal Advisers in Gdańsk.[57]

- http://www.igg.pl/1/node/39
  Sąd Arbitrażowy przy Izbie Gospodarczej Gazownictwa. Court of Arbitration attached to The Chamber of the Natural Gas Industry.[58]

- http://www.ihk.pl/index.html?id=1635
  Sąd Arbitrażowy przy Polsko-Niemieckiej Izbie Przemysłowo-Handlowej. Court of Arbitration attached to the Polish – German Chamber of Commerce and Industry.[59]

- http://www.iph.krakow.pl/?a=page&id=31
  Sąd Polubowny przy Izbie Przemysłowo-Handlowej w Krakowie. Court of Arbitration attached to the Chamber of Industry and Trade in Krakow.[60]

---

[53] Operation and accessibility of all websites were last checked on 17 November 2010.
[54] Website available in English, German, French, Polish and Russian.
[55] Website available in Polish.
[56] Website available in English and Polish.
[57] Website available in English and Polish.
[58] Website available in Polish. Some basic information, especially about the Chamber, also available in English and German.
[59] Website available in German and Polish.
[60] Website available in Polish.

- http://www.iph.torun.pl/index.php?aid=113837484143da38b99fb66
  Sąd Polubowny przy Izbie Przemysłowo-Handlowej w Toruniu. Court of
  Arbitration attached to the Chamber of Industry and Trade in Torun.[61]

- http://isap.sejm.gov.pl
  Legal information (laws and regulations) system on the portal of the Sejm
  [Parliament] of the Republic of Poland.[62]

- http://www.kigm.pl/index.php?option=com_
  content&task=view&id=60&Itemid-65&lang=p
  Międzynarodowy Sąd Arbitrażowy przy Krajowej Izbie Gospodarki
  Morskiej. International Court of Arbitration attached to the Polish
  Chamber of Maritime Commerce in Gdynia[63].

- http://www.knf.gov.pl/regulacje/Sad_Polubowny/index.html
  Sąd Polubowny przy Komisji Nadzoru Finansowego. Court of Arbitration
  attached to the Polish Financial Supervision Authority[64].

- http://www.liph.com.pl/index.php?body=7
  Polubowny Sąd Łódzkiej Izby Przemysłowo-Handlowej. Court of
  Arbitration attached to the Chamber of Industry and Trade in Łódz[65].

- http://www.nig.org.pl/sa/pl1.html
  Sąd Arbitrażowy przy Nowotomyskiej Izbie Gospodarczej w Nowym
  Tomyślu. Court of Arbitration attached to the Chamber of Economy in
  Nowym Tomyśl[66].

- http://www.nsa.gov.pl
  Supreme Administrative Court[67].

- http://oirp.olsztyn.pl/content/blogsection/23/73
  Stały Sąd Arbitrażowy przy Okręgowej Izbie Radców Prawnych w
  Olsztynie. Permanent Court of Arbitration attached to the Regional
  Chamber of Legal Advisors in Olsztyn[68].

---

61 Website available in Polish. The portal also offers English version which, however,
was not available during our last visit [17 November 2010] (we cannot rule out technical
problems but we could not verify that before handing over this manuscript to CYArb
for printing).
62 Website available in Polish. See also http://sejm.gov.pl.
63 Website available in Polish. Some basic information available in English.
64 Website available in English and Polish.
65 Website available in Polish.
66 Website available in Polish.
67 Website available in Polish.
68 Website available in Polish.

- http://www.piit.org.pl/piit2/index.jsp?layout=1&news_cat_id=62&place=Menu01
  Sąd Polubowny ds. Domen Internetowych przy Polskiej Izbie Informatyki i Telekomunikacji w Warszawie. Arbitration Court for Internet Domains attached to The Polish Chamber of Information Technology and Telecommunications[69].

- http://www.polubowny.org/index.html
  Centrum Mediacyjne oraz Stały Sąd Polubowny przy Fundacji Adwokatury Polskiej i Ośrodku Badawczym Adwokatury im. adw. W. Bayera. Mediation Center and Permanent Court of Arbitration attached to the Donation of Polish Bar and Center for Bar Research of W. Bayer[70].

- http://www.pssp.org.pl/index.htm
  Polskie Stowarzyszenie Sądownictwa Polubownego – Polish Arbitration Association.

- http://www.riph.com.pl/index.php/Company/sub32
  Sąd Arbitrażowy przy Regionalnej Izbie Przemysłowo-Handlowej w Gliwicach. The Permanent Court of Arbitration at the Regional Chamber of Commerce & Industry in Gliwice[71].

- http://www.sadarbitrazowy.org.pl
  Sąd Arbitrażowy przy Polskiej Konfederacji Pracodawców Prywatnych Lewiatan. Court of Arbitration at the Polish Confederation of Private Employers Lewiatan[72].

- http://www.oirpwarszawa.pl/kategoria/pokaz/idk/612/ida/520/strona
  Stały Sąd Polubowny przy Okręgowej Izbie Radców Prawnych w Warszawie. Permanent Court of Arbitration Attached to the Regional Chamber of Legal Advisers in Warszawa[73]

- http://www.rig.katowice.pl/default.aspx?docId=30
  Sąd Arbitrażowy przy Regionalnej Izbie Gospodarczej w Katowicach. Court of Arbitration attached to the Chamber of Economy in Katowice.[74]

---

[69] Website available in English and Polish.
[70] Website available in Polish.
[71] Website available in Polish. Some basic information also available in English and German.
[72] Website available in English and Polish.
[73] Website available in Polish.
[74] Website available in Polish.

- http://www.sa.dig.wroc.pl/sa/index.php?option=com_content&task=view&id=69&Itemid=28
  Sąd Arbitrażowy przy Dolnośląskiej Izbie Gospodarczej we Wrocławiu. Court of Arbitration attached to the Lower Silesia Chamber of Economy in Wrocław[75].

- http://www.sejm.gov.pl
  Sejm Rzeczypospolitej Polskiej. Sejm [*Parliament*] of the Republic of Poland[76/77].

- http://www.senat.gov.pl
  Senat Rzeczypospolitej polskiej. The Senate of the Republic of Poland[78].

- http://www.sn.pl
  Supreme Court of the Republic of Poland[79].

- http://www.ssp.piph.pl
  Stały Sąd Polubowny przy Pomorskiej Izbie Przemysłowo-Handlowej w Gdańsku. Permanent Court of Arbitration attached to the See [*Maritime*] Chamber of Industry and Trade in Gdańsk[80].

- http://www.trybunal.gov.pl
  Constitutional Court[81].

- http://www.wib.com.pl/index.php?idkat=11
  Sąd Arbitrażowy przy Wielkopolskiej Izbie Budownictwa. Court of Arbitration attached to The Wielkopolska Chamber of Construction[82].

- http://www.wiph.pl/content/view/69/53
  Sąd Arbitrażowy Izb i Organizacji Gospodarczych Wielkopolski. Arbitration Court attached to the All Polish Chamber of Industry and Trade[83].

---

[75] Website available in Polish. Applicable Rules of proceedings available in English and German.

[76] Website available in English and Polish.

[77] See also http://isap.sejm.gov.pl – legal information system available through the portal of Sejm.

[78] Website available in English, French, German, Polish and Russian.

[79] Website available in English and Polish.

[80] Website available in Polish.

[81] Website available in English and Polish.

[82] Website available in Polish. Basic information, especially about the Chamber, available in English.

[83] Website available in Polish.

- http://www.zbp.pl/site.php?s=MGM0YzkzYWY1MTc3Nw
  Sąd Polubowny przy Związku Banków Polskich. Court of Arbitration attached to the Polish Bank Association (ZBP)[84].

- http://www.ziph.pl
  Polubowny Sąd Gospodarczy przy Zachodniej Izbie Przemysłowo-Handlowej w Gorzowie Wielkopolskim. Court of Arbitration attached to The Western Chamber of Industry and Commerce in Gorzow Wielkopolski[85].

XIV. [ROMANIA]

- http://arbitration.ccir.ro
  The Court of International Commercial Arbitration attached to The Chamber of Commerce and Industry of Romania[86].

XV. [RUSSIAN FEDERATION]

- http://www.iccwbo.ru
  ICC National Committee Russian Federation

- http://www.spbcci.ru/engarbitaltribunal
  The Arbitration tribunal at Saint-Petersburg Chamber of Commerce and Industry[87].

XVI. [SLOVENIA]

- http://www.sloarbitration.org
  The Permanent Court of Arbitration, although attached to the Chamber of Commerce and Industry of Slovenia [CCIS][88].

---

[84] Website available in English and Polish.
[85] Website available in Polish. Basic information and information about the Chamber also available in English, French, German and Russian.
[86] Website available in English and Romanian.
[87] Website available in English and Russian.
[88] Website available in English and Slovenian.

- http://www.sloarbitration.org/english/introduction/organization.html
  Nonofficial English translations of Slovenian law on or related to
  arbitration published on the portal of the Permanent Court of Arbitration,
  although attached to the Chamber of Commerce and Industry of Slovenia.
  (i) Code of Civil Procedure of Slovenia[89]. (ii) Private International Law
  and Procedure Act[90]. [Law on Arbitration].

---

[89] Published in the: Official Gazette of the Republic of Slovenia, No. 26/99.
[90] Published in the: Official Gazette of the Republic of Slovenia, No. 56/99.

Index

516 |

528 |

CALL FOR PAPERS FOR VOLUMES 2012 AND 2013

Did you find the articles in the first volume of the CYArb interesting?

Would you like to respond to a current article
or contribute to future volumes?

We are seeking authors for both
the Czech Yearbook of International Law (CYIL) and the
Czech (& Central European) Yearbook of Arbitration.

The general topics for 2012 and 2013 are the following:

CYIL 2012	**CYArb 2012**
Public Policy and Ordre Public	*Party Autonomy versus Autonomy of Arbitrators*
CYIL 2013	**CYArb 2013**
Regulatory Measures and Foreign Trade	*Borders of Procedural and Substantive Law in Arbitral Proceedings (Civil versus Common Law Perspectives)*

More general and contact information available at:

www.czechyearbook.org